POWER, POLITICS, AND SOCIETY: AN INTRODUCTION TO POLITICAL SOCIOLOGY

Betty A. Dobratz

Iowa State University

Lisa K. Waldner

University of St. Thomas

Timothy Buzzell

Baker University

Allyn & Bacon

Boston   Columbus   Indianapolis   New York   San Francisco   Upper Saddle River
Amsterdam   Cape Town   Dubai   London   Madrid   Milan   Munich   Paris   Montreal   Toronto
Delhi   Mexico City   São Paulo   Sydney   Hong Kong   Seoul   Singapore   Taipei   Tokyo

Publisher: Karen Hanson
Editorial Assistant: Christine Dore
Executive Marketing Manager: Kelly May
Marketing Assistant: Janeli Bitor
Production Manager: Kathy Sleys
Production Assistant: Caitlin Smith
Editorial Production and Composition Service: Revathi Viswanathan/PreMediaGlobal
Creative Art Director: Jayne Conte
Cover Designer: Karen Salzbach
Printer/Binder/Cover Printer: Courier Companies

Credits appear on Page 383, which constitutes an extension of the copyright page.

Library of Congress Cataloging-in-Publication Data
Dobratz, Betty A.
  Power, politics, and society: an introduction to political sociology / Betty A. Dobratz, Lisa K. Waldner, Timothy Buzzell.
    p. cm.
  Includes bibliographical references and index.
  ISBN-13: 978-0-205-48629-8 (alk. paper)
  ISBN-10: 0-205-48629-0 (alk. paper)
  1. Political sociology.   I. Waldner, Lisa K.   II. Buzzell, Tim.   III. Title.
  JA76.D598 2012
  306.2—dc22

                                                            2010052422

10 9 8 7 6 5 4 3 2 1 CRS 15 14 13 12 11

PEARSON
Education

1859665

Allyn & Bacon
is an imprint of

www.pearsonhighered.com

ISBN-10: 0-205-48629-0
ISBN-13: 978-0-205-48629-8

CONTENTS

TABLES AND FIGURES

PREFACE

Do you know that ancient Chinese proverb you get when you open a fortune cookie? "May you live in interesting times." That's not deep political sociology. But, the profound simplicity to capture our sociological moment is summarized in that phrase in so many ways. We live in one of the most fascinating periods in political and social history. Terrorism has pushed the global political landscape into different realms. In 2008 Americans elected the first African-American president. Today, we find ourselves struggling with economic hardships tipped into tensions created by deregulation of banking, ideological struggles that characterize the first decade of the twenty-first century, and all the economic and political uncertainty that comes with globalization. There is perhaps no better time to be a political sociologist.

While political sociology has often been described as divergent, abstract, and fragmented, it continues to be an important subfield in sociology because a number of themes consistently explored by political sociologists are particularly relevant to the development of a sociological perspective. We believe undergraduate sociology students should be exposed to these themes, so we have written this text and its supplementary materials with three central goals. First, *introduce undergraduate students to core concepts* and research in political sociology. Second, highlight how sociologists have *organized the study of politics into conceptual frameworks*, and how each of these frameworks fosters a sociological perspective on power and politics in society. This includes discussing how these frameworks can be applied to understanding current issues and other real-life aspects of politics. Third, connect with students by *engaging them in activities where they complete their own applications* of theory, hypothesis testing, and forms of inquiry. We hope that instructors find the Web-based data applications and other supplementary material useful toward meeting this goal.

The plan of the book unfolds around these three goals. We begin with a discussion of the central concept in political sociology: power. Chapter 1 explores the core concepts in the study of power not only in formal systems, but in informal contexts, all of which define the agenda in the study of power. The theoretical frameworks in political sociology organize the work of political sociologists, and each framework presents very different arguments about how to understand the connections among power, politics, and society. We outline these in Chapter 1, which then sets the agenda for the entire book. Chapter 2 examines how various sociological perspectives conceptualize the state and differentiate this political institution from nation. This chapter also considers the future of the state. In Chapter 3 we integrate the study of power and politics to align with the cultural turn in the field of sociology more generally. Here we examine the more traditional features of political culture, such as political values and ideology and the study of how these values are acquired. The chapter also presents more recent theorizing which mixes institutions and culture, and suggests that the two must go hand in hand in order to understand the nature of politics.

As Mills suggested, private concerns connect to public issues. In Chapters 4 and 5 we give special treatment to describing how political sociologists have come to understand this important facet of the politics–society nexus. Chapter 4 especially focuses on the interplay between politics and economics. When we first conceived this chapter we understood how the middle class was losing ground, but we did not foresee how the economic woes of banks and the stock market would so dramatically influence us all. We thus modified our focus to include the Wall Street versus Main Street issue. Here we discuss the politics surrounding individual and corporate taxes, our welfare system, bankruptcies, foreclosures, and our worsening infrastructure. Chapter 5 illustrates how the political process impacts the institutions of education, including No Child Left Behind legislation, and marriage, especially the controversial issue of same-sex marriage (still legal in only a few states). This chapter would not be complete without considering the politics surrounding medical care and the difficulties of passing major health care reform. The concerns of civil liberties and national security are addressed as well, and we end the chapter pointing out that the state is a racial state and clearly influences our immigration policy.

In Chapter 6 we move the analysis into a fairly comprehensive discussion of the nature of political participation. This area of political sociology is extensive and provides great insights into the ways in which individuals, political groups, the state, and other elements of the public sphere all come together in the contest for power. The typologies of political participation presented in this chapter are good examples of the many ways in which political sociologists have examined the question, what power do individuals have to shape the political and social events of the day? The chapters that follow look at specific kinds of political participation: voting, movements, and terrorism.

In Chapter 7 we analyze voting, which is likely the most direct way for a majority of individuals in a democracy to influence politics. Elections perform numerous roles for individuals and society as candidates are selected for political office. The United States has one of the lower turnout rates for elections and some of the reasons for this may be associated with our electoral system. We look at a number of social, demographic, economic, and political factors to explain why people vote for the candidates they do. The 2008 election is analyzed including a discussion of the possible meanings of the election of a biracial president. Finally we consider the rise of the Tea Party Movement and examine the results of the 2010 election.

In Chapter 8 we discuss the importance of social movements that use both institutionalized and noninstitutionalized political activities to achieve their goals. Old and new social movements are compared and contrasted, noting that some movements are more likely to focus on class issues whereas others are more concerned with identity politics. We identify how important concepts such as collective identity, framing, and emotions are for the study of movements. In detail we examine the life cycle of social movements, including emergence, mobilization, political opportunity structures, outcomes, and decline. After discussing why social movements matter, we conclude by arguing that social movements should be viewed as a key part of political sociology.

Political violence including war, genocide, and terrorism is the focus of Chapter 9. We begin by considering the political uses of hate that can result in genocide and other forms of state-sanctioned violence against state citizens. A variety of sociological causes of terrorism are considered as well as state responses, including the threat to democracy not only posed by terrorists themselves but by democratic states that attempt to keep citizens safe, as security measures are often in conflict with basic civil liberties.

A question first asked in Chapter 2, "what is the future of the state?" is the central theme of Chapter 10, which considers the political implications of the complex phenomenon called globalization. Sociologists are vigorously debating the meaning of globalization as well as what the future holds for the political institution we call the state, using a variety of theoretical perspectives that provide conflicting, yet stimulating views. We consider both the potential negative and positive impacts of globalization, including the exporting of democracy. In all of these chapters we hope to provide not only a current snapshot of both empirical and theoretical directions in political sociology but also to stimulate questions that will be asked and eventually answered by future political sociologists.

This book endeavors to foster and instill the sociological perspective and to encourage students to pursue even greater sociological insights into the many connections between power, politics, and society. The project in fact begins with what C. Wright Mills (1959) taught about *the Sociological Imagination*. The personal is indeed public:

- In the midst of a student movement Betty was involved in during the 1960s, Senator Robert F. Kennedy wrote *To Seek a Newer World*. Perhaps our book helps students realize how essential concepts such as power and politics are to understanding the world we live in. Along the way, Betty observed many who worked for a better world including Robert F. Kennedy, a politician; Richard M. Ragsdale, a courageous doctor; Arthur G. P. Dobratz, her father and a World War II veteran who served on the *U.S.S. Missouri*; Ronald A. Dobratz, her brother and a history teacher; and Patricia Keith, her friend and fellow sociologist.
- In 1938 First Lady Eleanor Roosevelt wrote *This Troubled World*, reflecting on the need for world peace and the failure of international organizations to sustain it. Lisa is reminded that over seventy years later, Roosevelt's words are still relevant. She hopes students will ask impertinent questions and critically examine the "taken-for-granted view" that is rarely challenged. Lisa is grateful for ordinary women and men who work every day for change in their own communities to bring about a more just and fair world. She is especially thankful for all the men and women of the U.S. armed forces who risk their lives, including Brandon Haugrud (Lisa's son), a former U.S. Marine who served three tours of duty in Iraq and Afghanistan and Ashley Wiser (Lisa's daughter), a former U.S. Army Sergeant who served for eight years, including a tour of duty in Korea. She hopes daughter Claryssa and grandson Cody will be able to live in a more peaceful and safer world.

- When Franklin D. Roosevelt was president, society experienced one of its greatest economic and political shifts. His presidency was marked by compassion for those in trouble. For Tim, hearing stories about the nature of politics and troubled times during the Great Depression, including reminiscences of Roosevelt's famous fireside chats, gave the impression that political leaders could make a real difference. Community in this period was built by people who had compassion, who were never hesitant to help people, who could benefit from the fruits of hard work on the farm, and just as importantly, community was built by a sense that the affairs of state required that you get involved at a local level. With the grandparents in his family, political conversations were allowed at the dinner table. Tim continued this tradition early by his involvement in the Iowa caucuses, work on political campaigns, and an incredible experience at the Drake Law School dedicated to civic education.

Of course, any endeavor like this is part of our families and those we love.

For Betty: extremely grateful to both her mother Helen and her father Arthur and like her brother wishes that his children Theresa and Patricia and his grandchildren Tyler, Stacy, and Faith experience a better world.

For Lisa: always grateful to parents Mike and Reva, and partner Rebecca.

For Tim: ever grateful to parents Delores and Darwin, always loving and never thanked enough; and to Cheryl and Dan, who know the fun of a crazy brother.

The success of a book involves the labors of so many people, catching the errors, pointing out the confusion, or just cheering us on:

At Iowa State University, special thanks go to Rachel Burlingame, Dwight Dake, Renea Miller, copy editor Denise Rothschild, and three undergraduate research assistants, Chris Reardon, Mark Nieman, and Michael Bragg for their assistance. Lisa gratefully acknowledges the Faculty Development Office at the University of St. Thomas for providing sabbatical support. Of course to all those colleagues at ISU, the University of St. Thomas, and Baker University, thanks for your encouraging words and understanding the costs of seeking a better world.

To those who reviewed earlier drafts of this work, thank you. Teaching and research colleagues in political sociology have provided extremely valuable guidance in helping prepare this introduction to the field.

Many thanks to the various members of the Pearson Education team for their help in turning our manuscript into a completed book. This project wouldn't be possible without them.

Finally, for Lisa and Tim, there is no more appropriate way to honor the work of many teachers through their sociological careers, including (but of course knowing there are many others) high school social studies teacher Wayne Hendershott and professors Barbara Keating, Gloria Jones-Johnson, Dean and Sue Wright, and of course, Betty Dobratz. There is no greater privilege for two former students than to get a chance to write a book with their mentor.

In the end responsibility for oversights and errors belong to us. If you have thoughts or comments, feel free to contact the authors:

Betty A. Dobratz, Ph.D.
Professor of Sociology,
Department of Sociology
Iowa State University
Ames, Iowa
bdobratz@iastate.edu

Lisa K. Waldner, Ph.D.
Professor of Sociology & Chair,
Department of Sociology
& Criminal Justice
University of St. Thomas
St. Paul, Minnesota
lkwaldner@stthomas.edu

Timothy Buzzell, Ph.D.
Professor of Sociology & Chair,
Department of History,
Culture & Society
Baker University
Baldwin City, Kansas
tim.buzzell@bakeru.edu

Power

C. Wright Mills (1959) set out to develop among all of us a self-consciousness that was inherently about power and politics in their social context. The sociological imagination, as taught in introductory sociology, connects us to essentially political themes: personal troubles, public issues, and the interplay between biography and social history. The troubles we hear about—for example, unemployment, providing mental health services to war veterans, and failures of our schools—all have a personal dimension, a human face, and very real biographies. What Mills wants us to understand is that these personal troubles are often really public issues that are the result of larger, social, and global forces. These forces are even more apparent at this point in social history, as technology and globalization push societies together, structuring interactions in ways never seen before. Mills was influenced by his own historical epoch in 1959 but, nonetheless, was offering timeless lessons for political sociology about the nature of power, and the role of biography and the public. Mills believed that the sociological perspective brought great "promise" to the study of politics and power, valuable to building insights into the study of power, politics, and society, ultimately distinguishing political sociology from other disciplines of study.

While Mills was captivated by the role of science—namely, social science—much of his work focused on how sociologists could most successfully explore the relationships between society and politics. This textbook is a summary of the very diverse scientific and humanistic understandings that make up political sociology today and, in many ways, celebrates Mills' ingenious perspective on the connections between society, politics, and power.

This text begins with a definition of power, bringing focus to recent attempts to define a very abstract concept about social life. The insights that come about through the use of two analytical tools commonly used in the study of power—politics and society—help us to engage our thinking about a fairly difficult concept. The strengths of theory and research behind a rich history of exploration are found in the three major theoretical frameworks in political sociology—pluralist, elite-managerialist, and social-class perspectives. These classical frameworks set the foundation for a number of new perspectives in political sociology, guided no doubt by the sociological imagination, in the study of power and politics. Political sociology has been instrumental in outlining the many contours of power in a variety of social spaces and social contexts. We discuss this in the next section. Our introduction to political sociology asserts power as the essential overriding idea behind the topics found in the pages ahead. As Mills observed—and we hope that you agree—the study of power is a summary of a tradition of "intellectual craftsmanship," which is known as political sociology. It invites students of sociology and politics to the "sociological imagination our most needed quality of mind" (Mills 1959: 13).

POWER: THE KEY CONCEPT IN POLITICAL SOCIOLOGY

If we begin with the idea that politics is "the generalized process by which the struggle over power in society is resolved" (Braungart 1981: 2), at the outset, then we can understand that power is at the core of the work of political sociologists. The goal is to explain the connections between social interactions, social structures, and social processes altered by struggle and resolution. We must define what we mean by power. Defining power is not as straightforward as one might think. Certainly we all have experienced power in some way, perhaps the influence of a friend who cajoles and pushes us to go to a political meeting, or the force of a mugger who confronts us, taking an iPod at gunpoint! Power is encountered every day and every hour. Let's take a look at several definitions, identifying as we go the differences that reflect debates on how power is conceptualized.

The works of Karl Marx and Max Weber serve as the classic foundations for defining power. Marx established that economic structures like corporations, owners of capital, and more immediately, the boss represent societal sources of power. The use of wages to influence worker performance or attendance is a significant creation of capitalist society. According to Marx, the relationship between worker, wage, and class interests was the source of alienating individuals not only from pursuing nonwork-related self-interests but also alienating individuals from each other. For Marx, power has an economic context rooted in the relationships between and among social classes. Weber picks up this theme and offers one of the first formal political sociological analyses of power. Unlike Marx, Weber located power in a variety of social spaces including both economic and noneconomic contexts. For Weber, power was rooted in formalized social systems such as organizations or bureaucracies, as well as in social institutions such as religion and law. Weber differed from Marx in that he argued that power was not simply just about economic relationships, but rather a function of social patterns, culture, and social organization. These early approaches to the study of power offer one of the first debates in political sociology about the nature of the society–politics relationship.

Weber developed many of the early formal statements about power and politics, defining power as: "the chance of a man or a number of men to realize their own will in a social action even against the resistance of others who are participating in the action" (1947: 152). This definition was launched after nearly a century of attempts at clarification, precision, and nuanced understandings of power. Since Weber's study of power in the early 1900s, social scientists have focused on what is meant by the distribution of power in society, as well as identifying what kinds of resources make some individuals and groups powerful or powerless. Others have extended the notion that politics is inherent in most if not all aspects of social action and expression in human interactions. Consider the many definitions summarized in Textbox 1.1. These definitions offer evidence of a field of study characterized by diverse views about power and social and political processes.

Specifically, these various definitions reveal the insights into the characteristics of power as related to political and social outcomes, interests, intents, capacities for action, and resources. Drawing from these many approaches, *we define power as individual, group, or structural capacity to achieve intended effects as a result of force, influence, or authority.*

Metaphors and Paradoxes: Sociological Tools in the Study of Power

Students studying power, politics, and society will find that insights developed thus far come from applications of the sociological imagination. These insights are typically conveyed through the use of metaphors and paradoxes. These are useful tools in sociological thinking.

TEXTBOX 1.1

Varieties in the Definition of Power

Power Defined as . . .	Author
the production of intended effects.	Bertrand Russell (1938: 2)
Power has to do with whatever decisions men make about the arrangements under which they live, and about the events which make up the history of their times . . . men are free to make history but some are much freer than others.	C. Wright Mills (1959: 181)
the generalized capacity to secure the performance of binding obligations, when the obligations are legitimized with reference to their bearing on collective goals and where, in the case of recalcitrance, there is a presumption of enforcement by negative sanctions.	Talcott Parsons (1967: 297)
all kinds of influence between persons or groups, including those exercised in exchange transactions, where one induces others to accede to his wishes by rewarding them for doing so.	Peter Blau (1964: 115)
the capacity of some persons to produce intended and foreseen effects on others.	Dennis Wrong (1979: 2)
the capability to secure outcomes where the realization of these outcomes depends on the agency of others.	Anthony Giddens (1976: 111–112)
In the end, we are judged, condemned, classified, determined in our undertakings, destined to a certain mode of living or dying, as a function of the true discourses which are bearers of the specific effects of power.	Michel Foucault (1980: 94)
the social capacity to make binding decisions that have far-reaching consequences for society.	Anthony Orum (1989: 131–132)
the ability to affect the actions or ideas of others.	Olsen and Marger (1993: 1)

Metaphors are analytical devices commonly used to depict ideas or concepts, especially when we as sociologists are "trying to make sense of mysteries" (Rigney 2001: 3). Rigney finds that sociologists frequently use metaphors, such as models or pictures, to illuminate what are otherwise abstract ideas about social life. Models or pictures are useful in describing how social forces like power influence interactions. For example, recall that functionalists typically describe societies as social systems. A metaphor for a social system might be a car. The car (society) is made up of certain components like the transmission, engine, or electronics (subsystems) that all operate together to make the car (society) move forward. Each subsystem in turn has its various parts that are required in order for the whole (car or society) to move forward. If we think of a society as made up of various components (Talcott Parsons talked about religious systems, governments, and education as various components of a society), we create a metaphor for describing the nature of social dynamics.

Metaphors have been constructed to explain in detail the nature of power in society. According to Hindess (1996), power has historically been described as a type of capacity for either action or obligation. He argues that action and obligation are central to the role power plays in political processes. The metaphor he uses to understand *power as capacity* comes from the science of physics. Recall the old dictum from physics or introductory courses in the sciences, "for every action there is an equal and opposite reaction." When a series of physical events are put into motion in nature, such as a bowling ball being hurled down the hallway of a college dorm, there will be a number of reactions from this initial force (e.g., the ball hits the RA's door at the end of the hallway and breaks the door or a roommate stumbles into the hallway and his toe is run over by the rolling ball causing great pain). Using this metaphor, we are prompted to ask what started the ball rolling. The capacity to *force* a bowling ball through a hallway represents an ability, a skill, or the wherewithal to set up a series of actions. It also suggests that someone had an *interest* or a desire to roll the ball down the hallway, and the command of the resources to get a bowling ball, pick it up, and use it as a way to act on these interests. The metaphor here describes power as capacity to achieve some outcome or act on a particular interest.

Capacity for action is distinct from capacity for obligation and duty. Hindess argues that here is where we find the essence of politics and power moving from the individual to the societal level. Obligation is hidden at a different layer of social interaction, and power is not always action on interests or desires but rather power is acquiescence or *duty*. In democratic societies, social order is achieved through duty to the law. Law is created by the sovereign or in many cases by a legislature or parliament that in principle represents the citizenry and their interests. When citizens follow the speed limit, or pay their taxes, or immunize their children before school begins each fall, they may grumble, but for the most part, they oblige the state through compliance. A useful metaphor for describing this second distinction is that of the parent. The state is a parent— it creates, monitors, and enforces rules, including punishing violators to keep things in order. The power of the state or parent derives from the fact that we come to understand the state as legitimate authority; we give it power by agreeing to obey. This dimension of power is perhaps more subtle but nonetheless effective in describing the concept of legitimate power in shaping social patterns.

Another analytical tool used in sociology is *paradox* (Crow 2005). For political sociology in particular, we find that life in a democratic society is sometimes characterized by contradiction or patterns of power that are contrary to expectations, public opinion, or values about democratic life. Political sociologists grapple with a number of paradoxes about the distribution of power in order to bring attention to significant research questions. This analytical tool, much like metaphor, is about explaining mysteries. Consider, for example, the paradox studied in a great deal of research on American society: Are all Americans politically equal as suggested by the

Constitution of the United States? Voting is a form of power in a democratic system. But are all votes *truly* equal? Only within the last century have women been given *more equal* power by being granted the right to vote in 1920. Women did not have this power in the political system prior to the Nineteenth Amendment to the Constitution. Or consider the argument made by some that the Iowa caucuses give Iowans *more influence* in the process of selecting a presidential candidate than citizens in states that vote later in the presidential nominating process. Much of this argument rests on the belief that the winner in Iowa gets more media attention, and thus can ride a bandwagon effect (the media call it a "bump" from winning early nomination primaries), resulting in more positive polls and campaign donations. Paradoxically, this means all votes are not equal in the sociological sense that early voting states may have more influence than later-voting states. Identifying paradoxes in social systems, social outcomes, and social interactions is an important analytical goal of political sociology.

What insights are gained from the exploration of metaphors, paradoxes, and the application of the sociological imagination to the study of power and politics? By focusing on the debates, mysteries, and contradictions about power in social life, we develop keen insights into the nature of politics in society. Moreover, political sociology makes use of sociological tools to map out its focus for research. Lewis Coser (1966) defined political sociology as

> that branch of sociology which is concerned with the social causes and consequences of given power distributions within or between societies, and with the social and political conflicts that lead to changes in the allocation of power. (1)

Political sociology thus in its most basic orientation focuses on two elements: power and conflict. This definition of political sociology reflects the "state" of sociology in the late 1950s and 1960s. According to Coser, the various topics of the study of political sociology include:

1. attention to the state and institutions,
2. organization of power,
3. competition and order among groups, and
4. development of political associations.

This approach stands in contrast to the work of political science, which typically focuses on the nature of the state and its various manifestations. Political sociology casts its analytical net more broadly to capture the nature of the many power-based relationships between social structures, culture, and individuals.

Metaphors of Power Arrangements

Political sociologists have revealed the forms and nuances of the abstract notion of power by creating typologies of power. These various typologies highlight the nature of power in situations or the characteristics of power as they play a role in the construction of capacity, exchange of resources, and distribution of power in society. These various typologies and conceptualizations of power share the notion that society shapes and is shaped by individuals, groups, organizations, governments, and other societies in a broadly interactive process. The classic and contemporary typologies point to at least three types of power of interest to the study of society and politics:

1. Coercive and dominant power
2. Authority and legitimate power
3. Privileged and interdependent power

Both pro-choice and pro-life activists demonstrate in front of the U.S. Supreme Court, December 4, 2002, as oral arguments are being heard inside on the National Organization for Women (NOW) vs. Scheidler case that won the first-ever nationwide injunction against anti-abortion violence. The Court was deciding on the issue of punishment against those activists that use violence to protest against abortion clinics

Source: JOYCE NALTCHAYAN/AFP/Getty Images

Political sociologists have consistently studied these forms of power and patterns of social–political interactions, beginning especially with the work of Max Weber. Weber launched the sociological analysis by claiming that power existed in two forms: coercion and authority. Textbox 1.2 summarizes the variety of typologies that have been presented to better understand the contours of a rather abstract concept. We turn our focus to three typologies that have been central to the work of political sociology.

COERCIVE AND DOMINANT POWER   When we think of power, we most likely start with metaphors or pictures of coercion and dominance. For instance, coercive power in the form of physical force is clearly exercised as one nation-state invades and conquers another. The resources used to coerce may include brute force, military prowess, and the strength of large armies. Perhaps this type of power is the raw or most pure form. *Dominance* also reflects the use of resources with consequences for others in society. In this regard, Parenti (1978) reminds us that, "To win a struggle is one thing, but to have your way by impressing others that struggle would be futile, that is power at its most economical and most secure" (78). Coercion and dominance share a central tenet of command of resources with immediate and future submission by subjects to this form of power.

As we will see in Chapter 9, war and terrorism are important societal dynamics related to the brute use of dominance and coercion. The nature of coercion and dominance in totalitarian regimes has also been studied. Hannah Arendt, in *The Origins of Totalitarianism* (1958), studied the social and cultural influences that gave rise to Nazi Germany. The influence of economic

---

TEXTBOX 1.2

Typologies in the Study of Power

Power Conceptualized as ...	Types/Characteristics	Author
exerted through command of resources	utilitarian coercive persuasive	Etzioni (1968)
varying by resources and intent of the actor	force dominance authority attraction	Olsen (1978)

influence either unintended or intended (power)	force
	  physical (violent or
	  nonviolent)
	  psychic
	manipulation
	persuasion
	authority
	  coercive
	  induced
	  personal
	  competent
	  legitimate
		Wrong (1979)

relational, resource-driven, and socially organized	force authority influence dominance	Marger (1987)
defined in terms of its intended outcome	destructive or threat (stick) productive or economic (carrot) integrative (hug)	Boulding (1989)

the absence or presence of domination and influence	egalitarian
	  (no dominance/no
	  influence)
	coercive
	  (dominance/no influence)
	persuasion
	  (no dominance/influence)
	authority
	  (dominance/influence)
		Knoke (1990)

---

hardship, fear of outgroups, control of political party apparatus, use of propaganda, and creation of a military state are common to the creation of such regimes. Although totalitarianism as a form of political rule seems to be on the wane, the documentation of coercive forms of power is important to understanding the nature of power in alternative ruling systems. Since the Al Qaeda attacks on New York City and the Pentagon, considerable attention has been given to finding what causes terrorism, especially as a tool designed to advance political demands and claims. The nature of modern-day terrorism may usher in yet another field of study in which questions of coercion and domination through military excursions or political violence must be better understood.

The use of coercion for political gain or outcome is an important aspect of power not limited to studies of conquering figures in history. The modern democratic state uses coercion in several ways. Marger (1987: 12) equated coercion with *force*, which is based on "the threat or application of punishment or the inducement of rewards to elicit compliance." Periodically, we are reminded that the police power that we extend to specific agencies of the state is inherently coercive. Police power to control rioting, protests, or dissent is not uncommon, as seen during the civil rights protests of the 1960s or with dissent in North Korea, Cuba, or Pakistan. The coercive nature of police work in a free society can test the boundary between freedom to act or seek changes in the nature of rule through protest, while also attempting to maintain a semblance of social order through enforcing the law. The study of coercion and dominance is an important part of political sociology.

AUTHORITY AND LEGITIMATE POWER   Authority is a form of power that emerges from the acquiescence of individuals and groups based on a sense of *legitimacy and obedience* or duty. Individuals and groups within society create order by recognizing the power of law, tradition, or custom. They behave based on the belief that the power of the state protects members of society while preserving community interests. Consider the legitimate power of a police officer in the United States. Police act with authority, which is distinguished in the general population by a uniform and badge. The authority is strong as police officers are one of few agents in the United States who can stop free individuals, ask them questions, and apprehend them. The extent of police power is best symbolized by the fact that police officers carry weapons that can be used to force compliance with the law. The legitimacy of this power is found in the idea of representative lawmaking and the duty to obey as a member of the community.

Weber wrote extensively about the nature of authority in industrial society. In particular, he focused on the authority that would come from individuals and offices in large-scale organizations created to structure interactions based on law and procedures. He identified three types of authority:

- *Charismatic authority* emanates from the personality or character of leaders. Weber suggested that charismatic power and influence flow from an individual's heroic status or other achievements. Thus, the people follow, swayed by the conviction, style, and projection of the leader. Martin Luther King, Jr., was a charismatic leader, and his influence in a time of significant social unrest was important to bringing about changes in civil rights law in the United States. Even though he held no formal political office, he retained national influence in efforts related to social justice for racial-ethnic minorities as well as the poor.
- *Traditional authority* gains its legitimacy through custom and tradition. There is a certain sacred dimension to these traditions or appeals to customs that results in acquiescence to authority. Monarchies are a good example of traditional forms of governance in some societies. The Queen of England, for example, retains authority through appeals to tradition and custom, typically enacted through symbolic and ritualistic dramas that reinforce her authority. Similarly, the Pope, as the leader of the Roman Catholic Church, retains power through appeals to custom and tradition, holding influence over Church policy.
- *Rational-legal authority* is grounded in rules by which people are governed. Legitimacy stems from an appeal to law, commands, and decision making that is regarded as valid for all in the population. A good example is the Constitutional order of the United States. Recall the election in the year 2000, when George W. Bush won the electoral vote, but Al Gore won the popular vote. The outcome of the election was contested in Florida, and

legal claims about voting were made by both sides. Eventually the U.S. Supreme Court made a ruling that resulted in the election of Bush to the presidency. The legitimacy of law and rational-legal authority was seen in this acceptance of the outcome. In societies where there was no rational-legal authority to make such decisions, riots may have broken out, or revolution. Life went on in the United States—order was maintained as a result of the legitimate exercise of power by constitutional authorities.

As we will see in Chapter 2, the power of the democratic state is defined by its legitimacy to rule in contrast to authoritarian states. Weber's work marks an important beginning in the study of authority and rule in political sociology. All forms of power are better understood by examining the state, law in everyday life, and political socialization, as well as attempts to shape coalitions to legitimize state rule.

INTERDEPENDENT POWER   Power can operate in more subtle ways, resulting in dramatic changes in social interactions and the distribution of power in society. Certainly the typologies that focus on coercion or authority share this view, but this third body of research in political sociology encourages us to dig deeper into power relationships in society. In many ways, political sociology advanced beyond the simplicity of thinking of power as coercion or authority. As research on power evolved, especially in the 1960s, power came to be understood as quite complex. The idea of *interdependent power* depicts power relationships between individuals and social groups as reciprocal. That is, power is a two-way street where actors, even though they may think they have no influence, actually do, given the way in which the social system is set up. One insight from this approach explores power that quietly wraps around systems of inequality that constructs differences in who has what, when, and how.

Recently, Piven and Cloward (2005) urged political sociologists to consider more fully the role of rule breakers in the study of power. Their analysis highlighted how most of political sociology has focused on "rulemaking," which would include lawmakers or administrative bodies that create laws or policies to direct social interactions. Sometimes these rules are challenged. When societies experience protest and challenges to the distribution of power, political authority can be undermined. These forms of challenge by rule breakers may not be coercive but rather, much like the bumper sticker says, seek to "subvert the dominant paradigm." In other words, the power exercised in certain social contexts is intended to be disruptive to bring attention to claims.

The model of power that Piven and Cloward suggest advances current political sociology about power in an alternate direction. Most studies begin with the assumption that power is about the distribution of resources among individuals, groups, and social structures. Piven and Cloward believe that power is more complex than the mere distribution of resources (e.g., wealth, knowledge or skills, and property). Their notion of power is based on the idea that power is meaningful in social connections, or "interdependencies." In other words, power derives its significance when individuals exchange resources of many kinds in these interdependencies.

Complex organizations are stages for seeing the power as a function of social interdependencies. For example, a university in many ways is a small social system where each part of the system (e.g., the food service staff, faculty, financial aid office, and campus security) contributes to the order of the larger system called a university. Traditionally, models of power would have focused on the distribution of resources to understand who is powerful. For example, students pay tuition, which brings in financial resources that help pay the salaries of the vice presidents. The administrators, as the university elite (much like society), hold more wealth in comparison to the food service staff or hall janitors. If the food service staff become angry about their pay, they can go on strike, or negotiate for a wage increase. Or, they could walk off the job and most likely be replaced with new employees who might in fact be paid a lower wage as they come into entry-level positions. Thus, the distribution of resources would change again.

But, what if all the faculty at a university stopped teaching? Given the shortage of professors in some fields, would the university be able to offer majors or continue to offer degrees? Piven and Cloward would point to this type of *leverage in an interdependent system* as an example of power not extensively considered in political sociology:

> People have potential power, the ability to make others do what they want, when those others depend on them for the contributions they make to the interdependent relations that are social life. Just as the effort to exert power is a feature of all social interactions, so is the capacity to exert power at least potentially inherent in all social interaction. And because cooperative and interdependent social relations are by definition reciprocal, so is the potential for the exercise of power. (2005: 39)

Their argument is that protests, or challenges to the core purpose of an interdependent relationship (e.g., faculty teaching courses is a core purpose of the interdependencies that constitute the organization we call a university) are how power can be wielded in the social structure. If all middle-class Americans agreed not to pay income taxes for one year as a protest against unethical behaviors in Congress, would they wield power? Piven and Cloward suggest considering these interdependent social connections. Political sociologists can study power under this model by identifying leverage points in social embeddedness, connections that build trust, strengthen relationships, or achieve goals. The focus shifts from *who controls* the resources in society, who has the most education, and what groups compete for votes, to what *power comes from the connections themselves* and what systems collapse or are changed if the connections are severed?

Recent work by Alan Johnson (2006) highlights the nature of power in social interdependencies. His work focuses on how privilege is constructed in interdependencies using *privilege* to describe the nuances of power. He links privilege to the various ways society makes differences important or significant in use, allocation, and access to resources. Johnson identifies "unearned advantage" and "conferred dominance" as forms of power that create privilege in society. Unearned advantage emerges when one group in society is rewarded or benefits over another. One unearned advantage in society is found in hiring into the occupational structure; for many jobs, white males gain easier access than, say, minority females. This preserves white male privilege in job opportunities. This group reaps the gains, while the other is left out. Dominance takes a more active form, indicating that the privilege is solidified when one group pressures another group into conformity to privilege. Privilege that comes from interdependencies based on gender, race, sexuality, or social status can sustain institutional patterns of social difference.

THE CONCEPTUALIZATION OF POWER IN POLITICAL SOCIOLOGY

Political sociologists have traditionally organized the study of the relationships between society, politics, and power into three frameworks: the pluralist, the elite-managerial, and the social-class perspectives. These frameworks represent very different views of how power is distributed in society, how politics is socially organized, and how significant individuals, groups, organizations, and the state are. In this section, we examine the basic assumptions of each framework. The discussion also looks at the works of classical and contemporary thinkers associated with each framework. Finally, we consider recent criticisms of each framework as these are important to the development of new ways of conceptualizing the nature of power in society.

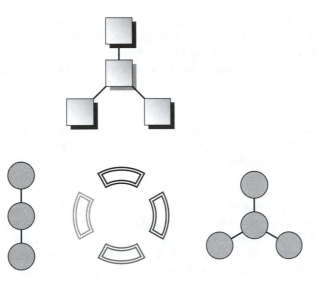

FIGURE 1.1   The Pluralist Metaphor of Power: Groups and Coalitions at the Political Table

Source: Figure created by Tim Buzzell

Pluralist

The pluralist approach to the study of politics and society is based on the assertion that power is distributed throughout society among a "plurality" of power centers. These power centers include political parties, interest groups, voters, associations, and a variety of other social actors. According to pluralism, these various centers within society compete for power. Thus, pluralism finds that power is fragmented, often changing as one group wins and another loses, and that coalitions are formed only to fall apart over time. The pluralist framework essentially views power as balanced as a result of the multitude of groups bargaining for roles in the political processes, including the policy-making process that affects the distribution of resources in society (Figure 1.1).

The groups that compete for power vie for control of the state, that is, the governing apparatus of society. Pluralists view the state as a structure that retains legitimate power (authority) to guard the rules of the political process, especially as they involve access to the governance structure, selection to office, or maintenance of order throughout society. The state itself is characterized by checks and balances, with groups or individual citizens serving as an ultimate check on the potential concentration of power. Pluralists also have understood the state as a collection of various power centers, such as different branches of government, or a system of federalism. Chapter 2 will provide a more extended discussion of pluralist views of the state.

CLASSICAL AND CONTEMPORARY PLURALIST APPROACHES   One of the earliest studies of politics in the United States brought attention in a unique way to the social nature of how power was structured in the newly created republic. After completing his own studies of the French Revolution of 1789, Tocqueville (1805–1859) was intrigued by the ways in which the government of the United States created equality in contrast to the ruling aristocracy found in France. During his famous travels throughout the United States in the 1830s, Tocqueville recorded what would come to be understood as aspects of American character, or culture, contributing to basic democratic processes. His observations were the basis for his two-volume study called *Democracy in America* (1945[1835]).

The historical and ethnographic insights in this work make a significant contribution to understanding American democracy in the 1800s as well as offer insights that are still relevant. The key to American democracy, Tocqueville claimed, was the ability of citizens to create associations of many kinds, including trade organizations and civic groups, or to gather in town-hall meetings. He concluded:

> In no country in the world has the principle of association been more successfully used or applied to a greater multitude of objects than in America. Besides the permanent associations which are established by law under the names of townships, cities, and counties, a vast number of others are formed and maintained by the agency of private individuals. (198)

In this passage, we find a number of sociological insights. First, Tocqueville offers an understanding that association in a social sense has different levels. Not only is association understood as a function of individuals taking initiative (agency) to form private groups but association also has a broader social characteristic, as individuals are organized into townships and cities. Second, he suggests that association has been paramount to the functioning of social order and the advancement of the common good. This is viewed as an essential principle of social life guaranteed in the Constitution of the United States. This associational nature of the early American republic reflects the pluralist argument that power is found in organizing. Tocqueville also advanced the basic pluralist assumption that social groupings constitute power centers in society to accomplish civic outcomes.

A century later, social scientists began to rigorously test the assumptions of the pluralist view of power in the United States. In a classic study of politics in the city of New Haven, Connecticut, Robert Dahl (1961) found that groups and coalitions in the city would compete for victory in elections for city office, or coalitions would be formed to address city issues of concern. Community life, Dahl would suggest, was indicative of the nature of power in the United States. He found that while the citizens of the community participated in elections to select city leaders, the business of governing was dispersed into sectors reflecting economic, social, and political interests. Each sector in the community was made up of groups and associations with the requisite resources (e.g., wealth or prestige) to influence decision-making processes. Dahl reported an image of a division of labor in governance whereby power was dispersed among interest centers within the community. There was no concentration of power per se, assured by a process characterized by negotiation and exchange of "this for that" in order to make decisions that affected the larger community. New Haven was essentially a mirror of the larger social pattern that Dahl and other pluralists believed best described American democracy in the 1950s and 1960s.

Following Dahl, various research projects (Hunter 1953; Polsby 1963) advanced knowledge about power at the local level and were key tests of basic pluralist assumptions. Studies of New York City (Sayre and Kaufman 1960) and Chicago (Banfield 1961) and Miller's (1970) cross-cultural study of Seattle, Bristol (England), Cordoba (Argentina), and Lima (Peru) confirmed a pattern of shared power across groups rather than concentrations of power. The studies of power in the 1960s came to be known as the community power studies. The pluralist conceptualization of power was supported by these early studies of local politics.

However in the 1970s, the focus would shift as the social upheaval of the 1960s prompted political sociologists to examine social movements, collective behavior, and eventually the state. The idea that power was dispersed across groups and sectors would be tested amidst a social backdrop of social conflict and change. Pluralist assumptions were challenged as segments of society asked whether power in society was truly equal and whether individual citizens, as well as those organized into interest groups and associations, could exercise power to achieve policy outcomes. Women, youth, and racial and ethnic minorities organized collective protests to demonstrate that power was not equal. But as pluralists would acknowledge, as a result of protest and collective action, the system of governance responded and accommodated change. For example, the civil rights movement in the 1950s and 1960s resulted in changes in election laws and employment laws, and in 1972, the voting age was lowered to 18 as a result of protest. The revolution was seen as a response to demands of organized citizens. Traditional pluralists would claim that the governance in the United States demonstrated its responsiveness to organized coalitions and collective efforts to change.

In the 1990s, explorations of pluralism took different directions. The focus shifted to what some argued was the disappearance of engagement in collective political action found in the 1960s and 1970s. This suggests a paradox that pluralists could not explain. In a discussion of "civic engagement," Skocpol and Fiorina (1999) observed that:

> Even as more voices speak up on behalf of social rights and broad concepts of the public interest, millions of Americans seem to be drawing back from involvements with community affairs and politics. Most prominently, voting rates have dropped about 25 percent since the 1960s. Moreover, the proportion of Americans who tell pollsters that they "trust the federal government to do what is right" has plummeted from three-quarters in the early 1960s to less than a third at the turn of the twenty-first century. American civil society may also be weakening. (2)

The decline of civil society struck a theme in pluralist research and was connected to the weakening of social ties that Tocqueville celebrated as a strength of American democracy. Researchers turned to explaining how citizens build trust and social solidarity through a variety of associations and social connections. Research on what came to be called *social capital* suggests that individuals who are more connected in groups and associations (e.g., PTA, soccer club, and Rotary) are more likely to participate in politics (Coleman 1990; Putnam 2000). Membership in social groups, according to this pluralist line of analysis, fosters a sense of the collective, which, Durkheim argued a century earlier, contributes to the ability of the community to solve problems in cooperative, collaborative ways. This sense of civil connection is an important claim in the pluralist approach.

CRITICISMS OF PLURALIST THEORY   The pluralist explanation of power and politics in society is not without criticism. The pluralist framework has in many ways stood as the baseline for counterargument and paradox in political sociology. Much of this has to do with the fact that pluralism in many ways aligns best with the assumptions of a U.S. democratic society. There are a number of ways this framework is weak in accounting for the social bases of power in society, in some cases failing altogether to explain some phenomena. A number of weaknesses in the pluralist model of power have been identified:

1. Much of the research that had gone into building the pluralist framework was based on U.S. democratic society; few tests of the pluralist model in a global context exist (Marger 1987).
2. The emphasis on groups assumes that individuals participate in political processes as a result of their group memberships. This assumes that individuals in the social system have equal access to political groups and associations across the horizon of state and public spheres. Some research indicates that this is not the case (Skocpol and Fiorina 1999).

3. There is also evidence that individuals who join politicized groups and associations tend to come from high-status segments of the population. This is also true for individuals who participate through voting. Thus, pluralism cannot account for significant differences in associational and political activity based on wealth, gender, or race.

4. These social cleavages in turn can create polarization and not a consensus of values as pluralism maintains. In many ways, the winner-take-all election rules exclude those who lose in the political game: typically those with fewer resources (Piven and Cloward 1988).

5. As will be seen in the following section, some argue that bureaucracy trumps democracy (Alford and Friedland 1985). In other words, the reality of politics is such that experts, bureaucrats, and policy professionals influence the state more so than the masses who typically participate on a cyclical (elections every two or four years) or periodic basis.

Elite/Managerial

The elite perspective in political sociology stands in stark contrast to the pluralist perspective. The focus here is on the concentration of power in society in the hands of few who are distinguished by shared background characteristics such as expertise, personality, social ties, or membership in select strata of society (Figure 1.2). The elite perspective explains the concentration of power in society by focusing on social groups, organizations, bureaucracies, and elite circles of interaction. It is the elite power center that controls the distribution of resources in society through its various structures and complex organizations.

The elite perspective thus places significant emphasis on how the concentrated power centers of society control the state and its governing apparatus. Studies of the state based on the elite framework focus on the bureaucracy in particular. Much of this emphasis is founded on Weber's classic argument that postindustrial life would rely on complex organizations and rationalization processes to manage social order. The ways in which a social elite controls these complex organizations and ultimately uses bureaucracies to exercise power are a principal focus of traditional elite approaches in political sociology.

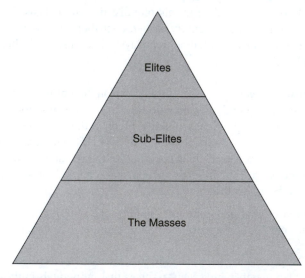

FIGURE 1.2   The Elite/Managerial Metaphor of Power: Dominance at Top

Source: Figure created by Tim Buzzell

CLASSICAL AND CONTEMPORARY ELITE/MANAGERIAL APPROACHES   The elite-managerial perspective has its first detailed articulations in the works of four European scholars heavily influenced by their observations and experiences of the Industrial Revolution: Max Weber, Vilfredo Pareto, Gaetano Mosca, and Robert Michels. While each described society as made up of the ruling elite and the ruled masses, they contributed very different observations about the characteristics of elite rule.

The contributions of Weber to the elite-managerial framework are perhaps the most significant. His writing served as the foundation for a great deal of work not only in political sociology but also in sociology more generally. Briefly, his work on the nature of bureaucracies in the creation of a truly "managerial" elite, the nature of leadership within these complex organizations, and the exercise of power in society are three important concepts he contributed to the elite framework in political sociology. Because Weber demonstrated how bureaucracy emerged as a part of the modern state to manage the complexities of industrial society, we will address the state more fully in Chapter 2. Suffice it to say here that Weber's central contribution to the elite-managerial framework in political sociology is that complex organizations and bureaucracies are at the heart of elite rule in society. These are the instruments of power, especially in industrial and postindustrial societies. In other words, Weber teaches us that bureaucracies are social systems that harness the resources in society—financial, technocratic, and legal—over long periods of time. The result is a concentration of power in upper social strata.

Pareto (1935) described emerging Italian society, and European society for that matter, as made up of elites and masses. At the pinnacle of social interaction, with control of key organizations—military, educational, financial—was an elite that emerged as a result of achievement or placement in key social positions of power. Pareto argued that elites exercised power through "force and fraud." He described the elite strata of society through analogy—that of lions (those who use force) and foxes (those who rule by fraud). Power was realized through the exercise of force or through cunning. Moreover, Pareto found that individuals could move or circulate from the governing to the nongoverning elite or they could move out of the elite and be replaced by members of the non-elte. This suggests a dynamic within the elite structure dictated by connections among lions and foxes in the ruling elite.

Mosca (1962[1915]) also, in observing Italian and European societies during the Industrial Revolution, described the elite as made up of its own layers of membership circles, with control of the pinnacles of power based on struggle between the various substrata of the elites. He suggested that while power was concentrated in the top positions of rule in society, there was a group of civil servants, bureaucrats, and military operatives all retaining a certain expertise that shapes understandings of social problems, political issues, and the interests, on occasion, of the masses. Mosca argued that the elite structure in society is made up of layers and that each layer contributes to periodic ebbs and flows in the exercise of power, rather than viewing elite rule as a matter of personality or achievement as suggested by Pareto. Shifts in the ability to exercise power are based on social conditions, the nature of organizational structure, and at times, the abilities of leaders within the elite structure.

Michels (1915) offered a fourth variant in the early conceptualization of the elite framework. His contribution comes from his rather famous observation still relevant to the study of why organizations and groups emerge within the elite: *oligarchy*. We refer to his "iron law of oligarchy" to describe the fact that a few typically tend to run organizations and groups. He draws upon the sociological notion of a division of labor to explain why this occurs. Simply stated, elite rule is reinforced by the fact that experts and specialists are rewarded in advanced industrial societies as legitimate leaders in a group or an organization. These are the individuals the masses defer to because the masses have little interest in the complexities of state leadership, policy creation, or more generally stated, solving the problems of society. This elite formation assured that power was concentrated in the hands of a few, predisposed toward preserving power in the oligarchy, and resistant to changing over to rule by others within the elite.

From these important foundations in the work of the elite-managerial perspective emerge a variety of contemporary applications. The work of C. Wright Mills was influential in building insights into the nature of elite rule in the United States, the largest democracy in the world. Mills (1956) coined the term *power elite* to describe the upper strata where top politicians, top military leaders, and corporate executive interacted to exercise power over the government, military, and corporate institutions of society. What Mills revealed in his study of the power elite of 1950s was that America was governed by a cohesive body of rulers, who were at times able to trade positions (e.g., military leaders who became politicians or corporate leaders from wealthy families who became politicians) to create a power center in the United States. This research challenged the metaphors of power found in the community power studies by Dahl, Polsby, and others.

The study of elites in the United States today focuses on the connections between concentrations of wealth, military power, or political power at the top, and various aspects of political life. Mintz (2002) concludes that research on two aspects of elite rule—corporate elites and upper-class elites—shows how power is indeed exercised by a few. Her summary of research looks at the network or organizational approach to the study of elites and shows how these concentrations of networks within the upper strata exercise significant power. Evidence suggests that elites have power through financing of electoral campaigns, participation in policy groups or think tanks, and the creation of interest groups to lobby policy-making bodies. Studies of elite power have been dedicated to understanding how these networked concentrations of membership work and to mapping the extent to which elites exercise influence throughout the civil sphere (e.g., media, political associations, education, and religion). Higley and Burton (2006) show how elite patterns of rule have emerged alongside global patterns of political change. They argue that within democracies around the world, elite power has emerged as a dominant force of rule:

> Elite theory holds that those who have serious and sustained effects on political outcomes are practically always few in number, are fairly well situated in society, and are mainly individuals who see some clear personal advantage in political action, despite its risks. These individuals and the tiny groups they form—elites—mobilize large numbers of people into more or less reliable blocs of supporters for various measures and causes. *In this respect, all politics, whether autocratic or democratic, are elitist in character.* (202; emphasis added)

This conceptualization of regimes throughout the world is a good example of how the elite framework continues to be a dominant model in describing, explaining, and predicting political outcomes in society.

CRITICISMS OF THE ELITE/MANAGERIAL THEORY   This framework has not fully explained all aspects of the society–politics relationship. Marger (1987) identified three major criticisms of the elite-managerial argument:

1. It is ambiguous as to whether or not elites are in fact cohesive enough to rule as a single unity. There is evidence that members in the elite circulate among positions and offices, much like Michels suggested. Thus, with membership in the elite changing, can we pinpoint a group with leadership that sets the agenda for power and governance? Moreover, as

we will see from the research by Domhoff (2010), it is unclear if the elite is a ruling segment of society or in fact a social class.

2. Another argument especially relevant for the United States is that masses still have some power to challenge elites, especially given the diversity of both. One line of research that raises questions about the ability of the masses to participate is the role the Internet plays in dissemination of political information through Web sites or political blogs. Are these controlled by the elite or is this an example of how elite rule is challenged through the adaptation of Internet technology for the expression of political interests by the masses? This implies too that the masses may include a new layer of technologically savvy, regulation- and law-focused experts who hold a higher-participatory position in the upper end of the triangle where the masses have traditionally been relegated. For instance, Figure 1.2 suggests that a subelite made up of experts, technocrats, and lawyers serves elite rule by working with the masses.

3. Related to this idea is that the old elite–masses model is too simple and it may not be dichotomous; is there room here for other layers? As the masses have become more educated since the Industrial Revolution, and as the middle class has grown to include financial assets that correlate with participation, additional layers of power may be found just below the elites, further distinguishing the masses into strata not previously identified by the research.

Social Class and Politics

The class perspective in political sociology, to some extent, is consistent with the elite framework, arguing that power is concentrated in the hands of a few. But the class framework suggests that the basis for the concentration of power is not necessarily based on characteristics of individuals who hold power. Rather, the traditional class argument suggests that *economic interests* are the basis for power in society. More directly, the class perspective studies how control of capital, labor, markets, and raw materials is maintained by the capitalist classes. This framework is based on Marxist theories, that power rests in the classes that control the means of production.

The class approach would thus consider politics and associated structures as "captured" by the capitalist class. The governing apparatus, the bureaucracy, political parties, and methods of selecting individuals for political office are shrouded in class interests. Variations on this basic argument are numerous and will be discussed throughout this textbook. At this point, remember that the class framework, much like Marx suggested, which originally sees the state as a social structure that grows out of economic interests in society, ultimately serves the interests of those who control the means of production. Thus, the state plays a key role in the distribution of resources in society, usually to advance economic demands of the owners of capital, or to placate the periodic uprisings of laborers.

CLASSICAL AND CONTEMPORARY CLASS APPROACHES   The essence of Marx is best summarized by a key statement in his work, *A Contribution to the Critique of Political Economy* (1970[1859]):

> In the social production which men carry on they enter into definite relations that are indispensable and independent of their will; these relations of production correspond to a definite stage of development of their material powers of production. The totality of these relations of production constitutes the economic structure of society—the real foundation, on which legal and political superstructures arise and to which definite forms of social consciousness correspond. The mode of production of material

life determines the general character of the social, political and spiritual processes of life. It is not the consciousness of men that determines their being, but, on the contrary, their social being determines their consciousness. (Bottomore 1973: 51)

These dynamics stand in contrast to societies organized around the principles of feudalism or slavery. Marx's historical analysis was an important advance in developing an empirical theory of power in societies as they stood during that period in history known as the Industrial Revolution. This historical analysis was comparative (capitalism compared to feudalism), and Marx pinpointed the paradoxes of what was at the time thought to be advances in the democratic experience. For Marx, power in capitalist society was to be understood as broad social forces and social structures created through the relations of production, the economic structure of society, and the superstructures.

Marx refers to the *relations of production* in a society as the day-to-day interactions between individuals along several dimensions. This concept rests on the notion that such day-to-day interactions are based on materialism, or on the basic needs of human life. The *relations of production* refer to the relationships between workers and their products and workers and submission to authority, and how facets of production are owned and distributed in a society. The modes of production are the technologies used in production such as coal, crops, steam engines, or farmland. Marx argued that the relations and modes of production constitute the "substructure" of a society, which contributes to social conflict.

The "superstructures" are those institutions arising out of the substructures. Once these superstructures evolve, they work to maintain the oppression of the working class. In other words, political organizations, ideology, religion, and other superstructures contribute to the dominance-characterizing relations of production. The superstructures generate the necessary conditions to assure that the working class is subservient to the owners of capital through control over the means of production, influencing the relationships among workers and dominating workers, and through the ownership and distribution of labor-based outcomes (material goods) distributed in a society for profit. The extent of this dominance is significant. Based on the concept of materialism, Marx and Engels wrote:

> The production of ideas, conceptions of consciousness, is at first directly interwoven with the material activity and the material intercourse of men, the real language of life . . . The class which has the means of material production at its disposal has control at the same time over the means of mental production, so that thereby, generally speaking, the ideas of those who lack the means of mental production are subject to it. (Marx and Engels, in Collins 1994: 4–5)

This dominance based on materialism and ideology, Marx concluded, was characteristic of the nature of power in advanced capitalist societies. This dynamic is the key variable in exploring how economic structures dictate the conscience of members of society.

The struggle between the classes in a capitalist society occurs as a result of the inequality in the ownership of scarce resources and the means of production. The bourgeoisie, through private ownership, controls these resources, as well as the means of production. The result of the capitalist superstructures is the exploitation of the labor sold by the proletariat in exchange for what amounts to a minimal wage. The profits taken by the capitalists are the surplus value of those goods produced by the exploited workers. The superstructures that develop as a result of this aspect of capitalist society serve to maintain control by the bourgeoisie. Such dominance continues until, according to Marx, the proletariat is enlightened and asserts its interests, thus overthrowing the dominant class through revolution. The conflicting interests of these two classes are the focus of Marxist notions of inequality. This conflict emerges from the materialist tendencies of humans; thus, Marx asserts that all social action is determined by economic structures and not by the consciousness of man.

According to the basic class argument, the essential characteristic of all social relationships in society is conflict. Simply stated, as substructures change, new superstructures emerge, and as superstructures are destroyed, new relationships between substructures are developed. This cyclical characteristic is how Marx accounts for patterns of social change. More specifically, he argues that the conflict inherent in a capitalist society occurs between classes. This moving force of history, which arises out of industrial production as owned by the bourgeoisie and produced by the labor of the proletariat, is the essence of Marx's concept of class conflict and the resulting political patterns.

Weber made a number of significant contributions to the study of power and society that built on the works of Karl Marx. As mentioned earlier, Weber developed a typology of power, descriptions of bureaucracy and the state, and, for the class perspective, a political sociology based on the interactions between what he called "class, status, and parties." He argued that classes were "clearly the product of economic interests" (Runciman 1978: 45). The term *class* is appropriately used when: "(i) a large number of men have in common a specific causal factor influencing their chances in life, insofar as (ii) this factor has to do only with the possession of economic goods and the interests involved in earning a living, and furthermore (iii) in the conditions of the market and conditions of labour" (Runciman 1978: 44). Throughout his analysis of classes, Weber, like Marx, demonstrates how the control of property or other economic interests is the basis for social associations of interests. He suggests that these associations contribute to the emergence of a phenomenon described by Marx as "class consciousness."

The term *status* is defined by Weber as a distinct phenomenon and, for the most part, unrelated to class. Status "means a position of positive or negative privilege in social esteem which in the typical case is effectively claimed on the basis of (a) style of life, (b) formal education, whether based on empirical or rational instruction, together with the corresponding forms of life, and (c) the prestige of birth or occupation" (Runciman 1978: 60). Status can transcend economic conditions, and thus, power in a status position may flow from prestige, occupation, or expertise. However, as Weber demonstrates, each of these elements is often related to economic conditions. As he notes, class is often associated with the relations of production while status can be associated with the principles of consumption.

The concept of "parties" was used by Weber to describe power relationships within society. He observed that class is based on economic order, status is based on social order, and parties are concerned with social power. The purpose of parties is to influence communal action by forming associations around a common interest. In this sense, party differs from class and status in that it is intentionally established to exert power over the apparatus of state or economic order. The party has an objective plan of action with specific goals to be achieved. Implementing this plan requires that members of the party be placed in positions of control and influence in a bureaucracy.

Weber's analysis of class is agreeable with Marx's notions of class in that both find economic forces dictating the emergence of certain associations within society. The notion of status provides clarification of how workers may be detached from the outcomes of production as well as how consumption patterns in a society contribute to differentiation between the bourgeoisie and proletariat. Finally, Weber's use of the concept of party suggests how those who dominate the structures of a society control it. This notion is similar to Marx's argument that those who control society are those members exercising power over the forces of production. In these and other ways, Marx clearly influenced the analysis offered by Weber.

From the foundations of Marx and Weber, the class perspective in the study of politics and society has taken divergent paths. In some ways, the class perspective has fragmented into so many different directions that it is difficult to claim that the framework offers a unified conceptualization of power. We include Weber in our discussion of the class perspective (he serves as a foundational thinker in the elite framework too) because his approach to politics included, much like Marx, an emphasis on the role of power differences and how these differences affected individuals, groups, classes, and the status structures of society. At least three distinct approaches to the study of politics have emerged from the Marx–Weber traditions. This collection of approaches in the class tradition suggests that the framework is composed of many different versions of the original teachings, including class conflict and political structures, the nature of class consciousness and views of power, and the effects of inequality for different groups in society. The latter reveals how power in society is used to exclude persons from politics.

CLASS, POLITICS, AND STRUCTURALISM   The first track of inquiry in the class tradition has emphasized how the class conflicts described by Marx and Weber are the social roots of political structures, including a state controlled by ruling-class interests. These "structuralists" place an emphasis on understanding how the state itself, political groups, and policy outcomes represent ruling-class interests. The basic assertion by structuralism is that the ruling class protects and preserves its position by dominating less powerful interests in society. The state is a superstructure that is created in capitalist societies in order to use law and policy to advance the interests of the capitalist class.

In an ongoing research focus on social class and politics, Domhoff (1967, 1970, 1978, 1996, 2010) has elaborated on earlier findings to describe in great detail a "ruling class" in the United States. By studying power as who benefits, who governs, and who wins, Domhoff provides evidence of what he calls a "class-domination theory of power" (2002: 181). Consistent with the class perspective, Domhoff traces power to those holding dominant positions in corporations and economic institutions. The ruling class in turn creates a unified effort to capture positions of political, cultural, and economic power in the United States. The upper class benefits as it controls the state to assure protection of economic and cultural interests.

CLASS AND POLITICAL CONSCIOUSNESS   The second line of work in the class framework has examined how, as Marx observed, consciousness is changed by class dynamics. Here the emphasis has been on describing the nature of distractions from the pursuit of self-interest. Recall that Marx believed that once workers understood the nature and extent of their exploitation, they would rise up in revolution. Historically this has not played out as Marx predicted. One explanation for this is that the consciousness-changing power of advanced capitalism continues to blind the working class from exerting power in society.

Much of the work in political consciousness stems from the assertion by Marx and Engels in *The German Ideology* (1947[1886]) that "The ideas of the ruling class are in every epoch the ruling ideas . . . its ruling intellectual force" (39). Political sociology in the class tradition has described this societal capture of ruling ideas as "hegemony." Antonio Gramsci advanced this notion as a world outlook that workers incorporate into their own thinking much to their disadvantage. Hegemonic power is based on ruling class culture, ideology, law, and everyday practices (routines). Carnoy (1984) defines hegemony as follows:

> Hegemony involves the successful attempts of the dominant class to use its political, moral, and intellectual leadership to establish its view of the world as all-inclusive and universal, and to shape the interests and needs of the subordinate groups. (70)

A modern extension of this apparatus is the media, which are corporate entities. Modern campaigns are geared toward the manipulation of candidate images and themes, and thus, candidates from the ruling class use the media to advance world views consistent with ruling-class ideas rather than working-class needs. For example, Mantsios (1995) argues that the media help to hide a basic understanding of the class structure in the United States, noting that since 1972, on average, 80 percent of the respondents in the General Social Survey identify themselves as members of the middle class. Images or language in society that places a greater value on being a part of the great American middle class—even though the gaps in wealth are significant—is an example of hegemonic thinking about class distinctions in the United States.

THE CRITICAL CLASS THEORISTS AND POWER IN SOCIETY   Thirdly, the work of Marx has given rise to an emphasis on understanding the significance of using power to exclude persons from power. Here we can look at political sociologists who study the role of gender, race and ethnicity, and sexual orientation, or the nature of citizenship in the modern political era as sources of social difference used to exclude some from holding power in various social contexts. Research on feminism, racism, citizenship, and the nature of upper-class dominance and power in society can be considered extensions of what came to be known as "critical class theory." The focus of this tradition has been on challenging power centers in society and utilizing knowledge of class inequalities to expose the hidden divisions of power. Early critical theory was associated with the work of scholars at the Institute for Social Research in Frankfurt, Germany, in the early 1920s. These scholars would conceptualize power differently from traditional Marxist notions, emphasizing instead the nature of human relationships in language, cultural symbols, ways of life, and daily interactions. The Frankfurt School developed a program of study that endeavored to expose how power was used to create social inequalities, social differences, and paths of exclusion.

T. H. Marshall (1950) explored how modern political life was changing the nature of citizenship. In his work on citizenship and social class, he argued that the evolution of capitalism changed the definitions of citizenship. He conceptualized citizenship as legal and political rights that would grow out of class and economic interests reflective of their historical era. The eighteenth-century rights were focused on individual freedoms (e.g., free speech). Debates over these rights changed with the Industrial Revolution to political rights, characterized mostly by voting (e.g., the suffrage movement in the United States). In the twentieth century, citizenship was framed in economic terms as rights related to social welfare and economic security. The significance of Marshall's work is that he cast citizenship—a political sociological concept—in terms of social evolution, following a historical progression that in each era revealed that certain groups in the society were excluded from citizenship. Questions of citizenship and social inequality remain an important part of the agenda in political sociology (Kivisto and Faist 2007; Turner 1993).

A great deal of work in political sociology has been done using the feminist perspective on the nature of power in society. In their recent global analysis of women holding positions of power, Paxton and Hughes (2007) concluded that "Although women have made remarkable inroads into both higher education and traditionally male occupations, the political sphere remains an arena where women have far to go" (3). Their research shows that despite progress in increasing the presence of women in political authority structures, this increase has only marginally affected power differentials. For example, in their study of 185 countries, 36 percent of the nations have women holding 10 percent of the seats in the national parliamentary body—this is the highest proportion of female representation. While representation brings voice to feminist concerns, for most parliamentary systems 10 percent is insufficient to exercise broader power in the political process.

The politics of race also holds a significant place in the study of power differences in society. Omi and Winant (1994), for example, trace the role of the state in changing the nature of how race is contested in the civil sphere. They argue that the civil rights movement of the 1960s offered one way that society conceptualized race (political rights). After the 1960s and 1970s, race was conceptualized as policies of equal employment, or job discrimination (economic rights), which Omi and Winant suggest continued ruling-class (white capitalist) dominance in economic spheres. Political questions of race were transformed from one struggle to another, with power being maintained by the white ruling class.

Criticisms of the Class Perspective

Some have argued that social class is a dead concept in political sociology, and more generally in sociology. This is a major criticism of the basic assumptions of the class perspective. In summarizing the weaknesses, Marger (1987) suggests that the class approach fails in the following ways:

1. One of the strongest cross-currents in the class perspective right now is that the traditional class model does not give attention to influences of key social factors such as sex, age, or issue politics. A recent study of populist politics suggests this pattern. Frank (2004) asks, "What's the Matter with Kansas?" to highlight how voters and political groups are distracted by single issues such as abortion or gay rights, often to the detriment of their own social-class positions. Why would laborers and farmers squelch their own economic interests in the political process to contribute to the success of political coalitions that in the end support policies to their detriment?

2. Politics are not simply influenced by economics, and can be shaped by other aspects of social change and social life. Religion, for example, has had significant influence in political change, in some cases revolution, and this appears to be a global phenomenon. Much like Weber observed about status, the role of technology and expertise can create what Derber, Schwartz, and Magrass (1990) called a "mandarin class" of experts whose power is found in their bureaucratic, legal, and scientific expertise.

3. Groups emerge that cannot be accounted for by the class model, such as a new class or elites of managers who do not necessarily emerge from the modes of production. As Marger (1987: 49) states, the class model is unable to fully explain the pattern that "The few dominate the many regardless of the nature of property relations." From this perspective, elites, rather than upper classes, have power. This criticism highlights the fact that much research in the class tradition fails to distinguish between a ruling elite and a ruling social class.

THE TRADITIONAL FRAMEWORKS TODAY

The three frameworks we know as pluralist, elite-managerial, and the social-class perspectives are at the foundation of the ways in which political sociology has conceptualized power. As theories have been tested through research, addressing unexplained paradoxes and political realities not captured by the metaphor of a particular theory, revisions have been proposed. The struggle in political sociology to explain political processes has created debates among proponents of the frameworks. A good example of the debates created by the three frameworks is found in the 1974 study of power by Lukes. His analysis of politics in society—which he revised in 2005 to elaborate on some of these tensions created by competing models of politics—highlights the differences between pluralist and elite/class approaches. Lukes builds a three-dimensional understanding of politics. The first dimension guides us to see politics as the observable exertion of power with tangible outcomes of decisions. For example, the first dimension would focus on how voters concerned about health care policy choose between Republicans and Democrats. The second dimension of politics would ask the question: How does health care become an issue of concern in an election, and just as important, how do we explain when the issue is ignored during an election by political candidates? The second dimension of politics, according to Lukes, requires us to uncover the less visible role of agenda setters who exert influence over what is on the table for deliberation. Democratic Party leaders may encourage candidates they fund to avoid discussing health care because it is too complex for voters to understand. The third dimension is even more subtle, according to Lukes. The third dimension is invisible, where cultural and hegemonic forces are at work shaping the beliefs and values in society that alter decision outcomes and choices in agenda setting. Health care is never addressed because the upper-middle and upper classes in the United States for the most part enjoy basic health care coverage. The belief that employers can sustain private health care insurance is sustained in a capitalist belief system that perpetuates the argument that government-funded health care is "evil" or "inefficient and wastes money." Often, candidates do not even spell out their arguments against government-funded health care; they just label it "socialized medicine" as if this in and of itself is sufficient to dismiss it as a policy option.

Lukes' purpose with his study of power is to suggest that the first dimension (pluralist) and the second dimension (elite) do not fully explain political outcomes. He points to a persistent question in the study of power: What happens when we think of power as acquiescence or non-decision where outcomes are a function of subjective forces (socially constructed) rather than objective (rational) forces? To extend this criticism of commonplace assumptions about democratic societies in particular, Egan and Chorbajian (2005) identified what they call "vernacular pluralism" (xvii). Much like Lukes pushes us to think beyond tacit assumptions and unchecked beliefs, these authors argue that:

> As long as there are social classes and other social divisions, there will be different and opposing class interests. Vernacular pluralism conceals this and contributes to making people naïve or apathetic and ultimately easier to manipulate and control. In this sense it is dangerous and holds back rather than promotes the strengthening and extension of democracy. (xviii)

As a result of these ongoing paradoxes in current studies of power and politics, political sociology has turned to a number of alternative frameworks to describe the nature of the relationship between society and politics.

Lukes warns that the few who make up the elite may use modern political processes to generate fears, guilt, and/or jealousy within the larger democratic community, and ultimately disrupt doing what is best for the community as a whole. In other words, Lukes explains that power will continue to be concentrated in the hands of a few when the few convince if not dissuade citizens to act in ways that are in fact not in the interests of the community as a whole. This work and others have pushed political sociology to address failures in the pluralist notion of democracy, or the inability of the elite-managerial framework to account for changes in political regimes, to construct new theories of power. Perhaps, this is admittedly an oversimplification. But questions posed by political sociologists have resulted in new directions in conceptualizing power and politics in society, building on the research of the past century.

NEW DIRECTIONS AFTER THE TRADITIONAL FRAMEWORKS

After a comprehensive assessment of the state of political sociology, Janoski, Alford, Hicks, and Schwartz (2005) argued that the debates between proponents of the different frameworks helped to identify yet unexplained patterns in politics and power. In particular, they identified three "challenges" that confronted political sociologists at the beginning of the twenty-first century.

The first challenge is "where to put culture" in the study of politics. Increasingly in the last two decades, sociologists have given more attention to the study of culture. While there are many definitions of culture used, we find that as political sociologists incorporate the study of culture into their work, they focus on topics associated with culture—values, beliefs, customs, traditions, symbols, and knowledge found in society.

The second challenge has to do with other research that more and more embrace the model that individuals and social groups act in rational ways, seeking to maximize benefits in certain outcomes. For political sociologists, this means understanding how groups in society use power to bring greater benefits to the group and its members.

The third challenge focuses on the growing theoretical tradition commonly referred to as *postmodernism* in sociology. While some may argue that this framework has its roots in social critique and the work of Marxist or conflict sociology, postmodernists argue it avoids labels and instead attempts to identify the ways in which power in society is subtly structured by dominant social forces. This framework is associated with the influences of Michel Foucault (1977, 1980), who traced through time the ways by which society maintains differences in power through language, ideas, inherited practices, or social "narratives."

As any field completes its research agenda, it develops theoretical revisions. Contemporary political sociology builds on the successes and failures of past understandings of power in society and has developed a number of new perspectives. Some of these incorporate lessons from the past. For example, there is now a more solid connection between the elite-managerial perspective and some aspects of the social class approach. Domhoff's (2010) work is a good example of how the class framework and elite/managerial framework have been tied together to understand the nature of a ruling elite. We identify four frameworks that are building interesting alternative metaphors for the social bases of power in society: the rational choice approach, studies of political culture, the institutionalist approach, and postmodern sociology.

RATIONAL CHOICE   Rational choice theories begin with the assumption that individuals and groups are moved to action by articulated desires and goals. In this sense, choices made reflect actions that are assumed to reflect the group's efforts to achieve certain goals. Criminologists have applied rational choice theory to explanations for crime by depicting certain criminal acts as a function of motivations and goals of an offender, the likelihood of detection or even arrest, and how these rewards and risks change given certain opportunities for crime (Cohen and Felson 1979; Felson 1987). In simplest terms, an offender might rob a business if he or she thinks that the cash take would be high with low likelihood of being caught. The outcome in this case might yield high dollar rewards with low risk. Rational choice theorists in political sociology suggest similar assessments of the risk–reward–opportunity in the political landscape. Are there potential rewards for an interest group going to the expense of organizing a get-out-the-vote campaign to gain a majority on a city council, or to lobby Congress to change policies that might benefit the group?

Using an economic model of human behavior, rational choice situates the study of power in the incentive-based connections between individuals, groups, and institutions. Participation in politics is assumed to be linked to reward structures. For example, one question addressed by this perspective is, which is more powerful, Congress or bureaucracies? Individuals and advocacy groups lobby government agencies that award grants or set regulations, much in the same way they try to influence members of Congress. Grants and entitlements are incentives for policy outcomes, and the details of how these are given may sometimes thwart congressional intent behind legislation creating the program. Rational choice research would focus on the flow of incentives from these agencies and the creation of groups that behave according to bureaucratic power rather than congressional.

Are interest groups motivated to achieve rewards from the government? Most likely so, and they have organized to see that their interests are in fact recognized in policy outcomes. Are there costs or risks to pushing interest-group agendas? One could say yes, that the risk may be inherent in a game that has limited resources, such as a state budget. What political opportunities arise to see that rewards are maximized and risks or loss minimized? Interestingly, political opportunities for interest groups may emerge when new political majorities gain power in Congress or the state legislature, or when interest groups work together to create coalitions to lobby a bill through Congress (opportunities for action). The old saying "politics makes for strange bed fellows" perhaps captures this idea that when interests are realized, the rational thing to do is align with others to achieve those interests. For example, the American Civil Liberties Union (ACLU) worked with groups from the pornography industry to oppose congressional attempts in the 1990s to regulate pornography on the Internet. The alliance was perhaps an odd combination on the surface, but the shared goal of the ACLU and pornographers was similar enough to create a coalition to support claims to First Amendment rights. On the other side was an even stranger coalition of feminists and religious conservatives opposed to the acceptance of pornography of any kind. The rational choice approach would understand these coalitions as an outcome of rational group behavior designed to bring about success in policy decision making in the policy arena.

Rational choice theories depict much of the political process as a game, with different interests competing in the game, which is constrained by certain rules and, in some situations, laws. Individuals, organizations, and nation-states all are players in an arena where there is competition for scarce resources. Nation-states as rational actors may compete in a foreign policy game over oil. We know that the competition for oil can in fact become intense enough to result in war or armed conflict. A war requires an army of individuals, in some cases paid for a career in the armed services, or in other situations drafted into service by the nation-state. Thus, the risk of life is seen as a willing expenditure on the part of nation-states that go to war to protect or control interests in the Middle East. Rational choice perspectives or game theory would understand the exercise of power by studying the self-interests of actors.

POLITICAL CULTURE   As the study of culture has flourished, so have explorations in the role of culture in the society–politics relationship. When Weber defined culture as a "switchman" on a train track of life directions, he was highlighting just how significant culture is in shaping social interactions, including the nature of political interactions at the individual, group, organizational, and societal levels. At first glance, the study of politics and culture has focused as one may expect on the nature of values, beliefs, knowledge systems, and political symbolism in society. Almond and Verba (1963) describe in their study of civic culture that democratic forms of governance flourish in societies with higher levels of educational achievement. This early argument in the study of political culture brought culture to the study of power.

Interest in the interconnections between culture and politics is organized around a number of themes (Berezin 1997; Jasper 2005). In broadest terms, the study of political culture currently focuses on (1) values and belief systems in society that affect politics; (2) the nature of ritual, symbolism, and the construction of meaning in political systems; and (3) the nature of agency in shaping political culture, which stems from individual understandings of power in society. As will be seen throughout the text, culture now plays an important role in sociological descriptions of power in social and political systems.

When we are introduced to sociology, we typically develop an understanding of culture as a system of norms, values, and beliefs assumed through socialization processes across the life course. The ways in which values and beliefs about power and politics are shaped have been studied in a number of ways. Inglehart (1990, 1997), for example, has found that historical events such as wars, periods of scarcity or wealth, and the experiences of generations throughout history can result in variations in belief systems about lifestyles as well as politics. He suggests that prior to World War II, individuals had a materialist conceptualization of the world as a result of experiencing World War I and the Great Depression. As a result, their political preferences were oriented toward pragmatism. In contrast, he found that the postmaterialists were influenced by periods of sustained economic growth. As a result, political action was understood as a way to achieve rights to protect certain lifestyles. For example, debates about legal recognition of intimate partners (e.g., gay marriage) or regulations about what constitutes a suitable family environment for children (e.g., adoptions by same-sex couples) reflect contemporary lifestyle choices that have become politicized.

Political groups and organizations typically stage rituals and symbolic expressions of meaning attached to political agendas. These rituals may be helpful in communicating throughout society what one group or political party believes is an important theme about the nature of power in society. Current research on far-right-wing political groups focuses on the role of ritual and symbolism in constructing a political agenda that in some cases seeks separation from the U.S. government, or a social reorganization of power based on race, gender, or sexual orientation. For example, sociologists have found that the Ku Klux Klan and neo-Nazi groups have staged rallies and protests to bring attention to their demands for white separatism (Dobratz and Shanks-Meile 1997). The use of staged rituals or rallies on state capitol steps or courthouse lawns, where leaders wear Nazi uniforms and swastikas, is a protest technique that uses Nazi symbolism to bring attention to the political demands of the group as part of what is called "new social movements" (Jenness and Broad 1997). These rituals are found in both the United States and Europe. Political sociologists who study these rallies examine the nature of the protest rituals, or what Tilly (1986) calls "repertoires of contention," that is, techniques or methods of challenging current power arrangements inevitably rooted in the cultural stock of the society.

If values and worldviews shape individual perceptions of power, and ritual and symbolism are further manipulated to project political demands or beliefs, then one is left with questions about what impact these cultural influences have on individual and group political actions. The nature of agency, or the ability of individuals to shape culture, to push back as it were, becomes an important question in the study of political culture. Giddens (1990), for example, has written extensively on the role of state power and authority in the lives of modern citizens. He argues that all individuals retain a "dialectic of control" where even in the most dire situations they can exercise some power against formalized rules or authority. For example, Best (2002) uses this concept to suggest that an individual being imprisoned can exert control against the authority through suicide, through a hunger strike, or by refusing to leave the prison cell. Albeit small, the individual has *agency* in this sense, shaping the influences around him by, at the very least, not complying.

INSTITUTIONALIST   Sociologists define institutions as enduring or lasting patterns of social organization, usually significant in shaping not only individual actions but also larger social outcomes. Similarly, the institutionalist approach in political sociology argues that there are significant enduring, stable, historical patterns related to struggles over power in society. As a result, there are patterned political outcomes. As the name suggests, institutionalists examine what creates these patterns of organized political processes. This theoretical approach follows several paths of analysis (Amenta 2005). At one level, institutionalists rely on the study of *structures*, namely interest groups, unions, organizations, international corporations, and parties, as well as the state and other associated structures typically with a political focus. At another level, institutionalists understand political processes as patterned by political norms, practices, belief systems, and traditions. Thus, political outcomes such as public policy or political move- ments are understood as a combination of organizational influences as well as cultural influ- ences. We believe the institutionalist framework seems especially comprehensive when it is combined with the political culture approach.

The concentric circles in Figure 1.3 depict the relationships suggested by the institutional- ists. The overlaps between the state, interest groups, and culture suggest areas where political sociologists find concurrent influences in politics that in the traditional frameworks were treated as separate concepts. For example, we can think of routines or political phenomena associated with the work of certain groups in society, advocacy organizations, or social institutions (the left circle in Figure 1.3), such as religious organizations. Groups in society may seek limits on be- haviors, and thus policies are created by the state, reflecting demands by the polity for address- ing a particular concern (the top circle in Figure 1.3). Some policies are likely to emerge under certain cultural conditions or as a result of values or attitudinal influences in the legislative body where policy is made (the right circle in Figure 1.3). Institutionalists would hypothesize that a policy, such as banning gay marriage, emerges as a result of the work of advocacy groups around changing definitions of marriage, how groups over time elect legislators that share this view or shape the work of a particular political party, and that groups and legislative leadership on gay marriage prohibition evolve out of a cultural pattern associated with religious, economic, and po- litical conservatism in the polity. The point is that institutionalists attempt to bring these concepts together to explain political outcomes, political structures, and aspects of political culture.

A recent example of research extending the institutionalism framework suggests that a vast global system of organizational networks and groups provides an international cultural context for the creation of policy. Beckfield (2003) finds evidence that policy ideas, such as educational change, regulation of same-sex relationships, laws related to population change and others, can be influenced by "policy scripts" that are dominant in "rich, core, Western societies" (401). He uses the concept of "world polity" as a global cultural backdrop of sorts where tracks about what con- stitutes effective policies in these areas are enacted as a result of international nongovernmental organizations' influences on societies throughout the world. In other words, interest groups

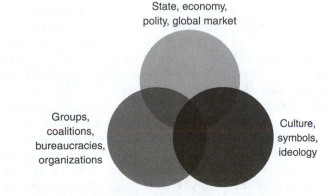

FIGURE 1.3 The Institutionalist's Metaphor of Power

Source: Figure created by Tim Buzzell

working throughout the world will tend to follow similar paths of creating policy regardless of the system of government in a particular country. What institutionalists study is this path of policy creation, such as identify the policy problem, document the problem through the use of experts or research, prepare model legislation, activate aligned interest groups in the society to gain local support, and approach appropriate state actors for policy implementation. This institutionalist approach demonstrates that culture, policy ideas, organizational actions, and policy outcomes blend together to reveal the institutionalist model in explaining global politics. Studies using this framework will be reviewed in our discussions of the state, political organizations, and policy.

POSTMODERN POLITICAL SOCIOLOGY   A distinct alternative path in the study of the relationship between society and politics is that represented by the influences of what we call here postmodernism. Rooted in the philosophical and empirical challenges to sociology as science in the 1960s and 1970s, the postmodern turn in political sociology has generated a unique perspective on the study of power.

Because postmodern thought takes many different forms, it is difficult to summarize its central argument. There are several themes running through this body of work. We highlight what postmodernism has to say about the nature and study of power. The first theme found in this work is that power must be understood in the subtle, hidden aspects of everyday life. For example, research on what is referred to as the *surveillance state* (Marx 2004; Staples 2000) documents how power has shifted to those who control forms of watching the behaviors of others, such as cameras on ATMs or cameras installed on street corners and traffic signals (see Textbox 1.3). The nature of being watched shifts power over the body, movement, and privacy to other authorities. The second theme in this work emphasizes that power will no longer be understood merely as a function of social structures per se. The emphasis shifts from the study of the state or social groups to the construction of individual identities in the face of social resistance. Here language becomes important. Power is found in the discourse about human sexuality, for example, and in the nature of making others less powerful by enacting historical scripts about homosexuality or sexual expression in general. The third theme found in this work emphasizes power in a global context. The nature of communication and social interaction in a postmodern era is such that human connections take electronic forms and transcend geographical and time boundaries. In this regard, power is exercised in the command of information or technologies to shape global awareness about groups. We will explore these themes throughout the text, finding that the postmodern turn in political sociology casts a very different light on understanding the nature of power.

One of the key figures in this perspective is French scholar Michel Foucault who wrote extensively on the nature of power. His insights are intriguing. In fact, he might be critical of our attempts to define power as we did at the onset of this chapter; he suggests that power "can be identified better by what it does than what it is" (quoted in Fiske 1993: 11). In this sense, power is a part of everything social, and the social consequences of power relations are, according to postmodernists, to be exposed and revealed. Postmodern analysts trace the nature of societal power throughout history, finding that many consequences of power relationships are subtle and hidden. Such was Foucault's (1977) study of discipline and punishment in society, which demonstrated how, through time, the exercise of state authority to punish through public executions in the town square was transformed by the state into controlled, private, nonpublic spaces away from the masses. When the eyes of the masses are unable to see the exercise of punishment, what happens to legitimacy or authority? Foucault argues that it becomes even more dominated by experts such as "corrections officials" or experts cloaked in the traditions of psychiatry. Because punishment was moved by the state from public venues to hidden prison cells, Foucault

TEXTBOX 1.3

Surveillance and Types of Power

As we have seen in this chapter, some sociologists who study power in its various forms at the end of the twentieth century argue that technology has played a significant role in changing the ways power is expressed/exercised in our day-to-day interactions. These sociologists see power as taking the form of *surveillance,* and they suggest that everywhere individuals are watched by different power centers in society.

"Eye" in the pyramid on the one dollar bill

Source: Thinkstock

French philosopher Michel Foucault concluded that science had come to be used in many different ways to control different categories of people. The diffusion of techniques of surveillance benefited significantly from this technology. For example, the science of criminology was eventually used to design "state-of-the-art" prisons that would use forms of "rehabilitation" as well as architectural designs to control individual routines and interactions. Often justified as a form of crime control or security, science to promote surveillance expanded the tools available to armies, law enforcement, school resource officers, deans of students, and parents! Foucault talked of the "gaze" or that knowing we are being watched causes us to reflect on our actions and behaviors. Power systems often use surveillance without our awareness. The state often utilizes surveillance to control citizens. College students are no exception!

Conduct an inventory of your day-to-day interactions and note which aspects of your person are being watched by others. Look for the following:

- cameras mounted on university buildings or in classrooms;
- images and interactions on Facebook, MySpace, or Web pages;

(Continued)

- cameras on street corners or buildings in town;
- ways ATMs monitor transactions;
- ways students are tested for things other than material learned in class (e.g., drinking habits in college and psych-metrics to measure motivation to learn);
- cell phones that record still or moving images;
- geographical positioning systems (GPSs) in cars.

When you start to inventory the various ways a person can be observed, watched, monitored, or tracked, or that someone can know where you are at all times, you are clearly subject to surveillance. But who is watching? What figures of power (authorities and nonauthorities) are monitoring your behaviors?

Warning sign at a metro bus stop

Source: Photo by Lisa K. Waldner

Do you think that being watched is a form of coercive, legitimate, or interdependent power? Is your conclusion based on "who" is watching?

Using Lukes three-dimensional understanding of power, how would you explain the role of surveillance in contemporary society? Does monitoring behavior represent an informed rational willingness by citizens to promote social order? Or does monitoring and tracking of behavior suggest manipulation through fear and increased distrust, mostly as a way to preserve power in the hands of a few? Discuss.

claimed that the philosophy of self-rule through diligent citizen monitors was given up to social control by experts watching the once-diligent citizenry. Clearly, Foucault has offered an important way of understanding power in the modern civil society.

Other contemporaries have taken postmodernist views of politics in similar directions, building on this theme that all things social are political—all things societal are about power. Anthony Giddens (1985), a prominent British sociologist, considers power to be at the heart of relationships between politics and social institutions including family, religion, education, and the economy. One theme that runs throughout much of his work is that the modern state blurs the lines between the state, public, private, and market spheres as we described earlier in this chapter. The exercise of power in this sense is all around us as resources are allocated by social systems (e.g., physical things) or as authoritative resources (e.g., supervision of employees) are allocated by social systems. In this regard, and much like Foucault, Giddens treats power relations as ubiquitous. Political sociology using this approach studies the nature of state control over allocation or exercise of authority in all aspects of life.

These frameworks each reveal different dynamics in society–politics relationships. Pluralist approaches to politics will ask different questions about the nature of power than the elite approaches do. And now we ask, what role does culture play in shaping elite preferences, or class-based expressions of resistance. In this regard, the various frameworks represent continuing debates about politics in society, highlighting a number of questions that will be addressed in the decades ahead. These many metaphors for power are built around resolutions to paradoxes of political and social life. Clearly the work of political sociology is not complete. The chapters that follow explore the many questions being studied today.

CONCLUSION

A conceptual mapping of the various paths in political sociology is helpful for visualizing the analytic territory of this introduction to political sociology. We are in a position to take advantage of research on the social bases of politics over the past hundred years. Coser offered an important conceptual baseline of sorts when he identified the four core topics of political sociology. But our understanding of power in its social context has greatly advanced in just the past fifty years. As a result, we can conceptualize the work of political sociology as that described recently by Hicks, Janoski, and Schwartz (2005):

> The very nature of the field that makes political sociology sociological comes from civil society in the broadest sense—everything about society that is either not the state or whether the state has overlapped into other arenas. (21)

Thus, the study of power takes in a variety of directions, arenas, or spheres of social and political interaction. Power is exercised through the authority and legitimate rule in the state sphere. Power is dynamic and conflictual in the public sphere as social groups compete for attention or control of the state. Power is economic and rational perhaps in the market sphere, where rules of capitalist economies dictate the allocation of resources. And in modern times, the private sphere, the day-to-day social place of interaction among family members, friends, and intimates, also becomes subject to the exercise of power by the state, the market, and the actors in the public sphere. These spheres constitute "civil society" and map the terrain for the study of power in political sociology.

Civil society then presents a stage where paradoxes are played out. These paradoxes emerge perhaps from belief systems that guide actors in the civil society. For example, societal discourse about abortion represents one issue where we find conflict between the private sphere (family, sexual relations), the public sphere (social movements, voluntary associations), and the state (judicial branch, police). Thus, the work of political sociologists is in several domains of the civil society. Researchers may turn their attention to studies of pro-life advocacy associations, the impact of abortion laws on teens and their families, or the ideological backgrounds of members of the judiciary. All of these areas of analysis constitute the focal points for political sociology.

We conclude this chapter by identifying three major themes that continue to characterize the study of power in political sociology. Some of these themes emerge as a result of challenges to our commonsense views of politics in democratic societies, or the tensions and conflicts created locally by global influences:

1. Power is concentrated in democratic societies;
2. Power operates not only in direct but also in indirect ways; and
3. Politics is not just about the state but imbues all social relations.

These themes are important to how much of the research in political sociology is organized. This is not to suggest that all of political sociology is about just three concepts; it's more complex than that to be sure. Rather, we suggest these ideas as we close the first chapter of this textbook and challenge students of political sociology to orient their thoughts to ideas ripe for inquiry. Debates among conceptual frameworks and emerging theories are the focus of this text as we prepare to move into more detailed considerations of the pluralist, elite/managerial, and social-class frameworks, especially considering attempts to synthesize these frameworks into a more unified political sociology, and to consider these frameworks in light of emerging research pushing the field into new vistas of understanding.

Power is concentrated, even in democratic societies. The Enlightenment thinkers like Hobbes, Locke, and Rousseau believed that freethinking rational individuals could engage in self-governance. This was in contrast to the pre-Enlightenment thinking that created a power structure in society based on divine right of the monarch. The experiences of the Industrial Revolution were the focus on sociological attention in what is considered the founding writings of the discipline. Marx brought attention to the ways in which class conflict and the concentrations of wealth created a paradox in Enlightenment hopes of self-governance. How could a parliament of elected citizens self-govern when the representatives in the parliament were owners of property, industry, and capital? Has the Enlightenment philosophy of self-governance met its ideal expression? Or have the struggles over power and the resolution of these struggles favored a few instead of the many?

Power operates in direct and indirect ways. The early studies of power focused on the direct exercise of power usually in the form of capacity for action as described in the previous paragraph. We can all think of obvious examples of direct forms of power—coercion, for example—where force is used to bring about compliance with interests or desires. Weber documented the role of bureaucracies in organizing human action into outcomes that would be legitimated through something as simple as writing things down in a procedures manual. His concept of rationalization would highlight the paradox of constrained will in democratic societies. Rationalization of society, according to Weber, was the transformation from informal exchanges between social groups to interactions and exchanges that more and more were governed (power) by the appeal to procedures and rules. The forces of rationalization including the creation of "more law" to govern an increasingly complex society after the Industrial Revolution would become part of the social mindset. Weber would highlight how deep into social interactions these rules would go, suggesting power is understood in its many subtle, more indirect forms found in the values, beliefs, and customs (culture) of complex societies.

For political sociologists, *power is about more than overt forms of governance* found in political institutions. Early works of political scientists focused on the nature of governmental systems. But these works were criticized for being too systems focused. Consider the work of feminist sociologists in the last forty years. While they focus on the impact of governmental structures on policy outcomes for women, or the fact that women do not hold a majority of the seats in Congress, the work of feminists has also identified the nature of power in all social interactions. Power in the workplace has typically been exercised by men, which has resulted in a "glass ceiling," a discriminatory barrier to women's advancement into key positions of corporate governance. Prior to the 1980s, the idea of "sexual harassment" had no form in law or in describing the nature of sexist language that creates oppressive environments for women and men through language. Identifying barriers, impediments, language, norms, and structures that differentiate people into social groups with power and social groups without power is a key task of political sociology. The field offers a deeper understanding of politics by emphasizing the role of social status and social institutions, in addition to politics, culture, and global influences.

Politics and power are central concerns of sociology and have been since the birth of the discipline. The ways in which power is played out in social networks of all kinds constitute one of the core areas of study. This chapter has shown how Marx, Weber, and Durkheim called our attention to the questions of social order and, how it was maintained through the exercise of power—as manipulated masses, or as moralists following the need for order in the community. The chapter also suggested that the exploration of political sociology assumed a significant place in the discipline of sociology thanks to the work of C. Wright Mills, who, in the 1950s, called our attention to age-old themes in the study of who wins and who loses as essential to the work of sociology. His application of the sociological imagination to power-based relationships in society marked a significant shift in how sociologists would study politics. Throughout the text, we will come to understand the role of the sociological imagination in understanding current debates about the nature of politics in contemporary society.

The tools political sociologists bring to the study of power have offered much insight and understanding about things that sometimes challenge our commonsense beliefs about the nature of politics. As a result of these analytical approaches, political sociology is rich with metaphors that reveal greater insights into the nature of power at many levels of society. Moreover, these tools have been helpful in identifying the nature of social paradoxes related to power. This chapter builds upon these ideas that are intricately part of the sociological imagination found in political sociology. With this brief introduction to power in mind, the chapter has described in more detail the ways in which political sociology has defined power and the typologies (metaphors) constructed to help understand the forms of power studied. The second portion of the chapter presented the three theoretical traditions (metaphors) that have evolved in political sociology. These traditions and others that are now developing tackle head-on the paradoxes that generate the questions and work for the field of political sociology. These theoretical approaches to understanding power are taking new forms as a result of debates and controversies in how power is understood in contemporary society.

References

Alford, Robert and Roger Friedland. 1985. *Powers of Theory: Capitalism, the State and Democracy.* New York: Cambridge University Press.

Almond, Gabriel and Sidney Verba. 1963. *The Civic Culture: Political Attitudes and Democracy in Five Nations.* New Jersey: Princeton University Press.

Amenta, Edwin. 2005. "State-Centered and Political Institutional Theory: Retrospect and Prospect." Pp. 96–114 in *Handbook of Political Sociology*, edited by T. Janoski, R. Alford, A. Hicks, and M. Schwartz. New York: Cambridge University Press.

Arendt, Hannah. 1958. *The Origins of Totalitarianism.* Ohio: World Publishing Company.

Banfield, Edward. 1961. *Political Influence.* New York: Free Press.

Beckfield, Jason. 2003. "Inequality in the World Polity: The Structure of International Organization." *American Sociological Review* 68: 401–424.

Berezin, Mabel. 1997, "Politics and Culture: A Less Fissured Terrain." *Annual Review of Sociology* 23: 361–383.

Best, Shaun. 2002. *Introduction to Politics and Society.* London: Sage Publications.

Blau, Peter. 1964. *Exchange and Power in Social Life.* New York: Wiley.

Bottomore, Tom (editor). 1973. *Karl Marx.* New Jersey: Prentice Hall.

Boulding, Kenneth. 1989. *Three Faces of Power.* California: Sage Publications.

Braungart, Richard. 1981. "Political Sociology: History and Scope." Pp. 1–80 in *Handbook of Political Behavior*, edited by S. Long. New York: Plenum.

Carnoy, Martin. 1984. *The State and Political Theory.* New Jersey: Princeton University Press.

Cohen, Lawrence and Marcus Felson. 1979. "Social Change and Crime Rate Trends: A Routine Activities Approach." *American Sociological Review* 44: 588–608.

Coleman, James. 1990. *Foundations of Social Theory.* Cambridge, MA: Belknap Press of Harvard University Press.

Collins, Randall. 1994. *Four Sociological Traditions.* New York: Oxford University Press.

Coser, Lewis (editor). 1966. *Selected Essays.* New York: Harper & Row Publishers, Inc.

Crow, Graham. 2005. *The Art of Sociological Argument.* London: Palgrave Macmillan.

Dahl, Robert. 1961. *Who Governs? Democracy and Power in an American City.* Connecticut: Yale University Press.

Derber, Charles, William Schwartz, and Yale Magrass. 1990. *Power in the Highest Degree: Professionals and the Rise of a New Mandarin Order.* New York: Oxford University Press.

Dobratz, Betty and Stephanie Shanks-Meile. 1997. *"White Power, White Pride!" The White Separatist Movement in the United States.* New York: Twayne Publishers.

Domhoff, G. William. 1967. *Who Rules America?* New Jersey: Prentice Hall.

_____. 1970. *The Higher Circles.* New York: Random House.

_____. 1978. *The Powers That Be.* New York: Vintage.

_____. 1996. *State Autonomy or Class Dominance: Case Studies on Policymaking in America.* New York: Aldine de Gruyter.

_____. 2010. *Who Rules America? Challenges to Corporate and Class Dominance.* 6th Edition. Boston: McGraw Hill.

Egan, Daniel and Levon Chorbajian. 2005. *Power: A Critical Reader.* New Jersey: Pearson Prentice Hall.

Etzioni, Amitai. 1968. *The Active Society.* New York: Free Press.

Felson, Marcus. 1987. "Routine Activities, Social Controls, Rational Decisions, and Criminal Outcomes." *Criminology* 25: 911–931.

Fiske, John. 1993. *Power Plays, Power Works.* New York: Verso Books.

Foucault, Michel. 1977. *Discipline and Punish: The Birth of the Prison.* New York: Pantheon Books.

_____. 1980. *Power/Knowledge: Selected Interviews and Other Writings, 1972–1977*, edited by Colin Gordon. New York: Pantheon Books.

Frank, Thomas. 2004. *What's the Matter with Kansas: How Conservatives Won the Heart of America.* New York: Henry Holt Publishers.

Giddens, Anthony. 1976. *New Rules of Sociological Method: A Positive Critique of Interpretive Sociologies.* New York: Basic Books.

_____. 1985. *The Nation State and Violence: Volume Two of a Contemporary Critique of Historical Materialism.* Cambridge, England: Polity.

_____. 1990. *The Consequences of Modernity.* Cambridge, England: Polity.

Hicks, Alexander, Thomas Janoski, and Mildred Schwartz. 2005. "Political Sociology in the New Millennium." Pp. 1–30 in *Handbook of Political Sociology*, edited by T. Janoski, R. Alford, A. Hicks, and M. Schwartz. New York: Cambridge University Press.

Higley, John and Michael Burton. 2006. *Elite Foundations of Liberal Democracy.* Lanham, Maryland: Rowman & Littlefield Publishing Group, Inc.

Hindess, Barry. 1996. *Discourses of Power: From Hobbes to Foucault.* Cambridge, MA: Blackwell Publishers, Inc.

Hunter, Floyd. 1953. *Community Power Structure.* Chapel Hill, NC: University of North Carolina Press.

Inglehart, Ronald, 1990. *Culture Shift in Advanced Industrial Societies.* New Jersey: Princeton University Press.

_____. 1997. *Modernization and Post-Modernization: Cultural, Economic, and Political Change in 43 Societies.* New Jersey: Princeton University Press.

Janoski, Thomas, Robert Alford, Alexander Hicks, and Mildred Schwartz. (editors*).* 2005. *Handbook of Political Sociology.* New York: Cambridge University Press.

Jasper, James. 2005. "Culture, Knowledge, Politics." Pp. 115–134 in *Handbook of Political Sociology*, edited by T. Janoski, R. Alford, A. Hicks, and M. Schwartz. New York: Cambridge University Press.

Jenness, Valerie and Kendal Broad. 1997. *Hate Crimes: New Social Movements and the Politics of Violence.* New York: Aldine De Gruyter.

Johnson, Allan. 2006. *Privilege, Power, and Difference.* New York: McGraw-Hill.

Kivisto, Peter and Thomas Faist. 2007. *Citizenship: Discourse, Theory, and Transnational Prospects.* Boston, Massachusetts: Blackwell Publishing.

Knoke, David. 1990. *Political Networks: The Structural Perspective.* New York: Cambridge University Press.

Lukes, Steven. 1974. *Power: A Radical View.* London: Macmillan.

_____. 2005. *Power: A Radical View.* London: Palgrave Macmillan.

Mantsios, Charles. 1995. "Media Magic: Making Class Invisible." Pp. 409–417 in *Race, Class and Gender.* 3rd Edition. edited by Paula Rothenberg. New York: St. Martins.

Marger, Martin. 1987. *Elites and Masses.* Belmont, CA: Wadsworth.

Marshall, T.H. 1950. *Citizenship and Social Class and Other Essays.* Cambridge: Cambridge University Press.

Marx, Gary. 2004. *Windows into the Soul: Surveillance and Society in an Age of High Technology.* Chicago: University of Chicago Press.

Marx, Karl. 1970 [1859]. *A Contribution to the Critique of Political Economy.* New York: International Publishers.

Marx, Karl and Frederick Engels. 1947 [1886]. *The German Ideology.* New York: International Publishers.

Michels, Robert. 1962 [1915]. *Political Parties.* Translated by Eden and Cedar Paul. New York: Free Press.

Miller, Delbert. 1970. *International Community Power Structures: Comparative Studies of Four World Cities.* Bloomington: Indiana University Press.

Mills, C. Wright. 1956. *The Power Elite.* New York: Oxford University Press.

_____. 1959. *The Sociological Imagination.* New York: Oxford University Press.

Mintz, Beth. 2002. "Elites and Politics: The Corporate Elite and the Capitalist Class in the United States." Pp. 53–80 in *Theoretical Directions in Political Sociology for the 21st Century*, volume 11 *Research in Political Sociology*, edited by B. Dobratz, T. Buzzell, and L. K. Waldner. London: Elsevier Science.

Mosca, Gaetano. 1939. *The Ruling Class.* New York: McGraw-Hill.

Olsen, Marvin. 1978. *The Process of Social Organization: Power in Social Systems.* New York: Holt, Rinehart and Winston.

Olsen, Marvin and Martin Marger (editors). 1993. *Power in Modern Societies.* Boulder, Colorado: Westview Press.

Omi, Michael and Howard Winant. 1994. *Racial Formation in the United States from the 1960s to the 1990s.* London: Routledge.

Orum, Anthony. 1989. *Introduction to Political Sociology.* 3rd Edition. New Jersey: Prentice Hall, Inc.

Parenti, Michael. 1978. *Power and the Powerless.* New York: St. Martin's.

Pareto, Vilfredo. 1935. *The Mind and Society: A Treatise on General Sociology.* New York: Dover.

Parsons, Talcott. 1967. *Sociological Theory and Modern Society.* New York: Free Press.

Paxton, Pamela and Melanie Hughes. 2007. *Women, Politics, and Power: A Global Perspective.* Los Angeles, California: Pine Forge Press.

Piven, Frances Fox. 2008. "Can Power from Below Change the World?" *American Sociological Review* 73: 1–14.

Piven, Frances Fox and Richard Cloward. 1988. *Why Americans Don't Vote.* New York: Pantheon Books.

_____. 2005. "Rulemaking, Rulebreaking and Power." Pp. 33–53 in *Handbook of Political Sociology*, edited by T. Janoski, R. Alford, A. Hicks, and M. Schwartz. New York: Cambridge University Press.

Polsby, Nelson, 1963. *Community Power and Political Theory.* New Haven, CT: Yale University Press.

Putnam, Robert. 2000. *Bowling Alone: The Collapse and Revival of American Community.* New York: Simon and Schuster.

Rigney, Daniel. 2001. *The Metaphorical Society: An Invitation to Social Theory.* Boston, MA: Rowman & Littlefield.

Runciman, W.G. (editor). 1978. *Weber: Selections in Translation.* Cambridge: Cambridge University Press.

Russell, Bertrand. 1938. *Power: A New Social Analysis.* London: George Allen and Unwin.

Sayre, Wallace and Herbert Kaufman. 1960. *Governing New York City: Politics in the Metropolis.* New York: Russell Sage Foundation.

Skocpol, Theda and Morris Fiorina (editors). 1999. *Civic Engagement in American Democracy.* Washington, DC: Brookings Institution Press and New York: Russell Sage Foundation.

Staples, William. 2000. *Everyday Surveillance: Vision and Visibility in Post-Modern Life.* Lanham, Maryland: Rowman & Littlefield Publishing Group.

Tilly, Charles. 1986. *The Contentious French.* Cambridge, Massachusetts: Harvard University Press.

Tocqueville, Alexis de. 1945 [1835]. *Democracy in America.* New York: Vintage Books.

Turner, Bryan (editor). 1993. *Citizenship and Social Theory.* Newbury Park, California: Sage Publications.

Weber, Max. 1947. *The Theory of Social and Economic Organization.* Translated by A. Henderson and T. Parsons. Glencoe, IL: The Free Press.

Wrong, Dennis. 1979. *Power: Its Forms, Bases, and Uses.* New York, NY: Harper.

Role of the State

It is undeniable that the state influences many different aspects of our lives (Olsen and Marger 1993) through what Michael Mann (1988, 1993) identifies as infrastructural power, or the ability of the state to penetrate civil society.

> The state can assess and tax our income and wealth at source, without our consent . . . (which states before 1850 were *never* [emphasis Mann's] able to do); it stores and can recall immediately a massive amount of information about all of us; it can enforce its will within the day almost anywhere in its domains; its influence on the economy is enormous; it even directly provides the subsistence of most of us (in state employment, pensions, in family allowances, etc.). The state penetrates everyday life more than did any historical state. Its infrastructural power has increased immensely. (Mann 1993: 315)

Similarly, the state has the power to regulate (Skrentny 2006) the most intimate aspects of our lives including whom we can marry, which sex acts between consenting adults are permissible,[1] and how parents may discipline their children. A functioning state, regardless of type, has the ability to restrict anyone under its jurisdiction. The state is a political institution because it wields power and for that reason is a focus for political sociologists.

Historically, the state has not always been the primary political institution (Bottomore 1979; Tilly 1985) nor is it clear that it will continue to occupy such a central role. This is not to say that political institutions will disappear; to the contrary, the institution that manages political power may be transformed into something very different from the traditional state. Meanwhile, the state and the nation-state are still considered important concepts by political sociologists. The focus of this chapter is, what is the state and how does it differ from a nation; how is the state different from government; what are various state forms; how do different sociological theories view the state; and what does the future hold?

WHAT IS THE MODERN NATION-STATE?

Defining the state is problematic because there are two conceptually different issues involved: What does the state look like and what does the state do or what are the institutional and functional dimensions (Mann 1988)? What we call "the state" is in reality a number of interacting institutions and organizations (Miliband 1993) comprising people occupying defined positions with specific responsibilities. The "modern nation-state" is a group sharing a common history, identity, and culture, with a monopoly on the legitimate use of force linked to a specific territory recognized as sovereign by other nation-states. The modern nation-state, with a centralized structure and elaborate bureaucracy, is a relatively recent human innovation (Bottomore 1979) having been in existence for only about 6,000 years (Berberoglu 1990).

Prior to the rise of the state, authority was determined by kinship relations or religious rituals with no specific group charged with decision-making responsibility (Bottomore 1979). For example, the decision to make war or peace with a neighboring tribe might be made by all the adult members or by only some members, although one person is the undisputed leader. Bureaucracy and rationalization, or the adoption of consistent practice and procedures rather than capricious decision making, are the hallmarks of the modern nation-state. While the concepts of nation and state are linked, there are important distinctions.

Defining the State

Max Weber contends that "a state is a human community that (successfully) claims the *monopoly of the legitimate use of physical force* [emphasis Weber's] within a given territory (Gerth and Mills 1946: 78). The state, then, has the ability to make and enforce laws and is run by those occupying positions in the state bureaucracy (Nagengast 1994). In short, the state has power over the lives of its citizens as well as persons currently residing within its borders.

COMPULSORY   Weber views the state as "a compulsory association with a territorial basis" (Heydebrand 1994: 26). The compulsory nature of the state is clear in that short of revolution, we have no choice but to submit to state authority as long as we physically reside within its borders. For example, a U.S. citizen traveling in Russia cannot refuse to obey Russia's laws because he or she is under Russian jurisdiction.

MONOPOLY   The state has a monopoly on the use of legitimate force within its borders (Runciman 1978). This does not mean that the state *must* use force. State domination is evidenced by the ability to have commands followed without the need to resort to coercion (Skrentny 2006). Recall the earlier metaphor of parent for understanding the state. Parents do not always need to threaten children with a spanking for compliance. Children usually comply because they accept the right of parents to punish even if they do not agree with the punishment.

As described by Michael Mann (1988), there are two types of state power: despotic and infrastructural. *Despotic power* is the use of physical force or coercion administered by the military or police as agents of the state. *Infrastructural power* is a more modern power and refers to the ability of the state to influence and control major spheres of our lives without using physical force. Consistent with a Weberian view of state (Gerth and Mills 1946), Robert Dahl (1963) argues that only the state decides who can use force, under what circumstances, and the type of force that is allowed. The state does not have to use force nor does a monopoly mean that *only* the state can use force, however, only the state decides when force is permissible.

LEGITIMACY   A driver obeys a police officer not only because a police officer carries a gun but also because citizens recognize the *right* of a police officer to make traffic stops on behalf of the state. For Weber, "If the state is to exist the dominated must obey the authority claimed by the powers that be" (Gerth and Mills 1946: 78). However, the force that is being used must be "permitted or prescribed by the regulations of the state" (Runciman 1978: 41). What is defined as permissible varies between nations and, within the United States, between jurisdictions. What is constant across all is that only the state determines legitimacy.

In Texas, one is allowed to use lethal or deadly force to protect one's life and, under some circumstances, property, including that of one's neighbors (Texas Penal Code: http://tlo2.tlc. state.tx.us/statutes/pe.toc.htm). In other jurisdictions, lethal force may be used only to protect one's life and the danger must be imminent. This means that within the United States, someone who kills an intruder may be treated differently depending upon local laws.[2] Weber observed that fathers sometimes physically discipline their children. Their ability to do so is limited by the state. Some modern nation-states severely restrict corporal punishment to prevent child abuse (e.g., Sweden). In the United States, parents cross the line between discipline and abuse when physical punishment leaves a mark such as a bruise or a handprint (Wallace 1999).

Citizens believing that the state has overstepped its boundaries may take action against the state through civil disobedience, protest, or even revolution. Ultimately, it is collective society that delegates legitimacy to the state and this means that it can also be taken away, as was the case with the American Revolution. Grievances must be extreme before groups will take on a more powerful state, yet, antistatist movements are on the rise and weaken not only a specifically targeted state but also all states (Wallerstein 2003).

Emergence of States

Consistent with Weber's view, Tilly defines the state as "relatively centralized, differentiated organizations the officials of which more or less successfully claim control over the chief concentrated means of violence within a population inhabiting a large, contiguous territory" (1985: 172). Where Tilly departs from Weber and others is in his view on state emergence. Rather than taking the Hobbesian view that equates the rise of the state with the need for a social contract, or trading submission to the state for protection, he argues that wars make states and that both war making and state making more closely resemble organized crime as those involved are "coercive and self-seeking entrepreneurs" (1985: 171). Tilly contends that just as a racketeer creates danger and then provides protection for a price, the state protects citizens against threats, both real and imagined, that are the consequences of the state's own activities. Citizens tolerate this because the benefits of other state services (e.g., fire and police protection and public schools) outweigh the costs.

In the past, professional soldiers and tax collectors held the right to use violence on behalf of kings. Kings eventually recognized the threat posed by private armies and roving bands of decommissioned soldiers and acted to consolidate power by disarming private armies and maintaining a standing one under monarch control. This approach was especially useful for keeping internal rivals in check.

Tilly contends that war making and capital accumulation created states because those controlling specific territories needed to extract resources from populations under their control to fund these efforts. Those in power warred to check or overcome their competitors. Capital accumulation through taxation provided a more permanent solution for financing wars than temporary measures such as selling off assets, coercing capitalists, or acquiring capital through conquest.

One of the advantages of Tilly's thesis is that he accounts for the variety in state forms and the different routes to state building (Goldstone 1991). Tilly (1990) identifies two settings in which states emerge: "capital intensive" and "coercive intensive." In the first setting, resources are in the form of money, are controlled by capitalists, and are often concentrated in cities. In the latter setting, resources are in the form of raw materials (e.g., grain and timber) and land. Because settings differ, the ways that states are organized and developed are a function of the setting. In capital-intensive settings, states are smaller, more commercialized, and city centered. Here, trade links are strong, resulting in a weaker state structure as capitalists collaborate with state building. In coercive-intensive settings, large empires tended to develop because with fewer cities, trade links are weaker, necessitating "high-level coercion structures" (Scott 2004: 5 of 10) as states developed without the cooperation of local capitalists.

For Tilly (1985), the activities of war making and other uses of state violence, such as *state making* or neutralizing rivals inside a power holder's base, and protection, or eliminating threats to citizens, are interrelated with and dependent upon extraction (i.e., taxing) or acquiring the resources to carry out the first three activities. Due to the interdependent nature of extraction, war making, and state making, these activities depend on a centralized organization and increasingly large bureaucracy. For example, efficient extraction of resources in the form of taxes necessitates a bureaucratic apparatus (e.g., Internal Revenue Service), which in turn increases state making. External pressure to create states increases as territories organize into states to defend against other global powers.

While Tilly's discussion concerns European states, he notes that decolonized, independent territories (e.g., 1947 partitioning of British India into India and Pakistan) acquired their military from outside. As a result, these states did not go through the process of negotiation between the rulers and the ruled, which expands civil or nonmilitary aspects of the state. Furthermore, these newer states are more dependent on others for arms and expertise. As a result, the military comprises a larger proportion of the newer state apparatus. The recognition of the sovereignty of these states by influential nations such as the United States or Russia provides an incentive for ambitious individuals to use the military to take over the state.

Pakistan has a history of the military subverting the democratic process. General Perez Musharraf's 1999 takeover was preceded by several previous military coups divided by periods of democratically elected governments. While Pakistan currently is a democracy, it remains to be seen whether another military leader will again wrest control and reinstall a more authoritarian state. For states where the military dominates the state apparatus, such as Pakistan, Tilly argues that the analogy between organized crime, state making, and war making is even more accurate.

Goldstone argues that although Tilly's analysis is groundbreaking, his "war-centered framework" (1991: 178) oversimplifies state formation by ignoring other factors that contribute to state making, including ideology and revolution. Goldstone points to the example of England and the role of the Reformation and religious conflict in shaping the state, or the role of nationalism in Italy.

Bruce Porter (1994) contends that the timing and type of war shaped the different paths of state development. The *Continental* path of state building created absolutist states and resulted first in civil war and then international war. A *Constitutional* path of state formation created constitutional monarchies with deliberating bodies but leaner administrative bureaucracies. This path was followed when a state was able to avoid international war but still had to contend with internal pressure and conflict. The *Coalitional* path is the result of states that were able to avoid civil war but were often involved in international conflicts. These states avoided pressure to centralize and tended to build more republican forms of government. Finally, states that experienced both internal and international conflicts, often simultaneously, tended to form *dictatorships*. Although an important contribution, Porter's work is criticized for overemphasizing military determinants of state formation at the expense of other variables (Kestnbaum 1995).

Differentiating Government from the State

The state is not a single entity but a network of organizations. Following the lead of Tilly and Skocpol, Ann Orloff describes the state as "*potentially* [emphasis Orloff's] autonomous sets of coercive, extractive, judicial, and administrative organizations controlling territories and the populations within them" (1993: 9). Because the state is made up of various units with various degrees of autonomy, Bottomore (1979) reminds us that the state is not a unified force. For example, the United States has an independent judiciary where judges make decisions that may conflict with the policies of the executive branch. In the 1930s, the U.S. Supreme Court ruled some of the New Deal programs designed by the Franklin D. Roosevelt administration to combat the Great Depression as unconstitutional. Ralph Miliband (1993) provides a detailed description of the types of organizations that comprise the state. He subdivides the state into the following categories: government, administration, military and police, judiciary, subcentral governments, and legislative or parliamentary bodies.

GOVERNMENT   The state is often confused with government because the latter speaks on behalf of the state (Miliband 1993). Government is "the specific regime in power at any one moment" (Alford and Friedland 1985: 1). In the United States, power switches back and forth between political parties with political appointees occupying important positions of power, yet government is less permanent because the state endures regardless of which party captures the presidency (Olsen and Marger 1993; Stepan 1988).

ADMINISTRATION OR BUREAUCRACY   Administration is the sphere that manages the day-to-day affairs of the state. Political appointees head U.S. departments such as State and Homeland Security, but civil servants remain regardless of which political party is in power. Richard Clarke, a former counterterrorism czar for both former U.S. presidents Bill Clinton and George W. Bush, served seven different presidents in a variety of posts. In light of his claims that the George W. Bush administration did not take his concerns about Al Qaeda seriously (Clarke 2004), he may be an administrator who should have had more influence over U.S. counterterrorism policy. Generally though, administrators are not simply instruments of government, but they take an active role in formulating policy (Miliband 1993). Perhaps this recognition is why some government officials allow political considerations to influence which persons are selected for nonpolitical government appointments. In 2007, hearings over the firing of nine U.S. attorneys revealed that politics influenced hiring decisions at the U.S. Department of Justice, which is a violation of civil service laws. One job candidate was allegedly rejected for a prosecutor job because she was perceived as a lesbian while another received favorable reviews because he was conservative on the three big Gs: God, guns, and gays (Lichtblau 2008).

Miliband asserts that the administrative feature of the state extends far beyond the traditional state bureaucracy and includes public corporations, central banks, regulatory commissions and other bodies "enjoying a greater or lesser degree of autonomy . . . concerned with the management of the economic, social, and cultural and other activities in which the state is now directly or indirectly involved" (1993: 278). Miliband's definition is broader than state bureaucracy but the latter is necessary as a "material expression of the state" and is an outcome of public policy shaped by politics (Oszlak 2005: 483). Furthermore, the state bureaucracy uses a myriad of resources including human, financial, technological, and material to produce programs or services, regulations, and even national symbols (Oszlak 2005). One example is the programs associated with what political sociologists call the welfare state.

MILITARY AND POLICE   Kourvetaris (1997) contends that there is little consensus among political sociologists regarding whether the military and police are considered part of the state system or a separate institution. Given that both act at the behest of the state and are under the authority of a political leader who occupies a government position (e.g., mayor, governor, or president), it seems reasonable to consider both aspects of the state. Miliband agrees, calling police and military forces as the branch concerned with the "management of violence" (1993: 279). Skocpol's (1993) definition of the state also includes the police and military. Finally, Tilly (1975) argues that the repressive features of the state including taxation, policing, and the armed forces were historically essential for the making of a strong state. For an authoritarian or nondemocratic state, the military either controls the state or is in charge of its coercive capabilities (Stepan 1988).

For democracies, there is concern regarding the role of military and intelligence organizations. Nations need a strong defense, but when the military and state security apparatus is not accountable to civilian authorities or when "security organizations . . . attempt to act with secrecy and autonomy, democratic control of policy is severely challenged" (Stepan 1988: ix). While Stepan was writing in the aftermath of the Iran–Contra scandal,[3] the current "war on terror" waged by the United States and its allies against Al Qaeda renews these concerns because of the more controversial aspects of the USA PATRIOT (Uniting and Strengthening America by Providing Appropriate Tools Required to Intercept and Obstruct Terrorism) Act. In the United States, an independent judiciary is a check on other components of the state, but Stepan also advises the development of the capacity within civil society "to speak with knowledge and authority on complex matters of geopolitics, arms, security, and peace" (1988: x). Political sociology is ideally suited to prepare individuals who take seriously Stepan's call to action.

JUDICIARY   Skrentny (2006) argues that the United States is a legal state with political actors using the law and courts to meet political ends. Courts have a substantial impact through policy making regardless of whether jurists are conservative or liberal. Not only is the U.S. judiciary independent from politicians heading the government, but it also acts to protect persons under state control. A recent example is the two U.S. Supreme Court decisions regarding the fate of enemy combatants held at the U.S. Naval base in Guantánamo Bay, Cuba. The Court rejected the position (of the George W. Bush administration) that enemy combatants are beyond the jurisdiction of American courts and allowed detainees the right to challenge their captivity before a federal judge (Gearan 2004; Savage 2008). Sociologists need to pay more attention to the role of both law and the courts in state building and the making of public policy (Skrentny 2006).

TEXTBOX 2.1

Undemocratic Practices of American Democracy

George W. Bush has been criticized by civil libertarians for the detention of enemy combatants outside of the United States as well as for the PATRIOT Act, which allows for warrantless wiretaps and other civil rights infringements. He is hardly the first American president with the cooperation of the U.S. Congress to suspend or impede civil liberties in the name of safety and security. The internment of Japanese citizens ordered by Franklin D. Roosevelt on the advice of the War Department after the attack on Pearl Harbor was considered by the American Civil Liberties Union "the worst single wholesale violation of civil rights of American citizens in our history" (Goodwin 1994). Other examples are described in the following paragraphs.

John Adams: The Alien and Sedition Acts of 1798 were passed during a time of fear of rebellion. The residency period for citizenship was increased from five to fourteen years. The president was granted the right to expel any foreigner deemed "dangerous" although Adams did not expel anyone. The Sedition Act "made any 'false scandalous, or malicious' writing against government, Congress, or the president, or any attempt 'to excite them . . . the hatred of the good people of the United States, or to stir up sedition,' crimes punishable by fine and imprisonment" (McCullough 2001: 505). Historian David McCullough notes that this was clearly a violation of the First Amendment of the Constitution. Several were fined and/or imprisoned including Congressman Matthew Lyon of Vermont.

Abraham Lincoln: Lincoln suspended the writ of habeas corpus, meaning that persons could be held indefinitely without trial. In the beginning, this was restricted to smaller geographical areas but later became nationwide and had a chilling effect on public dissent. Lincoln biographer David Donald writes "Editors feared that they might be locked up in Fort Lafayette or the Old Capital Prison if they voiced their criticisms too freely" (1995: 380). He also writes that Clement Vallandigham, an Ohio peace Democrat, was arrested and imprisoned for the duration of the civil war for giving a speech where he referred to the president as "King Lincoln." Previously, in a speech made in the House of Representatives, he had charged Lincoln with creating "one of the worst despotisms on Earth" (1995: 416).

Dwight D. Eisenhower: George W. Bush is criticized for circumventing the Geneva Convention protocols by classifying captured Taliban fighters and other insurgents from Iraq and Afghanistan as enemy combatants. He is not the first to circumvent the Geneva Convention. In the aftermath of World War II, Eisenhower served as the military governor of the U.S. Occupation Zone. He reclassified German Prisoners of War (POWs) as Disarmed Enemy Forces (DEFs), which allowed ignoring Geneva Convention protections. The advantage of this was the ability to lower the food rations to DEFs (History News Network 2003). In fairness, it should be noted that much of Europe was facing massive food shortages and starvation.

SUBCENTRAL   Miliband's fifth element is defined as "an extension of central government and administration, the latter's antennae or tentacles" (1993: 279). This component not only communicates and administers from the center to the periphery but also functions as the voice of the periphery to the center. Despite centralization, these units are also power centers in and of themselves as they "affect very markedly the lives of the population they have governed" (1993: 280). Miliband does not give specific examples but branch offices of federal agencies fit this category. The FBI, Immigration Customs Enforcement (ICE), and the Department of Justice all have regional offices that not only communicate and administer federal mandates from Washington but also communicate to the same local concerns and issues. These regional offices are examples of "diffusion of control" or having a national presence that is diffused throughout the country (Oszlak 2005).

Subcentral units of government may manifest themselves differently in other democratic societies as a result of cultural differences. One example is a rural village located in central Chhattisgarh (a state of India) that is cut off from the mainstream due to inaccessible roads and the lack of electricity. Residents have little interaction with lower state officials,[4] and what does occur is mediated by the *Patel* (village chief) or the most powerful village elder who is associated with divine legitimacy or a belief that this individual is chosen by the gods (Froerer 2005). This may place the Patel above the law. For these villagers, their experience with the tentacles of central government is influenced by a figure that is endowed with traditional authority as well as divine legitimacy.

LEGISLATIVE OR PARLIAMENTARY   Miliband characterizes the relationship between the legislative body of a state and its administration or the chief executive as both cooperation and conflict. Similar to subcentral units of government, legislative bodies are independent power centers that are often in conflict with the chief executive. Like subcentral units, these bodies also serve a communication function by articulating to the state the needs and concerns of the populations they represent and in addition they communicate information from the center to the periphery.

Features of Stateness

Oszlak (2005) contends that features of "stateness" include diffusion of control, externalization of power, the institutionalization of authority, and the capacity to reinforce a national identity. Diffusion is subdivided into two processes: (1) the ability to extract necessary fiscal resources for performing state functions and reproducing the state bureaucracy and (2) the development of a professional group of civil servants that has the expertise necessary to carry out administrative functions. Externalization of power is the recognition of a nation-state by others. The institutionalization of authority refers again to Weber's ideas regarding the monopoly on coercion. Finally, the capacity to reinforce a national identity requires producing symbols that inspire loyalty to a nation-state as well as a sense of belonging and unity. This sense of shared culture, belonging, and unity is captured in the concept of nation.

Differentiating Nation and State

The concepts of nation and state are often confused or considered synonymous. These concepts are distinct as *nation* refers to a shared culture, identity, and a desire for political self-determination (Bottomore 1979), while the *state* is a legal entity. Nation and state may coincide as the United States is recognized as a nation-state, because there is both a shared sense of national unity and a distinct geographical area controlled by U.S. laws that other nation-states recognize. Political sociologists have contributed to this confusion by overemphasizing the organizational character of the state at the expense of the importance of nation (Vujačić 2002). Perhaps because of the rise of ethnic nationalism and conflict, only recently have sociologists recognized the political importance and value placed on the perception of nations by citizens (Greenfield and Eastwood 2005).

NATIONALISM   Nationalism is "a 'perspective or a style of thought,' an image of the world, 'at the core of which lies . . . the idea of the nation' which we understand to be the definition of a community as fundamentally equal and sovereign" (Greenfield and Eastwood 2005: 250) with sentiments such as "we the people" capturing the essence of nation. While nation and state are often linked, a sense of nation can independently exist where there is no state, such as in Gaza or

Palestine. In some cases, a region might prefer to secede and create a separate nation-state that coincides with nationalist views, such as the Kurdish portion of Iraq or the Basque region of Spain. In *The Kurds: A People in Search of Their Homeland,* Kevin McKiernan (2006) argues that the Kurds have achieved a homeland in Northern Iraq in all but name. While the process of separation is oftentimes bloody (e.g., Yugoslavia), it need not be, such as with the more or less peaceful breakup of the former Soviet Union and Czechoslovakia (Vujačić 2004).

Not all nationalist expression necessarily leads to separation, because a culturally distinct group might prefer to maintain its sense of national identity within a multinational state, such as French-speaking Québec, which is considered a nation within a state. State and nation can be mutually reinforcing but need to be distinguished as separate entities (Vujačić 2002). The state is a legal creation while the attachment to nation is emotional.

When nationalism coincides with a specific territory that is recognized as an autonomous political unit, it is termed a *nation-state.* Nationalist ideology that coincides with a state is advantageous because it provides "the state with a new source of legitimacy and dramatically increase[s] its mobilization potential in comparison to traditional state structures" (Vujačić 2002: 136).

An important question for political sociologists is whether nationalism is a cause or a consequence of the increased fragmentation of larger political units or the breaking of states into smaller units (e.g., Yugoslavia into Bosnia and Herzegovina, Croatia, Kosovo, Macedonia, Montenegro, and Serbia). Schwarzmantel (2001) argues that it is both, but this depends on the nature of the nationalist movement in question. For example, nationalism based on ethnicity is more fragmentary, as its appeal will be limited to members of that ethnic group. Nation-building in areas where a variety of ethnic groups coexist cannot rely on a nationalism that is primarily based on ethnic identity. Nationalism that comes at the expense of another ethnic, race, or religious group may result in political violence including genocide.

CIVIL RELIGION   Nationalism is often an expression of civil religion or "attaching sacred qualities to certain institutional arrangements and historical events" (Scott and Marshall 2005: 71), which celebrates state or civil society and serves the same function as religion, including social cohesion and value socialization. In *The Elementary Forms of Religious Life,* Emile Durkheim distinguishes between the sacred and the profane. "Sacred things are things protected and isolated by prohibitions; profane things are those things to which the prohibitions are applied and that must keep at a distance from what is sacred" (Durkheim 1995 [1912]: 38). The profane is ordinary and the sacred extraordinary. When the profane transitions to the sacred, the *totius substantiae* or total substance is transformed (Durkheim 1995 [1912]). Durkheim writes "at that moment, the young man is said to die, and the existence of the particular person he was, to cease—instantaneously to be replaced by another. He is born again in a new form" (1995 [1912]: 37). Both people and inanimate objects[5] can be transformed and when that happens:

> the powers thereby conferred on that object behave as if they were real. They determine man's conduct with the same necessity as physical force . . . If he has eaten the flesh of an animal that is prohibited, even though it is perfectly wholesome, he will feel ill from it and may die. The soldier who falls defending his flag certainly does not believe he has sacrificed himself to a piece of cloth. (Durkheim 1995 [1912]: 229)

There are many examples of civil religious symbols in the United States, with the flag being the most common. There are prohibitions concerning how the flag is displayed, handled, and disposed including "don't let the flag (sacred) touch the ground (profane)." One of the

Constantino Brumidi's fresco, "Apotheosis of George Washington," in the Rotunda of the U.S. Capitol building

Source: Architect of the Capitol

most dramatic U.S. examples is Constantino Brumidi's fresco "*The Apotheosis of George Washington*" depicting Washington ascending into the heavens and is painted on the interior ceiling of the capitol dome. In writing about Brumidi's *Apotheosis,* Dove and Guernsey (1995) claim "the religious connotation was clear: here was a man so virtuous and beloved that he surely had ascended to heaven, escorted honorably by classical personifications of freedom and liberty." The ascension is both a symbolic as well as the literal rebirth of Washington from ordinary man to extraordinary and is but one of many examples of the deification of Washington that occurred after his death. This association of Washington with virtue continues with a national myth involving an axe and a cherry tree.

Vujačić (2002: 137) argues that this "sacralization of the political sphere remain[s] a permanent feature of modern nationalism." Greenfield and Eastwood (2005) take issue with equating nationalism with civil religion arguing that, by definition, religion excludes the secular. Yet we believe that Durkheim's concepts of the sacred and profane are applicable to understanding the cultural meaning and significance of national symbols.

Emergence of Nations

Greenfield and Eastwood (2005) argue that nationalism is cultural and not a structural phenomenon, yet there are a variety of views on what leads to the emergence of nations and whether modernity is required. In their review, Greenfield and Eastwood note that the "modernists" have become popular since the 1980s, and scholars in this group believe that nation is a result of specific social and economic processes including capitalism, industrialization, and the rise of the bureaucratic state. For the modernists, a bureaucratic state is one of several conditions necessary for the emergence of nation, suggesting that the state must come first. As anthropologist Carole Nagengast writes in summarizing various views about nations, "nations do not produce states, but rather states produce nations . . . In short, the integrative needs of the modern state produced nationalist ideology, which created the

TEXTBOX 2.2

The Alamo: An Example of Texas Nationalism

Texas was for a short time an independent country and that sense of regional pride and identity are still felt today. Texans fly the state flag at the same height as the American flag and celebrate their history of independence. One example is the Alamo shrine located in San Antonio, Texas. Approximately 3 million persons annually visit the Alamo also known as the "cradle of Texas liberty." Since 1905, the site has been operated by the Daughters of the Republic of Texas (DRT) who according to Texas law "must preserve the historic site as a sacred memorial to the heroes who immolated themselves upon that hallowed ground" (visit http://www.thealamo.org). The mission was built in 1718 and originally housed Spanish missionaries. It is also the site where a few hundred men, including Davey Crockett, Jim Bowie, William B. Travis, and others, held out for thirteen days against the Centralist army of General Antonio López de Santa Anna. The Alamo fell on March 6, 1836. Approximately a month later, the Texan Army under Sam Houston shouted, "Remember the Alamo!" when the Texan Army defeated Santa Anna at the battle of San Jacinto on April 21, 1836. The Alamo complex contains several buildings, including the mission. Upon entering, there are several signs reminding visitors of the sacredness of the building. Besides referring to the Alamo as a shrine, a plaque placed by the DRT reads "Blood of heroes hath stained me; let the stones of the Alamo speak that their immolation be not forgotten." Another sign reads "Quiet. No Smoking. Gentlemen Remove Hats." A plaque on another wall reads "Be Silent Friend. Here Heroes Died to Blaze a Trail for Other Men." The message is unmistakable. This is sacred ground that was transformed by the blood of the men who died defending it. Inside the great hall are several tables with glass tops that display and protect artifacts. Lines of people snake around these tables to get a glimpse of a wooden peg from the Crockett cabin and a locket with a snippet of Crockett's hair. This is no ordinary piece of wood or hair. These have become sacred objects. Signs forbid the taking of pictures or talking in loud voices as this is hallowed ground.

Plaque placed at the Alamo by the Daughters of the Republic of Texas

Source: Photo by Lisa K. Waldner

nation" (1994: 118). Therefore, the state comes first and the need to unify society necessitates the creation of nationalist symbols and other common cultural markers.

While there can be no doubt that nationalism serves the state by providing a unifying cultural force, the view that the state must precede the development of nation is disputed by the real sense of nation that exists independent of a state such as the Kurdish homeland in northern Iraq, and Palestine. If either the Kurds or the Palestinians achieve their dream of an independent state, it will be an example of a nation that existed prior to the legal creation of a state. Vujačić (2002) disagrees with the primacy of the state and challenges state-centered theories of nationalism. Perhaps there are multiple paths to the emergence of nation-states, and it is not necessary for state to precede nation.

Different Forms of the Nation-State

Political sociologists recognize several different nation-state forms. Tilly's analysis of western Europe suggests that when citizens contested war making and state making, leaders made concessions resulting in the expansion of civil liberties and other practices associated with democracy. In contrast, newer states created after World War II, where the military dominates the state apparatus, are more likely to fit an authoritarian model. The three basic models of the modern state include democracy, totalitarianism, and authoritarian. Before discussing distinctions amongst these types, it is important to understand that these taxonomic categories do not mean that regimes are static and unchanging. Furthermore, regimes may be a hybrid with a mix of democratic and undemocratic practices with concepts like democracy or authoritarianism referring to specific "phases or episodes through which politics evolve, allowing for a shift of our attention from essential characteristics and stable structures to differences, transitions, and change" (Brachet-Márquez 2005: 462).

Democracy

A democracy is a "political system in which the opportunity to participate in decisions is widely shared among all adult citizens" (Dahl 1963: 8). Markoff (2005) contends that there is a great deal of variation in "democratic" nations, with some having widespread violations of civil liberties despite holding free elections and others so inefficient at providing basic government services that they are termed *low quality* democracies. Three basic types of democracy—direct, representative, and liberal—are not mutually exclusive.

TYPES OF DEMOCRACY   Examples of *direct democracy,* where citizens participate in decision-making, include the ancient Greeks as well as New England town hall and rural township meetings. This type is best suited for small geographical areas and local politics where citizen input can be gathered efficiently and decisions do not have to be made quickly. A more common form is *representative democracy,* where citizens elect someone to vote and voice concerns on their behalf in a type of legislative body such as the U.S. Congress or the British Parliament.

The last type, *liberal democracy,* is characterized by freedoms including expression, assembly, political participation, and property ownership. Some term the last type "liberal capitalist" because of the freedoms associated with private property ownership and pursuit of profit (Babu 2006; Callinicos 2006; Spanakos 2007). Liberal democracies are usually representative democracies.

Using Dahl's definition, democracy exists on a continuum as the opportunity for citizen participation varies. The ancient Greeks did not allow women or slaves to participate, and historically, women and minorities have been disenfranchised. Only since the addition of the Twenty-Sixth Amendment to the U.S. Constitution in 1971 have adults younger than twenty-one been allowed the right to vote. Currently, some states prevent felons from voting after their release from prison. This disproportionately impacts African-Americans; some believe this has affected election outcomes since the 1970s (Manza and Uggen 2006).

Democracy is a process that can be undone and often involves serious conflicts between parties, including state social control agents such as the police (Markoff 2005). Markoff notes that sociologists such as Seymour Lipset and Barrington Moore see democracy not as a process but as a state of affairs associated with economic development (Lipset) and the accumulation of wealth (Moore). Markoff also suggests that there may be many different paths to democracy and diverse starting points, which are not well understood. Viewing democracy as a process and the potential "undoing" of democracy is a recognition that sometimes democracies engage in practices that violate democratic principles.

Democracy and Undemocratic Practices

Brachet-Márquez (2005) illustrates two categories of undemocratic practices:

> when democratic procedures are used as a legitimate cover in order to send out un-
> democratic messages [and] when democratic procedures are made to systematically
> misfunction for some groups (black, immigrants, women, the poor), thereby cover-
> ing up prejudice, exclusion, or downright aggression. In the first case, democracy
> lets in undemocracy by extending its legal mantle too far, whereas in the other, it
> fails to extend it far enough. (480)

Brachet-Márquez's systematic misfunction or the failure to extend the legal mantle is easy enough to understand. Examples include lack of equal protection before the law and the failure to provide services such as adequate police protection, sanitation, or education in low-income or impoverished areas. Brachet-Márquez challenges sociologists and others not to think of these examples as mere inefficiencies but rather as a lack of democracy. Using John Markoff's (2005) phrasing, systematic misfunction is allowing a "low-quality" democracy that affects only certain disadvantaged groups while those with privilege experience all the rights and advantages such as safe neighborhoods and quality public schools. Sudhir Venkatesh's book *Gang Leader for a Day* (2008) describes the real and very personal implications of systematic misfunction affecting residents of Chicago's Robert Taylor Homes. He describes residents who do not bother calling the police or an ambulance because no one responds. As a result, residents are forced to create informal networks to meet basic needs including relying on crack-dealing gang members for security and bribes to the Chicago Housing Authority (CHA) to take care of broken appliances or apartment repairs. Some of these informal arrangements involved exchanging sex for a needed service. Venkatesh explains:

> Then there were all the resources to be procured in exchange for sex: groceries from
> the bodega owner, rent forgiveness from the CHA, assistance from a welfare bureau-
> crat, preferential treatment from a police officer for a jailed relative. The women's
> explanation for using sex as currency was consistent and pragmatic: If your child was in
> danger of going hungry, then you did whatever it took to fix the problem. The women
> looked pained when they discussed using their bodies to obtain these necessities; it was
> clear that this wasn't their first—or even their hundredth—preference. (2008: 215)

Those of us who live middle- or upper-class lives cannot fathom and certainly would not tolerate such a complete lack of government service and protection. Charles Tilly suggests that citizens accept the danger posed by the state in exchange for other services such as hospitals, libraries, and parks. The fact that "low-quality" democracy exists within "real" democracies, where some citizens actually receive something in return for being subjugated while others do not is something that needs more attention from sociologists.

Brachet-Márquez's first case, extending the legal mantle too far, occurs when a democratic state uses its authority to promote undemocratic practices such as holding elections to establish an undemocratic regime that does away with the rights of women or some other group, legally tolerating child pornography as "free speech" but failing to protect the rights of minors, and including undemocratic principles in democratic constitutions such as the right of the military to take over when the nation is deemed at risk (Brachet-Márquez 2005).

Historical examples applicable to the United States include the Kansas–Nebraska Act of 1854 that allowed settlers to vote to determine whether or not to permit slavery. The logic behind voting is popular sovereignty or will of the people. The problem with popular sovereignty is what Tocqueville (1945 [1835]) has termed the *tyranny of the majority* which trumps the rights of the minority. It is paradoxical that the democratic process of voting was used to decide something undemocratic—whether or not whites in a specific territory could own other human beings. This trampled on inalienable rights—or rights that exist by virtue of being human and thus are not conferred by a benevolent state. Some might argue that this practice continues today with some states holding constitutional referendums to decide whether to bar gay citizens from marriage.

Is voting on gay marriage an example of extending the legal mantle too far? Answering yes depends on three premises: (1) the United States is a democracy; (2) voting is a democratic practice; and (3) banning gays from marriage is undemocratic. Most would agree with the first two premises with the third being contentious. Undoubtedly, there are important differences between the fight to end slavery and the struggle regarding gay marriage. And while Brachet-Márquez does not use the gay marriage debate as an example, we believe her insights could be used to critically examine this issue and others, including some of the more controversial aspects of the "war on terror." At minimum, these ideas are a call to action for those living in democracies to be vigilant and not take civil rights for granted.

Finally, any examination of democracy should consider the concept of *polyarchy*. The term originates from Robert Dahl (1956), and as modified by Robinson refers to "a system in which a small group actually rules on behalf of (transnational) capital and mass participation in decision-making is limited to choosing among competing elites in a tightly controlled electoral process" (2004: 442). Robinson argues that this type of democracy is promoted by U.S. foreign policy because it circumvents more radical social change that might undermine capitalism. In other words, the pretense of democracy exists but it is not real democracy as the process is controlled by elites. Robinson's arguments are considered more fully in Chapter 10.

Undemocratic State Forms

Markoff and Brachet-Márquez's ideas underscore that, in practice, democracies are far from perfect. Significantly though, this type does allow for dissent and possible revision of state practices. The following text summarizes undemocratic state forms such as totalitarianism and authoritarianism that are characterized by an absence of civil liberties and protection from state violence. Like democracies, these undemocratic state forms are not static; these labels are best used to describe a regime at a specific point in time rather than a permanent, stable category.

TOTALITARIANISM   In contrast to democracy, totalitarian states allow for no meaningful citizen participation; political expression is severely limited. For example, the former Soviet Union held elections but only members of the communist party were on the ballot. According to Brachet-Márquez, most scholars agree on three components of totalitarianism: (1) a comprehensive ideology detailing all aspects of social life with those opposed exterminated as enemies of the state; (2) a centrally controlled state bureaucracy that promotes this ideology via complete control of the communication and information infrastructure and a terror system for identifying and eliminating state enemies; and (3) a state-controlled political party that involves mass participation, whether willing or forced. Other scholars include components such as a sole political party with one leader and a focus on militarist expansion (Brachet-Márquez 2005).

The distinction between totalitarianism and other nondemocratic forms of government is not always completely objective but subject to political concerns and propaganda. During the height of the cold war, there was a tendency to label any fascism or communism as totalitarianism. Currently, the distinction is more nuanced,with some suggesting that the only true examples of totalitarianism were Nazi Germany and Stalin's Soviet Union (Brachet-Márquez 2005).

What is the distinction between fascism and totalitarianism? According to Brachet-Márquez, the difference is the degree of ruthlessness used in the pursuit of the ideological program and the degree of control exercised with fascist states having less of both. Brachet-Márquez uses Mussolini's Italy as an example of fascism as there was less control with the state needing some cooperation from preexisting institutions and elites.

AUTHORITARIANISM   This category reflects the degree of variation in political systems that are neither wholly totalitarian nor wholly democratic as authoritarianism occupies a mediating position. While authoritarian systems have less control over a society than a totalitarian system, this does not mean there is less death and violence inflicted on citizens. For Stepan (1988), the distinguishing feature is the presence or absence of civil society (voluntary civic and social organizations), which is nonexistent in totalitarian regimes. These organizations are present in an authoritarian state albeit restricted. Unfortunately, the repressed nature of civil society inhibits an authoritarian state from transitioning toward democracy (Brachet-Márquez 2005).

Another distinction is the lack of an overarching ideology guiding societal transformation. Markoff (2005) finds that authoritarian states are more pragmatic and pluralistic in their ideology. Similar to totalitarian regimes, authoritarian governments also rely on bureaucratic structures and technology for citizen repression (Brachet-Márquez 2005).

Saudi citizens do not elect their rulers and have limited civil liberties, with men having more rights than women. Despite ranking ninth overall in authoritarianism[6] (Kekic 2007), Saudi Arabia lacks some of the characteristics of a totalitarian regime such as a comprehensive state terror network. Pakistan is another example of nation-state with limited civil liberties and where the military at times dominates the state apparatus. In 2007, Pakistan President General Musharraf declared a state of emergency, imposed press restrictions ("Pakistan says more than 3000 freed" 2007), and had over 4,500 persons arrested, including his political opponents (Perlez 2007). Although Musharraf was victorious in the 2007 election, the election was boycotted by his political opponents. The Pakistani Supreme Court subsequently ruled this election invalid. Musharraf responded by dismissing the Supreme Court judges and filling judicial posts with his supporters who dismissed election challenges (Gall 2007). Then President George W. Bush called on Musharraf to "have elections soon, and you need to take off your uniform" (Rohde 2007), voicing disapproval for a military leader controlling the state apparatus. Musharraf's Pakistan better fits the category of an authoritarian state than totalitarianism regime despite military control and repression of civil rights and mass political arrests. Musharraf was ousted from the presidency of Pakistan in 2008 with the election of Asif Ali Zardari, the husband of former prime minister and assassinated opposition party leader Benazir Bhutto (Perlez and Masood 2008). Since then, the Pakistani Supreme Court has ruled Musharraf's actions invalid, including the installation of judges supporting his emergency rule, laying the foundation for possible treason charges against the former head of state (Shahzad and Toosi 2009).

Does this mean that Pakistan is now a democracy? Using Latin American countries in the 1970s and 1980s as examples, Stepan (1988) describes an important distinction between democratization and liberalization, which can be applied to Pakistan. Under liberalization, media censorship may be lifted, political prisoners released, and perhaps some free speech tolerated. In contrast, democratization involves the right for open and free elections where any qualified adult can run for political office. Whether the current democratically elected regime will be allowed to govern without another military takeover remains an open question. At best, Pakistan is currently considered a hybrid or a cross between a weak democracy and an authoritarian regime (Economist Intelligence Unit 2008).

China is another example of a state that cannot be considered totalitarian. The Tiananmen Square massacre is a powerful reminder of extreme political repression with thousands killed including those protesting in several Chinese cities besides Beijing between April 15 and June 4, 1989. Yet, this massacre is usually considered an example of authoritarianism rather than totalitarianism because it occurred after the death of Chairman Mao when the Chinese government made some economic and political changes including offering minority factions a token presence in government in exchange for unconditional regime support (Brachet-Márquez 2005). More recently, the Chinese government has enacted some economic reforms but it has been slower to bring about political reform that would allow an entity other than the Communist Party control of the government. Perhaps because of some lessening of societal control, China is a hybrid state that is not purely totalitarian (Orum 2001).

Complicating the ability to differentiate between democracies and authoritarian regimes is the tendency for some Western democracies to accept authoritarian regimes as democracies merely because elections are held. Human Rights Watch (HRW) (http://www.hrw.org), an independent, nongovernmental organization, has charged Western democracies with failing to hold regimes such as Pakistan, Kenya, and Russia accountable ("U.S. Is Too Quick to Accept Nations as True Democracies, Rights Group Says" 2008). According to the HRW, false democracies hold elections but fail on other measures including the right of assembly, a free press, and a strong civil society. Kenneth Roth, the executive director of HRW, argues that the willingness of Western democracies to ignore authoritarian practices is related to how strategically or commercially important an authoritarian regime is rather than the actual abuse of political and civil rights. This is related to Robinson's (2004) charge that the United States supports polyarchy rather than democracy because it benefits the transnational elite, or those from across the globe who are wealthy and powerful. Whether or not elites dominate the political process is only one of the issues debated by dueling theoretical perspectives on the state.

THEORETICAL VIEWS ON THE STATE

Sociological theories of the state have attempted to answer four basic questions: "(1) in whose interests does the state act?; (2) who influences and controls the state?; (3) to what extent do the masses hold political elites accountable?; and (4) how do states change?" (Olsen and Marger 1993: 252). Alford and Friedland (1985) recognized three basic models of power summarizing state–societal relations including pluralist, elite (managerial), and class or Marxist views of the state. Rather than championing one specific theoretical model, these political sociologists argue that all three theories are useful depending on the level of analysis, with pluralism for the individual, elite for examining the state as a set of networked organizations, and the class model for society. Additionally, there are newer perspectives such as institutionalism, rational choice, and postmodernism.

Pluralism

Alford and Friedland (1985) contend that pluralists do not really refer to *the state* per se. Instead pluralists substitute phrases such as *political system, the polity,* or *the pluralist system.* Nonetheless, pluralists have a view of the state with important distinctions when compared to other theorists, including worldview, the nature of political institutions, and the relations between them. Some of these distinctions will be discussed later but it is important to remember that there are important nuances between different theorists operating under the same theoretical umbrella, which cannot possibly be captured in a brief overview.

Pluralism is associated with sociologists Talcott Parsons and Seymour Lipset as well as political scientists Robert Dahl and Ted Gurr. According to Marvin Olsen (1993), one of the basic premises of pluralism can be traced back to Tocqueville who argued for the creation of voluntary associations to combat the potential for "tyranny of the majority." Tocqueville believed that the latter was an outcome of mass equality occurring in the absence of a hierarchical power structure that typifies feudal societies. The growth in voluntary associations leads to the development of a strong civil society that functions independent of the state. By virtue of this independence, voluntary associations have their own power base. Olsen (1993) mentions several characteristics these organizations share, including voluntary membership based on shared interests and concerns, limited sphere in the lives of members, being private or not connected to government, an ability to connect grassroots activism to the national level, and sufficient resources to influence political leaders.

Olsen acknowledges that some of these organizations are political, such as political parties and nonpartisan political action groups. However, these groups may also be nonpolitical in nature, such as professional associations or religious or civic groups termed "parapolitical actors" (1993: 147) that become involved only when their direct interests are at stake. Pluralism, then, involves an arena of competing organizational actors that attempt to influence the state. The state favors no particular set of actors. Although individuals independently do not have a great deal of power and influence, their concerns are heard through their membership in these voluntary associations.

According to pluralists, the core function of the state is to "achieve consensus and thus social order through continuous exchanges of demands and responses by social groups and government" (Alford 1993: 260). In contrast to elite and class perspectives, the pluralist model rejects that the state represents one dominant group at the expense of others or that the state is controlled by elites. For pluralists, the state is "an impartial arbitrator among competing pressure groups" (Alford and Friedland 1985; Olsen and Marger 1993: 255). Pluralists recognize the state as an institution that deals with power but oppose the idea that the state has any interests of its own (Olsen and Marger 1993). If the process works as intended, the state and society's interests are one and the same (Alford and Friedland 1985). This is in direct opposition to state-centrics who view the state as having its own interests. Pluralists also oppose Marxists regarding the importance of social class. For pluralists, social class is only one of many competing interest groups (Alford 1993).

Olsen is quite right when he remarks that pluralism is "the unofficial political philosophy of the United States" (1993: 150) as pluralism sounds very similar to what grade school children are taught about democracy. In fact, democratic is one of the many terms writers have used when writing about pluralism (Alford and Friedland 1985). Class theorists take this a step further and argue that pluralism is a deliberate falsehood taught to hide the real source of power in any capitalist democracy: big business. In comparing the pluralist perspective to others, Alford and Friedland write "In both managerial [elite] and class perspectives, popular identifications with the state or with local political party organizations are products of elite manipulation or false consciousness deriving from the illusory universality of the capitalist state" (1985: 24).

Regardless of which theory is correct on this latter point, the pluralist paradigm suffers from some important weaknesses. Expanding on more general criticisms summarized in Chapter 1, six weaknesses of this model are viability, harmony of interest, difficulty of new organizations to enter the political process, iron law of oligarchy, lack of sufficient power resources, and the lack of viable political channels (Olsen 1993). Viability refers to the question of whether individuals really are connected to and involved with voluntary organizations. While one might be a card-carrying member, this does not equal participation. This is an important criticism because one of the premises of pluralism is that voluntary associations provide an opportunity to develop the skills necessary to become more politically effective. Furthermore, without active member participation, organizations will not be effective conduits between society and government. With Robert Putnam's book *Bowling Alone* (2000) concluding that involvement in voluntary associations is declining, there is little evidence of viability.

Harmony of interests assumes that despite competing interests there is a basic consensus on core values. Olsen (1993) contends that when this is not the case, pluralism may result in societal paralysis and even destruction. In Chapter 1, we found that those with less power resources typically lose in the political process (Piven and Cloward 1988). Resource procurement is difficult for newer organizations undercutting the ability to participate in the society–state mediation process (Olsen 1993). At worse, these groups become simply mouthpieces for government as they lack resources needed to maintain autonomy. Further, even with resources, if there is no mechanism for influencing the state, effectiveness is limited. In other words, pluralism "specifies the role that intermediate organizations should enact in political affairs, but says nothing about how this role should be carried out" (Olsen 1993: 151). Olsen's final criticism concerns Robert Michels' "iron law of oligarchy" or the tendency for all organizations to become centralized and controlled by only a few (Zeitlin 1981). If this is the case, it would seem that civic organizations and other voluntary associations are not really a training ground for future leaders as folks do not join, and of those who do, most will not have the opportunity to assume a leadership role.

Elite Views of the State

Alford and Friedland prefer *managerial* to *elite* or *bureaucratic* to describe this perspective as they emphasize the "organizational base of elites and their control of the state" (1985: 161). We use the term *elite* because this is the more common label. Prewitt and Stone (1993) contend that elite theory is based on two principles: (1) society can be divided into two groups, the masses and the smaller number that rule them; and (2) the nature and direction of any society can be understood by understanding the composition, structure, and conflicts of those who rule.

The core function of the state is maintaining the dominance of existing elites (Alford 1993). Like class theorists, elite theorists believe that power is concentrated but disagree that it is based on class position. For elite theorists, managerial control is more important than property ownership (Alford and Friedland 1985) as power is the result of holding positions of authority in bureaucracies that control resources, and these complex organizations manage every important sphere of social life. Important bureaucracies may be political or governmental institutions but can also be banks, corporations, religious organizations, or the media, to name only a few (Alford 1993).

Unlike pluralists who believe that ordinary citizens can be influential through voluntary associations, elite theorists view those controlling the state bureaucracy "as relatively insular and rarely influenced by other members of society" (Olsen and Marger 1993: 255). What makes elites inaccessible also explains why elite control is so successful. "The combination of expertise, hierarchical control, and the capacity to allocate human, technological, and material resources gives the elites of bureaucratic organizations power not easily restrained by the mechanisms of pluralistic competition and debate" (Alford 1993: 259).

While elite theorists argue that real power rests with those who occupy positions within dominant organizations, this does not mean that elites are unified. Quite the contrary, elites compete with other elites for control and influence and use their positions to manipulate information and frame public opinion. In short, they manipulate the masses. There are a variety of different "flavors" of elite theory but key types include classical elite, power elite, and class domination views.

CLASSICAL ELITE THEORY   Theorists including Robert Michels, Vilfredo Pareto, and Gaetano Mosca are often lumped together under one rubric when ignoring important distinctions in their social theorizing. Yet, as discussed in Chapter 1, there are some important commonalties including the view that elite rule is necessary. Michels takes a less negative view of the masses by leaning more toward the ideas of Max Weber, including Weber's view of bureaucratic structure by noting the inevitability of such organizations as well as potential negative outcomes. Marger (1987) argues that compared to his contemporaries, Michels is the most sociological, and for this reason, we focus on his ideas.

Michels believed that the real power struggle was not between the elites and the masses, but between old elites and newer ones challenging the former for leadership positions. Michels' "iron law of oligarchy" was based on his analysis of the German Social Democratic (GSD) party. The GSD was deliberately chosen to illustrate that iron law, or rule by only a few, occurs even when an organization is governed by democratic principles (Marger 1987).

POWER ELITE   Unlike some classical elite views, C. Wright Mills was critical of elite control and bureaucracy, believing that they undermined democracy. Like Michels, he believed that society was controlled by elites, specifically, "the power elite" comprising three interlocking groups: corporate, political, and military. Elites can use their position in one domain to become dominant in another. An example is the number of past U.S. presidents who were military generals (e.g., Washington, Grant, Jackson, and Eisenhower) or wealthy Americans who translate wealth into political power (e.g., Kennedy, Rockefeller, and Bush). Unlike classical theorists, Mills also conceptualized a mediating level between "the power elite" and the masses termed *middle levels of power* or organized special interest groups. The third level is the unorganized masses (Mills 1956).

Mills believed that three factors explained the cohesive and unified nature of the power elite: common socialization as a result of similar career paths and educational experiences; the maintenance of continued personal and business ties (e.g., marriage and business arrangements); and the interdependent nature of the triangle of power (Olsen and Marger 1993).

CLASS DOMINATION THEORY   G. William Domhoff is an intellectual heir of C. Wright Mills and also credits E. Digby Baltzell, Paul M. Sweeney, and Robert A. Dahl as important influences (Domhoff 1993). While some describe Domhoff as an "empirical Marxist" (Lo 2002), he explicitly rejects this label (Domhoff 1993) and criticizes elite theory and prefers what he calls "class domination theory" (Domhoff 2006). We include him under the elite rubric because he shares with other elite theorists a belief that there is a dominant group in society with elite membership based on both having wealth and holding a position of power. He is best known for his analysis of four intertwining power structure networks: policy planning, candidate selection, special interests, and opinion shaping (Domhoff 2006).

Domhoff argues that the power elite are a "corporation-based upper class" comprised of both owners and top-level corporate executives. The power elite control enough money and wealth, occupy enough positions of power, and win enough of the time to conclude that the federal government is dominated—though not necessarily totally controlled, by the power elite.

While Mills emphasizes similar socialization experiences and current interpersonal ties through business and family connections, Domhoff emphasizes the similarity of social backgrounds by investigating social club membership, private school membership, and attendance at prestigious universities (Domhoff 2006). For example, though Bill Clinton was not born wealthy, he shares with other elites his membership in prestigious organizations, social clubs, and educational experiences (e.g., Yale Law School, Georgetown University, and Oxford).

Critics of elite theory question whether elites are truly cohesive enough to rule, whether the masses are really dominated by elites, and whether elite models are too simplistic. Domhoff criticizes other elite theorists for not acknowledging the ability of the corporate elite to dominate political elites such as elected officials. Furthermore, he argues that others fail to see the class bias built into the policy-planning network, rendering the leaders of nonprofits vulnerable to the corporate community. Finally, the failure to acknowledge class bias misrepresents the relationship between the corporate community and union leaders with the union usually defeated (Domhoff 2006). Although Domhoff encourages us to consider the importance of class domination, he does not hold to other tenets of Marxism such as the primacy of class struggle and the means of production (Domhoff 1993).

Class-Based Views of the State

While class-based theories are more a theory of society than a specific theory of state (Alford and Friedland 1985), Olsen and Marger (1993) contend that the ideas of class theorists represent "one of the most comprehensive explanations of the state and its power" (252). As previously discussed, there are a variety of neo-Marxian perspectives on the state, but these perspectives share some core concepts and assumptions.

For Marxists, economics determines the actual nature of the state and the role played in influencing other aspects of social life. All institutions are shaped by the mode of economic production. For this reason, class theorists use the term *capitalist state* rather than only *state* to underscore the role of capitalism. Under capitalism, "the state is controlled by and acts in the interests of the productive property-owning class" (Olsen and Marger 1993: 252).

The core function of the state is to maintain and reproduce the existing class relationships using both formal (law and the courts) and informal (socialization of children in schools and families) means (Alford 1993). Skocpol argues that "the crucial difference of opinion is over which means the political arena distinctly embodies: fundamentally consensually based legitimate authority, or fundamentally coercive domination" (1993: 307). Class-based theorists believe the latter and that the state emerged as a mechanism for controlling the masses. Class conflict is managed by both force and control of ideology (Nagengast 1994).

Viewing the state as shaped by economic forces and dominated by the capitalist class challenges the pluralist view of an institution that arbitrates between competing interest groups and an autonomous state that acts on behalf of greater society. However, neo-Marxists disagree on the exact nature of the relationship between the dominant capitalist class and the form and functioning of the state. According to Gold, Lo, and Wright (1975), there are three Marxist theories of capitalist states—instrumental, structural, and Hegelian–Marxist—that seek to answer two basic questions: "Why does the state serve the interests of the capitalist class?" and "How does the state function to maintain and expand the capitalist system?" (Gold, Lo, and Wright 1993: 269).

INSTRUMENTAL   Ralph Miliband is perhaps the most well-known proponent of this view that gives primacy to understanding the ties between the ruling class and the state (Gold et al. 1993). Quite simply, the state serves the interests of the capitalist class because the state is an instrument or tool used by this class to dominate society. This does not mean that dominant-class members directly rule by holding office; rather, they rule indirectly by exerting control over state officials (Olsen and Marger 1993).

This perspective has driven a research agenda that has examined the direct ties between members of the capitalist class and the state as well as other related institutions such as political parties and how the capitalist class shapes government policy to fit their interests (Gold et al. 1993). This shaping can be direct through the development of state policy or indirect through pressure and influence. Gold and colleagues argue that this view has been important for the development of the sociology of the capitalist class. Research from this perspective documents both the existence of a dominant class and the connections between members and the state apparatus. Nonetheless, there are criticisms of instrumentalism, including a failure to consider state autonomy, historical exceptions, and causation.

The failure to include autonomy includes two types: that of the state and other related institutions. As Gold and colleagues argue "There are also state policies which cannot easily be explained by direct corporate initiatives but which may come from within the state itself" (1993: 271). For example, to preserve the capitalist state, the state may need to enact policies such as social security payroll taxes or import restrictions that are opposed by capitalists (Block 1993). This would not be possible without an autonomous state. Furthermore, culture and ideology are promoted by the state and not simply manipulated by the capitalist class (Gold et al. 1993). As Block argues, this view "neglects the ideological role of the state. The state plays a critical role in maintaining the legitimacy of the social order, and this requires that the state appear to be neutral in the class struggle" (1993: 296). Even if the instrumentalists are correct, the fact that the state must appear neutral calls for a more nuanced and complicated framework for analyzing state policy (Block 1993).

Related to the argument of state autonomy is the criticism of historical exception. This argument suggests that not all policies enacted by a capitalist state are interests of the dominant class. Gold et al. (1993) note that business leaders were opposed to Franklin D. Roosevelt's New Deal programs. In fact, these leaders considered Roosevelt, a member of the upper class, a "class traitor." Gold et al. (1993) also note that even if some of the reforms implemented by the state on behalf of the working class ultimately co-opt the working class, to assume that all reforms are a co-optation denies the possibility of class struggle over reform.

Finally, the issue of causation challenges the assumption that state policy can be explained by the voluntary acts of powerful persons rather than an acknowledgment that the actions of the ruling class can be limited by structural factors. Gold et al. (1993) contend that this view of causation is the result of an instrumentalist view that rose to challenge a pluralist view of the state. Both views contend that social causes are due to actions of dominant actors that act on behalf of their own interests. The difference is that instrumentalists see one dominant actor, the ruling class, whereas pluralists believe there are many groups attempting to control the state. This view of a dominant class that acts in a manner consistent with its own interests assumes that the ruling class is cohesive and unified (Block 1993). In Fred Block's "The Ruling Class Does Not Rule", he argues that a "viable Marxist theory of the state depends on the rejection of the idea of a conscious, politically directive, ruling class" (1993: 305). This alternative view is a structural theory of the state.

STRUCTURAL   Just as Miliband is associated with an instrumental view of the state, Nicos Poulantzas is a main proponent of the structural view. The historical Miliband–Poulantzas debate was the dueling neo-Marxists' perspectives of instrumentalism and structuralism. While agreeing that the state acts to maintain capitalism, Poulantzas rejects instrumentalism, arguing that state functioning is a direct consequence of both structure and the contradictions of capitalism.

Because society is dependent on a functioning economy, state officials must protect the economy and, in doing so, serve the interests of the dominant class (Olsen and Marger 1993) According to Gold et al., structuralists are interested in "how the state attempts to neutralize or displace these various contradictions" (1993: 271) in order to maintain the capitalist system. In Poulantzas' (1975) influential book, *Political Power and Social Classes,* he argues that there is a contradiction between the social character of production and the private appropriation of surplus product, threatening the current system through working-class unity and capitalist-class disunity.

Capitalist-class disunity is fostered by competition. Far from being unified, capitalists compete with each other for surplus, and therefore do not always share economic and political interests. The only way to protect the long-term interests of the capital class, as opposed to short-term individualized interests of specific capitalists, is to have a state that maintains some autonomy, even if the state, from time to time, enacts working-class concessions such as minimum-wage laws. The long-term survival of capitalism is dependent upon providing these concessions in an attempt to prevent working-class unity. Without such concessions, workers might band together and overthrow the capitalist state.

In summarizing the structuralist view, Gold et al. (1993) note that the degree of state autonomy varies depending on the degree of conflict between classes, the intensity of divisiveness within classes, and which factions constitute a dominant-class power bloc. Gold et al. argue that the lack of any discussion that might explain how these functional relationships are regulated weakens this approach to understanding the capitalist state.

HEGELIAN–MARXIST   This final neo-Marxist perspective begins with the question, "what is the state?" The answer is a mystification or an institution that serves the interests of the dominant class though it appears to serve the interests of society as a whole. This shows that the state is an illusion, with most writers exploring how this mystification process occurs. Most writers emphasize the role of ideology, consciousness, and legitimacy. Although these ideas have advanced the understanding of politics, they are not a coherent theory of the state much less of the relation between the state and society (Gold et al. 1993). Thinkers associated with this perspective (e.g., Herbert Marcuse, Jürgen Habermas, and Georg Lukacs) include what is called the Frankfurt School of Critical Theory. The *Frankfurt School* refers to the first generation of critical theorists who were located in Frankfurt, Germany, and relocated to the United States after the Nazis rose to power.

Updated Marxist Theories of the State

In reviewing Marxist theories of the state, twenty-five years after the classic description of Gold et al. (1975), one of the original authors, Clarence Lo, argues there are four "currents" of Marxist theories of state that he labels empirical Marxism, socialist democracy, postcolonial Marxist political theory, and critical theory of the capitalist state. This section is based predominantly on this summary (Lo 2002).

EMPIRICAL MARXISM   Scholars working in this area have transcended the famous Miliband–Poulantzas debate by incorporating both perspectives. Lo argues that Domhoff's research on the American power structure fits under this rubric because class domination and class conflict are the foci of Domhoff's analysis of power. Work that "analyzes class power in its situational, institutional, and systemic forms" is also classified under this label (2002: 198), including examinations that theorize the role of class power both on the formation of the welfare state and its impact on social classes. Lo believes that empirical Marxism has made several contributions to Marxist thought by demonstrating why state policies benefit capitalism and by the precise measurement of concepts and causal models developed by the analytical Marxist, Erik Olin Wright.

SOCIALIST DEMOCRACY   Lo describes this current as that which criticizes the structural approach of Poulantzas and others. This Marxist model theorizes a socialist democracy where political practice and protest are motivated toward creating a society characterized by democratic practices, egalitarianism, meeting of basic needs, and a production cycle free from the need for profit maximization. Those working within this tradition reject the notion of a working class organized around only economic issues and see individuals with multiple identities such as gender, race, and ethnicity. Because the classic Marxian idea about the inevitability of class struggle is rejected, Lo contends that a major problem for both theorists and practitioners is specifying under what conditions individuals could be unified and organized, given their shifting conflicts and multiple identities.

POSTCOLONIAL MARXIST POLITICAL THEORY   This strand is the heir of the early Hegelian–Marxist model as it relies on some of the earlier writings of Karl Marx and also sees the state as a false universal. Marx's earlier writings are combined with postcolonial theories of literature that critically examine the colonizer's view and interpretation of third-world culture and the construction of race and ethnic identities. One of the more influential works to come out of this theoretical thread is Michael Hardt and Antonio Negri's *Empire*.

Specifically, *empire* is a political organization of global flow and exchanges that has no geographical boundaries (Hardt and Negri 2001). Sovereignty is exercised through transnational institutions (e.g., NATO, the World Trade Organization [WTO], and the G8[7]), the dominant military power of the United States and its allies, and international control of monetary funds by elites through other transnational organizations such as the International Monetary Fund (IMF) and the World Bank. Although Hardt and Negri rely on a variety of theoretical traditions, Lo argues that *empire* is framed within a Marxist tradition for several reasons, including the belief that "the sovereignty of Empire is interrelated with the processes of capital accumulation . . . that global sovereignty is a false universal, . . . that the cultural prerequisites for labor activate the facilitative power of persons that will undermine empire" (Lo 2002: 313).

CRITICAL THEORY OF THE CAPITALIST STATE   While drawing on the writings of those associated with the Frankfurt School of critical theory, Lo associates this strand with Claus Offe (1996), whose work demonstrates that pressure outside of the capitalistic system intensifies internal conflict, which poses three challenges to the state: political sovereignty, popular legitimacy, and economic effectiveness. Offe argues that the economic inefficiency of the state is due to weakening state sovereignty and political legitimacy. Lessening state sovereignty is evidenced by the inability of the state to intervene in either the economy or other aspects of social life. The state capacity for regulation has been weakened by globalization as well as lack of legitimacy. As Lo explains, "people simply do not trust the state to act to reflect the general will; rather they see the state as pursuing particularistic aims of interest groups, experts, bureaucrats, or clients" (2002: 219). Like many questions posed by political sociologists, this view of the state is hotly contested. One of the alternatives to a class-based approach is a state-centric view that became popular because of inadequacies with all three basic perspectives (Amenta 2005).

State-Centric

Theda Skocpol's influential introduction to the edited volume *Bringing the State Back In* summarizes this approach (Evans, Rueschemeyer, and Skocpol 1985) in which the state and other large political institutions are situated at the center of political sociology (Amenta 2005). Her work is influenced by Max Weber and conceptualizes the state as a "set of organizations with unique functions and mission" with "state structures and actors having central influence over politics and states" (Amenta 2005: 96–97). In the words of Skocpol, this "organizational" or "realist" view of the state "refuses to treat states as if they were mere analytic aspects of abstractly conceived modes of production, or even political aspects of concrete class relations and struggles. Rather it insists that states are actual organizations controlling (or attempting to control) people and territories" (1993: 311–312).

This is a departure from Marxist, elite, and pluralist views of state that respectively give primacy to class domination, ruling elite, and interest groups. Quite simply, this more Weberian approach advocates that the state is an independent actor not beholden to class interests or merely an arena for political mediation (Skocpol 1985). This does not mean that class or dominant groups are unimportant. To the contrary, "linkages to class forces" and "politically mobilized groups" along with the structure of state organizations and their location within the state apparatus are deemed important especially for those attempting to explain state stability as well as revolution or change (Skocpol 1993).

While Skocpol acknowledges the diversity of neo-Marxian views on the "role of the capitalist state," she argues that this perspective also suffers from a society-centered view that cannot account for the role of a state as an independent actor. She writes:

> virtually all neo-Marxist writers on the state have retained deeply embedded society-centered assumptions, not allowing themselves to doubt that, at base, states are inherently shaped by classes or class struggles and function to preserve and expand modes of production. Many possible forms of autonomous state action are thus ruled out by definitional fiat. (1985: 5)

According to Skocpol, even the neo-Marxist structuralist perspective that considers the "relative autonomy of the state" falls short of considering true autonomy necessitated by a need to maintain order, the international orientation of states, and an organization that creates a capacity for state officials to develop and implement their own policies. She further criticizes neo-Marxists for ignoring variations in state structures that lessens the utility of these approaches in comparative research (Skocpol 1985, 1993). For example, Skocpol asserts that neo-Marxist models are better at comparing states "*across* [emphasis Skocpol's] modes of production, rather than across nations within capitalism" (1985: 33). In other words, neo-Marxist models have less utility for understanding contrasts between advanced capitalistic states with concentrated technologies (e.g., Japan, United States, and Germany) and other capitalistic states whose economies may be more based on agriculture and resources extraction (e.g. mining and logging).

Skocpol (1985) contends that even the United States can be shown to have state autonomy despite its fragmented system of dispersing authority throughout the federal system, division of sovereignty among the various branches, and lack of a centralized bureaucratic structure. Most important, the degree of state autonomy is not a fixed feature but varies as a result of structural transformations due to both internal and external factors including crises necessitating a response from elites and administrators. Autonomous state action is most likely when career bureaucrats occupying positions within the state bureaucracy are insulated from external pressure.

A state-centric approach considers both state autonomy and state capacity, which are not synonymous. As Orloff explains "state capacities are based on financial and administrative resources; stable access to plentiful finances and a loyal and skilled body of officials facilitates state initiatives" (1993: 9–10). Pedriana and Stryker (1997) suggest that state capacity is also linked to statute interpretation with a more liberal interpretation linked to a greater capacity for state action.

While *capacity* refers to resources available to state managers, *state autonomy* refers to independence or the ability of state actors to act freely from interference from outside forces. In writing about state autonomy, Skocpol contends that "states conceived as organizations claiming control over territories and people may formulate and pursue goals that are not simply reflective of the demands or interests of social groups, classes, or society" (1985: 9). The implication of this view is to see the state as a "structure with a logic and interests of its own not necessarily equivalent to, or fused with, the interests of the dominant class of society or the full set of member groups in the polity" (Skocpol 1993: 308).

While Skocpol and associates brought "the state back in" to deal with an overly Marxist view that equated state control with class domination, this has not gone unchallenged. In theorizing about the rise of a global capitalist class brought about as a result of globalization, Robinson argues that "the case for 'bringing the state back in' has been overemphasized, tending to equate states with the institutional form they have taken in the nation-state. In contrast, a new transnational studies requires that analysts 'take out' the crippling nation-state framework into which states, social classes, political systems and so have been pigeonholed" (1998: 565).

Political Institutional or Institutionalist

State-centered scholars created the way for a political institutional theory. This perspective emphasizes both the state as well as other political institutions, including the social, economic, and ideological factors precipitating policy formation (Orloff 1993). While *state-centric* was the initial phrase, *institutionalist* is the preferred terminology (Amenta 2005) as it is less likely to convey the idea that factors external to the state are unimportant (Orloff 1993). In his review of the institutional approach, Amenta describes several varieties of political institutional theory. We limit our discussion here to whom he terms the *new institutionalists* (2005: 103) or those who view states as organizations and thus apply organizational theory.

The scope is not limited to the state as other major political organizations are also considered, including electoral systems and political parties. A political institutional approach places more emphasis than the state-centric approach on "the impact of political contexts on politics more so than the role of bureaucratic state actors" (Amenta 2005: 104). For example, in the United States, issues that appeal to a wide variety of constituents from all over the country are more likely to be dealt with in a system that elects congressional representatives based on geographical distribution. A related political context, fragmentation, includes the lack of integrated vertical or horizontal political authority. As explained by Amenta:

> The United States has a presidential and non-parliamentary system that allows intramural conflict. Members of Congress from the same party can defect from the President's legislative program without risking loss of office and can initiate competing programs . . . Any laws that make it through this [legislative] maze can be declared unconstitutional by the U.S. Supreme Court. (2005: 108)

Fragmentation, then, is an example of a political contextual factor that affects the formation of state policy, including what sociologists call "the welfare state." The political institutional approach considers this as well as other contextual factors. See Figure 2.1 for a comparison of the four main theories of the state (pluralist, elite, Marxist, and state-centric/institutional).

	Pluralist	Elite	Class	State-Centric/ Institutionalist
Whose interests does the state serve?	The state is an impartial arbitrator. The interests of state and society are the same	Those holding elite positions	The ruling class	The state bureaucracy
What is the source of power?	Voluntary organizations autonomous from the state	Occupying an elite position in an organization that controls resources	Owning capital	Occupying a position in the state bureaucracy associated with power
What comprises the state?	A multiplicity of overlapping jurisdictions	Cluster of large organizations based on separate institutional sectors	Capitalist state is not specified by its structure and function. It is influenced by capitalism	Organizations claiming control over territories
What are core state functions?	A neutral arbitrator that mediates between competing social actors	Maintaining dominance of elites	Maintaining the capitalist state	Maintaining the state bureaucracy
Who are the major political players?	Voluntary associations or interest groups and voters	Elites	The ruling class	State officials

FIGURE 2.1 Differences between Major Models of the State

OTHER EMERGING VIEWS OF THE STATE

Rational Choice

Rational Choice Theory (RCT) views all political entities as rational actors. Lobbying, foreign policy, or the relations between other nation-states, as well as domestic policy, are seen in terms of a game where various players vie for scarce resources, including power. Kiser and Bauldry (2005) argue that RCT has only recently become influential in political sociology and that this is due to the development of a *sociological* version that bypasses earlier criticisms by incorporating the influence of history, culture, and institutions. Because RCT has only recently emerged as a viable perspective for political sociologists, there is not a fully developed theory of the state. Yet, researchers have applied this theory to actions of political actors, including the state. Examples of substantive areas of research guided by RCT include nationalism, congressional policy making, and the existence of red tape in bureaucracies (Kiser and Bauldry 2005). RCT has also been applied to social movement participation (Chapter 8) and the state response to terrorism (Chapter 9). Despite the promise of RCT, it still needs to synthesize several different approaches to develop a more general theory and is not useful in situations where there is a high degree of uncertainty about the benefits and costs of actions or when both costs and benefits are low (Kiser and Bauldry 2005).

Postmodern

Some postmodernists may claim that politics is dead, or rather "politics is secret, veiled, or now even subpolitical" (Agger and Luke 2002: 162), with the study of politics moving from traditional power centers such as parliament or congress to the capitalist economy and culture. Agger and Luke embrace the postmodern turn in political sociology, believing that it challenges all political theorists to "rethink politics" (2002: 160), which will result in a broadening research agenda.

Postmodernism is heavily influenced not only by Marx and critical theory thinkers but also by philosophers and other humanities scholars. This broad perspective is not bound to a single discipline or to a narrowly focused question such as, "what is the state?" Postmodernists seem more interested in describing the consequences of the state or declaring the state obsolete, rather than defining the state itself. While Lo (2002) characterizes Hardt and Negri's work as an example of what he terms a *postcolonial* Marxist perspective, their work shares with a postmodern view a look at the political beyond the state to *empire* as well as power in a global context.

Many of the themes examined in subsequent chapters are influenced by a postmodern perspective. Chapter 9 reviews some of the implications of the "surveillance state" related to the implementation of the PATRIOT Act and the creation of what Giorgio Agamben (2005) calls the "state of exception." Chapter 10 considers the causes and consequences of globalization, including predictions for the future of the nation-state. Although there may not be a postmodern theory of the state per se, the ideas of many key philosophers connected to this perspective, such as Foucault's, are currently being used to address key concerns of both political sociology and political science (Torfing 2005). Both rational choice and postmodern theories will continue to influence political sociology but will most likely be combined with "rather than [used] as a replacement for, the neopluralist, conflict, and state-centric" approaches (Hicks, Janoski, and Schwartz 2005: 17).

We began with a closer look at what the state is and various sociological theories of the state. The rest of this discussion is more concerned with the question "what does the state do?"

Part of this answer involves examining the "welfare state." Many different theoretical perspectives have been used to explain the welfare state (Hicks and Esping-Andersen 2005), but this has been an especially important topic for those using a state-centric or institutional approach. Future chapters will also examine what the state does by reviewing issues such as immigration, education, business, and the "politics of everyday life."

THE WELFARE STATE

The *welfare state* refers to the social and economic managerial role of a nation-state (Melling 1991). In "state corporatism," social and economic organizations are controlled by the state. This dictatorial rule is a feature of state–society relations under totalitarianism. In contrast, "liberal corporatism" involves the state sharing space with other groups that are organized voluntarily and are recognized as representing various sectors of society such as gun owners, business, labor, or specific occupational groups that are recognized as a channel of political representation. These groups work with the state to negotiate competing interests. Not all democracies are corporatist states, but in states that are both corporatist and democratic, corporatist groups are recognized in exchange for submitting to the primacy of the state (Streeck and Kenworthy 2005).

In their review of public policy and the welfare state, Hicks and Esping-Andersen (2005) describe three types of welfare states—liberal, social democratic, and conservative—differentiated by population coverage, role of the private market, target population, decommodification, defamilialization, recommodification, and poverty reduction through redistribution of income. It is important to note that these concepts are ideal types with specific nations perhaps illustrating hybrids of two or more types.

Types of Welfare States

All welfare states vary in terms of the types of social programs that are enacted as a function of state capacity. States with a higher degree of capacity will initiate social welfare programs earlier than those with a more limited capacity (Orloff 1993). The types of welfare states or "welfare regimes" differ by the degree of state capacity as well as cultural values that define who is considered worthy of receiving state support and the role that family is supposed to play in supporting its members.

LIBERAL   The United States has avoided corporatism and has opted for a liberal-market state where there is little state control over the economy and where there are many competing interest groups. Liberal states initiate programs in reaction to market and family failures and also initiate their programs later than social democratic or conservative welfare states (Orloff 1993). The welfare state is much more restricted and conceived more as a safety net targeted toward the needy through the use of means tests. Private market solutions are preferred over broad policies that might extend universal health care coverage or family benefits such as paid maternity or paternity leave. Calls to privatize social security are an example of a proposed private market solution.

Liberal welfare states tend not to "defamilialize" or to encourage the shift from the family to paid providers of responsibilities such as child care or elder care. This means that the state does not subsidize the cost of day care for young children or the elderly, with the exception of welfare mothers participating in job training or other required employment programs as a condition of receiving benefits. Liberal welfare states also do not support women-friendly employment policies such as paid maternity leave or efforts to recommodify individuals with job training or other programs designed to ensure full employment for adults. Compared to the other two types of welfare regimes, liberal market states have a lower capacity for proactive public policy as these states initiate their welfare policies much later than other welfare states (Orloff 1993).

SOCIAL DEMOCRATIC   The social democratic welfare state as illustrated by some Scandinavian countries is an example of a democratic corporatist state. These nations have a more extensive welfare state that is more inclusive and not only includes the poor or some other narrowly defined groups but also universal programs that attempt to provide "cradle-to-grave" security such as health care, subsidized day care for children and elders, as well as minimum-income guarantees. Private market solutions are rejected in favor of government-run programs covering all citizens. There is a strong commitment to gender equality through defamilialization or providing external resources for traditional family obligations such as day care. High tax rates mean that income is redistributed to fund social welfare programs with a high commitment to poverty reduction including recommodification, which maximizes the market power of the individual in the labor market through income guarantees and opportunities for job training and retraining. These states have also tried to buffer workers from volatile markets through decommodification. All of the benefits provided by this type of welfare state means that a worker need not accept just any job.

Korpi (2003) notes that structural changes in the economy such as postindustrialization or the shift to a more service sector base have led to a retrenchment or scaling back of the welfare state in western Europe. In addition to economic factors, Orloff (1993) adds demographic changes and international economic competition as other reasons for cutting back on services and eligibility. Whether globalization causes welfare state retrenchment is hotly contested and will be examined more fully in Chapter 10.

CONSERVATIVE   This type of welfare state practices corporatism based on occupational groups, such as unionized coal miners or dock workers, which target male breadwinners for social welfare programs. These programs are based on the primacy of the male breadwinners and the need for families to look after their members, both young and old. Like social democratic welfare states, the private market is not embraced as a solution for meeting typical welfare needs such as pensions or health care. Similar to liberal states, there is low commitment to poverty reduction, income redistribution, and defamilialization. Examples of nations classified as having this type of state include Germany, France, Italy, and Spain (Hicks and Esping-Andersen 2005).

Role of Race and Gender

The U.S. welfare state provides some respite from poverty by redistributing income, but at the same time, it also acts to reinforce a stratification system (Esping-Andersen 1990) that reflects class, race, and gender bias as minorities and poor women are overrepresented in the public assistance sphere (e.g., foods stamps and public housing) while white men are more often found in the more generous social insurance sphere with private pension and health insurance (Misra 2002). Misra calls on sociologists to explore how welfare policy has been shaped by bias. For example, in the United States, some programs using a means test such as income eligibility have often excluded African-Americans entirely or paid out smaller benefits in order to ensure an adequate supply of low-paid agricultural workers (Quadagno 1988). Gender stereotypes are also reinforced through welfare policy as a conservative welfare state targets only male bread-winners and defamilialization is rejected as families should take care of their own. This rein-forces more traditional gender roles of the female homemaker and male breadwinner.

FUTURE OF THE STATE

In recognizing the era of government deregulation and the increasing privatization of traditional state functions, Oszlak (2005) asks, "Does this mean that the state is no longer necessary?" Oszlak cites Ohmae (1995) who argues that the nation-state will be replaced by a supranational state be-cause it has lost its capacity to generate real economic activity in an era of increasing globalization. The rise of transnational corporations and international nongovernmental organizations is a global-ization outcome, which may further weaken the nation-state (Haque 2003; Lauderdale and Oliverio 2005). Robinson (1998, 2001) argues that nation-states are being replaced by national states that are part of a transnational state apparatus. The authors of *Empire,* Hardt and Negri (2001), also contend that a supranational entity will succeed the state, with the process well under way.

There have been several criticisms of the *Empire* thesis, including the failure to provide empirical data (Arrighi 2003; Tilly 2003), not distinguishing politics and the state from the econ-omy (Steinmetz 2002), and not being historically grounded. Despite Oszlak's empathy for the weak-state thesis, he himself argues that the state plays a role that cannot be delegated and that the size of the state, as measured by the number of agencies, its budget, and the percentage of the labor force employed by the state, means that the state will not be disappearing anytime soon.

Yet many scholars debate the impact of globalization on the state. Important state func-tions such as waging war are believed to be shifting from nation-states to larger sociocultural en-tities (Huntington 1996) such as North Atlantic Treaty Organization (NATO) and the European Union. The state's role in formulating social policy is largely influenced by economic forces that are less and less under the control of a nation-state (Falkner and Talos 1994).

As discussed earlier, Tilly (1985) views security as one of the main functions of the state. Globalization is linked to declining state legitimacy, which impacts security by delegitimizing the state further. Wallerstein (2003: 65) explains, "The more they do so the more there is chaotic vio-lence, and the more there is chaotic violence, the more the states find themselves unable to handle the situation, and therefore the more people disinvest the state, which further weakens the ability of states to limit the spiral." In areas where the state is already weak, the elite may hire and pay their own security forces, threatening the state's monopoly on the legitimate use of force.

For Wallerstein, the loss of state legitimacy is caused by changes in the world capital-ist system (1998, 2003). He challenges the view that states are autonomous entities with un-limited power but rather are institutions of a larger world system. While Wallerstein is adamant that the world is transitioning from the current capitalist order to something else, and that this period of transition will be difficult, he does not argue that the state will neces-sarily disappear. What he does argue is, (1) it is impossible to know definitively what the fu-ture will look like; and (2) those with privilege will do what they can to ensure that the new world order will perpetuate their advantage by "replicate[ing] the worst features of the ex-isting one—its hierarchy, privilege, and inequalities" (Wallerstein 2003: 270).

CONCLUSION

It is clear that political sociologists have a long list of potential hypotheses that need empirical testing before deciding whether the state survives or is on the decline. Just as Tilly (1985) and Bottomore (1979) contend that the state has not always been the main regulator of power with a monopoly on the legitimate use of force, we see no reason to assume it will always be.

While many of the ideas on the future of the state are theoretical and need empirical verification, what cannot be denied is the importance of political institutions and the ways in which these entities impact every facet of social life. Whether future political sociologists will study the effects and interactions of the nation-state, the transitional state apparatus, or *Empire*, we expect that there will continue to be rich diversity in both theoretical perspectives and empirical approaches. That diversity will be a direct result of the past and current debates taking place among pluralist, elite, Marxist, and political institutionalists who continue to refine their arguments to overcome weaknesses identified by competing perspectives. Rational choice and postmodern views will also continue to be influential. Future chapters will take a closer look at the impact of the state on our everyday lives, theoretical contributions for understanding other political processes such as voting and other forms of political participation, and the many globalization debates.

Endnotes

1. The federal government and most of the fifty states do not currently recognize gay marriage. Historically, there have been statutes that prohibit sex acts between consenting adults such as premarital sex, extramarital sex, same-sex sexual behavior, and even certain sex acts between spouses such as oral sex. While many of these statutes are not currently enforced, the exception has been gay sex acts. Both U.S. Supreme Court cases *Lawrence v. Texas* (2003) and *Bowers v. Hardwick* (1986) began when law enforcement arrested persons engaging in consensual same-sex sexual acts in the privacy of their homes. Until *Lawrence,* which overturned *Bowers v. Hardwick*, states could prohibit same-sex sexual behavior while considering similar behavior in heterosexual couples as legal (e.g., oral sex). *Lawrence* is based on the right of sexual privacy or that sex acts between consenting adults are off limits to state regulation. Note though that the state, through the judiciary, is in the position of deciding what does and does not come under state regulation.

2. On November 14, 2007, after calling 911, sixty-two-year-old John Horn, a resident of Pasadena, Texas (a Houston suburb), killed two men he suspected were burglarizing a next-door neighbor. While the 911 operator pleaded with Horn to stay inside and wait for the police, he replied "I am going to kill them." He redialed 911 and said "They came in the front yard with me, man. I had no choice. Get somebody over here quick." A Texas grand jury refused to indict Horn (Lozano 2008). In contrast, Kyle Huggett, a 32-year-old Danbury, Wisconsin, resident was initially bound over for trial for the January 2009 killing of John Peach, who broke through the front door of Huggett's residence to confront him. The two had been exchanging harassing text messages. Peach was the ex-boyfriend of Huggett's girlfriend who was pregnant with Huggett's child. Huggett testified that he was afraid of Peach and what he might do to his girlfriend and their unborn child. Burnett County District Attorney, Kenneth Kutz, denied that the accused was facing imminent danger arguing "I think Mr. Huggett panicked and shot John Peach when he came into the house—a reasonable person wouldn't have reacted that way" (Beckmann 2008: 6A). Homicide charges were eventually dismissed by a Wisconsin judge who ruled that Burnett County officials denied the defendant due process by failing to listen to or transcribe voice mail messages left by John Peach (Xiong 2009). The Burnett County district attorney appealed the ruling (Rathbun 2009). The Wisconsin Supreme Court refused to hear the appeal, meaning that Huggett will not have to stand trial (Beckmann 2010).

3. The Iran–Contra affair was a political scandal during the Reagan administration in which weapons were sold illegally to Iran and were used in Iran's war with Iraq while the latter was a U.S. ally. Weapon sale proceeds were used to fund the Contras' (anti-communist) fight against the Nicaraguan Sandinista government. The Sandinistas or the Sandinista National

Liberation Front is a Nicaraguan political party based on Marxist ideology.

4. The national government of India controls the harvest of *tendu* leaves that are used to make Indian cigarettes. The tendu committee is a local group that oversees the harvest on behalf of the forest department. The harvest is a major source of cash income for locals with an opportunity to earn five to ten times the average daily wage. The committee appoints a *munshi* who is responsible for organizing the leaf collection, keeping harvest and payment records, and distributing cash payments to the villagers. In the situation described by anthropologist Peggy Froerer (2005), the munshi for a specific village was also the *Patel* or traditional leader who had been cheating the villagers out of their entitled share of the proceeds for several years. The villagers were hesitant to approach the tendu committee and request a new munshi. Her description of how the villagers were eventually able to override the Patel and have a new munshi appointed illustrates how those holding traditional authority in order to maintain their power use the state and also how those villagers were able to use that external state power to remove someone who abused his authority.

5. In his classic work, *The Elementary Forms of Religious Life*, Durkheim notes that no object is inherently incapable of being transformed and in a footnote he refers to scholarship on the religious quality of excrement.

6. The *Economist*'s index of democracy uses five criteria including electoral process and pluralism, civil liberties, the functioning of government, political participation, and political culture. Nations are divided into four categories including full democracies, flawed democracies, hybrids, and authoritarian. The index ranges from 10 to 1 with Sweden the top-rated democracy with a score of 9.88 and North Korea the least democratic nation with a score of 1.03. Out of twenty-seven nations categorized as full democracies, the United States ranks 17 with a score of 8.22. For more information on methodology, see http://www.economist.com/media/pdf/DEMOCRACY_INDEX_2007_v3.pdf (Kekic 2007).

7. The G8 is an international forum represented by the governments of Canada, France, Germany, United Kingdom, Italy, Japan, Russia, and the United States.

References

Agamben, Giorgio. 2005. *State of Exception.* Translated by Kevin Attell. Chicago: University of Chicago Press.

Agger, Ben and Tim Luke. 2002. "Politics in Postmodernity: The Diaspora of Politics and Homelessness of Political and Social Theory." Pp. 159–196 in *Theoretical Directions in Political Sociology for the 21st Century*, volume 11, *Research in Political Sociology*, edited by B.A. Dobratz, T. Buzzell, and L.K. Waldner. Amsterdam: Elsevier (JAI).

Alford, Robert. 1993. "Paradigms of Relations between State and Society." Pp. 258–267 in *Power in Modern Societies*, edited by M.E. Olsen and M.N. Marger. Boulder, CO: Westview Press.

Alford, Robert and Roger Friedland. 1985. *Powers of Theory.* Cambridge: Cambridge University Press.

Amenta, Edwin. 2005. "State-Centered and Political Institutionalist Theory: Retrospect and Prospect." Pp. 96–114 in *The Handbook of Political Sociology*, edited by T. Janoski, R. Alford, A. Hicks, and M.A. Schwartz. Cambridge: Cambridge University Press.

Arrighi, G. 2003. "Lineages of Empire." Pp. 29–42 in *Debating Empire*, edited by G. Balakrishnan. New York: Verso Books.

Babu, B. Ramesh. 2006. "The Liberal Capitalist West as the New 'Global State.'" *International Studies* 43: 291–304.

Beckmann, Todd. 2008. "Huggett to Face Murder Charge." *Burnett County Sentinel* July 23: 1A, 6A.

_____. 2010. "A Final Dismissal." *Burnett County Sentinel* August 18: 1A, 6A.

Berberoglu, Berch. 1990. *Political Sociology: A Comparative/Historical Approach.* Dix Hills, NY: General Hall, Inc.

Block, Fred. 1993. "The Ruling Class Does Not Rule." Pp. 295–305 in *Power in Modern Societies*, edited by M.E. Olsen and M.N. Marger. Boulder, CO: Westview Press.

Bottomore, Tom. 1979. *Political Sociology.* 2nd Edition. Minneapolis, MN: University of Minnesota Press.

Bowers v. Hardwick. 1986. 478 U.S. at 219.

Brachet-Márquez, Viviane. 2005. "Undemocratic Policies in the Twentieth Century and Beyond." Pp. 461–481 in *The Handbook of Political Sociology*, edited by T. Janoski, R. Alford, A. Hicks, and M.A. Schwartz. Cambridge: Cambridge University Press.

Callinicos, Alex. 2006. "Confronting a World without Justice: Brian Barry's Why Social Justice Matters." *Critical Review of International Social and Political Philosophy* 9: 461–472.

Clarke, Richard A. 2004. *Against All Enemies: Inside America's War on Terror.* New York: Free Press.

Dahl, Robert A. 1956. *A Preface to Democratic Theory.* Chicago: University of Chicago Press.

_____. 1963. *Modern Political Analysis.* New York: Prentice Hall.

Domhoff, G. William. 1993. "The American Power Structure." Pp. 170–182 in *Power in Modern Societies*, edited by M.E. Olsen and M.N. Marger. Boulder, CO: Westview Press.

_____. 2006. *Who Rules America.* 5th Edition. Boston: McGraw-Hill.

Donald, David H. 1995. *Lincoln.* London: Jonathon Cape.

Dove, Laura and Lisa Guernsey. 1995. "The Apotheosis of George Washington: Brumidi's Fresco and Beyond." Retrieved November 12, 2007 from http://xroads.virginia.edu/~CAP/gw/gwmain.html.

Durkheim, Emile. 1995 [1912]. *The Elementary Forms of Religious Life.* Translated by Karen E. Fields. New York: Free Press.

Economist Intelligence Unit. 2008. "The Economist Intelligence Unit's Index of Democracy 2008." *Economist.* Retrieved July 22, 2009 from http://graphics.eiu.com/PDF/Democracy%20Index%202008.pdf.

Esping-Andersen, Gøsta. 1990. *The Three Worlds of Welfare Capitalism.* Cambridge, UK: Polity.

Evans, Peter B., Dietrich Rueschemeyer, and Theda Skocpol. 1985. *Bringing the State Back In.* Cambridge, UK: Cambridge University Press.

Falkner, Gerda and Emmerich Talos. 1994. "The Role of the State within Social Policy." *Western European Politics* 17: 52–71.

Froerer, Peggy. 2005. "Challenging Traditional Authority: The Role of the State, the Divine, and the RSS." *Contributions to Indian Sociology* 39: 39–73.

Gall, Carlotta. 2007. "Pakistan's Court Dismisses Election Cases." *New York Times* November 20. Retrieved November 20, 2007 from http://www.nytimes.com/2007/11/20/world/asia/20pakistan.html?_r=1&ref=todayspaper.

Gearan, Anne. 2004. "Government Struggles to Deal with Fallout from Supreme Court's Guantanamo Decision." *Associated Press* June 30. Retrieved November 20, 2007 from http://www.nytimes.com/2007/11/20/world/asia/20pakistan.html.

Gerth, H.H. and C.Wright Mills (editors and translators). 1946. *From Max Weber: Essays in Sociology.* New York: Oxford University Press.

Gold, David L., Clarence Y.H. Lo, and Erik Olin Wright 1975. "Recent Developments in Marxist Theories of the Capitalist State" *Monthly Review* 27: 29–43.

_____. 1993. "Marxist Theories of the Capitalist State." Pp. 268–276 in *Power in Modern Societies*, edited by M.E. Olsen and M.N. Marger. Boulder, CO: Westview Press.

Goldstone, Jack. 1991. "Review: States Making Wars Making States Making Wars. . . ." *Contemporary Sociology* 20: 176–178.

Goodwin, Doris Kearnes. 1994. *No Ordinary Time: Franklin and Eleanor Roosevelt: The Home Front in World War II.* New York: Simon and Schuster.

Greenfield, Liah and Jonathan Eastwood. 2005. "Nationalism in Contemporary Perspective." Pp. 247–265 in *The Handbook of Political Sociology*, edited by T. Janoski, R. Alford, A. Hicks, and M.A. Schwartz. Cambridge: Cambridge University Press.

Haque, M.S. 2003. "The Role of the State in Managing Ethnic Tensions in Malaysia." *American Behavioral Scientist* 47: 240–266.

Hardt, Michael and Antonio Negri. 2001. *Empire.* Cambridge: Harvard University Press.

Heydebrand, Wolf (editor). 1994. *Max Weber: Sociological Writings.* The German Library, volume 60. New York: Continuum.

Hicks, Alexander M. and Gøsta Esping-Andersen. 2005. "Comparative and Historical Studies of Public Policy and the Welfare State." Pp. 509–525 in *The Handbook of Political Sociology*, edited by T. Janoski, R. Alford, A. Hicks, and M.A. Schwartz. Cambridge: Cambridge University Press.

Hicks, Alexander M., Thomas Janoski, and Mildred Schwartz. 2005. "Political Sociology in the New Millennium." Pp. 1–32 in *The Handbook of Political Sociology*, edited by T. Janoski, R. Alford, A. Hicks, and M.A. Schwartz. Cambridge: Cambridge University Press.

History News Network. 2003. "HNN Debate: Was Ike Responsible for the Deaths of Hundreds of Thousands of German POW's? Pro and Con." February, 17. Retrieved November 16, 2007 from http://hnn.us/articles/1266. html#bacque.

Huntington, Samuel P. 1996. *The Clash of Civilizations and the Remaking of World Order.* New York: Touchstone: Simon and Schuster.

Kekic, Laza. 2007. "The Economist Intelligence Unit's Index of Democracy." *Economist.* Retrieved January 2, 2008 from http://www.economist.com/media/pdf/DEMOCRACY_INDEX_2007_v3.pdf.

Kestnbaum, Meyer. 1995. Review of *War and the Rise of the State: The Military Foundations of Modern Politics* by Bruce D. Porter. *Contemporary Sociology* 24: 360–361.

Kiser, Edgar and Shawn Bauldry. 2005. "Rational-Choice Theories in Political Sociology." Pp. 172–186 in *The Handbook of Political Sociology*, edited by T. Janoski, R. Alford, A. Hicks, and M.A. Schwartz. Cambridge: Cambridge University Press.

Korpi, Walter. 2003. "Welfare-State Regress in Western Europe: Politics, Institutions, Globalization and Europeanization." *Annual Review of Sociology* 29: 589–609.

Kourvetaris, George A. 1997. *Political Sociology: Structure and Process.* Boston: Allyn & Bacon.

Lauderdale, Pat and Annmarie Oliverio. 2005. "Introduction: Critical Perspectives on Terrorism." *International Journal of Comparative Sociology* 46: 3–10.

Lawrence v Texas. 2003. 539 U.S. 558.

Lichtblau. Eric. 2008. "Report Faults Aides in Hiring at Justice Dept." *New York Times* July 29. Retrieved

July 29, 2008 from http://www.nytimes.com/2008/07/29/washington/29justice.html.

Lo, Clarence Y.H. 2002. "Marxist Models of the Capitalist State and Politics." Pp. 197–231 in *Theoretical Directions in Political Sociology for the 21st Century*, volume 11, *Research in Political Sociology*, edited by B.A. Dobratz, T. Buzzell, and L.K. Waldner. Amsterdam: JAI Press/Elsevier.

Lozano, Juan A. 2008. "Texas Man Cleared of Shooting Suspected Burglars." *Associated Press* July 1. Retrieved July 28, 2008 from http://nl.newsbank.com/nl-search/we/Archives.

Mann, Michael. 1988. *States, War, and Capitalism*. New York: Basil Blackwell.

_____. 1993. "The Autonomous Power of the State." Pp. 314–327 in *Power in Modern Societies*, edited by M.E. Olsen and M.N. Marger. Boulder, CO: Westview Press.

Manza, Jeff and Christopher Uggen. 2006. *Locked Out: Felon Disenfranchisement and American Democracy.* New York: Oxford University Press.

Marger, Martin N. 1987. *Elites and Masses*. 2nd Edition. Belmont, CA: Wadsworth.

Markoff, John. 2005. "Transitions to Democracy." Pp. 384–403 in *The Handbook of Political Sociology*, edited by T. Janoski, R. Alford, A. Hicks, and M.A. Schwartz. Cambridge: Cambridge University Press.

McCullough, David. 2001. *John Adams*. New York: Touchstone.

McKiernan, Kevin. 2006. *The Kurds: A People in Search of Their Homeland.* New York: St. Martin's Press.

Melling, Joseph. 1991. "Industrial Capitalism and the Welfare of the State: The Role of Employers in the Comparative Development of Welfare States. A Review of Recent Literature." *Sociology* 25: 219–239.

Miliband, Ralph. 1993. "The State System and the State Elite." Pp. 277–285 in *Power in Modern Societies*, edited by M.E. Olsen and M.N. Marger. Boulder, CO: Westview Press.

Mills, C. Wright. 1956. *The Power Elite*. New York: Oxford University Press.

Misra, Joya. 2002. "Class, Race, and Gender and Theorizing Welfare States." Pp. 19–52 in *Theoretical Directions in Political Sociology for the 21st Century*, volume 11, *Research in Political Sociology,* edited by B.A. Dobratz, T. Buzzell, and L.K. Waldner. Amsterdam: JAI Press/ Elsevier.

Nagengast, Carole. 1994. "Violence, Terror, and the Crisis of the State." *Annual Review of Anthropology* 23: 109–136.

Offe, Claus. 1996. *Modernity and the State: East, West.* Cambridge, MA: MIT Press.

Ohmae, Kenichi. 1995. *The End of the Nation-State: The Rise of Regional Economies*. New York: Free Press.

Olsen, Marvin E. 1993. "Sociopolitical Pluralism." Pp. 146–152 in *Power in Modern Societies*, edited by M.E. Olsen and M.N. Marger. Boulder, CO: Westview Press.

Olsen, Marvin E. and Martin N. Marger. 1993. *Power in Modern Societies.* Boulder, CO: Westview Press.

Orloff, Ann Shola. 1993. "The Role of State Formation and State Building in Social Policy Developments: The Politics of Pensions in Britain, the United States, and Canada, 1880s–1930s." *Political Power and Social Theory* 8: 3–44.

Orum, Anthony. 2001. *Introduction to Political Sociology*. 4th Edition. New Jersey: Prentice Hall.

Oszlak, Oscar. 2005. "State Bureaucracy." Pp. 482–505 in *The Handbook of Political Sociology*, edited by T. Janoski, R. Alford, A. Hicks, and M.A. Schwartz. Cambridge: Cambridge University Press.

"Pakistan Says More than 3000 Freed." 2007. *Associated Press* November 20. Retrieved November 20, 2007 from http://www.nytimes.com/aponline/world/AP-Pakistan.html.

Pedriana, Nicholas and Robin Stryker. 1997. "Political Culture Wars 1960s Style: Equal Employment Opportunity—Affirmative Action Law and the Philadelphia Plan." *American Journal of Sociology* 103: 633–691.

Perlez, Jane. 2007. "Musharraf in Talks on Exiled Rival." *New York Times* November 20. Retrieved November 20, 2007 from http://www.nytimes.com/2007/11/21/world/asia/ 21pakistan.html?ref=world.

Perlez, Jane and Salman Masood. 2008. "Bhutto's Widower, Viewed as Ally by U.S., Wins the Pakistani Presidency Handily." *New York Times* September 7. Retrieved September 8, 2008 (http://www.nytimes.com/2008/09/07/world/asia/07pstan.html).

Piven, Frances Fox and Richard Cloward. 1988. *Why Americans Don't Vote*. New York: Pentheon Books.

Porter, Bruce. 1994. *War and the Rise of the State: The Military Foundations of Modern Politics*. New York: The Free Press.

Poulantzas, Nicos. 1975. *Political Power and Social Classes*. London: Verso Books.

Prewitt, Kenneth and Alan Stone. 1993. "The Ruling Elites." Pp. 125–136 in *Power in Modern Societies*, edited by M.E. Olsen and M.N. Marger. Boulder, CO: Westview Press.

Putnam, Robert F. 2000. *Bowling Alone: The Collapse and Revival of American Community*. New York: Simon and Schuster.

Quadagno, Jill. 1988. "From Old Age Assistance to Supplemental Security Income: The Political Economy of Relief in the South, 1935–1972." Pp. 235–264 in *The Politics of Social Policy in the United States*, edited by M. Weir, A.S. Orloff, and T. Skocpol. Princeton, NJ: Princeton University Press.

Rathbun, Andy. 2009. "Burnett County Judge Dismisses Homicide Charge against Minneapolis Firefighter." *Pioneer Press* June 3. Retrieved August 5, 2009 from http://m.twincities.com/twincities/db_11032/contentdetail.htm;jsessionid=6B158843F3AB3D4FD89E423A1CEEA601?full=true&contentguid=QuVjbQpN&pn=0&ps=5.

Robinson, William I. 1998. "Beyond Nation-State Paradigms: Globalization, Sociology, and the Challenge of Transnational Studies." *Sociological Forum* 13: 561–594.

_____. 2001. "Social Theory and Globalization: The Rise of a Transnational State." *Theory and Society* 30: 157–200.

_____. 2004. "What to Expect from US 'Democracy Promotion' in Iraq." *New Political Science* 26: 441–447.

Rohde, David. 2007. "U.S. Prods Musharraf to End Emergency Rule." *New York Times* November 8. Retrieved November 8, 2007 from http://www.nytimes.com/2007/11/08/world/asia/08pakistan.html.

Runciman, W.G. 1978. *Weber: Selections in Translation.* Translated by Eric Matthews. Cambridge: Cambridge University Press.

Savage, David G. 2008. "In Historic Ruling, Gitmo Detainees Win a Day in Court." *Star Tribune* June 13: A1, A3.

Schwarzmantel, John. 2001. "Nationalism and Fragmentation since 1989." Pp. 386–395 in *The Blackwell Companion to Political Sociology*, edited by K. Nash and A. Scott Malden, MA: Blackwell Publishers.

Scott, Alan. 2004. "The Political Sociology of War." Pp. 183–194 in *The Blackwell Companion to Political Sociology*, edited by K. Nash and A. Scott. Blackwell Publishing, Blackwell Reference Online. Retrieved August 18, 2009 from http://www.blackwellreference.com/subscriber/tocnode?id=g9781405122658_chunk_gs978140512265819.

Scott, John and Gordan Marshall. 2005. *Oxford Dictionary of Sociology.* 3rd Edition. Oxford: Oxford University Press.

Shahzad, Asif and Nahal Toosi. 2009. "Pakistan's Top Court Rules Musharraf's 2007 Declaration of Emergency Rule Unconstitutional." *Star Tribune* July 31, 2009. Retrieved August 5, 2009 from http://www.startribune.com/world/52192243.html.

Skocpol, Theda. 1985. "Bringing the State Back In: Strategies of Analysis in Current Research." Pp. 3–37 in *Bringing the State Back In*, edited by P.B. Evans, D. Rueschemeyer, and T. Skocpol. Cambridge: Cambridge University Press.

_____. 1993. "The Potential Autonomy of the State." Pp. 306–313 in *Power in Modern Societies*, edited by M.E. Olson and M.N. Marger. Boulder, CO: Westview Press.

Skrentny, John D. 2006. "Law and the American State." *Annual Review of Sociology* 32: 213–244.

Spanakos, Anthony P. 2007. "Adjectives, Asterisks and Qualification, or How to Address Democracy in Contemporary Latin America." *Latin American Research Review* 42: 225–237, 279.

Steinmetz, George. 2002. *Empire* by Michael Hardt and Antonio Negri. *American Journal of Sociology* 108: 207–210.

Stepan, Alfred. 1988. *Rethinking Military Politics: Brazil and the Southern Cone.* Princeton, NJ: Princeton University Press.

Streeck, Wolfgang and Lane Kenworthy. 2005. "Theories and Practices of Neocorporatism." Pp. 441–460 in *The Handbook of Political Sociology*, edited by T. Janoski, R. Alford, A. Hicks, and M.A. Schwartz. Cambridge: Cambridge University Press.

Tilly, Charles. 1975. *The Formation of National States in Western Europe.* Princeton, NJ: Princeton University Press.

_____. 1985. "War Making and State Making as Organized Crime." Pp. 169–191 in *Bringing the State Back In*, edited by P.B. Evans, D. Rueschemeyer, and T. Skocpol. Cambridge: Cambridge University Press.

_____. 1990. *Coercion, Capital, and European States, AD 990–1990.* Oxford and Cambridge, MA: Basil Blackwell.

_____. 2003. "A Nebulous Empire." Pp. 26–28 in *Debating Empire*, edited by G. Balakrishnan. New York: Verso Books.

Tocqueville, Alexis de. 1945 [1835]. *Democracy in America.* New York: Vintage Books.

Torfing, Jacob. 2005. "The Linguistic Turn: Foucault, Laclau, Mouffe, and Žižek." Pp. 153–171 in *The Handbook of Political Sociology*, edited by T. Janoski, R. Alford, A. Hicks, and M.A. Schwartz. Cambridge: Cambridge University Press.

"U.S. Is Too Quick to Accept Nations as True Democracies, Rights Group Says." 2008. *Associated Press* February 1.

Venkatesh, Sudhir. 2008. *Gang Leader for a Day.* New York: Penguin Press.

Vujačić, Veljko. 2002. "States, Nations, and European Nationalism: A Challenge for Political Sociology." Pp. 123–156 in *Theoretical Directions in Political Sociology for the 21st Century*, volume 11, *Research in Political Sociology*, edited by B.A. Dobratz, T. Buzzell, and L.K. Waldner. Amsterdam: JAI Press/Elsevier.

_____. 2004. "Perceptions of the State in Russia and Serbia: The Role of Ideas in the Soviet and Yugoslav Collapse." *Post Soviet Affairs* 20: 164–194.

Wallace, Harvey. 1999. *Family Violence: Legal, Medical, and Social Perspectives.* 2nd Edition. Boston: Allyn & Bacon.

Wallerstein, Immanuel. 1998. *Utopistics.* New York: The New Press.

_____. 2003. *The Decline of American Power.* New York: The New York Press.

Xiong, Chao. 2009. "Firefighter's Homicide Charges Dropped." *Star Tribune* June 2: A1, A4.

Zeitlin, Irving M. 1981. *Ideology and the Development of Sociological Theory.* 2nd Edition. Englewood Cliffs, NJ: Prentice Hall.

CHAPTER 3

Politics, Culture, and Social Processes

T.S. Eliot once observed that culture is made up of those things that make life worth living (1948). *Culture* in this sense refers to things we call "high taste," or artifacts such as classical music, expensive art, or gourmet food. As sociologists, we understand that culture has both material and nonmaterial dimensions. For example, *material forms of culture* are displayed in museums and archives. The Constitution and the Declaration of Independence on display in the National Archives in Washington, DC, are examples of highly symbolic forms of material culture, including the architecture of the temple-like National Archives building. *Nonmaterial forms of culture* include music played or speeches given on the Fourth of July to celebrate the principles in those documents. As the study of culture has grown in sociology, it has confirmed the fact that culture is essential to the functioning of society and its component social structures and groups.

Over the past three decades, sociologists have made great strides in refining their understanding of the role of culture in guiding social and personal interactions. Much of this work represents the return to key concepts originally outlined by Weber, Durkheim, and to some extent, Marx. Political sociology has built on much of this work in the study of culture, and more recently returned to the study of the various nuances of the relationship between culture, power, and the nature of political arrangements in society. In this chapter, we explore just a few ways in which culture and politics intertwine. The goal here is to briefly describe how political beliefs, values, ideologies, and other symbolic systems in society are related to the exercise of political power in its many different forms, such as formations of political groups and associations, or participation in political action.

CULTURE AND POLITICS

What is culture? C. Wright Mills (1959) observed that "the concept of 'culture' is one of the spongiest words in social science" (160). While there are many approaches typically connected to various disciplines, we conceptualize culture as comprised of values, knowledge, beliefs, symbols, language, and artifacts found in all societies. Culture is essential to the facilitation of social interaction. Weber described the concept in a fascinating observation about the nature of religion and culture in guiding social action:

> Not ideas, but material and ideal interests directly govern men's conduct. Yet very frequently the "world images" that have been created by "ideas" have, like switch-men, determined the tracks along which action has been pushed by the dynamic of interests. (Weber 1946: 280)

Weber's insight is that images and ideas shape interests and guide social interactions.

In his treatment of culture, Talcott Parsons (1951) identified three elements of culture, all of which are transmitted, learned, and shared—knowledge, values, and symbolic expressions. Knowledge is the store of experiences, findings, facts, and ways of comprehending the world. For instance, since the Enlightenment, science has evolved into a tradition of knowledge. Schools obviously play an important role in preserving this knowledge and sharing it with successive generations. Values are made up of beliefs or mental benchmarks for assessing the world. In a classic study of values in the United States, Williams (1970) concluded that freedom, equality, democracy, individual success, progress, work, material comfort, efficiency, morality, science, patriotism, and the superiority of some groups over others have consistently served as guides to social interactions in the United States. Parsons also suggested that norms, including folkways and mores, were part of this element of culture. In addition, Parsons brought to our attention the significance of symbolic expression as an element of culture. This includes art, music, poetry, rituals, and religions as manifestations of emotions and tastes. Language too is an essential symbolic expression especially for facilitating interaction. It gives human beings a mechanism for expression through utterances, words, verbalizations, and signs.

Ann Swidler (1986) defined culture as a "tool kit" of habits, skills, and styles from which people construct strategies of action. The tools we are given in the socialization process help us navigate social interactions as we move through social groups and social institutions. Understanding culture as a tool kit for interaction in society, and as made up of elements that help forge the tools, provides an important analytic tool for considering the role of culture in politics. As revealed in the study by Williams (1970), values play a significant role in deciding power relations in society. As Weber argued so persuasively in his early work, culture governs social actions, including social conflicts, be it conflicts among social classes, status groups, or other structures in society. The mechanisms for transmitting information about political candidates, or how individuals learn about citizenship, are examples of forms of political knowledge linked to socialization processes of many kinds. Certainly we can think of politics as having symbolic expressions too. The more obvious are associations with nationalism or patriotism, such as flying a flag. Language can also play a role in legitimizing power relationships, or quite literally, creating a criterion for citizenship. In this case, the tools in the kit are labeled in such a way that we access them when considering aspects of power and politics.

The work on culture has advanced considerably within the last twenty years. Granted, culture at one level is about a complex of values and attitudes that in turn influence social interactions. But the sociological understanding of culture goes beyond that. Hall, Neitz, and Battani

(2003) build on the classical sociological, anthropological, and historical treatments of culture and define culture to

> encompass: (1) *ideas, knowledge* (correct, wrong, or unverifiable belief), and *recipes* for doing things; (2) humanly fabricated *tools* (such as shovels, sewing machines, cameras, and computers); and (3) the *products* of social action that may be drawn upon in the further conduct of social life (a dish of curry, a television set, a photograph, or a high-speed train for example). (7)

Contemporary approaches to the study of culture focus on these concepts. Moreover, as this definition suggests, culture is more than just values and belief systems. The study of values and beliefs, however, constitute an important part of research in political sociology. The study of political culture offers a different view of politics, asking questions such as:

1. How do citizens develop ideas about power?
2. Where does political knowledge come from and what effect does it have on politics?
3. What role do the media play in the creation of political ideas or knowledge?
4. Is symbolism embedded in political structures used to manipulated citizen beliefs about power?

As we shall see in this chapter, these and many other questions about the connections between culture and politics make a "terrain" of a relatively new focus for political sociology (Berezin 1997).

Coronation of Elizabeth II, Westminster Abbey, London, June 1953
Credit: PhotoLibrary

POLITICS, CULTURE, AND THEORETICAL FRAMEWORKS

Early works in political sociology made references to culture and especially the significance of cultural contexts to the social psychology of politics. For example, Bendix and Lipset (1966) suggested that "interaction among individuals occupying the same economic position is also conditioned by cultural, social-psychological and situational determinants" (27). In building the research agenda of the growing field of political sociology in the 1960s, Coser (1966) advanced the argument that power had a number of cultural dimensions worthy of greater research:

> While political science had concentrated mainly on the specifically political sphere, political sociology claimed that to understand the political process fully one had to relate politics to the entire social structure. These sociologists emphasized the ways in which a particular political order as well as specific instances of political behavior—for example voting—must be studied with reference to ostensibly non-political factors such as the socialization of the young, the formal and informal patterns of association in which men are variously enmeshed, or the complicated ways in which systems of beliefs and ideologies color the perspective of political actors. (2)

This description of the nature of power in society reinforced the claim that socialization, values, beliefs, and ideologies should be studied in order to understand better the distribution of power and conflict. The major theoretical frameworks over time would address each of these "nonpolitical factors" in unique ways. The various conceptual perspectives in political sociology highlight different aspects of the nature of values, beliefs, and orientations and how these are connected to politics in society.

Pluralist

Culture has always played an important role in pluralist thinking about politics and power. Pluralists view culture as the seedbed for the beliefs, values, symbols, and orientations necessary to support the political process. For example, children learn in school that being a good citizen involves obeying the law as well as active participation in the governing processes, especially voting. These values, as Parsons would say, are important to the maintenance of the political system.

Tocqueville (1945[1835]) conducted one of the earliest studies of the new political system in the United States, highlighting the pluralist nature of the new American republic. He viewed nineteenth-century America as one of the most democratic countries in the world. Intrigued by the notion that democracy in America brought to its citizens (i.e., White adult males) social, economic, and political equality, Tocqueville's focus was especially on the participatory nature of the new democracy and how individuals would be engaged not only in voting, but also be active in civic groups and associations. Tocqueville predicted great success for the new nation. He offered five conclusions about American democracy that would assure its success:

1. a division of authority throughout society which would enhance individualism and diversity of viewpoints
2. a federal system that divided power among three branches of government as well as a division of power between state and federal governments
3. a sense of local control which would check outsiders as a threat
4. the right to a free press and
5. the right to freely associate, preventing the centralization of economic or social functions beyond government.

In many ways, these five observations from Tocqueville reflect pluralist assumptions about politics and power. Power is viewed as dispersed among groups and associations of citizens, not concentrated, but rather balanced as a result of fair elections and exchanges of opportunities to govern. Values and beliefs are supported by the cultural structures, and in some cases, these values are reflected in the language of the Constitution itself.

One of Tocqueville's most important observations dealt with the frequency with which Americans tended to organize into voluntary associations for social, economic, and political purposes. He believed that this tendency grew out of the value given to equality and the social contract—that is, the set of expectations that come from living in a community where the individual also gains from the collective life of the community. Tocqueville brought attention to the fact that political participation grows out of association and group formation oriented around political goals. Tocqueville recognized that conflict was an important source of social evolution, however, he was optimistic about American society's ability to handle this conflict. Conflict, he believed, would be balanced by giving emphasis to local governance and solving communal problems, and strengthened by voluntary association. As American democracy emerged, collective action through association was equated with power.

In *Civic Culture*, Almond and Verba (1963, 1989) made one of the earliest arguments for emphasizing the role culture played in shaping politics. From their study of citizens from the United States, Great Britain, Germany, and Italy, they concluded that political culture is the cement that holds together democratic societies in a number of ways. First, culture is "the political system internalized in the cognitions, feelings, and evaluations" (1963: 27) of the citizenry that fosters a healthy tension of sorts between full participation on every policy decision (pure democracy) and no participation at all. In other words, political culture creates a social context in which the business of governance occurs as a result of consensus. This allows a cadre of political leaders to act in the best interests of the society based on consensus about essential social values, such as equality, individualism, or achievement. Second, citizens learn that trust is crucial to the business of governing. A plurality of groups or coalitions of interest are created to address the concerns of society. Consider for example, the significance of a peaceful transition of power in the United States. The president's term of office is limited, and when a term ends, the power of the presidency is peacefully handed over from one individual to the next. Despite the contentious election of 2000, when the U.S. Supreme Court ruled in favor of the plaintiff in *Bush v. Gore*, George W. Bush was peacefully sworn in as the forty-third president of the United States. Almond and Verba (1989) would argue that political culture creates trust in these processes of governance. Consensus is maintained around the value of peaceful transitions of power and recognition by citizens that the party or majority elected in a fair electoral process has a legitimate claim to rule.

Consensus about the nature of political rule is another feature of the role of culture in politics. Equality is clearly a key theme in democratic systems. Individuals are considered to have certain rights that provide them access in the competition for power. Pluralists treat culture as an essential component to the understanding of how the masses offer support for the political system, or how changes in values and beliefs result in corresponding changes in configurations of political coalitions that result in changes in who rules. As we shall see in this chapter, a great deal of work has been done to highlight the connections between governance and mass belief systems.

Elite/Managerial

In contrast to the pluralist framework, the elite/managerial approach shifts the emphasis from conceptualizing politics to conceptualizing power as held in the hands of a few, because the competition among interest groups is guided by the rules of a fair process. The elite framework treats political culture as a source for values resulting in acquiescence to elite rule. The simple argument for this perspective is that the elites construct the political culture to reinforce elite rule.

Weber played a significant role in identifying what role culture would play in sustaining patterns of institutional rule, namely through bureaucracies. Two contributions are worth noting here in our study of politics and culture: the role of religion in fostering capitalism and associated patterns of government, and the impact of rationalization on values about interactions between citizens and larger organizations.

Weber argued that religion and systems of power were associated in ways that created a value system in a society which supported institutional arrangements. Weber's analysis of how capitalism emerges in societies alongside Protestant beliefs in particular was a critical contribution to a cultural understanding of social inequality and stratification. He suggested that Protestant attitudes contributed to the rise of capitalism in several ways. These aspects of Protestant doctrine included the idea of predestination or being God's chosen people, the notion that wasting time was a sin, or that work and occupational choice were a calling divinely inspired (Collins 1985). The strength of these attitudes, according to Weber, created a cultural system that would foster adherence to a managerial system of work and politics. Those with higher status conclude that their position in society is "providence": "This internal situation gives rise, in their relations with other strata, to a number of further characteristic contrasts in the functions which different strata of society expect religion to perform for them" (Runciman 1978: 183). For those with lower status, the hopes for salvation in the afterlife maintain a sense of complacency and acceptance of their social situation.

By understanding culture as a way of life, Weber also shed light on the structural ways in which the Industrial Revolution was changing the power of elites and their everyday existence. Weber's description of large organizations and bureaucracy contributed to understanding how what he called the *forces of rationalization* changed social patterns and social arrangements, especially power and politics. Weber found that rules, procedures, laws, and the formality of social interactions were becoming institutionalized. As a result of the forces of rationalization, value is placed on efficiency, predictability, and adherence to procedure. Culture shaped by these forces would foster the expansion of bureaucracies and the impersonal nature of law and procedures. Lawyers, bureaucrats, scientists, and experts would hold positions in the elite and assure adherence to this way of life.

The works of Mosca also extended the elite framework's argument that those who rule craft a ruling ideology. Mosca wrote of a "political formula" which the elite used to "justify its power on the ground of an abstraction" (Meisel 1962: 55). Mythological references to providence, divine right, or perhaps vision for leadership are formulas that justify political actions. Mosca wrote of this symbolic system of beliefs that resulted in elites electing elites to positions of authority, or using intellectual justification to assure elite appointment to positions in governing bodies. Mosca saw the formula as a cultural element as a distraction from the reality that power was not "of the people" (political formula) but rather in the hands of a few.

Fifty years later, in his analysis of politics and social change, Daniel Bell (1960, 1973, 1976) came to the conclusion that elites dominated the political culture of the 1970s by creating distinct belief patterns. He argued that elites would preserve power through the creation of what he called more "inclusive identities." These psychological attachments would trump social-class divisions in many ways, for example, shifting individual orientations to perhaps focus on geography, nationalism, or gender identity. Related to this shift, he argued that elites would play a role in redefining what equality meant in the modern state. Moreover, identities linked to work would change with the onset of postindustrial life, as knowledge and education would become more important. Thus elites would command the right skills or credentials required for rule. As a result of these and other global forces, Bell was one of the first to argue that political ideological struggles would be reduced to whether or not capitalism or socialism was the best model for social political economic systems. Bell argued that the "end of ideology" meant that social life was being transformed into managed life, where values would be redefined by an elite made up of diffuse centers of power.

Class Perspective

Marx originally treated the notion of culture as a superstructure, that is, culture emerged out of the economic relationships of society as well as preserved social-class divisions. In this regard, political culture would include those values, beliefs, and ideologies that preserved capitalism, the concentration of wealth in the capitalist class, the obedience of the laboring class, and the psychological power of money. For conflict theorists, culture has an important role to play in the preservation of unequal distributions of power in society.

Marx and eventually Engels concluded that each class had its own worldview in the history of class struggle, and its resulting tradition. This outlook was described as "class consciousness," which for Marxists is the source of political ideology. Class consciousness reflects economic interest. For political sociologists grounded in the class or Marxist perspective, political culture is understood as a function of ruling interests weaved into ideology and worldviews. The symbolic aspects of culture are controlled to promote economic gain for capitalist leaders. The capitalist ideology (or consciousness) is reproduced and distributed in books, letters, church pulpits, and media of all forms. The extent of this control assumes that the upper class, often with the assistance of the intelligentsia, can produce ideas to maintain or legitimize inequalities.

The essence of Marxist notions of culture, especially ideology as we shall consider it later in this chapter, is best summarized by a key statement made in Marx's 1859 work, *A Contribution to the Critique of Political Economy*:

> In the social production which men carry on they enter into definite relations that are indispensable and independent of their will; these relations of production correspond to a definite stage of development of their material powers of production. The totality of these relations of production constitutes the economic structure of society—the real foundation, on which legal and political superstructures arise and to which definite forms of social consciousness correspond. The mode of production of material life determines the general character of the social, political and spiritual processes of life. It is not the consciousness of men that determines their being, but, on the contrary, their social being determines their consciousness. (Bottomore 1961: 51)

Because property is the basis for economies, which creates classes, Marx believed that the role of the state was to protect the property interests of the owners of production. Property is owned because the state creates "rights" to ownership. The state and associated structures would create the requisite ideologies to support these outcomes.

In his efforts to describe *Who Rules America* (2006), Domhoff identifies what he calls "Americanism" as a unique mix of values which support the capitalist system and its associated governing structures. Based on decades of refining a class-based model of power in the United States, Domhoff argues that the unique ideological make-up of the United States has fostered the creation of the corporate ruling class through history. Specifically, he argues that individualism and a corresponding support for free enterprise yields at the least acquiescence to political outcomes favorable to the ruling class. As a result, few individuals challenge what are considered to be taken-for-granted assumptions in a capitalist society. This ideological characteristic of U.S. culture is one of the elements of American social history that Domhoff identifies as a component of the foundation for ruling-class dominance of politics in the United States.

A second cultural dimension found in Domhoff's (2006, 2010) research focuses on the creation of cohesion among individuals in the ruling class. Early in his research, he identified the role of the Bohemian Club and its camp north of San Francisco in creating literally a retreat for America's wealthy and elite. Interestingly, this retreat has become a place for corporate, political, and social elites to gather for fun and relaxation. Cohesion is fostered in this environment. Interestingly, Domhoff describes a number of rituals which contribute to the cohesion. One of the most intriguing of these rituals takes place near the beginning of the annual retreat when the responsibilities of corporate, political, and social leadership are symbolically burned in the "cremation of care." In this elaborate ritual, responsibility and care are personified in a muslin-wrapped wood skeleton placed in a coffin; later the coffin is burned on an altar before a large carved owl, the symbol of the Bohemian Club and Bohemian Grove camp. This symbolic letting go of the affairs of banking, corporate finance, the affairs of state, or cares that go with being a celebrity, creates cohesion among the membership much like rituals found in other groups. According to Domhoff, this ritual and the various activities found at the retreat foster interaction, loyalty, and cohesion among the ruling-class members attending.

Derber (2006) recently proposed that the history of political rule in the United States has been what he calls a series of regimes. One of the "pillars" of regime rule is the role of ideology, or political culture, manipulated to create "hidden power." Derber poses an interesting challenge to the pluralist thinking about fair and open governance in the United States:

> Do you believe in black magic? You should, because the regime survives through its own amazing form of it. All regimes weave hegemonic myths and stories that help to win the allegiance of the people and keep the regime in power. These can be called regime ideology or, more bluntly, propaganda. In democratic societies, the role of propaganda is to partly cloak what Teddy Roosevelt called the "invisible government" of the regime itself. (121)

In his historical analysis of regimes in the United States, especially since the Industrial Revolution, Derber argues that intellectual centers, corporate leaders, and the media have all played a significant role in weaving what the people come to believe is true about the state of political affairs. The goal of this belief system is to preserve wealth and power in the hands of a few. Regimes create a ruling-class hegemony, that is, a belief system that diverts people from acting in their own economic self-interest and instead becoming loyal to nationalistic or moral beliefs that ultimately do nothing to advance the causes of those who suffer or are excluded from the societal systems of power.

Rational Choice

Ideology, political values, hegemony, or symbolic systems of power that foster adherence to political rule are themes in the pluralist, elite, and class frameworks. In many ways, political culture has been an important topic for political sociologists and has never been removed from the agenda of research in political sociology, especially as sociologists have recently brought new life to the study of culture in general. Rational choice theory has come to occupy a prominent position in current explanations of power and political outcomes. It emphasizes treating politics as outcomes of interest based on rational actors operating within the bounds of a system, shaped by the social allocation of resources or the distribution of power in the community, which ultimately results in political action understood as a matter of choice. In other words, political institutions as well as political individuals act in their best interests based on the resources they have or come to earn. Following the assumptions of rational choice theory in the study of politics, we could make the case that values and orientations, no matter what the source, guide the choices of individual citizens (e.g., voting choices, action to address a community problem).

Kiser and Bauldry (2005) identify six ways in which current research in the rational choice tradition is making use of concepts in political culture. First, they note work on a concept called "focal points" which researchers argue constitutes information, values, and beliefs in an organization that become a point for agreement. This creates a basis for coordinating action within the organization and marshalling resources directed at certain goals. Second, they note that information and knowledge play a role in rational choices in organizational or institutional dynamics. As an element of culture, knowledge can guide choices. In this sense, political sociologists are now studying what role information sources play in directing actions of bureaucracies as well as political activists. The role of norms in political groups and the creation of ways to maintain membership in the groups is the third cultural dimension to the rational choice approach to the study of politics. Fourth, legitimacy to authority is an important dynamic in emerging rational choice models of politics. Related to the role of norms is the idea that some power centers in the game of politics command greater credibility to rule than others. This line of research would examine how legitimacy is created by political groups acting in the political arena. This connects to a fifth theme identified by Kiser and Bauldry, the role of ritual in pulling together collectives for political action. Political rituals can reinforce membership and loyalty to a group, thus affecting the ability of organizations to again marshal the resources necessary for achieving political goals. Sixth, more recent rational choice approaches have started to examine the role of nationalism as a cultural component to coordinating political action. As we will see later in this chapter, the rational choice approach raises interesting questions for political sociologists who consider cultural dimensions in their research as some find nationalistic tendencies to be powerful motivators for political action. As we will see in other chapters, the impact of culture continues to appear in the work of political sociologists reinforcing the role cultural elements play in politics.

Institutionalist

As mentioned in Chapter 1, we believe that the new institutionalist theories in the social sciences are in many ways a hybrid of theories of politics that have focused on structures such as organizations, bureaucracy, and the state, and have incorporated aspects of culture that emphasize culture as habits, symbolic guides to political processes, or traditions in politics. Because the institutionalist approach emphasizes the effects of culture, it's important to consider what role culture plays in politics when contrasting the various frameworks in political sociology. There are many concepts associated with this approach: the role of social ideas that affect political outcomes, the role of experts in influencing political processes, and the reliance on scripts or narratives as norms that also guide political action.

An important question in political sociology is "How is public policy made?" A cultural turn in answer to this question suggests that there are ideas, or what Burstein (1991) calls "policy domains"—"a component of the political system that is organized around substantive issues" such as education, crime, or welfare (328). These domains make up arenas of action where citizens, politicians, interest groups, parts of the bureaucracy, courts, and legislators come together with a particular policy focus. In this sense, a variety of structures are moved to address policies in these domains or areas of interest. These domains are focused on determining how issues become part of the public agenda, or how policy options are chosen. Burstein's notion of policy domains gives a focal point for analyzing what political institutions are at work, such as political actors, rules, and eventual policy outcomes. The policy domain as a clustering of structural activity around an idea explains the influence that interest groups, protest organizations, or even judicial actors have when they come together in a pattern of social action around issues like public education, defense, or health care.

Similar to the notion of the policy domain is another cultural concept referred to as a normative context for politics. Norms play a role in guiding the work of policymakers, lobbyists, or civil servants. One way of thinking of these contexts, or fields as suggested by Campbell (2002), is as "taken-for-granted world views of policy makers" that "constrain the range of policy choices they are likely to consider when formulating economic, welfare, national security, and other public policies" (22). These are typically important normative assumptions about the nature of work or family or education. For example, there may be normative boundaries in policymaking that follow the "get tough on crime" norm typical of campaigns which emphasize to legislators the taken-for-granted cultural expectations regarding punishment of crimes that are considered particularly harmful to society.

Policymakers as well as candidates seeking office often turn to experts for advice on political processes. The role of experts as retainers of knowledge and experiences in political action is another field of research in the institutionalist framework. Manza (2000) studied, for example, a constellation of experts that played a critical role in the creation of the New Deal reforms initiated by President Roosevelt in the 1930s and 1940s. He finds that "At the center of the efforts of these reformers were advocacy organizations such as the American Association for Labor Legislation and the American Association for Old Age Security. These organizations provided intellectual and political leadership for early pension reform campaigns, and eventually at the national level during the New Deal" (312). As an element of culture, knowledge in this regard is seen as an important variable in explaining actions of the state. A cadre of intellectuals or experts typically plays an important role in bringing areas of specialty to bear on political processes, including policy processes and electoral activities of campaigns (e.g., pollsters or campaign strategists).

Another stream of inquiry associated with institutionalist political sociology has explored "narratives" in politics. Jacobs and Sobieraj (2007) describe narratives as "templates for orienting and acting in the world: by differentiating between good and evil, by providing understandings of agency and selfhood, and by defining the nature of social bonds and relationships" (5). In this sense, political culture is a source for ways in which stories about public problems or concerns are told, with situations, actors, even scripts for telling the story. In their research, they study how members of Congress weaved what the researchers called "a masquerade narrative" to shed light on fake or illegitimate nonprofit groups. The power of these stories is revealed by how public perceptions were molded by members of Congress who wanted to maintain their image as champions protecting legitimate nonprofit groups that help people, and at the same time criticizing the nonprofit sector for taking advantage of the taxpayer through tax exemptions or high salaries paid to CEOs of nonprofit groups. Narratives in this regard originate in the power of storytelling as a way to persuade voters or describe groups in context of a political debate or conflict. We will revisit the importance of narrative and the story creation to motivate political participation.

Postmodern

The postmodern analyses of politics, political structures, and political processes in society are perhaps in essence cultural in their approach. This body of work focuses on inherently cultural themes, such as the power of language and social discourse in creating exclusion of segments of society, the emergence of social identities related to values and beliefs unique to postmodern life, the understanding of history as culture, as well as the evolution of political configurations of symbols, meanings, and structures across time. Torfing (2005) summarizes this approach, concluding that "Poststructuralist discourse theory is a tool for analyzing the more or less sedimented rules and meanings that condition the political construction of social, political and cultural identity" (153). The postmodern framework as we describe in this text is a collection of works perhaps not as unified as the previous traditions but nonetheless significant to studies of political culture.

A key feature of the postmodernist notions of power is that language structures reality. Thus, power distributions in society are understood as what is commonly referred to in this framework as narratives. These narratives are (to oversimplify perhaps) patterns of social actions created as/by systems of power. They reflect the "sedimented rules and meanings" in language and interaction that Torfing describes. Two key works by Foucault shaped this approach. In his study of mental illness, *Madness and Civilization* (1973), he proposed the idea that some groups of people can be separated because they are not adherents to reason. Separation was created not only physically, but also through narratives. For example, society created a named category of persons with mental problems—the mad. Eventually, the narrative of mental illness was commanded by doctors and scientists, who described these conditions as medical conditions. In *Discipline and Punish* (1975), Foucault traces the narratives of punishment. Prior to the 1800s, societies created spectacles of pain and torture often in the name of the monarch or church. Science changed this narrative with the invention of a science of punishment. The modern prison, invented in the early 1800s, was structured to allow the "gaze" of the watchful state, maintaining control and surveillance of those convicted with large prisons designed to control every move of the body as well as watch every aspect of daily prisoner routines. The science of punishment would also invent narratives related to reform and rehabilitation, again with the idea that criminality was sickness, or bad choices, which could be changed. The language of these forms of control in society was changed by science, experts, and the state. Narratives mark these shifts in thinking about control of deviant populations.

Another example of the postmodern approach to politics and culture is found in the work of Laclau and Mouffe (1985; Mouffe 1991) who offer a framework where citizenship is redefined in terms of the creation of discourse to describe a cultural guide of sorts to steer individuals to come together to tackle common problems. Mouffe suggests that individuals create a common bond when they share a concern or problem. They draw upon cultural rules and manners of talking relevant to conceptualizing problems in order to get things done. Mouffe refers to the cultural sources that guide manners, talk, and conceptualizations of social issues as citizenship emerging from the res publica:

> Those rules prescribe norms of conduct to be subscribed to in seeking self-chosen satisfactions and in performing self-chosen actions. The identification with those rules of civil intercourse creates a common political identity among persons otherwise engaged in many different enterprises. This modern form of political community is held together not by a substantive idea of a common good but by a common bond, a public concern. It is therefore a community without definite shape, a definite identity, and in a continuous reenactment. (1991: 77)

In this sense, the exercise of political power can appear and disappear depending on the public concern addressed, as well as on the makeup of any given community that expresses its concerns and at the same time is motivated to act against the political authority. Politics is not thought of as interest group against interest group (pluralism), elites against the masses (elitism), or upper class against working class (class), but rather politics is constructed by citizens working together using cultural resources (e.g., discourse, symbolism, cohesion of a community) to create civic bonds that once forged, are useful in addressing public concerns.

This approach to understanding politics requires the political sociologist to see the exercise of power by collectives in its civic context, or consistent with the terminology of this approach, politics occurs in certain social spaces. For example, in his study of AIDS activism in Canada, Brown (1997) found that individuals in urban areas came together to address the public concern of how to care for AIDS patients. Political action was not just about lobbying the state for resources to help AIDS patients, but it was also about creating groups of volunteers in neighborhoods to care for patients or to educate the community about AIDS. In addition, Brown discovered that activism also involved families in a way to create care networks of sorts for individual patients. What Brown discovered was that the "radical democracy" that Mouffe and Laclau talked about was revealed in the way of life associated with the particular city studied. The res publica was a cultural basis for the norms and rules of action involving the state (national and urban), community (neighborhoods), and families (the private sphere). Politics emerged to address the concern of AIDS. Urban life fostered this new space of political action.

According to this approach, culture and structure foster the emergence of political action. Political action at any given moment can appear as individuals define political concerns through discourse, and find a configuration of collective action that works for the problem. Culture is the sources of rules about forming action, beliefs about what is valuable action or what issue is in need of concern, and ideas for solving problems. This action may then disappear once it's felt it has been addressed. Thus, because of the heavy influence of culture in this approach outlined by Laclau and Mouffe, political action is always changing. Although complex, this conceptualization of politics and culture is a good example of the postmodern orientation to politics and power.

POLITICAL SOCIALIZATION

How does an individual learn about the practices of politics in society or tools for citizenship? How is knowledge transferred or language practiced? We call the social process by which members of the social group acquire the tools, skills, and beliefs for political action and the exercise of power, *political socialization*. The acquisition of political knowledge, comprehension of political symbols, or manipulation of values for political ends is better understood if we consider how society transmits culture to future generations. This is referred to as the *process of political socialization*.

The early studies of political socialization focused on the nature of political learning, especially in childhood and adolescence. Greenstein (1965) defined political socialization as "the deliberate inculcation of political information, values and practices by instructional agents who have been formally charged with this responsibility" (5). Reflecting a systems orientation, political socialization was understood as a process for schools, as organizations of the state are assigned the responsibility of fostering political learning. Easton and Dennis (1969) concluded that a child's attachment to political systems revolves around three "attitude objects." All children first understand the political community, that is, the localized social group brought together through political influences. For example, children in early elementary grades learn about their city or community and the actors in it, namely police officers, fire safety officials, or the postmaster. The second set of objects is political authorities. Occupants of key political roles, such as George Washington or Abraham Lincoln, who occupied the political role of president, are studied. The third object is the regime, which although a bit more abstract for children, is the focus of law, rules, duty, and obligation connected to the notion of citizenship. Good citizens follow the rules, and participate in political institutions by voting in elections. Mock elections, where children are encouraged to vote, are examples of learning processes where political roles such as voter are learned.

Much of what we know about political socialization is that it is developmental, meaning that the acquisition of attitudes, values, and orientations about politics and power takes place throughout the course of life (Braungart and Braungart 1990). This model of political socialization is a process not limited to childhood or adolescence (see Textbox 3.1). It explains the dynamics of values and understandings as occurring throughout life. Generally, the transmission of knowledge, values, and symbolic expressions from one generation to another has been suspected of having significance to a society's political systems. The patterns of socialization culturally create a basis for generalized support of democratic structures in society. As Easton and Dennis (1969) noted, these patterns develop "diffuse support" for the political system as the individual critically analyzes the political world. This diffuse support contributes to the forces necessary for acceptance of the political order and its institutions. The "benevolent leader hypothesis" confirms this by showing how the positive image of the president developed during childhood influences subsequent beliefs about political institutions and leaders (Greenstein 1960). This may take the form of looking to the president as a problem solver or person responsible for addressing social ills or as a source of protection in times of threat. According to Dawson, Prewitt, and Dawson (1977), the significance of the stages of development in political knowledge and values was that "adult political behavior is the logical expression of values, knowledge, and identification formed during childhood and youth" (73). This assertion, however, was never fully supported as much of the research on political socialization died out since few links between childhood attitudes correlated with adult political behavior.

The socialization process is constructed by what are called *agents of socialization*. These social structures play an important role in learning about politics and culture. The impact agents of socialization have on political values, beliefs, and symbols of politics is an important part of the research efforts in the study of political socialization. Research on political socialization has thus focused in particular on family, school, and social groups, with some attention to the role of workplace in the formation of attitudes, values, and knowledge about politics (Jennings and Niemi 1981).

Families play an important role in the early inculcation and development of political beliefs, values, and attitudes. The primary function of the social institution of family is to transmit norms, roles, and statuses to children. Roles related to power and authority are some of the first learned in the family environment. For example, working-class parents tend to display more authoritarian patterns of discipline with children (Kohn and Schooler 1969). These patterns are learned and then associated with persons in positions of leadership or authority. Families are where children also learn about identification with political parties, which in most cases lasts into adulthood. Republican parents tend to raise Republican-identifying children. The more visible parents are in voting or participating in politics, the more their children seem to learn that participation is important.

Schools play an important role in the process of political socialization. There is clearly an explicit role for the social institution of education in that it claims a social mandate to instruct and

---

TEXTBOX 3.1

Political Socialization through the Life Course

In the 1960s and 1970s, studies of political socialization applied advancing psychological and educational models about learning. Dawson, Prewitt, and Dawson (1977) identified a number of dynamics that occur at different stages in what Braungart and Braungart (1990) would later call the "life-course understanding" of political socialization. Erikson, Luttbeg, and Tedin (1988) identified the following stages in political socialization:

- *Preschool (ages three to five)*   Children become aware of a political world in very simple terms. They are aware of the authority of the state, namely through role models, and they are aware of a political community fostered by saying the Pledge of Allegiance or becoming familiar with the flag.
- *Early Childhood (ages six to nine)*   Children begin to understand in very basic terms that government and the president have power which is similar to the hierarchy found in many families. Interestingly, children start to develop a party identification mostly as a result of familial identification. Hess and Torney (1969) reported that 55 percent of the children in a 1963 sample of grade school children were able to identify themselves as being a Democrat or Republican. The child is capable of labeling himself or herself but is unable to articulate the meaning of a political party.
- *Late Childhood (ages ten to twelve)*   The child begins to learn about voting for the person not the party as a political value in democracy. Interests in public affairs, voting, and getting others to vote are viewed by the child as definitions of good citizenship (Hess and Torney 1969). Children develop the capability to distinguish between persons and institutions. The president is now known as an individual who holds an institutionalized position of authority.
- *Adolescence (ages thirteen to eighteen)*   This stage is characterized by a great deal of change and for all practical purposes, the crystallization of political views. Adelson and O'Neil (1966) note that the child is now able to distinguish self-interest from community interest. Policy conceptions at this stage are more coherent and the child is able to think in terms of ideology. Adolescents in their early teens hold a positive view of government and the Constitutional structure in general.
- *Political Adulthood*   The effects of life-course experiences after high school are notable in the political socialization process. Understanding and commitment to the regime, authority, and politics can be influenced by life experiences, group membership, and aging. Partisan attachment is generally stronger during middle to late adult years. Abramson (1983) found that the electorate tends to "Republicanize" as it becomes older. Taking stands on political issues could be affected by some events such as a war, a corrupt administration, or others. During one's life, events such as these could change basic political views. Social forces are capable of changing the party orientations acquired during childhood as one ages. Early patterns of socialization may be influenced by experiences later in the life cycle, and so early patterns have little subsequent effect on political behavior.

teach children about the nature and characteristics of government, and the more generalized role of citizenship. In early grades, the benevolence of public servants is reinforced with visits from law enforcement officers or trips to the state capitol to meet legislators or the governor. Children view authority as looking out for the interests of the community. In adolescence, the focus of the socialization process shifts to preparation for citizenship. Most direct is enrollment in civics courses designed to provide instruction in the characteristics and operations of the state apparatus. Students may be engaged in community service projects that emphasize the role of the citizen or seek out volunteer roles in campaigns or community organizations. These connections between the school and the political apparatus are designed to reinforce aspects of citizenship that are assumed to carry through to adulthood. Education beyond the K-12 experience increases the likelihood that an individual will become more active in politics (Dalton 2008). Whether this is a function of "greater knowledge" or other factors is unclear. Nonetheless, years of schooling correlate strongly with civic activism and growth of democratic forms of governance.

Social groups also play an important role in shaping political values and orientations. Drawing on findings from other fields of study that conclude that peers matter, this body of knowledge confirms that peers play an important role in shaping political ideas among citizens. For adolescents in particular, peer groups can serve as a reference point for political information by communicating about political events such as elections, as well as a place to explore defining role behaviors related to citizenship. These patterns carry into adulthood.

The media have also played an increasingly important role in political socialization processes, but Dawson, Prewitt, and Dawson (1977) noted early on that this role is secondary in contrast to the power of the three socializing agents described previously. Since the 1960s, the role of television, especially in politics and campaigning, has grown remarkably. Since the 1990s the Internet has also launched important changes in the nature of media-oriented politics. Obama's campaign for president made very effective use of the Internet, including the solicitation of significant campaign contributions. For children, the media are an important source of imagery and information. Children and adolescents are more likely than adults to

Barack Obama gives election victory speech on BBC News TV screens on audio floor of John Lewis department store

Credit: © RichardBaker/Alamy

report getting their understanding of political events or issues from TV sources. This may be changing as the Internet and other media forms take on a significant role in the lives of adolescents especially. What impact this has on socialization processes related to information sharing or the construction of political orientations or images is unclear. Clearly, we cannot ignore the role of TV in the last forty years, especially in conveying a political understanding to the youngest citizens. For example, presidential and vice-presidential debates continue to generate considerable interest among the TV-viewing public. Thanks to technology and changes in the media industry, this all may be changing.

Research from the disciplines of psychology, political science, education, and sociology have fine-tuned our understanding of what factors seem to influence the development of political values, attitudes, and beliefs. For example, research in the field of psychology now suggests that schemas or "cognitive mailboxes," are constructed to retain and analyze information about political occurrences (Torney-Purta 1990, 1995). Renshon (2004) identified three questions of interest that build on more than forty years of research. He argues that contemporary social changes are behind three new orienting questions in political socialization research:

1. What impact does globalization have on nationalist identities? For example, the September 11, 2001 terrorist attacks in the United States appear to have significant impact on nationalist identities in the United States. What aspects of the socialization process are crucial in shaping these types of identities?
2. How will immigration and changing demographic patterns in the United States influence socialization processes? As the population of the United States becomes even more diverse, interactions among individuals of differing ethnic and racial backgrounds will become more frequent, much like those during the Industrial Revolution. The ways in which citizens adapt to these changes will no doubt be found in the socialization processes associated with schooling in particular.
3. How have changes in civic education in the last decade influenced socialization outcomes? For example, some research notes declining levels of civic literacy, suggesting that schools have not lived up to the expected role of socializing future citizens into informed roles (Niemi 1999).

Much of the focus has shifted to exploring what impact social structures, like schools or group memberships, have on shaping attitudes and values about politics. Moreover, as we shall see in Chapters 6, 7, and 8 on political participation, some argue that culture shifts have had important effects on youth civic involvement, community activism, and ultimately, voting.

POLITICAL VALUES

Political socialization entails many mechanisms by which members of a society or social group understand the formalized operations of power in society, namely the ways in which the state works. Knowledge is conveyed regarding the nature of government, the duties and obligations associated with the role of citizen, as well as the skills necessary for participating in the political process. At another level, political socialization affects the values and political orientations of individuals. These values shape the ways in which individuals make judgments about the distribution of power in society, or the acceptability of certain policies advocated by the state (Halman 2007, Weakliem 2005). Political values are shaped not only by the agents of socialization described earlier but also by what political sociologists describe as period effects or influences associated with societal events at a particular period in history.

Almond and Verba (1963, 1989) and Huntington (1968, 1991) argued that certain cultural patterns that emphasize well-being and education give rise to democratic forms of government. The groundbreaking work *The Civic Culture* (Almond and Verba 1963) concluded that democratic societies would evolve out of changing societal milieu, namely one characterized by higher levels of industrialization and education. Politics would be changed as citizens in societies characterized by modernization would embrace forms of participation, self-governance, and government led by principles of civil service rather than elite dominance. The exploration of social change and its effects on politics has yielded insights into the connections between cultural elements (knowledge, values, symbolic systems) and political outcomes. In 1997, Inglehart concluded that:

> The political culture approach today constitutes the leading alternative to rational choice theory as a general explanatory framework for political behavior. The political culture approach is distinctive in arguing that (1) people's responses to their situations are shaped by subjective orientations, which vary cross-culturally and within subcultures, and (2) these variations in subjective orientations reflect differences in one's socialization experience, with early learning conditioning later learning, making the former more difficult to undo. Consequently, action can not be interpreted as simply the result of external situations: Enduring differences in cultural learning also play an essential part in shaping what people think and do. (Inglehart 1997: 19)

What Inglehart does here is advance the sociological agenda in connecting politics and culture. This argument suggests that it is not economic or political outcomes that dictate choices (the assumption of rational choice theories), but rather, politics, economics, and social structures in general change and adapt as a result of culture. This chapter now takes a detailed look at the work of Inglehart, and examines how processes of socialization, generational experiences, and economic conditions shape values and political beliefs.

The Shift from Materialist to Post-Materialist Values

One of the most comprehensive projects dedicated to studying how social change affects political culture and thus, political dynamics in society, is the project led by Ronald Inglehart (1977, 1990, 1997). His studies of political culture in the United States and more recently worldwide (Inglehart and Welzel 2005) focus on explaining how historical, socioeconomic changes in the last one hundred years have fostered changes in the values of citizens. Inglehart defines culture as "a people's strategy for adaptation." That is, the toolkit that includes ways of understanding political events, cognitive skills for making political decisions, and values that would influence political choices, is altered by structural and historical forces. These strategies are altered in response to economic, technological, and political shifts, and ultimately affect politics. This study of political culture has highlighted how economic effects experienced by different generations change political values and attitudes.

Inglehart's initial studies in the United States hypothesized that economic changes since World War II (WWII) have resulted in changes in values and personal skills. Specifically, he observed that cultural change in Western society is "deemphasizing economic growth as a dominant goal" with a corresponding decline of economic criteria as the standard for rational behavior. By studying two cohorts (individuals born before and after WWII), Inglehart found differences in value orientations and what he described as "skills" related to work and political

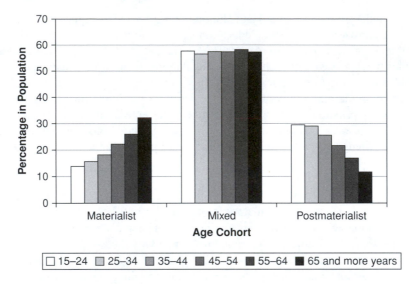

FIGURE 3.1   Materialist, Mixed, and Postmaterialist Population in Britain, France, West Germany, Italy, Belgium, The Netherlands, and the United States by Age Group

Source: World Values Survey 1981–2008 Official Aggregate v.20090901, 2009. World Values Survey Association (www.worldvaluessurvey.org). Aggregate File Producer: ASEP/JDS, Madrid. This graph was created using the World Values Online Data Analysis, http://www.worldvaluessurvey.org/.

involvement. He referred to these cohorts as *materialists* (those born before WWII) and *postmaterialists* (those born after WWII). As seen in Figure 3.1, a greater percentage of older persons reported holding materialist values, while a greater percentage of younger persons reported postmaterialist values. Those with mixed value patterns did not vary by cohort.

Industrialization and socioeconomic change since WWII has resulted in a change in what Inglehart refers to as the *political community*. He suggests that individuals require different skills for social and political interaction, which reflects how people conceptualize political community. The postmaterialist political community is national, complex, and driven by technology. Postmaterialists (those in the post-WWII cohort) acquired skills that facilitate participation in a national political community. Inglehart suggested that generational differences existed in what he called, "cognitive mobilization" or essentially, the skills needed for political action in modern political communities. These skills include education, information, and participation in organizations or networks. These are elements we associate with modern mass societies. Inglehart argues that these mechanisms of social transition may raise the potential for political participation.

Postmaterialists as social idealists are redirecting their energies toward social activities that go beyond mere physical or economic security. Pursuit of lofty social goals leads to opportunities for greater participation, according to Inglehart, as postmaterialists are driven by idealism. Cognitive skills create opportunities for value reflection and critical examination of personal priorities. As a result of postmaterialist political culture, Inglehart concludes that inequality between elites and masses has generally diminished, and education has become the basis of power for the masses, who in turn could become elites. He points to data showing that for the postmaterialist generation, education and unconventional participation are strongly associated. He also points to general declines in gender-based inequalities in Western societies. This model argues that education is washing out the effects of gender discrimination in voting or political participation in general.

According to Inglehart, the value sets common to the post-WWII generation focus on lifestyle issues (e.g., aspects of sexuality, religious and spiritual pursuits, environmentalism). The appeal to social class is no longer significant as economic development has equalized much of the individual's need to feel economically secure. Change in orientations toward state authority and legitimacy of national institutions have also been significant. As a result of relative prosperity, individuals shift their emphasis, from economic and physical security to belonging, self-expression, and quality-of-life issues. This shift follows the expansion of the welfare state and economic growth after WWII, which by the 1970s had turned into post-materialist support for exploration of differing lifestyles especially in contrast to the values of the pre-WWII generation.

The changes in political values and behavior were also significant. Shifts were noted in the prevailing types of participation. Specifically, Inglehart finds changes in loyalties to political parties. No longer does party identification represent class or socioeconomic status (SES) cleavages. Postmaterialists transcend traditional labels, and tend to support change parties in general. Postmaterialists are far more likely to engage in protest politics such as petition drives, demonstrations, strikes, or boycotts. And according to Inglehart, postmaterialists gained access to elite groups in the United States. Those with postmaterialist values are now achieving positions of authority in society. Members of this cohort now serve in parliaments or congress, and hold occupations in the elite occupational groups (e.g., educators, lawyers, labor leaders, media reps).

In their most recent project, Inglehart and Welzel (2005) have identified similar shifts in other countries, again connected to global economic modernization. Based on surveys of values from 120 societies, Inglehart and Welzel have created a model of political culture that emphasizes a connection between economic growth, human choice, and strength of democratic processes. Specifically, they conclude that

> Each of the three components of human development is a distinct manifestation of a common underlying theme: autonomous human choice. Socioeconomic development increases people's resources, giving people the objective means that enable them to make autonomous choices. With self-expression values, people give high priority to acting according to their autonomous choices. And democracy provides civil and political liberties, granting people the rights to act according to their autonomous choices. (Inglehart and Welzel 2005: 287)

Inglehart's studies have tested this claim and provided evidence that the relationship between cultural shifts and political attitudes and behavior is strong.

Inkeles and the Modern Personality

Much like the model of cultural change and politics outlined by Inglehart, Alex Inkeles has conceptualized political culture emerging from social change resulting in what he calls "modern values" (Inkeles 1983; Inkeles and Smith 1974). Societies that become economically complex in the modern era would modernize further as a result of individuals retaining values including:

- openness to new experience
- independence from traditional authority
- belief in science and medicine for solving human problems
- educational and occupational ambition
- punctuality and orderliness and
- interest in civic affairs. (Schooler 1996)

One key factor in modernizing these values in contrast to traditional value systems held by older generations in society was the advancement of education. He too concluded that each generation experiences a number of historical and structural changes reflected in the socialization processes of society. The result is a shift in individual value patterns among citizens.

Religion and Political Values

Interest in the connections between religion and politics is not new. In fact, one can easily argue that prior to the Enlightenment, religion, as Weber suggested, was the social base for the legitimization of power. Think for example about the concept of divine right of kings. Rule of the monarch was justified by appeals to the intentions of God. Enlightenment thinking and the age of revolution changed this basic philosophy of rule. Political power would move from a religious base to a focus on the ability of free persons to think and choose rulers and policies. The role of religion in politics since then has changed. In the last two centuries, appeals to religious thinking have been used to justify political acts such as wars, declarations of independence, the abolition of slavery, and the intervention of the state in human reproduction and death.

In very recent history, American politics in particular entered an era where religion played an important role in shaping political outlooks thus organizing citizens into various forms of political action. The 1980s and 1990s were described by some political sociologists as polarized, suggesting significant divisions between a variety of citizen groups. Hunter (1991) coined the term *culture wars* to describe the intensity of what emerged as a debate about the perceived morality of American society and the role of the state and religious organizations in defining social values. Why is religion important to our understanding of politics? It serves as a basis for structuring moral imperatives about the nature of life, and thus, social conflicts that may become political questions.

In the United States, the social institution of religion has undergone three significant changes in the past century:

1. decline in size of mainline denominations with growth in conservative denominations;
2. decline in denominationalism (ecumenical, cross church); and
3. emergence of "direct action, special purpose" groups.

As a result of these changes, the role of religion in politics has taken on new forms. Hunter describes this as a key influence in the culture wars, because the purpose of many of the emergent religious groups is "about power—a struggle to achieve or maintain the power to define reality" (1991: 52). It is within this environment that groups like the Moral Majority marshaled political resources including money and churchgoers, and the presidential candidacies of Pat Robertson, a tele-evangelist who placed a surprising second in the 1988 Iowa Caucuses, and Mike Huckabee, a former Arkansas governor and minister in the Southern Baptist Church who won the Iowa Caucuses in 2008.

Some scholars have argued that the current religious critique of culture and morality is a direct attack on modernity and everyday life as the twentieth century came to a close (Marty and Appleby 1995). The growth of fundamentalist religious beliefs is worldwide, involving especially two of the largest global religious traditions: Islam and Christianity. The shift to fundamentalist thinking at the end of the twentieth century was important to national and global politics. The key point is that religion serves as a significant source of values that in turn construct political orientations and dispositions that foster variations in individual and group values, attitudes, and resulting political actions. Manza and Wright (2003) find that these values create "religious cleavages" in voting patterns in the United States. For example, they conclude

TEXTBOX 3.2

Religion, Ideology, and Political Extremism

Religion has historically been a powerful force in shaping the motivations and eventual acts of kings, crusaders, revolutionaries, and activists. The role of religion in serving as a catalyst for political actions such as terrorism or war has been studied. Even today we find examples of religious frameworks transformed into what some believe are justifiable acts of political violence. Because values and religious beliefs are involved, there is controversy in defining the exact relationship between religion and politics. Some bristle at the label "political extremism" based on religious ideology.

In May 2009, abortion provider Dr. George Tiller was murdered while attending services at his home church in Wichita, Kansas. Scott Roeder, a self-proclaimed anti-abortion activist in Kansas who had created an anti-abortion Web site and had participated in protests at Planned Parenthood clinics in the Kansas City area, was convicted of the murder. Law enforcement officers also linked Roeder with a right-wing movement known as the "Freemen," which was an antigovernment movement in the Midwest claiming to operate under its own system of common law. Roeder has claimed that his use of deadly force was "justifiable" to defend unborn children. There are clues in this case that religion and beliefs in conspiracy shaped Roeder's beliefs about abortion.

In an effort to examine the role of religion in contemporary politics, some groups monitor the acts of religious groups organized around political agendas. Abortion has become a highly politicized topic in the last fifty years. In one recent study, entitled *Toxic to Democracy: Conspiracy Theories, Demonization, and Scapegoating* Chip Berlet (2009) claims that religion helps form outgroups in politics and establishes social divisions that rationalize the use of political violence. He observes:

> Right-wing pundits demonize scapegoated groups and individuals in our society, implying that it is urgent to stop them from wrecking the nation. Some angry people in the audience already believe conspiracy theories in which the same scapegoats are portrayed as subversive, destructive, or evil. Add in aggressive apocalyptic ideas that suggest time is running out and quick action mandatory and you have a perfect storm of mobilized resentment threatening to rain bigotry and violence across the United States.

According to the study, there are four "tools of fear" commonly used by groups and individuals associated with what we know as right-wing political movements. These tools include: (1) dualism, (2) scapegoating, (3) demonization, and (4) apocalyptic aggression. The report also details how each of these goals are commonly pursued by various groups that make up far-right followings. Many of these groups are part of a larger social and political ideological movement in the United States.

Go to the link listed in the source to download your copy of this study. Then using these four goals and news reports on the Roeder case, identify how religion and conspiracy are used to construct a justification for political violence. Find specific examples of statements or law enforcement testimony or reports that demonstrate dualist thinking about abortion, blaming and demonization of abortion doctors, and the use of violence and aggression.

Source: Chip Berlet. "Toxic to Democracy: Conspiracy Theories, Demonization, & Scapegoating." Public Eye.Org, the Web site of Political Research Associates, retrieved July 29, 2009 from http://www.publiceye.org/conspire/toxic2democracy/media.html.

that denominational membership and a commitment to dogma or religious teaching influence how people vote for president. Others have identified the role of religious values in structuring more radical forms of political protest and extremism as we will see in Chapters 8 and 9. Sociologists studying radical forms of political protest, rallies, and the emergence of extremist Web sites have found that religion plays an important role in the construction of attitudes and beliefs that are used to justify racism, anti-Semitism, and homophobia. Textbox 3.2 provides an example of this research.

IDEOLOGY, BELIEFS, AND PUBLIC OPINION

The concept of ideology is used to conceptualize the arrangement of values and belief systems that citizens, policymakers, leaders, and even nonparticipants create about power and power structures. The study of ideology has held a prominent position in social and philosophical inquiry since the concept was described by Destutt de Tracy in the late eighteenth century. Influenced by Enlightenment philosophers, this French citizen charged with rebuilding French intellectualism after the revolution used the term *ideology* in a plea for a science, or logic, of ideas. In the fields of philosophy and social psychology, ideology has emerged as a concept related to the individual's interpretation of various events or aspects of the environment. The writings of Karl Marx focused on ideology as a superstructure, its expression in various forms of the division of labor, in the forces of economic history, and its use by the ruling class. Marx suggests that ideology emerges from the superstructures creating false consciousness among the working class. Mannheim (1936) argued as did Marx that ideology was a historically captured notion, representing the thinking of the times. Specifically, he suggested that ideology was expressed by individuals as particularistic, or ideology was totally emanating from the forces of culture and social history. Oakeshott (1962), a philosopher aligned with the British idealists, treated ideology in yet another vein. He as well as his students, argued that ideology be conceptualized as a connection with the practical, day-to-day actions of the human being. For example, citizens would find interest as rational actors in how political parties would treat minimum-wage policies or tax credits as incentives to buy an energy-efficient car. Politics, in this sense, is an appeal to social action, bringing about change in the routine existence rather than some unattainable ideal. Goran Therborn (1980) cast ideology as a set of attitudes, values, and beliefs about the distribution of power in society and the resulting social actions that flow from this set of views. It is useful to construct arenas of research that treat ideology as mental pictures as well as social actions. Larrain (1979) concludes that:

> Ideology is perhaps one of the most equivocal and elusive concepts one can find in social sciences; not only because of the variety of theoretical approaches which assign different meanings and functions to it, but also because it is a concept heavily charged with political connotations and widely used in everyday life with the most diverse significations. (13)

The Faces of Ideology

Because defining ideology has been problematic, the ways by which political sociologists have conceptualized ideology have varied. One useful way of thinking about the many approaches to the concept of ideology is by categorizing the vast research on ideology in four ways that highlight the interplay between culture, power, and social action: (1) ideology understood as an ability to comprehend the political environment, (2) political attitudes and beliefs that make up a constellation or collection of orientations about power, (3) beliefs about issues and politics changed by deliberation or talking about politics, and (4) ideology as a function of historical and social-class influences that conceal or distort to assure power. Each of these research traditions has to date generated a great deal of understanding about the interactions between individual citizens, their political thinking, and structural influences that have effects on the nature of power in society.

IDEOLOGY AS POLITICAL "SOPHISTICATION"   Early studies of ideology were designed to test the basic assumptions of democracy that voters are informed, keen decision makers. In other words, social scientists were interested in the assertion that democracy required citizens to be informed using what they understood about issues and candidates to come to logical conclusions to make decisions. Much of the early work on ideology in American politics began as a result of two studies. In 1964, Converse asserted that most American voters had little ideological sophistication. Rather, understanding politics was a function of "constraints" that had little to do with comprehension of issues, or thinking in a critical way about the pros and cons of policy positions held by political candidates. In the classic study of American voting, this lack of sophistication was confirmed. Campbell, Converse, Miller, and Stokes (1960) found that indeed, a larger portion of American voters did not vote based on what was then described as *a sophisticated* view of political positions. These studies, combined with the arguments of sociologists at the "Columbia School" of voting, indicated that other influences were important to vote choices, and launched decades of study around the nature of ideology and what were called "mass belief systems." Converse defined a mass belief system as "a configuration of ideas and attitudes in which elements are bound together by some form of constraint or functional interdependence" (Converse 1964: 478). Ideology was understood as a system of ideas among the citizenry that was shaped, or "constrained" by idea elements.

Political sociologists have examined this argument about ideological thinking and sophistication in very interesting ways. The research has continuously focused on determining whether the American electorate could be characterized as sophisticated in its reasoning about politics. In 1990, Luskin concluded:

> . . . a person is politically sophisticated to the extent to which his or her political cognitions are numerous, cut a wide substantive swath, and are highly organized or "constrained." Some psychologists write in this vein of cognitive complexity, meaning the extent to which a person's cognition of some domains are highly differentiated (roughly, numerous and wide-ranging) and highly integrated (organized or constrained). Others refer equivalently to expertise, meaning the extent to which the person's knowledge of the domain is both extensive and highly "chunked." Political sophistication is political cognitive complexity, political expertise. (115)

Dalton (2008) more recently concluded that although citizens may not be rational and logical experts on politics, they are "reasonable thinkers" using what information they have to make relatively stable decisions. Dalton proposes that mass belief systems be understood as a "hierarchy" of policy opinions based on (1) general orientations to politics shaped by group memberships, religious views, or economic conditions; and (2) principles or values connected closely to fundamental notions about how politics should look. For example, ideological thinking about health care may emerge from principles related to the role of government in helping people or furthering the free market. These give rise to orientations focused on government-sponsored insurance in certain circumstances or for certain populations. These general orientations may in turn shape specific opinions on a particular proposal, such as universal health care insurance, support for caps on Medicare payments to doctors, or other specific policy outcomes. What Dalton suggests is a model of ideology in an electorate that comes to "reasonable" conclusions about political things rather than highly sophisticated conclusions based on idealized forms of civic thinking.

IDEOLOGY AS A SET OF POLITICAL BELIEFS   After the 1960s and 1970s, research on political ideology tended to measure this orientation of value sets and attitudes as a spatial concept, with ideology understood as a place on a continuum between liberal and conservative (Gerring 1997; Knight 2006). Not only were individuals found to have fairly consistent political orientations on this continuum but the measure of conservative–liberal was applied to understanding office-holders as well as political groups. This "spatial" notion of ideology finds that individuals and groups can hold a number of positions on selected beliefs about the nature and role of government, power, civil liberties, foreign policy, and the relationship between state and citizen in a pattern consistent with liberal or conservative philosophies. About a third of the participants in the General Social Survey have consistently identified themselves as "moderates" over the past four decades (see Figure 3.2).

However, how individuals see themselves ideologically can differ from their actual cognitions to how they respond to political questions. The so-called objective measures of ideology, in contrast to those that measure self–placement, have been developed to give ideology a "spatial" (Knight 2006) characteristic along the liberal–conservative continuum. When individuals are asked to assess specific policy outcomes, such as support for foreign interventions in global markets, or agreement with the statement that prayer in schools should be banned, the American polity tends to look a bit

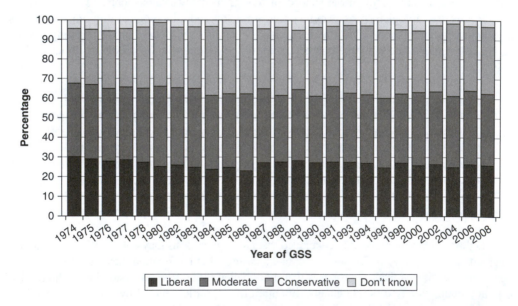

FIGURE 3.2   Respondents Who Identify Themselves as Liberal, Moderate, or Conservative in the GSS, 1974 to 2008

Source: Davis, James A., Tom W. Smith, and Peter V. Marsden. GENERAL SOCIAL SURVEYS, 1972–2008: [CUMULATIVE FILE] [Computer file]. Chicago, IL: National Opinion Research Center [producer], 2009. Storrs, CT: Roper Center for Public Opinion Research, University of Connecticut; Ann Arbor, MI: Inter-University Consortium for Political and Social Research, Berkeley, CA: Computer-Assisted Survey Methods Program (http://sda.berkeley.edu), University of California [distributors], 2009.

different when asked to rate themselves as conservative, moderate, or liberal. For example, in a study of twenty years of survey data measuring respondents' positions on key ideological issues, the Pew Research Center (2009) found slight shifts to liberal ideology on certain issues. Respondents in 2009, in contrast to respondents studied in 1987, were more supportive of programs for the "needy" and those "who can't care for themselves." In addition, support for "old fashioned values about marriage and family" and homosexuality were less of a concern to respondents in the 2009 survey than to those surveyed in 1987. These signs of shifts away from right-ideological positions may be early signs of changes in the political culture associated with the election of President Obama in 2008.

IDEOLOGY AS DELIBERATION AND DISCOURSE   Another approach to ideology draws upon the idea that citizens are engaged in conversation or dialogue about the nature and distribution of power found in society (Eliasoph 1996). Marx and Hegel observed that this dialogue was constructed by the ruling classes to assure that the outcome of the dialogue would favor preservation of wealth in the capitalist class. The concept of dialectic was used here to describe societal understandings created by each human being gaining some experience, then observing and comparing this to other experiences, and then making a judgment. There is a mental dialectic characterizing all such interactions between the person and the object in the environment.

Billig et al. (1988) suggested that ideology be viewed as a mindset about politics constructed for contrasting sometimes conflicting themes encountered in daily life, placing an emphasis on thesis and antithesis, or ideology created through dialectic processes. These authors argue that dilemmas emerge out of shared beliefs and social values. The response of the person to the dilemma, however, according to this framework is a function of the preconditions of the decision if one is involved. Out of the contrary themes that emerge from daily interactions is the need for argumentation and discourse. Billig et al. propose that dilemmas around common sense result in thinking processes. Social beliefs are the foundation for these debates. The shared beliefs lead to new forms of thought or beliefs, as patterns of discourse dissuade the utility of older value sets, or reinforce the stance of the common sense that the individual has grown with. Discourse and argument are at the foundation of the theory of ideology described by Billig. The individual's expressions in discourse or debate may reflect the challenge between a lived and intellectual ideology. Ideology based on this model is a dynamic, fluid concept that is a function of historical influences on the contextual interactions of the human existence.

Billig et al. (1988) have developed a typology of ideology based on these frameworks of thought. The *lived ideology* refers to a "society's way of life." Billig et al. admittedly treat ideology in many ways as synonymous with culture. This type of thinking about power in everyday social patterns is contrasted with *intellectual ideology*. This refers to specifically articulated frames of reference. Often, as the name implies, intellectual ideology is associated with great thinkers or philosophical advocates who have formalized their interpretations or demands. The lived and intellectual ideologies are often the source of the dilemmas that Billig et al. argue make up the dialectic of social action.

IDEOLOGY AS HEGEMONY AND HISTORY   The traditional class perspective has analyzed ideology more in terms of historically relevant views of politics, economics, and daily human interactions. Marx saw ideology as that giving rise to the legitimation of the relations of production and continued exploitation of labor. Others conceptualize ideology as a function of historical forces and experiences related to economic determinism and resulting positions in the class structure.

In his study of the emergence of Protestantism and socialism through the Enlightenment, Wuthnow (1989) found that how societies constructed views of power could be connected to a culture and social structure. His historical analysis demonstrated how Protestantism, the Enlightenment, and Socialism emerged from cultural movements as a result of periods of "exceptional economic growth" (9). Periods in history were also characterized by a unique process of cultural development. Ideology grows out of the social processes of cultural production. He suggested that ideology be thought of as "an identifiable constellation of discourse" connected to social groups, patterns of social interaction, and institutions. He is suggesting here that ideology comes from three forces in society bound up in their historical era—environmental, institutional, and action sequences. Ideology is created, torn down, and then recreated through cycles in history. As Mannheim (1936) concluded, every epoch or age has an ideology unique to that frame in time.

Wuthnow concludes that socialism comes from an ideology made by its environmental conditions, institutional contexts, and actions connected to each. The environmental conditions include the social, political, or economic conditions of a particular period in history. For example, wars or famine can create shifts in how resources in society are distributed. Institutional contexts shape this distribution process. By institutional contexts, Wuthnow is describing the work of organizations or bureaucracies. The masses connect to these contexts in schools or universities, governmental agencies, reading or scientific societies, newspapers, or political parties. Action sequences flow from environmental conditions and institutional contexts. That is, ideas associated with ideological movements (e.g., socialism) are produced in these settings and at the same time seek changes in the institutional contexts and eventually environmental conditions. Imagine for example how wars in nineteenth-century Europe were a focal point of conversations in coffee shops or cafés in France or Germany. Ideas about the effects of the war, such as what to do with those who fought in these wars and lost their livelihood, might eventually become the ideological basis for creation of social insurance programs such as pensions for the aged or medical care. This cyclical nature of historical conditions giving rise to ideas about power and the distribution of resources in society, according to Wuthnow, characterizes how ideology changes historically.

Another approach to political culture developed by proponents of the class perspective addresses the more subtle influences of culture on ideas and values. Antonio Gramsci (1971) used the term *hegemony* to describe that general cultural milieu created by the ruling classes, where ideas and values are shaped in compliance with ruling-class objectives. The intent with this cultural dimension of ruling-class dominance is to preserve through the power of ideas, emotions, loyalties, and beliefs the stability of class differences. Thus power is exercised through the manipulation of ideas. Gramsci used the concept to explain why the upper economic classes maintained power even when compliance with upper-class demands was against the best interests of the working class.

One example of how hegemony works is found in the work of political sociologists who study power differences between and among men and women. Masculine hegemony is described as made up of a set of ideas such as aggression, competition, winning in a game, or deceit in order to attain interests. In their global analysis of women's representation and participation in political systems, Paxton and Hughes (2007) find that hegemonic influences in countries described as patriarchal create cultural barriers to women attaining positions in the political system. They conclude that cultural forces such as attitudes in society about roles of men and women, especially those shaped by religion, "matter for women's acquisition of political power" and can "influence women's decision to run for political office" (120).

Contemporary work exploring the emergence of hegemonic power in other ways has grown significantly with the study of globalization. As an oversimplification perhaps, globalization argues that the beliefs and ideas associated with U.S. capitalist culture have been extended to all parts of the globe. As a result, ideas influence consumer choices in nations characterized as newcomers to capitalist life. For example, as China has embraced some forms of capitalist market activity in the past several years, consumer choices for things like McDonald's products or Western music have become hallmarks of change in a traditionally anticapitalist society. In his recent study of the impact of the Internet and digital technologies on societies throughout the world, Drori (2006) suggests that Internet communications represent "a totalizing and individualizing form of power, allowing each person a voice while also imposing on individuals a hegemonic structure" (121). Although people are led to believe that the World Wide Web offers a forum for free speech or communication, the truth is that the communication is virtual and typically becomes a place for the distortion of identities (e.g., gender-bending in a chat room, faking a profile). We believe we can anonymously communicate using these digital communications, but the rules of online interaction are structured by the creators of the device being used. If this replaces face-to-face communication, intent or genuineness is more difficult to test. Drori concludes, "In the age of globalization, where the global is regarded as the homogenizing force and the local as a unique scene, technology—like other forms of knowledge—is an instrument of power" (121). Hegemonic influences are practiced through the structure of the World Wide Web, which is made real in the small space of the computer screen throughout the world.

POLITICAL CULTURE AND MEDIA

The mass media have assumed a unique role in the dynamics of modern political culture. On one hand, the media have been treated as a source of information and knowledge about political candidates, political events, and global political changes. The media have also been studied as a significant actor in the processes of political socialization described earlier in this chapter. For social constructionists, the media have been understood as key players in the manipulation of political symbols and expressions related to deliberation, ritual, and outright political mythologies. Textbox 3.3 explores another direction of research which tests the claim that the media has a liberal bias in its treatment of candidates and issues. The holy grail of sorts in the study of media effects on political attitudes and behavior is being able to identify the direct impact of TV ads, or exposure to images, or time spent reading on specific political outcomes. After decades of research, few studies have been able to make such direct links (Preiss et al. 2006). What we understand now about the role of media in shaping elements of political culture is that sociological variables are important—education of the viewer, economic status of target audiences, predispositions created by other societal influences or reference groups, and group membership more generally. Needless to say, the connections between media and political outcomes are complex.

Political sociologists typically focus on the role of the media as a social institution; that is a type of social organization created for reasons of profit, or to claim a voice in political discourse. For example, Domhoff's study (2006) of the ruling class in the United States finds that:

> The media can say what people think is important, but the news they stress reflects the biases of those who access them—corporate leaders, government officials, and policy experts. Even here, there is ample evidence that the views of liberal critics make frequent appearances in newspapers and magazines, and that corporations and establishment politicians are regularly criticized. (117)

TEXTBOX 3.3

Is There a Liberal Media Bias?

The perception that the media is biased is widespread. A Google Internet search found 2.2 million hits for "liberal media bias" compared to 1.5 million for "conservative media bias." This perception is backed with opinion poll data revealing that 45 percent of Americans believe that the media are too liberal compared to 35 percent who say the media are about right and 15 percent who believe the media are too conservative (Gallup Organization 2009). Partisanship influences perception. In other words, Republicans perceive liberal bias while Democrats perceive a conservative slant (Morris 2007). Sixty-three percent of Americans believe that news stories are inaccurate and 74 percent believe that news organizations are influenced by powerful people and organizations (Pew Research Center 2009). Not surprisingly, the majority of Americans (55 percent) report having little to no trust and confidence in the mass media (Gallup 2009). How accurate are these perceptions?

Those advocating that a liberal media bias exists cite studies showing that journalists have more left-of-center views on social issues (e.g., Dye 2002) and that when researchers ask reporters to make hypothetical journalistic decisions, the reporters choose responses consistent with their partisan views (e.g., Patterson and Donsbach 1996). However, responses to hypotheticals do not prove actual bias in reporting (Niven 1999). Gans (1980) points out that reporters do not have control over headlines or story placement and editors are careful to weed out any trace of political bias.

In their review of media bias research, Covert and Wasburn argue that past studies fail to ask "More or less conservative (or liberal) than what other specific news sources" and assume that bias does not vary over time or by the issue (2007: 690). In a comparison of twenty-five years (1975–2000) of news magazine coverage, mainstream sources such as *Time* and *Newsweek* are centrist in their coverage of crime, environment, gender, and poverty compared to the markedly more conservative *National Review* or liberal *Progressive* (Covert and Wasburn 2007). Niven (1999) also found, using an objective baseline, no liberal bias in his analysis of newspapers.

In contrast, other studies have found that Fox News, self-promoted as an alternative to the "liberal media," has become friendlier to Republican views since its inception (Morris 2005), with news coverage more supportive of the Bush invasion of Iraq (Aday, Livingston, and Hebert 2005). Fox News viewers were also more likely than others to believe incorrectly that there was a link between Al-Qaida and Saddam Hussein and that weapons of mass destruction were found after the 2003 invasion (Kull 2003). Fox viewers also underestimated the number of U.S.–Iraq war casualties compared to other viewers (Morris 2005).

G. William Domhoff (2010) argues that media bias is not influential because consumers gravitate toward media sources that fit their ideological views. For example, Republicans tend to choose Fox News as their primary source (Morris 2007), so any relationship between news viewing and behavior is probably more a function of previously established political attitudes. However, a more fragmented media market may result in a more polarized public, making consensus building more difficult. Morris contends that previously, a more homogenized news environment exposed viewers to different points of view. In today's more fragmented media, viewers choosing news consistent with own point of view reduce their exposure to alternative ideas.

Morris (2007) contends that Fox News benefits from the persistent perception of liberal bias, having become one of the most popular news sources in the United States, as those who believe that the media have a liberal slant are also more likely to report Fox News as their primary news source. A larger audience share means increased advertising revenue. This raises an important question: Is there really a liberal media bias or is this only a gimmick to attract viewers and advertising dollars?

Political sociologists approach the study of mass media in many different ways. We organize this vast body of research around the basic notions of political culture in that, culture, given our use of a fairly simple definition, includes values, knowledge, and symbolic systems in society. In this sense, we have learned that the mass media play a powerful role in influencing political values, political knowledge, and the symbolic dimensions of American politics in particular. The mass media, which we define to include here the news gathering and reporting organizations, the entertainment industry, and most recently, the Internet, are a collection of organizations that are outside the formal apparatus of the state (although in countries other than the United States, the mass media can be an arm of the state). The media are part of the civil sphere in that they may target not only citizens or popular audiences (mass), but typically the work of the mass media can influence the behavior of state actors.

Media and Political Knowledge

We begin with the work on the relationship between exposure to mass media and citizen behavior. This is where much of the research has focused. We can connect this long-standing research agenda to the early voting studies in the 1940s, 1950s, and 1960s, which basically painted a picture of a fairly unsophisticated American electorate, as described earlier. As the media emerged to hold a greater presence in society by the 1960s—only fifty years ago—studies of what impacts the mass media had on changing the relative sophistication of the American electorate became more common.

One critical assumption in American democracy follows the dictum of Thomas Jefferson, who argued that educated citizens would be active participants in the processes of governance. At first glance, we do find a connection between the use of various forms of media and news and forms of political participation. As Figures 3.3 and 3.4 show, individuals who participated in the National Election Studies reported a greater use of television as a source of political information than newspapers but both television viewership and newspaper readership have increased between 1974 and 2004. The impact of media on citizen's knowledge about politics is at best described in the research as a complex pattern (Bishop 2004; Glynn et al. 1999; Markus 2007; Norris 2000). The link between information from media sources and political participation or interest in politics is trumped by other influences. For example, the relationship between watching C-SPAN and CNN or reading the *New York Times* and *Time* magazine tends to be a function of interest in politics to begin with. In other words, the effects of this vast potential for gathering political information at the mass level has not resulted in increased mass participation or mass interest in politics. Reading newspapers or news magazines has over time become less prominent a source of news for many, and the rise of the Internet as a source of political information is only now being studied.

In a recent review of this body of research, Goldstein and Ridout (2004) suggested that TV advertising in political campaigns actually creates knowledge as a "by-product" (211). In other words, the intent of political ads is to persuade voters to choose one candidate over another, or to convince citizens to support a particular proposition. Brians and Wattenberg (1996) found that even for individuals watching TV news and reading newspapers, TV political ads contributed more to political learning. Others who tested a similar hypothesis did not find support for the notion that political ads contribute to the knowledge of voters. Rather, the effect is present only under certain conditions, such as if the ad is sponsored by a political candidate, or the audience has low interest or low information to begin with (Just et al. 1996; Pfau et al.

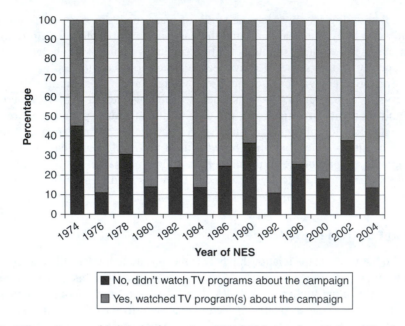

FIGURE 3.3 TV as a Source of Political Information, 1974–2004, American National Election Studies

Source: The American National Election Studies (www.electionstudies.org). The ANES Guide to Public Opinion and Electoral Behavior. Ann Arbor, MI: University of Michigan, Center for Political Studies [producer and distributor]. This graph was created at the Computer-Assisted Survey Methods Program (http://sda.berkeley.edu), University of California [distributors], 2009. (These materials are based on work supported by the National Science Foundation and a number of other sponsors.)

2002). Therefore, there is not a clear picture of the extent of the overall effect of media on knowledge about politics and under what conditions this effect consistently appears. More research needs to be conducted.

As we discussed earlier, the Internet and World Wide Web are a new form of mass media communication. Only recently have researchers started to examine what role the Internet plays in political sophistication and knowledge (Margolis 2007). Given the relative youth of this form of mass media (only twenty years), researchers have yet to untangle the many influences hypothesized to have effects, especially on younger citizens who have grown up with this new form of political communication. Bimber (2003) finds that much like other media sources, the Internet has relatively little impact on political knowledge or information for the general population. Rather, cyberspace has become a place for activists to post information about political events (e.g., posting comments on a blog after a president's speech). These sites tend to be visited by activists rather than the mass public seeking information by which to evaluate political outcomes. Yet, data collected by the National Election Studies (Figure 3.5) from voters in the last four national elections does show that more voters reported accessing the Internet for information. More research will be done for sure as sociologists continue to sort out what the Internet means to activists, voters, and the public at large.

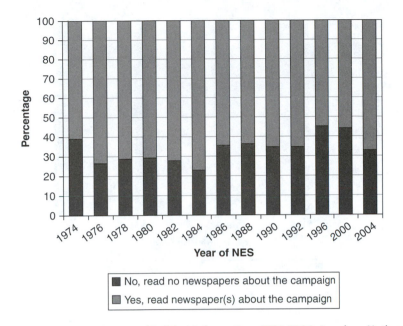

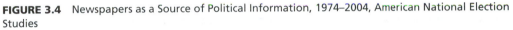

FIGURE 3.4   Newspapers as a Source of Political Information, 1974–2004, American National Election Studies

Source: The American National Election Studies (www.electionstudies.org). The ANES Guide to Public Opinion and Electoral Behavior. Ann Arbor, MI: University of Michigan, Center for Political Studies [producer and distributor]. This graph was created at the Computer-Assisted Survey Methods Program (http://sda.berkeley.edu), University of California [distributors], 2009. (These materials are based on work supported by the National Science Foundation and a number of other sponsors.)

Media and Political Values

One popular notion is that the media shapes values about politics as well as moral concerns, and as a result, the media are typically a source of scrutiny by interest groups seeking regulation of media images or even vocabulary. Research on attitudes and values suggests that for the most part, these are relatively stable in adulthood, and the media have only minor effects on major shifts in these attitudes and values. Political values are not likely to change for the greatest portion of individuals in society. As we saw earlier from the research on postmaterialism and the personality of modernity, values tend to be altered as a result of cohort or generational effects, including crises such as war, or economic depressions. The media do not significantly change political values per se. If anything, values tend to dictate what kinds of media are sought out or accessed by politically aware individuals.

In her review of the vast literature in this field, Graber (2006) finds that individuals tend to pay attention to news media sources such as TV or print media as a result of existing dispositions. For example, individuals predisposed to liberal or conservative values seek out sources that confirm these positions (Ansolebehere and Iyengar 1995; Becker and Kosicki 1995; Erikson and Tedin 2005; Glynn et al. 1999).

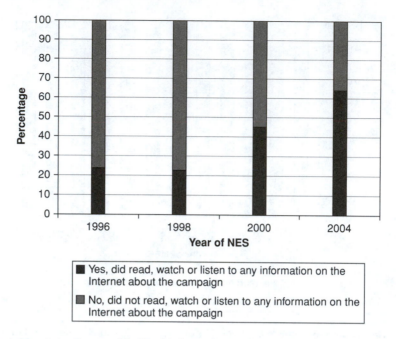

FIGURE 3.5 Internet as a Source of Political Information, 1996–2004, American National Election Studies

Source: The American National Election Studies (www.electionstudies.org). The ANES Guide to Public Opinion and Electoral Behavior. Ann Arbor, MI: University of Michigan, Center for Political Studies [producer and distributor]. This graph was created at the Computer-Assisted Survey Methods Program (http://sda.berkeley.edu), University of California [distributors], 2009. (These materials are based on work supported by the National Science Foundation and a number of other sponsors.)

Graber (2006) arranges this mixed picture on media effects into three frameworks of research. These three camps in media research have evolved in an attempt to explain and describe patterns of media use based on values, lifestyles, and personal dispositions:

Uses and Gratification—This research suggests that individuals seek out media stories that fit personal uses or interests. "Put simply, proponents of this approach contend that individuals ignore personally irrelevant and unattractively presented messages. They pay attention to the kinds of things that they find useful and intellectually or emotionally gratifying if time and effort constraints permit it" (Graber 2006: 190). As some point out, these uses of information or media sources can vary across time and across experiences in life. What may be attractive for a college student participating in a political campaign for the first time may change as the student leaves the campaign and joins other causes.

Selective Exposure—Individuals tend to avoid unpleasant things, and if one ever watches the evening network news, it tends to be filled with stories of death, destruction, war, disease, corruption, murder, and other negative topics! Moreover, people tend to listen to those who hold similar attitudes. "Selectivity reduces the already slim changes that exposure to different views will alter an individual's established beliefs, attitudes, and feelings. Selective exposure therefore helps to explain the considerable stability that exists in orientations, such as party allegiance or foreign policy preferences" (Graber 2006: 192).

Agenda Setting—This body of research challenges the other two frameworks and suggests that the media does change values and attitudes through a process of agenda setting. "When people are asked which issues are most important to them personally or to their communities, their lists tend to correspond to cues in the news sources that they use in their communities" (Graber 2006: 194). Thus media sources can, in some ways, alter what groups of people value as political priorities or issue concerns. But, Graber warns that this influence "varies in potency." New concerns, for example, are more likely to be influenced by the media polls or reports as well as information required for understanding new issues.

These three perspectives are examples of competing findings in the current research on the impact of the media on citizens. The results are complex and tend to vary from social group, social context, and historical environment.

Media and Political Symbols

As we know from sociological work in the field of symbolic interaction, symbols are powerful mechanisms for building interpersonal understanding, the formation of social connections, the formation of group cohesion, and using symbolic cues to identify belonging to a group as well as individual differences. The symbolic system studied most extensively is language. Think about how words, phrases, tones, or inflections are used to connect to others. Early in the study of power, Deutsch (1955) identified at least five symbolic systems significant to the ways in which power is understood by individuals, and in some cases, manipulated in political processes:

1. abstractions (e.g., ideas, sayings, chants)
2. pictures (e.g., flags, animals, buildings, relics)
3. people (e.g., heroes, presidents from the past, saints)
4. places (e.g., national shrines, parks, tombs) and
5. organizations and institutions (e.g., courts, synagogues, military).

These symbolic systems are sources for influencing political values, knowledge, or more abstractions about power. The media use imagery to invoke emotions that can construct important political belief systems through the depiction of symbols. Television, print media, and more recently, the Internet, all use technology to convey images about elections, world politics, war, political candidates, political groups, and political power generally. What these images mean to the viewer is of interest to political sociologists.

In a series of works beginning in 1964, Edelman (1964, 1971, 1988) suggested that for the most part, American politics was about spectators watching the symbolic manipulation of governance by the elites. He suggested that the spectators, for the most part, played little role in actual decision making in the rule of the country. Rather, they were placated as spectators of sorts, reassured by the symbolic expression of the ruling elite. For example, Edelman described what symbolic expressions are used in the modern political convention. American politics in particular was about the manipulation of nationalist symbols. If you watch the Democratic or Republican National conventions on TV, you witness a highly choreographed event. You will see symbols used to invoke party loyalty and bring attention to the candidate nominated for president that are organized around patriotic themes (e.g., red, white, and blue balloons or flags and banners), or you will hear speeches filled with symbolic phrases that may end up as sound bites on the evening news or become campaign slogans (e.g., in 2008 Barack Obama, the Democratic nominee for president, invoked change). These "spectacles" as Edelman describes them, were common dramas in the modern media age created to portray the American political process as open and inviting the participation of the masses.

POLITICAL CULTURE AND PLACE

The study of political culture has also revisited Durkheim's classical argument that values and social orientations are a function of social context. Researchers are exploring the connections among values, attitudes, ideologies, political action, social context, and place. More specifically, one path in this line of work explores the distribution of various political communities throughout society. As we will see in this section, place and social context have also been connected to nations and the development of nationalism.

Political Subcultures

One of the first major projects dedicated to understanding the link between place and political institutions as well as values was that of Daniel Elazar (1984, 1994). He proposed a model of state–federal institutional relationships based on a configuration of political value patterns found in the United States. He described political culture as "the particular pattern of orientation to political action in which each political system is embedded" (1984: 112). The importance of these patterns is manifest in the ways in which government and citizens interact in the creation of the public good. This theme is important not only to Elazar's work but also to the early writings on civic culture (Almond and Verba 1963, 1989). The purpose of this work was to find what roles local contexts, patterns of values, and attitudes play, and in which ways political power was used.

Elazar's theory of political culture established an explanation for how "patterns of orientation" affect power in the geographical structures created as states. He concluded that three influences were at work. Specifically, political culture affected state politics as a result of:

> (1) the set of perceptions of what politics is and what can be expected from government, held by both the general public and the politicians; (2) the kinds of people who become active in government and politics, as holders of elective offices, members of the bureaucracy, and active political workers; and (3) the actual way in which the art of government is practiced by citizens, politicians, and public officials in light of their perceptions. In turn, the cultural components of individual and group behavior in the various political systems make themselves felt at three levels: in the kind of civic behavior dictated by conscience and internalized ethical standards; in the character of law-abiding-ness displayed by citizens and officials; and, to a degree, in the positive actions of government. (Elazar 1984: 112)

According to Elazar, these cultural dimensions of political life were especially significant to patterns of federalism in the United States. Specifically, localized political cultures played a role in fostering national unity while at the same time contributing to tensions as a result of conflicts between regionalized political cultures.

Elazar went on to suggest that three traditions of political values were found in regions throughout the United States, and in subregions within the fifty states. His early work identifies three distinct political cultures: moralism, individualism, and traditionalism.

Moralist—values that see the state as a way to achieve communal good; healthy civic competition with all citizens participating is a way to articulate this desire for the common good; the state serves a higher communal moral interest; associated with the upper New England states and northern tier of states continuing through Oregon and Washington.

Individualist—approaches the state as an arena for the fair exchange of ideas dedicated to the smooth operation of governmental functions; government is like a business in that rewards of hard work and competition are shared with participants; political competition is seen as a contest between organizations rather than ideas; confined to lower New England and the industrial Midwest.

Traditionalist—the state preserves the existing social order; political participation is associated with the interests of a political elite dedicated to "taking care of" the affairs of public policy on behalf of the current social order; participation is based on family connections or social ties within the community; predominant in the South.

According to Elazar, states and regions of the country could be characterized by these dominant patterns of value and political orientations. He also suggested that within states and regions, there were variations or pockets of variant beliefs. For example, while the northern tier of states from Maine to the northwest were predominantly moralist in their cultural configurations, these states also typically blended individualist cultural characteristics as well. Within each state, more localized subcultures were also distinguishable such as the moralist and traditionalist locales in the desert southwest.

While much of the work was criticized for failing to operationalize "political culture" so it could be measured consistently, a number of researchers have taken up the challenge of developing very detailed models of political culture in the United States. Lieske (1993, 2007) has found using county-level measures of religious, racial, economic, educational, and immigrant diversity, that distinct communities of political culture can be mapped throughout the United States. His work has suggested that there are "regional subcultures" with predominant normative patterns that affect political behaviors, party identification, and political attitudes. He pinpoints eleven distinct localized political subcultures in the United States:

- Heartland—creates a belt from Kansas through Iowa, Illinois, Ohio through Pennsylvania
- Latino—southwest including south Texas and New Mexico and parts of California and identified with the Catholic Church
- Nordic—along the north Dakota and Minnesota northlands with identity linked to the Lutheran church and church organizations
- Border—throughout California and Arizona with heavy concentrations of immigrant populations
- Mormon—concentrated in Utah
- Global—scattered throughout the United States; concentrated in urban areas associated with cosmopolitan and urban lifestyles
- Blackbelt—south and through the Appalachia communities
- Native-American—pockets in the west
- Germanic—scattered through the Nebraska, Northern Iowa, and Wisconsin through Pennsylvania

- Rurban—scattered throughout states west of the Mississippi with concentrations of rural and highly educated communities
- Anglo-French—upper New England, especially Maine

Clearly, as Lieske suggests, these subcultures are not marked by easily identifiable borders but rather, are best described as fluid pockets or concentrations of groups of people based on ethnicity, rural/urban environments, economic orientations, and religious identities.

An important question in the research on political subcultures and political geography is, does it matter to political processes or the distribution of power? A few studies have started to examine this (Miller, Barker, and Carman 2006). One significant argument is that these various expressions of political subcultures create regionalisms in the United States. This has historically been significant to electoral outcomes. Recall that the balance of power in the creation of the United States Congress, for example, was to some extent an issue of geography. Seats in the U.S. House of Representatives were apportioned to states based on population, and seats in the Senate were apportioned equally to each state—two per state. Thus, policy in Congress can be changed when a southern bloc of conservative senators hold up a nomination for the U.S. Supreme Court, or when "blue dog" Democrats (fiscal conservatives primarily from the Midwest and the South) in the House of Representatives effectively block ways to fund health care reform. In this sense, the political values of the regions in the United States are expressed in the policy-making process and have impact on policy outcomes.

The manifestations of state and regional political subcultures go beyond voting blocs in Congress. Some fear that as the country changes demographically, ideological differences rooted in more local settings will create greater social division. As we will see in Chapter 6, Putnam (2000) predicted that these divisions would result in greater civic disengagement over the long term. Textbox 3.4 explores the depth of these subcultures at the community and neighborhood level, where Bishop (2008) traces the impact of cultural pockets of settlement to what he fears to be further political polarization in the United States. These projects would suggest that another impact of the political culture arising out of geographical settlement is fragmentation.

Nationalism

One could conclude from the previous section that the United States is a nation divided. Certainly, those who argue that the "culture wars" have pitted the Northeast against the South and West suggest that political culture in the United States is dispersed. What holds us together then? An interesting track in the study of political culture has only recently examined the nature of nationalism, not only in the United States but in other parts of the world. Nationalism is in many ways how we conceptualize the cultural dimensions of the nation-state. Some scholars treat the state as a structural element, and view nationalism as a cultural element. Values and beliefs about the state or national identity result in patterns of behavior associated with loyalty or even patriotism.

According to Greenfield and Eastwood (2005), the study of nationalism has taken two basic paths. Early works were described as "structural." Citing the works of Earnest Gellner, they describe nationalism as a "form of consciousness" (248) that surrounds state structures, especially those that enforce or create social order. Gellner theorized that nations retained a "shared culture" (248) inherent in the nation as community or group: "a very distinctive species of patriotism, and one which becomes pervasive and dominant only under certain social conditions, which in fact prevail in the modern world, and nowhere else" (quoted by Greenfield and Eastwood 2005: 248). Using a similar cultural approach, Anthony Smith defined nationalism emerging out of "a named human population which shares myths, memories, a mass public culture, a designated homeland,

TEXTBOX 3.4

Political Birds of a Feather?

Emile Durkheim used the term *homophily* to describe forms of social cohesion driven by interests, jobs, religion, neighborhood, and social interests. He believed that people with similarities tended to settle together in communities. Some would argue that political interests may be reflected in this pattern of settlement or place. Recall in this chapter that Elazar and others suggested that there were distinct political cultures in the United States based on a geographical diffusion of political values and ideologies. In a recent book, Bill Bishop (2008) summarizes evidence that there is a "clustering of like-minded" Americans who he fears will create a triumph of localism over a unified national political community.

In commenting on the book, columnist Robert Samuelson made a number of observations recognizing this sociological pattern:

> People prefer to be with people like themselves. For all the celebration of "diversity," it's sameness that dominates. Most people favor friendships with those who have similar backgrounds, interests and values. It makes for more shared experiences, easier conversations and more comfortable silences. Despite many exceptions, the urge is nearly universal. It's human nature.
>
>   The increasing segregation of America by social and cultural values—not just by income—helps explain America's growing political polarization, Bishop argues in his new book (naturally: "The Big Sort"). Because prosperity enables more Americans to live where they please, they gravitate to lifestyle ghettos—and that has significant political implications. Citing studies of social psychology, Bishop says that group consciousness actually amplifies likes and dislikes. Views become more extreme. People become more self-righteous and more suspicious of outsiders.

Samuelson argues that the effects of this segregation will make it more difficult to create the "great middle" or centrist majority necessary for governance in the United States:

> What Arthur Schlesinger Jr. called "the vital center" is being slowly disenfranchised. Party "bases" become more important than their numbers justify. Passionate partisans dislike compromise and consensus. They want to demolish the other side. Whether from left or right, the danger is a tyranny of true believers.

What impact does political culture have on the ability of the state to create majorities necessary for governing? What effect might political cultural clustering have on democratic processes in the future? Does place matter to political culture?

Credit: Robert J. Samuelson. 2008. "Political Perils of a 'Big Sort'?" *Washington Post* Wednesday, August 6: A17.

economic unity and equal rights and duties for all members" (quoted by Greenfield and Eastwood 2005: 248). Nationalism, according to structuralist views, connected cultural elements to structures of state, nation, and territory.

Greenfield and Eastwood call the second approach to nationalism "constructivist." Citing the works of Benedict Anderson, they find that this body of analysis casts nationalism as a projection of sorts of the members of the nation-state: "because the majority of inhabitants or members of any given nation do not know each other and do not meet face to face, they cannot be, presumably, a 'real' community but can only constitute an imagined one" (Greenfield and

Eastwood 2005: 249). Using this approach, we can understand nationalism as reliant on symbols or myths that construct a sense of belonging or membership. For example, it has become a tradition to begin sporting events in the United States with the national anthem. As audience members sing along we assume that membership in a nation is constructed through that sense of the moment.

The cultural roots of nationalism are varied. One source is the collective memory of the people in a given territory, who over time craft a symbolism and imagery that creates national heroes or principles celebrated in the collective memory. For example, in his studies of President's Day and the mythology surrounding George Washington and Abraham Lincoln, Schwartz (2008: 78) shows us how ritual constructs societal recollections:

> Collective memory, whose content holidays sustain, refers to the social distribution of beliefs, feelings, and moral judgments about the past. The primary vehicles of collective memory are history—the establishing and propagating of facts about the past through research, monographs, textbooks, museums, and mass media—and commemoration; the process of selecting from the historical record those facts most relevant to society's ideals and symbolizing them by iconography, monuments, shrines, place-names, and ritual observance. Mediating the relation between history and individual belief, holidays are major parts of all commemorative repertories.

In other words, members of the group draw upon the collective representations found in the elements of culture (e.g., art, mass media, architecture, museums, knowledge) and incorporate themes into enacted rituals. Nationalism is created through this social context.

Another variable in understanding nationalism springs from the intricacies related to membership as related to the territory and state. The creation of the community requires boundaries or definitions of who belongs, and consistent with social history, who doesn't belong. Research on nationalism has also typically grappled with the role and significance of ethnicity (Lane and Ersson 2005; Vujačić 2002). On one hand, ethnic identities (especially race and religion) have served as the basis for creating a unified group that resulted in the creation of a nation-state. For example, separations of the former USSR (Union of Soviet Socialist Republics) into distinct nations were guided by ethnic and regional identities. On the other hand, identities force separation of the state—the Union of Soviet Socialist Republics are no longer united. The example of the USSR shows that ethnicity can also serve as the basis for challenges to nationalism. Moreover, history is filled with what results when ethnic identity reaches extremism, as found in Hitler's Nazi Germany. Nationalism in this regard resulted in ethnoviolence and genocide. The role of ethnicity in defining our conceptions of nationalism, including cultural nuances, and especially as nationalism is cast as inclusion or exclusion of groups, will play a significant role in future research in an emerging field of political sociology.

A third way of characterizing contemporary dynamics of nationalism focuses on current debates and reactions related to globalization. As patterns of social organization create global interconnections and result in embracing Western values and beliefs (culture), where does nationalism fit? One argument is that the forces of globalization may in fact reinforce nationalist identities. For example, while China appears to embrace Western capitalist practices in the global economy, and McDonald's and the Internet find their way into Beijing, China is finding ways to resist these influences. (See Chapter 10 for an extended discussion of the relationship between nationalism and globalization.) As Vujačić (2002) observes, global economic interests eventually prevailed over some hardline nationalist interests when the European Union (EU) was created. The interactions between nationalism and globalization will no doubt continue to be of interest to political sociologists.

CONCLUSION

Culture plays many roles in the social processes associated with the distribution of power in society. As you can see from this chapter, political sociologists have examined the role of culture in politics in different ways. These various paths of research take us in different directions. What is exciting is that more research is being done to further refine our understanding of what role culture plays in political processes. For example, the field of political socialization has been relatively dormant for thirty years. Only recently have social scientists begun to revisit early findings in light of advances in research related to developmental psychology, political cognition and value formation, and generational studies of political attitudes. Revisiting political socialization processes seems likely in the work ahead.

Some of the work on how people develop political values and attitudes has been advanced by innovations in research. The study of world values and contrasts in how people view power and politics has gained much from comparing citizens from different countries around the world. By comparing belief systems, ideologies, the role of subcultures, or the impact of media on systems of political values, cross-cultural studies will develop much needed insight into the significance of culture to politics in societies throughout the world. Here too advances in the study of the many forms of mass media further highlight the nature of culture and politics in the modern world. As we conclude that TV has "mixed effects" on values, attitudes, and beliefs but that these effects vary by social group, the door opens to future research. Only recently have political sociologists begun to track what impact the Internet and emerging forms of mass media and mass communication have on politics. These are fascinating times indeed for political sociologists.

The significance of political ideology to the study of politics and culture has not died out in spite of continued struggles over how to define ideology. We know that broad-based political orientations in society play a role in patterns related to political systems, as well as in choices of political groupings and affiliations. This research has reminded us that social context matters. We also know that political culture and place have an apparent connection. Social groups, including peer groups, workplace groups, communities, and larger geographical units such as towns and counties, follow Durkheim's principle of homophily—birds of the same social feather do tend to flock together.

In the chapters ahead we continue to explore the significance of culture to politics. The discussions ahead move us to consider the politics of everyday life and political participation, including voting, policy outcomes, politics and corporations, and globalization. As we will see, aspects of culture play a role in all of these key concepts.

References

Abramson, Paul. 1983. *Political Attitudes in America: Formation and Change.* San Francisco: Freeman.

Aday, Sean, Steven Livingston, and Maeve Hebert. 2005. "Embedding the Truth: A Cross-Cultural Analysis of Objectivity and Television Coverage of the Iraq War." *Harvard International Journal of Press/Politics* 10: 3–21.

Adelson, Joseph and Robert O'Neil. 1966. "Growth of Political Ideas in Adolescence: The Sense of Community." *Journal of Personality and Social Psychology* 4: 305–306.

Almond, Gabriel A. and Sidney Verba. 1963. *The Civic Culture: Political Attitudes and Democracy in Five Nations.* Beverly Hills, CA: Sage.

_____. 1989. *The Civic Culture Revisited.* Thousand Oaks, CA: Sage Publications.

The American National Election Studies (www.electionstudies.org). The ANES Guide to Public Opinion and Electoral Behavior. Ann Arbor, MI: University of Michigan, Center for Political Studies [producer and distributor].

Ansolabehere, Stephen and Shanto Iyengar. 1995. *Going Negative: How Attack Ads Shrink and Polarize the Electorate.* New York: Free Press.

Becker, Lee and Gerald Kosicki. 1995. "Understanding the Message-Producer/Message-Receiver Transaction." *Research in Political Sociology* 7: 33–62.

Bell, Daniel. 1960. *The End of Ideology*. New York: Free Press of Glencoe.

_____. 1973. *The Coming of Post-Industrial Society*. New York: Basic Books.

_____. 1976. *The Cultural Contradictions of Capitalism*. New York: Basic Books.

Bendix, Reinhard and Seymour M. Lipset. 1966. "The Field of Political Sociology." Pp. 9–47 in *Political Sociology: Selected Essays*, edited by Lewis Coser. New York: Harper & Row Publishers.

Berezin, Mabel. 1997. "Politics and Culture: A Less Fissured Terrain." *Annual Review of Sociology* 23: 361–383.

Berlet, Chip. 2009. "Toxic to Democracy: Conspiracy Theories, Demonization, and Scapegoating." PublicEye.Org, the Web site of Political Research Associates Retrieved July 29, 2009 from http://www.publiceye.org/conspire/toxic2democracy/media.html.

Billig, Michael, Susan Candor, Derek Edwards, Mike Gane, David Middleton, and Lan Randly. 1988. *Ideological Dilemmas: A Social Psychology of Everyday Thinking*. Thousand Oaks, CA: Sage Publications.

Bimber, Bruce. 2003. *Information and American Democracy: Technology in the Evolution of Political Power*. New York: Cambridge University Press.

Bishop, Bill. 2008. *The Big Sort: Why the Clustering of Like-Minded America Is Tearing Us Apart*. Boston, MA: Houghton Mifflin Company.

Bishop, George. 2004. *The Illusion of Public Opinion: Fact and Artifact in American Public Opinion Polls*. Lanham, MD: Rowman and Littlefield.

Bottomore, T.B. 1961. *Karl Marx: Selected Writings in Sociology and Social Philosophy*. New York: McGraw-Hill Book Co.

Braungart, M. and Margaret Braungart. 1990. "The Life Course Development of Left- and Right-Wing Youth Activist Leaders from the 1960s." *Political Psychology* 11: 243–282.

Brians, C. and Martin Wattenberg. 1996. "Campaign Issue Knowledge and Salience: Comparing Reception from TV Commercials, TV News, and Newspapers." *American Journal of Political Science* 40: 172–193.

Brown, Michael. 1997. *Replacing Citizenship: AIDS Activism and Radical Democracy*. New York: Guilford Press.

Burstein, Paul. 1991. "Policy Domains: Organization, Culture and Policy Outcomes." *Annual Review of Sociology* 17: 327–350.

Campbell, Angus, Phillip Converse, Warren Miller, and Donald Stokes. 1960. *The American Voter*. New York: Wiley & Sons, Inc.

Campbell, John. 2002. "Ideas, Politics and Public Policy." *Annual Review of Sociology* 28: 21–38.

Collins, Randall. 1985. *Three Sociological Traditions*. New York: Oxford University Press.

Converse, Philip. 1964. "The Nature of Belief Systems in Mass Publics." Pp. 206–261 in *Ideology and Discontent*, edited by D. Apter. New York: Free Press.

Coser, Lewis (editor). 1966. *Political Sociology: Selected Essays*. New York: Harper & Row Publishers, Inc.

Covert, Tawnya, J. Adkins and Philo C. Wasburn. 2007. "Measuring Media Bias: A Content Analysis of Time and Newsweek Coverage of Domestic Social Issues, 1975–2000." *Social Science Quarterly* 88: 690–706.

Dalton, Russell. 2008. *Citizen Politics: Public Opinion and Political Parties in Advanced Industrial Democracies*. 5th Edition. Washington, DC: CQ Press.

Davis, James A., Tom W. Smith, and Peter V. Marsden. General Social Surveys, 1972–2008: [Cumulative File] [Computer file]. Chicago, IL: National Opinion Research Center [producer], 2009. Storrs, CT: Roper Center for Public Opinion Research, University of Connecticut; Ann Arbor, MI: Inter-university Consortium for Political and Social Research; Berkeley, CA: Computer-Assisted Survey Methods Program (http://sda.berkeley.edu), University of California [distributors], 2009.

Dawson, Richard, Kenneth Prewitt, and Karen Dawson. 1977. *Political Socialization*. 2nd Edition. Boston: Little, Brown and Company.

Derber, Charles. 2006. *Hidden Power: What You Need to Know to Save Our Democracy*. San Francisco: Berrett-Koehler Publishers, Inc.

Deutsch, Karl. 1955. "Symbols of Political Community." In *Symbols and Society: Fourteenth Symposium of the Conference on Science, Philosophy and Religion*, edited by L. Bryson, L. Finklestein, H. Hoagland, and R. Maciver. New York: Harper & Brothers.

Domhoff, William. 2006. *Who Rules America? Power, Politics & Social Change*. 5th Edition Boston: McGraw-Hill.

_____. 2010. *Who Rules America? Challenges to Corporate and Class Dominance*. 6th Edition. Boston: McGraw Hill.

Drori, Gili. 2006. *Global E-Litism: Digital Technology, Social Inequality, and Transnationality*. New York: Worth Publishers.

Dye, Thomas R. 2002. *Who's Running America? The Bush Restoration*. 7th Edition. Upper Saddle River, NJ: Prentice Hall.

Easton, Dennis and J. Dennis. 1969. *Children in the Political System*. New York: McGraw-Hill.

Edelman, Murray. 1964. *Symbolic Uses of Politics*. Champaign, IL: University of Illinois Press.

_____. 1971. *Politics as Symbolic Action: Mass Arousal and Quiescence*. London: George Allen & Unwin.

_____. 1988. *Constructing the Political Spectacle*. Chicago: University of Chicago Press.

Elazar, Daniel. 1984. *American Federalism*. 3rd Edition. New York: Harper & Row.

_____. 1994. *The American Mosaic: The Impact of Space, Time, and Culture on American Politics*. Boulder, CO: Westview.

Eliasoph, Nina. 1996. "Making a Fragile Public: A Talk-Centered Study of Citizenship and Power." *Sociological Theory* 14 (3): 262–289.

Eliot, T.S. 1975 [1948]. "Notes towards a Definition of Culture." Pp. 292–306 in *Selected Prose of T.S. Eliot*, edited by Frank Kermode. New York: Harcourt, Inc.

Erikson, Robert and Kent Tedin. 2005. *American Public Opinion: Its Origins, Content and Impact*. 7th Edition. New York: Longman.

Erikson, Robert, Norman Luttbeg, and Kent Tedin. 1988. *American Public Opinion: Its Origins, Content and Impact*. 3rd Edition. New York: Macmillan Publishing.

Foucault, Michel. 1973. *Madness and Civilization*. New York: Vintage.

_____. 1975. *Discipline and Punish: The Birth of the Prison*. New York: Pantheon.

Gallup Organization, August 31–September 2, 2009. Retrieved January 22, 2010 from the iPOLL Databank. The Roper Center for Public Opinion Research. University of Connecticut (http://www.ropercenter.uconn.edu/ipoll.html).

Gans, Herbert. 1980. *Deciding What's News*. New York: Vintage.

Gerring, John. 1997. "Ideology: A Definitional Analysis." *Political Research Quarterly* 50: 957–994.

Glynn, Carroll, Susan Herbst, Garrett O'Keefe, and Robert Shapiro. 1999. *Public Opinion*. Boulder, CO: Westview Press.

Goldstein, Kenneth and Travis Ridout. 2004. "Measuring the Effects of Televised Political Advertising in the United States." *Annual Review of Political Science* 7: 205–226.

Graber, Doris. 2006. *Mass Media and American Politics*. Washington, DC: CQ Press.

Gramsci, Antonio. 1971. *Selections from the Prison Notebooks*. London: New World Paperbacks.

Greenfield, Liah and Jonathan Eastwood. 2005. "Nationalism in Comparative Perspective." Pp. 247–265 in *The Handbook of Political Sociology: States, Civil Societies and Globalization*, edited by T. Janoski, R. Alford, A. Hicks, and M. Schwartz. New York: Cambridge University Press.

Greenstein, F. 1960. "The Benevolent Leaders: Children's Images of Political Authority." *American Journal of Political Science* 20: 773–779.

_____. 1965. *Children and Politics*. New Haven: Yale University Press.

Hall, John, Mary Jo Neitz, and Marshall Battani. 2003. *Sociology on Culture*. New York: Routledge.

Halman, Loek. 2007. "Political Values." Pp. 305–322 in *Oxford Handbook of Political Behavior*, edited by R. Dalton and H. D. Klingemann. New York: Oxford University Press.

Hess, R. and Judith Torney. 1969. *The Development of Political Attitudes in Children*. Chicago: Aldine.

Hunter, James. 1991. *Culture Wars: The Struggle to Define America*. New York: Basic Books.

Huntington, Samuel. 1968. *Political Order in Changing Societies*. New Haven: Yale University Press.

_____. 1991. *The Third Wave: Democratization in the Late Twentieth Century*. Norman, OK: Oklahoma University Press.

Inglehart, Ronald. 1977. *The Silent Revolution: Changing Values and Political Styles among Western Publics*. New Jersey: Princeton University Press.

_____. 1990. *Culture Shift in Advanced Industrial Society*. New Jersey: Princeton University Press.

_____. 1997. *Modernization and Post-Modernization: Cultural, Economic, and Political Change in 43 Societies*. New Jersey: Princeton University Press.

_____ and Christian Welzel. 2005. *Modernization, Cultural Change, and Democracy: The Human Development Sequence*. Cambridge, UK: Cambridge University Press.

Inkeles, Alex. 1983. *Exploring Individual Modernity*. New York: Columbia University Press.

_____ and David Smith. 1974. *Becoming Modern: Individual Change in Six Developing Countries*. Cambridge: Harvard University Press.

Jacobs, Ronald and Sarah Sobieraj. 2007. "Narrative and Legitimacy: U.S. Congressional Debates about the Nonprofit Sector." *Sociological Theory* 25(1): 1–25.

Jennings, M. and Richard Niemi. 1981. *Generations and Politics*. New Jersey: Princeton University Press.

Just, M.A. Crigler, D. Alger, T. Cook, M. Kern, and D. West. 1996. *Crosstalk: Citizens, Candidates, and the Media in a Presidential Campaign*. Chicago: University of Chicago Press.

Kiser, Edgar and Shawn Bauldry. 2005. "Rational Choice Theories in Political Sociology." Pp. 172–186 in *The Handbook of Political Sociology: States, Civil Societies and Globalization*, edited by T. Janoski, R. Alford, A. Hicks, and M. Schwartz. New York: Cambridge University Press.

Knight, Kathleen. 2006. "Transformations of the Concept of Ideology in the Twentieth Century." *American Political Science Review* 100(4): 619–626.

Kohn, Melvin L. and Carmi Schooler. 1969. "Class, Occupation, and Orientation." *American Sociological Review* 34: 659–678.

Kull, Steven. 2003. *Misperceptions, the Media, and the Iraq War*. Research paper Conducted by the Program on International Policy Attitudes (PIPA) and Knowledge Networks. Available at http://www.pipa.org.

Laclau, Ernesto and Chantel Mouffe. 1985. *Hegemony and Socialist Strategy*. London: New Left Books.

Lane, Jan-Erik and Svante Ersson. 2005. *Culture and Politics: A Comparative Approach*. London: Ashgate Publishing Ltd.

Larrain, J. 1979. *The Concept of Ideology*. London: Hutchison.

Lieske, Joel. 1993. "Regional Subcultures of the United States." *Journal of Politics* 55(4): 888–913.

———. 2007. *The Changing Political Subcultures of the United States and the Utility of a New Cultural Measure*. Paper presented at the annual meeting of the Midwest Political Science Association, Chicago, IL.

Luskin, Robert. 1990. "Explaining Political Sophistication." *Political Behavior* 12: 331–362.

Mannheim, Karl. 1936. Ideology and Utopia. New York: Harvest Books.

Manza, Jeff. 2000. "Political Sociological Models of the U.S. New Deal." *Annual Review of Sociology* 26: 297–322.

Manza, Jeff and N. Wright. 2003. "Religion and Political Behavior." Pp. 297–314 in *Handbook of the Sociology of Religion*, edited by M. Dillon. Cambridge: Cambridge University Press.

Margolis, Michael. 2007. "E-Government and Democracy." Pp. 765–782 in *Oxford Handbook of Political Behavior*, edited by R. Dalton and H.D. Klingemann. New York: Oxford University Press.

Markus, Prior. 2007. *Post-Broadcast Democracy: How Media Choice Increases Inequality in Political Involvement and Polarizes Elections*. New York: Cambridge University Press.

Marty, Myron and Scott Appleby. 1995. *Fundamentalisms Comprehended*. Chicago: University of Chicago Press.

Marx, Karl. 1970 [1859]. *Contribution to the Critique of Political Economy*. New York: International Publishers.

Meisel, James. 1962. *The Myth of the Ruling Class: Gaetano Mosca and the Elite*. Ann Arbor: University of Michigan Press.

Miller, David, David Barker, and Christopher Carman. 2006. "Research Note: Mapping the Genome of American Political Subcultures: A Proposed Methodology and Pilot Study." *Publius: The Journal of Federalism* 36(2): 303–315.

Mills, C. Wright. 1959. *The Sociological Imagination*. London: Oxford University Press.

Morris, Jonathon S. 2005. "The Fox News Factor." *Harvard International Journal of Press/Politics* 10: 56–79.

——— 2007. "Slanted objectivity? Perceived Media Bias, Cable News Exposure, and Political Attitudes." *Social Science Quarterly* 88:708–728.

Mouffe, Chantel. 1991. "Citizenship and Political Community." Pp. 70–82 in *Community at Loose Ends*, edited by the Miami Theory Collective. Minneapolis: University of Minnesota Press.

Niemi, Richard. 1999. *Civic Education: What Makes Students Learning?* New Haven: Yale University Press.

Niven, David. 1999. "Partisan Bias in the Media? A New Test." *Social Science Quarterly* 80: 847–857.

Norris, Pippa. 2000. *Virtuous Circle: Political Communications in Postindustrial Societies*. New York: Cambridge University Press.

Oakeshott, M. 1962. *Rationalism in Politics and Other Essays*. London: Methuen.

Parsons, Talcott. 1951. *The Social System*. New York: Free Press.

Patterson, Thomas and Wolfgang Donsbach. 1996. "News Decisions: Journalists as Partisan Actors." *Political Communication* 13: 455–468.

Paxton, Pamela and Melanie Hughes. 2007. *Women, Politics, and Power: A Global Perspective*. Los Angeles, California: Pine Forge Press.

Pew Research Center for the People and the Press and Princeton Survey Research Associates International, July 22–July 26, 2009. Retrieved January 22, 2010 from the iPOLL Databank, The Roper Center for Public Opinion Research. University of Connecticut (http://www.ropercenter.uconn.edu/ipoll.html).

Pfau, M., Holbert R., Szabo E., and Kaminksi, K. 2002. "Issue Advocacy Versus Candidate Advertising: Effects on Candidate Preferences and Democratic Processes." *Journal of Communications* 52: 301–315.

Preiss, Raymond, Barbara Mae Gayle, Nancy Burrell, Mike Allen, and Jennings Bryan (editors). 2006. *Mass Media Effects Research: Advances through Meta-Analysis*. New York: Routledge.

Putnam, Robert. 2000. *Bowling Alone: The Collapse and Revival of American Community*. New York: Simon and Schuster.

Renshon, Stanley. 2004. "Political Socialization in a Divided Society and Dangerous Age." Pp. 427–456 in *Encyclopedia of Government and Politics*, edited by M. Hawkesworth and M. Kogen. New York: Routledge.

Runciman, W.G. 1978. *Weber: Selections in Translation*. Cambridge: Cambridge University Press.

Samuelson, Robert J. 2008. "Political Perils of a 'Big Sort'?" *Washington Post*, August 6: A17.

Schooler, Carmi. 1996. "Cultural and Social-Structural Explanations of Cross-National Psychological Differences." *Annual Review of Sociology* 22: 323–349.

Schwartz, Barry. 2008. "Collective Memory and Abortive Commemoration: President's Day and the American Holiday Calendar." *Social Research* 75(1): 75–110.

Swidler, Ann. 1986. "Culture in Action." *American Sociological Review*. 51: 273–286.

Therborn, Goran. 1980. *The Ideology of Power and the Power of Ideology*. New York: Verso.

Tocqueville, Alexis de. 1945 [1835]. *Democracy in America*. New York: Vintage Books.

Torfing, Jacob. 2005. "Poststructuralist Discourse Theory: Foucault, Laclau, Mouffe, and Zizek." Pp. 153–171 in *The Handbook of Political Sociology: States,*

Civil Societies and Globalization, edited by T. Janoski, R. Alford, A. Hicks and M.A. Schwartz. New York: Cambridge University Press.

Torney-Purta, Judith. 1990. "From Attitudes and Knowledge to Schemata: Expanding the Outcomes of Political Socialization Research." Pp. 98–115 in *Political Socialization, Citizenship Education, and Democracy*, edited by O. Ichilov. New York: Teachers College Press.

_____ 1995. "Psychological Theory as a Basis for Political Socialization Research: Individuals' Construction of Knowledge." *Perspectives on Political Science* 24: 23–33.

Vujačić, Veljki. 2002. "States, Nations, and European Nationalism: A Challenge for Political Sociology." Pp. 123–156 in *Theoretical Directions in Political Sociology for the 21st Century*, volume 11: *Research in Political Sociology*, edited by B. Dobratz, T. Buzzell, and L. K. Waldner . London: Elsevier.

Weakliem, David. 2005. "Public Opinion, Political Attitudes, and Ideology." Pp. 227–246 in *The Handbook of Political Sociology: States, Civil Societies, and Globalization*, edited by T. Janoski, R. Alford, A. Hicks, and M. Schwartz. Cambridge, UK: Cambridge University Press.

Weber, Max. 1946. *From Max Weber: Essays in Sociology*. Translated and edited by H.H. Gerth and C.W. Mills. New York: Oxford University Press.

Williams, Robin. 1970. *American Society: A Sociological Interpretation*. New York: Alfred A. Knopf.

World Values Survey 1981–2008 Official Aggregate v.20090901, 2009. World Values Survey Association (www.worldvaluessurvey.org). Aggregate File Producer: ASEP/JDS, Madrid.

Wuthnow, Robert. 1989. *Communities of Discourse: Ideology and Social Structure in the Reformation, the Enlightenment and European Socialism*. Cambridge, MA: Harvard University Press.

The Politics of Everyday Life: Political Economy

In this chapter and in Chapter 5, we are especially interested in pointing out how certain key institutional features in our society have political aspects that influence our lives. What we identify are certainly not things that are on every person's mind all the time, but they have the potential to influence most of us during important parts of our lives. According to their book *Sociology in Everyday Life,* Karp, Yoels, and Vann (2004: 1) believe that a key ingredient of sociology's importance lies in its "power to let you see everyday behaviors and situations in a new way." Sociologists frequently study how people behave and analyze how ordered and predictable people's everyday lives may be.

One of the major concepts that helps us better understand everyday life is power. In Chapter 1 we pointed out C. Wright Mills' contributions to the study of power, and here, too, we examine his ideas about the connections of individuals' everyday lives to what is happening in society currently and also how our lives intersect with global world history. Mills (1959: 3) argues, "Neither the life of an individual nor the history of a society can be understood without understanding both." For example, when a war happens, an insurance salesperson may become a marine, a spouse may live alone, a child may grow up without a parent, and a person in the National Guard may be activated and go to the front several times. Developing the sociological imagination enables people to understand the connections between their everyday lives and the course of history (4, 6).

An individual troubled by war used political graffiti to express his or her concern. C. Wright Mills would consider stopping war a social issue.

Credit: Thinkstock

For Mills it is important to distinguish between troubles and issues. Troubles are private or personal problems regarding the individual's biography, whereas issues are public matters going beyond the limited environment of the individual. Mills uses the example of unemployment: If one person is unemployed in a community of 100,000, it is a personal trouble, but if 15 million people in a country of 50 million jobseekers are unemployed, this is an issue that many would argue the government should be responsive to.

Dividing society into the public and private spheres of life places the state and thus politics into the public sphere, distinct from other major social institutions like the family, religion, education, economics, and the media. This separation has made it more difficult to recognize the politics in our everyday lives. Yet politics is changing at least in part due to basic alterations in our economic and social life such as the development of postindustrial capitalism, global transportation, advances in medical technology, the rise of mass culture, and the growth of the media and the Internet, and possibly, as some argue, a decline in religion. Agger and Luke (2002: 162) suggest that "politics has been dispersed" more so than the postmodern claim that politics has ended. The 2008 U.S. government bailouts of major financial institutions such as Bear Stearns, Fannie Mae, Freddie Mac, and the insurance conglomerate American International Group Inc. (AIG) by the U.S. Treasury and the Federal Reserve illustrate just how politics, the state, and the economy are tightly linked. House Speaker Pelosi questioned "how these captains of the financial world could make millions of dollars in salary, and yet their companies fail and then we have to step in to bail them out" (Andrews 2008).

Our goal in this chapter and in Chapter 5 is to show how politics plays an important role in our major institutions of economy, education, and family, and in other aspects of our lives related to the infrastructure, health care, civil liberties, and race and ethnic relations. Throughout we look at public opinion to help us understand what the "typical" American may be thinking on various issues and what their values may be. Our examples illustrate how politics affects our everyday lives in various ways. In this chapter we consider politics and the economy, including a look at the infrastructure that affects the economy and society.

The term *political economy* has been coined to refer to the relationship between politics and economy. Perhaps the relationship between the state and the economy is the most influential in people's lives and involves the most significant displays of power in our society. Marger (1987: 92) argues that "political power in a society can be understood only as a synthesis of the actions of governmental and economic institutions. . . . The consequences of the actions of business and government leaders affect all people" including jobs, taxes, prices, public services, and war and peace.

CAPITALISM AND DEMOCRACY

Technically, the U.S. economic system has been labeled "mixed," suggesting the involvement of both private and public institutions. To Marger (1987) a significant feature of the U.S. economy is how major corporations dominate. In a capitalist economic system there is private ownership of property, private and competitive pursuit of profits, and inequality in the distribution of society's resources. Ideally the competition for profit makes society stronger and more efficient and motivates individuals to work hard, although in reality things may not always work that way.

As an economic system the United States is a capitalist system, and politically it is regarded as a democracy. Although ideally in the political system citizens are entitled to vote, have equal rights before the law, and have access to their politicians, their economic resources influence these aspects. Robertson (1981) points out that part of the possible dilemma about understanding the complex relationship between politics and economy revolves around differing interpretations of *freedom*, a value most of us strongly endorse. More specifically, some emphasize liberty in their definition of freedom while others stress freedom as promoting equality. Robertson believes that both liberty and equality are important values in American society, but the two concepts are not very compatible because the exercise of liberty may negatively affect the degree of equality in society, and vice versa. In the United States, liberty is emphasized, and that results in inequality, but socialist countries value equality at the expense of individual liberty. Somewhat similarly, Marger (2008) identifies the contradiction of capitalism and democracy, with capitalism founded on liberty that creates inequality and democracy grounded in equity (fairness for everyone).

In 2009 the Government Accountability Office (GAO) identified a new high-risk area that called for "modernizing the outdated U.S. Financial Regulatory System," proclaiming, "Having a vibrant, healthy financial sector is critical to the United States" (2009: 11). The report recognized that the Gramm-Leach-Bliley Act of 1999 reversed restrictions that were a key part of the financial regulatory system created in the 1930s as a response to the Great Depression. Also the "largely unregulated investment bank securitization of mortgage loans" and the "nonbank mortgage lenders, which generally are not subject to direct federal oversight" (13) were important in subprime mortgage lending that resulted in "the worst financial crisis in more than 75 years" (12). During the five presidential administrations before Obama's, fewer restrictions were placed on branch banking, and loan restrictions were abandoned. The deregulation of banking not only expanded the availability and types of credit but also helped to facilitate disturbing, and sometimes fraudulent, lending practices (Leicht and Fitzgerald 2007).

THEORETICAL FRAMEWORKS

The various theoretical frameworks give us differing views of the relationships between politics and economy. In addition to our discussion of the pluralist, elite/managerial, class/Marxist, postmodern, rational choice, and institutionalist frameworks, we also consider Domhoff's class-domination theory of power.

Pluralist

In the pluralist interpretation of society and politics the key focus is on the relationship between the political system and democracy. Pluralists recognize that some maldistribution or inequality of economic resources exists, but the inequities can be corrected. The social values in the United States support a capitalist system, extolling the virtues of free enterprise and hard work. The profit that corporations make is generally deserved and is a return for investing and engaging in some risk. Typically workers are not exploited but are rewarded on the basis of their work ethic and skills (Alford and Friedland 1985). Generally the government develops Social Security (SS), employment, and other welfare policies to benefit its citizens and reduce social inequality. The state is typically pictured as neutral, trying to determine the policies that are in the best interest of voters and consumers while helping businesses that are contributing to the welfare of the society (Neuman 2005).

Elite/Managerial

In the elite/managerial perspective, C. Wright Mills identified the power of the corporate, military, and political elites, stressing how power was being centralized so that "the economy . . . has become dominated by two or three hundred grant corporations, administratively and politically interrelated, which together hold the keys to economic decisions" (1956: 7). The major source of bureaucratic power rests in the control of significant institutions, especially the corporation and the executive branch of the government. The power elite is generally cohesive, with the state typically operating to protect the institutional arrangements that benefit the dominant elite (Marger 1987). Drawing on data from 1980 to 1981 Dye (2002) identified three sectors of the power elite. The corporate sector, composed of industrial corporations, banks, insurance, and investment companies, had nearly 60 percent of the power elite leadership positions. This is followed by the public interest sector, which is comprised of mass media, law, education, private foundations, and civic and cultural organizations, with around 37 percent. The government sector had less than 4 percent of the power elite leadership positions.

While an elite and a subelite exist, the masses, generally most people, are being manipulated and taken advantage of by the elite. The classical conservative elite theorists like Michels and Pareto distrust the masses, who have generally been viewed as apathetic and wanting others to lead them. The masses are typically viewed as unable to make rational decisions, incompetent, and either not willing or not capable of governing or participating thoughtfully in politics. The more contemporary or radical version of elite theory suggests that the masses are not being provided with adequate information that would enable them to make educated economic and political decisions and thus they are being taken advantage of by the power elite (Marger 1987).

If the masses do express their discontent on economic issues, they may be granted minor reforms or symbolic changes that tend to placate them.

Class/Marxist

Instead of viewing power as being in the hands of major government and economic organizations as in the elite/managerial perspective, in the class/Marxist perspective, power is viewed as being in the hands of the capitalist class. Class theory is extremely critical of the capitalist economic system and the capitalist state that supports it. The key power group according to this theory is the ruling class, which can be defined as those who own and control the means of production (Marger 1987). To make a profit, the ruling class exploits the working class who has only its labor to sell. A person's class position significantly influences many aspects of his or her life. Many workers feel alienated from the work they do, as their labor creates wealth for the capitalists. Workers, though, ultimately develop a sense of class consciousness and move toward an overthrow of the capitalist system. Some class theorists believe the capitalist system will experience crisis after crisis that will ultimately result in the collapse of capitalism and the triumph of the working class.

Berberoglou (2001) points out that certain Marxist theorists support the view that "the state in capitalist society is *both* controlled by *and*, at the same time, relatively autonomous from the various fractions of the capitalist class" (41). Other Marxist theorists recognize that the state needs to consider more than the ruling class when it makes its policy. According to Szymanski, "State policy is always influenced to some extent by the various classes, even while it is normally under the domination of the [ruling] class" (quoted in Berberoglou 2001: 56). Textbox 4.1 describes differing interpretations of corporate involvement in the political process.

Postmodern

Postmodernism emphasizes what is going on within the economic system of capitalism and the development of a consumer culture as people try to find their identity and sense of self while questioning science and rationality. Postmodernism is placed "in the context of the 'disorganized capitalism' of the consumer society and cultural mass production of the late 20th century. . . . The world now has a messy and highly uncertain feel to it" (Best 2002: 42). This uncertainty especially affects economic life. Instead of developing class consciousness, people "create their own thoughts and their own bonds of community" in a fragmented society that is undergoing numerous changes (266). Without the economic interests of classes, politics becomes irrational and unpredictable. Power is not rooted in class domination but rather power is seen in the "micro-process invading the bodies, discourses, habits of people in their everyday lives" (Agger and Luke 2002: 181).

Rational Choice

Rational choice theories are rooted in ideas from economics (Neuman 2005). *Macroeconomics* refers to that area of economics that focuses on theories and methods that deal with relationships among government policies and expenditures, inflation, unemployment, and income. The government's fiscal policy involves how it spends money to provide goods and services and what methods it uses, including taxes and borrowing, to finance its expenditures (Leicht and Fitzgerald 2007). Leicht and Fitzgerald point out that only Keynesian and supply-side economics have had a major influence on government policy. A typical Keynesian presidential candidate would stress

---

TEXTBOX 4.1

Corporate Involvement in Politics

A topic of major debate focuses upon how much business is and should be involved in shaping politics. Ideally the government should be functioning to maintain society to benefit the people it serves, and the marketplace should be operating to provide and distribute needs, goods, and services to its customers. The state serves as an arbiter between those with conflicting interests as it decides "who gets what, when, and how" (Robertson 1981: 485). Lehne (2006) examines the advantages and disadvantages of involvement of business in politics.

Those who are supportive of corporate involvement argue that the corporate community's political agenda favors economic growth and supports basic social and political values, especially those related to free enterprise, individualism, and democracy. Lehne (2006) identified three particular benefits corporate activity has provided to the political system. First, corporations have given their employees and others a very good standard of living. In order to do this the corporate sector needs to have favorable governmental policy so that it can offer employment and returns on people's investments. If corporations could not participate in politics, the government might not implement policies that promote a successful economy.

Second, business involvement in politics helps document the success of pluralism in the American system. Business is one of the "multiple power centers within a diverse society but the expanding influence of government in American life jeopardizes the autonomy of other social institutions" (Lehne 2006: 137). Corporations are certainly one of the more powerful nongovernmental organizations in society, but they also function as potential allies for other groups to form coalitions or to fight against too much government power.

Third, corporations can help protect individual liberties by defending their own rights to freedom of association, due process, and freedom of speech. Such a defense could also help strengthen people's claims for these same rights.

Those concerned about too much corporate power argue that corporate resources are used to dominate the process and hinder other groups from significant influence. Corporate influence advances their own interests often at the expense of most people in society, especially the poor. Inequities become even more accentuated. In addition, they suggest business involvement does not limit possible abuse of power by government or protect societal diversity. Most business contributions to politicians tend to support people already in office (Lehne 2006).

Kinloch (1989) too argues that the economic institution promotes inequality, and economic interests are overrepresented in politics. The tremendous lobbying influence and political power of corporations negatively affects political and legal policies. For example, tax laws are formulated that benefit those with greater economic resources, whereas welfare and social services budgets may be reduced. Elected officials may be indebted to those who have made substantial campaign contributions.

---

his interest in "getting America working again" and "maintaining the economic integrity of working Americans" (45). The fiscal policy would likely include incentives for income maintenance programs like unemployment insurance, SS benefits, and interest deductions for consumer debts. Tax cuts and investment in public works programs may also be used to stimulate the economy. President Obama's advisors tend to be Keynesian. A presidential candidate using supply-side economics would likely stress "getting the government off of people's backs" and "getting America to invest, save, and work" (45). The fiscal policies would likely include tax cuts and deregulation actions also intended to stimulate the economy. President Ronald Reagan's and President George W. Bush's administrations serve as prototypes for supply-side economics.

Institutionalist

In his assessment of political institutional theory Amenta (2005) points out how this framework overlaps with other sociological ones including political culture, pluralist, elite/managerial, and class/Marxist. Institutionalist theorists often use a comparative historical approach to examine political phenomena. For example in her work on the welfare state Skocpol (1992) uses a "structured polity" perspective that emphasizes how politicians and administrators are influenced by political organizations. In addition to cultural patterns and socioeconomic relations, state and party structures shape how groups organize and develop consciousness. In the late 1800s and early 1900s in the United States working-class consciousness was relatively weak and patronage party officials and legislators influenced social welfare policies. For example Civil War pensions provided benefits for veterans and their dependents. Moral and political criteria were used to guide that policy rather than socioeconomic criteria. Veterans were seen as having made sacrifices for the good of the nation and worthy of reward. Many poor people, however, were seen as undeserving. As pointed out in Chapter 2 of our book, political values thus play a key role in determining who is worthy of benefits. In other Western welfare states, officials in government bureaucracies employed socioeconomic standards to formulate labor regulations and policies to benefit workingmen, and the working class developed a stronger sense of consciousness than in the United States (Skocpol 1992).

Class-Domination Theory of Power

G. William Domhoff has dedicated numerous years to the study of power and class, especially the upper class and power elite, in American society. His class-domination theory, though certainly related to Marxist, institutionalist, and power elite frameworks, deserves separate treatment here in the discussion of the economy and everyday life. Domhoff (2006) sees two major coalitions: a corporate–conservative coalition and a liberal–labor coalition. The leaders of the corporate–conservative coalition are top executives and corporate heads who are supported by many patriotic, antitax, and single-issue organizations. There is also an uneasy alliance of the corporate leaders with the Christian Right. For the liberal–labor coalition, unions remain the largest and best-financed segment even though they have lost considerable influence. Other segments of this coalition include liberal university communities, liberal churches, most minority communities, and local environmental organizations.

The majority of people are not strongly loyal to either of these coalitions although the coalitions are competing for people's support. Domhoff believes that the reason for the majority's lack of attention to policy issues is that these people often concentrate on their everyday life concerns including their families and job challenges. Although some describe such people as being apathetic or ignorant about politics, Domhoff argues that their behavior actually makes sense because of the "many time-consuming necessities and pleasures of everyday life" (2006: xviii), the problems in reaching consensus on policy issues, and the amount of time and patience needed to bring about change.

We might add, though, that the corporate–conservative coalition does certainly influence people's everyday lives. The following issues Domhoff (2006) identifies as class or economic conflicts certainly affect us all: (1) concern about the distribution of profits and wages, (2) rate and progressivity of taxation, (3) the role of labor unions, and (4) the degree of government regulation of business. Domhoff recognizes how well organized those who wield the most power are. He describes their influence as "dominant" because of their great power; however, he also recognizes there are limits to corporate power.

In Chapter 3, concerning culture, we noted the importance of values in politics. Domhoff (2006: 112) identifies the following key principles of an American value system that structure class relations in the United States: individualism, equality of opportunity, free enterprise, competition, and limited reliance on government in our everyday lives. The power elite engage in the opinion-shaping process that uses an individualistic ideology that emphasizes personal effort and responsibility as well as benefitting the successful and blaming the victims. Many people blame themselves rather than the system even though they intellectually realize that there are many injustices and barriers to equal opportunity. Most people accept the power of the dominant class because that class has shaped "the rules and customs through which everyday life is conducted" (199).

WALL STREET VERSUS MAIN STREET

At the end of 2007, the United States entered a recession that some suggest may be the worst since the Great Depression. Although in many ways one could argue that there had been a huge division between Wall Street and Main Street for a long time, the phrase *Wall Street vs. Main Street* was certainly given greater attention near the end of the first decade of the twenty-first century. On the one hand, Wall Street represents the very rich, the powerful, large corporate organizations, banks, financiers, and other capitalists or what Dye refers to as the *national institutional elite* and Domhoff as the *ruling class.* Main Street comprises most everyone else but especially the hard-working men and women struggling either to maintain a decent standard of living or just to survive.

While many were losing their jobs, the value of stock was declining rapidly, many financial institutions and corporations were receiving bailouts, and Wall Street continued to hand out bonuses. White (2009) reports that "despite crippling losses, multibillion-dollar bailouts and the passing of some of the most prominent names in the business, employees at financial companies in New York . . . collected an estimated $18.4 billion in bonuses for the year [2008]." White also

Members of the Bailout the People Movement protest in front of the New York Stock Exchange on Friday, October 24, 2008. The group wants the government to help homeowners facing foreclosure and other people affected by the debt crisis as opposed to financial institutions.

Credit: Richard B. Levine/Newscom

reports that as if this wasn't enough, outside the financial industry, many corporate executives received fatter bonuses while the economy lost 2.6 million jobs. For top executives other than CEOs, the average supposedly performance-based bonus was $265,594 (White 2009). People on Main Street typically make much less than that as yearly income, let alone bonuses.

Perhaps the most frustrating case regarding bonuses involved the AIG, which had received over $170 billion in taxpayer bailout money but announced in March 2009 that it was planning to give about $165 million to executives in the business unit who had led the company to near collapse in 2008. AIG defended its position, arguing that the bonuses had been promised much earlier and thus it was legally bound to provide them. Also, the bonuses were needed to retain high-quality executives (Andrews and Baker 2009). Because of growing pressures, AIG Chief Liddy asked employees with bonuses over $100,000 to return them. Although much of the anger was directed at AIG because of the huge bailout it received, other companies were doing much the same.

While many were losing jobs, those who had jobs also had problems. For example, many companies, including FedEx, Eastman Kodak, Motorola, General Motors (GM), and Resorts International, cut their contributions to worker 401(k) retirement plans at the same time workers were seeing the value of their retirement accounts drop drastically. Cutting back on retirement contributions makes it more difficult to retire securely (Williams and Bernard 2009). In addition, those working may feel great stress and want to change jobs. One study by Hochwater has found 55 percent of bosses or supervisors had become more demanding of their workers and more than 70 percent of employees indicated that their stress levels had grown since the recession began. Many employees felt that they were doing the work of employees who had lost their jobs, as well as their own work. Employers realized that with the high unemployment rate it would be easy to fill open positions if someone left (Bruzzese 2009).

Thousands line the streets outside Madison Square Garden near the Empire State Building for the Twin Towers Job Expo in New York, October 25, 2001. Lines stretched around the block and many were turned away from the job fair created in the wake of the World Trade Center attacks.

Credit: Doug Kanter/AFP/Newscom

Not only was the jobless rate increasing at mid-year 2009; for those with jobs, wages were declining due to furloughs, pay freezes, and pay cuts (Aversa 2009). Several states had implemented or were considering implementing furloughs to deal with their budget problems. Furloughs may be particularly problematic for states. Private companies that use furloughs often have a decrease in workload; however, when state agencies use furloughs, typically government services are delayed. In addition, government services are in greater demand when the economy is doing poorly (Seelye 2009).

In January 2009, President Obama labeled Wall Street bankers giving themselves bonuses of nearly $20 million in the face of government bailouts and the rapidly worsening economy as "shameful." Then in February, the Obama administration proclaimed a $500,000 cap on bonuses for top executives of corporations obtaining the largest shares of the bailouts. He declared that this was not only being fair but also reflecting "basic common sense." The public, though, was not appeased, and two weeks later Congress passed a $787 billion stimulus package that included tougher restrictions on those in top positions in the most troubled corporations ("Executive Pay" 2009). In July 2009, the House Financial Services Committee, in support of the Obama White House's proposal, approved a bill that gave shareholders the right to vote on executive salaries and bonuses, although their vote would not be binding. Regulators were to have authority to stop inappropriate or risky compensation packages for regulated financial companies (Labaton 2009a).

The media devoted considerable attention to the anger felt by ordinary citizens. *Newsweek*'s cover story on March 30, 2009, was entitled "The Thinking Man's Guide to Populist Rage." In that issue, historian Michael Kazin defines the core of populism as "a protest by ordinary people who want the system to live up to its stated ideals—fair and honest treatment in the marketplace and a government tilted in favor of the unwealthy masses" ("The Outrage Factor" 2009: 24). In 1892 populists created their own political party, but it didn't survive very long. Also in the 1930s at the time of the Great Depression "populist movements challenged elected officials to serve the hard working majority instead of the 'plutocrats' " (24). Kazin believes that the current "widespread disgust" (24) gave the Obama administration an opportunity to reshape politics that would include placing strict regulations on the financial industry.

A debate sponsored by Intelligence Squared U.S. focused on the proposition "blame Washington more than Wall Street for the financial crisis." Historian Niall Ferguson supports the proposition and argues that, while it is easy to blame the bankers for everything, he blames the politicians even more. He blames the following four key components of government in particular:

- The Federal Reserve Board, which allowed the housing market to get out of control.
- The Securities and Exchange Commission, which allowed the banking system to spiral out of control.
- Congress, which didn't supervise Fannie Mae and Freddie Mac very well.
- The White House under the G. W. Bush administration, which made statements like "We want everybody in America to own their own home" ("Who's to Blame: Washington or Wall Street?" 2009: 30).

In the debate, Nell Minow, editor of The Corporate Library, a corporate-governance research firm, partially challenged the proposition that blamed the government more. He countered that Wall Street relied too much on poor statistics and had a bad incentive program that should have been based on the quality of transactions rather than quantity. He also blamed shareholders, especially big shareholders who supported "insane pay packages" ("Who's to Blame: Washington or Wall Street?" 2009: 31). Finally Minow identified Washington by asking whether the large amount of money (more than $600 million from 1998 to 2008) spent by lobbyists to eliminate regulations and capital requirements on banks influenced the government (31).

It appears that there was justifiable anger at bankers, corporations, and the government, but what could and should the government have done about this? We can't answer that question completely, and it will possibly take several years to understand what actually occurred, but what happens with future federal budgets will shed light on the issue as well as how the public views spending. According to Fineman (2009: 34), "While the Beltway is getting its populist freak over AIG, a bigger, more fateful drama . . . [involves] whether the Obama administration can reverse a generation's worth of skepticism about the role of government in our lives." Rahm Emanuel, the former White House chief of staff, supported an affirmative role for the administration in shaping the budget, stating, "Not 'active' for its own sake, but affirmative in the sense of being a force for good in everyday lives—education, health, a lessening of economic and social schisms in society" (34). As we are seeing in this chapter and as we will see in Chapter 5, government plays a key role in our everyday lives whether we are angry with it, supporting it, challenging it, or disagreeing with it.

MIDDLE CLASS

As Marger (2008) points out, most people identify themselves as members of the middle classes, which represent the large majority of the population. Also he recognizes that at various times parts of government policy have indeed benefitted the middle classes. For example, compulsory public schools have been regarded as an important way to promote an equal opportunity structure as has been the establishment of land-grant colleges and universities. The establishment of a progressive income tax in 1913 was also ideally to help equalize the income distribution. In the face of the Great Depression, the SS system was created to provide a safety net for those who retired or were no longer able to work in the paid labor force. The Wagner Labor Relations Act of 1935 allowed industrial workers to organize into labor unions, and the G.I. Bill of Rights after World War II and other legislation encouraged returning veterans to attend college and made home ownership more available. What became quite apparent in the first decade of the twenty-first century, however, was how the middle classes were declining even in the face of increasing productivity and high rates of profitability.

Forgrave (2008) documents how the middle class is being squeezed especially in terms of household income, gas prices, medical insurance, and college cost. The median household income has declined 1 percent between 1999 when it was $50,641 and 2007 when it was $50,233 (adjusted for inflation). The average annual payment made by workers for medical insurance is $3,354, illustrating a 65 percent increase since 1999. The average cost for a public school education has also increased 35 percent from 1999 to 2007 (1A, 11A).

Pew Research Center (2008) conducted a survey in January and February 2008 that also documented a middle-class squeeze.[1] The survey reported "middle-class blues" with 78 percent of the middle class indicating that, compared with five years ago, it was more difficult to maintain their standard of living. When asked who or what was responsible for the middle-class squeeze, the responses were quite diverse, but the government, at 26 percent, was the most frequently mentioned. Remembering that G. W. Bush was president at the time, note that 35 percent of the Democrats named the government as the reason, while only 16 percent of the Republicans did. Also middle-class Republicans were much more likely to blame the people themselves (17 percent of Republicans and 8 percent of Democrats).

In *America's Forgotten Majority,* Teixeira and Rogers (2000: xi) identify a strong decline in the public's trust of government by white working-class Americans (from almost 80 percent in 1964 to slightly less than 30 percent in 1996). Teixeira and Rogers argue that "The changes that these voters really want—and that aren't being offered in sufficient quantities by either of the major parties at present—are improvements in basic aspects of their lives." Their list includes health insurance, secure retirement, proper education, tensions between work and family, and competing in a global economy.

Recent data from the Pew values survey suggest disenchantment with government also although the young, blacks, and Hispanics were more positive than others. In addition, one's political affiliation and which party is in power in Congress and the presidency do influence one's views on the government. Table 4.1 confirms this statement, as differences between Republicans and Democrats essentially reversed themselves between 2007 (when George W. Bush was president) and 2009 (when Obama became president) on the question of whether government is run for the benefit of all (Pew Research Center for the People & the Press 2009). The responses to the question of whether the government controls too much of our daily lives are also clearly influenced by one's party affiliation and which party is in power, especially in 2009. The survey found 72 percent of Republicans, 57 percent of Independents, and 42 percent of Democrats agreed that government has too much influence (Pew Research Center for the People & the Press 2009).

Postindustrial Peasants: The Illusion of Middle-Class Prosperity by Leicht and Fitzgerald (2007) focuses especially on the difficulties of the middle class[2] and compares the current situation of middle class with that of peasants in past agrarian societies. Doing research on the middle class, supposedly "the bedrock on which economic prosperity is based" (xv), enables one to see how increasingly precarious life has become for much of society. The authors provide compelling documentation to support their argument about the struggles of the middle class that have led to a "general politics of displacement" due to "tax cuts for the wealthy, deregulation,

Table 4.1	Republicans, Democrats Change Views about Whether Government Is Run for Benefit of All (Depending on Which Political Party the President Affiliates With)					
	Year					
	1987	**1994**	**1999**	**2003**	**2007**	**2009**
	Percentage of People Who Agree					
Total	57	42	49	52	45	49
Republicans	67	37	49	69	61	41
Democrats	55	50	54	44	40	60
Independents	53	37	48	47	40	44
R–D (Republican–Democratic) gap	+12	−13	−5	+25	+21	−19

Source: Pew Research Center for the People & the Press, 2009

Credit: "Republicans, Democrats Change Views about Whether Government Is Run for Benefit of All," taken from "Independents Take Center Stage in Obama Era." The Pew Research Center for the People & the Press, 2009. A project of the Pew Research Center.

corporate tax avoidance, and an overall shifting of tax burdens onto earned income" (13). The consequences of the continuing deterioration of the middle class are great, resulting in an "overall coarsening of American life" (128) that encourages a "we versus they" outlook that divides Americans. Citizens' trust in government has declined. Members of the middle class develop a cynicism toward politics, seeing "little support from politicians and other elites, believing they don't understand the realities of everyday life" (133). Leicht and Fitzgerald (138) maintain that neither Republicans nor Democrats seem attentive to the cultural and economic issues facing the middle class.

Leicht and Fitzgerald (2007) offer several suggestions for improving the situation of the middle class and society at both the individual and collective levels. We consider only three here. First, middle-class prosperity needs to be reconnected to the accumulation of capital. Workers need to be rewarded when economic times are good. It is not simply about giving bonuses to those at the top of the corporate ladder. Second, if American society values families, a strong economic base is needed for those families. Good jobs with fair wages would help improve the tensions over money in the family. Taxes need to be progressive rather than regressive. Third, people need to recognize and understand that inequality is truly a social problem and society needs to do something about it. Rather than debating whether inequality motivates people to work hard, the focus needs to be on ways to reduce the extreme levels of inequality. If politicians and economic elites are held accountable for creating policies that support economic health for the nation, this may result in greater confidence in government also.

TAXATION

One of the slogans of the American Revolution was "no taxation without representation," which suggests how strong people's concern was about paying unfair taxes. Benjamin Franklin is the likely source of the statement, "In this world nothing is certain but death and taxes" (McKenna and Feingold 2004), which suggests the pervasiveness of taxation. As already noted, tax policy is a basic tool available to governments to help administer the economy. The U.S. Constitution states in Article I, Section 8 that "Congress shall have Power to lay and collect Taxes, Duties, Imports and Excises, to pay the Debts and provide for the common Defence and general Welfare of the United States" (Blum et al. 1963: 814). In 1912 the Sixteenth Amendment gave Congress the power to tax incomes without apportionment, and Congress then adopted a graduated income tax on individuals and businesses.

While few would ever say they enjoy paying taxes, many might well agree with Supreme Court Justice Oliver Wendell Holmes that "taxes are what we pay for civilized society" (McKenna and Feingold 2004: 230). Taxes go for services people need in order to function in a complex society, including public education, fire and police protection, roads, military defense, and social welfare programs. Despite desiring essential services from the government, citizens frequently express concerns about how much they pay in taxes.

Key questions about taxation are who pays taxes and how taxes are spent. As shown in Figure 4.1, the Internal Revenue Service (IRS) (2009: 90) reports that for fiscal year 2008, personal income taxes made up 39 percent of the nation's income, followed by 30 percent of income from SS, Medicare, unemployment, and other retirement taxes. Corporate income taxes made up only 10 percent of the income. The largest expenditure (37 percent) was for SS, Medicare, and other retirement programs for the disabled and medical care for the elderly. The next largest category (24 percent) was for national defense, veterans, and foreign affairs. The smallest category was money spent for social programs (20 percent) including Medicaid,

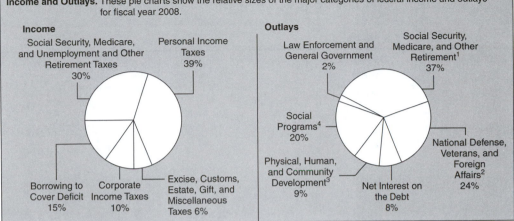

Income and Outlays. These pie charts show the relative sizes of the major categories of federal income and outlays for fiscal year 2008.

Federal income was $2.524 trillion and outlays were $2.983 trillion in fiscal year 2008 (October 1, 2007–September 30, 2008).

[1]Social security, Medicare, and other retirement. These programs provide income support for the retired and disabled and medical care for the elderly.

[2]National defense, veterans, and foreign affairs. About 20 percent of outlays were to equip, modernize, and pay our armed forces and to fund the Global War on Terrorism and other national defense activities; about 3 percent were for veterans benefits and services; and about 1 percent were for international activities, including military and economic assistance to foreign countries and the maintenance of U.S. embassies abroad.

[3]Physical, human, and community development. These outlays were for agriculture; natural resources; environment; transportation; aid for elementary and secondary education and direct assistance to college students; job training; deposit insurance, commerce and housing credit, and community development; and space, energy, and general science programs.

[4]Social programs. About 14 percent of total outlays were for Medicaid, food stamps, temporary assistance for needy families, supplemental security income, and related programs; and the remaining outlays were for health research and public health programs, unemployment compensation, assisted housing, and social services.

FIGURE 4.1 Major Categories of Federal Income and Outlays for Fiscal Year 2008

Source: Internal Revenue Service 2009: 90

Temporary Assistance for Needy Families (TANF), health research, unemployment compensation, and other social services.

Individual Taxes

To get some idea of how much the public pays for government, the Tax Foundation, a fiscal group, calculates when "tax freedom day"[3] occurs each year. Total tax collections for the country are divided by the total income, providing a very crude measure of what percentage of the public's income goes toward all forms of taxes (Musante 2008). Table 4.2 shows the findings from 1900 to 2008. The Tax Foundation's findings generally indicate an increase in the number of work days required for people to pay their taxes, although the year 2000 showed the highest number of days. There are five different tax categories used to calculate the tax freedom day. It would take forty-two days to pay for federal, state, and local taxes, twenty-eight to cover payroll taxes for SS and Medicare, sixteen days for sales and excise taxes, and twelve days for property taxes. The final tax to cover corporate income taxes is based on the assumption that this tax is passed on to customers paying higher prices, employees receiving smaller paychecks, and shareholders receiving less value for their shares. Given this, it would

Table 4.2	One Hundred Years of Taxes Showing When Tax Freedom Day Has Occurred		
Year	Tax Freedom Day	Number of Days	Rate (%)
1900	January 22	22	5.9
1910	January 19	19	5.0
1920	February 13	44	12.0
1930	February 12	43	11.7
1940	March 7	66	17.9
1950	March 31	90	24.6
1960	April 11	101	27.7
1970	April 19	109	29.6
1980	April 21	111	30.4
1990	April 21	111	30.4
2000	May 3	123	33.6
2008	April 23	113	30.8

Source: The Tax Foundation (taken from Musante 2008)

Credit: The Tax Foundation recalculates each year's tax freedom day annually based on new government data; therefore, the date of any year's tax freedom day may change from year to year. For the latest information, see www.taxfoundation.org/taxfreedomday/.

take thirteen days to pay off the corporate taxes. In comparison, the Tax Foundation reports it takes sixty days to pay for housing, fifty days to cover health and medical care, and thirty-five days to pay for food (Musante 2008).

Although federal taxes take the largest sum of money from most people, this tax rate is graduated or progressive; as one's income increases, one's tax rate rises proportionately. Economist John Kenneth Galbraith points out that "the only effective design for diminishing the income inequality inherent in capitalism is the progressive income tax" (quoted in Marger 2008: 246). Since 1955, federal taxes on income have actually declined as a means of taxation for the middle class; however, this decrease has been more than compensated for by increases in payroll taxes and state and local taxes. State and local taxes tend to be regressive; they place a heavier burden on those with lower income.

Government tax policies influence the patterns of inequality in the nation. While corporations and the wealthy have seen their taxes decline, those whose income is near the median family income have seen theirs increase. Drawing on the work of Piketty and Saez, who have analyzed tax return data, Johnston (2007: 272) points out that the wealthiest 300,000 citizens had nearly as much income as the 150 million citizens at the bottom of the income distribution. Johnston compared the income distribution pattern to slices in a pie. From the time of the Reagan administration, that is, from 1980 to 2005, the income pie grew by 79 percent, while the population increased by one-third. In 1980 the income of the great majority of people represented about two-thirds of the pie, but this declined to just over half of the pie in 2005. The top 10 percent saw their slice of the pie increase from about one-third in 1980 to nearly half in 2005. Even more, the top 0.1 percent (30,000 persons) saw their share increase from 1.3 percent to a little more than 5 percent in 2005 with incomes of at least $9.5 million in 2005. This means that the average income of the great majority of people *dropped* slightly from $29,495 in 1980 to $29,143 in 2005 (272–274). In addition to the increase in income for the rich, the tax rates on the top incomes have actually declined (278).

The George W. Bush-era tax cuts have benefitted the rich much more than those in other classes while at the same time government spending created very high budget deficits (Leicht and Fitzgerald 2007). Leicht and Fitzgerald believe that because the tax system is biased against the middle class who seem to be paying more than their fair share, cynicism about politics has grown among the middle class. More specifically they argue that the elites, in the form of what they call a new landlord class, dominate political life by using political action committees and their special access to politicians who have modified the tax system and regulations to benefit the upper class (132). As we have already discussed, this results in "middle-class alienation" where people "suspect something is wrong and that the system is rigged against them, but coherent political action to combat these trends seems to be beyond their reach" (13).

Corporate Taxation

Corporations have contributed a much lower percentage of their income than have individuals to tax revenue. Corporate taxes have made up a declining proportion of total federal government revenue throughout the twentieth century (Hurst 2010: 355). Indeed a study by the GAO revealed that 1.2 million U.S. companies, or two-thirds of U.S. corporations, did not pay any federal income taxes between 1998 and 2005. About 38,000 (68 percent) of foreign companies that did business in the United States also did not pay corporate taxes. Combined these companies had $2.5 trillion in sales (Kerr 2008: 5A).

U.S. corporations have increasingly used a technique called "inversions" that became legal under U.S. law in 2002. U.S. companies have incorporated parts of their businesses as subsidiaries in certain countries such as the Cayman Islands possibly to avoid paying corporate taxes. Subsidiaries could also be created to take advantage of sales opportunities or favorable labor situations. These countries are called tax havens because they have little or no taxes, limited effective sharing of information with foreign tax authorities, and no transparency in legislative, administrative, or legal provisions (GAO 2008). The IRS estimated that in 2001 about $70 billion may have been lost in taxes due to tax havens (Hurst 2010). The 2008 GAO study identified that eighty-three of the one hundred largest publicly traded U.S. corporations had subsidiaries in jurisdictions labeled as tax havens. Also, sixty-three of the one hundred largest publicly traded U.S. federal contractors had subsidiaries in tax havens (GAO 2008). Some of the companies with subsidiaries in tax havens have received federal bailouts. For example, Bank of America Inc., Citigroup Inc., and Morgan Stanley were part of the $700 billion financial bailout approved by Congress, and insurance company AIG received about $150 billion in bailout money (Thomas 2009). U.S. Senator Carl Levin (D-Mich.), who requested the 2008 GAO report, estimated that at least $100 billion a year is now being lost due to abusive tax havens and offshore accounts (Thomas 2009). In May 2009, President Obama argued for legislation that would limit offshore tax havens and corporate tax breaks. He estimated that the changes would result in $210 billion increase in tax revenues over the next ten years. This would help compensate for the tax cuts he was proposing for the middle class. The president of the Business Roundtable, however, countered that Obama's plan would hinder the ability of U.S. corporations to compete abroad (Calmes and Andrews 2009).

International Comparison Regarding Taxation

The U.S. taxation policy is different from many OECD (Organisation for Economic Co-operation and Development) countries in that the overall tax burden as percentage of Gross Domestic Product (GDP) tends to be lower than that of many developed nations. More specifically, according to 2004 OECD data, the U.S. tax revenue was 25.4 percent of GDP, whereas countries like

Sweden, France, Italy, United Kingdom, Germany, Canada, and Australia had tax revenues ranging from 31.6 percent to 50.7 percent of GDP. Japan's percentage was very similar to that of the United States (Marger 2008: 249). Since 1980, U.S. corporations' corporate taxes as a percentage of GDP have been less than the average for other OECD nations. In the early 2000s, the U.S. corporate tax percentage was only 1.5 to 2 percent of GDP (Leicht and Fitzgerald 2007).

Summary

We have seen that a larger part of the individual tax burden has been shifted toward the middle class. This clearly affects most U.S. citizens because more of our income goes to pay taxes while the government loses possible revenue from the upper classes. In the twenty-first century this has resulted in budget deficits and the inability of the government to provide all the services society needs. The loss of money from corporations adds further to the government's problems of providing services to the public. Also corporations creating subsidiaries abroad may be looking for cheap labor so they can reduce their higher paid labor force in the United States. As Leicht and Fitzgerald (2007) have suggested, as the public realizes they are losing ground and other individuals and corporations are not paying their fair share, they become increasingly alienated and lose their trust in politicians and government.

THE WELFARE STATE

Although the word *welfare* makes many people picture the poor and may even evoke the welfare recipient who takes advantage of the system, it is important to realize that social welfare in the United States comprises a number of different social programs. Some of these are called social insurance programs such as SS and Medicare, which may be paid for through payroll taxes. All people in American society may benefit from these programs. The other part of the welfare system has been referred to as *public assistance programs* that are funded through general government revenues. The phrase *means-tested* indicates that recipients have to prove their need according to certain criteria. Before we turn to a discussion of public assistance programs we will consider benefits that have helped corporations, and then examine the SS system, which has benefited and likely will continue to benefit millions of people.

Corporate Welfare

Corporate welfare is sometimes called *wealthfare* or *phantom welfare*. As we have already seen, many corporations do not pay taxes at all. Corporate tax loopholes are great, and tax havens have also helped corporations avoid or reduce taxes. Certain industries and companies such as airlines, commercial agriculture, and defense contractors are provided considerable subsidies to help them. For example, the sugar industry has received $1.4 billion annually (Marger 2008: 252–253). Indirect subsidies include highway construction, which helps the trucking industry, and airport construction, which helps the airlines. Trade restrictions against foreign imports by means of tariffs also benefit certain industries. In the early 1990s, Huff and Johnson estimated the benefits from phantom welfare to be $150 billion to $200 billion per year (Hurst 2010: 364).

In addition, government has a history of bailing out major industries when those industries encounter financial problems. For example, in the late 1980s the bailout of the savings and loan industry cost taxpayers billions of dollars. The multibillion-dollar rescue of financial institutions in 2008–2009 also illustrates government support of the elite (Hurst 2010). The interesting question is why most people focus on the benefits given to the poor rather than on corporate welfare.

Social Security

The Social Security Act was signed in 1935 during the Great Depression; the first taxes were actually collected in 1937. Currently SS provides retirement, disability, family, and survivor benefits. Both the employer and the employee (for most occupations) contribute to SS through payroll taxes. The self-employed pay both the employer's and the employee's contribution. One must normally be sixty-two years or older to receive retirement benefits. The amount of an individual's earnings determines the amount of monthly benefits, and an individual must have forty credits or quarters to qualify. The retirement benefits were to provide a foundation for one's retirement but were never intended to be the sole source of support.

SS has been quite effective in limiting the number of elderly who are in poverty (Center on Budget and Policy Priorities 2009). Using a three-year average for 2000–2002 the data suggest that nearly half of the elderly would have incomes below the poverty line if one did not count SS benefits. As shown in Figure 4.2, when one takes into account the SS income, only one in twelve are poor according to the Center on Budget and Policy Priorities (CBPP) (Sherman and Shapiro 2005). Using 2002 SS data, Sherman (2005) documented how children have benefitted, as 1 million children under eighteen were lifted above the poverty line. Except for the earned income tax credit (EITC), no other government program has helped children to rise above the poverty line as much as SS. Using 2008 U.S. Census data, Van de Water and Sherman (2010) reported that without SS benefits, 45.2 percent of the elderly would be in poverty, but with SS benefits, only 9.7 percent of the elderly were officially listed as poor.

At various times the government has encountered the issue of how to preserve SS for future generations. Because the baby boom generation will begin to retire soon, this will add financial strain to the SS system. In May 2009, Robert Greenstein reported that SS is not facing an immediate crisis; however, it does need to be changed and it is best to make the changes now. The 2009 trustees report on SS identified 2037 as the last projected date when SS will be able to pay full benefits. After 2037 it will be able to pay out about 75 percent of payments. Greenstein suggests that

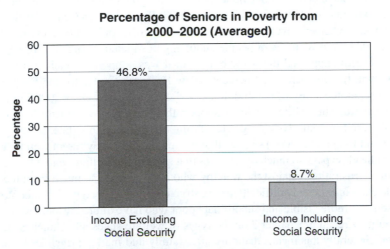

Percentage of Seniors in Poverty from 2000–2002 (Averaged)

FIGURE 4.2   Social Security Reduces Number of Seniors in Poverty

Source: Sherman and Shapiro 2005

Credit: Arloc Sherman and Isaac Shapiro 2005, taken from Center on Budget and Policy Priorities (CBPP). February 24, 2005. "Social Security Lifts 13 Million Seniors above the Poverty Line: A State-By-State Analysis". Data are based on CBPP's tabulations from the U.S. Census Bureau's Current Population Survey for March 2001, 2002, and 2003.

these facts pointed out the importance of passing Obama's initial proposal that the tax cuts for those making more than $250,000 expire after 2010. He argued that "members of Congress cannot legitimately claim that the tax cuts for people at the top are affordable while the Social Security shortfall constitutes a dire fiscal threat" (Greenstein 2009). However, in December 2010, Democrats and Republicans compromised and legislation was passed continuing tax cuts for all social classes, reducing SS contributions, and extending unemployment benefits.

The G. W. Bush administration pushed for privatization of part of the SS system, but they were not successful. Feldstein (2005) argues for an investment-based component in the form of personal retirement accounts that he believes will likely increase benefits. Kloby (2004) offers a class/Marxist interpretation of the campaign to privatize SS. While there is a tremendous concentration of wealth among the richest Americans, there is also a shortage of profitable investment outlets. Capitalists try to expand their markets, so they search for new areas of profitability. Privatizing SS would have meant expansion of the brokerage business and an increase of billions of dollars in broker's fees.

Hiltzik (2005), who strongly opposed privatization, documented Gallup Poll results that found that the majority surveyed are opposed to private accounts that would sharply cut their basic benefits from the current pay-as-you-go arrangement. By a 2-to-1 margin they supported raising the payroll tax ceiling and limiting benefits for wealthy retirees. Also only 30 percent felt that investing in stocks and bonds with their private accounts would give them better benefits (218). Congress discovered many people seemed to mistrust Wall Street even around 2005, well before the stock market problems of 2008–2009. People worried that market volatility that could tear a major hole in the social safety net and make the system financially less stable (Diamond and Orszag 2005; Hiltzik 2005). Diamond (2004) believes Congress will pass legislation that lowers benefits relative to those in effect now and also provides additional revenue to finance benefits.

Public Assistance

At times there is heated debate about what should be the role of government in the welfare state. For example, two surveys (Pew Research Center 2008; Pew Research Center for the People & the Press 2009) asked whether government should take care of people who can't take care of themselves. Since 1987 the percentage of people endorsing this idea has ranged from 57 to 71 percent. In 2009, 63 percent supported this view but again it was supported much less by Republicans (46 percent) than by Democrats (77 percent) (Pew Research Center for the People & the Press 2009). In the separate survey of the middle class (Pew Research Center 2008) 56 percent of the middle class agreed. Thus while a majority support the idea that government should care for people who can't care for themselves, a significant minority question this statement.

Leicht and Fitzgerald (2007) suggest that the middle class may resent welfare recipients because the middle class pays so much of the taxes that support the welfare state. For the middle class to channel their frustrations against the wealthy who have profited so much from the productivity of the middle class is extremely difficult; the tax structure is basically out of their control. It is much easier to resent the more visible and subordinate poor who have limited resources.

As you may recall in Chapter 2 on the types of welfare states, the United States is a liberal welfare state. Generally this means that only after family and market principles break down does public intervention occur. Assistance is limited, short term, and frequently stigmatizing or punitive (Myles 1996). Put another way, the U.S. policy is relatively inexpensive and basically incomplete in the services it provides (in comparison to many Western European nations) (Weir, Orloff, and Skocpol 1988). Such programs limit the chances of people on traditional welfare to get off welfare.

Many people and some researchers think that those on welfare use the ideas of rational economic choice theory. They believe that potential welfare recipients calculate the relative benefits and costs of participation weighed against other choices (Van Hook and Bean 2009). Often, too, these supporters of rational choice believe that inequality plays a key role in motivating people to improve their positions by working hard, obtaining the appropriate education and training, and so on. Inequality is a powerful incentive (Smeeding 2006). Drawing on U.S. Census data from a Current Population Survey, Hoynes, Page, and Stevens (2006: 63–64) found that

> government programs do have a modest effect on poverty [for the nonelderly], even though many of them are not accounted for in the official rate. More to the point, these programs may have a substantial effect on the poverty *gap,* the sum of the differences between families below the poverty line.

One estimate by other researchers is that the gap was reduced by 72 percent for all persons, and TANF alone reduced it by 5 percent. Still it can be argued that the goal should be for people to get off welfare.

As noted earlier, in liberal welfare states it is often difficult for people to get off welfare because the program is quite limited. Would more generous welfare policies help fight poverty and improve the chances of people to get off welfare? Some theorists view welfare expansion as a means to extend social and political rights and thus promote good citizenship (Fording 2001: 120). In that sense, a strong welfare system may provide certain benefits for all of us in society as it promotes social solidarity and reduces tension. A weak welfare system may promote social discord. As an example, Fording cites studies that found that a decline in welfare generosity is associated with a rise in incarceration rates. A rise in prison rates leads to more costs as the inmate population increases and demand for building new prisons increases. Currently incarceration rates are at unprecedented high levels and greater than in other nations (Schram et al. 2009). As the United States deals with the enormous costs of poverty one may ask whether it is better to establish and maintain a strong welfare system or pay higher costs for such things as incarcerating prisoners.

Empirical studies have documented that political leaders frequently respond to mass unrest by expanding the welfare state (Fording 2001). For example, Piven and Cloward (1979) in their analysis of the welfare rights movement in the 1960s found that the welfare system was vulnerable to protest and disruption by the poor. The disruption of the welfare system followed by an electoral crisis would likely encourage leaders to promote policies to limit the polarization of the electorate over the protests concerning the welfare system.

An important theoretical issue is why the state responds the way it does. Fording (2001) tested whether a social control perspective that has been advanced by neomarxists, or a neopluralist perspective best explains this theoretical issue. In the social control model, the state acts in the long-term interests of elites or the ruling class to limit or reduce the effects of the insurgency. The state can do this in two ways: repressing the protest (coercive) and increasing the benefits of the welfare system (beneficent). Neopluralists, on the other hand, view the insurgency as an effort of the relatively powerless to secure access to the policy-making government agenda. The protest gives them increasing visibility so that they can "effectively compete and bargain with other interests to obtain policy changes favorable to their interests" (115). Using black insurgency data including Aid to Families with Dependent Children

(AFDC) recipient rates and state imprisonment records (to measure repression), Fording finds strong support for the social control perspective (illustrated in Figure 4.3). The state responds to reduce the protest or insurgency that threatens the stability of the system by offering more welfare benefits. It also becomes more punitive by increasing the incarceration rates, which serves to limit the protest. However, Fording also recognizes that conventional electoral channels contribute to welfare reform as well. The two theoretical frameworks and Fording's findings help us understand better why government may respond as it does to providing welfare benefits.

In addition to the costs of incarceration, another issue that also has consequences for taxpayers is how poverty influences the ability and achievement of children. Duncan and Brooks-Gunn (2000) point out several key statistics about social and also financial costs of poverty. Poor children are:

- at 1.7 times higher risk for child mortality
- at 2.0 times higher risk for a short stay in the hospital
- at 2.0 times higher risk for grade repetition and dropping out of school
- 4 times as likely to have a learning disability
- 1 time as likely to have teenage out-of-wedlock births
- at 6.8 times higher risk for reported cases of child abuse and neglect

Statistics like these help illustrate why there are significant concerns about the welfare system particularly as the debate has shifted to family and child well-being (Lichter and Jayakody 2002).

At the micro level, Clark-Kauffman, Duncan, and Morris (2003) have found some support for the generosity idea as it affects young children. They examined data on more than 30,000 achievement reports on children in families that participated in fourteen welfare and work

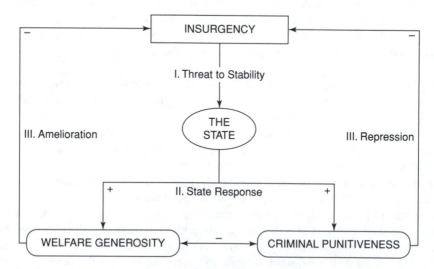

FIGURE 4.3   The Social Control Model of State Response to Insurgency

Source: Fording 2001:116

Credit: The Political Response to Black Insurgency: A Critical Test of Competing Theories of the State, by Richard C. Fording © 2001 American Political Science Association. Reprinted with the permission of Cambridge University Press.

programs. All types of programs were able to increase the parents' employment; however, only the programs that had generous welfare packages to make work more financially rewarding were able to increase both the parents' employment and the family income. If one pools all the programs, they positively affect only the very young.

Remember that at the beginning of this chapter we discussed C. Wright Mills' view about the significance of social issues rather than the concerns of a few people. We argue that poverty and the welfare state policies should be everyone's issues. Brady (2009) documents that poverty is the result of politics more than individual characteristics and abilities. He used data from eighteen countries over more than thirty years to provide an institutionalized power relations explanation rather than examine individual problems or labor markets. Variation in poverty rates is shaped by variation in the generosity of countries' welfare policies. Where leftist political organizations and parties along with coalitions supporting egalitarianism are able to shape welfare policies, poverty is less and support for equality has been institutionalized. In the United States, poverty is widespread and support for equality has not been institutionalized.

Early in this chapter we identified a possible conflict over the meaning of freedom: emphasizing liberty or equality. Esping-Andersen (2007) examines the relationship between the U.S. welfare state and equal opportunity, a value many Americans endorse. He finds the income distribution in the United States is unusually unequal. The United States ranks very high in poverty as well as inequality. Smeeding (2006) documents that cross-national comparisons show U.S. poverty rates to be at or near the top when compared with other rich nations. Esping-Andersen (2007) points out that the 19 percent of children living in poverty in the United States is twice that of Germany and five times that of Sweden. Further, he notes research by economists that documents less equality of opportunity, less mobility, and more inheritance in the United States than in Germany, Canada, or Scandinavia. He labels the United States as an equal-opportunity underachiever (23).

Although education is a key to social mobility, Esping-Andersen (2007: 23) argues that the "seeds of inequality are sown prior to school age on a host of crucial attributes such as health, cognitive, and noncognitive abilities, motivation to learn, and more generally school preparedness." Recent research documents that "early child investments matter most" (25). Heckman estimates that for every dollar invested in early-childhood programs, the return is $5.70. Esping-Andersen argues that "if we care about fairness and seriously subscribe to an equal-opportunities standard, the case in favor of corrective measures is strong indeed" (27). He further maintains that the United States needs a comprehensive family policy in its welfare program. As part of this plan, access to affordable and high-quality childcare would limit inequalities of employment and income as well as narrow the learning gap among children. This would result in less wasted human talent. Thus Esping-Andersen makes a strong case for the U.S. government to expand its welfare program even though many nations have instituted or are considering retrenchment.

DEBT AND BANKRUPTCY

There are at least three different types of debt that are relevant in the discussion of the politics of everyday life. They are government debt, business debt, and household debt. Because the state has great power and resources, including the ability to print money, it is highly unlikely that the government will go broke even though it is in debt and pays interest on the debt. Since 2000, though, great concern has been expressed about the accumulation of debt. With the recession that started late in 2007 and the government bailouts, even greater concerns about the federal deficit are being expressed. In July 2009 the federal deficit grew to $1.27 trillion. That month was the fifteenth consecutive month that receipts by the government were lower than the same month in the prior year (Associated Press 2009a).

The second type of debt is incurred by businesses. The bailout program of the U.S. Treasury may have helped stabilize the banking system but has been quite costly. Bush's treasury department paid about $350 billion mainly in the form of direct investments in financial companies. Obama's secretary of the treasury Geithner's plan proposed up to $2.5 trillion that would create a new federal entity to draw private investors into a partnership with the government, which would eventually buy as much as $1 trillion of the assets that were in trouble and harming the banking industry ("Credit Crisis—Bailout Plan" 2009). The Big Three U.S. automakers (GM, Chrysler, and Ford) asked the government for emergency bailouts. Ford ultimately decided it could function on its own. Americans, especially those unemployed or experiencing hard times and possible bankruptcy, may feel the government has done much more to save financial institutions and certain automakers than individuals. At the same time, if the financial institutions had not been stabilized, the situation for many individuals could have become much worse.

Household Debt and Bankruptcy

While clearly the federal government under the G. W. Bush and Obama administrations has supported the financial sector and corporations, there has also been some support for individuals in debt and/or going through bankruptcy. The $789 billion stimulus package as a recovery measure "seemed almost trifling compared with the possible $2.5 trillion rescue plan for the financial system" ("Economic Stimulus" 2009). The bill provided $507 billion for spending programs and $282 billion in tax relief. It included more than $150 billion for public work programs for transportation, technology, and energy and $87 billion to help states with their rising Medicaid costs, but it restricted funds for provision of health insurance to the unemployed. It has helped car companies as well as individuals in its cash-for-clunkers project that provided rebates of up to $4,500 for people trading in gas-guzzling cars. The program though has been criticized for taking operating cars off the street that could have been purchased by the working poor. It has also provided a form of corporate welfare to companies and in many cases helped those who bought the gas-guzzling cars rather than those who purchased more fuel-efficient cars in the first place.

Consumer debt is a major problem in the United States although by mid-2009 consumer debt was actually declining, to $2.5 trillion according to the Federal Reserve. Revolving credit, mainly credit cards, was $917 billion while nonrevolving credit such as car loans was $1.59 trillion in June 2009 (Associated Press 2009b). People were paying off debt and trying to save in the face of increasing job losses, reduced home values, and declining stock portfolios. Morgenson (2008) believed "the lucrative lending practices of America's merchants of debt have led millions of Americans—young and old, native and immigrant, affluent and poor—to the brink." In October 2010 Ben S. Bernanke, the Federal Reserve chairman, announced that the central bank was taking steps to pour more money into the economy. Although the recession had officially ended in June 2009, the unemployment rate was still at 9.6 percent and economic growth was slow. The plan was to make credit cheaper so that consumers and businesses would borrow and spend leading eventually to lower rates of unemployment (Chan 2010).

In the early 2000s interest rates were low and many people bought homes, with the homeownership rate rising to 69.2 percent. Home prices jumped, especially on the coasts and in the Southwest, followed by a rapid drop in the values of homes ("Mortgages and the Markets" 2009). Some people reacted by defaulting; they simply stopped making payments on their credit cards or on mortgage loans when their homes became worth less than their debt. There also were foreclosures. Defaulters face low credit scores, possible lawsuits, and hostile calls from collection agencies. Collectors, though, noted that people were less willing to pay, possibly due to the bailouts the government was giving the banks and others (Streitfeld 2009).

Average student debt has increased, although about one-third of students receiving a bachelor's degree have no student debt. The median student debt was $19,999 in 2007–2008 for bachelor's degree graduates, an increase of 5 percent from 2003 to 2004. These figures from the College Board, however, did not include parents' borrowing, credit card debt, informal loans from relatives or friends, or loans for graduate school (Lewin 2009).

Because many consumers were in serious debt and angry at the extreme punitive changes and high interest rates, Congress passed legislation to place restrictions on the credit card industry. Some of the rules of the Credit Card Accountability Responsibility and Disclosure Act took effect in August 2009 and others in 2010. In 2009 provisions were added increasing the required notice of rate increase from fifteen days to forty days and allowing cardholders the right to decline a rate increase by closing the account and agreeing to pay off the balance at the current rate within five years. Other reforms, like the requirements banning retroactive rate increases and requiring adult cosigners for applicants under age twenty-one, took effect in 2010 ("Credit Card Industry" 2009; Pugh 2009). Credit card companies created new ways to generate revenue such as charging customers a surcharge to receive their statements by mail. Morgenson (2010: 1) claimed such practices were "Proof, yet again, that if you close the door, they will come in through the window. And if you close the window, they blow through the door." In general there has been a great deal of concern about credit card and mortgage companies using deceptive practices.

Who Goes Bankrupt and Why?

One of the issues frequently debated and to which there does not appear to be consensus is the question of who goes bankrupt and why. As with explanations of poverty, there are both individual and structural frameworks to guide us. Perhaps somewhat surprisingly the middle-class family is more likely to end up in bankruptcy in the first decade of the twenty-first century than ever before (Leicht and Fitzgerald 2007; Warren and Tyagi 2003). The families in the worst financial trouble are neither the elderly nor the very young. Rather they are parents who have children at home. Indeed what Warren and Tyagi find from examining data from the 2001 Consumer Bankruptcy Project is that "having a child is now the single best predictor that a woman will end up in financial collapse" (6). They also conclude that "bankruptcy has become deeply entrenched in American life" (6) and foreclosures of homes have more than tripled in less than twenty-five years (7). In addition, these families are in greater debt than those of the 1980s (7). Also, based on the criteria frequently used to define middle-class status, 90 percent or more of those filing bankruptcy could be classified as middle class (7).

The 2001 Consumer Bankruptcy Project asked those who filed for bankruptcy why they went bankrupt, and 87 percent of them named only three reasons for bankruptcies: family breakup or divorce, medical problems, and job loss (Warren and Tyagi 2003). The authors reject what they label as the *overconsumption myth* or the *myth of the immoral debtor.* Warren and Tyagi believe that instead of being immoral or overconsuming, there are great societal pressures on the family, and if something, at least in part, beyond the family's direct control goes wrong, it could face financial disaster.

Himmelstein et al. (2009) surveyed a random sample of 2,314 bankruptcy filers in 2007 and from the 2001 survey and found an increase in the percentage of bankruptcies associated with medical bills. A conservative estimate is that 62.1 percent of the bankruptcies stem from medical bills. Most of these bankruptcy filers had middle-class occupations, were well educated, and owned homes. Between 2001 and 2007 health care costs increased, the number of uninsured and underinsured increased, and Congress passed stricter bankruptcy laws. In 2003, collection agencies contacted 37.2 million people about their medical bills and there were 15.6 million underinsured, but this grew to 25.2 million in 2007. Twenty-nine percent of low- and middle-income households that had balances on their credit cards used the credit cards to pay off medical expenses over time (Himmelstein et al. 2009). The authors conclude that "the U.S. health care financing system is broken, and not only for the poor and uninsured. Middle-class families frequently collapse under the strain of a health care system that treats physical wounds, but often inflicts fiscal ones" (745–746).

The Bankruptcy Abuse Prevention and Consumer Protection Act (BAPCPA) contained procedural barriers to make filing for bankruptcy more expensive and difficult. The credit card industry supported these changes including placing an income means test on those who could file using Chapter 7 bankruptcy where debts could be eliminated (Himmelstein et al. 2009; Leicht and Fitzgerald 2007). Lawless et al. (2008) tested whether the change in the law, which was supposed to protect against abuse of the bankruptcy process by "high-income deadbeats," is effective. Their findings support the beliefs of some legal scholars that while stopping those who were unfairly taking advantage of the system was used as the rationale for the law, it was instead "a general assault on all debtors" (1).

Juliet Schor (1999) examines American culture and how individuals are conducting their lives. She argues for a change in people's relationship to consuming goods so that the focus is on "quality of life, not just quality of stuff" (2). For her, a key problem is "the new consumerism," which she defines as "an upscaling of lifestyle norms: the pervasiveness of conspicuous, status goods and of competition for acquiring them; and the growing disconnection between consumer desires and incomes" (2). People try to compete or at least keep up with the social group with which they identify, which tends to be the upper middle class or the rich. She rejects what she labels as the *conventional view* that consumers are rational, well informed, and have consistent and independent (of other consumers) preferences. Challenging the image of the rational and in-control approach, she points out that most people with credit cards do not intend to borrow on them but two-thirds do, and there has been an "explosion of personal bankruptcies" (4). She recommends a politics of consumption that in addition to stressing quality of life calls for a distinction between needs and desires. She advocates a "decent standard of living," democratizing consumption practices (e.g., Martha Stewart's brand at K-Mart), and a consumer movement to "articulate a vision of an appealing and humane consumer sphere" (8). Holt (1999) believes Schor's new politics of consumption idea would not influence social inequality. Holt argues from a postmodern perspective that "postmodern market conditions lead to overconsumption problems" (17). The market promotes a sense of freedom from constraint that results in the personal debt crisis and environmental problems.

Warren (2006, 2007) clearly disagrees with Schor about overconsumption and maintains that it is not about designer clothes, restaurant meals, or Michael Jordan athletic shoes like Schor claimed. Rather it focuses on what is safe for the family, educating children, paying for transportation, childcare, and other things that are necessary for work. Warren (2006: 4) further suggests there may be "a politics of living on the edge" and "everyday, middle-class families carry higher risks that a job loss or a medical problem will push them over the edge." Warren recognizes that individuals certainly bear some responsibility and make mistakes, but there are other considerations that could be improved.

Indeed, there can be no doubt that some portion of the credit crisis in America is the result of foolishness and profligacy. Some people are in trouble with credit because they simply use too much of it. Others are in trouble because they use credit in dangerous ways. But that is not the whole story. Lenders have deliberately built tricks and traps into some credit products so they can ensnare families in a cycle of high-cost debt. (Warren 2007: 11)

Warren (2007) and Bar-Gill and Warren (2008) recommend the formation of a Financial Product Safety Commission to regulate the financial products. Tangible physical products like toasters, infant car seats, and drugs are inspected and regulated for safety, but credit products such as mortgage loans and credit cards are mainly unregulated despite the fact they can be unsafe and lead to financial distress, foreclosure, and bankruptcy. In part, disclosure about financial products has turned out to be a means to obfuscate with incomprehensible language rather than inform. The current regulatory system is more of a patchwork of agencies, but this proposal would halt the regulatory competition that poses dangers to consumer safety.

In the face of the severe crisis in the world financial system and the deregulation of the U.S. financial system as well as the outrage about credit card rates and the subprime mortgage problems, the Obama administration in June 2009 proposed a new regulatory structure in part to protect the rights of consumers and to give the Federal Reserve more authority over the powerful financial institutions. In addition a new regulatory agency was suggested to supervise credit card companies, mortgages, and other types of consumer debt. The Federal Reserve would lose some of its regulatory powers to the new agency; other agencies, like the Federal Deposit Insurance Agency and the nation's financial system, objected ("Financial Regulatory Reform" 2009). In September 2010 President Obama appointed Elizabeth Warren whose work is cited earlier in this chapter to oversee the establishment of the new Consumer Financial Protection Bureau.

There is little to encourage mortgage companies to provide much assistance to consumers to help consumers out of their debt, even though in 2009 there was a $75 billion program to help homeowners prevent foreclosures. The mortgage companies collect high fees on delinquent loans so the longer the loan is delinquent, the better the opportunities to collect fees (Goodman 2009). According to a *New York Times* (2010) editorial 4.2 million loans were currently in or near foreclosure. The antiforeclosure efforts by the Obama administration had resulted in less than 500,000 loan modifications in eighteen months. Labaton (2009b) points out how both large and small banks and their trade associations are involved in strong lobbying attempts to kill or weaken any new agency trying to both write and enforce new regulations.

INFRASTRUCTURE

The GAO (2009) not only identified the U.S. financial structure as high risk but also identified the U.S. infrastructure as high risk beginning in 2007. As the GAO points out, "The nation's economic vitality and its citizens' quality of life depend significantly on the efficiency of its surface transportation infrastructure" (67). The director of the Congressional Budget Office, Peter R. Orszag (2008: 1), noted that "infrastructure is notoriously difficult to define because it can encompass such a wide array of physical assets," but in testimony before two House of Representative committees he included transportation, utilities, and some other public facilities. Transportation expenditures made up almost three quarters of the approximately $60 billion federal spending on infrastructure in 2004. Highway expenditures alone were half the total. At the state and local government levels, much of the spending in 2004 was for highways, water systems, and schools. The private domain spends most of its money on energy and telecommunications.

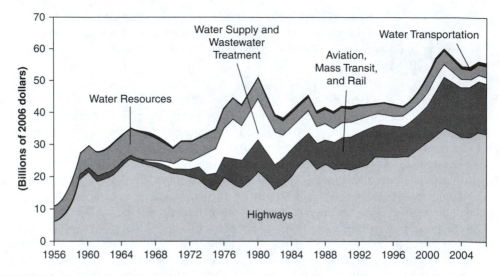

FIGURE 4.4   Federal Capital Spending on Transportation and Water Infrastructure, 1956 to 2007
Source: Congressional Budget Office, taken from Orszag 2008: 7

Capital spending on infrastructure, according to Orszag's testimony, included $232.6 billion in public money and $173.5 billion in private money. Figure 4.4 provides an indication of federal spending on infrastructure from 1956 to 2007. Current spending for highways is $66.7 billion, but maintaining current levels will cost $78.8 billion and the amount that is economically justifiable is $131.7 billion, about twice the current expenditure. For mass transit the figures are $15.5 billion, $15.8 billion, and $21.8 billion, respectively (8).

The American Society of Civil Engineers' (ASCE) plan for 2008 pointed out that poor road conditions are very expensive; they cost U.S. motorists $67 billion a year in operating costs and repairs—$333 per motorist. Further, Americans stuck in traffic lose 4.2 billion hours at a cost of $78.2 billion a year to the economy. Transit ridership is growing more quickly than is highway use and also needs additional support (ASCE 2007). Textbox 4.2 provides a case study of the social justice concerns that communities need to contend with when creating more transit options.

In 2009 ASCE unveiled a new report that increased its estimate of the investment needed in the next five years to keep the infrastructure in good condition to $2.2 trillion. Dr. Wayne Klotz, the president of ASCE, commented, "Crumbling infrastructure has a direct impact on our personal and economic health, and the nation's infrastructure crisis is endangering our future prosperity" (Cooper 2009: 1). He cited possible benefits from investing in infrastructure including declining traffic congestion, better air quality, protection against natural hazards, and clean and abundant water supplies.

Leicht and Fitzgerald (2007) argue that the condition of public infrastructure including roads, bridges, dams, and airports declined as spending for their maintenance was reduced. This decrease was a political effect of supply-side economics that called for cuts in government spending and taxes as well as deregulation. Herbert (2007), in a *New York Times* editorial, cited "politics and ideology" as the major reasons for the government not investing in infrastructure due to pressures for small government and not raising taxes. We will now briefly look at two key examples of infrastructure, bridges and levees, to illustrate the problems that exist.

TEXTBOX 4.2

Light Rail and the Politics of Everyday Life

Sociologist Robert Merton qualifies functionalist theory by asking "functional for whom?" recognizing that "items may be functional for some individuals and subgroups and dysfunctional for others" (1949: 51). Herbert Gans continues this thread by arguing that in diverse and heterogeneous societies there are "few phenomena [that] are functional or dysfunctional for the society as a whole, and most result in benefits to some groups and costs to others" (1972: 277). Government agencies at the national, regional, and local levels make decisions every day that not only impact the quality of everyday life of citizens but may benefit one group of citizens at the expense of another.

In an attempt to improve public transit, the Metropolitan Council of the Twin Cities (Minneapolis and St. Paul, Minnesota) has been making plans to build a new Light Rail Transit (LRT) system. This new thoroughfare, called the Central Corridor, will run from downtown Minneapolis to downtown St. Paul, passing the University of Minnesota, the state capitol, shopping districts, residencies, and places of employment. Like many governmental projects, this one affects a large number of people including those who live in the neighborhoods through which the LRT travels. While many aspects of the LRT plan are being scrutinized, there is one issue that has garnered the most public input and debate.

Over three miles of the eleven-mile rail route run through working-class and immigrant neighborhoods along University Avenue in St. Paul. There are over thirty-six thousand people living in neighborhoods within a half-mile of the proposed rail (Bailey 2007: 4). The LRT is designed to stop once every mile in this corridor. Transit use is greatly increased when both origin and destination reside along the rail line (Parsons Brinckerhoff Quade & Douglas, Inc. 1996). A 2000 study found that 31 percent of workers along University Avenue also reside in the corridor (Bailey 2007).

These neighborhoods are currently served by Route 16 buses, which stop at every block along the avenue. Records show that many people use this route for short trips (Bailey 2007). In the neighborhoods north and south of University Avenue, 29 percent of households are without vehicles compared to about 18 percent city-wide. Some of the neighborhoods surrounding University Avenue have as high as 33 percent of residents living at or below the poverty line compared to about 17 percent city-wide (Ramsey County Regional Rail Authority 2006). Low income and households without vehicles are two of the highest contributors to transit ridership (U.S. Department of Transportation 2004). When the LRT project is complete, Route 16 bus stops will be significantly cut in order to reduce total transit costs (Bailey 2007). Thus, University Avenue residents will see a reduction in short-distance public transit service as a result of the Central Corridor LRT.

Neighborhood councils, community organizations, and many local lawmakers are demanding three additional stops along University Avenue, making the LRT stops one-half mile apart instead of the proposed one mile. Studies have found that transit ridership suffers a significant drop when stops are over one-half mile apart—averaging a 0.65 to 2 percent drop in ridership for every 100 feet a stop is from the rider's residence (Cervero et al. 2004; Kuzmyak, Pratt, and Douglas 2003; Parsons Brinckerhoff Quade & Douglas, Inc. 1996). According to its own standards, the Twin Cities Metropolitan Council (2006) defines appropriate walking distance as just over one-third mile in their "Guide to Transit Oriented Development" (2006).

The great majority of those involved acknowledge three additional LRT stops are important; however, the Metropolitan Council maintains that it is a simple dollars-and-cents issue. To qualify for federal funding, a project must meet cost-effectiveness standards. Using certain models, the number of riders gained does not justify the additional cost of the extra stations. The Metropolitan

(Continued)

Council has agreed to put in the underground infrastructure for the stops and "rough-in" later if surplus money becomes available as the project moves forward.

The Civil Rights Act of 1964, Title VI, and President Clinton's 1994 Executive Order 12898, *Federal Actions to Address Environmental Justice in Minority Populations and Low-Income Populations* (Federal Register 1994), explicitly prohibit the intentional or unintentional discrimination and unequal impacts when public money is used. Those opposed to the LRT plan as-is perceive an instance of geographic institutionalized racism and classism. University Avenue neighborhoods have minority populations of over 50 percent compared to the city average of 36 percent, and these neighborhoods have some of the highest poverty rates in St. Paul (Ramsey County Regional Rail Authority 2006).

Many community leaders are calling for equitable development. They argue that the characteristics of these neighborhoods and their populations are being used as an argument for the project, yet are being served by it the least. This sentiment is echoed by some of the residents who publically commented on the LRT proposal. One of the residents Veronica Burt explains:

> What [Metropolitan] Council is doing with community participation is symbolic. . . . Here you are coming through a community with environmental justice stakeholders and they are using our statistics—*our* incomes, *our* lack of automobiles, *our* lack—to get approval from the FTA [Federal Transportation Administration]. They are using *our* lives, *our* backs, but we will be losing transit in the process. They will limit bus 16 stops every eighth mile and not put light rail stops at Victoria and Western? What are they thinking? (Arbit, Nightingale, and Ton 2007: 8)

While the new LRT will bring local economic development along the corridor, it will also likely bring gentrification, pushing many residents out of the area. Additional burdens on University Avenue neighborhoods include construction-related issues such as increased noise, street closures, and more congestion on residential streets while the LRT is being built. Resident Linda J. Winsor argues that "light rail needs to *serve* [emphasis speaker's] the neighborhoods not just pass through it" ("Central Corridor LRT Stations at Western, Victoria, and Hamline: Community Report" 2008: 12). As already noted, postconstruction losses include a reduction in both rail and bus transit service as those wanting to use LRT will have to walk more for access and Route 16 bus stops will be cut by more than half. This means that a person could wait as long as half an hour to get on a bus to connect them to the LRT or to their destination along the corridor (Bailey 2007). Who benefits and who pays? Neighborhood groups affected by the reduced service are arguing that while the Central Corridor LRT brings much to the Twin Cities as a whole, its impact is bore most heavily by minority and lower-class populations along University Avenue. In the language of Robert Merton and Herbert Gans, the current LRT proposal is more functional for those who live and/or work by LRT stops and dysfunctional for those whose transit options are already limited due to poverty. Gans' insight is that it is the latter who give up more, thus subsidizing the functionality of the system for the rest.

LRT Update:

> Three additional stations were added to the line thanks to efforts of local activists and a change in the funding formula (Federal Transit Administration) that is used to determine the federal share of transit projects and additional monies from local and foundation sources. ("Three More Train Stations Coming to St. Paul" 2010)

Author Randy Hade majored in sociology and justice and peace studies while an undergraduate student at the University of St. Thomas. While doing a semester with Higher Education Consortium for Urban Affairs (HECUA), he had an internship with a local community organization working on local issues such as the LRT.

Bridges

ASCE (2005, 2007, 2009a) has given bridges higher grades than it has assigned other parts of the infrastructure although that grade was only a C. ASCE's (2009b) report on bridges revealed that more than 26 percent of the nation's bridges are either functionally obsolete or structurally deficient. The number of bridges in rural areas that are deficient is declining but the number of deficient urban bridges is not. This is particularly significant because bridges in urban areas have greater passenger and freight traffic. The average bridge is now forty-three years old and most of them have been built to last fifty years. The cost of eradicating all bridge deficiencies as they develop in the next fifty years is estimated at $850 billion (2006 dollars), which means an average annual investment of $17 billion (ASCE 2009b).

The tragic collapse of the busy interstate I-35W bridge that dropped 108 feet into the Mississippi River occurred in Minneapolis on August 1, 2007. It resulted in thirteen deaths and 145 injured. The state of Minnesota has paid more than $37 million to the families of victims and survivors (Associated Press 2009c). The state of Minnesota and some victims have filed lawsuits against the engineering firm, the URS Corporation. The National Transportation and Safety Board released its final report in November 2008 proclaiming that the gusset plates that were used to hold the steel beams together were not the proper size and gave way when a contractor placed tons of equipment and repair material in one location (Diaz 2008a; Wald 2008). The new I-35W bridge with a one hundred-year life span opened on September 18, 2008, about three months earlier than scheduled (Minnesota Department of Transportation n.d.). Textbox 4.3 discusses the I-35W bridge collapse in greater detail.

TEXTBOX 4.3

I-35W Bridge Collapse: Does Government Bear Any Responsibility?

On August 1, 2007, a 1,907-foot forty-year-old bridge that spanned the Mississippi River linking Minneapolis and St. Paul collapsed during rush hour, sending fifty to sixty cars into the river (Levy 2007) with thirteen fatalities and approximately 145 injuries. Tapes of the 911 calls reveal the horror as people described vehicles on fire and bloodied and injured victims. Brian Sturgill was in Minneapolis driving on I-35W having just flown in from San Diego. In an interview with the *Star Tribune*, he describes the horror of seeing the road break in front of him and the feeling of terror as his car falls into the water and his struggle to escape. He sees people covered in both blood and oil and wonders what could have happened to him had he been just a few feet in front or behind (McKinney and Smetanka 2007).

According to Tilly (1985), we allow the state to exert coercive control in exchange for protection. Although initially this protection was from invaders, we also rely on the state to protect us from other dangers including terrorists, bad food, and unsafe business practices. Much of what the state does is through regulation but the state also provides much of the infrastructure we need to stay healthy and safe, including clean water, sanitation, and transportation. Unlike the situation in many developing countries, we do not worry about the safety of a bridge or road. We assume it is safe because government has the responsibility to build and maintain it using tax dollars for both.

What then caused the I-35W bridge to collapse and why didn't the Minnesota Department of Transportation (MnDOT) know this bridge was unsafe? According to the report released by the National Transportation Safety Board (NTSB), a design flaw led to a failure of the gusset plates

(Continued)

that are used to connect beams to load-bearing columns. Specifically, the designers failed to do the proper math calculations, which resulted in undersized plates that were not designed to carry the extra weight (Diaz 2008b). At the time of the collapse, there were 287 tons of construction materials on the center span that were needed for a repaving project. NTSB members were surprised that neither the contractors nor the state officials had considered whether the bridge could hold the additional weight (Diaz 2008b). According to NTSB director of the Office of Highway Safety, Bruce Magladry, "had the gusset plates been properly sized, this bridge would still be there" (Diaz 2008b). This bridge had been labeled structurally deficient since 1991; yet the NTSB did not find that the age, corrosion, or poor rating was a factor in the collapse. According to NTSB Chairman Mark Rosenker, "A structurally deficient bridge is not ready to fall down" (Diaz 2008c). Others, though, place some responsibility on MnDOT. A study commissioned by the Minnesota State Legislature blamed lack of funding and a confusing chain of command at MnDOT (Kaszuba 2008a). Minnesota Governor Tim Pawlenty, a Republican, appointed his Lt. Governor, Carol Molnau, to also serve as the state transportation commissioner. This was considered by some as "inappropriate" and a "huge mistake" (Kaszuba 2008a). Molnau was later removed as transportation commissioner by the DFL-controlled (Democratic-Farmer Labor party) state legislature. Also, earlier that year, the governor vetoed a nickel gas tax increase wanted by the state legislature to pay for road and bridge upkeep. While passing a tax increase in May would not have prevented the August collapse, others argue that there were warning signs ignored by the state. In 2000, a consulting firm trying to drum up a state contract recommended "supplemental plates" and "a new oversized gusset" (Kaszuba 2008b). Instead, MnDOT went with the consulting firm URS Inc., which recommended less costly strategies. URS had recently hired a former MnDOT state bridge engineer (Kaszuba 2008b). In Ohio, a bridge of similar design collapsed in 1996 because of undersized and corroded gusset plates; yet MnDOT officials were unaware of the incident despite subscribing to civil engineering journals and attending a conference where the Ohio incident took place (Kaszuba 2008a). Finally, photos taken four years prior to the collapse showed that the gusset plate connections were bowed (Kennedy 2008), suggesting that MnDOT should have known the gusset plates were failing. Democrats, then, fault the Republican administration for not spending enough money on maintenance and the NTSB for giving "short shrift to concerns about bridge maintenance, aging, and corrosion" (Diaz 2008c). Although the NTSB is nonpartisan, agency head Mark Rosenker was a George W. Bush appointee, and a lifelong Republican raising concerns that NTSB findings were in some part politically motivated (Diaz 2008b). The probe authorized by the Minnesota State Legislature was also criticized as politically motivated because the DFL controls the legislature and has been a sharp critic of both Governor Pawlenty and MnDOT (Kaszuba 2008a).

Levees

Levees have also been a key concern, although it was not until 2009 that ASCE included levees in its report card. ASCE's (2009c) grade for levees was a D: "the state of the nation's levees has a significant impact on public safety. . . . Many levees are integral to economic development in the protected community." While there is no accurate record of how many levees are in the United States let alone their current condition, the Federal Emergency Management Agency (FEMA) believes that 43 percent of the U.S. population lives in counties with levees (ASCE 2009c). A summary of the hearing on "Recommendations of the National Committee on Levee Safety" by the House of Representatives Subcommittee on Water Resources and Environment Staff (2009) documented that more than two thousand levees under the auspices of the U.S. Army Corps of Engineers (Corps) covered more than 14,000 miles. Although unknown, undocumented levees may cover more than 100,000 miles. The Corps has identified 114 levees that have been given an unacceptable rating based on inspections since February 1, 2007. ASCE (2009c), though, suggests 177 levees or about 9 percent as of February 2009 are likely to fail in a flood.

HURRICANE KATRINA   Hurricane Katrina is believed to have killed more than 1,600 people in Louisiana and Mississippi and damaged property worth an estimated $40 billion (Associated Press 2009d). The tragedy of Hurricane Katrina involved the breakdown of New Orleans' levees. Although certainly not all the damage of the August 2005 hurricane was due to breaches of levees, the ASCE estimated that damages from flooding in levee-related areas amounted to almost $16.5 billion. The human costs are difficult to evaluate. After more than three years of "nomadic uncertainty" for those without permanent homes in the Renaissance Village trailer park, students were behind in school, they acted out, and they experienced extraordinary rates of illness and mental health problems (Dewan 2008). Parents also had problems coping. Although victims from the hurricane were told they had to abandon their FEMA trailers by the end of May 2009, the Obama White House staff announced that victims could buy the FEMA trailers for $5 or less. The Obama administration promised additional money for case managers to assist people in obtaining permanent housing. Hurricanes Katrina and Rita were so severe that temporary housing lasted longer than expected. Nearly two-thirds of the people still living in the trailers were trying to finish repairs on their homes (Dewan 2009).

The reaction of government agencies including the G. W. Bush administration to the hurricane was at best questionable. Tierney (2006: 207) discussed how people were "astonished by the sheer incompetence of the government response to the largest catastrophe to strike the nation in the last one hundred years." Further, people became angry when they realized the terrible devastation in the Gulf had been predicted, contrary to G. W. Bush's statement that the flooding could not have been anticipated. Tierney, who uses a vulnerability sciences approach, sees the Katrina disaster as similar to other disasters. The catastrophic effects resulted from failures in protective systems, structural factors that led to high vulnerability for many, and emergency systems that didn't properly care for or protect the victims (208).

Political finger-pointing occurred with a Democratic governor and a Republican White House administration: each blamed the other for failing to act appropriately. Krugman (2007) expressed his concern that "there's a powerful faction in this country that's determined to draw exactly the wrong lesson from the Katrina debacle—namely, that the government always fails when it attempts to help people in need." Krugman fears this cynicism about government may aid conservatives who argue for limited federal government involvement. Yet Krugman feels that the issue is more about the type of beliefs and practices of a particular government and it also influences governmental response rather than calling for a broad generalization about the effectiveness of government involvement. Obama has been praised by both Democrat and Republican officials and others in the Gulf area for his actions. Governor Bobby Jindal (R-La.) believes Obama is providing a more practical and flexible policy dealing with the devastation, stating, "There is a sense of momentum and a desire to get things done" (Associated Press 2009d). The National Committee on Levee Safety called for consistent comprehensive national leadership combined with new state levee programs to address the levees (ASCE 2009c). The ASCE (2009c) concluded:

> Due to their impact on life and safety issues, and the significant consequences of failure, as well as the financial burden of falling property values behind levees that are not safe and are being decertified, the nation must not delay addressing levee issues.

There are significant costs of failure for all aspects related to the infrastructure, and infrastructure maintenance and improvement are vital for the economy and people's lives in general. Whether the money in the stimulus package for infrastructure will be sufficient to mitigate the general crisis in infrastructure is an important question that will take years to answer. How the economy and the infrastructure intertwine with politics is a major example of how politics affects our everyday lives.

CONCLUSION

We began this chapter discussing C. W. Mills' idea that to understand the life of a person or our own life we need to be able to understand the history of the society and how it relates to the individual. We focused on politico-economic issues of our times to show how they affect our everyday lives regardless of what social class we are in. Corporations may downsize, outsource, or lay off workers. Another way to decrease labor costs is to employ undocumented workers. Those with limited skills in the United States may find it difficult to make a living wage as their wages likely suffer or they become unemployed. Between 1976 and 2007 the average inflation-adjusted hourly wage dropped by more than 7 percent (Frank 2010). In September 2010 the U.S. Census Bureau reported one in seven people are living in poverty; this is the highest number in the half century the government has kept such records (Morello 2010). Those who are employed become concerned about the high taxes they think they are paying to help the unemployed and others on welfare. Corporations are sometimes able to pay taxes on only a small percentage of their profits and/or find tax havens, thus limiting revenue that would enable the government to support social programs. A rich person may be concerned about possible increases in taxes and the government introducing more regulations on his or her business. Tax cuts have greatly benefitted the upper class, and businesses have been able to find tax havens to protect themselves. Businesses have often benefited from government welfare and CEOs have often benefited from large bonuses. Most persons, though, consider themselves part of the middle class, and the middle class in general has lost ground. Bankruptcies and foreclosures happen frequently in the middle class. The poor receive certain benefits from government assistance programs, but the benefits are not as great in comparison to other advanced societies. For the nation and the economy to thrive, a strong infrastructure is also needed, but as we enter the second decade of the twenty-first century our infrastructure faces numerous problems.

Chapter 3 discussed how culture influences political beliefs and politics. A key value that helps explain our attitude about government centers around individualism or autonomy. Individual hard work and achievement is valued, and material rewards are needed to motivate people. Such a belief is generally associated with a laissez-faire or hands-off approach to government involvement in economic affairs. Yet in complex societies, government always plays a role in our lives. Even if there aren't many regulations on the economy, some people benefit but others lose out. Current research shows the middle class has been losing out for decades. A collectivist rather than an individualist orientation likely favors more government and community involvement on behalf of its citizens, but this too requires that the state act in a democratic fashion. Whether government involvement in our lives will intensify and if so who is most likely to benefit is certainly an important societal issue. Chapter 5 examines the politics of everyday life involving social institutions and social relations.

Endnotes

1. The Pew Research Center (2008) results are based on a nationally representative sample of 2,413 adults. Their use of the label *middle class* is interesting. The survey asked respondents to put themselves in one of five groups—upper class, upper middle class, middle class, lower middle class, and lower class. About half (53 percent) classified themselves as middle class while another 19 percent indicated upper middle class and another 19 percent lower middle class. However, the Pew Research Center combined upper middle with upper class and lower middle with lower class to form a three-class stratification profile.

2. Leicht and Fitzgerald (2007) define the middle class mainly as based on socioeconomic status (SES) characteristics, but they also consider cultural factors. Typically middle-class people have incomes between $35,000 and $75,000 annually and tend to work as upper- and lower-level managers, professionals, and small business owners. They have graduated from or at least attended a four-year college. Further, their major source of wealth is home ownership.

3. The idea of a tax freedom day is theoretical and should not be taken literally. The Tax Foundation is a taxpayer advocacy group according to Musante (2008).

References

Agger, Ben and Tim Luke. 2002. "Politics in Postmodernity." Pp. 159–195 in *Theoretical Directions in Political Sociology for the 21st Century*, volume 11, *Research in Political Sociology*, edited by Betty A. Dobratz, Timothy Buzzell, and Lisa K. Waldner. Amsterdam: Elsevier.

Alford, Robert and Roger Friedland. 1985. *Powers of Theory*. Cambridge: Cambridge University Press.

Amenta, Edwin. 2005. "State-Centered and Political Institutionalist Theory: Retrospect and Prospect." Pp. 96–114 in *The Handbook of Political Sociology*, edited by T. Janoski, R. Alford, A. Hicks, and M. A. Schwartz. Cambridge: Cambridge University Press.

American Society for Civil Engineers (ASCE). 2005. "2005 Grades Infrastructure." Retrieved January 21, 2009 from http://www.asce.org/reportcard/2005/page.cfm?id=103.

_____. 2007. "Raising the Grades: Small Steps for Big Improvements in America's Failing Infrastructure. An Action Plan for the 110th Congress." Retrieved January 21, 2009 from http://www.asce.org/reportcard/2005/actionplan07.cfm.

_____. 2009a. "Report Card for American Infrastructure." Retrieved August 20, 2009 from http://www.infrastructereportcard.org/.

_____. 2009b. "Report Card for American Infrastructure: Bridges." Retrieved August 20, 2009 from http://www.infrastructereportcard.org/fact-sheet/bridges.

_____. 2009c. "Report Card for American Infrastructure: Levees." Retrieved August 20, 2009 from http://www.infrastructereportcard.org/fact-sheet/levees.

Andrews, Edmund. 2008. "Vast Bailout by U.S. Proposed in Bid to Stem Financial Crisis." *New York Times* September 19. Retrieved June 22, 2009 from http://www.nytimes.com/2008/09/19/business/19fed.html?pagewanted=print.

Andrews, Edmund L. and Peter Baker. 2009. "A.I.G. Planning Huge Bonuses After $170 Billion Bailout." *New York Times* March 15. Retrieved December 4, 2010 from http://www.nytimes.com/2009/03/15/business/15AIG.html.

Arbit, David, Kimberly Nightingale, and Hoang Ton. 2007. "A Central Corridor Light Rail Study: Making the Case for Three Additional Stops at Hamline, Victoria, and Western Avenues: Restorative Justice, Urban Design, TOD, Transit Dependency, and a Culture of Transit." Hubert H. Humphrey Institute of Public Affairs, University of Minnesota.

Associated Press. 2009a. "Federal Deficit Increases to $1.27 Trillion in July." *Des Moines Register* August 13: 4A.

_____. 2009b. "Consumer Debt Declined in June for a 5th Month." *New York Times* August 7. Retrieved August 15, 2009 from http://www.nytimes.com/2009/08/08business/08credit.html?scp=7&sq=Debt&st=cse.

_____. 2009c. "Two Years after Minneapolis Bridge Collapse, Some Survivors Struggle to Move on." *New York Times* August 1. Retrieved August 20, 2009 from http://www.nytimes.com/2009/08/02/us/02minneapolis.html.

_____. 2009d. "Obama Praised on Katrina Recovery." *Des Moines Register* August 28: 10A.

Aversa, Jeannine. 2009. "Wages Shrank Even as Rate of Joblessness Rises in U.S." *Des Moines Register* July 3: 10B–11B.

Bailey, Mary Kay. 2007. "The Case for Stations at Western, Victoria, and Hamline Avenues, Executive Summary." District Councils Collaborative of Saint Paul and Minneapolis. Retrieved November 14, 2007 from http://www.districtcouncilscollaborative.org.

Bar-Gill, Oren and Elizabeth Warren. 2008. "Making Credit Safer." *University of Pennsylvania Law Review* 157(November): 1–101.

Berberoglou, Berch. 2001. *Political Sociology.* Dix Hills, NY: General Hall.

Best, Shaun. 2002. *Introduction to Politics and Society.* London: Sage.

Blum, John, Bruce Catton, Edmund S. Morgan, Arthur Schlesinger, Jr., Kenneth Stampp, and C. Vann Woodward. 1963. *The National Experience.* New York: Harcourt, Brace, and World.

Brady, David. 2009. *Rich Democracies, Poor People: How Politics Explain Poverty.* New York: Oxford University Press.

Bruzzese, Anita. 2009. "Stress Is So Bad Workers Want to Change Jobs." *Des Moines Register* June 8: 6E.

Calmes, Jackie and Edmund Andrews. 2009. "Obama Calls for Curbs on Offshore Tax Havens." *New York Times* May 5. Retrieved May 21, 2009 from http://www.nytimes.com/2009/05/05/business/05tax.html.

Center on Budget and Policy Priorities. 2009. "Social Security Reduces Number of Seniors in Poverty." Retrieved July 5, 2009 from www.cbpp.org/research/?fa=topic&id=38.

"Central Corridor LRT Stations at Western, Victoria, and Hamline: Community Report." 2008. District Councils Collaborative of Saint Paul and Minneapolis.

Cervero, Robert et al. 2004. "TCRP Report 102: Transit-Oriented Development in the United States—Experiences, Challenges, and Prospects." Washington, DC: National Academy Press. Retrieved December 31, 2008 from http://www.ulisacramento.org/documents/tod/4.Implementation/IM7.pdf.

Chan, Sewell. 2010. "Bernanke Weights Risks of New Action." *New York Times* October 15. Retrieved October 17, 2010 from http://www.nytimes.com/2010/10/16/business/economy/16fed.html?scp=4&sq=The%20Fed&st=cse.

Clark-Kauffman, Elizabeth, Greg Duncan, and Pamela Morris. 2003. "How Welfare Policies Affect Child and Adolescent Achievement." *American Economic Review* 93: 299–303.

Cooper, Michael. 2009. "U.S. Infrastructure Is in Dire Straits, Report Says." *New York Times* January 27. Retrieved August 20, 2009 from http://www.nytimes.com/2009/01/28/us/politics/28projects.html?_r=1.

"Credit Card Industry." 2009. *New York Times Topics.* Updated May 20, 2009. Retrieved August 31, 2009 from http://topics.nytimes.com/topics/reference/timestopics/subjects/c/credit_and_money_cards/index.html.

"Credit Crisis—Bailout Plan." 2009. *New York Times Topics.* Updated August 11, 2009. Retrieved August 14, 2009 from http://topics.nytimes.com/topics/reference/timestopics/subjects/c/credit_crisis/bailout_plan/index.html.

Dewan, Shaila. 2008. "Katrina Victims Will Not Have to Vacate Trailers." *New York Times* June 3. Retrieved August 20, 2009 from http://www.nytimes.com/2009/06/04/us/04trailers.html.

_____. 2009. "Many Children Lack Stability Long After Storm." *New York Times* December 4. Retrieved August 22, 2009 from http://www.nytimes.com/2008/12/05/us/05trailer.html.

Diamond, Peter. 2004. "Social Security." *American Economic Review* 94: 1–24.

Diamond, Peter and Peter Orszag. 2005. "Saving Social Security." *Journal of Economic Perspectives* 19(2): 11–32.

Diaz, Kevin. 2008a. "The NTSB Findings: Bridge's Fatal Flaw: Gusset Plates, but Other Factors Cited in Collapse." *(Minneapolis) Star Tribune* November 14: A1, A8.

_____. 2008b. "NTSB's Final Bridge Report Due Today." *Star Tribune* November 14. Retrieved November 14, 2008 from http://www.startribune.com/politics/state/34404129.html?elr=KArksUUUoDEy3LGDiO7aiU.

_____. 2008c. "Tragedy of Bridge May Yield New Rules." *Star Tribune* November 15. Retrieved November 15, 2008 from http://www.startribune.com/politics/state/34454549.html?elr=KArksUUUoDEy3LGDiO7aiU.

Domhoff, G. William. 2006. *Who Rules America? Power, Politics, & Social Change.* Boston: McGraw-Hill.

Duncan, Greg J. and Jeanne Brooks-Gunn. 2000. "Family Poverty, Welfare Reform, and Child Development." *Child Development* 71: 188–196.

Dye, Thomas. 2002. *Who's Running America? The Bush Restoration.* 7th Edition. Upper Saddle River, NJ: Prentice Hall.

"Economic Stimulus." 2009. *New York Times Topics.* Updated August 13. Retrieved August 14, 2009 from http://topics.nytimes.com/top/references/timestopics/subjects/u/united_states_economy/economic_stimulus/index.html.

Esping-Andersen, Gøsta. 2007. "Equal Opportunities and the Welfare State." *Contexts* 6(3): 23–27.

"Executive Pay." 2009. *New York Times Topics.* Updated June 17. Retrieved July 28, 2009 from http://topics.nytimes.com/top/reference/timestopics/subjects/e/executive_pay/index.html.

Federal Register. 1994. "Presidential Documents. Executive Order 12898 of February 11, 1994." *Federal Actions to Address Environmental Justice in Minority Populations and Low-Income Populations.* Vol. 59, (32). Retrieved December 31, 2008 from http://www.archives.gov/federal-register/executive-orders/pdf/12898.pdf.

Feldstein, Martin. 2005. "Structural Reform of Social Security." *Journal of Economics Perspectives* 19(2): 33–55.

"Financial Regulatory Reform." 2009. *New York Times Topics*. Updated August 6, 2009. Retrieved August 15, 2009 from http://topics.nytimes.com/topics/reference/timestopics/subjects/c/credit_crisis/financial_regulatory_reform/index.html.

Fineman, Howard. 2009. "Living Politics: Big Ideas = Bags of Cash." *Newsweek* March 30: 34–35.

Fording, Richard C. 2001. "The Political Response to Black Insurgency: A Critical Test of Competing Theories of the State."*American Political Science Review* 95: 115–130.

Forgrave, Reid. 2008. "How the Middle Class Is Being Squeezed." *Des Moines Register* October 12: 1A, 10A.

Frank, Robert H. 2010. "Income Inequality: Too Big to Ignore." *New York Times* October 16. Retrieved October 17, 2010 from http://www.nytimes.com/2010/10/17/business/17view.html?_r=1&hpw.

Gans, Herbert J. 1972. "The Positive Functions of Poverty." *American Journal of Sociology* 78: 275–289.

Goodman, Peter. 2009. "Lucrative Fees May Deter Efforts to Alter Loans." *New York Times* July 29. Retrieved August 14, 2009 from http://www.nytimes.com/2009/07/30/business/30services.html.

Government Accountability Office (GAO). 2008. "Highlights International Taxation." GAO-09-157. Retrieved July 22, 2009 from www.gao.gov/highlights/d09157high.pdf.

_____. 2009. "Report to Congress: High-Risk Series an Update." January GAO-09-271. Washington, DC: Government Accountability Office.

Greenstein, Robert. 2009. "Statement: Robert Greenstein on Trustees' Social Security Report. Report Shows Social Security Doesn't Face an Immediate Crisis but Does Require Changes, and the Sooner They're Made the Better." Center on Budget and Policy Priorities, May 12. Retrieved July 5, 2009 from http://www.cbpp.org/cms/index.cfm?fa=view&id=2813.

Herbert, Bob. 2007. "Our Crumbling Foundation." *New York Times* April 5. Retrieved August 20, 2009 from http://www.nytimes.com/2009/05/26/opinion/26herbert.html.

Hiltzik, Michael. 2005. *The Plot Against Social Security.* New York: Harper Collins.

Himmelstein, David, Deborah Thorne, Elizabeth Warren, and Steffie Woolhandler. 2009. "Medical Bankruptcy in the United States, 2007: Results of a National Study." *American Journal of Medicine* 122: 741–746.

Holt, Douglas B. 1999. "Postmodern Markets." *Boston Review* Summer. Retrieved August 14, 2009 from www.bostonreview.netBR24.3/summer99.pdf.

House of Representatives Subcommittee on Water Resources and Environment Staff. 2009. Letter on "Hearing on 'Recommendations of the National Committee on Levee Safety' " to Members of the Subcommittee on Water Resources and Environment, May 18. Retrieved August 22, 2009 from http://transportation.house.gov/Media/file/water/20090519/SSM_WR.pdf.

Hoynes, Hilary W., Marianne E. Page, and Ann Huff Stevens. 2006. "Poverty in America: Trends and Explanations." *Journal of Economic Perspectives* 20: 47–68.

Hurst, Charles E. 2010. *Social Inequality*. 7th Edition. Boston: Pearson.

Internal Revenue Service. 2009. *1040A Instructions 2009*. Washington, DC: Government Printing Office.

Johnston, David Cay. 2007. *Free Lunch*. New York: Penguin.

Karp, David, William Yoels, and Barbara Vann. 2004. *Sociology in Everyday Life*. Long Grove, IL: Waveland Press.

Kaszuba, Mike. 2008a. "MnDOT Missed Opportunities to Note Bridge Flaws, Study Finds." *Star Tribune* May 21. Retrieved June 6, 2008 from http://www.startribune.com/politics/state/19133569.html?elr=KArksUUUoDEy3LGDiO7aiU.

_____. 2008b. "In 2000, a Focus on Those Critical Gussets." *Star Tribune* June 14. Retrieved June 14, 2008 from http://www.startribune.com/local/19932304.html?elr=KArksUUUoDEy3LGDiO7aiU.

Kennedy, Tony. 2008. "Old Photos Show Flaws in Steel of I-35W Bridge." *Star Tribune* March 26. Retrieved June 6, 2008 from http://www.startribune.com/local/16927626.html?elr=KArksUUUoDEy3LGDiO7aiU.

Kerr, Jennifer C. 2008. "Study: Most U.S. Firms Avoid Paying Income Tax." *Des Moines Register* August 12: 5A.

Kinloch, Graham. 1989. *Society as Power.* Englewood Cliffs, NJ: Prentice-Hall.

Kloby, Jerry. 2004. "Overaccumulation and the Drive for School Reform." *Political Sociology: States, Power, and Societies* Summer (newsletter): 3–5.

Krugman, Paul. 2007. "Katrina All the Time." *New York Times* August 31. Retrieved August 23, 2009 from http://select.nytimes.com/2007/08/31/opinion/31krugman.html.

Kuzmyak, Richard, Richard H. Pratt, and G. Bruce Douglas. 2003. *Traveler Response to Transportation System Changes: Transit Cooperative Research Program 95*. Transportation Research Board. Retrieved December 31, 2008 from http://onlinepubs.trb.org/onlinepubs/tcrp/tcrp_rpt_95c15.pdf.

Labaton, Stephen. 2009a. "House Panel Approves Restraints on Executive Pay." *New York Times* July 28. Retrieved July 28, 2009 from http://www.nytimes.com/2009/07/29/business/29pay.html.

_____. 2009b. "Regulators Spar for Turf in Financial Overhaul." *New York Times* July 24. Retrieved September 28, 2009 from http://www.nytimes.com/2009/07/25/business/economy/25regulate.html?_r=1&hp.

Lawless, Robert M., Angela K. Littwin, Katherine M. Porter, John Pottow, Deborah Thorne, and Elizabeth Warren. 2008. "Did Bankruptcy Reform Fail? An Empirical Study of Consumer Debtors." *American Bankruptcy Law Journal* 82: 349–406. Retrieved August 15, 2009 from http://ssrn.com/abstract=1286284.

Lehne, Richard. 2006. *Government and Business.* Washington, DC: CQ Press.

Leicht, Kevin T. and Scott T. Fitzgerald. 2007. *Postindustrial Peasants: The Illusion of Middle-Class Prosperity.* New York: Worth.

Levy, Paul. 2007. "4 Dead, 79 Injured, 20 Missing after Dozens of Vehicles Plummet into River." *Star Tribune* August 2. Retrieved June 6, 2008 from http://www.startribune.com/local/11593606.html?elr=KArksUUUoDEy3LGDiO7aiU.

Lewin, Tamar. 2009. "Study Shows Rise in Average Borrowing by Students." *New York Times* August 11. Retrieved August 15, 2009 from http://www.nytimes.com/2009/08/12/education/12college.html?scp=1&sq=Debt&st=cse.

Lichter, Daniel and Rukmalie Jayakody. 2002. "Welfare Reform: How Do We Measure Success?" *Annual Review of Sociology* 28: 117–141.

Marger, Martin. 1987. *Elites and Masses.* Belmont, CA: Wadsworth.

_____. 2008. *Social Inequality.* 4th Edition. New York: McGraw-Hill.

McKenna, George and Stanley Feingold (editors). 2004. *Taking Sides: Clashing Views on Controversial Political Issues.* 13th Edition. Guilford, CT: McGraw-Hill/Dushkin.

McKinney, Matt and Mary Jane Smetanka. 2007. "911 Calls: Horror after Bridge Fell." *Star Tribune* August 24. Retrieved June 6, 2008 from http://www.startribune.com/local/11593896.html?elr=KArksUUUoDEy3LGDiO7aiU.

Merton, Robert King. 1949. "Manifest and Latent Functions." In *Social Theory and Social Structure.* Glencoe, IL: Free Press.

Metropolitan Council. 2006. "Guide to Transit-Oriented Development." Retrieved December 12, 2008 from http://www.metrocouncil.org/planning/tod/tod.htm.

Mills, C. Wright. 1956. *The Power Elite.* New York: Oxford.

_____. 1959. *The Sociological Imagination.* New York: Oxford.

Minnesota Department of Transportation. n.d. "I-35W St. Anthony Falls Bridge: The New I-35W Bridge." Retrieved August 20, 2009 from http://projects.dot.state.mn.us/35wbridge/index.html.

Morello, Carol. 2010. "One in Seven Americans Is Living in Poverty, Census Shows." *Washington Post* September 16. Retrieved September 16, 2010 from http://www.washingtonpost.com/wp-dyn/content/article/2010/09/16/AR2010091602698_pf.html.

Morgenson, Gretchen. 2008. "Given a Shovel, Americans Dig Deeper Into Debt." *New York Times* July 20. Retrieved August 15, 2009 from http://www.nytimes.com/2008/07/20/business/20debt.html.

_____. 2010. "Credit Cards and Reluctant Regulators." *New York Times* January 17. Copied January 17, 2010 from http://www.nytimes.com/2010/01/17/business/17gret.html?sq=creditcards topic&st=cse&scp=48pagewanted=print.

"Mortgages and the Markets." 2009. *New York Times Topics.* Updated July 29. Retrieved August 15, 2009 from http://topics.nytimes.com/top/reference/timestopics/subjects/m/mortgages/index.html.

Musante, Kenneth. 2008. "Pay Off Your Tax Bill—In 113 Days." CNNMoney.com March 25. Retrieved March 26, 2008 from http://money.cnn.com/2008/03/25/pf/taxes/tax_freedom/index.htm.

Myles, John. 1996. "When Markets Fail: Social Welfare in Canada and the United States." Pp. 116–140 in *Welfare States in Transition*, edited by Gøsta Esping-Andersen. London: Sage.

Neuman, W. Lawrence. 2005. *Power, State, Society.* New York: McGraw-Hill.

New York Times. 2010 "Editorial: The Foreclosure Crises." October 14. Retrieved October 17, 2010 from www.nytimes.com/2010/10/15/opinion/15fril.html?ref=credit_crisis.

Orszag, Peter. 2008. "Statement of Peter A. Orszag, Director Current and Future Investment in Infrastructure before the Committee on the Budget and the Committee on Transportation and Infrastructure, U.S. House of Representatives." May 8. Washington, DC: Congressional Budget Office. Retrieved August 21, 2009 from http:// www.cbo.gov/ftpdocs/91xxx/doc9136/05-07-Infrastructure_Testimony.pdf.

"The Outrage Factor." 2009. *Newsweek* March 30: 23–29.

Parsons Brinckerhoff Quade & Douglas, Inc. 1996. *Transit and Urban Form.* TCRP Report 16. Washington, DC: National Academy Press.

Pew Research Center. 2008. *Inside the Middle Class: Bad Times Hit the Good Life.* Washington, DC: Pew Research Center.

Pew Research Center for the People & the Press. 2009. "Independents Take Center Stage in Obama Era." May 21. Retrieved August 1, 2009 from http://people-press.org/report?pageid=1517.

Piven, Frances Fox and Richard A. Cloward. 1979. *Poor People's Movements.* New York: Vintage/Random House.

Pugh, Tony. 2009. "Some Credit Card Rules Take Effect." *Des Moines Register* August 19: 7B–8B.

Ramsey County Regional Rail Authority. 2006. *Central Corridor Alternatives Analysis and Draft Environmental Impact Statement.*

Robertson, Ian. 1981. *Sociology.* New York: Worth.

Schor, Juliet. 1999. "The New Politics of Consumption." *Boston Review* Summer. Retrieved August 14, 2009 from www.bostonreview.net/BR24.3/summer99.pdf.

Schram, Sanford F., Joe Soss, Richard C. Fording, and Linda Houser. 2009. "Deciding to Discipline: Race, Choice, and Punishment at the Frontlines of Welfare Reform." *American Sociological Review* 74: 398–422.

Seelye, Katherine Q. 2009. "To Save Money, States Turn to Furloughs." *New York Times* April 23. Retrieved July 5, 2009 from http://www.nytimes.com/2009/04/24/us/24furlough.html.

Sherman, Arloc. 2005. "Social Security Lifts 1 Million Children Above the Poverty Line." Center on Budget and Policy Priorities May 2. Retrieved August 3, 2009 from http://www.cbpp.org/cms/index.cfm?fa=view&id=296.

Sherman, Arloc and Isaac Shapiro. 2005. "Social Security Lifts 13 Million Seniors Above the Poverty Line: A State-by-State Analysis." Center on Budget and Policy Priorities February 24. Retrieved August 3, 2009 from http://www.cbpp.org/cms/index.cfm?fa=view&id=1111.

Skocpol, Theda. 1992. *Protecting Soldiers and Mothers.* Cambridge: The Belknap Press of Harvard University Press.

Smeeding, Timothy. 2006. "Poor People in Rich Nations." *Journal of Economic Perspectives* 20: 69–90.

Streitfeld, David. 2009. "Tight Mortgage Rules Exclude Even Good Risks." *New York Times* July 10. Retrieved July 11, 2009 from http://www.nytimes.com/2009/07/11/business/11housing.html?_r=1&th&emc=th.

Teixeira, Ruy A. and Joel Rogers. 2000. *America's Forgotten Majority: Why the White Working Class Still Matters.* New York: Basic Books.

Thomas, Ken. 2009. "Report: Over 8 in 10 Corporations Have Tax Havens." Yahoo! News January 16. Retrieved January 16, 2009 from http://news.yahoo.com/s/ap/20090116/ap_on_go_co/tax_havens/print.

"Three More Train Stations Coming to St. Paul." 2010. *Star Tribune* January 26. Retrieved from http://www.startribune.com/local/stpaul/82601562.html?elr=KArks:DCiUUUU.

Tierney, Kathleen. 2006. "Review: Foreshadowing Katrina: Recent Sociological Contributions to Vulnerability Science." *Contemporary Sociology* 35(3): 207–212.

Tilly, Charles. 1985. "War Making and State Making as Organized Crime." Pp. 169–191 in *Bringing the State Back In*, edited by P.B. Evans, D. Rueschemeyer, and T. Skocpol. Cambridge: Cambridge University Press.

U.S. Department of Transportation. 2004. "Status of the Nation's Highways, Bridges, and Transit: Conditions and Performance Report to Congress." Retrieved December 12, 2008 from http://www.fhwa.dot.gov/policy/ 2004cpr/chap14.htm.

Van de Water, Paul and Arloc Sherman. 2010. "Social Security Keeps 20 Million Americans Out of Poverty: A State-By-State Analysis." Center on Budget and Policy Priorities August 11. Retrieved October 17, 2010 from http://www.cbpp.org/cms/index.cfm?fa=view&id=3260.

Van Hook, Jennifer and Frank Bean. 2009. "Explaining Mexican-Immigrant Welfare Behaviors." *American Sociological Review* 74: 423–444.

Wald, Matthew. 2008. "National Briefing, Washington: Bridge Collapse Is Laid to Design Flaw." *New York Times* November 14. Retrieved August 21, 2009 from http://www.nytimes.com/2008/11/14/us/14brfs-BRIDGECOLLAP_BRF.html.

Warren, Elizabeth. 2006. "The Middle Class on the Precipice." *Harvard Magazine* January–February. Retrieved August 17, 2009 from http://harvardmagazine .com/2006/01/the-middle-class-on-the.html.

———. 2007. "Unsafe at Any Rate." *Democracy* Summer (Issue #5): 8–19.

Warren, Elizabeth and Amelia Warren Tyagi. 2003. *The Two-Income Trap: Why Middle-Class Parents Are Going Broke.* New York: Perseus Books.

Weir, Margaret, Ann Shola Orloff, and Theda Skocpol (editors). 1988. *The Politics of Social Policy in the United States.* Princeton, NJ: Princeton University Press.

White, Ben. 2009. "What Red Ink? Wall Street Paid Hefty Bonuses." *New York Times* January 29. Retrieved January 30, 2009 from http://www.nytimes.com/2009/01/29/business/29bonus.html.

"Who's to Blame: Washington or Wall Street?" 2009. *Newsweek* March 30: 30–31.

Williams, Mary Walsh and Tara Siegel Bernard. 2009. "In Need of Cash, More Companies Cut 401(k) Match." *New York Times* December 21. Retrieved from http://www.nytimes.com/2008/12/21/your-money/401ks-and-similar-plans/21retire.html.

5

The Politics of Everyday Life: Social Institutions and Social Relations

Mills (1959: 135) pointed out in his book *The Sociological Imagination*, "In terms of power . . . the most inclusive unit of social structure is the nation-state. The nation-state is now the dominating form in world history and, as such, a major fact in the life of every man [*sic* human]." Mills continued by discussing how power and decision making, our institutions, and where we live our public and private lives are all organized within the nation-state. Brewer (2003: 37) suggests that Mills really saw a fourfold interaction "between the social structure, individual biography and experience, historical events and constraints, and the political process." The major purpose of this chapter is to unravel some parts of these interactions and thus make one aware of how the state specifically and politics in general significantly influence people's lives in ways one may not have previously considered. There are multiple institutions and topics we could analyze; however, in order to provide some detail about the complex processes involved, we focus on how politics plays a crucial role in the major institutions of education and family, and health care, civil liberties, and race and ethnic relations. We look at public opinion to help us understand what the "typical" American may be thinking on various issues.

EDUCATION

Like the economy, education is a major institution in our society, and various government bodies play a key role in how education operates. While many countries see education as a national enterprise, in the United States the various states and communities, including local school boards, are quite important. At the elementary and secondary grades, less than 8 percent of funding comes from federal sources (U.S. Department of Education 2009a). One estimate suggests that $1 trillion is spent nationwide on all levels of education. Another estimate suggests that 49.8 million students were attending public elementary and secondary schools in fall 2009. Expenditures for school year 2009–2010 for public elementary and secondary schools are estimated at $543 billion. Roughly $631 billion is spent on elementary and secondary schools, whereas $386 billion is spent for all postsecondary degree-granting institutions. The American Recovery and Reinvestment Act that President Obama signed in 2009 allocated $98.2 billion for the U.S. Department of Education (2009b).

Pluralists tend to emphasize the roles of parents, teachers, and interest groups in shaping schools that teach pride in country and democratic skills as well as prepare students for the workplace. Elite theorists emphasize the role of school administrations that serve to maintain dominance of elites and inequality in society. Class theorists point out how social class influences both the quantity and the quality of one's education (Alford and Friedland 1985; Kinloch 1989; Neuman 2005). From a postmodern perspective, education may be constantly in flux due to uncertainty and chaos, but if students are properly indoctrinated, they should be able to control their own behavior without much direct government intervention. For theorists like Foucault, extra-political venues like education and family are important places for the production and distribution of power (Agger and Luke 2002). Rational choice theorists likely support

A father and his daughter wait their turn to speak in favor of the charter school proposal at a Los Angeles Unified School District (LAUSD) board meeting to vote on a LAUSD resolution that would invite private charter school operators, local communities, and even the mayor's office to submit proposals for operating fifty new schools as well as two hundred existing underperforming schools.

Credit: Newscom

the need for students to plan for their future, including obtaining the proper credentials to succeed in the workplace. Those using the institutionalist framework likely focus on the interactions among local school boards and state and federal governments.

Greater education may increase people's cognitive skills, including their ability to understand politics. It may improve their political participation in part because it enhances their sense
of civic duty and responsibility and helps them understand the procedural matters involved in
voting and in other political processes (Orum and Dale 2009).

Miliband (1969) points out that although teachers generally avoid appearing partial to a particular political party or cause, schools do engage in political socialization "mostly in terms which
are highly 'functional' to the prevailing social and political order" (239). Miliband believes that
nationalism is typically used to promote national allegiance that supports the existing order.
Further, Best (2002: 8), drawing on the ideas of Anthony Giddens, points out how power relations
characterize our institutions and that "institutions such as schools, attempt to control the lives of
individual people by the use of rules, which become deeply embedded in our everyday lives."

In part because property taxes often form part of the available resources for school districts, social class plays a key role in one's educational opportunities (Robertson 1981).
Conservatives who focus on liberty likely argue that parents should be free to use whatever
resources are at their disposal to benefit their children. Liberals tend to be more concerned about
employing resources to promote equity and prefer to distribute tax revenues more equally among
rich and poor school districts (Marger 2008).

Bowles and Gintis (1976, 2002, 2004; Bowles, Gintis, and Meyer 2004[1975]) offer a
class analysis as they examine the relationship between education and the economy. Bowles
et al. (2004[1975]) refer to the hierarchical structural similarity between education and economic
life that helps explain how the educational system reproduces an obedient "amenable labor
force" (114). It is the "lived experiences of daily life" (115) learned in school and the family
where the young are taught "cooperation, competition, dominance, and subordination" (116).
Bowles and Gintis (1976) suggest that by being taught to compete for rewards, children are
being socialized for economic activities in a capitalist society.

The social relations that develop in schools are associated with the different social-class
backgrounds and race and ethnic composition of the entire school and the individual classes.
Schools with more arbitrary and coercive authority structures that emphasize behavioral control
and rule-following tend to be associated with working-class and minority student bodies, whereas
more open systems that encourage student involvement, student electives in courses, less direct
supervision, and internal motivational control tend to characterize more affluent white-collar and
white schools (Bowles et al. 2004[1975]). Schools also "immerse children in a structure of rewards and sanctions" (Bowles and Gintis 2002: 13). Students are rewarded for prosocial attitudes
such as doing something to help the school even when it may not be advantageous for the student. In an article in *Enriching the Sociological Imagination,* Bowles and Gintis (2004) affirm
their earlier findings and argue again for the importance of "embedding the analysis of education
in the evolving structure of the economy and the polity, and giving attention to the non-cognitive
as well as conventional effects of education" (111).

No Child Left Behind

In January 2002 the legislation optimistically known as the No Child Left Behind (NCLB) Act
was signed with bipartisan support. Indeed Senator Edward M. Kennedy (D-Mass.) was one of
the four legislators to join George W. Bush on a twelve-hour tour of three states promoting what
President Bush called "a new era, a new time in public education" (Mantel and Greenblatt

2008: 1). The law extended the role of the federal government into the management of local schools. Ideally it was to hold those receiving federal funds accountable for improving the achievement scores of all students in part by expanding funds for schools that had many poor students. NCLB was to make sure that teachers in all classrooms were to be "highly qualified," meaning they have a college degree and are licensed or certified by the state. A deadline of 2014 was established for all students to be at grade level in reading and math. To reach this goal, schools would be sanctioned if they didn't meet state benchmarks two years in a row. If a school fails to reach "adequate yearly progress" (AYP) for two years in a row, the state and district designate the school as "in need of improvement" and determine a plan to help it. Students have the right to transfer to other schools if they desire. If in the third year the school does not meet its AYP, it must pay for tutoring, after-school programs, and summer school for low-income students who remain. In addition to improving overall test scores both in math and in science, achievement differences between various subgroups are to be reduced. This includes four major subgroups: (1) economically disadvantaged, (2) major racial and ethnic groups, (3) those with disabilities, and (4) those with limited English proficiency (Dworkin 2005; Karen 2005; Mantel and Greenblatt 2008; Popham 2004).

Although NCLB initially had strong bipartisan approval, support has dissipated as criticisms that the program is underfunded, poorly implemented, and mismanaged have emerged. Congress appropriated $27 billion less than what was authorized in 2005 to fund the program. In 2006 G. W. Bush requested only $13.3 billion for funding Title I programs out of the $22.8 billion that was authorized. In 2005 the largest teachers' union, the National Education Association, and the state of Connecticut each sued the Department of Education over funding issues (Mantel and Greenblatt 2008).

One of the key provisions required annual testing of students in grades 3–8 in reading and math and also at least one additional test in grades 10–12. Each state can develop and adopt its own tests. One problem is that most states started systematic testing only ten to fifteen years ago and several have changed their tests, making comparisons difficult (Mantel and Greenblatt 2008).

NCLB is trying to establish educational accountability through "high-stakes tests," which have serious consequences for the students, the teachers, the schools, the states, and so on (Popham 2004). There are a number of concerns related to accountability issues:

> Critics of accountability systems involving high-stakes testing have contended that these systems narrow the curricula to what is tested, promote teaching to the test, encourage school personnel to cheat, produce heightened test-taking skills without the actual learning of content, place too much emphasis on a single indicator in violation of test theory, discriminate against students who have trouble with multiple-choice tests, harm poor and minority-group members, and increase the dropout rate (Heubert and Hauser 1999; McNeil 2000). These analyses suggest that high-stakes testing could widen the achievement gaps among groups of students. (Dworkin 2005: 170)

Although there are concerns, some studies suggest that high-stakes testing can narrow the achievement gap between groups.

RESULTS OF TESTING THUS FAR   The U.S. Department of Education has measured student achievement scores since 1969 through its National Assessment of Education Progress (NAEP). In general the data suggest that minorities as well as whites are making gains and there is some narrowing of the gap (Mantel and Greenblatt 2008). Most of the declines, though, occurred in the 1970s and 1980s for minorities and younger students, which was before NCLB was passed

(Dillon 2009a). A 2009 NAEP report on the achievement gaps for fourth and eighth graders through 2007 generally documented the declining gap (U.S. Department of Education 2009c), but such findings do little to explain what factors in schools, the home, and the community contribute to the gap (Mantel and Greenblatt 2008).

While one of NCLB's goals was to reduce the gap, the U.S. Department of Education acknowledged that few students were receiving free tutoring if their school was failing. Also, no state had met the goal of having "highly qualified" teachers in all classrooms (Clemmitt 2008). In addition, school dropout problems frequently exist with low-income and minority students. It is particularly revealing that almost 50 percent of African-American students, 40 percent of Latino/a students, and 11 percent of white students are in schools where graduation is not the norm (Clemmitt 2008). In other words, NCLB, or any new initiative, faces major issues that need to be improved, but education reform likely needs to be part of an even more extensive change.

Reauthorization of NCLB or developing new legislation is part of the Obama agenda. Education Secretary Duncan has discussed improving national academic standards and making sure high-quality teachers are distributed equally among schools in poor and rich neighborhoods (Dillon 2009b). Some have seriously considered renaming the law Quality Education for All Children while others more humorously have suggested names like All Children Are Above Average Act and the Act to Help Children Read Gooder ("No Child Left Behind Act" 2009). Whatever is ultimately decided, all U.S. citizens—students, teachers, administrators, parents and relatives of students, and so on—will be influenced by the quality of education.

MARRIAGE AND FAMILY

In addition to education, the family serves as a major socializing institution. Pluralists would focus on the diverse types of families and that families and marriage promote balance, political order, and harmony in society. The political socialization of children (Ferrante 2008; Kinloch 1989) means that political preferences and values are to some extent passed down from one generation to the next. Elite and class theorists are particularly interested in how social inequality is passed down from one generation to the next. Social class, region, race, religion, and other factors associated with the family shape one's voting and political attitudes. Children of the elite are socialized to achieve positions of power and influence in society (Domhoff 2006). Laws are formulated by the state to maintain social control of families. Elite theorists especially recognize the power arrangement in families, with men dominating both women and children and thus representing "the basis of political authority" and "of economic stratification in terms of age, sex, and social origins" (Kinloch 1989: 215). From a class perspective,

> the *family,* not the individual, is seen as the basic unit of class membership. People all begin life in the class of their parents. This reality is further reflected in the fact that most people marry within their class. . . . And it is through families that property is passed on. (Liazos 1982: 33, drawing on the ideas of Paul Sweezy)

For class theorists who draw on social reproduction theory, parents' class position tends to be reproduced or recreated in their children. The class structure in society remains, so the ruling class continues to rule (Hurst 2010).

Drawing on a comparative study of childhood, society, and development in Nordic nations, Dencik (1989: 155) considers "the transformations of the everyday life of parents and children" in postmodern society. Dencik points out that there is an "eternal triangle" that includes the state as well as parents and children (163). It is the state that provides benefits, and possibly legal assistance, for children. Laws against certain forms of corporal punishment or abuse and laws to provide an education or nurturance for children are significant. Representatives of the state, such as teachers and medical professionals, are expected to report potential problems in child–parent relationships.

For Dencik (1989: 172) "the family is fragile in the post-modern epoch" as it tries to provide a zone of stability and an intimate sanctuary under chronic uncertainty and the quickening pace of everyday life. Dencik believes the younger generation may be "less willing to accept things as they are, more open-minded and outspoken, and perhaps a good deal less conscientious" (176) and concludes that "life is beginning to look like a never-ending examination situation" (177). This uncertainty likely influences children's worldviews. If Dencik is correct, more open-minded and outspoken children could influence and possibly bring about political change.

TEXTBOX 5.1

Politics, Major League Baseball (MLB) and the National Football League (NFL)

Historically, the great pastime for American families has been watching MLB. While we may debate whether the most popular sport is now baseball or football, we should not lose sight of the fact that politics plays a significant role in sports. Although politics affects many aspects of MLB and the NFL, we will limit our discussion to three specific illustrations: the political economy of the sport especially as it relates to the use of the public's resources, the steroid issue, and the antitrust exemption. Johnston (2007: 21) maintains that "while some teams are profitable, overall the sports-team industry does not earn any profit from the market. Industry profits all come from the taxpayers."

The first issue discussed here is the political economy of the sport. Neil deMause (2007), coauthor of *Field of Schemes: How the Great Stadium Swindle Turns Public Money into Private Profit,* testified to the House Subcommittee on Domestic Policy that government subsidies for Major League stadiums and minor league facilities from 1995 to 2006 totaled more than $10 billion and may now be averaging more than $2 billion a year. DeMause (2) estimates that job creation is actually very costly ($250,000 per new job) and stadiums do not revitalize urban neighborhoods. He (7) identifies "sports industry's dirty little secret: New stadiums don't make money."

Further, deMause testified that team owners claim their stadiums are obsolete and threaten to move if demands aren't met. In the 1980s, teams used to pay rent and share their ticket and concession revenue so the public's investment could be returned, but now there are often rent rebates and possible revenues are often forgone from future parking, property taxes, construction, sales tax, and so on. For the fans, new baseball parks have resulted in ticket prices being raised by an average of 41 percent (5). The so-called cheap seats often end up being fewer and farther from the field since the corporate boxes push the upper decks higher. DeMause (8) recommended that Congress "close the loophole that allows teams to use federally subsidized tax-exempt bonds for private sports stadiums . . . drastically restrict the business-entertainment deduction for luxury box and club seat purchases . . . [and] put on the brakes for not just sport teams, but all industries holding cities hostage for tax subsidies."

Second, we note that certainly all sports have been involved in illegal drug use, but Congress has particularly been concerned about steroids in MLB. Fay Vincent, MLB's commissioner in the early 1990s, sent all the teams a memo stating illegal drugs were prohibited by law and their use could lead to discipline or expulsion. However, when Bud Selig succeeded Vincent, he and the players' union downplayed the issue ("Steroids" 2009). As the twenty-first century dawned though, it was clear there was a major problem, and drug testing of players began in 2003 followed by a Congressional investigation in 2005.

(Continued)

The 2005 hearings before the House Committee on Government Reform were entitled "Restoring Faith in America's Pastime: Evaluating Major League Baseball's Efforts to Eradicate Steroid Use." The committee's chair representative Tom Davis explained that MLB did not respond quickly to steroid use and that Congressional pressure had been applied to get MLB to adopt a testing policy. Davis proclaimed, "Our responsibility is to help make sure Major League Baseball strategy, particularly its new testing program, gets the job done" (Committee on Government Reform 2005: 3).

U.S. Senator Jim Bunning, a MLB Hall of Fame member, felt the new drug policy was "a baby step forward" with "puny" penalties (16) and that if the policy doesn't fix the scandal, then Congress should amend the labor laws or repeal "the outdated anti-trust exemption that baseball alone enjoys" (16). In 2007 former Senator George J. Mitchell released an independent report for MLB that identified the issue as "a collective failure to recognize the problem as it emerged and to deal with it early" (Wilson and Schmidt 2007: 2). In the Congressional hearings, Mitchell report, and the media, many famous players and record breakers like Sammy Sosa, Barry Bonds, Manny Ramirez, Roger Clemens, Jason Giambi, and Andy Petite were alleged to have used steroids (Committee on Government Reform 2005; Schmidt 2010; "Steroids" 2009; Wilson and Schmidt 2007). Schmidt (2010) credited Congress for helping Selig convince the players' union to support tougher testing procedures. In 2009 Manny Ramirez was suspended for fifty games for violating the drug policy. In 2010, after Mark McGwire's acknowledgment of drug use, Selig reported only two positive steroid tests in 2009 and declared the steroid era "a thing of the past" (Schmidt 2010: 1).

The third issue is that of baseball's exemption from antitrust legislation that Bunning and others have often threatened to try to repeal. Supreme Court decisions first in 1922 and then in 1953 provided and reinforced MLB's exemption from competition. MLB thus has decision-making power over who owns teams and where they play. The exemption also aids the team owners in obtaining subsidies. Although individual teams are not tax exempt, MLB is. While Johnston (2007: 69) suggests that other sports leagues "are effectively exempted from most of the laws of business competition" the issue is not so clear-cut. For example in the NFL Raiders owner Al Davis successfully won a legal case that allowed him to move his team in the 1980s.

In January 2010 the Supreme Court heard a case brought by American Needle that had manufactured hats of NFL teams until the NFL sold an exclusive license to Reebok. The lower-level courts ruled against American Needle, but the NFL was hoping for a Supreme Court ruling that could be interpreted as a blanket antitrust exemption giving them advantages of a single corporate entity (Pearlstein 2009). One entity cannot be found guilty of forming a monopoly with itself to harm consumers (Barnes 2010). Such a broad ruling could have led to the NFL transferring all its broadcasts to its own network, killing free agency, dictating ticket prices, and enhancing subsidies for the building or renting of stadiums. The players' union is opposed to any such exemption. Late in May 2010 the Supreme Court unanimously ruled against the NFL in its request for broad antitrust immunity. Justice John Paul Stevens described the teams as "separate, profit-maximizing entities" rather than a single entity (Liptak and Belson 2010). The specific case involving American Needle was referred back to the lower courts.

Family Law

Drawing on English common law tradition, a marriage is a contract or voluntary agreement between a man and a woman. Similar to education, many of the laws regulating marriage are state laws. For example, many states require a couple to have a marriage license issued by a county clerk or clerk of the court before they can marry. Some states have stopped requiring blood tests,

Scoreboard at AT&T Park San Francisco, illustrating corporate advertising during San Francisco Giants versus Los Angeles Dodgers game, August 10, 2009

Credit: Photo by Lisa K. Waldner

but some require tests for venereal disease. Civil ceremonies are usually performed by judges, whereas religious services are frequently conducted by pastors or other religious leaders. All states limit people to one spouse at a time. Most states require the two partners to be of the opposite sex ("Marriage" n.d.).

If a person is getting married again, he or she needs to be legally released from the previous marriage through death of the spouse, annulment, or divorce before he or she can marry ("Marriage" n.d.). States permit divorces in order to serve the public good, but individuals do not have a constitutional or legal right to divorce. Before laws were passed to promote more equalized property allocation, the wage-earning spouse, typically a male, received a more favored property distribution. Now the courts tend to recognize marital property acquired during the marriage and separate property acquired before the marriage that did not change substantially in value. The judge typically tries to divide the assets equitably, which may not be equally. The court may or may not grant alimony in a divorce. If children are involved, there may be child support ("Divorce" n.d.).

When children are involved in divorces, child custody becomes an issue as the court tries to decide "the best interests of the child," which can be quite complex. Joint legal custody gives parents equal rights in decision making regarding the child. If only one parent has custody, the other parent receives visitation rights unless that person is deemed harmful to the child(ren) ("Child Custody" n.d.).

Adoption occurs when an adult other than a child's biological parent becomes the guardian of the child and takes on the responsibilities of a parent. The Constitution does not provide a fundamental right to adopt. States have various policies regarding who may adopt. People who have physical or mental disabilities, criminal histories, or unstable employment, or who are gay or lesbian or single may be disqualified. There is an investigation of potential adopters followed by a report from the state adoption agency ("Adoption" n.d.).

All these laws help illustrate the roles of government, especially the states, in marriage and the family. We will now turn to the very controversial issue of gay marriage that clearly illustrates the importance of the national and state governments in defining who may or may not marry.

Same-Sex Marriage

In the United States and generally elsewhere, heterosexuality is more valued and accorded higher status than is homosexuality, and in some places homosexuality is viewed as an aberration and those who are gay or lesbian are stigmatized. One manifestation of the dominance of heterosexism is the political controversy centered on gay marriage (Hurst 2010). Masci (2009a) suggests that since the 1960s some gay Americans have been advocating the right to marry or have formalized legal arrangements, but same-sex marriage has developed as a national issue in the last twenty years. An important spark for the debate was in 1993 when the Hawaii Supreme Court ruled that the state legislature needed to demonstrate a compelling reason for banning same-sex marriage. The Hawaii legislature then passed a bill in 1994 that marriage was intended for "man–woman units" capable of procreation (Masci 2009a).

Legislatures in more than forty states followed, passing acts that defined marriage strictly as a union between a man and a woman. Although a few of these laws have been struck down, most are still in effect. In 1996 President Clinton signed a federal Defense of Marriage Act (DOMA). Congressional sponsors stated the law was devised "to define and protect the institution of marriage" and "to make explicit what has been understood under federal law for over 200 years; that a marriage is the legal union of a man and a woman as husband and wife" (Hurst 2010: 1361). Supporters of the DOMA attempted to frame the legislation in moral terms as preserving traditional family values, as they realized most people perceive homosexuality as immoral. The DOMA declares that no state has to recognize a same-sex union from another state as legal. Benefits such as family medical leave and Social Security (SS) were not allowed for gay couples. Indeed the General Accounting Office (1997) identified 1,138 federal rights associated with marriage. SS survivor benefits, veterans' benefits, estate taxes, family leave, living together in nursing homes, and so on are all benefits associated with marital status (Hurst 2010; Peplau and Fingerhut 2007).

In 2003 the highest court in Massachusetts ruled that same-sex marriages were guaranteed by the state's constitution. The G. W. Bush administration pushed for a U.S. Constitutional amendment prohibiting same-sex marriage across the country. However, in both 2004 and 2006 the proposed amendment did not receive the requisite two-thirds majority in both houses of Congress (Hurst 2010; Masci 2009a).

President Obama has stated that as a Christian he opposes same-sex marriage but also that he is a "fierce advocate of equality" for gays. Obama has declared his support for a legislative repeal of the DOMA ("Same-Sex Marriage, Civil Unions, and Domestic Partnerships" 2009). In June 2009 Obama extended certain benefits to domestic partners of federal workers, such as long-term care insurance; however, he said under current federal law same-sex couples

A gay couple is being married in a religious ceremony. In many states such marriages are not recognized or legal.

Credit: © Queerstock, Inc./Alamy

cannot be provided the full range of benefits that heterosexual couples enjoy. He called on Congress to enact legislation regarding this. While some gay rights supporters welcomed the changes, other activists felt these were very small steps and were frustrated by the lack of progress (Stone 2009).

Peplau and Fingerhut (2007) reviewed the literature on same-sex couples, noting that with the increasing visibility of same-sex couples, more studies are conducted. Still, research is hampered as some gays and lesbians are reluctant to indicate their sexual orientation, and there is a lack of public records on same-sex marriages and divorce. The 2000 U.S. Census identified about 600,000 same-sex couples living together.

In 2009, five states, four in New England (Massachusetts, Connecticut, Vermont, and New Hampshire) and one in the Midwest (Iowa), allowed gay marriage. Because Iowa is the only state not on the East Coast, gays from other states, especially in the Midwest, have married in Iowa. In the first three months after same-sex marriages were initiated, approximately 45 percent of the 676 known gay marriages were for out-of-state couples (Olson 2009). From 2001 to mid-2009 seven countries (the Netherlands, Belgium, Spain, Canada, South Africa, Norway, and Sweden) have legalized gay marriage (Masci 2009a).

PUBLIC OPINION ON SAME-SEX MARRIAGE   Loftus (2001) found that people surveyed are likely to support civil liberties of gays and lesbians but at the same time perceive homosexuality as immoral. Positive attitudes toward gays and lesbians tended to increase somewhat from 1973 to 1998, although the pattern was not entirely consistent. According to Peplau and Fingerhut (2007), a Kaiser Family Foundation survey found more than two-thirds of Americans favor provisions such as SS, health insurance, and inheritance rights for same-sex couples. Also, 74 percent of lesbians and gay men would like to marry in the future. Same-sex couples engage in commitment ceremonies, and a growing number of employers offer domestic partner benefits to same-sex partners.

The Pew Center surveys of attitudes toward same-sex marriage since 1996 have consistently found more people opposed to same-sex marriage than supporting it. The percentage opposed has ranged from 65 to 49 percent while support for same-sex marriage has ranged from 27 to 39 percent. In the April 2009 survey 54 percent opposed same-sex marriage while 35 percent supported it (Masci 2009b). Opinions about same-sex marriage are associated with political party identification and other political attitudes. Republicans (77 percent) are much more likely than Democrats (41 percent) to oppose same-sex marriage. Another Pew Center survey of 2,900 adults in 2008 (before the presidential election) found that more people who indicated they were McCain voters than Obama voters saw gay marriage (38 to 22 percent) and moral values (71 to 55 percent) as very important to their vote (Pew Forum on Religion & Public Life and Pew Research Center for the People & the Press 2008).

Figure 5.1 shows the results of a 2009 survey in some detail. Republicans, older people, those who attend religious services at least once a week, and white evangelical Protestants are most likely to oppose gay marriage. As Figure 5.2 shows, the 2009 survey reported that a slight majority of those surveyed favor civil unions (54 percent versus 35 percent, with 11 percent "don't know"), but followed the same patterns as those opposed to gay marriage (Masci 2009b).

PRO AND CON ARGUMENTS   Often supporters of same-sex marriage frame their argument by stating that marriage should be a civil right for all, whereas those who oppose it often see same-sex marriage as a religious and/or morality issue (Hurst 2010). The latter point out that various religions, including Christianity and Islam, condemn homosexual relationships and that the homosexual lifestyle is immoral (Hurst 2010; White 2009). Those who advance the civil rights argument have sometimes compared same-sex marriage to the Civil Rights Movement's struggles for racial equality in the 1960s. Opponents, though, tend to argue that homosexuality is a choice, unlike one's race, but the scientific literature, while not conclusive, suggests that one's sexual orientation may be determined before birth or shortly thereafter (White 2009).

In the 2004 election campaign, President G. W. Bush was quoted as stating, "The union of a man and a woman is the most enduring human institution, honored and encouraged in all cultures and by every religious faith." Those who oppose same-sex marriage believe that marriage traditionally has been and should continue to be a committed relationship between a man and a woman. They feel changing marriage would greatly contribute to the erosion of the institution of marriage, which is already threatened by the high divorce rate (White 2009). Sprigg (2009), for example, claims same-sex relationships are not by definition eligible for marriage because marriage is the union of a man and a woman. Others have argued a type of slippery-slope approach, suggesting if same-sex marriage is allowed, polygamy, incest, and even bestiality could follow (Rimmerman 2008). Hurst (2010: 135) summarizes part of the argument of those opposing same-sex marriage: "It is feared that unless gays and lesbians are held in check, traditional

Views on Gay Marriage

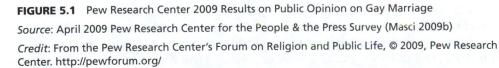

	% Favor	% Oppose	% Don't know
Total	35	54	11
Republican	17	77	7
Democrat	50	41	8
Independent	34	55	12
Age			
18–29	43	45	12
30–49	38	51	11
50–64	29	61	10
65+	24	64	12
Attend church...			
At least weekly	21	69	10
Less than weekly	43	45	12
Total Protestant	24	67	10
White evangelical	13	81	6
White mainline	33	55	12
Black Protestant	30	56	14
Total Catholic	39	45	16
White non-Hispanic	42	46	11
Unaffiliated	67	25	8

FIGURE 5.1 Pew Research Center 2009 Results on Public Opinion on Gay Marriage

Source: April 2009 Pew Research Center for the People & the Press Survey (Masci 2009b)

Credit: From the Pew Research Center's Forum on Religion and Public Life, © 2009, Pew Research Center. http://pewforum.org/

morality and family structure as foundations of our society will become contaminated and seriously weakened."

Negative stereotypes of gays and lesbians, although not supported by the empirical social science literature, include the beliefs that gays are more likely than heterosexuals to be serial predators of children or that children will be damaged or be pushed into homosexuality (Hurst 2010).

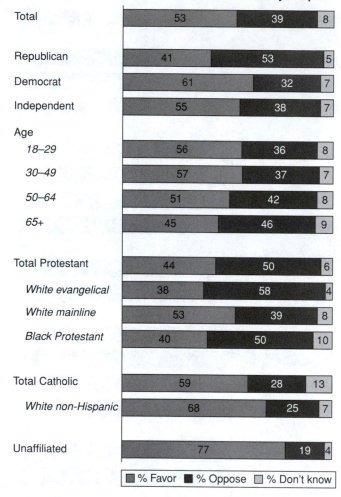

FIGURE 5.2 Pew Research Center 2009 Results on Public Opinion on Civil Unions

Source: April 2009 Pew Research Center for the People & the Press Survey (Masci 2009b)

Credit: From the Pew Research Center's Forum on Religion and Public Life, © 2009, Pew Research Center. http://pewforum.org/

Former U.S. Senator Rich Santorum (R-Penn.) argues how popular culture and the media condemn those like him who oppose same-sex marriage: "We know that the American public doesn't approve of same-sex marriage, but they are uncomfortable about it because, again, the public perception is if you feel that way, you're a bigot or a hater" ("An Argument against Same-Sex Marriage: An Interview with Rick Santorum" 2008).

Part of the argument for same-sex marriage is a practical one based on the substantial economic advantages that are associated with legal marriage, including items noted previously such as joint filing of tax returns, surviving spouse SS benefits, and health insurance. Another supportive argument is that in a truly democratic society there should be equality for all citizens. Also there may be tremendous psychological benefits, including increased self-esteem, from achieving the right to marry. Some argue that gaining this right could benefit both the lesbian and gay communities and society in general by enhancing the stability of gay relationships and encouraging monogamy (Rimmerman 2008).

A study of 288 gays and lesbians sheds some light on possible advantages and disadvantages of same-sex marriage. Almost all of those surveyed thought legalization of same-sex marriage would be an indicator of first-class citizenship, illustrating fairness and equal rights (Peplau and Fingerhut 2007). From their point of view the positive side would also include the following:

1. Marriage could strengthen their relationships, helping couples feel closer.
2. It would also create structural obstacles to dissolving a relationship, possibly encouraging couples to work harder to improve their relationships.
3. Marriage could reduce the strains that same-sex couples experience by increasing the couples' legal rights, reducing societal prejudice, and diminishing any internalized homophobia.

The gays and lesbians surveyed also expressed possible disadvantages, including the idea that legalization might pressure gays to get married or create status hierarchies that would value marriage and stigmatize those who do not marry. In addition some feared that legalization of same-sex marriage could result in pressures to assimilate and thus follow heterosexual family norms that could alter the special and unique features of the gay–lesbian community (Peplau and Fingerhut 2007).

SAME-SEX FAMILIES AND CHILDREN   One important focus of the same-sex marriage debate has been on the welfare of children. While certainly some same-sex couples who would marry (if same-sex marriage were legalized) would not have children, some would, using adoption, artificial insemination, surrogacy, sperm donation, and so on. Even without legal marriage, these practices are used, and many children who live with same-sex parents were born within heterosexual marriages that ended in divorce or separation. For some opponents of same-sex marriage, the fact that same-sex couples cannot reproduce biological children eliminates same-sex couples from the definition of marriage and thus these opponents tend to believe that same-sex relationships do not contribute to society. However, supporters of same-sex marriage argue that some heterosexual couples voluntarily remain childless, whereas others may be sterile. Still, though, they are married (Friedman 2006).

Individual states determine the rules for adoption. As of mid-2009, twenty-two states allowed gays or lesbians to adopt, depending on other rules governing adoption. Eighteen of those twenty-two states, though, allow gay and lesbian adoption only in certain parts of the state. Those who support same-sex marriage likely believe children will do well in families with one or more gay or lesbian parent. If a couple has a child through artificial insemination, the birth parent is the legal guardian. Some states, though, allow second-parent adoption where the legal guardian retains custody, but the other person gains legal rights as well. Those who oppose gay and lesbian adoption disapprove of the gay and lesbian lifestyle and thus question whether gays and lesbians would make excellent parents. Some are concerned that children with gay or lesbian parents will experience ridicule and harassment (Belge n.d.). In 2004 the American Psychological Association's (APA) Council of Representatives adopted a resolution that stated, "The APA opposes any discrimination based on sexual orientation in matters of adoption, child custody and visitation, foster care, and reproductive health services" (2009[2004]: 195). The council concluded that social science research has not supported any of the negative stereotypes that promote concerns about children of lesbian and gay parents (APA 2009[2004]). Public opinion on the issue of gay and lesbian adoption is quite divided and tends to follow a pattern similar to that on same-sex marriage.

Stacey and Biblarz (2001) point out that social scientists have in part tended to emphasize a no-differences approach in comparing children with lesbian or gay parents with children having heterosexual parents. Researchers are politically sensitive to the fact that those who oppose lesbian and gay parental rights are looking for evidence that children with lesbian or gay parents are at greater risk for negative outcomes. The authors reviewed twenty-one psychological studies that generally reported no or few differences in parenting or child outcomes. Among the few differences, they found that children, especially daughters of lesbian parents, were less likely to conform to sex-typed cultural norms. For boys the relationship was quite complex because on some measures sons of lesbian parents were less traditional in masculine behavior but on others they showed gender conformity. One study found a moderate level of parent-to-child transmission of sexual orientation. Regarding mental health, the children of lesbian mothers tend to do at least as well as children of heterosexual members and sometimes better.

In addition, children with lesbian or gay parents seem more open to homoerotic relationships and are less traditionally gender-typed. Stacey and Biblarz (2001: 178) point out the possible political effects of such findings:

> We recognize the political dangers of pointing out that recent studies indicate that a higher proportion of children with [lesbian or gay] parents are themselves apt to engage in homosexual activity. In a homophobic world anti-gay forces deploy such results to deny parents custody of their own children and to fuel backlash movements opposed to gay rights. . . . It is neither intellectually honest nor politically wise to base a claim for justice on grounds that may prove falsifiable empirically. Moreover, the case for granting equal rights to nonheterosexual parents should not require finding their children to be identical to those reared by heterosexuals. Nor should it require finding that such children do not encounter distinctive challenges or risks, especially when these derive from social prejudice.

Not surprisingly, Sprigg (2009), who is against adoption by gays and lesbians, cites certain findings of Stacey and Biblarz as he argues that children raised by homosexual couples are different from other children. Dailey (2009) argues that few homosexual relationships actually include children and most homosexual relationships are not really committed and stable. He maintains that engaging in a social experiment redefining marriage and family would do great harm to children "by denying them both a mother and a father in a committed marriage" (201).

It is likely that the political debate on same-sex marriage and gay and lesbian adoption within the individual states and at the national level will continue to be contentious for some time. Jonathan Rauch, an openly gay advocate, argues that same-sex marriage would have positive unifying effects for society:

> Far from hastening the social decline of marriage, same-sex marriage shores up the key values and commitments on which couples and families and society depend. Far from dividing America and weakening communities, same-sex marriage, if properly implemented, can make the country both better unified and truer to its ideals. (Rauch, quoted in White 2009: 122–123)

For the time being though, the courts, legislatures, and the public seem deeply divided and unity on the issue in the short run seems unlikely. We now turn to health care, another divisive issue that affects people's everyday lives.

HEALTH CARE

Approximately 46 million people in the United States do not have health care insurance (Begley 2009) and others are underinsured. Many argue that health care costs have spiraled out of control. Indeed on February 23, 2009, President Obama referred to the rising cost of health care as "the single most pressing fiscal challenge we face by far" ("History: Presidential Statements Barack H. Obama—2009" 2009). According to the National Coalition on Health Care, the typical American family has seen their premiums for employer-sponsored coverage doubled from $5,791 in 1999 to $12,680 in 2008 when figures are adjusted for inflation ("Plan Gives Insurance Firms Time to Change" 2009: 3A). Consumer Reports National Research Center survey of January 2009 found almost 70 percent of 2,004 adults who regularly took prescription drugs followed certain dangerous strategies often to reduce their health care costs. For example 23 percent put off a doctor's visit, 18 percent put off a procedure, and 16 percent skipped filling a prescription ("Dangerous Strategies for Saving Health-Care Dollars" 2009: 1).

Turner (2004) applies Mills' (1959) sociological imagination framework to medical care by trying to connect individuals' personal experiences of illness to a larger frame of issues related to political economy, health inequality, and the power of the medical elites in society. He argues, "The private narratives of illness tell a powerful story about the public issues of wealth, power, and status" (Turner 2004: 313). It is also crucial to understand that the autonomy of the medical profession is "owed to its relationship to the sovereign state from which it is not ultimately autonomous" (Freidson 1970: 24).

Theoretical Frameworks

PLURALIST   Both the pluralist and elite frameworks consider a similar list of organizations as relevant for health care issues although they interpret their roles somewhat differently. These include the American Medical Association (AMA), a major professional society and lobbying group that represents physicians; the pharmaceutical companies that manufacture drugs; the insurance companies; manufacturers of medical devices; profit and nonprofit hospitals; health maintenance organizations; and patient advocate groups. For pluralists these represent interest groups that lobby to influence policy. Cunningham and Cunningham (1997: 142) describe the passage of Medicare in the mid-1960s as "the cumulative product of what Odin Anderson called 'the riotously pluralistic policy-making system of the United States.'"

ELITE/MANAGERIAL   Although somewhat simplistic, it can be claimed that physicians represent part of the elite and patients the masses. Brint (1994: 59) notes the scientific training of doctors and how doctors are taught to objectify their patients to a much greater degree than are other human services professionals. While discussing some astute statements of his patients, Toth (2007: 148) commented, "Patients are indeed smarter than we often give them credit for." This statement seems to suggest that many doctors do not view their patients as particularly intelligent. Another physician, Groopman (2007: 25) acknowledged that while patients often recognize a physician's negativity, they don't understand how it affects their medical care. "Rather, they often blame themselves for complaining and taxing the doctor's patience." The power relationship between doctor and patient that the state sanctions can thus at times end up harming patients. Cockerham (2007: 249–250) suggests that the "professional dominance" of the doctor in general is declining due to (1) increasing government regulation, (2) managed care, (3) doctors being hired as employees by corporations and thus losing some of their autonomy as these companies control more of the medical marketplace, and (4) patients educating themselves as they desire more "consumer-oriented health care" and wish to participate in the decision-making process.

In 1980, physician Relman (2007: 28) used the term *new medical–industrial complex* to call attention to the increasingly commercialized face of U.S. medicine. Wilensky (2009) is concerned about the high administrative costs of the medical–industrial complex and the chaos resulting from the complicated combination of private and public regulations of the health care system. He identifies insurance companies as the dominant political barrier to national health insurance.

CLASS   According to class analysis, the medical profession, insurance companies, and drug companies struggle to maintain and/or expand their power, financial resources, and profit by influencing and possibly decreasing government regulation. Drawing on the *Fortune* 1000 reports, in 2007 health groups earned $71 billion. There has been a rapid increase in the annual profits of the top fifteen health insurance companies from $3.5 billion to $15 billion from 2000 to 2007. Pharmaceuticals and medical equipment were third and fourth on the list of fifty-two industries in terms of profits as a share of revenue (Goldhill 2009). Lupton (1994) maintains that good health includes having access to both material and nonmaterial resources that help sustain or promote life. Under capitalism, a primary focus of health care is to make sure workers and consumers are healthy enough to contribute to the capitalist system. Health care is viewed "as a commodity in which the seeking of profit is a major influencing factor" (9).

POSTMODERN   Foucault argues, "Power is embodied in the day-to-day practices of the medical profession within the clinic" (Turner 1997: xi–xii). Doctors in clinics and hospitals tightly control information and knowledge about medicine and their patients. The patient is expected to follow the knowledgeable doctor's recommendations. From the postmodernists' point of view, knowledge is a form of power that is not always used to benefit patients or the general public (Kendall 2007).

RATIONAL CHOICE   The rational choice framework embraces the idea of rationality and the value of scientific research and study. Rational choice theory emphasizes how doctors use their scientific knowledge to calculate risks in the management of diseases and decide on treatments. This knowledge gives them power. The concept of the marketplace can be applied to health care. For example, patients (or buyers) ideally make rational choices based on the medical information received, their ability to compare alternative doctors (or sellers), and their evaluation of the price and quality of medical care in a competitive environment.

INSTITUTIONALIST   Frenk and Durán-Arenas (1993: 29) point out that the state, the medical profession, and bureaucratic organizations form a complex triangle of relationships that need to be studied. The state plays an important role in licensing doctors and in malpractice suits. The medical profession gains a grant of monopoly from the state as only members of the profession can treat patients, order certain medical tests, and write prescriptions (Starr 1982). Physicians interact not only with complex bureaucracies such as hospitals, clinics, drug companies, and insurance agencies but also with federal agencies such as the Food and Drug Administration and the National Institute of Health. Large health care conglomerates provide employment, offices, equipment, hospital privileges, and possibly salary guarantees to physicians. Working for the corporation reduces the doctors' autonomy and shapes their pace and routines of work. The corporate culture values maximizing profits, offering efficient services, and controlling costs. Such changes modify the doctor–patient relationship (Cockerham 2004).

U.S. Health Care Uniqueness

Wilensky (2009) documents how the United States' health care system is distinct from that of other rich democracies. Other rich democracies have centralized budget control using compulsory contributions from employers and individuals and/or government revenues to provide national heath care. They also allow private purchase of health services to supplement the government health care programs. In contrast, the United States lacks national health insurance and has a very large private sector involved in health care and a uniquely expensive arrangement based in part on a poor cost-benefit ratio with the United States paying a much larger percentage of its gross domestic product (GDP) for health care than other countries.

Wilensky (2009) examined three possible reasons for the United States' uniqueness. The first is that its public policy has historically focused more on technologically intensive health care rather than raising the number of people who have access to that health care. According to Wilensky the second and most important reason is the U.S. government's structure, including federalism, that has resulted in a decentralized and fragmented system. This includes electoral laws that make it difficult for third parties to exist, let alone push for health care reform, and also the unique policy of the Senate that allows a political party with minority support of 41 percent to filibuster an issue so that it cannot be voted upon. For example, in December 2009 Democrats and two independent senators were able to break a filibuster and pass health care legislation. While Congress was attempting to find compromises between the health care bills passed in the Senate and House, Republicans gained a forty-first Senate seat in a special election in Massachusetts to replace the late Edward M. Kennedy. This meant that if all Republicans acted together, they could possibly filibuster in the Senate to prevent a new vote on any compromise legislation on health care. To avoid the filibuster in the Senate in 2010, there was a reconciliation process where the House accepted the Senate version of the health care bill, and later some modifications were made.

Wilensky is more critical of the third explanation advanced by some for the uniqueness of health care in the United States. That explanation points to American culture and values such as free enterprise, individualism, and concern about too much government involvement in society. Mechanic (2006: 22) believes that there are two currently competing worldviews about health care reform that can be identified with the two major political parties. The Republican Party and its supporters tend to see health care as similar to other commodities or products and services, best handled in the competitive marketplace with limited regulation. They do not see health care as a right and they support private insurance companies, fee-for-service medicine, and cost sharing that supposedly would foster prudent decision making in using the health care system. The Democratic Party and its supporters are more likely to see health care as an individual right and a public service instead of a commodity like many goods and services. They believe health care service does not do well in the profit-oriented marketplace with limited regulations and favor a public option or national health care.

At the individual level, health care reform seems to evoke powerful emotions including fear, anger, and hate so "people are unable to balance their emotional reactions with rational ones" (Begley 2009: 43). Begley further believes that such situations are not helped when political figures express their concerns about end-of-life counseling that some have labeled *death panels.* Town hall meetings and tea parties helped fuel populist emotions including one person's demand to "keep your government hands off my Medicare" (43). The reality is that Medicare is a government program and misinformation complicates attempts at reform.

In a historic vote in March 2010 the House of Representatives supported a health care bill that had been passed by the Senate on Christmas Eve 2009. No Republican supported the legislation that was estimated to help 24 to 30 million people without health insurance to afford such insurance ("Health Care Reform" 2010; Murray and Montgomery 2010). According to the legislation, people who refuse to buy insurance will face fines. Insurance companies will not be able to impose lifetime limits on patient benefits or drop people who develop major illnesses. The Medicare program will be changed ideally to provide care at a reduced cost but more efficiently. Possibly 16 million people will be added to the Medicaid rolls and government could help subsidize private coverage for many people in the lower and middle classes. The Congressional Budget Office estimated the new law would cost $938 billion over the next ten years but this would result in decreasing the federal budget by $138 billion over the same period ("Health Care Reform" 2010). President Obama signed the bill a couple of days after the House had passed it. This was followed by the passage of several modifications of the bill that had been agreed upon earlier. As previously noted, the passage of the legislation involved a reconciliation process because the Democrats lacked a sixtieth vote to break a potential Senate filibuster.

How much of a role should and will the government play in health care is likely be an ongoing discussion for some time in Congress and throughout the country. Debates will likely focus on the government's role in promoting social justice by working toward equal access to health care and whether health care is a right and if so whether that right should be extended to undocumented workers. Another major focus will center around the issue of cost containment including the failure of the bill to grant the Medicare program the right to negotiate with pharmaceutical companies to reduce the costs of drugs for those eligible for Medicare. Attorney generals in various states are also challenging the constitutionality of the health care legislation.

CIVIL LIBERTIES

Provisions and guarantees for civil liberties characterize democratic societies. Although in the abstract people give support to democratic values, they often may not "translate abstract principles into democratic patterns of behavior" (Dye and Zeigler 1972: 131). There is a rather long history of debate surrounding civil liberties. Difficulties exist when conflict may be perceived between the demands for national security and for civil liberties or between possibly protecting society and the rights of the individual. Farber (2008: 1–2) defines civil liberties as including "issues relating to freedom of expression, due process, restrictions on government surveillance, and the discrimination against minority groups" and "national security as involving a perceived violent threat that implicates either the stability of the government (subversion), the general safety of large numbers of members of society, or the government's ability to engage successfully in armed conflicts."

Law professor Geoffrey R. Stone wants a balance between civil liberties and security. He argues "our nation needs citizens who have the wisdom to know excess when they see it and the courage to stand for liberty when it is imperiled" (Ojeda 2004: 15). In examining the relationship between liberty and security, Holmes (2008) argues it is important to distinguish between private or individual liberty and public liberty of citizens who examine, criticize, and work to change policy and leaders. Further he believes, "That we may increase our security by giving up your privacy makes at least some sense. What makes no sense at all is the government's implicit boast that it will do a better job of protecting national security if it is never criticized or forced to give an informed audience plausible reasons for its actions" (216).

It can be argued that freedom of expression—freedom of speech, press, association, assembly, or petition—forms the cornerstone for civil liberties and is essential to maintain a free society (American Civil Liberties Union [ACLU] 2004[1997]). This commitment to freedom of expression has been sorely tested since the adoption of the Bill of Rights, including the First Amendment guaranteeing freedom of expression. Indeed the Constitution was drafted without the Bill of Rights. Particularly in times of "national stress, like war abroad or social upheaval at home, people exercising their First Amendment rights have been censored, fined, even jailed" (30).

People with unpopular views have been repressed at numerous times. In a dissenting opinion in *Abrams v. U.S.*, Supreme Court Justices Oliver Wendell Holmes and Louis D. Brandeis argued that speech should be punished only if it presents "a clear and present danger" of imminent harm. Ultimately this was accepted as the standard. Defining clear and eminent danger may be quite difficult, however. There are important exceptions to the rules including libel, defamation, words of conspiracy, and so forth (Delgado 2004).

Students may be wondering why in the politics of everyday life civil liberties are discussed, because many people haven't directly felt that their civil liberties are being threatened. That doesn't mean it won't happen or that other liberties valued by students won't be threatened. The frequently cited[1] lines from Martin Niemöller, a German Protestant pastor, help explain the importance of civil liberties for all. During the time of the Nazis in Germany he stated that the Nazis came for various groups such as the Jews, the Communists, the labor leaders, and the socialists and he did not object. Then when they came for him, no one remained who could protest ("Niemöller, Martin" n.d.). Put simply, if some of us may be threatened, others may be in the future. Even if not threatened, maintaining democratic values is important.

Gerry Spence, the lawyer for Randy Weaver in the controversial Ruby Ridge case, tries to make it clear how civil liberties issues involve all of us when he states: "When the rights of our enemies have been wrested from them, our own rights are lost as well, for the same rights serve both citizen and criminal" (1995: 7). Textbox 5.2 discusses the Ruby Ridge case in greater detail.

TEXTBOX 5.2

Civil Liberties and Ruby Ridge: Any Heroes? Any Costs?

A little-known example of a civil liberties dispute is a shootout frequently labeled the "Ruby Ridge" tragedy. Among those on law enforcement's side were the U.S. Marshal Service, the FBI, and a hostage rescue team that was called in. The challengers included Randy Weaver, his wife Vicki, and their children as well as Kevin Harris. U.S. Marshal Degan, Sammy Weaver, the fourteen-year-old son of Randy and Vicki Weaver, Vicki Weaver herself, and a family dog were killed. The details include the following:

Randy and Vicki Weaver were considered by law enforcement to be white supremacists. Randy Weaver accepted that they were white separatists based on his interpretation of the Bible that the races should be separate. The Weavers attended some events at Aryan Nations (AN) but were never formal members. In 1990 federal agents asked Weaver to spy on AN and other movement supporters. Previously one of the informants had enticed him to sell sawed-off shotguns. Government officials suggested that law enforcement would go easy on him for having sold sawed-off shot guns if he agreed to become an informant. Weaver refused and through a ruse was caught by government officials when he left his isolated cabin. He faced a magistrate who incorrectly told him if convicted he could possibly lose his land that he was putting up for bail. Weaver then decided to hole up and refuse to come down from his mountain cabin. On August 21, 1992, a surveillance mission watching him and the cabin was "bungled" (Miller 1992: A6). Supposedly the marshals got too close to the cabin, and a family dog caught their scent and chased after the marshals. Probably wondering what was bothering the dog, Randy Weaver went on one path and his son Sammy and family friend Kevin Harris went on another. The dog, Sammy, and Kevin caught up with the marshals. A shootout ensued and U.S. Marshal Degan, Sammy Weaver (shot in the back), and the dog died. Once this incident occurred, the FBI took over the investigation and brought in the hostage rescue team, which surrounded the cabin. Not knowing they were surrounded since no one had asked them to surrender, Randy, his oldest daughter, and Kevin Harris left the cabin and were fired

(Continued)

upon. Randy and Kevin were wounded and Vicki was killed opening the door for the retreating individuals. Several days later the Weavers and Harris surrendered. Several investigations of the event occurred. Senator Charles Grassley (R-Iowa) criticized the culture of law enforcement finding fault with the new "swashbucklers" who preferred hostile solutions over negotiations stating: "At Ruby Ridge this culture led to a military buildup that would have impressed Saddam Hussein" (Subcommittee on Terrorism 1997: 10–11). In this case it is important to note that in federal court Randy Weaver was convicted only of failure to appear in court and having committed a crime (carrying a gun) while on pretrial release. Kevin Harris was not convicted of anything.

There are many ways to describe a situation according to Zald (1996: 269), who discusses how different sides take part in a competitive process to define the situation. Goffman (1974: 21) used the idea of framing as "schemata of interpretation" that help people "locate, perceive, identify and label" grievances. Certain coercive actions by authorities can be seen as simply enforcing the law and doing what is needed to protect people in society while others may view it as oppression of those who disagree with the government. (For a detailed discussion of framing, see Chapter 8.) Gamson, Fireman, and Rytina (1982) examine a legitimating frame in which people do not question the authority of the person in charge and an injustice frame that suggests authority could indeed operate unfairly. Dobratz, Shanks-Meile, and Hallenbeck (2003) argue that what authorities did during the investigations of Ruby Ridge was to "yield ground" in order to maintain the legitimacy frame. As Gamson (1968: 114) has pointed out, "by giving a little at the right time, authorities may prevent later more important modifications."

The U.S. government settled two civil suits out of court regarding the deaths and woundings at Ruby Ridge. In the first, the three remaining Weaver children each received $1 million and Randy Weaver $100,000. Later Kevin Harris received $380,000. In neither case did the government admit any wrongdoing (Associated Press 2000; Dobratz et al. 2003). At the end of the second case, the U.S. Assistant Attorney General declared: "This settlement resolves this long-pending case in a way that is fair to the United States and all those involved."

The investigation by the Subcommittee on Terrorism (1997: 1105) concluded the marshals approached the Weaver residence too closely and unnecessarily made noises that risked a response without having any specific plan for retreat. Also, why the three people retreating to the cabin were fired upon was questioned. While two government reports did not challenge the "second shot" that went through Kevin Harris and killed Vicki Weaver, the Subcommittee on Terrorism believed the shot was indeed unconstitutional and inconsistent with the FBI's standard deadly force policy and the rules of engagement.

The subcommittee's investigation was done not only to discover what happened but to show that the government was interested in justice and accountability. "This country can tolerate mistakes made by people like Randy Weaver, but we cannot accept serious errors made by federal law enforcement agencies that needlessly result in human tragedy" (Subcommittee on Terrorism 1997: 1097). The report noted "a disturbing absence of leadership" from many law enforcement officials and "the unwillingness of some high ranking people in every agency to accept responsibility . . . . Accountability is essential to public confidence" (1097).

These government officials want to assure the American people that they were accountable and that government could be trusted. Gerry Spence (1995: 47), Randy Weaver's lawyer, stressed:

> The lesson of the Weaver trial must never become the vindication of Weaver's beliefs, but instead the need of all Americans freely to believe as they will without risk of persecution by a government or by a majority or by a power clique.

On the one hand, the investigation of the Senate Subcommittee on Terrorism and the out-of-court settlements may be viewed as a means to ensure us of government's accountability, encourage us to trust the government, and convince us of government's legitimacy. On the other hand, these events could lead us to question government's accountability, weaken our trust, and view elements of government as unjust or opposed to dissent.

Twenty-First Century: War on Terror

Activities by the government against terrorism in the twenty-first century have clearly been shaped by the terrorist attacks in 2001. On September 11, 2001, terrorists hijacked four airplanes and attacked the World Trade Center and the Pentagon. Thousands were killed and billions of dollars of damage resulted. Chapter 9 discusses terrorism and USA PATRIOT (The Uniting and Strengthening America by Providing Appropriate Tools Required to Intercept and Obstruct Terrorism) Act. Therefore here we will focus only on how general concerns of civil liberties were generated after calls for Congress to provide new powers to law enforcement to fight terrorism. President G. W. Bush declared war on terrorism, especially Al Qaeda, and U.S. troops moved into Afghanistan against the Taliban and later invaded Iraq. By mid-2002 the G. W. Bush administration was divided between those associated with Secretary of State Colin Powell, who stressed coalition building and democratic initiatives, and Secretary of Defense Donald Rumsfeld, who argued for the invasion of Iraq. Rumsfeld won out, which resulted in the invasion of Iraq in 2003.

There are arguments for and against sacrificing some civil liberties in order to win the war on terror. For example, those favoring limits on civil liberties argue that the costs of not obtaining important information are great because thousands could be killed and great economic damage inflicted. Using new ways of surveillance and data collection may mean terrorists will have to change their tactics and could help law enforcement better determine who the guilty people are. Also the checks-and-balances system should prevent the government from becoming too extreme in their tactics ("Should We Sacrifice Some of Our Civil Liberties to Help Fight the War on Terror?" n.d.).

Those who argue we should not sacrifice civil liberties believe that the loss of civil liberties would harm our definition of what it means to be an American and such a loss thus would allow the terrorists to be victorious. Such sacrifices would likely violate our Constitution and its associated rights. Racial profiling, which enhances discrimination, would likely be used. They maintain that once it is clear to others that the United States abuses the rights of people, more and more citizens of the United States and other societies would lose faith in the U.S. government or enhance their negative views of it. Once some civil liberties are sacrificed, future administrations may want further sacrifices ("Should We Sacrifice Some of Our Civil Liberties to Help Fight the War on Terror?" n.d.).

In January 2006, the Pew Research Center for the People & the Press conducted a public opinion survey among 1,503 adults about the trade-off between fighting terrorism and protecting civil liberties. Only one in three surveyed indicated they had a major concern that the government has "gone too far in restricting civil liberties." A plurality of 46 percent believed that the government has not gone far enough to protect the country. These results were similar in 2004 and 2005 (Pew Research Center for the People & the Press 2006a, 2006b).

On the one hand, the debate between civil liberties and national security has followed certain patterns over time. Farber (2008) identifies three key similarities between terrorism in the twenty-first century and earlier. They are as follows: (1) presidents have concentrated on national security with little attention to civil liberties; (2) partisan politics also characterizes the response of opponents to the president as they emphasize civil liberties; and (3) disputes over national identity are frequently part of the conflict between civil liberties and national security (20–21). Holmes summarizes the war on terror as being almost as serious as the greatest of America's earlier wars and considers the Bush administration to be "not more restrained than its predecessors" (2008: 213).

On the other hand, there are differences, such as the current war on terror doesn't have an endpoint and that contributes to the difficulty of assessing how serious the threat actually is and how successful the United States is in dealing with it (Holmes 2008: 214). Further, the Bush administration relied on unprecedented levels of secrecy and limited itself to input from a small group of advisors. In addition the courts have shown a greater sense of judicial independence than previously, and finally, technological advances have provided opponents greater means to communicate secretly, organize, and use techniques of large-scale destruction (Holmes 2008; Farber 2008).

RACE AND ETHNIC RELATIONS AND THE RACIAL STATE

Ezekiel (1995: xxxiv–xxxv), who has studied African Americans and white racists, points out that

> the issue of race is absolutely central to American life. Our lives are deeply affected by the conceptions that segments of our society have of one another and by the institutions that have grown up over the years to embody these conceptions. Nothing more befogs the critical relationships of wealth, power, poverty, and the common good than the racism of our culture.

Thus racism is often a part of our everyday life whether we are more or less privileged according to race. The state plays a key role in fostering or hindering the perpetuation of racism.

The Frameworks

In spite of the strong connections between race and politics, there has been little dialogue until recently between the literatures on the social construction of race and on political sociology (James and Redding 2005). Pluralists tend to support normative theories that explain prejudice and discrimination within a perspective of values and beliefs and how people conform to the dominant views about minorities (Marger 2009). The state can be seen as both shaping and being shaped by the norms or basic guidelines of behavior people seem to follow. The pluralist framework emphasizes that either the assimilation of various ethnic and racial groups, so they are absorbed into mainstream society, or the coexistence of a variety of distinct racial and ethnic groups in society is acceptable. Thus current policies by the state should facilitate either assimilation or racial or ethnic pluralism (Kendall 2007).

The elite/managerial framework would emphasize how state-enforced racial policies contribute to the development of race identities. Unlike the pluralist view that sees the state as a neutral arbiter, the state shapes racial inequalities that tend to especially advantage elites (James and Redding 2005). Redding, James, and Klugman (2005: 546) point out that "race has always involved politics as both cause *and* effect." Further, the authors argue, "the color conscious policies of the past created race inequalities that are durable" (546). In the United States, race-conscious and race-neutral policies have especially been encouraged by "white elites in political arenas" (564).

The class theoretical perspective emphasizes the importance of class in explaining what has happened to ethnic and racial minorities. Marxist theorists maintain that capitalists advocate the principle of "divide and rule," and ethnic or racial antagonisms provide an important basis on which to divide the working class in America and thus hamper the development of any class solidarity. As Marger (2009: 74) summarizes:

> Ethnic prejudice, therefore, is viewed as a means of sustaining a system of economic exploitation, the benefits of which accrue to the capitalist class. Though capitalists may not consciously conspire to create and maintain racist institutions, they nonetheless reap the benefits of racist practices and therefore do not seek to completely dismantle them.

By passing and enforcing the policies, the state can help maintain or restrict institutional discrimination, "the day-to-day practices of organizations and institutions that have a harmful impact on members of subordinate groups" (Kendall 2007: 261).

According to James and Redding, the political sociology of race has failed to develop a theory of the racial state despite the pressing need to consider "how variation in the political institutionalization of racial practices affects racial inequalities and identities" (2005: 193). Yet they are encouraged by an emerging literature that links the political process to identity construction and inequality. Before we consider the important issues of the racial state raised by Omi and Winant (1994) and James and Redding (2005), who review an emerging political sociology of race, it is important to note that not everyone agrees with the continuing significance of race and the racial state perpetuating racism. William Julius Wilson's (1978) *The Declining Significance of Race* does not deny the importance of racism but does emphasize class issues. D'Souza (2009[1995]: 182) points out that "racism undoubtedly exists, but it no longer has the power to thwart blacks or any other group in achieving their economic, political, and social aspirations." Steele (2009[2005]: 220), like Bill Cosby, stresses the idea "that greater responsibility is the only transforming power that can take blacks to true equality." Steele believes that the Hurricane Katrina example we will discuss shortly portrayed "a poverty that oppression could no longer entirely explain" (218).[2]

Explaining the Racial State

Omi and Winant (1994) see the state as comprising institutions or agencies that carry out policies that are supported by various rules and conditions. In addition, the state is embedded in the ongoing social relations in the society. According to them, every state institution is a racial institution although each state institution does not operate in the same way and may even be working at cross purposes: "Through *policies* which are explicitly or implicitly racial, state institutions organize and enforce the racial policies of everyday life. . . . They organize racial identities by means of education, family law, and the procedures for punishment, treatment, and surveillance" (83). For example, the state formulates and enforces discrimination policies including its agencies like the Department of Housing and Urban Development (HUD) that handles concerns about residential segregation.

Concerning the historical development of the racial state in the United States, Omi and Winant (1994: 81) argue that "for most of U.S. history, the state's main objective in its racial policy was repression and exclusion." The Naturalization Law of 1790 defined the eligibility of American citizenship as limited to only free "white" immigrants. In counting people for the purpose of representation and direct taxes, the Constitution defined nonfree persons (especially slaves) as three-fifths of a person. Omi and Winant (96) also argue that "race is not only a matter of politics, economics, or culture, but of all these 'levels' of lived experiences simultaneously" so it is a social phenomenon affecting a variety of aspects including individual identity, family, community, and the state. The 1950s and 1960s marked major transformations in racial identity and the racial state in the civil rights era (97). Major civil rights laws were passed in the 1960s including the Civil Rights Act of 1964 and the Voting Rights Act of 1965 that resulted in a huge increase in black voter registration.

James and Redding (2005) take an interesting and different position than Omi and Winant, specifying that a state is considered a racial state only if it uses race as a criterion for the enforcement of state policies. James and Redding are explicit in maintaining that a racial state designation is not defined by policy outcome, and point out that their definition differs from past conceptualizations like Omi and Winant's. James and Redding (187) critique Omi and Winant's stance that states are racial "because all states have effects on racial inequalities" in part because such views provide no understanding of how states create racial inequalities or identities or the variations between "racist" and "race-neutral" states.

Color-Blind Policies

Despite their criticisms, James and Redding praise Omi and Winant for illuminating "how states in racially divided societies produce racially unequal effects whether the state policy being enforced is explicitly racial or not" and note that "color-blind policies often create, maintain, or exacerbate racial inequalities" (2005: 194). Because color-blind policies ignore the effects of past discrimination thereby safeguarding white privilege (Bonilla-Silva et al. 2003), color-blind policies are racist. State practices are influenced by citizen attitudes and those occupying positions of power. For example, one of the themes of color-blind racism is *abstract liberalism,* which refers to those who in principle support equal opportunity but are not supportive of governmental programs like affirmative action to help eliminate racial disadvantage (Bonilla-Silva et al. 2003).

Racial Identity and Equality

Individuals perceive racial identities and act on them in both exclusionary (Jim Crow segregation) and inclusionary (affirmative action) ways. In the case of a state that has a policy of equal opportunity, there is a mechanism for policy enforcement such as the U.S. Equal Employment Opportunity Commission (EEOC). The EEOC is a federal agency charged with enforcing fair employment laws and investigating claims of discrimination. If race discrimination did not occur, the state would not need an EEOC. This view takes racial categories and the impact of those categories on individuals as something that the state responds to rather than seeing the state as a cause of racial categories. While the former is certainly true, James and Redding (2005) argue that the role of the state in shaping racial identities also bears scrutiny. In other words, state policies should be viewed not just as an effect of racial identity and inequality but also as a cause. Using the U.S. Census as an example, they argue that developing and labeling certain racial categories is significant because it attributes a certain characteristic to some individuals and further it enhances the likelihood that such people will then identify themselves as belonging to that group, which has implications for political mobilization as well as the application of practices that either enable or disable racial inequality.

While the state has a powerful role in the creation and maintenance of racial categories, groups also influence the state. Changes to the 2000 census, including a failed attempt to add a multiracial category, came from those who resisted official classifications and did not see themselves simply as "white" or "Asian" or "black." James and Redding conclude that institutional arrangements matter, and theorizing about the relationship between state making and race making should guard against both dismissing the importance of race and overemphasizing it to the detriment of other factors, including gender and social class.

Environmental and Natural Disasters

It may seem somewhat strange to discuss the racial state in the context of environmental hazards and natural disasters because it is difficult to limit environmental hazards and impossible to prevent natural disasters in our complex society. However, we argue that certain patterns emerge that involve various levels of the racial state. In a symposium on natural disasters including environmental toxins, Tierney (2006) used a vulnerability science approach to study natural disasters and argued that population vulnerability, including proximity to disaster, impacts race and ethnicity, one of three key factors that explain why people in a particular area are more likely to experience disasters than people in other areas.

Bullard (2000) examines environmental racism and argues that whites benefit more from the actions of polluting industries. He identifies Executive Order 12898, *Federal Actions to Address Environmental Justice in Minority Populations and Low-Income Populations*, signed by President Clinton as a key one that calls for government agencies to consider the disproportionate negative influence of human health and environmental effects on minorities. Bullard (2000) finds that some states have subsidized polluting industries in return for promised jobs. These states argue that tax breaks help create jobs, but the few jobs really created are done so at a very high cost. Toxic dumping and facilities have occurred disproportionately in poor and minority areas that have few citizens that lobby against them. Bullard argues that environmental policies and decision making often follow a pattern similar to the power arrangement in the general society.

We previously dealt with the case of Hurricane Katrina and the government response in Chapter 4, but we continue our discussion here as it relates to the racial state as well. Tierney (2006) believes that the relief agencies dealing with Katrina cared little about the needs of many of the people. She describes the "social triage process" as "driven by negligence, incompetence, and perhaps even malice" (207). She believes that "members of the elite evidently hope that many among the over 1 million residents who have been displaced will eventually exhaust their options and give up their efforts to return" (208). Certain elites seem to have wanted a "smaller, whiter, richer, Disneyfied replica" of New Orleans (208). A study by Brown University sociologist Logan shows how African Americans in the region lived disproportionately in damaged areas. Also, they were dependent on institutional evacuations and resettled at great distances from their community (Petterson et al. 2006; Wise 2008). This led Petterson et al. (2006) to conclude "Katrina has initiated profound ethnic shifts" (652).

Like Tierney, Wise (2008) identifies certain key racist events like the media attention to the looters and the mostly white National Guard threatening to blow people's heads off as they aimed their guns at people in the Convention Center who were trying to get food from a locked pantry. He argues that the New Orleans story is about a political system dominated by white elites and government at all levels and both political parties that would not prioritize the lives of black and poor people. Wise lived in New Orleans earlier, "when state Democrats and Republicans both bowed to big business" (185).

Wise (2008) argues that instead of the problems after Katrina being a "system failure" (185), it is normal for the black community to be exposed to dangerous situations and for their homes to be moved or destroyed for projects like the construction of an interstate, the Superdome, malls, office parks, and so on. He feels what occurred in New Orleans is an example of "institutional white supremacy" (184) and suggests "We must see our fates as linked to theirs. We must see them as family. We must demand that their needs be prioritized at all levels of government, and we must refuse to lend our support to candidates who fail to do so" (190).

In summary, while one may think natural disasters are rare, often the patterns of institutional racism make minorities and the poor particularly vulnerable to these patterns and drastically interrupt their everyday lives. As Mills has suggested, such examples of the racial state may surely affect us all whether we are the privileged or the disadvantaged.

Immigration: A Major Ethnic and Racial Issue Facing the United States

Waldinger (2008: 306) clearly identifies how political and controversial the issue of immigration is when he states, "Immigration is roiling American politics, with controversy continuing and no clear solution in sight." He explains how governments at various levels "create differences between the people *of* the state and all other people *in* the state" (306) such as the divide between citizens and noncitizens. Illegal immigrants may not be able to obtain a driver's license or other benefits reserved for American citizens, they can be deported if convicted of a felony, and they cannot vote. He points out how our democratic values are being sacrificed: "The damage, rather, is to the American democracy, decreasingly a government of and for the people, when barely a third of all foreign-born persons living on U.S. soil are eligible to vote" (306). Waldinger contrasts the approaches to citizenship in Canada and the United States. In the United States the government follows a laissez-faire or neutral approach with no impediments to vote for legal immigrants, but individuals have to obtain citizenship on their own. In Canada the state actively supports and encourages citizenship and has multicultural policies helping citizens retain ties to their country of origin.

Janoski and Wang (2005) examine Gimpel and Edwards' (1999) work that suggests that by 1982 political parties had become intensely polarized on the issue of immigration policy. Those who favor expansion of immigration on the basis of expanding citizenship rights are more likely to be Democrats. The mainly Republican "free-market expansionists" are less interested in citizenship aspects but want to ease labor shortages and thus also support increasing immigration. Some of those who want to restrict immigration do so because they focus on doing what is best for labor and African Americans rather than for new immigrants. Others want to protect American–European culture and thus want to restrict immigration. Some social scientists emphasize that state elites shape the immigration policy often to benefit themselves or corporate elites (Janoski and Wang 2005).

A brief look at U.S. immigrants based on 2007 Census Bureau data reveals that 54 percent of the 38.1 million foreign-born are from Latin America, 27 percent from Asia, 13 percent from Europe, and 4 percent from Africa. A total of 11.7 million came from Mexico. Those from India make up 4 percent of the foreign-born and are the best educated, earning an average of $91,195 per year. Concerning language, 97 percent of immigrants from Mexico and the Dominican Republic do not speak English at home. In addition, roughly 52 percent of the foreign-born residents report they speak English less than very well (Roberts 2009). Immigrants are now 12.6 percent of the population, higher than any time since the 1920s (Greenblatt 2008: 99). Jenness, Smith, and Stepan-Norris (2008) point out that estimates of illegal immigrants range from 7 to 20 million, but most scholars tend to agree on about 12 million.

The terrorist attacks on September 11, 2001 greatly stirred up the debate over immigration although none of the terrorists were immigrants per se. They were from Middle Eastern countries and generally held tourist or student visas. The numbers of legal immigrants from Middle Eastern or mainly Muslim countries are not large. However, shortly after the terrorist attacks more than twelve thousand Middle Easterners were rounded up by federal agents. Most were released or deported by August 2002 (Katel, Marshall, and Greenblatt 2008). Marger (2009) points out that being Arab and being Muslim are not the same thing. Americans had viewed Arabs with suspicion even before 9/11 due in part to the oil crisis, but the suspicions and negative images grew considerably after that. Marger (350) argues that the "government-induced environment of fear, following the September 11 attacks" has created and sustained the negative images of Muslims. Tumlin (2004: 1175) supports Marger's view by stating, "A hallmark of terrorism policy's control over immigration policy since 9/11 is the institution of what I call an immigration-plus profiling regime which targets immigrants of certain national origins and presumed Muslim religious identity for increased scrutiny."

Recent comprehensive national legislation on immigration has been debated but not passed. Therefore some states stepped in, passing 206 immigration-related acts in 2008. Most of these laws tried to limit illegal immigration by restricting access to public benefits, driver's licenses, and so on. Some laws, though, tried to help immigrants learn English and become more integrated into certain features of mainstream society (Greenblatt 2008; "Immigration and Emigration" 2009). President Obama has been working on a comprehensive immigration reform package that would include a plan for illegal immigrants to gain legal status and a markedly improved detention system ("Immigration and Emigration" 2009; Thompson and Lacey 2009).

Officials of Immigration and Customs Enforcement (ICE) started immigrant raids on factories and communities in 2006 and steadily increased them. Workplace raids were increased tenfold between 2003 and 2008 with 6,287 actual arrests in 2008 (Hastings 2009: 1AA). By fiscal year 2008 nearly 350,000 immigrants were deported for various reasons ("Immigration and Emigration" 2009). Raids in Postville, Iowa, and Laurel, Mississippi, typify the crackdown on illegal immigrants. In May 2008 nearly four hundred workers at a meatpacking plant in Postville were detained and taken for processing to a temporary court facility on the grounds of the National Cattle Congress in Waterloo, Iowa. Nearly three hundred of them were imprisoned for several months on charges of using false documents, and then deported. An interpreter was very critical of the process, saying many of those who pleaded guilty did not really understand the charges. In Laurel the largest raid thus far was conducted at a factory manufacturing electrical transformers, and so forth. About five hundred workers were initially detained in August 2008; many of them were processed for deportation (Liptak and Preston 2009). In both cases the communities, local churches, and families were disrupted. During the Laurel raid blacks and whites at the factory reportedly applauded and jeered when the Hispanics were led away (Hastings 2009).

ADVANTAGES AND DISADVANTAGES OF IMMIGRATION   An important consideration of the debate on the issue of immigration, especially illegal immigration, revolves around the economic benefits and costs. Clearly the most important reason the majority of immigrants come to the United States is to better their economic position. Those who support increasing immigration argue that there is a demand for certain types of labor. While we focus on the demand for unskilled labor, note that many of the newest immigrants may have important skills in areas such as computer technology and medicine that are needed to fill positions for which it appears there are not enough qualified citizens (Marger 2008). Evaluating the economic effect is indeed as controversial today as it has been in the past. The effects vary in part with the rate of unemployment and the health of the economy in the United States as a whole. Clearly what benefits business does not necessarily help less-skilled workers.

There is some agreement that immigrants filling slots for unskilled labor may be driving down the wages of native workers. The disagreement though is on how strong this effect is (Lowenstein 2006; Marger 2008). Light (2006) in *Deflecting Immigration* argues that the effect is substantial. In his study of low-skilled workers immigrating to Los Angeles from Mexico and Central America in the 1980s, wages were driven down, housing supply decreased, and housing prices increased (Calavita 2008). A 2002 study of illegal workers in Chicago found that two-thirds worked low-wage jobs, with wages depressed by 22 percent for men and 36 percent for women (Katel et al. 2008). AFL-CIO's Avendano does not want the AFL-CIO to have to choose between domestic workers and foreign workers, but he recognizes illegal immigrants push wages down (Katel et al. 2008).

Hanson, a senior fellow at the Hoover Institution, argues that the connection between undocumented workers and high unemployment needs to be recognized. Employers are aware that in illegals they have cheap labor that will not organize and can often be paid in cash with few government deductions and little expense. He advocates strongly enforcing existing laws and stiff employer sanctions (Katel et al. 2008). Tilove (2007), a reporter from Newhouse News Service, supports Hanson, pointing out how this pliant immigrant labor force benefits employers. He is concerned that blacks are becoming marginalized among those supporting immigration. He argues that "because immigrants who are hired instead are also not white, employers run little risk of running afoul of antidiscrimination laws or their own sense of shame" (215). Swain (2007: 12) too makes it clear that disadvantaged groups in the labor force suffer disproportionately: "Moreover, immigrant-supporters do themselves and their country a disservice when they fail to consider all aspects of the problem and the national obligations to historically disadvantaged groups such as Native Americans, African Americans, poor whites, and legal Hispanics and Asians."

In spite of these arguments about the costs of immigration, Lowenstein concludes with a rather positive view about the economic effects of immigration:

> The economic effects generally tend to be perceived as positive though since they provide scarce labor, which lowers prices in much the same way global trade does. And overall, the newcomers modestly raise Americans' per capita income. But the impact is unevenly distributed; people with means pay less for taxi rides and household help while the less affluent command lower wages and probably pay more for rent. (2006: 1)

Not only do immigrant workers expand the supply of labor, they also consume products and services, which helps businesses.

Myers (2007) in *Immigrants and Boomers* tends to support this view using a "demographic lag" approach that as the current baby boomer generation ages, we need more younger people, including immigrants, to help the economy including buying homes and contributing to SS (Jenness et al. 2008). In 2007 it was estimated that undocumented immigrants improved SS's cash flow by $12 billion (Van de Water 2008).

The health of the economy is linked with the issue of immigration. On the one hand, when there is a recession or depression creating unemployment, like the one starting in late 2007, many citizens want less immigration. On the other hand, if the economy is doing well, concerns about immigration are defused (Janoski and Wang 2005). Latino/a immigration patterns also seem to support the idea that recession has negative effects as well. According to a Pew Hispanic Center analysis of Census Bureau data between 2007 and the third quarter of 2008 there has been a small but significant decrease in Latino/a immigration during the recession that officially started in December 2007. Among foreign-born Latino/a immigrants, 71.3 percent were working in the paid labor force at the end of the third quarter of 2008 while 72.4 percent were working a year earlier. While this decline seems small, the labor-force participation rate had been steadily increasing since 2003 (Kochhar 2008).

Drawing on several sources, Passel and Cohn (2009) conclude that the flow of Mexican immigrants to the United States has declined rather sharply from 2006 to 2009. On the other hand, one might expect that some of these immigrants would return to Mexico, but the data do not support the notion of an increase in outflow during this period. We will now turn to a consideration of how public education has been affected by increasing immigration.

In addition to the economy, education has been greatly influenced by immigration. Using the 2006 American Community Survey, Fry and Gonzales (2008) report that the number of Latino/a students in public schools nearly doubled between 1990 and 2006. A large majority of the Hispanic children (84 percent) were born in the United States. Thus while certainly not all this growth can be attributed to current immigration, the public education issue is complicated by immigration patterns. More than half of the Hispanic students are enrolled in the public schools in California and Texas, and the highest percentage of Hispanic students is Mexican (69 percent). A much higher percentage of Hispanic students (28 percent) are in households labeled poor compared to non-Hispanic students (16 percent). Foreign-born Hispanic students are much more likely to live in poverty and to speak English with difficulty.

In addition to education, we note one more effect on the family that often is not considered. While there has been substantial work describing the positive effects of migration on origin communities, Frank and Wildsmith (2005) introduce a concern related to the dissolution of marital unions when one person, typically the female, remains in the place of origin and the male leaves for the United States. For those who remain in Mexico, their improved economic position is likely to be accompanied by divided families, tension, and at times, dissolution of the marital relationship.

In addition to economic, schooling, and family issues, the general social implications of immigration are important for society. Some American citizens see that immigrants are having a positive effect on society by contributing to multiculturalism, but others perceive that the new immigrants threaten the social order and the shared culture of the American way of life that unites people (Bloemraad 2008; D'Angelo and Douglas 2009). Bloemraad (2008: 298) argues that "although economic considerations are important, the politics of race, social cohesion, and culture cannot be ignored." Edwards (2007: 60), an adjunct fellow at the Hudson Institute, argues that the largest problem cannot necessarily be expressed in dollars and cents but rather "the greatest harm . . . may be to our ability to preserve a sense of common culture and community in a rapidly changing world."

Huntington (2009[1996]) argues that the United States should not turn into two different communities or civilizations. Further he warns:

> Unlike past immigrant groups, Mexicans and other Latinos have not assimilated into mainstream U.S. culture, forming instead their own political and linguistic enclaves—from Los Angeles to Miami—and rejecting the Anglo-Protestant values that built the American dream. The United States ignores this challenge at its peril. (quoted in Massey 2007: 146)

Taking the opposite point of view, Etzioni (2007) argues that Mexican immigrants help strengthen the community because of their dedication to their family and community as well as respect for authority and moderate moral views (Bloemraad 2008). In addition Legrain (2009: 35) argues that "diversity also acts as a magnet for talent," suggesting that research indicates diverse groups of talented people actually perform better than nondiverse ones. According to him opening U.S. borders would benefit our society, including our culture and economy, while spreading freedom and increasing opportunity. Etzioni supports this view as well, arguing that the traditional black/white identity politics will change due to the added multiethnic and racial backgrounds of immigrants, and this should help normalize American politics:

> One should expect that Hispanic (and Asian) Americans will contribute to the depolarization of American society. They will replace African Americans as the main socially distinct group and will constitute groups that either are not racial (many Hispanics see themselves as white or as an ethnic group and not as a member of a distinct race, black or brown) or are of a race that is less distinct from the white majority (as in the case of Asian Americans). By increasing the proportion of Americans who

> do not see themselves as victims and who intermarry with others, these immigrants will continue to "normalize" American politics. (Etzioni 2007: 203–204)

While Etzioni seems optimistic about a possible decline in the politics of race, we suggest that the racial state would continue to deal with the issues raised by black–white tensions and with the increasing concerns about immigration.

PUBLIC OPINION   Fetzer (2000), in a comparative study of attitudes toward immigration in the United States, France, and Germany, concluded that in the United States concerns about economic interests were not as important as social issues: "U.S. immigration politics seems to bring into question the ascendancy of the traditionally dominant majority's cultural values" (107). Those who are well educated, have higher occupational prestige, or are Catholic are more tolerant toward immigrants.

A major political values survey by Pew Research Center in 2007 (Doherty 2007) found a majority of people surveyed favored giving undocumented immigrants the possibility of citizenship (59 to 37 percent), but at the same time a strong majority favored restricting immigration more than what was being done in 2007. Responses were much more evenly divided over the issues of building a fence along 700 miles of the border with Mexico (46 percent favored, 48 percent opposed) and whether immigrants are a threat to traditional American values (48 percent agreed, 46 percent disagreed). Those who identified with the Democratic Party were more likely to give undocumented immigrants a chance at citizenship while Republicans were more likely to want to build a long fence, restrict immigration, and see immigrants as a threat to traditional values (Doherty 2007).

In a Pew Forum on Religion & Public Life and a Pew Research Center for the People & the Press survey in 2009, participants were asked if there is a lot of discrimination against certain groups. Nearly 60 percent of those surveyed believed Muslims experienced a lot of discrimination. The only group that was identified by more people was gays and lesbians. Hispanics were named by just slightly more than a majority of people. Another 2009 Pew survey (Morin 2009) asked about perceived conflicts between different types of social groups. A higher percentage of people believed there were strong conflicts between immigrants and people born in the United States than any other group named.

SUMMARY   Immigration is clearly both a significant sociopolitical and political economy issue. Economically, there is the problem of "absorbing new, generally non-English-speaking populations into an economy that may have to provide increasing public support" for them, and socially there is a concern about whether society's "traditions and values clash with those of the newcomers" (McKenna and Feingold 2009: 277). There are also political and ethical consequences in how the United States is viewed by other countries and peoples if immigration is strongly restricted.

CONCLUSION

We began this chapter discussing C. Wright Mills and his concept of the sociological imagination. Lacking a sociological imagination may encourage individuals to blame themselves or other individuals for their troubles (Ferrante 2008). However, as Charon (1987: viii) points out, "Our individual lives and our personal problems are part of a much larger history and are embedded in a society." In this chapter we identified a number of issues defined as matters "that can be explained only by factors outside an individual's control and immediate environment" (Ferrante 2008: 9).

When one marries, one may not fully comprehend the rights and responsibilities attached to marriage. Extending those rights to gay and lesbian couples has occurred in a small percentage of states, but this issue is quite contentious in society. Schools with limited budgets face difficulties getting students to perform at grade level in reading and mathematics. The state tries to apply pressure to schools to improve test scores, and schools may be sanctioned if students fail to improve. Children who are not proficient in English also may need special resources to help them learn the language and adjust. Health care issues, especially related to cost and availability, continue to concern this country. The state's policies regarding civil liberties clearly have the potential to affect our freedoms to express ourselves as guaranteed by the Bill of Rights. Maintaining our civil liberties and also making sure that citizens are safe from both domestic and international terrorists is a difficult job for the government. The state is clearly a racial state as it formulates policy related to racial and ethnic issues. Immigration policies, like health care, clearly affect us all, in terms of both economic and social consequences.

In this chapter we examined some of the significant ways that the state as well as more local units of government make decisions every day that impact virtually every aspect of our lives. The ways we live our lives, including our political participation, also shape politics and the policies of government. In Chapter 6 we turn to a discussion of political participation.

Endnotes

1. The exact text of these lines is quite controversial as Pastor Niemöller evidently quoted various versions at different occasions (Marcuse 2008; "Niemöller, Martin" n.d.).

2. For various sources regarding the persistence of racism in the state, see D'Angelo and Douglas (2009), especially issues 9 and 11.

References

"Adoption." n.d. Wex. Sponsored and hosted by the Legal Information Institute at the Cornell Law School. Retrieved August 28, 2009 from http://topics.law.cornell.edu/wex/adoption.

Agger, Ben and Tim Luke. 2002. "Politics in Postmodernity." Pp. 159–195 in *Theoretical Directions in Political Sociology for the 21st Century*, volume 11, *Research in Political Sociology*, edited by Betty A. Dobratz, Timothy Buzzell, and Lisa K. Waldner. Amsterdam: Elsevier.

Alford, Robert and Roger Friedland. 1985. *Powers of Theory*. Cambridge: Cambridge University Press.

American Civil Liberties Union (ACLU). 2004[1997]. "Limits Should Be Placed on Freedom of Expression." Pp. 19–28 in *Civil Liberties: Opposing Viewpoints*, edited by Auriana Ojeda. San Diego: Thomson (Greenhaven).

American Psychological Association. 2009 [2004]. "APA Policy Statement on Sexual Orientation, Parents, & Children." Pp. 193–197 in *Taking Sides: Clashing Views in Gender*. 4th Edition, edited by Jacquelyn White. Boston: McGraw-Hill.

"An Argument against Same-Sex Marriage: An Interview with Rick Santorum." 2008. Pew Research Center: Pew Forum on Religion and Public Life. Interview April 24. Retrieved September 4, 2009 from http://pewforum.org/events/?EventID=180.

Associated Press. 2000. "U.S. Settles Final Civil Lawsuit Stemming from Ruby Ridge Siege." *New York Times* September 23. Retrieved September 17, 2009 from http://www.nytimes.com/2000/09/23/national/23RUBY .html.

Barnes, Robert. 2010. "Supreme Court Seems Disinclined to Give NFL Antitrust Exemption." *Washington Post* January 14: A03. Retrieved January 21, 2010 from http:// www.washingtonpost.com/wp-dyn/content/article/2010/01/13/AR2010011304394_pf .html.

Begley, Sharon. 2009. "Attack: The Truth about Obamacare." *Newsweek* August 24 and 31: 40–43.

Belge, Kathy. n.d. "Both Sides of the Issue: Lesbian and Gay Adoption Rights." Retrieved September 7, 2009 from http://lesbianlife.about.com/cs/families/a/adoption_2.htm.

Best, Shaun. 2002. *Introduction to Politics and Society.* London: Sage.

Bloemraad, Irene. 2008. "Analyzing and Affecting Immigration Politics: Can Sociologists Influence Opinions?" *Contemporary Sociology* 37: 295–298.

Bonilla-Silva, Eduardo, Tyrone A. Foreman, Amanda E. Lewis, and David G. Embrick. 2003. "It Wasn't Me!: How Will Racism and Race Work in 21st Century America." Pp. 111–134 in *Political Sociology for the 21st Century*, volume 12, *Research in Political Sociology*, edited by B. A. Dobratz, L. K. Waldner, and T. Buzzell. Amsterdam: Elsevier.

Bowles, Samuel and Herbert Gintis. 1976. *Schooling in Capitalist America.* New York: Basic Books.

_____. 2002. "Schooling in Capitalist America Revisited." *Sociology of Education* 75(1): 1–18.

_____. 2004. "Comments on 'The Long Shadow of Work.'" Pp. 107–111 in *Enriching the Sociological Imagination*, edited by Rhonda F. Levine. Leiden, The Netherlands: Brill.

Bowles, Samuel, Herbert Gintis, and Peter Meyer. 2004[1975]. "The Long Shadow of Work: Education, the Family, and the Reproduction of the Social Division of Labor." Pp. 113–132 in *Enriching the Sociological Imagination*, edited by Rhonda F. Levine. Leiden, The Netherlands: Brill.

Brewer, John D. 2003. *C. Wright Mills and the Ending of Violence.* New York: Palgrave Macmillan.

Brint, Steven. 1994. *In an Age of Experts.* Princeton, NJ: Princeton University Press.

Bullard, Robert. 2000. *Dumping in Dixie.* Boulder, CO: Westview Press.

Calavita, Kitty. 2008. "Deflecting the Immigration Debate." *Contemporary Sociology* 37: 302–305.

Charon, Joel (editor). 1987. *The Meaning of Sociology: A Reader.* 2nd Edition. Englewood Cliffs, NJ: Prentice-Hall.

"Child Custody." n.d. Wex. Sponsored and hosted by the Legal Information Institute at the Cornell Law School. Retrieved August 28, 2009 from http://topics.law.cornell.edu/wex/child_custody.

Clemmitt, Marcia. 2008. "Fixing Urban Schools." Pp. 25–47 in *Issues for Debate in American Public Policy* (Selections from CQ Researcher). 8th Edition. Washington, DC: Congressional Quarterly.

Cockerham, William C. 2004. *Medical Sociology.* 9th Edition. Upper Saddle River, NJ: Pearson, Prentice Hall.

_____. 2007. *Medical Sociology.* 10th Edition. Upper Saddle River, NJ: Pearson, Prentice Hall.

Committee on Government Reform. 2005. "Restoring Faith in America's Pastime: Evaluating Major League Baseball's Efforts to Eradicate Steroid Use." Hearing Before the Committee on Government Reform, House of Representatives, March 17, Serial No. 109-8. Available via the World Wide Web: http://www.gpoaccess.gov/congress/index.html; http://www.house.gov/reform. Retrieved October 22, 2010 from http:www.diamondfans.com/archive/house_hearing_109-8_steroids.pdf.

Cunningham III, Robert and Robert M. Cunningham, Jr. 1997. *The Blues: A History of the Blue Cross and Blue Shield System.* DeKalb: Northern Illinois Press.

Dailey, Timothy J. 2009. "State of the States: Update on Homosexual Adoption in the U.S." Pp. 198–202 in *Taking Sides: Clashing Views in Gender.* 4th Edition, edited by Jacquelyn White. Boston: McGraw-Hill.

D'Angelo, Raymond and Herbert Douglas. 2009. *Taking Sides: Clashing Views in Race and Ethnicity.* 7th Edition. Boston: McGraw-Hill.

"Dangerous Strategies for Saving Health-Care Dollars." 2009. *Consumer Reports on Health* 21(6): 1.

Delgado, Richard. 2004. "Exceptions to the First Amendment." P. 39 in *Civil Liberties: Opposing Viewpoints*, edited by Auriana Ojeda. San Diego: Thomson (Greenhaven).

deMause, Neil. 2007. "Testimony of Neil deMause to Subcommittee on Oversight and Government Reform." March 29. Retrieved January 18, 2010 from http://oversight.house.gov/images/stories/documents/20070329144749-35526.pdf.

Dencik, Lars. 1989. "Growing Up in the Post-Modern Age." *Acta Sociologica* 32: 155–180.

Dillon, Sam. 2009a. "'No Child' Law Is Not Closing a Racial Gap." *New York Times* April 29. Retrieved August 27, 2009 from http://www.nytimes.com/2009/04/29/education/29scores.html?_r=2.

_____. 2009b. "Education Standards Likely to See Toughening." *New York Times* April 14. Retrieved August 27, 2009 from http://www.nytimes.com/2009/04/15/education/15educ.html.

"Divorce." n.d. Wex. Sponsored and hosted by the Legal Information Institute at the Cornell Law School. Retrieved August 28, 2009 from http://topics.law.cornell.edu/wex/divorce.

Dobratz, Betty A., Stephanie L. Shanks-Meile, and Danelle Hallenbeck. 2003. "What Happened on Ruby Ridge: Terrorism or Tyranny?" *Symbolic Interaction* 26: 315–342.

Doherty, Carroll. 2007. "The Immigration Divide." Pew Research Center, April 12. Retrieved September 25, 2009 from http://pewresearch.org/pubs/450/immigration-wedge-issue.

Domhoff, G. William. 2006. *Who Rules America? Power, Politics, & Social Change.* Boston: McGraw-Hill.

D'Souza, Dinesh. 2009[1995]. "The End of Racism." Pp. 182–189 in *Taking Sides: Clashing Views in Race and Ethnicity.* 7th Edition, edited by Raymond D'Angelo and Herbert Douglas. Boston: McGraw-Hill.

Dworkin, A. Gary. 2005. "No Child Left Behind Act: Accountability, High-Stakes Testing, and Roles for Sociologists." *Sociology of Education* 78(2): 170–174.

Dye, Thomas R. and L. Harmon Zeigler. 1972. *The Irony of Democracy.* Belmont, CA: Wadsworth.

Edwards, James R., Jr. 2007. "A Biblical Perspective on Immigration Policy." Pp. 46–62 in *Debating Immigration,* edited by Carol M. Swain. Cambridge, UK: Cambridge University Press.

Etzioni, Amitai. 2007. "Hispanic and Asian Immigrants: America's Last Hope." Pp. 189–205 in *Debating Immigration,* edited by Carol M. Swain. Cambridge, UK: Cambridge University Press.

Ezekiel, Raphael S. 1995. *The Racist Mind.* New York: Viking/Penguin.

Farber, Daniel. 2008. "Introduction." Pp. 1–23 in *Security v. Liberty,* edited by Daniel Farber. New York: Russell Sage.

Ferrante, Joan. 2008. *Sociology: A Global Perspective.* Belmont, CA: Thomson Higher Education.

Fetzer, Joel. 2000. *Public Attitudes toward Immigration in the United States, France, and Germany.* Cambridge, UK: Cambridge University Press.

Frank, Reanne and Elizabeth Wildsmith. 2005. "The Grass Widows of Mexico: Migration and Union Dissolution in a Binational Context." *Social Forces* 83: 919–947.

Freidson, Eliot. 1970. *Professional Dominance: The Social Structure of Medical Care.* New York: Atherton Press.

Frenk, Julio and Luis Durán-Arenas. 1993. "The Medical Profession and the State." Pp. 25–42 in *The Changing Medical Profession,* edited by Frederic W. Hafferty and John B. McKinlay. New York: Oxford University Press.

Friedman, Lauri S. (editor). 2006. *Gay Marriage: Opposing Views.* Farmington Hills, MI: Greenhaven Press.

Fry, Rick and Felisa Gonzales. 2008. "One-in-Five and Growing Fast: A Profile of Hispanic Public School Students." Pew Research Center, August 26. Retrieved September 21, 2009 from http://pewresearch.org/pubs/937/one-in-five-and-growing-fast-a-profile-of-hispanic-public-school-students.

Gamson, William. 1968. *Power and Discontent.* Homewood, IL: Dorsey.

Gamson, William, Bruce Fireman, and Steven Rytina. 1982. *Encounters with Unjust Authority.* Homewood, IL: Dorsey.

General Accounting Office. 1997. "Letter and Enclosures from Barry Bedrick, Associate General Counsel to Representative Henry J. Hyde, Chair Committee on the Judiciary." Dated January 31, 1997. Retrieved May 10, 2009 from http://www.gao.gov/archive/1997/og97016.pdf.

Gimpel, James and James Edwards. 1999. *The Congressional Politics of Immigration Reform.* Boston: Allyn & Bacon.

Goffman, Erving. 1974. *Frame Analysis.* New York: Harper and Row.

Goldhill, David. 2009. "What Washington Doesn't Get about Health Care." *Atlantic* 304(21): 38–55.

Greenblatt, Alan. 2008. "Immigration Debate." *CQ Researcher* 18(5): 97–120.

Groopman, Jerome. 2007. *How Doctors Think.* Boston: Houghton Mifflin Company.

Hastings, Deborah. 2009. "The Have-Nots War." *Des Moines Register* January 25: 1AA–2AA.

"Health Care Reform." 2010. Times Topics. Updated March 26, 2010. Retrieved May 3, 2010 from http://topics.nytimes.com/top/news/health/diseasesconditionsand healthtopics/health_insurance_and_managed_care/health_care_reform/index.html.

Heubert, Jay P. and Robert M. Hauser. 1999. *High Stakes: Testing for Tracking, Promotion, and Graduation.* Washington, DC: National Academy Press.

"History: Presidential Statements Barack H. Obama—2009." 2009. Retrieved July 11, 2009 from www.ssa.gov/history/Obamastmts1.html.

Holmes, Stephen. 2008. "Conclusion." Pp. 208–227 in *Security v. Liberty,* edited by Daniel Farber. New York: Russell Sage.

Huntington, Samuel P. 2009[1996]. "The Clash of Civilizations and the Remaking of World Order." Pp. 75–79 in *Taking Sides: Clashing Views in Race and Ethnicity.* 7th Edition, edited by Raymond D'Angelo and Herbert Douglas. Boston: McGraw-Hill.

Hurst, Charles E. 2010. *Social Inequality.* 7th Edition. Boston: Pearson.

"Immigration and Emigration." 2009. *New York Times Topics.* Updated August 11. Retrieved September 19, 2009 from http://topics.nytimes.com/top/reference/timestopics/subjects/i/immigration_and_refugees/index.html.

James, David R. and Kent Redding. 2005. "Theories of Race and State." Pp. 187–198 in *The Handbook of Political Sociology,* edited by T. Janoski, R. Alford, A. Hicks, and M. A. Schwartz. Cambridge: Cambridge University Press.

Janoski, Thomas and Fengjuan Wang. 2005. "The Politics of Immigration and National Integration." Pp. 630–654 in *The Handbook of Political Sociology,* edited by T. Janoski, R. Alford, A. Hicks, and M. Schwartz. New York: Cambridge.

Jenness, Valerie, David A. Smith, and Judith Stepan-Norris. 2008. "Editor's Note: The Politics of Immigration." *Contemporary Sociology* 37: vii–viii.

Johnston, David Cay. 2007. *Free Lunch.* New York: Penguin Group (Portfolio).

Karen, David. 2005. "No Child Left Behind? Sociology Ignored!" *Sociology of Education* 78: 165–169.

Katel, Peter, Patrick Marshall, and Alan Greenblatt. 2008. "Illegal Immigration." Pp. 339–365 in *Issues for Debate in American Public Policy.* Washington, DC: CQ Press.

Kendall, Diana. 2007. *Sociology in Our Times: The Essentials.* 6th Edition. Belmont, CA: Thomson.

Kinloch, Graham. 1989. *Society as Power.* Englewood Cliffs, NJ: Prentice-Hall.

Kochhar, Rakesh. 2008. "Latino Workers in the Ongoing Recession: 2007 to 2008." Pew Research Center, December 15. Retrieved September 21, 2009 from http://pewresearch.org/pubs/1054/latino-workers-in-the-ongoing-recession-2007-to-2008.

Legrain, Philippe 2009. "The Case for Immigration: The Secret to Economic Vibrancy." Pp. 34–39 in *Taking Sides: Clashing Views in Race and Ethnicity,* edited by R. D'Angelo and H. Douglas. Boston: McGraw Hill.

Liazos, Alexander. 1982. *People First: An Introduction to Social Problems.* Boston: Allyn & Bacon.

Light, Ivan. 2006. *Deflecting Immigration.* New York: Russell Sage Foundation.

Liptak, Adam and Julia Preston. 2009. "Justices Limit Use of Identity Theft Law in Immigration Cases." *New York Times* May 4. Retrieved September 19, 2009 from http://www.nytimes.com/2009/05/05/us/05immig.html.

Liptak, Adam and Ken Belson. 2010. "N.F.L. Fails in Its Request for Antitrust Immunity." *New York Times* May 24. Retrieved May 29, 2010 from www.nytimes.com/2010/05/25/sports/football/25needle.html?scp=1&sp=sports%20anti-trust&st=cse.

Loftus, Jeni. 2001. "America's Liberalization in Attitudes toward Homosexuality, 1973 to 1978." *American Sociological Review* 66: 762–782.

Lowenstein, Roger. 2006. "The Immigration Equation." *New York Times* July 9. Retrieved September 19, 2009 from http://www.nytimes.com/2006/07/09/magazine/09IMM.html.

Lupton, Deborah. 1994. *Medicine as Culture.* London: Sage.

Mantel, Barbara and Alan Greenblatt. 2008. "No Child Left Behind." Pp. 1–24 in *Issues for Debate in American Public Policy* (Selections from CQ Researcher). 8th Edition. Washington, DC: Congressional Quarterly.

Marcuse, Harold. 2008. "Martin Niemöller's Famous Quotation: 'First They Came for the Communists.'" Updated November 6. Retrieved September 14, 2009 from www.history.ucsb.edu/faculty/marcuse/niem.htm.

Marger, Martin. 2008. *Social Inequality.* 4th Edition. New York: McGraw-Hill.

_____. 2009. *Race and Ethnic Relations.* 8th Edition. Belmont, CA: Wadsworth Cengage Learning.

"Marriage." n.d. Wex. Sponsored and hosted by the Legal Information Institute at the Cornell Law School. Retrieved August 28, 2009 from http://topics.law.cornell.edu/wex/marriage.

Masci, David. 2009a. "Pew Forum: A Contentious Debate: Same-Sex Marriage in the U.S." Pew Center's Forum on Religion and Public Life, July 9. Retrieved September 4 from http://pewforum.org/ docs/?DocID=422.

_____. 2009b. "Pew Forum: Public Opinion on Gay Marriage: Opponents Consistently Outnumber Supporters." Pew Center's Forum on Religion and Public Life. July 9. Retrieved September 4 from http://pewforum.org/docs/?DocID=424.

Massey, Douglas. 2007. *Categorically Unequal.* New York: Russell Sage.

McKenna, George and Stanley Feingold. 2009. *Taking Sides: Clashing Views on Political Issues.* 16th Edition. Boston: McGraw-Hill.

McNeil, Linda M. 2000. *Contradictions of School Reform: Educational Costs of Standardized Testing.* NY: Routledge.

Mechanic, David. 2006. *The Truth about Health Care.* New Brunswick, NJ: Rutgers University Press.

Miliband, Ralph. 1969. *State in the Capitalist Society.* London: Camelot Press.

Miller, Dean. 1992. "FBI Links Bullet That Killed Degan to Harris' Rifle." *The [Spokane] Spokesman Review.* September 16: A1–A6.

Mills, C. Wright. 1959. *The Sociological Imagination.* New York: Oxford.

Morin, Rich. 2009. "What Divides America? Immigration and Income—Not Race—Are Seen as Primary Sources of Social Conflict." Pew Research Center, September 24. Retrieved September 25, 2009 from http://pewresearch.org/pubs/1354/social-conflict-in-america.

Murray, Shailagh and Lori Montgomery. 2010. "House Passes Health-Care Reform Bill Without Republican Votes." *Washington Post* March 22: A01. Retrieved March 22, 2010 from www.washingtonpost.com/wp-dyn/content/article/2010/03/21/AR2010032100943_pf.html.

Myers, Dowell. 2007. *Immigrants and Boomers.* New York: Russell Sage Foundation.

Neuman, W. Lawrence. 2005. *Power, State, Society.* New York: McGraw-Hill.

"Niemöller, Martin." n.d. Retrieved September 14, 2009 from http://www.holocaust-history.org/questions/niemoller.shtml.

"No Child Left Behind Act." 2009. *New York Times Topics.* Updated April 29. Retrieved August 27, 2009 from http://topics.nytimes.com/topics/reference/timestopics/subjects/n/no_child_left_behind_act/index.html

Ojeda, Auriana (editor). 2004. *Civil Liberties: Opposing Viewpoints.* San Diego: Thomson (Greenhaven).

Olson, Gunnar. 2009. "Wedding Unites 9 Gay Pairs at Church in D.M." *Des Moines Register* August 30: 1B, 4B.

Omi, Michael and Howard Winant. 1994. *Racial Formation in the United States: From the 1960s to the 1980s.* 2nd Edition. New York: Routledge and Kegan Paul.

Orum, Anthony M. and John G. Dale. 2009. *Introduction to Political Sociology.* New York: Oxford University Press.

Passel, Jeffrey and D'Vera Cohn. 2009. "Recession Slows—but Does Not Reverse—Mexican Immigration." Pew Research Center, July 22. Retrieved September 20, 2009 from http://pewresearch.org/pubs/1288/mexican-immigrants-recent-inflows-outflows.

Pearlstein, Steven. 2009. "Trust-busting the NFL." *Washington Post* October 21. Retrieved October 21, 2010 from http://www.washingtonpost.com/wp-dyn/content/article/2009/10/20/AR2009102003698_pf.html.

Peplau, Letitia A. and Adam Fingerhut. 2007. "The Close Relationships of Lesbians and Gay Men." *Annual Review of Psychology* 58: 405–424.

Petterson, John S., Laura Stanley, Edward Glazier, and James Philipp. 2006. "A Preliminary Assessment of Social and Economic Impacts Associated with Hurricane Katrina." *American Anthropologist* 108: 643–670.

Pew Forum on Religion & Public Life and Pew Research Center for the People & the Press. 2008. "Some Social Conservative Disillusionment: More Americans Question Religion's Role in Politics." Pew Forum on Religion and Public Life, August 21. Retrieved September 6, 2009 from http://pewforum.org/newassets/images/reports/summer08/survey.pdf.

———. 2009. "Muslims Widely Seen as Facing Discrimination: Views of Religious Similarities and Differences." Retrieved September 21, 2009 from http://pewresearch.org/pubs/1336/perceptions-of-islam-religious-similarities-differences.

Pew Research Center for the People & the Press. 2006a. "Americans Taking Abramoff, Alito and Domestic Spying in Stride: About This Survey." Retrieved September 9, 2009 from http://people-press.org/report/?pageid=1032.

———. 2006b. "Americans Taking Abramoff, Alito and Domestic Spying in Stride: Summary of Findings." Retrieved September 9, 2009 from http://people-press.org/report/267/americans-taking-abramoff-alito-and-domestic-spying-in-stride.

"Plan Gives Insurance Firms Time to Change." 2009. *Des Moines Register* September 4: 3A (Metro edition).

Popham, W. James. 2004. *America's "Failing" Schools.* New York: Routledge.

Redding, Kent, David R. James, and Joshua Klugman. 2005. "The Politics of Racial Policy." Pp. 546–565 in *The Handbook of Political Sociology,* edited by T. Janoski, R. Alford, A. Hicks, and M. Schwartz. New York: Cambridge.

Relman, Arnold S. 2007. *A Second Opinion: Rescuing America's Health Care.* New York: Public Affairs.

Rimmerman, Craig A. 2008. *The Lesbian and Gay Movements: Assimilation or Liberation.* Boulder, CO: Westview Press.

Roberts, Sam. 2009. "Government Offers Look at Nation's Immigrants." *New York Times* February 20. Retrieved September 19, 2009 from http://www.nytimes.com/2009/02/21/us/21census.html.

Robertson, Ian. 1981. *Sociology.* 2nd Edition. New York: Worth.

"Same-Sex Marriage, Civil Unions, and Domestic Partnerships." 2009. *New York Times Topics.* Updated August 3. Retrieved September 4 from http://topics.nytimes.com/top/reference/timestopics/subjects/s/same_sex_marriage/index.html.

Schmidt, Michael S. 2010. "Selig Says Steroid Era Is Basically Over." *New York Times* January 12. Retrieved January 22, 2010 from http://www.nytimes.com/2010/01/12/sports/baseball/12steroids.html?pagewanted=print.

"Should We Sacrifice Some of Our Civil Liberties to Help Fight the War on Terror?" n.d. Retrieved September 7, 2009 from http://www.balancedpolitics.org/civil_liberties.htm.

Spence, Gerry. 1995. *From Freedom to Slavery.* New York: St. Martin's Griffin.

Sprigg, Peter. 2009. "Questions and Answers: What's Wrong with Letting Same-Sex Couples 'Marry?'" Pp. 183–189 in *Taking Sides: Clashing Views in Gender,* edited by Jacquelyn White. New York: McGraw Hill.

Stacey, Judith and Timothy Biblarz. 2001. "(How) Does the Sexual Orientation of Parents Matter?" *American Sociological Review* 66(April): 159–183.

Starr, Paul. 1982. *The Social Transformation of American Medicine.* New York: Basic Books.

Steele, Shelby. 2009[2005]. "Witness: Blacks, Whites, and the Politics of Shame in America." Pp. 218–221 in *Taking Sides: Clashing Views in Race and Ethnicity.* 7th Edition, edited by Raymond D'Angelo and Herbert Douglas. Boston: McGraw-Hill.

"Steroids." 2009. *New York Times Topics.* Updated July 30, 2009. Retrieved January 22, 2010 from http://topics.nytimes.com/top/news/health/diseasesconditionsandhealthtopics/steroids/index.html.

Stone, Andrea. 2009. "Gay Activists: Federal Benefits Still Lacking." *USA Today* June 18: 4A.

Subcommittee on Terrorism, Technology and Government Information of the Senate Committee on the Judiciary. 1997. *The Federal Raid on Ruby Ridge, ID* (Hearings). Washington, DC: Government Printing Office.

Swain, Carol (editor). 2007. "Introduction." Pp. 1–14 in *Debating Immigration,* edited by Carol M. Swain. Cambridge, UK: Cambridge University Press.

Thompson, Ginger and Marc Lacey. 2009. "Obama Sets Immigration Changes for 2010." *New York Times* August 10. Retrieved September 19, 2009 from http://www.nytimes.com/2009/08/11/world/americas/11prexy.html.

Tierney, Kathleen. 2006. "Review: Foreshadowing Katrina: Recent Sociological Contributions to Vulnerability Science." *Contemporary Sociology* 35(3): 207–212.

Tilove, Jonathan. 2007. "Strange Bedfellows, Unintended Consequences, and the Curious Contours of the

Immigration Debate." Pp. 206–219 in *Debating Immigration*, edited by Carol M. Swain. Cambridge, UK: Cambridge University Press.

Toth, Peter P. 2007. "Editorial: Avandia and Risk for Acute Cardiovascular Events: Science or Sabotage?" *Journal of Applied Research* 7(2): 147–149.

Tumlin, Karen. 2004. "Suspect First: How Terrorism Policy Is Reshaping Immigration Policy." *California Law Review* 92: 1173–1239.

Turner, Bryan. 1997. "From Governmentality to Risk: Some Reflections on Foucault's Contribution to Medical Sociology." Pp. ix–xxi in *Foucault: Health and Medicine*, edited by Alan Petersen and Robin Bunton. London: Routledge.

———. 2004. *The New Medical Society*. New York: W.W. Norton.

U.S. Department of Education. 2009a. "Overview: The Federal Role in Education." Retrieved August 24, 2009 from http://www.ed.gov/about/overview/fed/role.html?src=ln.

———. 2009b. "Fiscal Year 2010 Budget Summary—May 7, 2009." Retrieved August 24, 2009 from http://www.ed.gov/about/overview/budget/budget10/summary/edlite-section1.html.

———. 2009c. "Achievement Gaps: How Black and White Students in Public Schools Perform in Mathematics and Reading on the National Assessment of Education Progress." Statistical Analysis Report, July 2009, NCES 2009-455. Retrieved August 29, 2009 from http://nces.ed.gov/nationsreportcard/pdf/studies/2009455.pdf.

Van de Water, Paul. 2008. "Immigration and Social Security." Center on Budget and Policy Priorities, November 20. Retrieved July 11, 2009 from http://www.cbpp.org/files/11-20-08socsec.pdf.

Waldinger, Roger. 2008. "The Border Within: Citizenship Facilitated and Impeded." *Contemporary Sociology* 37: 306–308.

White, Jacquelyn (editor). 2009. *Taking Sides: Clashing Views in Gender*. Boston: McGraw Hill.

Wilensky, Harold L. 2009. "U.S. Health Care and Real Health in Comparative Perspective." *Forum* 7: Issue 2, Article 7. DOI:10.2202/1540-8884.1312. Available at http://www.bepress.com/forum/vol7/iss2/art7. From Berkeley electronic press. Retrieved January 28, 2010 from www.bepress.com.proxy.lib.iastate.edu;2048/cgi/viewcontent.cgi?article=13128&context=forum.

Wilson, William Julius. 1978. *The Declining Significance of Race*. Chicago: University of Chicago Press.

Wilson, Duff and Michael S. Schmidt. 2007. "Steroid Report Cites 'Collective Failure.'" *New York Times* December 14. Copied January 22, 2010 from http://www.nytimes.com/2007/12/14/sports/baseball/14mitchell.html?_r=1&pagewanted=print.

Wise, Tim. 2008. *White Like Me*. Brooklyn: Soft Skull Press.

Zald, Mayer N. 1996. "Culture, Ideology, and Strategic Framing." Pp. 261–274 in *Comparative Perspectives on Social Movements*, edited by D. McAdam, J. D. McCarthy, and M. N. Zald. Cambridge: Cambridge University Press.

CHAPTER 6

Political Participation

In this chapter, we look at the various ways in which individuals and groups participate in the processes of governance. We know from decades of research that there is a great deal of variation in the ways and degrees to which individuals participate in political processes. The chapter opens with a discussion of citizenship as a social role of sorts in a system of politics. We have found there are many acts associated with citizenship as well as acts associated with exclusion from rights, privileges, or expectations associated with citizenship. Many of these role behaviors have been organized into quite useful typologies of political participation. The chapter then looks at these types of political participation in detail, including current research. This is followed by a discussion of a contemporary debate around what some call the decline of civic engagement in the United States, and the role of what sociologists call "social capital" in this process. Finally, the chapter ends by looking at two recent studies that conclude political participation is changing as a result of broad social forces. This chapter prepares us to move into more detailed chapters that follow regarding voting and electoral processes, the extensive research on political and social movements, and terrorism as political violence.

POLITICAL PARTICIPATION AS POWER

Political participation is important to the field of political sociology because it addresses fundamental characteristics of politics, the state, and organization of power in society. Who participates in the political decision making of the community? Is this participation even and equal for all members of the social group; is it divided, or concentrated in the hands of a few? Do some participate more than others? What are the boundaries of legitimate participation encouraged or fostered by the institution of politics and its associated structures? Are certain forms of participation considered illegitimate, beyond the role the nation conceptualizes for citizens? These are a few of the many questions that political sociologists address in the study of political participation. Much of the work begins with the study of citizenship.

The concept of citizenship is both a political and a social artifact (Kivisto and Faist 2007; van Steenbergen 1994). It is a creation of the state and at the same time provides structure to individual roles in society; it takes on different forms of action, expression, symbolism, and social organization. Thus, the concept of citizenship is important to political sociology. *Citizenship* refers to the participation in or membership in a community. Marx noted that citizenship is the creation of the modern state, a superstructure that emerges from the dynamics of a class-based society. Citizenship as a political creation obscures the class inequalities created in the capitalist system:

> The state in its own way abolishes distinctions based on birth, rank, education and occupation when it declares birth, rank, education and occupation to be non-political distinctions, when it proclaims that every member of the people is an equal participant in popular sovereignty regardless of these distinctions, when it treats all those elements which go to make up the actual life of the people from the standpoint of the state. (Marx 1992[1843]: 219)

Parsons approached the concept by emphasizing the function of citizenship in maintaining societies. Citizenship is recognition of membership in a community. Thus, with membership in the larger social group of citizens and civil society we identify certain roles and norms for behavior. Citizenship is essential for social order according to the functionalist model. Legitimacy to rule and assumptions of authority are reinforced through participatory rulemaking. From the elite power perspective, we are interested in understanding whether this notion of "membership in a political community" is inclusive or exclusive. What are the bases for citizenship? What power does citizenship offer to those who hold membership? Is citizenship the basis for distributing power among all members of the community? How is membership reproduced?

One of the first studies of citizenship was the historical analysis developed by T. H. Marshall (1950). By treating citizenship as rights-based and created through the rules and procedures developed formally by the state, Marshall saw rights as moving through a number of stages since the great revolutions of the 1700s. His approach to understanding citizenship was designed to explain how democracy and capitalism could work together as it evolved in the eighteenth, nineteenth, and twentieth centuries. Marshall suggested a paradox. Adam Smith argued that naked power in society could be checked by the presence of a political system alongside a system of commerce. A minimalist state could act as a watchman to preserve economic growth. Similarly, Immanuel Kant viewed the state as an instrument of security, preserving social peace. Liberal governments in consort with trade and the involvement of people normally considered outside the process of governance would create a balance between democratic institutions and capitalism. But T. H. Marshall's mid-century study of this relationship offered a different conclusion, especially after examining the historical evidence of the Industrial Revolution, the Great Depression, and World Wars I and II. Marshall argued that capitalism and democracy were incompatible for two reasons. First, capitalism required a "set of practices" we associate with competition and define primarily in economic terms, whereas democracy emphasized equality, cooperation, and free access. Second, capitalism survives only in an environment where those who command the resources are deemed worthy, or perhaps competent, whereas democracy assumes an equal distribution of power among members of the community or society. This creates an inherent tension in society, which seeks to extend citizenship and maintain the wealth of commerce.

According to Marshall, rights associated with modern citizenship could only be understood in the context of what we know as the modern welfare state. He concluded that social actions the civil sphere created in tandem with the welfare state revolved around three axes of tension where social conflict would have to be balanced or transformed to create some semblance of social order. These axes of citizenship were known as the civil, political, and social axes. In the civil axis, rights would be developed to assure necessary or fundamental individual freedoms. As these first appeared in the eighteenth century, civil citizenship took the form of laws where society would put principles of acceptable boundaries of citizenship into constitutional form. Political citizenship focused on extensions of participation and sharing of political power with the masses. Here a relationship was created between citizen and parliament, with tensions created in direction of rule or allocation of resources always in check by those voting. Social citizenship, according to Marshall, was about defining a standard of life and the social heritage of one's community or society. Broad-based social relationships were built between the individual and services offered by the state (education, welfare, etc.).

Emphases on one dimension over another are associated with different eras of history, as well as different social institutions. The individual is thus placed in a context of history and social structure. Thus, Marshall suggested that citizenship evolved and changed as a result of social conflict and struggle. Class struggles of the feudal period resulted in changes in the extension of rights and legal protections (e.g., Magna Carta, common law in England). The constitutional changes of previous periods in history were altered yet again in the 1800s as economic inequality prompted demands for participation in democratic processes traditionally run by the ruling class (e.g., enfranchisement of working-class populations in England and the United States). According to Marshall, once political rights were achieved, class struggle manifested itself in the conflict over demands for certain standards of living, and this reflects the real class war. Although social rights have reduced some inequalities, the conflict continues.

Bryan Turner's work (1993) is a good example of how Marshall's theory of citizenship was extended. Turner suggests that modern citizenship especially be thought of as "that set of practices (juridical, political, economic, and cultural) which define a person as a competent member of society, and which has consequences for the flow of resources to persons or social groups" (2). He treats citizenship as more than just the formal extension of rights by the state. The political sociology of citizenship in this regard emphasizes a number of advances beyond Marshall. First, Turner highlights social practices connected to group (social) membership. Historically, one of the essential practices of citizenship has been to participate in the decision making of the community. This is an important tenet of democratic systems of rule as well. Under authoritarian forms of rule, the practices of citizenship are restricted to obedience to the commands of those in power. Second, Turner suggests that social practices unfold in a number of social arenas including those related to the laws of society, and the political and economic organizations and rules, as well as the normative and cultural spheres of social life. Thus, to conceptualize citizenship fully we must look for social practices other than just the political. Citizenship can be enacted in a number of social contexts. Third, Turner highlights how social practices influence the distribution of power in society. In his view, power is understood in a more traditional model of resource allocation and scarcity of resources in society. Nonetheless, the enactment of the social role of citizen can change the flow of resources in the social group.

In many ways, current political sociologies of citizenship are shaped by tensions between the traditional pluralist model of politics, and the class-elite models that argue citizenship is not equal by any means. Citizenship and subsequent political participation was tied to Enlightenment philosophy that moved societies from monarchies to democracies. The essential argument was

Detroit, Michigan, voters cast ballots in a presidential election

Credit: Jim West/Alamy Images

this: Human beings could rule themselves based on reason, knowledge, and understanding of the social condition. In the Age of Revolution, the notion of rule through divine right was transformed. We associate the emergence of citizenship in the nineteenth and twentieth centuries with the philosophy of liberalism and the changing nature of the relationship between individual and the state. As Hall and Ikenberry (1985) note in their study of citizenship, liberalism, and the state, "the individual is held to be the seat of moral worth" (5).

THEORETICAL FRAMEWORKS

Each framework in political sociology approaches the study of political participation with different assumptions and perspectives. Nonetheless each examines the classic assumptions about democracy, the role of participation by the masses, as well as the role of political action in the public sphere in different ways. This work and its many directions over the past one hundred years offers a detailed political sociology of political participation in its many forms, as we shall see.

Pluralist

The pluralist framework places a heavy emphasis on political participation, as it argues that participation by the masses and competition among interest groups are the essence of democratic society. The plurality of power in society in fact includes individual citizens influencing the allocation of societal resources in a number of different ways. The pluralist view of political participation links it closely to the creation of the state, and thus sees participation by individuals and groups as critical to its survival. Participation is one way to understand how societies deal with the pressures of modernization. Participation is also a way to bring about consensus and integration. Elections are taken as the final arbiter of political decisions and conflicts over values. "Majority rule" is never challenged to the point where the society crumbles.

In their outline of the pluralist approach to understanding political participation, Alford and Friedland (1985) identified forms of citizen action at different levels of social organization. For example, widespread changes at the societal level typically involve organization of citizens into sociopolitical movements. The Civil Rights Movement of the 1960s is a good example of a watershed movement resulting in changes in the distribution of power at many levels of state action. Numerous policies and practices would eventually change as a result of this movement's concentrated efforts to reform voting rights and employment practices, and raise societal concern about racial, gendered, and age-based prejudice in society.

At another level of social organization, political parties structure participation in governance by organizing citizens into party activities and party voting. Parties may sometimes attempt to pull in social movements into their political work, as the Democrats did with the Civil Rights Movement. In the United States, participation in the work of a political party is a mechanism for exercising influence over policy. Interest-group work and lobbying are examples of the kinds of efforts that formalized organizations use to create other channels of participation. Interest groups typically activate citizens over single-policy issues. For example, the American Association of Retired Persons (AARP) keeps its members informed of federal and state legislation changing policies on Social Security (SS), Medicare, or health care reform. The AARP works with both political parties in the United States to create favorable policy outcomes for persons who approach retirement as defined by law, or to support programs designed to help aging segments of the population. Members are typically encouraged to send letters or contact their representatives in Congress when policies concerning this segment of the population become a concern.

One of the more interesting statements of liberalism, citizenship, and political participation in the modern era was that offered by Theodore Lowi (1969). He argued that liberalism is a product of capitalism, but through history this has evolved into new forms of citizenship. Traditional capitalism was the seedbed of American civic ideas about political participation: "The United States is a child of the Industrial Revolution. Its godfather is capitalism and its guardian Providence, otherwise known as the 'invisible hand' " (3). It created a political culture or liberal philosophy that civic life in America was a function of beliefs in individualism, rationality, and nationalism. Thus, early American liberalism accentuated the basic tenets of capitalism. These ideas went hand in hand in defining citizenship.

Lowi argues that in the nineteenth century, the United States was characterized by pure capitalism. In the early twentieth century, four factors changed the public's ideological orientations toward capitalism:

1. increased division of labor with a multiplication of roles;
2. specialization in the units of production and distribution systems;
3. multiplication of the units of social control; and
4. spatial differentiation, urbanization, and population shifts.

In the late nineteenth century and after the Industrial Revolution, the progressive and populist reforms placed a greater emphasis on state protection of interests. Emphasis moved away from the capitalist philosophies of self-regulation and the invisible hand, and shifted to the state that defined citizenship in a manner that would foster social control.

The post-industrial period marks the entrance of activist government, which is found in the modern liberal state. Lowi describes what emerged as "interest-group liberalism." After the Industrial Revolution especially, the state was characterized by greater emphasis on interest groups influencing the incremental development of public policies and associated governmental agencies and civil servants working to support what was a growing role for governmental regulation of social life. Social-class politics as witnessed in Europe did not play out in the United States. Lowi concluded that competition among interest groups would assure this, because class unity is avoided and replaced by pluralist forms of state. Thus, liberalism as a philosophy of the state and citizenship in the early twentieth century sought greater separation between the state and the economy, and treated politics as an arena for conflict with governance left to the bureaucrats and the emerging class of civil servants loyal to the ideals of the craft of governing.

As he witnessed the social changes of the 1960s, Lowi hinted at yet another shift in how citizenship would be defined in the United States, especially at the end of the twentieth century. But Lowi argued that the changes of the last half of the twentieth century would threaten earlier forms of the liberal state. He warned of dangers that would come from excessive interest-group liberalism. Some of these paradoxes have become central to the research agenda in political sociology:

1. atrophy of institutions of popular control, resulting in a tendency to turn things over to leaders. This atrophy would create a dominance of administration and bureaucracy in its negative sense with much greater complexity and barriers to true public participation in all public decisions and a lack of accountability for those who govern;
2. the maintenance of old and creation of new structures of privilege. In other words, failures in civic participation would result in the protection of leaders at the expense of the masses, and privilege preserved for the administrators. He feared that interest groups would become more specialized and deny public participation in the structures. Membership in interest groups is transformed as group membership focuses on volunteerism to a cause rather than loyalty to the agenda;
3. a weakening of popular government and the protection of privilege that are aspects of conservatism or the preservation of the status quo. Interest groups that capture public opinion would create administrative structures that resist change.

This conceptualization of citizenship at the end of the twentieth century suggests interactions with bureaucracies and large organizations captured by the modern administrative state. The consequences would include failures to address widespread social concerns and political fragmentation.

The pluralist understanding of political participation rests on a view that the state is a policy-making system that can be influenced by those who vote, organize or influence others into action, or express opinions. The framework treats participation as a prerequisite for making the system we call the state operate effectively. The balance of power is created through mass participation. That is, when citizens who have been granted the power to participate in decisions and self-govern, and actually participate as required, the policy outcomes create a consensus in the outcomes of governance. Thus, equilibrium and social order is preserved. In states where mass participation is prohibited, competition between factions or military rulers results in frequent changes in the state and social disequilibrium. Mass participation is a key if not the principal orienting theme for pluralist theories in political sociology.

The assumptions of the pluralist notions of political participation are challenged by Marger (1987), who observes that the democratic requirement of mass participation has evolved into something quite different. He suggests that the assumptions fail in three regards. First, rates of participation vary significantly from one democratic state to another. Assuming high rates of participation could result in what Lipset (1981[1960]) called "working class authoritarianism" (102) fostered through the participation of middle- and working-class participants swayed by less than sophisticated or fully informed claims to how society should be governed. Second, the varieties of political participation make it difficult to simply claim that participation is a function of demands by the masses being translated into policy outcomes by those who rule the state. Political bodies such as legislatures or chief executives do not necessarily respond to the opinions of the electorate. This may be a function of knowledge, as legislators elected to office for long periods of time hold greater expertise than the electorate at large. These legislative experts may be challenged by forms of participation such as protests and social movements, or by letter-writing campaigns typically involving far fewer citizens. The fact that the masses engage in many forms of political influence, combined with the sometimes independent behavioral dynamics of bodies of the state, creates a political process that is more complex than pluralists describe. Third, Marger suggests that there is an uneasy marriage between the governing masses and electoral participation. But beyond that, the masses cannot participate in policy deliberations at all levels of the policy decision-making process. Thus, nonparticipation by virtue of the way the democratic state is designed creates points in the process that invite elite decision making. In other words, the complexity of policy creation may in fact foster elite concentrations of power at certain levels of the state because it's more efficient than mass participation. These observations are common to the critique of the pluralist framework and, as we shall see in the next section, are at the core of the elite views of how political participation should be studied.

Elite/Managerial

The elite/managerial perspective on participation suggests that avenues for the genuine influence over policy, allocation of resources in society, or influence over decision making is limited to a small group. Participation by the masses then is perhaps symbolic, or sufficient to generate legitimacy for the ruling elite to pursue selected actions. In 1943, Joseph Schumpeter observed:

> democracy is not a process of popular participation and representation; rather it is an institutional method for selecting leaders. It is not an outcome (representation of popular will) but a structure (elite competition). (quoted in Alford and Friedland 1985: 250)

In this sense, political participation involves various attempts by elites to manage the political tensions originating from the masses. In other words, participation of the masses matters little in light of the fact that the few who rule are the focus of attention. The elite framework treats the participation as the management of electoral competition between elite groups (e.g., political parties), or the interactions between citizens and bureaucracies, or co-opting the will of the masses into the agenda of competing elite groups.

Through extensive research the elite perspective reveals a compelling pattern in the institutional forms of political behavior. In the United States, about half of all citizens participate in the electoral process—usually fewer than half. Moreover, as we shall see in looking at the various typologies of political participation, the more sophisticated the form of participation (e.g., running for office, expressing an opinion to newspapers or elected officials, or participating in a campaign), the fewer the number of participants. In other words, democracy in America is not a democracy of mass participation. This is an important beginning point for the elite perspective. Clearly, the ideal form of mass participation suggested by a democratic state is just that—an ideal. The political decisions of the society are in the hands of a few.

One approach by theorists in this tradition stands in contrast to the pluralist interest-group model suggested by Lowi and mentioned in the previous section. As a way of contrasting these perspectives, we present the work of Ralf Dahrendorf who argued in the 1950s that participation in political decisions was essentially decision making among competing elite policy groups and not ordinary citizens: "There is a clear division between ordinary citizens who possess only the right to vote and the elites, who are in the position to regularly exercise control over the life chances of others by issuing authoritative decisions. . . . Citizens are not the suppressed class, but they are a subjected class" (Dahrendorf 1959: 293).

Dahrendorf (1959) suggested that politics in society be viewed in the context of conflict groups that are generated by the differential distribution of authority or power in society in what he called "imperatively coordinated associations" (ICAs). Building upon the works of Weber, Dahrendorf argued that organizations and groups are built around conflicting interests, or what amounts to contending associations for scarce resources in a society. A struggle between those who control and those who are controlled is always present. In industrialized societies, these ICAs serve as legitimations of authoritarian relationships. The ICA is a concept borrowed from Weber, which describes the organizations that focus on various social tasks, such as unions, schools, and government. Moreover, we see in this conceptualization the application of the Weberian view of legitimate power exercised in modern society. This model of power relationships suggests that social interests are structured according to an individual's relationships with various levels of social organization and a division of labor.

Dahrendorf argues however, that the basic structure of these relationships in the social order is a dichotomy between those in power and those under domination. When groups or organizations assert opposing interests and attempt to gain authoritarian status in a society, those dominating will resist, giving rise to social conflict. Once conflict emerges, authority within the social order is redistributed. Dahrendorf does not adopt Marx's notion that conflict is based on economic factors. Rather, conflict in society is based on competing ICA interests. Stratification in this view involves the organization of associations and competitions for power.

This framework studies participation in politics by examining the work of elites and how they control or subject the masses. Elite manipulation of campaigns or the roles of political parties in absorbing social conflict are typical topics of study. The two-party system in the United States is seen by elite theorists as an example of elite rule, with policy outcomes of Democrats and Republicans considered quite similar, inevitably protecting elite interests that are expressed through lobbying groups or corporate interests that cooperate with party leaders and campaigns. The masses have few choices in a two-party system where the winner takes all.

A good example of where political sociologists explore the elite's management of political participation is focused on money and politics. Much of this research follows the elite approach that finds that competing groups among the elites seek to influence politics by raising money and creating war chests to be made available to favorable candidates or parties. Manza, Brooks, and Sauder (2005) find the following patterns in this body of research:

1. political contributions to incumbents seeking re-election create a "signaling effect" that can deter others from running against the incumbent in races for Congress;
2. contributions to candidates build a war chest, which in turn can influence election to public office only in that elections require money. Money helps one get elected to office, whether it comes from private interest groups or party organizations; and
3. "there is little disagreement among analysts that PAC money buys access" (225). This suggests that interest groups that do contribute may have an advantage in opportunities to meet and discuss public policy.

In this regard, elites participate in the political process by influencing who runs for office, building resources for campaigns, and accessing policy processes. For the disengaged or the masses who participate in the electoral cycle only as voters, participation and influence are dwarfed by the flow of resources coordinated by competing elite interests.

Class

The class perspective concludes that political participation is allowed only as far as it preserves the interests of the capitalist classes. Marx and Engels in the 1848 *Communist Manifesto* suggest that the only genuine moment of mass participation by the working class was that found at the revolution as they predicted:

> The Communists disdain to conceal their views and aims. They openly declare that their ends can be attained only by the forcible overthrow of all existing social conditions. Let the ruling classes tremble at a communist revolution. *The proletarians have nothing to lose but their chains*. They have a world to win. Working Men of All Countries, Unite! (1961: 43–44)

But the workers' revolution predicted by Marx for the most part has not been realized as capitalism has advanced into many societies throughout the world. The class approach has consistently confirmed that the working class and the poor simply do not participate in large numbers in the many forms of giving voice in a democratic society (Piven and Cloward 1989; Verba, Schlozman, and Brady 1995).

The class framework argues that the power held by the upper class is significant for assuring that the state apparatus protects the interests of those with the most capital. The forms of participation in a class-stratified society may be symbolic, or may in fact pacify the masses to a level of acquiescence to ultimately preserve upper-class dominance. Such is the class view of participation in the political process. That is, at best, participation by the working and middle classes has miniscule impact on the reallocation of power, let alone policy. This is especially true for policies related to taxation, business, finance, banking, and commerce. As the Task Force on Inequality and American Democracy created by the American Political Science Association concluded, "ordinary Americans speak in a whisper while the most advantaged roar" (2004: 11).

Political sociologists continue to consider the significance of social class to the complexities of political participation. Some have argued that class-based participation has declined with the ascendancy of the modern democratic society since the Industrial Revolution. Seymour Martin Lipset (1981[1960]) argued that class differences in the structure of political parties in democratic societies have in fact become the hallmark of the "democratic translation of the class struggle" (320). In this sense, political participation as party activity represents one way in which the class perspective explains the absorption of labor political action into existing parties and unions rather than revolutionary movements. In other words, the unrest of exploited workers is transformed into a belief or sense that workers have a voice in the political process. As Lipset (1991) and others have pointed out, class-based participation declined toward the end of the twentieth century. We will examine this in detail in our discussion on voting. While socioeconomic status continues to be significant in explaining some differences in the various types of participation, the overall pattern in Western democracies has been a decline in political action based on class connections. Others (Hout, Brooks, and Manza 1995; Przeworski and Sprague 1986) have suggested that patterns in class-based political actions change over time and it is too early to declare the class perspective a theoretical dead end in the study of political participation. These researchers point to the role of class identity in the formation of attitudes and beliefs that in turn affect the ways in which individual citizens from the working and middle classes participate in various political actions. The class perspective continues to point to the significant influence that economic and educational differences have not only on voting but also on protesting, participating in social and political movements, and following politics.

Rational Choice

Rational choice models of political participation treat political action as derived from economic interest or social action that solidifies an agreed-upon or desired political outcome. In other words, persons, groups, or institutions exercise whatever power they can to influence political outcomes in their best interest. Recent rational choice approaches to the study of politics are known as "game theory," which suggests that individuals, interest groups, or even nation-states will make strategic choices given a certain set of circumstances. Game theory attempts to predict outcomes by knowing the interests of the actors and the strategies used for making decisions. In many ways, rational choice approaches to the study of political participation, especially voting, have become a staple in the research on participation.

The basic argument of the rational choice approach was best summarized by an early champion of the model, Anthony Downs, whose economic models of voting were significant to the development of rational choice theories. Downs (1957) observed: "Every rational man decides to vote just as he makes all other decisions: if the returns outweigh the costs, he votes; if not he abstains" (260). Downs offered five propositions about participation in voting that are exemplars in many ways of how rational choice theory conceptualizes participation:

1. when voting is costly, every citizen who is indifferent abstains, and every citizen who has any preference whatsoever votes.
2. if voting is costly, it is rational for some indifferent citizens to vote and for some citizens to abstain.
3. when voting costs exist, small changes in the perceived costs of voting (e.g., national holiday on election day, relaxed voter registration procedures, a ride to the polls) may radically alter the distribution of political power.
4. the costs of voting act to disenfranchise low-income citizens relative to high-income citizens.
5. it is sometimes rational for citizens to vote even when their short-run costs exceed their short-run returns, because social responsibility produces a long-run return. (266–271)

These assertions are typical of the kinds of variables rational choice theorists would study when looking at political participation: choice, costs or returns, resources, and abstaining or participating. As we will see in Chapter 7, rational choice models of voting are powerful explanations in determining whether an individual votes, and the model has been applied to other forms of participation as well.

Mancur Olson, Jr. (1965) offered another classic model of the rational choice approach moving toward participation based not on a calculation for voting but rather participation in politics equated with collective action. Individuals and groups would form into collective action around a desire to create or enhance what Olson called "collective goods." These creations of group action would emerge in the marketplace of political interests such as public sidewalks, schools, or a common defense. When individuals find some benefit to participation in the creation of the public good, they are likely to participate because benefits most likely will outweigh the costs. This approach to collective action suggested that participation in the collective was linked to incentives of some kind. The outcome gained was considered worth the participation required. Olson is famous for creating the concept of the "free rider problem" that emerges when individuals contribute nothing to the decision making yet experience equally high gains in contrast to all others in the group. Moreover, this early articulation of rational choice theory began to advance research on why individuals would volunteer in various groups and associations, including those with political goals.

Consider, for example, the recent concerns with declining voting rates in the United States as well as the alleged decline in joining various civic and community associations suggested by

Putnam's 2000 thesis in *Bowling Alone,* or what Dalton aptly refers to as *the crisis of democracy literature* (2009: 163). As we shall see later, this research laments the fact that over half of the eligible population in the United States fails to vote in each presidential election, leaves more active forms of participation to what amounts to less than one-fourth of the eligible voting citizenry, and has exhibited increasing civic isolation (Putnam 2000). Rational choice theorists would approach these patterns with an assumption that disengagement from political participation of many kinds is a sign that these forms of participation are too costly in terms of time, knowledge or skills, or other resources. In this regard, lack of participation is a rational choice based on the high costs of participation. Or equally as plausible according to this perspective would be the conclusion that nonparticipation is a choice reflecting satisfaction by citizens who require no political action or attention to issues!

Postmodern

The postmodern theorist approaches political participation in a rather unique way. Although perhaps an oversimplification, some of the postmodern approaches to political participation treat participation as freedom to explore the intersections between politics, everyday life, and social identity (Best 2002; Giddens 1992). Moreover, this framework is home to political sociologists who conclude that politics after the modern era is about redefining citizenship through the construction of new categories of inclusion, exclusion, identity, and political association. Social solidarity to create new political groupings around what some would call social narratives is designed to challenge more traditional conceptualizations of citizenship, including the nature of political participation.

We can begin to understand the postmodern view of political participation by considering the critical assumption that life at the beginning of the twenty-first century is guided heavily by consumerism, technology, globalization, and distrust in the traditional forms of political participation. One of the key figures in this framework is Zygmunt Bauman (1997), who has suggested that societies today are composed of individuals who move from one social context to another and fail to commit to the long-standing traditions of using politics or science to understand and act in the social world. He identifies four types of postmodern personalities migrating from one context or social situation to another:

1. the stroller—someone who perhaps is oriented by superficial things, especially related to fashion or looks;
2. the vagabond—the nomad who finds no particular social identity upon which to land or settle;
3. the tourist—seeks out social lives as a way to experience new or different things, perhaps even treating life as movement from one entertainment setting to the next; and
4. the player—it's about the social game and being strategic in how the social game itself is played; the player is never committed to an idea or goal or outcome, but rather just plays the game. (Bauman 1996)

These personality types created by the social conditions of the postmodern era are indicative of what Bauman describes in many works as the altered patterns of social interaction. Thus, politics is seen as politics of self-identity and one participates by playing the definitions of self projected into the public sphere.

What does this have to do with political participation? As we shall see in Chapter 8, some political sociologists argue that political and social activism around lifestyles, consumerism, feminism, race, and sexualities are all oriented by this exploration of multiple social identities.

These new social movements are forms of political activism not oriented around labor or social-class concerns, and the fight for civil rights per se, but rather are movements organized to construct challenges to what are perceived as dominant identities. Consider too, for example, how Internet technology provides a place for individuals to pose as gay or bisexual and take on this identity on a Web site or in a chatroom. They may play the game of advancing the identity, or pass from one chatroom to the next trying on new sexual identities. This is political participation in the postmodern sense in that power is personal and expressed in a sphere of public space. In other words, the technology for the new social movement provides a noninstitutional social context for use namely through the power of reconstructing identities. Bauman and others would note that the freedom that comes from the postmodern social condition is the freedom to exercise power around identity, everyday practices, or newly created social groupings and connections.

Another example of the postmodern treatment of politics is that offered by Jurgen Habermas (1989a, 1989b), a sociologist associated with the famous Frankfurt School in Germany. In many ways, Habermas is interested in preserving democracy by exposing ways in which advanced capitalism distorts more traditional notions of democracy. For example, he is critical of how dialogue about political issues in society is dramatically altered by corporate interests to make profit, rather than rationally discussed to solve social problems. This approach argues for a reconstruction of ways to participate in politics. In other words, this framework suggests that political participation is fluid, always changing as persons and groups in society seek out new social landscapes to challenge power.

The postmodernist argument outlined by Habermas is quite extensive and goes well beyond the scope of this summary. But his critical sociology argues in the postmodernist tradition: as politics, science, and religion lose their credibility in guiding people's everyday decisions, something must be reconstructed in its place. He argues for an interaction and discourse where members of society rebuild participatory democracy by coming to reasonable ideas about addressing social problems. The state may no longer be the arena for guiding decisions about how best to address problems of global warming, for example. And so, individuals politicize their everyday existence by being aware of the impact of carbon emissions on their environment, and choosing to ride their bikes rather than drive to work! This is a form of political participation that might catch on with others who also commit to riding their bikes as a political action. Large systems such as governments, or certainly corporations, fail in this regard. The discourse of global warming shifts to coming to agreed-upon conclusions about "what I can do in my everyday" life to participate in bringing an end to environmental problems.

What distinguishes the work of Habermas from Weber and Marx? Marx believed emancipation from alienation and social conflict brought on by capital accumulation would occur through enlightening the workers who would organize into eventual class-based revolution. Weber offered little optimism, describing instead the emergence of an "iron cage" of rationality, constructed through bureaucracy and demanding an adherence to formalized systems of law. Habermas, in the critical theory tradition, believes that emancipation from the postmodern condition occurs through the social interactions between people. Like many postmodern theorists, Habermas draws upon the psychoanalytic approach and suggests that individuals come to understand how their communicative rationality is taken from them when they adhere to a technocratic ideology. By realizing how communications are distorted by systems and structures, Habermas believes that individuals can regain their communicative competence—that is, a politics devoid of distortions created by traditional politics or ideologies. This is one example of the postmodernist view of political participation; redefinitions of self-identity against the monoliths of political and economic systems!

POLITICAL PARTICIPATION AND ITS MANY FORMS

Participation in the political processes of society can take many different forms. As suggested earlier, some of these forms are a function of rules or laws, others are formalized through social roles attached to the notion of citizenship, and we also find that participation can be less formalized as citizens participate at the everyday level in advocacy, resistance, and politicized talk. There is a wide range of social activities that we can connect to political participation.

Early Typologies of Political Participation

Political sociologists have developed a number of typologies to identify and measure various types of political participation. These typologies have not only proven useful in painting a picture of what people do when they act on political attitudes or demands, but the typologies have also been useful in organizing the large body of research on political participation, especially voting. The typologies of political participation have also helped make connections among ideology, attitudes, and values, which are assumed to be the basis for social and political actions as we saw in Chapter 3. In this section, we examine three early typologies that guided much of the later research on political participation, and then consider a number of more recent studies of types of political participation as updates of sorts to the earlier frameworks.

Lester Milbrath (1981) developed one of the first typologies of political participation in 1965. He suggested that political acts by citizens went beyond mere voting, and were typically patterned into clusters of behaviors. Later, Milbrath and Goel (1977) defined participation "as those actions of private citizens by which they seek to influence or to support government and politics" (2). These actions were thought of as political roles now understood as somewhat complex and multidimensional. Conceptualizing political participation as multidimensional highlighted the significance of individual intentions, resources, and skills. These roles emerged as a result of a person first deciding to get involved in the political process in some way, such as casting a vote on Election Day or attending a city council meeting. The action then was altered by a second characteristic of participation, what they called the *direction* of the action. Once a decision to participate (or not participate) was made, the action could be understood in terms of duration and intensity.

The roles Milbrath and Goel identified in their typology varied in terms of action, duration of the political act, and intensity of the political act. They suggested that American citizens could be categorized into three modes of political participation: (1) apathetics, or those withdrawn from the political process; (2) spectators, or those showing minimal involvement, who have decided to be engaged at a basic level; and (3) gladiators, or "active combatants" in the political system. This typology suggested that political participation was in fact arranged in a hierarchy, and thus, the typology offered an important systematic explanation for why a significant percentage of Americans simply did not participate in politics. Of course there was great interest in explaining not only why people did not vote or participate in political party meetings, but also what influenced those who did. Political participation was now understood as having many complex dimensions.

In addition to the three basic modes of participation (apathetics, spectators, and gladiators), Milbrath and Goel identified seven specific forms of participatory acts (these acts are listed in Table 6.1). These political acts represent behaviors that vary according to difficulty and styles of influence. Moreover, this typology helped researchers understand that political participation is not a set of distinct behaviors, but rather, political participation is a pattern of behaviors, much like the role set that sociologists describe for all members of society. Like other social roles, those associated with political participation are a function of skill, time, and energy. Clearly, the strength of this typology then was to identify the forms of participation common to democratic systems, and raise questions about what factors might change political participation. For example, what influences the likelihood that an individual will give the time and energy to protest or write a letter to the editor?

At about the same time, Verba and Nie (1972), on the heels of the major voting studies in the 1960s and 1970s, suggested an alternative typology. They argued that political participation was influenced mostly by individual goals for some political outcome. Verba and Nie defined political participation as "those activities by private citizens that are more or less directly aimed at influencing the selection of government personnel and/or the actions they take" (2). Modes of political participation were the result of what citizens believed they can change or influence, the extent to which the participation involved conflict, the time and energy required for the participation, and the need for cooperation with other political actors to achieve any objective (Verba, Nie, and Kim 1978). Verba et al. identified four common modes of political participation in the survey project they conducted: voting, campaign activity, community activity, and contact with political leaders.

The typology developed by Verba and Nie brought attention to the fact that political participation was seen as a mix of modes, much like Milbrath and Goel had concluded. But they also found that this process of mixing modes of participation was complex for some individuals. Some modes of participation require greater resources for mapping out an objective, such as getting a particular candidate elected to office, and being adept at engaging in activities that would achieve the goal. This typology suggested that the modes were not equal in terms of influence or energy required to change or show support for political goals. Participation oriented to affect policy in Congress, a state legislature, or local city council was understood as goal oriented, and modes of participation were activated to achieve those desired policies.

A third typology of political participation took a different approach. Marvin Olsen (1982) argued that such typologies focus on the political sociology of power, and emphasize the connection between political action and impact on various elements of the political system. In other words, Olsen's research examined just how much power was exercised by the corresponding mode or role associated with positions in the polity. At the top of the hierarchy he identified "political leaders," those government officials elected to office as well as civil servants who are able to affect policy on a day-to-day basis. Clearly, these roles have greater power than those outside the governing apparatus. "Activists" were also seen as having considerable power, but it tended to be highly focused on a single issue or cause. Most individuals play the role of citizen in the polity, and exercise a collective power in each election. In this regard, influence is limited to participation in choosing political leaders. Marginals and isolates were at the edges of participation in the political process, typically unaware of politics and uninterested in having an impact on the political system.

Table 6.1 presents the distribution of individuals participating in the various surveys along the modes and categories of participation identified by these researchers. While the comparison of typologies emphasizes different variables that create the modes, there is fair agreement among the typologies about the modes of participation in general. In addition, these surveys identified a common distribution of the population across different modes. Nearly one-fourth to one-third of those surveyed participate at the margins of U.S. political activity. The more complex the mode of participation, the smaller the proportion of the population participating. For example, less than 5 percent participate by seeking elected office.

This early research on types of political participation established two important patterns. First, as seen in the contrasts between models, a few individuals participate in the

Table 6.1	Contrasting Traditional Typologies of Political Participation				

Milbrath (1965); Milbrath and Goel (1977)		Percentage	Verba and Nie (1972); Verba, Nie, and Kim (1978)	Percentage	Olsen (1982)	Percentage
Gladiators	Protestors	5–7			Leaders	3
	Community activists		Complete activists	11	Activists	14
	Party and campaign workers		Campaigners	15		
Spectators	Communicators	60	Communalists	20	Communicators	13
	Contact specialists		Parochial participants	4		
	Voters and patriots		Voting specialists	21	Citizens	30
Apathetics	Inactive	33	Inactive	22	Marginals	18
					Isolates	22

more influential or powerful types of political action. Yet, most citizens are inactive or apathetic, and at the most, people vote, and that's about it. Using Olsen's conceptualization, the power found in participation rests with a small percentage of the populace. Second, these typologies created two distinct categories of political action that would stay with future research. Participation was considered to be either conventional or unconventional. The conventional forms were associated with the role of citizen, namely voting, contacting elected officials, or running for political office. Unconventional forms of participation would include protest and some activism. These were important findings for the sociology of politics and power.

In what types of political participation did citizens engage in 2008? Using responses from the 2008 National Election Studies (NES), the most recent survey of citizens and their political attitudes and behaviors, we can construct a sense of what percentage of the citizenry is involved in certain types of acts. The 2008 election appears to have generated a great deal of interest, and as a result, a strong percentage of citizens turned out to vote. The NES also asked respondents to report on other types of political behaviors they engaged in; many of those were reflected in these early typologies of political participation. The 2008 results suggest similarities with the past. A strong percentage of citizens vote, and as we see in Table 6.2, about half of those who responded to the NES survey reported having signed a paper petition or attended a local city board or school board meeting. One-third of the respondents indicated they had given money to a political organization, or had attended a political meeting. Less than one-fourth of the citizens had attended a protest or rally or invited others to a political meeting. These patterns are fairly consistent with prior patterns of participation reported in the typologies discussed in this chapter. Emerging forms of participation, such as those that use the Internet, are worth tracking in the years ahead.

Table 6.2	Types of Political Participation Reported in the 2008 National Election Studies		
Type of Political Participation		**% Likely to**	**% Who Have Ever**
Vote			76.1
Attend a city or school board meeting		71.6	50.9
Sign a paper petition		70.6	51.2
Attend a meeting about social/political issue		55.5	30.5
Give money to a social/political organization		53.2	36.8
Sign an Internet petition		48.8	21.8
Invite others to social/political meeting		41.5	19.2
Distribute social/political group info		40.7	19.4
Join a protest march or rally		36.5	19.4

Source: The American National Election Studies (www.electionstudies.org). THE ANES GUIDE TO PUBLIC OPINION AND ELECTORAL BEHAVIOR. Ann Arbor, MI: University of Michigan, Center for Political Studies [producer and distributor].

Emerging Typologies of Political Participation

Milbrath suggested that participation was more complex as individuals moved up the hierarchy of participation from apathetic to spectator to gladiator; factors that would foster higher levels of participation were assumed to be more complex. In an ingenious test of Milbrath's model of participation, Ruedin (2007) conducted a computer simulation to explore the hierarchical argument implied in Milbrath's original model. In moving from spectators to gladiators, Ruedin found that higher levels of participation are not easily explained by knowing a few simple factors, such as socioeconomic status or even hypothesized personality traits. Rather, this study argued that greater activity in politics may best be explained by multiple influences. For example, associating with individuals interested in politics and being connected to networks of political communication are just two of many factors that would predict gladiatorial type political involvement. Ruedin urges more studies that go beyond just analysis of voting as participation and focus on a range of influences in more complex forms of participation.

Zukin et al. (2006) more recently concluded that the role of citizen participation has changed significantly in recent decades as a result of technology and social structural changes around consumerism, community, and generational values. They argue that the result has not been a decline in the number of forms of political participation, but rather the emergence of new forms, especially for the youngest cohort they refer to as the *DotNets*. They find that participation for the youngest generation of citizens includes Internet activism such as blogging. Community service also holds a prominent role in the lives of this generation. In addition, they find that civic engagement follows patterns of consumer-related behavior, such as boycotts of products or support for those companies "going green" in the era of environmentalism. These researchers link these forms of political participation to values and attitudes that motivate young citizens in a different way than older cohorts.

In a large-scale study of British citizens, Li and Marsh (2008) classified civic participation as comprised of political activists, expert citizens, everyday makers, and nonparticipants. This framework seems consistent with prior studies that suggested that a large portion of the population failed to participate in politics (39 percent in their sample), and a small portion of the population was described as activists (8.4 percent). The research by Li and Marsh uncovers forms of participation in the middle of this range of behaviors. Expert citizens (14.5 percent of respondents in their study) were understood as problem solvers who would use social networks, knowledge, and skills to negotiate or persuade others without being activists or without being captured per se by a political party or political organization. Li and Marsh find that expert citizens were perhaps at one time activists who played a role in the political conversations of the polity. The everyday makers (37.3 percent) understand politics as local and tend to act on local concerns as duty, fun, or personal interest rather than loyalty to a political party, ideology, or national cause. Everyday makers, according to Li and Marsh, "typically think globally, but act locally" (251). This typology is a good example of contemporary classifications that regard political participation more broadly than as defined by Milbrath, Verba, and Nie, and others.

As the study of political participation has evolved, political sociologists now treat forms of political participation as either institutional or noninstitutional. Traditionally, political sociologists have divided political participation into two categories: conventional (voting, running for office, etc.) and unconventional, or what some call contentious politics (Tilly and Tarrow 2006), such as riots and protests. Anthony Orum argues that the main distinction between conventional and contentious political behavior is how these activities "*both treat themselves, and are treated by the established authorities and institutions of a society, in radically different ways* [emphasis Orum's]" (2001: 219). In other words, the actions of those engaging in contentious politics are perceived by both the participants themselves and the authorities, or those having legitimate power, as being outside of the boundary of conventional behavior. We follow the recent work of Marger (2008) who defines institutional forms of participation as "legitimate ways in which, presumably, people can make their views known and pursue their interests through the prevailing political system" (384). This includes voting, writing letters to elected representatives, or seeking elected office. But as Marger observes, "when people find that their political objectives cannot be met by using the conventional institutions, that is the electoral system with its attendant parties and interest groups, they may act outside the established political framework" (384). The contrast and terminology here is important in that it highlights citizenship as a role within a legitimate, institutional, conventional framework including the norms, rules, and laws associated with that role. The terminology here is significant in another way. As activism for objectives deviates from the rules of the political system, it is noninstitutional in the sense that it does not adhere to the traditions associated with the role. These forms of political action include protests, movements, and revolutions.

INSTITUTIONAL FORMS OF POLITICAL PARTICIPATION

Institutional political roles for members of society reflect the traditional expectations of behavior associated with citizenship. Traditional, formalized means of participating in decisions about the distribution of power in society have been studied extensively in political sociology. Voting is the institutional form of participation studied most intensively. In fact, we dedicate an entire chapter to the research on voting because it's a significant type of political action in the political system. In this section, we examine other institutional or conventional forms of political participation as they too explain how individuals interact with political groups and institutions to influence policy, political outcomes, and distributions of power. These types of institutional political action include engaging in political conversations, utilizing the Internet for political action, and getting involved in campaigns or being engaged in campaign work.

Political Talk/Political Discourse

The importance of talking about politics as a form of political participation was discovered in one of the first studies of political behavior in America. Berelson, Lazarsfeld, and McPhee (1954) concluded that people discussed politics with those holding similar viewpoints, which had the effect of "stabilizing" voting intentions. Early studies of political participation established the significance of talking about politics and political conversations and treated the frequency of political discussion as an important dependent variable, usually in the traditional measures of political participation (Campbell, Gurin, and Miller 1954; Lazarsfeld, Berelson, and Gaudet 1944). More recent inquiries have generally supported the conclusion that individuals frequently engaged in political conversations are more likely to be politically active (Dalton 2009).

Discourse has also been linked to other political sociological concepts, going beyond its historical treatment as merely one aspect of political behavior. Inglehart (1990) uses the frequency of engaging in political conversation as a measure of political skill. He finds that the rate of political discussion positively correlates with Protestantism and higher levels of education, and political conversations are more likely to occur in states with advanced levels of capitalist development. Huntington (1991) suggests that levels of political talk provide an important indicator of democratization in a society. Knoke (1992) concludes that engaging in political discourse is the medium by which social influence takes place in social networks. His analysis demonstrates that individuals who are frequently engaged in political talk are more likely to vote, persuade others to vote in favor of a particular candidate, give money, or attend a political rally. Koch (1995) reports that reference groups can in fact influence political attitudes as a result of conversational processes. Clearly, political discourse has held an important place in describing social interaction at different levels of social organization.

As a result of the importance of political discourse in research on political behavior and political sociology, a number of analysts have only recently started to examine what factors might quantitatively and qualitatively alter different aspects of discussion. Based on research focusing on political conversations in a variety of settings, MacKuen (1990) identified various characteristics of social interaction that influence the mere presence of political talk. These factors include the value the individual places on expressing opinion, the presence of opposing viewpoints, and the degree to which the individual perceives that viewpoints are skewed in a certain situation. Weatherford (1982) found that perceived consensus by the actors in a social exchange would also influence the overall "climate of political discussion" surrounding the individual. These interaction-based dynamics raise important questions about how rates of political discourse might be influenced by environmental or structural forces.

Conceptualizations of human political thinking and ideology suggest that there is a qualitative significance to engaging in political discourse in addition to the quantity of political discourse (Gamson 1992). Rosenberg (1988) as well as Billig et al. (1988) highlight the significance of discourse in the development of individual political worldviews, ideologies, and political thought in general as we saw in Chapter 3. Rosenberg in fact suggests that research has been helpful in identifying those environmental factors which might in some situations alter the nature of political conversations. The basic conclusion of analyses like these is that discourse represents an important process in reflective thinking, and reflective thinking is a key element in the formation of ideology. Therefore, the construction of attitudes and beliefs about the distribution of power in society or politics in general may be a function of contexts and conversations about politics or power-related themes.

Current discourse about the extent to which the United States should reform health care policy provides a timely example of how talk and conversation are important in shaping belief systems around this particular public policy. Throughout the fall of 2009, citizens attended town meetings sponsored by members of Congress and various interest groups to provide comments on what health care reform should look like. Interestingly, some of these town meetings turned violent as participants engaged in shouting matches were booed as they spoke in favor or against a particular position, or at some sites were assaulted by other participants.

Political Participation and the Internet

With the evolution of the Internet, political participation has changed. The technology of the World Wide Web, blogs, Twitter, and other forms of electronic communication, like any technological advances in society, has made an imprint on the nature of politics. Because the technology changes rapidly, research on what could be called e-politics (*e* for the electronic forms of communicating in a global system of networks) is only now beginning to catch up and create an empirical picture of just how technological change is at work in the relationship between society and politics. In many ways, e-politics creates new forms of political participation, including political talk and conversation, the acquisition of news and information about candidates or political issues, mobilization of participants, and as some have suggested, online voting.

Research to date has followed the view that the Internet represents a new medium for sharing information. Researchers of political communication focused on television and its effects on citizen knowledge and information and participation in politics, ultimately voting (see Bimber 2003 for a history of these "information revolutions" in American politics). One line of current research argues that the Internet is different in that it requires greater interaction than the one-way communication of TV. Individuals must search, select, and interact with Web sites on political candidates or issues. In his study of Internet campaigning, Klotz (2007) quotes author William Gibson in an interesting observation:

> Today's audience isn't listening at all—its participating. Indeed audience is as antique a term as record, the one archaically passive, the other archaically physical. The record, not the remix, is the anomaly today. The remix is the very nature of the digital. Today, an endless, recombinant, and fundamentally social process generates countless hours of creative product. (3)

Thus transmission of political information and knowledge online is different in that the online experience itself is participatory. Rather than receiving information as on TV, the Internet provides a social space for citizens to combine or actively engage information sources about candidates.

A number of studies find that in spite of the exponential possibilities for information shared through Internet interactions, the overall effect of the Internet on institutional political participation to date is minimal. Tolbert and McNeal (2003) studied recent NES to determine what impact online information had on voting. Those who reported gathering greater online information on politics were more likely to have voted in 1998 and 2000. But this may be because individuals who seek out online political information are more likely to vote anyway or are more politically engaged to begin with. In his studies of the NES, Bimber (2003) concludes that citizens who found information online "had not changed levels of engagements in any substantial way" (224). Early clues suggest, however, that the Internet may be a useful tool in mobilizing supporters for candidates or causes, and for increasing donations to the campaign or distributing information about rallies and meetings.

Other researchers are looking at the effects of Internet political activity on factors associated with political participation, such as trust in the political system or feelings of overall political efficacy. Shah, Kwak, and Holbert (2001) found a relationship between information gained on the Internet and increased feelings of trust and efficacy. Bimber's (2003) study extended these findings and revealed that persons who get political information online are more likely to mistrust traditional news sources (e.g., TV or newspapers) and place greater stock in personal exchanges of information from online sources. His analysis of the 2000 NES found that this was especially true for those with higher education and for younger voters.

Campaigning and Canvassing

One of the assumptions behind the activation of citizens is that policy can be influenced as a result of mobilizing voters to select a certain candidate, or collect signatures on a petition to support a policy by a local city council. Verba et al. (1995) suggested that individuals pulled into efforts at mobilizing citizens to work on behalf of political parties, candidates, or issues were motivated by what Verba et al. called the "civic voluntarism model." This model for explaining party activism, going door-to-door for a cause, or giving time to a political party draws heavily on sociological and psychological influences to explain participation. Dalton (2008) finds, "people participate because they can, they want to, or someone asked them" (58).

Participating in a political campaign or working for a political party as a volunteer requires a motivating interest in the candidate, issue, or loyalty to a party. In his analysis of election studies from a number of countries, Dalton (2008) finds that individuals who are older, hold strong party attachments, and report high political efficacy are more likely to engage in campaign activity of various kinds. People who describe themselves as partisans are surprisingly not more likely to expend the time and energy to work in a campaign.

Components of campaign work include engaging in direct contact with other citizens to raise money, supporting a candidate or cause, or voting. But direct contact with others on a political matter can also take the form of contacting a member of the state legislature or Congress to support a certain position. Persons with higher education were more likely to engage in direct contact with other citizens through door-to-door work or canvassing. Much like involvement in campaign activity, older persons and those reporting stronger party allegiances are more likely to engage in direct-contact forms of political participation. This is especially true if one has worked on a campaign where access to the elected official may come with greater ease as a result of localized contact.

Age and party attachments are important determinants to these more direct forms of canvassing and campaign activity. As Dalton suggests, as one gets older, policies related to taxation, quality of education, or health care and SS have direct impact on daily life, thus perhaps fostering greater interest and willingness to get involved. Moreover, those who hold strong beliefs about the ability of one political party to address these issues as opposed to another are an important motivating force for involvement. These are social psychological factors at work. Sociologically, we know that having the resources to participate in various forms of politics is associated with occupational status and education level. Nie, Junn, and Stehlik-Barry (1996) conclude that education is a key factor in many forms of participation. They and others conclude that there is a link between cognitive skills and higher education, which seems necessary for more active forms of participation as well as the adherence to principles about democracy and citizenship. This is consistent with the civic voluntarism model posed by Verba et al. (1995) in that the higher good justifies political involvement.

Conway (2000) emphasizes an additional key point about participation in campaigns, direct contact, and canvassing. She notes that these forms of participation required more resources, including time and in some cases money. She argues that using the rational choice approach, individuals who are able to afford the costs of this level of participation are more likely to become engaged in these forms of political action. This might explain why older and more highly educated persons are engaged. The cost to them may be lower and the benefits may be higher given that certain policies like social security benefits or tax policies may affect individuals more as they progress through life.

NONINSTITUTIONAL FORMS OF POLITICAL PARTICIPATION

The modes of political participation that move outside the traditional legal or customary forms of influence are known as noninstitutional forms of political action. These include protest, political violence, and terrorism. In a study of political participation in European countries, Sabucedo and Arce (1991) found that citizens perceived unconventional forms of political action in broad categories that include legal and illegal actions. Unconventional legal acts include protests or strikes and boycotts. Unconventional illegal acts include unauthorized demonstrations or rallies, protests that disrupt local order, and in some cases, political violence. We look at political violence and terrorism in the chapters that follow because of their recent significance in U.S. domestic and global politics. In addition, we explore participation in social and political movements separately as this field of sociology has generated significant advances in explaining why people participate in both violent and nonviolent political movements of many kinds. As we will see in Chapters 8 and 9, sometimes individuals participate in movements and acts of political violence simultaneously. At this point, we introduce briefly the research on noninstitutional political participation to develop a sense of how power is resisted or challenged by individuals in society.

Graffiti

Typically, noninstitutional or unconventional political participation is thought of as riots, protests, mobs, or acts associated with the potential for physical violence as well as property damage. Certainly not all forms of contentious politics are necessarily violent. One form that has not received much attention from political sociologists is graffiti, although scholars in communication studies and rhetoric have examined strategies that graffiti writers use to advance their political arguments from sites as diverse as Moscow (Ferrell 1993), Northern Ireland (Sluka 1996), and Israel (Klingman and Shalev 2001), as well as Palestinian city walls (Peteet 1996) and Nigerian (Obeng 2000) and Ghanaian university student lavatories (Nwoye 1993).

Regardless of the culture or site, political graffitists have several things in common. First, graffiti is perceived as outside the course of normal or institutionalized political participation and may be criminalized. For example, in some U.S. cities, it is illegal for those under eighteen to possess spray paint (Peteet 1996). Ferrell (1993) argues that moral panic is often the response to graffiti and that the war on graffiti is similar to the wars on drugs and gangs. A moral panic is a process for raising concern over a social issue (Scott and Marshall 2005) where "folk devils" are implicated as the cause of a social problem. Folk devils are often powerless to challenge the accusations. Graffiti is often construed negatively by its association with vandalism and destruction (Klingman and Shalev 2001). More extreme responses occur when authoritarian regimes or occupying military forces perceive graffiti as a direct threat to authority. Writing on the walls in the occupied West Bank was treated as an illegal behavior by the Israeli military, which acted to erase graffiti and sometimes shot or beat writers (Peteet 1996). Somewhat less extreme are responses that view the appropriation of foreign imagery in graffiti as an assault on national identity.

Political graffiti is outside the institutionalized or accepted bounds of proper political behavior and those creating graffiti are often excluded from participating in mainstream politics.

University students in Ghana (Obeng 2000) and Nigeria (Nwoye 1993) write messages on lavatory walls because they lack other means to effectively influence the state. Anthropologist Julie Peteet contends that writing on the walls in the occupied West Bank during the height of the intifada (late 1980s to early 1990s) "was a sort of last-ditch effort to speak and be heard" (1996: 142) and "constituted a voice for those who felt voiceless in the international arena" (145). Although individuals who use graffiti may be powerless or outside the conventional political process, Peteet argues that graffiti is not merely a message of defiance, but a "vehicle or agent of power . . . to overthrow hierarchy" (140). It is an attempt to circumvent the power relationship between the dominant and the oppressed.

Besides being a form of political protest, graffiti has several other political functions, including communicating political ideologies and beliefs (Ferrell 1993; Sluka 1996) as well as creating a forum for debating political ideas (Nwoye 1993; Obeng 2000), socializing with a targeted group or teaching a targeted group political ideas and values (Ferrell 1993; Sluka 1996), creating cultural meanings (Ferrell 1993; Sluka 1996), and acting as a safety valve for releasing political tension that is much safer than directly challenging the state (Nwoye 1993; Obeng 2000).

A good example of sites where graffiti as protest can be seen is billboards, road signs, and other public signs that command attention from persons on a roadway. For example, the billboard in the following picture, which appears to be posted by individuals or groups opposed to

Billboards and signs become social spaces for graffiti as political contention. What emotions or beliefs are evoked by the example of a defaced billboard in this picture?

Credit: Photo by Lisa K. Waldner

abortion, is on a busy thoroughfare in an urban area where numerous passersby can view the message. But note the "Hitler" style mustache (we assume) on the billboard's photo. Is defacing a billboard in this particular manner outside the normal bounds of political expression? Is the political ideology about abortion countered by what we assume an attempt to depict this message as fascist? It's difficult to say for sure, but the allusion to one political ideology (fascism) on top of another (antiabortion) offers a good example of the ways in which graffiti takes on meanings in political protest.

Johnston (2006) contends that graffiti may appear to be the work of a single person but this is often misleading. We agree that graffiti is a collective activity for several reasons. First, while lavatories are often chosen by Nigerian and Ghanaian university students because of the privacy that allows a graffitist to write messages without fear (Nwoye 1993; Obeng 2000), it is far from a solitary activity. As Obeng (2000) points out graffiti is often sequential, with a statement followed by a response. Therefore, it is a type of discourse where participants take turns reacting to each other's messages. In situations where privacy is not possible, such as public walls, participants may organize in groups with members taking different roles such as provide supplies (e.g., purchasing spray paint), serve as a lookout, or write (Peteet 1996).

Orum (2001) notes that contentious politics is similar to conventional political activity in that both are organized and can involve well-educated and respected members of a community. Those who use graffiti as a form of contentious politics share a desire to change the social order but lack legitimate channels of power to do so. The lack of attention by political sociologists to the use of graffiti and other under-researched forms of protest adopted by the powerless and disenfranchised only serves to reify more conventional political behavior as legitimate, further stigmatizing those who fall outside more respectable forms of political participation. Often graffiti is associated with protest or political demonstrations that we discuss now.

Protest and Demonstrations

As Jenkins and Klandermans (1995: 8) point out, "Social protest is inherently a political act, because the state regulates the political environment within which protesters operate, and because social protest is, at least implicitly, a claim for political representation." The concept of protest has been used in various ways (Lofton 1985: 1). For example, *protest* can refer to the "unconventional and often collective action—taken to show disapproval of, and the need for change in, some policy or condition" (Frank et al. 1986: 228). Therefore, protest can be legal or illegal, peaceful or violent. Others view protest as one of the three major classes of action. According to this tripartite conceptualization:

> Protest struggle stands between polite and violent struggle, a kind of "middle force" . . . protest eschews or at least avoids the extensive physical damage to property and humans found in violent struggle on the one side and the restraint and decorum of staid politics on the other. (Lofton 1985: 261)

Eisinger (1973: 13) distinguishes between a generic definition of protest as "any form of verbal or active objection or remonstrance" and the more technical one that refers to a conceptually distinct set of behaviors, or a number of types of collective action that are "disruptive in nature, designed to provide 'relatively powerless people' with bargaining leverage in the political process." In protest, actors are trying to maximize their resources while minimizing the costs. For some scholars, then, protest can be distinguished from political violence by this attempt to minimize costs. Those engaging in violence could experience major costs such as death, serious injury, or loss of freedom. Protesters use the implicit threat of violence, whereas those using violence are explicit in their intention to harm.

Gamson's (1975) *The Strategy of Social Protest* seems to consider violence as a form of protest. The objective of social protest activities is to gain support for a movement's cause (Gamson 1975: 140). People typically engage in protest to achieve certain kinds of resources for the movement, such as attracting new members, reinforcing solidarity of current members, obtaining material rewards such as money or equipment, or gaining attention for a particular ideological position. At times protest activities hinder those opposed to the movement, for example, by making the opposition look bad (which can make the movement look good), destroying the opposition's resources, or eliminating key figures through political assassination.

As Gamson (1975: 140) notes, "The form that protest takes is viewed as the result of an interaction." Movement groups or individuals in the movement engage in a show of strength that may or may not be challenged by other groups, including law enforcement. Symbolic acts may be designed to challenge the power of another group or governmental authority (Tilly 1970 cited in Gamson 1975). For example, the American flag was burned at a white separatist protest rally in Pulaski, Tennessee, to challenge governmental authority. Protest demonstrations, which include sit-ins, rallies, marches, and pickets, are the most frequent form of publicly accessible movement activity. A demonstration is "an organized, noninstitutionalized, extraordinary form of political expression; a gathering of people (or a person if sponsored by or acting as a representative of an organized group) engaged in the act of making known by visible or tangible means a public display of group feeling" (Everett 1992: 961).

At times social protest activities may result in violence. In fact, violent activities of movements are a common form of political participation (Tilly 1973). Political violence can be viewed as "the result of reasoned, instrumental behavior" (Crenshaw 1992: 7). In general, those who are discontented or involved in some protest "are no more nor less rational than other political actors" (Gamson 1975: 137). Protest is now seen as an accepted form of engagement among groups with political standing rather than an activity of those at or near the bottom of the class system or on the political margins (Wallace and Jenkins 1995: 132). Gurr (1989: 13) identifies four significant changes in how group violence has been studied. First, most social scientists have come to recognize that group violence is typically a result of "real grievances over underlying social, economic, and political issues" rather than pathological acts of misfits in society. Second, choices are being made by the groups, their opponents, and authorities that all influence the likelihood and the type of violence. Third, "authorities have substantial responsibility for violence, either by their own action or through inaction in the face of private violence" (13). Fourth, violence is often an effective tactic in gaining recognition and concessions, particularly if it is the result of a prolonged social movement.

Social, Political, and Revolutionary Movements

In societies throughout history, we witness some of the more dramatic, widespread forms of participation—those dedicated to changing the political order through a social, political, or revolutionary movement. The "political order" in this sense is broadly defined, and can include anything from the political order shaped in public policies, order created through the extension or denial of civil rights, or changes in the structure of the state or regime itself. In recent decades, movements in the United States have brought about changes in voting and civil rights, as well as laws related to abortion, drunk driving, and human sexuality. In Chapter 8, we will look in detail at social movements and explanations for how movements arise. But in this chapter, we consider the nature of political participation in a noninstitutional sense, and highlight a few findings from what is an extensive tradition of study focused on social, political, and revolutionary movements.

Our understanding of participation in movements today faces a challenge in that, as Tilly (2005: 423) observed, "diverse forms of political contention—revolutions, strikes, wars, social movements, coups d'états, and others—interact." Some suggest there is no clear line to separate the broad spectrum of political actions categorized as "contentious politics" (McAdam, Tarrow, and Tilly 2001; Tilly 2005). This can range from organizing a movement to change policies or laws, building a movement to champion a social identity, overthrow the leadership of the state, or use violence and terrorism to bring attention to a group's political grievances.

Movements pose interesting questions at this point in our study of politics for the nature of citizenship. As mentioned earlier, Tocqueville marveled at the ability of Americans to create associations to address civil and political needs. The nature of social, political, and revolutionary movements suggests a path that may be characterized by conflict and tension (although not always). Thus, in the study of noninstitutional forms of political participation, it deserves attention. In Chapter 8, we focus on the nature of movements, and in Chapter 9, we focus on terrorism and political violence. At this point, however, we look briefly at the foundations for explaining participation in the politics of challenge.

In describing the logics of early explanations of movements, Jenkins and Form (2005) find that participation was explained by "strains, new resources, opportunities, and ideas" (335). These early studies of collective action broadly understood participation in agitations, crowds, or masses as a contagion of sorts fostered through irrational forces. In other words, participation in mass action was a function of aggression, hostility, or panic. Studies by Turner and Killian (1957) and Smelser (1962) changed this picture and suggested that movements in a society grew out of "emergent norms" and attempts to deal with social strains brought on by social change. This shift in the research viewed participation in collective acts as being connected to attempts to correct problems in society that were viewed as creating stress or strain, or as a way to meet changing values and norms in society.

An alternative explanation to participation in movements emerged in the 1970s, as these forms of challenges to the political order were understood to be purposeful. McCarthy and Zald (1973), for example, found that participation was a function of mobilization and leadership in movement groups' intent upon activating individuals and other resources. More recently, participation in contentious politics has been connected to systems of meaning (culture), definitions of grievances, and what C. Wright Mills described in 1940 as the "vocabularies of motive." A good example of how political sociologists have studied movement language is found in Textbox 6.1 where the vocabularies of motive used in the white supremacist movement are discussed. The research on hate groups highlights the connections between how movement participants use a logic of power in society and how this logic corresponds to forms of noninstitutional political action. The influences on participation in social, political, and revolutionary movements vary as do the theories developed by political sociologists to explain these forms of political action.

The nature and causes of institutional and noninstitutional political participation as introduced in this section reveal the many ways in which power is fluid and changing in society. The complexities of these various forms of participation will be discussed in Chapters 7–9. A number of recent theories on voting and electoral participation, as we will see, bring greater attention to the role of social division, the effects of legal changes, and demographic shifts in recent decades. As we will see in Chapter 8, various contemporary explanations for participation in contentious politics focus on social processes and structures, with some political sociologists concluding that social change and culture continue to be key factors in the construction of these movements. Before we conclude this chapter, we will consider a recent debate about the role of group membership and social networks in various kinds of political participation.

TEXTBOX 6.1

Hate and Violence in the White Separatist Movement

The label *hate groups* has frequently been applied to the white separatist movement and thus it is not surprising that the movement is thought of as very violent. Researchers (Dobratz and Shanks-Meile 1997; Kaplan 2000) have expressed concerns about studying this movement, given the media and watchdog images about its supporters. Kaplan (2000: xxiii) refers to the *demonization of the radical right* that makes it difficult for people to understand this movement. Indeed Kaplan, the author of many publications on the movement, including *Encyclopedia of White Power,* acknowledged that when he first started his research, he expected to find "angry, violent men, so consumed by hatred that they could scarcely have resembled human beings at all" (2000: xxx). Rather Kaplan (2000: xxxii) points out:

> What I found most puzzling was that the monsters of terra incognita, upon closer examination, were not really monsters at all. They held political views that were repugnant, and religious views based on fantastically eccentric interpretations of sacred text. But whatever their belief structure, these were not monsters. They were not the violent and hate filled people I had expected to find.

Ezekiel (1995) developed a typology of four kinds of movement members and their relation to violence:

1. The leaders often do not recognize the link between violence and a successful movement.
2. Typical members are not fanatical and do not want to harm nonwhites. They want to belong to a "serious" group and the possibility of violence suggests to them this is a serious organization.
3. The loose cannon is unpredictable and ready to explode. If that person disrupts, he is likely to be imprisoned. The movement can gain notoriety from this person's unpredictability and the idea that the movement can be violent.
4. Potential terrorists firmly support the movement's ideology. They need the comradeship of the tight terrorist cell to try to accomplish their goals.

Ezekiel (1995) suggests overall that the movement needs the aura of violence to help sustain it.

Like other movements, the white separatist movement has used a variety of strategies ranging from participation in violent activities to voting for political candidates who support their views. In the interviews of 113 white separatists (Dobratz, Shanks-Meile, and Waldner 2008), the majority (59) both believed that movement members should run for political office and believed that under certain circumstances violence is justified. Over 80 percent of the respondents answered yes when asked if violence was ever justified in the movement. When asked an open-ended question about under what circumstances violence might be justified, about 60 percent responded "in self-defense," whereas 22 percent mentioned violence would be justified when it helps the white race.

Major Donald V. Clerkin, B.S., L.L.B. of the Euro-American Alliance Inc., commented on the issue of self-defense "as a last resort in most cases, but always in self-defense. We oppose gratuitous violence—violence for its own sake, violence in order to terrify or intimidate. We don't allow members who merely want to inflict pain on someone else." Richard Barrett of the Nationalist Movement also expressed his position on self-defense and staying within the law: "We would encourage people to seek solutions that are peaceful but yet are self-defensive. So, be self-defensive. Be confrontational. Don't back down. Don't surrender your rights. But be aggressive only up to the point that you are still within the law" (Dobratz and Shanks-Meile 1997: 183).

Movement members have rather diverse views of the appropriateness and effectiveness of violence. For example, according to Barry Peterbuilt, a skinhead from Missouri: "It really depends on who you speak to and what their goals are. Right now we are in a transition period . . . and it is unclear as to whether or not violence will be necessary. Personally, I feel that violence is a very good motivation for governments and institutions to take any group seriously." Somewhat similarly John C. Sigler, aka "Duck" of the Confederate Hammer Skinheads argued: "Violence works, contrary to the nonsense of popular society, when the oppressed take up arms, the oppressor is forced to recognize and appease him" (Dobratz and Shanks-Meile 1997: 184–185). Nocmar 3 Clan Rock also commented on the appropriateness of violence, suggesting that its use can be effective at times, but it must be limited:

> People often specialize in different fields, I myself specialize in politics. When a problem such as the ones we feel are important is not addressed on a broad scale, violence is an excellent method to draw your views into the limelight. After this happens violence must be abandoned or you can not continue to pull support from the public. (Dobratz et al. 2008: 9)

Others in the movement do not think that the movement should be engaging in violence. For example, Jost (1993: 6) of NS Kindred pointed out how the movement had more than its share of characters potentially harming the movement, including those who believed now was an appropriate time for revolution:

> We all know that the White racial movement is adorned with a dismally large number of kooks, screwballs, sociopaths and government informers. But it is less known that there are a growing number who live in a fantasy world of revolution and guerrilla warfare. . . . At this time, revolution or guerrilla warfare is strictly for losers. The call to arms and revolution is completely irresponsible, very dangerous, and it plays right into the hands of our enemies.

From the statements shown here, it is apparent that there are mixed views within the white separatist movement about the timing of violence and whether to employ violence at all. Certainly, some believe that violence promotes success, some see it as effective if limited, and others are more questioning about whether violence is even an appropriate strategy.

POLITICAL ENGAGEMENT AND GROUP CONTEXT

Some of the earliest studies of political participation discovered that participation in politics was influenced by the associations of individuals in a number of group contexts (Berelson et al. 1954; Lazarsfeld et al. 1944). One of the first major studies of voting behavior reported in the now classic book *The People's Choice* (Lazarsfeld et al. 1944) discovered that variables such as socioeconomic status, religion, residence, and group membership were correlated with voting behavior. Replications of the analysis, however, led to serious revamping of the entire model. In 1952, social scientists at the University of Michigan proposed an alternative approach, focusing on three psychological variables: individual attachment to party, orientation toward issues, and orientation toward specific candidates. The findings suggested a strong link between party identification and support for candidates of the same party and issues often associated with the party. Interestingly, the significance of group membership, social networks, and associations would take center stage in debates about political participation in the new century.

Off and on since the Columbia studies of the 1940s and their emphasis on group influences on voting, social scientists have studied the role of group context in affecting many forms of political participation. Dennis (1987) offered an important discussion of the basic assumptions that characterize the group analysis of political behavior. Implicit in his work was that groups serve as some filter for the individual, or perhaps even as a yardstick by which political stimuli are considered. He observed that, "Membership, identification, commitment, likes and dislikes, and such, all filter the group through the prism of person-centered responses" (325). He also argued that considerable research showed how groups have personal meaning for individuals. Meaning in this case would include affective and rational dimensions. Finally, Dennis observed that groups are an important social-psychological source of attitudes and thus eventual behaviors. These themes would be picked up more broadly as Robert Putnam (1993, 1995) published a series of works in the 1990s that recognized the importance of group membership to participation in civic life. With his publication of *Bowling Alone: The Collapse and Revival of American Community,* Putnam generated significant academic and popular discussions around the apparent collapse of citizen engagement in civic life.

When Putnam (2000) introduced the notion of "bowling alone" as descriptive of American political culture and social malaise, he helped bring attention to long-standing sociological themes. The phrase *bowling alone* struck a chord similar to the terms *anomie, alienation,* and *the lonely crowd* and helped introduce discussions about how connected individuals are in modern society and what implications this lack of connectedness would have on democratic processes. The "bowling alone" thesis offers political sociologists, however, an opportunity to once again explore the significance of group cohesion and group membership and the influences of these aspects of social context on political participation. There is a long-standing research tradition in political sociology that explores the impact of group membership on political participation of many kinds. Specifically, attention was given to the connection between group-belonging and participation in civic and political life. This debate would bring a great deal of attention to the sociological concept of "social capital."

Politics and Social Capital

Early in this debate—and reminiscent of Toqueville's observations—the relationship between social capital and political participation was hypothesized to be central to the "health" of contemporary democracy in America (Foley and Edwards 1997; Miller 2009). Putnam (1995, 2000) initially linked social capital and political power as a result of his studies of Italian communities, and suggested that social capital in modern American communities was related to declines in political engagement. The subsequent research on social capital and civic engagement in many ways would build on the well-established work within political sociology that highlights the significance of social context to politics. This work shows that social connectedness in the form of networks (Knoke 1992), neighborhood identification (Huckfeldt and Sprague 1995), and group identity (Conover 1984; Miller et al. 1981) can influence ideology, political attitudes, and political participation. Timpone (1998) confirmed that forms of political participation and associated dynamics are affected by "social connectedness," which is conceptualized as anything from region of the country to neighborhood-level interactions. This notion of connectedness is an essential sociological argument in understanding political participation.

Interestingly, James Coleman observed years earlier that, "the concept of social capital constitutes both an aid in accounting for different outcomes at the level of individual actors and an aid toward making the micro-to-macro transitions without elaborating the social structural details through which this occurs" (1988: S101). Coleman (1988, 1990) originally outlined his conceptualization of social capital as a theoretical construct to describe what are essentially by-products of social interaction. In other words, his analysis of social capital treated the products of group memberships and ties between individuals as a transformation of sorts of social action into social currency (media) where exchanges of capital (financial, human, and cultural) constitute basic social processes. The various forms of social capital he identified include obligation and trust, information, and what he referred to as *effective norms* (1988). The forms of social capital reflect those aspects of human interaction that facilitate the achievement of a particular goal. What emerges from human interactions are "social-structural resources," which can be applied by individuals in different social contexts where action is directed toward a particular outcome. According to Coleman, social capital cannot be studied without consideration of social structures such as small groups, work settings, and organizational contexts. Coleman's framework places an emphasis on understanding social capital as having functions, forms, and contexts.

Coleman (1990) gave significant attention to voting in his original presentations of the social capital framework, mostly in an attempt to provide an alternative theoretical explanation to the rational school of voting. His work shifted the study of voting toward a normative model that was more closely aligned with sociological concepts. He makes several important observations regarding voting and nonvoting. First, he notes that voting is guided by emergent norms much like other choices in any given social context. Pressures from friends and other social connections can encourage or discourage an individual to vote. This model of voting suggests how social process explanations overcome the limits of the rational voting model, which asserts that if costs of voting outweigh rewards, the individual will not vote. Certain qualitative aspects of personal networks mean that in some situations ("differential application of the norm") (1990: 292), norms about voting may be a factor in the choice calculus for voting. Second, Coleman notes that, "Empirically, there is . . . a small positive correlation between social status and voting in modern democracies where voting is not compulsory. That correlation is very likely due to the fact that both interest in the election and social capital are lower among lower-status persons" (827). Voting rates vary according to level of social capital, and the eventual decision to vote can be changed by the context or situation surrounding lower-status individuals and categories of people.

Basing his work in a different set of theoretical assumptions, Bourdieu (1984, 1986) argues that there are three forms of capital—financial, cultural, and social—each caught up in the exercise of power: "resources . . . when they become objects of struggle as valued resources" (Swartz 1997: 74). These resources, much as Coleman suggests, emerge from the "possession of a durable network of more or less institutionalized relationships of mutual acquaintance and recognition" (Bourdieu 1986: 248–249). All forms of capital are developed, invested, accumulated, and spent in power relationships according to Bourdieu, and consequently, all forms of social capital vary in volume (accumulated or saved) and accessibility (opportunity to act); these variations ultimately create status differentials among individuals within society. Some researchers have used this theoretical perspective to study participation in social movements, and have found that networks provide the social and cultural capital that facilitates activism.

Bourdieu's theoretical conceptualization of social capital generally focuses on three social processes that have relevance to the study of civic engagement: transformation, fields, and stratification. All forms of capital represent a social currency of sorts, eventually transformed into social outcomes that Bourdieu suggests are practices, habits, and traditions. These transformations and transactions take place in "fields" or a "structured space of dominant and subordinate positions based on types and amounts of capital" (quoted in Swartz 1997: 123) where social interaction is structured into distinct patterns. One field Bourdieu (1990) studied is housing policy. Here, the landlord–tenant relationship—the dominant and subordinate—represents a pattern of capital exchange and transformation—rent for a unit and obligation for a lease. The repetition of capital transformation in these "structured spaces" creates more general forms of social stratification. Social class becomes apparent in this type of field, and is created by social processes, according to Bourdieu, out of repeated transformations of social, cultural, and financial capital in certain fields. Politics would constitute one such field of human action.

Both Coleman and Bourdieu conclude that the location of the individual in a context of social ties is a source of variations in different forms and volumes of capital. Coleman (1988) noted that there might be a "lack of social capital" (S103) in some social contexts, and offered an important observation that so far is under-researched. Specifically, he argued that "certain kinds of social structure . . . are important in facilitating some forms of social capital." More generally, those who live in these structures arguably retain less social capital, which inhibits participation in social processes like voting. Similarly, Bourdieu claims that social capital varies in volume as a result of context:

> The volume of the social capital possessed by a given agent thus depends on the size of the network of connections he can effectively mobilize and on the volume of the capital possessed in his own right by each of those to whom he is connected. (1986: 249)

Both theorists clearly give significance to structures, networks, and social context in creating forms and differences in social capital.

Themes in Research on Social Capital and Political Participation

A number of sociologists have argued that the study of social capital helps to account for the impact of variations in social context and structures on participation in politics, shaping policy, and political activism. Flora (1998) advances this argument, suggesting that researchers give greater attention to understanding social capital as emerging from "social embeddedness." He identifies one form of social embeddedness as "entrepreneurial infrastructures" where community leadership, political coalitions, and citizen support are found to vary, for example, in small rural towns. Mondak (1998) makes a similar point when he noted that "Social capital may inhere in the structure of all relations, but the form, character and consequences of that social capital vary. . . . We should endeavor to learn about the relative nature of social capital as it exists in various contexts" (435). Emphasis shifts to the structural and contextual rather than treating social capital as a resource. His observation extends the criticism often made that much of the social capital research on civic engagement has focused on "voluntary associations" (e.g., parent–teacher association , Lions Club) rather than on other social groupings (Greeley 1997). The embeddedness model of social capital creates a contrast to the rational choice models of social capital that cast the concept in terms of more economic explanations of social behavior and emphasize social capital exchange or accumulation.

To date most of the research has focused on explaining the connections between social networks, groups, and associations on traditional forms of political participation. As mentioned earlier, voting or engagement in campaign work can be linked to having friends so engaged or being a member of a group that urges these types of participation (Verba et al. 1995). Activism in a social or political movement has also been linked to network memberships (Snow, Zurcher, and Ekland-Olson 1980; Viterna 2006). Lim (2008) finds that the more social ties a person has to a variety of groups, the greater the likelihood that person is politically mobilized in a variety of political situations: "The key proposition in these studies is that people participate in political and civic activities because they are asked or encouraged by someone with whom they have a personal connection" (961). Lim's research finds that participation in a protest, community politics, or contact with elected officials can be realized even when the intensity of these personal connections varies from stranger, to indirect tie, to close friend.

Other research finds that social capital may not have such a direct role as that described earlier in recruiting, or cajoling friends to go vote (McClurg 2006). Walker (2008) summarizes current studies exploring this theme, finding that "associations are consequential for political participation because they promote political discussion (Eliasoph 1998), awareness of common interests (Fung 2003), psychological engagement about politics (Verba et al., 1995), and mobilization on issues of interest to community members (Barber 1984)" (117). Walker's own research shows that the nature and tone of the groups an individual belongs to are key to determining political activism. Similarly, McFarland and Thomas (2006) find that youth voluntary associations such as those promoted in high school (e.g., community service groups or public-speaking organizations) provide a context that seems to bolster political participation later in life. What this research tells us is that social ties matter to political participation as long as the ties seem to provide a social context for learning and reinforcing certain political skills. These studies of social capital, associations, and participation reveal another side to the social bases of politics.

We end this section by coming full circle of sorts, noting with interest that it was Tocqueville (1945) who traveled the United States in 1830 and 1831 and observed how the then new American republic was engaged in self-governance. Many of the scholars currently debating the importance of social capital, civic association, and social networks start their analysis with some reference to Tocqueville, because he hypothesized that the associational or group nature of the American "civil society" was one of its hallmarks. In light of the research summarized here, it was perhaps Tocqueville who captured something unique to the nature of democracy and political participation nearly two hundred years ago.

THE CHANGING NATURE OF POLITICAL PARTICIPATION

Recall from Chapter 3 that some political sociologists argue that demographic patterns and related value shifts in a society are particularly important to the ways in which political values and beliefs emerge, which in turn affect political participation including voting, involvement in political campaigns, activism, and social movement activity. Two recent studies took a comprehensive look at this thesis in light of what appeared to be a significant youth presence in the 2008 presidential election. This influence was a clue to what Dalton (2009) and Zukin et al. (2006) found as an important generational change in the nature of political participation in the United States.

Using survey data from two national surveys of citizens fifteen years and older, focus groups in four regions of the country, and interviews with experts working with youth in different settings, Zukin et al. (2006) affirmed a "new engagement" in the United States tied to different age cohorts. There were a number of significant findings from this comprehensive multiyear study that challenged the debate in political sociology whether citizens at the turn of the century were less engaged in civic groups and civic life (Putnam 2000). This group of political scientists found that civic participation was *not* in decline, but rather changing. We highlight three significant findings from this study that reveal how social forces are at work in altering the nature of political participation.

Zukin et al. (2006) on the one hand confirmed past research, showing that close to half of the citizenry (48 percent in their study) are disengaged from the civic life of society. On the other hand, they found that half of the citizens were engaged fairly consistently in two kinds of civic life, with one form ignored or underestimated in the older typologies. A large segment of the population studied was active in political engagement or what in the traditional definition was referred to as "activity that has the intent or effect of influencing government action—either directly by affecting the making or implementation of public policy or indirectly by influencing the selection of people who make those policies" (Verba et al. 1995, quoted in Zukin et al. 2006: 6). These institutional forms of participation as we described them earlier in this chapter include voting, writing letters to elected officials, or seeking elected office. Equally significant to the nature of political life in the United States is what Zukin et al. identified as civic participation. This segment of the population is engaged in "organized voluntary activity focused on problem solving and helping others" (7). Participation in the political life of the society closely aligns itself with what Tocqueville described in his observations of the American civic villages in the 1840s where individuals gathered in groups to address local problems as well as consider the challenges presented to a national civic body.

The second pattern revealed in their study of the new engagement was that citizens participated in twenty-four different dimensions of political life, which Zukin et al. (2006) organized into four distinct patterns of social action:

1. "Political engagement" included those actions described previously and consistent with past models of institutional participation: voting, contributions to campaigns, and displaying yard signs or bumper stickers for candidates.
2. "Civic engagement," as described previously, was action around local issues or problems. This form of participation involved joining a PTA to address school issues, or participating in town hall meetings about city or county tax issues.
3. "Cognitive engagement" described those citizens who basically indicated that they follow the news about politics at many levels. This form of engagement not only describes paying attention to media reports about political issues but also indicates a certain level of knowledge gained by the individual as a way to keep informed about politics and to comprehend political concerns.
4. Finally, Zukin and his colleagues described participation as creating "public voice", which refers to expressions through letters to the editor, signing petitions, boycotts of consumer items, or using the Internet for political expression.

As the authors conclude, these four forms of civic participation suggest a shift in previous forms of participation studied by social scientists in the 1970s and 1980s.

The third and most significant finding from the study of new engagement was the generational differences in the four forms of participation. In categorizing respondents in the study by age cohort, Zukin et al. (2006) found that "DotNets" (born after 1976) and "Gen-Xers" (born between 1965 and 1976) varied in their forms of participation in contrast to "Baby Boomers" (born between 1946 and 1964) and "Dutifuls" (born prior to 1946). Specifically, although patterns of involvement are complex in many ways, Zukin et al. found that DotNets are less active in traditional political forms overall, and equally as involved in forms of civic engagement as their parents. In addition, DotNets tend to find ways to engage political voice at similar rates of older cohorts, but in different ways. For example, DotNets are more likely to participate in a demonstration, sign an e-mail petition, or participate in a boycott than older citizens. Younger citizens are about equally as likely to go door-to-door canvassing, sign a written petition, or send a letter to the editor. The authors conclude that young citizens are not as disengaged as some may have previously thought. In other words, while fifteen- to twenty-eight-year-olds may not vote at levels similar to older citizens, younger individuals find alternative ways to participate at a rate equal to or greater than their parents or grandparents.

In another comprehensive study of political participation and social change, Dalton (2009) finds that the "norms of citizenship" are changing. Based on extensive use of the 2004 General Social Survey (GSS) as well as survey data collected by the Center for Democracy and Civil Society (CDCS), Dalton finds compelling evidence that suggests two kinds of norms emerging beyond the earlier traditional notions of citizenship and participation. He suggests that citizenship includes four dimensions. The first is participatory sense, where citizenship is defined in terms of what we traditionally think of as social actions of enfranchisement: voting or activity in political groups. The second he calls autonomy, where citizenship is thought of as keeping informed or paying attention to politics, much like Thomas Jefferson suggested when he believed that the informed citizen was the watchman of any democracy. The third dimension Dalton suggests is social order. This theme connects citizenship to political behaviors such as obeying the law or service on a jury or in the military. The fourth dimension of citizenship is solidarity, where citizenship calls upon a higher ethic or morality of the community or society, typically an appeal to altruism and helping people in the community.

From these dimensions, Dalton (2009) finds two norms of citizenship and political participation. The first norm he describes as the "duty-bound" notion. Participation in civic life is defined mostly in terms of traditional notions of political action as well as helping to maintain the social order. The "engaged citizen" is the second norm at work in contemporary society. This norm orients individuals to actions around solidarity and autonomy. Individuals engaged in this way are watchful, understanding, and altruistic, while at the same time likely to vote in elections. Dalton argues that these "two faces of citizenship" are distributed in varying ways across different groups in society, especially age groups. Younger-age cohorts—who are commonly referred to as Generations Y and X—are more oriented to the norm of the engaged citizen. Those born prior to World War II and the Baby Boomers are oriented to the norm of duty-bound participation. Dalton, much like Zukin et al., concludes that as the younger cohorts age, and as the older cohorts leave the population, the nature of political participation will most likely change from what traditional models have described.

What kinds of political participation are consistent with the norms identified in Dalton's study? Consistent with prior typologies of traditional modes of participation, Dalton (2009) finds that those adhering to the duty-bound notion of citizenship vote, work for a political party or campaign, and donate money to a campaign. In contrast, those adhering to the engaged citizen norm sign petitions, participate in demonstrations, engage in boycotts, and use the Internet for political activities.

The study by Dalton (2009) goes a step further and suggests a number of factors influencing this shift in how participation and citizenship are being defined. One of the most significant factors affecting this shift has been the growing level of education in the United States since World War II. He finds that the duty-bound norm is best predicted by "age, income, religious attachments, and Republican party identification" (51). In contrast, "Education, racial minority, and religious attachments significantly increase engaged citizenship, but age, income, and Republican party identification lower engaged citizenship" (51). Age was the strongest predictor of citizen duty; education was the strongest predictor of the engaged citizen. Interestingly, Dalton (2009) finds that these trends are similar to those found in other advanced industrial democracies:

> Generational change, educational effects, and the reshaping of life experiences are producing a similar norm shift across the affluent democracies. This is consistent with a large body of research on value change in advanced industrial societies, which argues that citizens are shifting to post-material and self-expressive values that are analogous to the norm shift described here. (171)

Again, these findings paint a picture of generational change and its impact not only on political participation but also on political culture.

Both studies presented here are indicative of the complex relationships between politics and social change. Social forces of modernization, affluence, changing gender roles, and demographic shifts are antecedents to underlying changes in the nature of political participation. Future research will no doubt continue to track how the age cohort we call DotNet participates in the political process at the national and local levels. How this cohort utilizes technology to apply certain political skills in the political process, as well as what issues or concerns attract attention, will be of particular interest. Moreover, political sociologists will follow with interest the trend hinted at in the last two presidential elections that suggested a turnaround in the decline in voting by younger voters.

CONCLUSION

The goal of this chapter was to provide a description of various ways in which political participation is conceptualized in political sociology. Each of the theoretical frameworks approaches the study of political participation with differing assumptions about the role participation plays in affecting the distribution of power in society. The various typologies, both classical and contemporary, suggest that we continue to find social spaces for forms of political participation as expressions of interest, roles related to social positions, and the interests in changing the nature of power. What follows is a detailed study of current fields of analysis in political sociology related to very specific forms of political participation:

- voting and electoral politics
- social and political movements
- terrorism

These particular areas constitute the focal points of political sociology where researchers have been most active in understanding how these particular forms of political participation affect power in society.

References

Alford, Robert and Roger Friedland. 1985. *Powers of Theory: Capitalism, the State and Democracy.* New York: Cambridge University Press.

The American National Election Studies (www.election-studies.org). THE ANES GUIDE TO PUBLIC OPINION AND ELECTORAL BEHAVIOR. Ann Arbor, MI: University of Michigan, Center for Political Studies [producer and distributor].

Bauman, Zygmunt. 1996. "From Pilgrim to Tourist—Or a Short History of Identity." Pp. 18–36 in *Questions of Cultural Identity*, edited by S. Hall and P. DuGay. London: Sage Publications.

_____. 1997. *Post-Modernity and Its Discontents.* Cambridge, UK: Polity.

Berelson, Bernard, Paul Lazarsfeld, and William McPhee. 1954. *Voting.* Chicago: University of Chicago Press.

Best, Shaun. 2002. *Introduction to Politics and Society.* London: Sage Publications.

Billig, Michael, Susan Candor, Derek Edwards, Mike Gane, David Middleton, and Lan Randly. 1988. *Ideological Dilemmas: A Social Psychology of Everyday Thinking.* Thousand Oaks, CA: Sage Publications.

Bimber, Bruce. 2003. *Information and American Democracy: Technology in the Evolution of Political Power.* New York: Cambridge University Press.

Bourdieu, Pierre. 1984. *Distinctions: A Social Critique of the Judgment of Taste.* Cambridge: Harvard University Press.

_____. 1986. "The Forms of Social Capital." Pp. 241–258 in *Handbook of Theory and Research for the Sociology of Education*, edited by John Richardson. New York: Greenwood Press.

Campbell, Angus, G. Gurin, and Walter Miller. 1954. *The Voter Decides.* New York: Row, Peterson.

Coleman, James. 1988. "Social Capital in the Creation of Human Capital." *American Journal of Sociology* 94(supplement): S95–S120.

_____. 1990. *Foundations of Social Theory.* Cambridge, MA: Harvard University Press.

Conover, Pamela Johnson. 1984. "The Influence of Group Identifications." *Journal of Politics* 46: 760–785.

Conway, Margaret M. 2000. *Political Participation in the United States.* Washington, DC: CQ Press.

Crenshaw, Martha. 1992. "Current Research on Terrorism." *Studies in Conflict and Terrorism* 15: 1–11.

Dahrendorf, Ralf. 1959. *Class and Class Conflict in Industrial Society.* California: Stanford University Press.

Dalton, Russell J. 2008. *Citizen Politics: Public Opinion and Political Parties in Advanced Industrial Democracies.* Washington, DC: CQ Press.

_____. 2009. *The Good Citizen: How a Younger Generation Is Shaping American Politics.* Washington, DC: CQ Press.

Dennis, Jack. 1987. "Groups and Political Behavior: Legitimation, Deprivation, and Competing Values." *Political Behavior* 9: 232–372.

Dobratz, Betty A. and Stephanie Shanks-Meile. 1997. *"White Power, White Pride!" The White Separatist Movement in the United States.* New York: Twayne/Simon & Schuster MacMillan.

Dobratz, Betty A., Stephanie Shanks-Meile, and Lisa K. Waldner. 2008. "White Separatist Movement Strategies: Institutionalized and Violent Forms of Activity." Paper presented at the American Sociological Association meetings, Boston, MA, August 2.

Downs, Anthony. 1957. *An Economic Theory of Democracy.* New York: Harper & Row.

Eisinger, Peter K. 1973. "The Conditions of Protest Behavior in American Cities." *American Political Science Review* 67: 11–28.

Everett, Kevin Djo. 1992. "Professionalism and Protest." *Social Forces* 70: 957–975.

Ezekiel, Raphael S. 1995. *The Racist Mind.* New York: Viking/Penguin.

Ferrell, Jeff. 1993. "Moscow Graffiti: Language and Subculture." *Social Justice* 20: 188–199.

Flora, Jan. 1998. "Social Capital and Communities of Place." *Rural Sociology* 63(4): 481–506.

Foley, Michael and Bob Edwards. 1997. "Escape from Politics? Social Theory and the Social Capital Debate." *American Behavioral Scientist* 40(5): 550–561.

Frank III, Arthur W., Richard Lachmann, David W. Smith, Janice V. Swenson, Richard Wanner, and Alan Wells. 1986. *The Encyclopedic Dictionary of Sociology.* Guilford, CT: Dushkin.

Gamson, William A. 1975. *The Strategy of Social Protest.* 1st Edition. Homewood, IL: Dorsey Press.

_____. 1992. *Talking Politics.* Cambridge: Cambridge University Press.

Giddens, Anthony. 1992. *Modernity and Self Identity.* Cambridge, UK: Polity.

Greeley, Andrew. 1997. "Coleman Revisited: Religious Structures as a Source of Social Capital." *American Behavioral Scientist* 40(5): 587–594.

Gurr, Ted Robert. 1989. "The History of Protest, Rebellion, and Reform in America." Pp. 11–22 in *Violence in America: Protest, Rebellion, Reform*, volume 2, edited by Ted Robert Gurr. Newbury Park, CA: Sage.

Habermas, Jurgen. 1989a. *The New Conservatism.* Cambridge, UK: Polity.

_____. 1989b. *The Philosophical Discourse of Modernity.* Cambridge, UK: Polity.

Hall, John and G. John Ikenberry. 1985. *The State.* Minneapolis: University of Minnesota Press.

Hout, Michael, Clem Brooks, and Jeff Manza. 1995. "The Democratic Class Struggle in the United States: 1948–1992." *American Sociological Review* 60: 805–828.

Huckfeldt, Robert and John Sprague. 1995. *Citizens, Politics, and Social Communication: Information and Influence in an Election Campaign.* Chicago: University of Illinois Press.

Huntington, Samuel. 1991. *The Third Wave: Democratization in the Late Twentieth Century.* Norman: Oklahoma University Press.

Inglehart, Ronald. 1990. *Culture Shift in Advanced Industrial Society.* Princeton, NJ: Princeton University Press.

Jenkins, J. Craig and Bert Klandermans. 1995. "The Politics of Social Protest." Pp. 3–13 in *The Politics of Social Protest*, edited by J. Craig Jenkins and Bert Klandermans. Minneapolis: University of Minnesota Press.

Jenkins, J. Craig and William Form. 2005. "Social Movements and Social Change." Pp. 331–349 in *The Handbook of Political Sociology*, edited by Thomas Janoski, Robert Alford, Alexander Hicks, and Mildred A. Schwartz. Cambridge: Cambridge University Press.

Johnston, Hank. 2006. "Let's Get Small: The Dynamics of (small) Contention in Repressive States." *Mobilization* 11: 195–212.

Jost. 1993. "Revolutionary Fantasies." *The WAR Eagle* 1(2): 6.

Kaplan, Jeffrey (editor). 2000. *Encyclopedia of White Power.* Walnut Creek, CA: Alta Mira.

Kivisto, Peter and Thomas Faist. 2007. *Citizenship: Discourse, Theory and Transnational Prospects.* Oxford: Blackwell Publishing.

Klingman, Avigdor and Ronit Shalev. 2001. "GRAFFITI: Voices of Israeli Youth Following the Assassination of the Prime Minister." *Youth & Society* 32: 403–420.

Klotz, Robert. 2007. "Internet Campaigning for Grassroots and Astroturf Support." *Social Science Computer Review* 25(1): 3–12.

Knoke, David. 1992. *Political Networks: The Structural Perspective.* New York: Cambridge University Press.

Koch, Jeffrey. 1995. *Social Reference Groups and Political Life.* New York: University Press of America.

Lazarsfeld, Paul, B. Berelson, and H. Gaudet. 1944. *The People's Choice.* New York: Duell, Sloan and Pearce.

Li, Yaojun and David Marsh. 2008. "New Forms of Political Participation: Searching for Expert Citizens and Everyday Makers." *British Journal of Political Science* 38: 247–272.

Lim, Chaeyoon. 2008. "Social Networks and Political Participation: How Do Networks Matter?" *Social Forces* 87(2): 961–982.

Lipset, Seymour Martin. 1981[1960]. *Political Man: The Social Bases of Politics.* Baltimore: Johns Hopkins University Press.

_____. 1991. "Why Americans Refuse to Vote." *Insight* (February): 24–26.

Lofton, John. 1985. *Protest: Studies of Collective Behavior and Social Movements.* New Brunswick: Transaction.

Lowi, Theodore. 1969. *The End of Liberalism: The Second Republic of the United States.* New York: W.W. Norton.

MacKuen, Micheal. 1990. "Speaking of Politics: Individual Conversational Choice, Public Opinion, and the Prospects for Deliberative Democracy." Pp. 59–99 in *Information and Democratic Processes*, edited by J. Ferejohn and J. Kuklinski. Chicago: University of Illinois Press.

Manza, Jeff, Clem Brooks, and Michael Sauder. 2005. "Money, Participation and Votes: Social Cleavages and Electoral Politics." Pp. 201–226 in *The Handbook of Political Sociology: States, Civil*

Societies, and Globalization, edited by T. Janoski, R. Alford, A. Hicks, and M. Schwartz. Cambridge: Cambridge University Press.

Marger, Martin. 1987. *Elites and Masses.* Belmont, CA: Wadsworth.

_____. 2008. *Social Inequality: Patterns and Processes.* Boston: McGraw Hill.

Marshall, T. H. 1950. *Citizenship and Social Class and Other Essays.* Cambridge: Cambridge University Press.

Marx, Karl. 1992[1843]. "On the Jewish Question." Pp. 211–242 in *Karl Marx: Early Writings*. New York: Penguin Classics.

Marx, Karl and Fredrick Engels. 1961[1848]. "The Communist Manifesto." In *Essential Works of Marxism.* New York: Bantam Books Inc.

McAdam, Doug, Sidney Tarrow, and Charles Tilly. 2001. *The Dynamics of Contention.* Cambridge: Cambridge University Press.

McCarthy, John D. and Mayer N. Zald. 1973. *The Trend of Social Movements in America: Professionalization and Resource Mobilization.* Morristown, NJ: General Learning Press.

McClurg, Scott. 2006. "The Electoral Relevance of Political Talk: Examining Disagreement and Expertise Effects in Social Networks on Political Participation." *American Journal of Political Science* 50(3): 737–754.

McFarland, Daniel and Reuben Thomas. 2006. "Bowling Young: How Youth Voluntary Associations Influence Adult Political Participation." *American Sociological Review* 71(3): 401–425.

Milbrath, Lester. 1965. *Political Participation: How and Why Do People Get Involved in Politics?* Chicago: Rand-McNally Publishing.

_____. 1981. "Political Participation." In *The Handbook of Political Participation*, edited by S. Long. New York: Plenum Books.

Milbrath, Lester and M. Goel. 1977. *Political Participation: How and Why Do People Get Involved in Politics?* Boston: Rand-McNally Publishing/University Press of America.

Miller, Melissa. 2009. "Debating Group Structure: How Local, Translocal, and National Voluntary Organizations Promote Democracy." *Social Science Journal* 46: 47–69.

Miller, Arthur, Patricia Gurin, Gerald Gurin, and Oksana Malanchuk. 1981. "Group Consciousness and Political Participation." *American Journal of Political Science* 25(3): 494–511.

Mills, C. Wright. 1940. "Situated Actions and the Vocabulary of Motives." *American Sociological Review* 6: 904–913.

Mondak, Jeffery. 1998. "Editor's Introduction." *Political Psychology* 19(3): 433–439.

Nie, Norman, Jane Junn, and Kenneth Stehlik-Barry. 1996. *Education and Democratic Citizenship in America.* Chicago: University of Chicago Press.

Nwoye, Onuigbo G. 1993. "Social Issues on Walls: Graffiti in University Lavatories." *Discourse & Society* 4: 419–442.

Obeng, Samuel Gyasi. 2000. "Doing Politics on Walls and Doors: A Sociolinguistic Analysis of Graffiti in Legon (Ghana)." *Multilingua* 19: 337–365.

Olsen, Marvin. 1982. *Participatory Pluralism.* Chicago: Nelson-Hall.

Olson Jr., Mancur. 1965. *The Logic of Collective Action: Public Goods and the Theory of Groups.* Boston: Harvard University Press.

Orum, Anthony. 2001. *Introduction to Political Sociology.* 4th Edition. Upper Saddle River, NJ: Prentice Hall.

Peteet, Julie. 1996. "The Writing on the Walls: The Graffiti of the Intifada." *Cultural Anthropology* 11: 139–159.

Piven, Francis Fox and Richard Cloward. 1989. *Why Americans Don't Vote.* New York: Pantheon Books.

Przeworski, Adam and John Sprague. 1986. *Paper Stones: A History of Electoral Socialism.* Chicago: University of Chicago Press.

Putnam, Robert. 1993. "The Prosperous Community: Social Capital and Public Life." *American Prospect* 13: 35–42.

_____. 1995. "Bowling Alone: America's Declining Social Capital." *American Prospect* 6: 65–78.

_____. 2000. *Bowling Alone: The Collapse and Revival of American Community.* New York: Simon and Schuster.

Rosenberg, Steven. 1988. *Reason, Ideology, and Politics.* Princeton, NJ: Princeton University Press.

Ruedin, Didier. 2007. "Testing Milbrath's 1965 Framework of Political Participation: Institutions and Social Capital." *Contemporary Issues and Ideas in Social Sciences* 3(3): 1–46.

Sabucedo, Jose Manuel and Constantino Arce. 1991. "Types of Political Participation: A Multidimensional Analysis." *European Journal of Political Research* 20: 93–102.

Scholzman, Kay Lehman, Sidney Verba, and Henry Brady. 1995. "Participation's Not a Paradox: The View from American Activists." *British Journal of Political Science* 25: 1–36.

Scott, John and Gordan Marshall. 2005. *Oxford Dictionary of Sociology.* 3rd Edition. Oxford: Oxford University Press.

Shah, Dhavan, Nojin Kwak, and R. Lance Holbert. 2001. "Connecting and Disconnecting with Civic Life: Patterns of Internet Use and the Production of Social Capital." *Political Communication* 18: 141–162.

Sluka, Jeffrey A. 1996. "The Writing's on the Wall: Peace Process Images, Symbols and Murals in Northern Ireland." *Critique of Anthropology* 16: 381–394.

Smelser, Neil J. 1962. *Theory of Collective Behavior.* New York: Free Press.

Snow, David, Louis Zurcher, and Sheldon Ekland-Olson. 1980. "Social Networks and Social Movements: A

Microstructuralist Approach to Differential Recruitment." *American Sociological Review* 45(5): 787–801.

van Steenbergen, Bart (editor). 1994. *The Condition of Citizenship.* Thousand Oaks, CA: Sage Publications.

Swartz, David. 1997. *Culture and Power: The Sociology of Pierre Bourdieu.* Chicago: University of Chicago Press.

Task Force on Inequality and American Democracy. 2004. "American Democracy in an Age of Rising Inequality." Washington, DC: American Political Science Association.

Tilly, Charles. 1970. "From Mobilization to Political Conflict." Center for Research on Social Organization. Ann Arbor: University of Michigan.

_____. 1973. "The Chaos of the Living City." Pp. 98–124 in *Violence as Politics.* New York: Harper and Row.

_____. 2005. "Regimes and Contention." Pp. 423–440 in *The Handbook of Political Sociology: States, Civil Societies, and Globalization*, edited by T. Janoski, R. Alford, A. Hicks, and M. Schwartz. Cambridge: Cambridge University Press.

Tilly, Charles and Sidney Tarrow. 2006. *Contentious Politics.* Herndon, VA: Paradigm Publishers.

Timpone, Richard. 1998. "Ties That Bind: Measurement, Demographics and Social Connectedness." *Political Behavior* 20(10): 53–77.

Tocqueville, Alexis de. 1945. *Democracy in America.* Volumes I and II. New York: Vintage Books.

Tolbert, Caroline and Ramona McNeal. 2003. "Unraveling the Effects of the Internet on Political Participation." *Political Research Quarterly* 56(2): 175–185.

Turner, Bryan S. (editor). 1993. *Citizenship and Social Theory.* Thousand Oaks, CA: Sage Publications.

Turner, Stephen and Lewis Killian. 1957. *Collective Behavior.* Englewood Cliffs, NJ: Prentice Hall.

Verba, Sidney and Norman Nie. 1972. *Participation in America: Political Democracy and Social Equality.* New York: Harper and Row.

Verba, Sidney, Norman Nie, and J. O. Kim. 1978. *Participation and Political Equality: A Seven-Nation Comparison.* New York: Cambridge University Press.

Verba, Sidney, Kay Schlozman, and Henry Brady. 1995. *Voice and Equality: Civic Voluntarism in American Politics.* Cambridge: Cambridge University Press.

Viterna, Jocelyn. 2006. "Pulled, Pushed, and Persuaded: Explaining Women's Mobilization into the Salvadoran Guerrilla Army." *American Journal of Sociology* 112(1): 1–45.

Walker, Edward. 2008. "Contingent Pathways from Joiner to Activist: The Indirect Effect of Participation in Voluntary Associations on Civic Engagement." *Sociological Forum* 23(1): 116–143.

Wallace, Michael and J. Craig Jenkins. 1995. "The New Class, Postindustrialism, and Neocorporatism." Pp. 96–137 in *The Politics of Social Protest*, edited by J. Craig Jenkins and Bert Klandermans. Minneapolis: University of Minnesota Press.

Weatherford, Stephen. 1982. "Interpersonal Networks of Political Behavior." *American Journal of Political Science* 26(1): 117–143.

Zukin, Cliff, Scott Keeter, Molly Andolina, Krista Jenkins, and Michael X. Delli Carpini. 2006. *A New Engagement? Political Participation, Civil Life, and the Changing American Citizen.* New York: Oxford University Press.

Elections and Voting

Most of us have learned from our government classes the importance of democracy, with free elections being the key ingredient. Harrigan (2000: 178) makes it clear just how essential the right to vote is: "Elections are the heart of democracy; they give the people a voice in how they are governed. Without meaningful elections there is no meaningful democracy." Budge and Farlie (1983: xi) point out that voting is the only time when most citizens can directly act to influence government decisions as elections provide a means to link government actions with public desires such as deciding whether to increase property taxes or fund a sports stadium. The 2010 U.S. election in which Republicans regained control of the House of Representatives and also gained numerous Senate seats provides an interesting example of how linkages between voting and government actions might work. In response to the message from the voters, President Obama and the Republican leadership discussed working together. Obama conceded there would be no legislation on greenhouse gases and indicated he would be willing to negotiate on issues like the extension of tax cuts for the rich. He was possibly willing to "tweak" health care legislation, but he would not "relitigate arguments" concerning major parts of that legislation (Baker and Hulse 2010).

Some authors suggest that elections perform symbolic or ritualistic roles, making voters feel they have fulfilled their civic duty and have contributed to society. Milbrath and Goel (1977: 12) argue that a person votes more out of a sense of civic duty than the belief that his or her vote will make a difference—voting may be a means for voters to define themselves as good members of the community. Milbrath and Goel contend too that one can vote without as much information or motivation as needed for other political activities. Those who focus only on the symbolic roles believe that voters "do not necessarily make intelligent, informed decisions. Few know anything about candidates . . . election results are uninterpretable" (Niemi and Weisberg 2001: 1–2).

Others suggest that nominated major party candidates are not that different from each other (Tweedledum and Tweedledee), that one vote does not matter, and elections are plagued by fraud (Niemi and Weisberg 1976, 2001). In Chapter 6, we considered the theoretical frameworks related to political participation, and here we will first examine how the various theoretical frameworks view voting and the electoral process. Then we will discuss two social scientists' evaluations of the functions of elections and look at electoral systems and turnout. These sections will be followed by considerations of the voting behavior research, the impact of social cleavages on voting, issue-based voting, and finally an examination of various U.S. presidential elections.

THEORETICAL FRAMEWORKS[1]

Pluralist

In the pluralist framework, voting and free elections are key ingredients of the democratic state. Voting is a key strategy of political action that enables one to influence government decisions and thus it demonstrates that the public has power. Casting a ballot is seen as a major mechanism, perhaps the single most important one, for individuals to express their political preferences. The voter should be informed about the multiple issues in an election, and the major political parties and candidates should appeal to the majority of the voters. According to Alford and Friedland (1985: 106), pluralists assume that

> *all* voters were available to respond to candidates, issues, or party appeals, that their behavior could be changed by the right appeals, and that moderate shifts of voting back and forth from left to right constituted the full range of political choice available.

It is expected that citizens trust their elected leaders and that the minority of voters are willing to accept the decision of the majority as legitimate. Should the electorate turn to an extremist political leader, ideally there would be checks and balances in place to return the system to greater stability and harmony. Pluralists are concerned if there is a surge in political participation; this may signal a lack of consensus or great disagreement that could be viewed as disruptive to society (Alford and Friedland 1985).

Elite/Managerial

The elite/managerial framework interprets voting and elections quite differently from pluralists. The heart of the issue is that elections are pictured as "a fiction, a legitimation of elite control, sometimes a recipe for political disorder" (Alford and Friedland 1985: 250). An elite theorist might view elections as a device to manipulate the masses into believing that they truly have a voice in government. Because political power and decision making are concentrated among elites, elections fail to offer meaningful alternative candidates. Elections tend to be viewed as contests between political elites whose views do not differ in significant ways as the system maintains elite control and power. Elections and other democratic features like political parties and legislatures have a symbolic function, suggesting that they provide a form of democracy without actual democratic content. Elections may also have a controlling function as they provide a mechanism for peaceful participation and an outlet to express one's preferences (259–260).

Elites may also feel that it is better to have an apathetic mass rather than citizens commit-ted to true participatory democracy. Having less committed citizens makes it less likely that there would be any attempts to make major system changes. The focus in this framework is more on elites and their strategies to maintain order and control, whereas issues of political participation like elections and voting are of lesser importance. Conservative elite theorists might well argue that the established elites serve as the guardians of democracy and are the responsible and compe-tent managers of politics and society (Hamilton 1972: vii).

Class

Class theorists like elite theorists tend to believe nonelite or lower-middle- and working-class political participation does not provide an effective means to influence or control political lead-ers. However, elections do function as a means to legitimate the existing system. Class theorists recognize the power potential of the lower classes but believe these classes have little impact on the current power structure. Democracy can be seen in a variety of ways according to a class per-spective. Therborn (1978: 248) identified a paradox in what he labeled "bourgeois democracy—a regime in which the exploiting minority rules by means of a system of legally free popular elec-tions." This perspective shares with the elite perspective the notion that elections mislead the lower classes into believing they have real power. Alternatively, democracy might be seen as something truly possible only if and when capitalism is overthrown.

Rational Choice

The central assumption of rational choice is that voters act to maximize their utility or to exhibit goal-oriented political behavior (Brooks, Manza, and Bolzendahl 2003: 142). Neuman (2005: 599) defined rational choice theory as follows: "Individuals make instrumental decisions about whether to invest time and effort into voting, and they vote if or when they believe it is likely to make a difference for their immediate personal situation." According to Downs (1957), the rational citizen looks at the political parties' policies and platforms to evaluate the value of par-ticipation in the long run and the expected value of change versus no change against the costs of voting. Simply put, if the benefits to the potential voter exceed the costs, the person will vote. Some argue it is irrational for most people to vote. Downs believed that the potential voter at times also considers how close the election will be.

Some argue it is rational to vote and thus fulfill one's civic duty (Niemi and Weisberg 1976: 26), but this is debatable. For example, some people may feel that as citizens they are obligated to vote, but instead of rationally considering the issues, they vote for the candidate with the most pleasing smile or because they shook hands with the candidate. The early work on the rational voter tended to emphasize mathematical modeling, but more recent work has focused on the role of issues in voting (Niemi and Weisberg 2001: 16).

Postmodern

Another framework is the postmodernist approach that emerged because modernist theories emphasizing the concepts of capitalism, industrialism, centralized administrative power in the state, and centralized control of military power could no longer effectively explain how the world works (Best 2002: 41). Instead, disorganized capitalism exists coupled with disorder, flux, and ambiguity. There tends to be no strong participatory democracy, and a decline in the impor-tance of the nation-state. Individuals are not actively involved in the political process, and politics exist without established rules (52). It seems that the people are no longer tied together by community, and they are trying to make sense of what is happening in the world. Social-class ties also weaken in a postclass society. Unlike the ideas surrounding the rational voter, political preferences lack any ordered means of predictability (266).

Institutionalist and Political Culture

Manza, Brooks, and Sauder (2005) identified a number of institutional factors affecting the turnout of voters. Their list included how difficult it may be to register to vote, negative campaigning and advertisements in the media, the costs of voting (e.g, whether the polls are open on a workday or weekend), and the range of ideological choices offered by the political parties. Such factors could easily interact with political culture ones including attitudes such as the public mood (Brooks et al. 2003). For example, the Tea Party Movement emerged to provide alternative candidates to traditional Republican and Democratic ones and captured some of the anger directed toward the economic stimulus package, environmental issues, and health care reform ("Tea Party Movement" 2010).

An additional example of how institutional and political culture issues influence elections is the ouster of three Iowa Supreme Court justices in the 2010 election in Iowa. In 1962 Iowa introduced a merit selection system for judges that called for periodic retention votes on justices. Justices serve for staggered eight-year terms and their names appear on election year ballots with voters having the option to vote "yes" or "no" regarding their retention. In 2009 the seven Iowa Supreme Court justices unanimously ruled that a law defining marriage as between a man and a woman was unconstitutional because it violated the constitution's provision for equal protection rights for minorities including same-sex couples who wanted to marry. In 2010 out-of-state organizations such as the National Organization for Marriage and the American Family Association contributed money to the campaign to remove the justices who were labeled "activist judges" in some negative ads. In the 2010 election, none of the three Iowa Supreme Court judges who were on the ballot were retained. Those against same-sex marriage saw it as a victory for the voice of the people while others saw it as severely challenging an independent judiciary and the role of the courts as a protector of minority rights (Sulzberger 2010).

We will now consider some more specific discussion of the functions of elections and then turn to the empirical work in political sociology that provides some insight on factors that influence both voting turnout and choice.

THE FUNCTIONS OF ELECTIONS

For a government to be democratic, "consent of the governed" is necessary, and elections give meaning to the idea of consent (Dye 2003: 249). A direct function of elections is to select officials who will occupy public office. Voters can pass judgment on current officeholders by reelecting them or by voting for someone else. Indirectly voters may be able to shape policy directions by choosing between or among candidates or parties with different policy goals (Dye 2003).

Ideally, for elections to direct the formulation of policy, four conditions need to be achieved:

1. Competing candidates provide concise well-explained policy options;
2. Citizens vote solely on the policy alternatives provided;
3. Election returns clearly reflect the voters' policy choices;
4. Elected officeholders abide by their campaign statements.

As Dye (2003) points out, none of these conditions are fully achieved in U.S. elections.

Domhoff (2006) acknowledges that elections have the potential for voters to influence public policy by their support for candidates who would represent their policy preferences. However, he believes that the U.S. electoral process has not allowed for as much input by critics and nonwealthy citizens as have most social democratic Western European procedures. For Domhoff, elections have four functions:

- Elections provide a way for "rival power groups, not everyday people" to resolve disagreements peacefully;
- Elections allow average persons to play a role in deciding which rival power groups will be the major leaders in government;
- Citizens in many nations can have some input on social and economic issues if they participate in electoral coalitions;
- Elections provide a means to introduce new policies if there are extreme domestic problems caused by social disruption. (135–136)

Domhoff believes that because the United States has only a two-party system and such systems do not facilitate parties offering clear policy alternatives, candidates tend to moderate their positions to appeal to voters in the middle. Thus, the personality characteristics of candidates become significant instead. The candidate-selection process is "in good part controlled by members of the power elite through large campaign contributions" (148). In addition to campaign contributions, the corporate community can financially support politicians by giving them corporate stock, purchasing some of their property at high prices, hiring them or their law firms, and paying them for giving speeches at corporate and trade association events.

According to Domhoff, the candidate-selection process in the United States tends to result in certain types of elected officials, including those frequently from the top 10 to 15 percent of the income and occupational hierarchies: lawyers and a number of "ambitious people who are eager to 'go along to get along' " (156). Most successful politicians are either conservative or quiet on controversial social issues and those in national positions tend to be probusiness conservatives. Given these views on elections and those elected, we will now turn to what seems to encourage voters to go to the polls to vote.

ELECTORAL SYSTEMS AND TURNOUT

Studying electoral systems is important because these systems define how the political system functions. "Metaphorically, electoral systems are the cogs that keep the wheels of democracy properly functioning" (Farrell 2001: 2). In addition, electoral systems ideally reflect the preferences of voters, facilitate strong and stable governments, create a sense of legitimacy, and elect qualified representatives. The design of both electoral laws and electoral systems impacts how the functions are carried out (3). For example, many regard a secret ballot as a significant provision for democratic elections. Figure 7.1 presents a device for ensuring secrecy even in absentee voting.

One key component of elections involves the complex process of translating votes into legislative seats based on proportional versus nonproportional systems. In the proportional system, the number of seats each party wins reflects as closely as possible the number of votes it has received. In the opposite system, much greater emphasis is given to ensuring whether one party obtains a clear majority of seats to increase the likelihood of having a strong and stable government (Farrell 2001: 4–6).

In the majoritarian system (nonproportional), a candidate must receive a majority (more than 50 percent) of the votes. This may mean two rounds or more of voting if no candidate receives

BALLOT SECRECY FOLDER

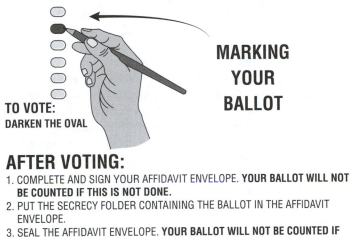

OPEN THIS FOLDER
FOR COMPLETE INSTRUCTIONS ON

**MARKING
YOUR
BALLOT**

TO VOTE:
DARKEN THE OVAL

AFTER VOTING:

1. COMPLETE AND SIGN YOUR AFFIDAVIT ENVELOPE. **YOUR BALLOT WILL NOT BE COUNTED IF THIS IS NOT DONE.**
2. PUT THE SECRECY FOLDER CONTAINING THE BALLOT IN THE AFFIDAVIT ENVELOPE.
3. SEAL THE AFFIDAVIT ENVELOPE. **YOUR BALLOT WILL NOT BE COUNTED IF THIS IS NOT DONE.**
4. ENCLOSE AFFIDAVIT ENVELOPE IN THE RETURN CARRIER ENVELOPE.
5. **POSTMARK BEFORE ELECTION DAY** OR DELIVER IN PERSON TO THE AUDITOR'S OFFICE BEFORE THE POLLS CLOSE ON ELECTION DAY.

FIGURE 7.1   Secrecy Folder for Absentee Voting in Iowa

More and more people vote absentee or in advance of Election Day. To provide for secrecy in returning absentee ballots, Iowa provided this folder and these instructions for the 2008 election.

a majority in the first round. If a second round takes place, voter turnout is often lower. The single-member plurality system used in the United States is another example of a nonproportional system. The contested seat goes to whoever has the highest number of votes. Proportional systems, on the other hand, often offer lists of candidates put forward by the political parties. The size of the lists depends on the number of seats to be filled with the proportion of votes each party receives determining the number of seats it can fill. Smaller parties thus have greater chances to gain representation than if under either the single-member plurality or majoritarian systems. Mixed systems combine both proportional representation and single-member plurality. Generally speaking, turnout is higher in proportional systems, perhaps in part because supporters of smaller parties see some benefit from voting.

Analyses of voter turnout are less common than studies of why people prefer a certain party or candidate. Kelley and Mirer (1974) examined "The Simple Act of Voting" but Dalton and Wattenberg's (1993) title "The Not So Simple Act of Voting" seems more appropriate. In the United States voter turnout has been characteristically low and until very recently seemed to be declining. Reasons for low turnout include individual, structural, socioeconomic environment, and political cultural factors (Blais 2006; Dye 2003: Chapter 5; Neuman 2005: Chapter 5). Studies on U.S. voting have conclusively documented that those who are older, have more education and higher income tend to vote more, whereas minorities vote less.

According to the socioeconomic environment perspective, economically advanced nations with high standards of living are more likely to have higher turnout rates. Yet, there seems to be no relationship between downturns in an economy and higher voter turnout. While a declining economy and hardships might encourage certain people to vote, others become alienated and withdraw from the political process (Blais 2006: 117). Other contextual factors such as living in small countries, discussing politics with friends and neighbors, and being contacted by a political party also contribute to turnout. Political cultural values including individualism, egalitarianism, and materialism, and participatory cultures may encourage voting. The subjective orientation of citizens to politics may facilitate efficacious feelings, thus leading to greater voter turnout. For example, individuals who trust their government may feel that their vote is important and therefore go to the polls.

Jackman (1987) stresses how political and legal institutional arrangements have significant impact on national rates of voter turnout. He examined nineteen industrial democracies in the 1960s and 1970s and postulated that nationally competitive electoral districts, unicameralism (power concentrated in one legislature), and compulsory voting laws that mandate voting tend to increase turnout. On the other hand, turnout is less when there are many parties and when minor parties must accumulate lots of votes to achieve a given degree of representation in the legislature. Jackman concludes that "where institutions provide citizens with incentives to vote, more people actually participate; where institutions generate disincentives to vote, turnout suffers . . . turnout figures offer one gauge of participatory political democracy" (419).

Blais (2006) disagrees with Jackman, suggesting that the impact of institutional variables may be overstated. More specifically he argues that the effects of unicameralism on turnout are mixed and that while compulsory voting increases turnout, it is unclear if light sanctions are effective in generating turnout. While research supports that proportional representation promotes turnout for well-established democracies, it is not clear why that is the case and the finding does not necessarily apply to other societies. For example, Morgenstern and Vazquez-D'Elia (2007) have found that standard electoral system variables did not predict different aspects of parties and party systems in Latin America. Further, studies suggest that sociologists do not have a very good understanding of the relationship between turnout and number of parties. For example, a study of fifteen East European countries (Kostadinova 2003) found that proportional representation increased turnout, but the number of parties decreased it. Voters may be confused when there are too many parties competing. Also, close competition between major parties did not predict turnout.

Table 7.1 shows U.S. voter turnout rates for the presidential elections from 1964 to 2008 with lower turnout for the years in which there are no presidential elections. Because the number of citizens is less than the total population, turnout percentages using number of *citizens* are always higher than turnout percentages using *total* population of age eighteen and above. Generally turnout has been declining, although it was higher in 1992 and increased somewhat in 2004 from the previous two elections.

Felon disenfranchisement, or the loss of voting rights following a felony conviction, also affects turnout. The laws concerning such disenfranchisement in the United States are unique in the democratic world because on Election Day

> there are . . . more than five million citizens who will neither vote nor voluntarily choose not to participate. These ineligible citizens are current and former criminal offenders. Only one-quarter of them are confined in prisons or jails. While some have committed violent offenses, most have been convicted only of nonviolent crimes. (Manza and Uggen 2006: v)

Table 7.1	Voters among the Total Population (Eighteen plus), Citizens, and Registered Voting-Age Populations 1964–2008 Presidential Elections				
	Total Voting-Age Population (in thousands)	**Percent Voting**		**Percent Registered**	
Year		**Total Population**	**Citizen Population**	**Total Population**	**Citizen Population**
2008	225,499	58.2	63.6	64.9	71.0
2004	215,694	58.3	63.8	65.9	72.1
2000	210,421	42.3	46.1	63.9	69.5
1996	193,651	54.2	58.4	65.9	71.0
1992	185,684	61.3	67.7	68.2	75.2
1988	178,098	57.4	62.2	66.6	72.1
1984	169,963	59.9	64.9	68.3	73.9
1980	157.085	59.3	64.0	66.9	72.3
1976	146,548	59.2	NA	66.7	NA
1972	136,203	63.0	NA	72.3	NA
1968	116,535	67.8	NA	74.3	NA
1964	110,604	69.3	NA	NA	NA

Source: http://www.census.gov/population/socdemo/voting/tabA-1.xls

The United States follows a system of federalism whereby the individual states have significant powers to pass laws that disenfranchise felons,[2] thus the rules vary considerably by state. Manza and Uggen (2006: 165–180) estimate that, in presidential elections from 1972 to 2000, 35 percent of disenfranchised felons would have voted, compared to 52 percent of the electorate. While the turnout rates of disenfranchised felons would certainly be lower than the rest of the electorate, over 1.5 million currently disenfranchised citizens would likely have participated in the 2000 and 2004 elections if they had been eligible. A variety of characteristics of the disenfranchised felon population suggest they are more likely to be African Americans than whites, have lower incomes and levels of education, come from poor or working-class backgrounds, and are more likely to support the Democratic Party (182–183).

TEXTBOX 7.1

Should Disenfranchised Felons Be Allowed to Vote?

Various states have different restrictions on the voting rights of felons and ex-felons. There has recently been some liberalization of laws for ex-felons, but there is significant debate about whether felons or ex-felons should be allowed the right to vote.

Pro

Disenfranchisement laws deprive citizens of their right to vote and thus their ability to participate in political and social institutions. This is counterproductive to the ideal of promoting democracy

(Continued)

and involving citizens in the political process, and it poses a threat to political equality. "Democracy rests on universal participation, even among those citizens who have committed criminal offenses. Their exclusion affects everyone and diminishes the democratic polity as a consequence" (Manza and Uggen 2006: 233).

Reenfranchising felons helps them reestablish connections as stakeholders in politics. Some evidence suggests that participating in elections reduces the rate of recidivism (Uggen, Manza, and Thompson 2006). Civic reintegration could serve as a link between voting and desisting from crime, thus benefiting society (Manza and Uggen 2006: 125). Stigmatizing felons makes it more difficult for them to fulfill the duties of responsible citizenship such as participating in the paid labor force, paying taxes, and raising children. Voting could promote respect for the law and for those who enforce the laws.

It is mainly poor people and people of color who are "locked out" of the democratic process, and this is unfair. According to Manza and Uggen (2006: 79), in fourteen states more than 10 percent of blacks have been disenfranchised, and in five of these states more than 20 percent of blacks are not eligible to vote. In the United States, 13 percent of black men have lost the right to vote and this percentage is seven times higher than the national average of those who have lost the right to vote (Wood and Trivedi 2007: 32). Poor people are also overrepresented as felons. When they are required to pay all fines, court costs, fees, restitutions, and other legal financial obligations before regaining the right to vote, permanent disenfranchisement is likely (31). Groups that are overrepresented among the disenfranchised may not be fully represented in the political process.

Con

Hull (2006) divides the arguments supporting disenfranchisement into three types.

The Pragmatic

1. Advocates of felon disenfranchisement argue that the possibility of losing one's vote helps deter people from actually engaging in crime, or discourages them from committing further crime.
2. Loss of voting rights fulfills a possible need for retribution to punish the guilty and thus help foster stability in the society.

The Principled

1. Citizens have certain obligations to the community and when they fail to fulfill their responsibilities, the community has a right to punish the criminal, including disenfranchising the felon.
2. Limiting or restricting the franchise helps the community define its own identity.

The Philosophical Theories

1. "Civic Republicanism" maintains that society's moral and physical health depends on the virtue of its citizens. Voting is a privilege awarded only to those who are worthy and loyal. Committing a felony defines a citizen as unworthy because criminals are less likely to be good citizens.
2. "Social contract" theorists argue that people give up some of their freedoms to live under a government's rules that protect them. When people violate the rules, they lose their right to participate in decisions affecting the community.

In addition Clegg (n.d.), general counsel of the Center for Equal Opportunity in Sterling, Virginia, points out that although it is true that blacks disproportionally comprise the felon population, there is no discriminatory intent to bar them from voting. Also because an overwhelming majority of states have disenfranchisement laws, it is unlikely that racial discrimination is the reason for these laws.

Piven and Cloward (2000) consider Americans' low turnout rate in depth as they focus on the Human Service Employees Registration and Voter Education (Human SERVE) project they initiated in 1983. They argue that Americans tend to see the United States as a model of democracy, "but in fact the United States is the only major democratic nation in which the less-well-off, as well as the young and minorities, are substantially underrepresented in the electorate" (3). Further they question the idea that nonvoting is a "tacit expression of satisfaction" with the current political situation (3) and are critical of the idea that too much participation burdens democratic institutions. They reject the pluralist view that a balance is needed between participation and nonparticipation.

Due in part to the work of groups like Human SERVE and Rock the Vote, the National Voter Registration Act (NVRA) was passed in 1993, which provided for voter registration at driver's license facilities and agencies providing public welfare benefits. Although NVRA resulted in an unprecedented increase in voter registration (11 percent from 1994 to 1998), voter turnout in general did not increase (Piven and Cloward 2000: 261). The increased registrations were offset by purging the voting registration lists. Turnout rates declined from 1994 to 1998 (years that did not involve presidential elections) by 2.8 percent (265). A partial explanation for this trend includes a decline in party loyalty, a weakening of citizen faith in politician responsiveness to voters, and even the Democrats seemed to be "at best reluctant allies" (269) in recruiting new voters. Piven and Cloward argue that "hotly contested elections about intensely felt issues" (266) and "a new surge of protest" (272) could generate increased turnout in the twenty-first century.

After the close election in 2000, turnout was higher in 2004 than in the previous two presidential elections. Mobilization efforts by organizations like Human SERVE and Rock the Vote may have become more effective. Rock the Vote (2006), a nonprofit, nonpartisan group trying to engage and build political power for young people, states that they registered 1.4 million voters. Young people ages eighteen to twenty-nine comprised 11 percent of the vote cast in 2002 but 13 percent in 2006. According to CIRCLE, a University of Maryland youth voter research institute, 4.6 million more young voters turned out in 2004 than in 2000 (Rock the Vote 2006). At times mobilization efforts seem to work, but whether there is a sustained increase in turnout remains to be seen in future elections.

VOTING BEHAVIOR RESEARCH

Two early traditions of voting behavior research emerged more than half a century ago. One of these, the Columbia University approach, offered a truly sociological approach to the study of voting by examining the flow of information during a campaign, individual decision making, group process variables, socioeconomic status (SES) indicators (e.g., education, income, class), and sociodemographic measures (e.g., race, ethnicity, religion, place of residence). Researchers concluded that most voters' party preferences were rather inflexible although a minority of voters frequently switched their preferences. Lazarsfeld, Berelson, and Gaudet (1968: 69) found that although they believed people who switch parties were very thoughtful and concerned about the issues in the election, such people actually had very limited involvement in politics and the campaign. The Columbia researchers thus were interested in "within campaign movement of voting intentions" (Scheingold 1973: 718) including how parties motivate their regular supporters to turn out and how they attract those who tend to switch parties frequently. The flow of political information through various social groups is key in a historical period of partisan realignment when individual and social group preferences may be in flux.

The second tradition is the University of Michigan school, which focuses on sociopsycho-logical variables or political attitudes. In *The American Voter,* Campbell et al. (1960) argued that voting is mainly the result of attitudinal forces and sociodemographic background, and parental characteristics are less influential at the time of voting.

> The elements of national politics—the presidential candidates, questions of group interest, the issues of domestic and foreign policy, the performance of the parties in the conduct of government—are not simply perceived by the individual; they are *evaluated* [emphasis added] as well. (66)

Knoke (1974) proposed a causal synthesis of American voting behavior based on these two tra-ditions by using both sociological and sociopsychological variables in his model. None of the so-cial variables (occupation, race, religion, social class, or father's party) had direct influence on voting, although the three issue variables (social welfare, civil rights, and foreign policy), party identification, and candidate evaluations did. Orum (1983: 229), in his survey of the literature on political sociology, concluded that in the late 1970s and early 1980s issues assumed a more prominent position in influencing voting behavior in the United States.

SOCIAL CLEAVAGES OR CHARACTERISTICS

While some studies may question the relevance of sociodemographic characteristics in influenc-ing turnout and specific voting preferences, others support the relevance of what Miller and Shanks (1996: 212) term the *nonpolitical variables* of "stable social and economic characteris-tics." Miller and Shanks find that current policy issues or the evaluations of candidates explain only minor elements of the effect of social and economic differences on voter choice in the elec-tions for the period 1980–1992. It should be pointed out that these cleavages are not only charac-teristics of individuals but based on group memberships, historical identification, and/or feelings of belonging that include a sense of linked fate (Manza et al. 2005: 205).

Social Class

Lipset's (1963) classic *Political Man* clearly documents the significance of social class for explaining both turnout and voting preferences in Western democracies. More recently, others, including Lipset, argue there has been an important decline in class voting in postindustrial soci-eties. Clark and Lipset (2001: 39) maintain that "class is an increasingly outmoded concept." Other authors like Evans (1999a: 1) challenged this by suggesting that the obituary on class voting is premature.

The argument for the decline in class voting has several different strands or types of expla-nations hinging on the significance of the shift of advanced societies to postindustrial or post-modern status. New social cleavages develop that tend to reduce class-based conflict and thus class-based voting. Various other identity groups, including gender, race, ethnicity, and public and private consumption sectors, become more significant collectivities. Postmaterialist values replace materialist or economic ones, become more important as a basis of party preferences, and crosscut the impact of social class. According to Inglehart (1997: 234), a change has occurred "from political cleavages based on social class conflict toward cleavages based on cultural issues and quality of life concerns."

Hout, Manza, and Brooks (1999) support the frequent finding that in the United States class positively influences voter turnout, and argue that there has been a significant realignment of class voting rather than a decline since 1960. There is a split in the salariat, or those receiving salaries. Managers tend to support Republicans who favor low taxes and deregulation, whereas professionals have shifted rapidly toward the Democrats who support civil rights, civil liberties, and the environment. Routine white-collar workers have slowly switched to the Democratic side. The working class, especially skilled workers, reflects a very volatile voting profile, swinging widely in their preferences. They were originally strong Democrats but often split their votes; in 1988 they were strong Republicans. The decline in union membership has harmed the Democratic Party, but the realignment in class voting is independent of union membership.

The influence of several social variables on voting preferences in the American elections of 2000, 2004, 2006, and 2008 is displayed in Table 7.2. The CNN exit poll data document the importance of income in predicting voting preference. Those with incomes under $15,000 were much more likely to vote for the Democratic candidate than those making over $100,000. If someone in his or her household was a union member, the voter was more likely to vote Democratic. Education is not an indicator per se of social class, but it does influence one's social class. Those with less education and also those with postgraduate training are most likely to support the Democrats.

Table 7.2 National Election Political Preference from 2000, 2004, 2006, and 2008 CNN Exit Polls (in Percentage) by Selected Sociodemographic Characteristics

	2000 Election		2004 Election		2006 Election		2008 Election	
	Bush	Gore	Bush	Kerry	Dems	Reps	Obama	McCain
Income								
Under $15,000	37	57	36	63	67	30	73	25
$15,000–30,000	41	54	42	57	61	36	60	37
$30,000–50,000	48	49	49	50	56	43	55	43
$50,000–75,000	51	46	56	43	50	48	48	49
$75,000–100,000	52	45	55	45	52	47	51	48
Over $100,000	54	43	NA	NA	NA	NA	NA	NA
$100,000–150,000	NA	NA	57	42	47	51	48	51
$150,000–200,000	NA	NA	58	42	47	51	48	50
$200,000 or more	NA	NA	63	35	45	53	52	46
Union Household Member								
Yes	37	59	40	59	64	34	59	39
No	52	44	55	44	49	49	51	47
Education								
No High School	39	59	49	50	64	35	63	35
High School Graduate	49	48	52	47	55	44	52	46
Some College	51	45	54	46	51	47	51	47
College Graduate	51	45	52	46	49	49	50	48
Postgraduate Study	44	52	44	55	58	41	58	40

(Continued)

| Table 7.2 | National Election Political Preference from 2000, 2004, 2006, and 2008 CNN Exit Polls (in Percentage) by Selected Sociodemographic Characteristics **(Continued)** |

	2000 Election		2004 Election		2006 Election		2008 Election	
	Bush	**Gore**	**Bush**	**Kerry**	**Dems**	**Reps**	**Obama**	**McCain**
Gender								
Male	53	42	55	44	50	47	49	48
Female	43	54	48	51	55	43	56	43
Race								
White	54	42	58	41	47	51	43	55
African American	9	90	11	88	89	10	95	4
Latino/a	35	62	44	53	69	30	67	31
Asian	41	55	44	56	62	37	62	35
Religion								
Protestant	56	42	59	40	44	54	45	54
Catholic	47	50	52	47	55	44	54	45
Jewish	19	79	25	74	87	12	78	21
Other	28	62	23	74	71	25	73	22
None	30	61	31	67	74	22	75	23
White Religious Right (2000) White Evangelical (2004) White Protestant Born Again/Evangelical (2006, 2008)	80	18	78	21	28	70	26	73
Church Attendance								
More Than Weekly	63	36	64	35	38	60	43	55
Weekly	57	40	58	41	46	53	43	55
Monthly	46	51	50	49	57	41	54	46
Few Times a Year/Seldom	42	54	45	54	60	38	59	39
Never	32	61	36	62	67	30	67	30
Lesbians, Gays, Bisexual (LGB)	25	70	23	77	75	24	70	27

NA: Not Available. Dems = Democrats, Reps = Republicans

Sources: CNN Exit Polls 2000, *N*=13,310 respondents, http://www.cnn.com/ELECTION/2000/epolls/US/P000.html

CNN Exit Poll 2004 U.S. President, National, *N*=13,660 respondents, http://www.cnn.com/ELECTION/2004/pages/results/states/US/P/00/epolls.0.html

CNN Exit Poll 2006, U.S. House of Representatives/National, *N*=13,251 respondents, http://www.cnn.com/ELECTION/2006/pages/results/states/US/H/00/epolls.0.html

CNN Exit Poll 2008 U.S. President, National, *N*=17,836 respondents, http://www.cnn.com/ELECTION/2008/results/polls/#USPOp1

Nieuwbeerta and DeGraaf (1999) analyzed twenty democratic industrialized societies from 1945 to 1990. There was a substantial decrease in the levels of class voting in most of the democratic nations. Denmark, Sweden, and Great Britain had high levels of class voting, whereas the United States and Canada had the lowest. Differences in voting preferences between the classes, though, varied considerably from country to country. About one-fifth of the changes in the levels of voting by blue-collar or white-collar classes within nations could be explained by changes in the actual composition of those classes, while the remaining four-fifths of the variation was due to changes in voting preferences of the subclasses in the manual and nonmanual classes. Nieuwbeerta and DeGraaf suggest that future studies need to focus on class-specific voting behavior such as that of professionals or managers as well as the overall levels of class voting.

Müller (1999) found no significant support for any class decline in voting for ten surveys in Germany from 1976 to 1994, while Ringdal and Hines (1999: 202) found that class voting declined in Norway from 1957 to 1989, but "Norway may simply be approaching an equilibrium level of class voting similar to that in many other West European nations." Using data from the 1930s to the early 1990s, Weakliem and Heath (1999) analyzed class voting in Britain, France, and the United States. There was no convergence in voting; rather there were differences in the levels of class voting and the trends. There was support for the postmodern argument in the United States and Britain but not in France. Weakliem and Heath argue that studies on class politics "should begin from the assumption that class is an enduring, but rarely or never a dominating influence on political behaviors" (133).

Clark (2001: 24) suggests that a key factor driving the decline of class voting is the decreasing size of the manual labor force while the size of the service workers labor force has increased. The middle class has grown in size but that does not mean class politics is declining because political parties "appealing to middle class interests is simply a new twist on an old theme" (Evans 1999b: 330). Left parties, for example, may try to widen their base of support by appealing more to middle-class interests. Further examination is needed of how the changing shape of the class structure influences parties' strategies. Intensive national case studies by researchers looking for common patterns are likely to contribute to theory building (332).

Typically much of the early research used the white-collar or nonmanual versus blue-collar or manual dichotomy as the measure of social class. Class needs to be reconceptualized to take into account the growing complexities and shifting of the social stratification system in postindustrial societies where manufacturing finished goods has been replaced by producing services and information. The numbers of service workers dominate over those in manufacturing (Marger 2008). According to Weakliem (2001: 201), researchers who have used more complex class measures tend to find that a substantial part of the change in class voting suggests realignment instead of decline, something that would not have been discovered using a dichotomy. Weakliem argues that the "decline of class" perspective is not well supported, but those who challenge it have not provided groundbreaking clear alternatives explaining political patterns in voting at the cross-national level.

Before turning to other types of cleavages, we should point out that class sometimes competes with and sometimes coexists with the other divisions such as race, religion, and gender for influence on voter preferences. For example, Brooks and Manza (1997) examined social cleavages for the U.S. presidential elections from 1960 to 1992. The racial cleavage has increased significantly since 1960, and the gender cleavage gained modestly, while the class cleavage seemed stable and the religious cleavage declined slightly.

More recently Brooks, Nieuwbeerta, and Manza (2006) looked at class, religion, and gender cleavage-based voting behavior in six postwar democracies from 1964 to 1998. Class is typically the largest social cleavage, but religion has larger effects in the United States and the Netherlands. Unskilled workers have declining attachments to leftist parties in Britain, Germany, the Netherlands, and the United States, but not in Australia or Austria. Gender cleavage has an important effect mainly in the United States. We will now look at gender, race, and religious cleavages separately and focus mainly on the United States.

Gender Gap

Although in the United States some states had previously granted women the right to vote, it was not until 1920 that women were given the right to vote through the Nineteenth Amendment to the Constitution. Only about one-third of eligible women voted in that election, compared to two-thirds of eligible men. The gap between turnout rates for men and women narrowed somewhat from the 1940s to the 1960s, but it was estimated by the University of Michigan National Election Studies to be about 10 percent (Burrell 2004: 92). The Bureau of the Census initiated its national survey of voting in 1964 and found a difference of 5 percent in turnout between eligible males and females. The year 1980 marked the first time a higher percentage of eligible women than men voted, though the difference was a mere 0.3 percent (93). By the 2004 election, the difference was 3.8 percent, with 56.3 percent of males and 60.1 percent of females voting (U.S. Census Bureau 2005). In general, younger women are more likely to vote than men, but once they are sixty-five or older, women are less likely to vote than men of the same age.

Manza and Brooks (1998: 1235) tested various hypotheses that could explain why a higher percentage of women tended to vote for Democratic Party candidates than men. Analyzing National Election Survey data from 1952 through 1992, Manza and Brooks found that the changing labor-force participation among women helped explain the gap. Working women's labor-force participation positively influences their views on social service spending, and this in turn influences how they vote. In the 1992 election, feminist consciousness emerged as an important variable and influenced women's voting behavior as well.

Women not only are more likely to vote than men, they also have been more likely to prefer the Democratic Party candidates and less likely to think of themselves as Independents. Exit poll data suggest that women are more likely than men to support female candidates in Congressional elections. For example, Hillary Rodham Clinton won the New York senatorial election in 2000 because women strongly favored her while men were split about equally between her and her opponent (Burrell 2004). According to CNN exit polls (Table 7.2), males supported Bush while females supported Gore and Kerry, but they favored Gore more than Kerry.

Kaufmann and Petrocik (1999: 866) argue that the gender gap between men's and women's voting behavior was due mainly to men's "dramatic conversion" to the Republican Party. Men's Democratic identification steadily declined after 1964, and since 1980 it has not been above 50 percent. Men were generally more conservative than women, especially on social spending and homosexuality. Women were more negative in their evaluations of the national economy and personal finances. Race and social-class differences stood out more than the gender gap, though, for predicting party preference.

Inglehart and Norris (2000) studied the gender gap in voting and left–right ideology in a comparative perspective using data from the World Values Survey conducted in various countries from the 1980s to the 1990s. They argue that in postindustrial societies, gendered relationships increasingly converge as more women enter the paid labor force and take advantage of educational opportunities. The family changes from more traditional to modern, and gender equality becomes more highly valued. The authors maintain that there is a realignment of political behavior with women moving toward the left of men in advanced industrial societies but not in developing or postcommunist nations.

On the other hand, Brooks et al. (2006) examined 112 nationally representative voter surveys in six Western democracies from 1964 to 1998. They found support for the growing partisan importance of gender only in the United States. Gender cleavage is basically nonexistent in Britain, Germany, Australia, and Austria, with recent data suggesting a small cleavage emerging in the Netherlands. More research seems needed, including in-depth considerations of gendered relationships, cultural influences, and historical factors in various societies, before sociologists can conclude much about a gender gap in voting, let alone explain it in a cross-national perspective.

Racial Cleavages

Racial cleavages are certainly significant in numerous societies, but this discussion concentrates on those in the United States where differences, especially between blacks and whites, have been pronounced. Whites have served as the norm from which the other races have been judged in the United States. According to the CNN election exit polls shown in Table 7.2, whites have tended to support Republican candidates, whereas racial minorities have favored Democrats. We will look particularly at African Americans, Hispanics, and East Asians.

BLACKS   Blacks have always tended to strongly favor one political party or the other, although it has not always been the same party. As part of President Lincoln's legacy of abolishing slavery, blacks strongly supported the Republican Party during the Reconstruction era following the Civil War. Orey and Vance (2003) claim that black voters played major roles in determining the presidential winners in 1868 and 1872. Since 1930 and Franklin D. Roosevelt's (FDR) presidency, blacks shifted toward the Democratic Party, because FDR's social programs contributed to their support, as did his creation of a "Black Cabinet," an informal mechanism comprising many black civic leaders who were unofficially appointed to advise the president. It is estimated about 85 percent of blacks voted for FDR in 1936 (208), and since then blacks have strongly supported the Democratic Party. In the 1960 election, John F. Kennedy received about two-thirds of the black vote. The Civil Rights Act of 1964 and the Voting Rights Act of 1965 were passed after Kennedy's assassination, during Johnson's presidency. Since 1964, black preferences for Democratic presidential candidates have not dipped below 80 percent (212).

While blacks were strongly supporting the Democrats, white dissatisfaction with the Democratic Party grew. Whites switched their allegiance to the Republican Party, especially in the South. This realignment favored Republican presidential candidates, who have won six of the nine contests between 1968 and 2000. Registration and turnout figures for blacks in the United States have increased substantially since 1965. In the 1970s civil rights workers mobilized many blacks in the South to register and vote.

Not surprisingly, blacks are more likely to turn out when a candidate is of the same race or strongly endorses racial inclusion. Black voter registration reached its highest level in 1984 when black minister Jesse Jackson was an African American candidate for president. In the 1988 presidential primaries, Jesse Jackson received 29.1 percent of the total Democratic vote, carrying five southern states and the District of Columbia, all of which had substantial black populations (Orey and Vance 2003: 234–235). Since the Voting Rights Act of 1965, the total number of black elected officials has risen substantially (1,469 in 1970 to 9,040 in 2000) even though it remains disproportionate to the black population. Interestingly, 34.5 percent of those elected officials in 2000 were female. For the 2004 election, 69 percent of blacks were registered to vote and 87 percent of the registered blacks actually voted. This was less than non-Hispanic whites, but more than Asians and Hispanics (U.S. Census Bureau 2006). Recent CNN exit polls (Table 7.2) show that 88 to 90 percent of blacks supported Democratic candidates. Democrat Barack Obama's candidacy did for race what Hillary Clinton's campaign did for gender by keeping both of the cleavages at the forefront during the 2008 presidential nomination process. As expected, Obama captured about 95 percent of the black vote in 2008. This is discussed in greater detail in the subsection on the 2008 election.

HISPANIC OR LATINO/A AMERICANS[3] Hispanic or Latino/a Americans comprise a particularly interesting grouping because they are now considered to be the largest American ethnic/racial minority and there are several ethnicities or subgroups within this category. Most Hispanics are considered white. According to the 2000 U.S. Census, 66 percent are Mexican, 15 percent Central and South American, 9 percent Puerto Rican, 4 percent Cuban, and 6 percent other Hispanic (Chavez 2004: 8). Generally speaking, Hispanics have lower political participation rates than non-Hispanic whites. Reasons for this include their lower SES, lower civic volunteerism in various organizations, fewer mobilization attempts (not being recruited by organized interests to be active or to register), and structural factors such as perceived discriminatory practices that involve issues of citizenship status, bilingual assistance, or intimidation at the polls (Garcia and Sanchez 2004: 123–131).

Citizenship of Latino/a Americans is a key concern because 41 percent of Hispanics of any race were not citizens in 2004; thus the voting rate for Hispanics is about 28 percent of the voting-age population and 47 percent of voting-age citizens. Among registered Hispanic citizens, 82 percent voted. In comparison, non-Hispanic white voting rates are much higher (U.S. Census Bureau 2006).

Traditionally Mexicans and Puerto Ricans have supported Democratic candidates, whereas Cubans have favored the Republican Party. Cubans tend to be better educated and have higher SES. A *Washington Post* 1999 survey that included 2,417 Latino/as found that a majority of all Hispanic subgroups had voted for Clinton in 1996, but Cubans had the lowest (57.3 percent) support for him while the support from other groups ranged from 71.9 to 97.1 percent (Garcia and Sanchez 2004: 140). In 1999 more than half of the Cubans surveyed expressed preference for Bush. A question about liberal–conservative ideology, though, found that most respondents considered themselves conservative with scores showing Puerto Ricans least conservative and Salvadorans most conservative (138).[4]

The exit polls for the 2000 election indicated that Gore won two-thirds of the Hispanic vote with the greatest support from Puerto Ricans and Dominicans, and more than 55 percent of support from voters of Mexican origin. One significant regional variation was that more than 60 percent of Mexican Americans in California voted for Gore, but about half of those in Texas supported Bush (Garcia and Sanchez 2004: 143). George W. Bush was the Governor of Texas prior to running for the presidency.

As seen in Table 7.2, CNN's 2004 exit poll found that 44 percent of Hispanics supported Bush while 53 percent supported Kerry. In the 2006 elections for the House of Representatives, 69 percent of Hispanics voted for Democrats and 30 percent for Republicans. Hernandez (2007) argues that Hispanics are playing more and more important roles in elections, especially in California, New York, Arizona, and Florida. Hispanics strongly supported Obama in the 2008 national election.

EAST ASIAN AMERICANS[5]   East Asian Americans are a particularly interesting minority group to examine politically because they have relatively higher incomes and higher education levels than most other minorities, yet have low political participation rates. One possible reason for low turnout is that Asian Americans have not joined either political party because they believe neither party has treated them very well (Chi 2005: 122). The Immigration Act of 1965 eliminated the discriminatory national-origin quota system that had favored European immigrants, and the number of East Asian immigrants rose substantially from 1.1 million in 1970 to 4.3 million in 2000 (6), with a major portion of this gain in the Korean population, which surpassed the Japanese population. Chinese Americans remain the largest East Asian ethnic group.

Nearly one-third (32.5 percent) of Asian Americans are not citizens (U.S. Census Bureau 2006: 6). Forty-four percent of the total Asian American citizen population vote, whereas 85 percent of those registered vote; these rates are somewhat similar to Hispanics. Two surveys of political attitudes of Asian Americans suggest a shift in political ideology away from the conservative and toward the more moderate or liberal view. Koreans remain the most conservative followed by the Japanese and then the Chinese. Party affiliations have changed as well, as might be expected, such that all three groups identified with the Democrats in 2001 (Chi 2005: 17–20). The CNN exit polls (Table 7.2) show Asian Americans (not only East Asians) favoring Gore, Kerry, and Obama as well as the Democratic candidates in U.S. House of Representative elections.

Religious Cleavages

Advocates of a postmodern or postmaterialist society, like Inglehart (1997), argue that the overall influence of religious group membership and involvement on voting may be declining. This is because of the growing secularization of societies whereby "fewer voters are integrated into religious networks and exposed to the religious cues than can guide the vote" (Dalton and Wattenberg 1993: 199–200). However, empirical results do not necessarily support this line of reasoning. For example, in three of six nations studied, Brooks et al. (2006) found stability in religious cleavages with two societies declining and one possibly increasing. Religion may be an enduring cleavage, but its form may also be changing with more attention to divisions between those who are religious versus those who are not and also between those involved in religious activities versus those not involved. Ideological differences on the basis of religious traditions may underlie certain current patterns of cultural conflict between and within many societies (Brooks et al. 2003: 163). For example, in Iraq differences between Shiites and Sunnis have made it difficult to form a unity government.

At times religion has played an important role in U.S. politics. It was not until 1960 that a Catholic, John F. Kennedy, was elected president. Protestantism consists of many denominational groups that, at times, complicate the voting picture. One helpful, yet simplistic classification for voting is that of mainline Protestants, evangelical Protestants, Catholics, Jews, and the nonreligious, with other religions' viewpoints sometimes considered. Miller and Shanks (1996) found that in terms of religious affiliation there were some dramatic shifts from 1980 to the early 1990s. The percentage of mainline Protestants dropped from 36 to 24 percent, while that of evangelical Protestants grew from 26 to 32 percent. The religious commitment of mainliners also declined, but it flourished for evangelicals and remained pretty much the same for Catholics.

Regarding trends in voter turnout from 1980 to 1992, both committed and nominal Catholic supporters increased but committed mainline Protestants and evangelicals declined. In 1992 nominal mainline Protestants and Catholics shifted to the Democrats more than those more committed. On the other hand, committed Catholics increased their party identification for the

Democrats more than did nominal supporters. Evangelicals marked a key shift from 1980 when they supported Democrat Carter, to favoring Republican G. W. Bush in 2000. This is particularly true of strongly committed evangelicals. Utter and True (2004: xii) identify three key trends in religious affiliation in the United States: (1) growing membership in fundamentalist denominations, (2) decline in mainline church supporters, and (3) growing numbers who do not identify with any religion. Those labeled *other*, *no religion*, or *Jewish* are a strong part of the pro-Democratic Party movement. Table 7.2 shows that those who frequently attend church are more likely to support Republican candidates.

According to the 2000 CNN exit poll (Table 7.2) 56 percent of Protestants voted for Bush, but 80 percent of the 14 percent who identified as white religious right supported him. In 2004, 59 percent of Protestants supported Bush, but 78 percent of white evangelicals did so, according to the CNN exit poll. The 2006 CNN election poll of voters for seats in the U.S. House of Representatives sheds even more light on the importance of the intersection of race with religion. Only 54 percent of Protestants voted for Republicans compared to 70 percent of white evangelicals and born-again Christians. Evangelicals and born-again Christians also supported McCain in 2008. Non-white, mainly black fundamentalists, seem loyal to the Democratic Party while white evangelicals support the Republicans.

Jewish voting has shifted somewhat to the right although still supportive of Democratic candidates. In 2000, Democratic presidential candidate Gore chose Jewish Senator Joseph Lieberman to be his vice presidential candidate, and they captured 78 percent of the Jewish vote (Medoff 2002: 181–209). CNN's 2004, 2006, and 2008 election exit polls show strong Jewish support for Kerry, Obama, and Democrats as well. Medoff (208) believes, however, that Jewish votes in mayoral and congressional races are changing in part because the size and influence of the less liberal elements of Jewry are increasing.

POLITICAL VIEWS AND ISSUE-BASED VOTING

The American Voter, a major landmark in early electoral research, proclaimed that voters were very unsophisticated in their views about policy concerns. According to Campbell et al. (1960: 543), "We do not find coherent patterns of belief. . . . [The public] is almost completely unable to judge the rationality of government actions." Dalton and Wattenberg (1993: 194) found that studies of other societies, particularly Western democracies in the mid-twentieth century, also support the idea of unsophisticated citizens.

Schulman and Pomper (1975) found that over time voting preferences have been less strongly shaped by social characteristics and traditional loyalties. Schulman and Pomper support Key's (1966: 7) conclusion, though, that the voter "behaves as rationally and responsibly as we should expect, given the clarity of the alternatives presented to it and the character of the information available to it." Nie, Verba, and Petrocik (1979: 319) point out that the issues and the way candidates present those issues have been important in shaping the electorate's vote: "If candidates offer clear issue alternatives, voters are more likely to make political issues a criterion for electoral choice." The traditional school of thought on rationality views voters' competence negatively, but a revisionist approach maintains that when parties take positions on the major issues, voters' decisions may well be rational. They vote for the candidate closest to them on the issues because they perceive greater benefits from such a vote (Downs 1957; Niemi and Weisberg 1976).

Budge and Farlie (1983) analyzed post World War II data for twenty-three democracies and developed an important issue-based theory that modified rational choice theory. They argue that voters evaluate political issues on the basis of their location in one of fourteen self-contained issues, but if more than six or seven issues are introduced into a particular election, confusion in the electors' voting decisions may result. The four major issues are (1) government record and prospects (current financial situation and prospects, economic prosperity, satisfaction with democracy in general, and economic stability), (2) candidate reactions (likes and dislikes about candidates), (3) foreign policy relationships (e.g., membership in NATO, entry to the European Community, and relations between Eastern and Western European nations), and (4) socioeconomic redistribution (e.g., issues of social justice, social service spending, and importance of social welfare).

According to Budge and Farlie (1983), political parties do not compete with each other by debating directly on focused issues; rather each party tries to make its own areas of concern most prominent. This is different from the rational choice notion of parties confronting each other with different policies on the same issues. The expansion of welfare is associated with leftist or socialist parties and law-and-order issues with bourgeois or rightist parties. The political parties devote most of their attention to the types of issues that favor themselves. Niemi and Weisberg (2001: 193–194) and Brooks et al. (2003: 140) conclude that recent studies suggest quite convincingly that issues make important contributions to voting decisions and therefore to electoral results.

Table 7.3 contains information on selected political attitudes and issue orientations related to voting preferences in CNN exit polls. In 2000, if voters believed either taxes or world affairs were the most important, they preferred Bush, whereas those who indicated education, economy/jobs, or health care as important supported Gore. Prior to this election the general model forecasting presidential victory relied on the argument "that voters support the incumbent (White House) party to the extent they favor its economic and non-economic policies" (Lewis-Beck and Tien 2002: 174). In 2004 Bush still benefited from those who believed taxes were most important, but those who believed terrorism or moral values were most important even more strongly supported him. Kerry strongly benefited from those who believed economy and jobs, health care, education, or Iraq was most important. In 2008 Obama also benefited from those who believed economy and jobs, health care, or Iraq were most important.

Liberalism and Conservatism

Although liberalism and conservatism are difficult concepts to define and measure, they include an evaluation of various types of political issues. Conservatism is defined as

> an ideological orientation that opposes social change, especially change away from traditional cultural values and mores, and justifies its actions and values on the basis of the presumed accumulated wisdom of the past inherent in traditional forms. (Theodorson and Theodorson 1969: 73)

Liberalism is defined as

> an ideological orientation based on a belief in the importance of the freedom and welfare of the individual, and the possibility of social progress and the improvement of the quality of life through change and innovation in social organization. . . . Liberals believe that the government must take positive steps to ensure each person's welfare. (Theodorson and Theodorson 1969: 230)

Table 7.3   National Election Political Preferences from 2000, 2004, 2006, and 2008 CNN Election Exit Polls (in Percentages) by Political Attitudes

Political Attitudes	2000 Election		2004 Election		2006 Election		2008 Election	
	Bush	**Gore**	**Bush**	**Kerry**	**Dems**	**Reps**	**Obama**	**McCain**
Most Important Issue								
Taxes	80	17	57	43	NA	NA	NA	NA
Education	44	52	26	73	NA	NA	NA	NA
Iraq	NA	NA	26	73	NA	NA	59	39
Terrorism	NA	NA	86	14	NA	NA	13	86
Economy/Jobs	37	59	18	80	NA	NA	53	44
Moral Values	NA	NA	80	18	NA	NA	NA	NA
Health Care	33	64	23	77	NA	NA	73	26
World Affairs	54	40	NA	NA	NA	NA	NA	NA
Ideology								
Liberal	13	80	13	85	87	11	89	10
Moderate	44	52	45	54	60	38	60	39
Conservative	81	17	84	15	20	78	20	78
Party ID								
Democrat	11	86	11	89	93	7	89	10
Republican	91	8	93	6	8	91	9	90
Independent	47	45	48	49	57	39	52	44

NA: Not Available. Dems = Democrats, Reps = Republicans

Sources: CNN Exit Poll National 2000, *N*=13,310 respondents, http://www.cnn.com/ELECTION/2000/epolls/US/P000.html

CNN Exit Poll 2004 U.S. President, National, *N*=13,660 respondents, http://www.cnn.com/ELECTION/2004/pages/results/states/US/P/00/epolls.0.html

CNN Exit Poll 2006, U.S. House of Representatives/National, *N*=13,251 respondents, http://www.cnn.com/ELECTION/2006/pages/results/states/US/H/00/epolls.0.html

CNN Exit Poll 2008 U.S. President, National, *N* = 17,836 respondents, http://www.cnn.com/ELECTION/2008/results/polls/USPOp1

Economic liberalism refers to the conventional issues of redistribution of income, status, and power among the classes (such as welfare state measures, higher wages, graduated income taxes, and support of trade unions), whereas *noneconomic liberalism* refers to support of, for example, civil liberties for political dissidents, civil rights for ethnic and racial minorities, internationalist foreign policies, and liberal immigration legislation (Lipset 1959: 485). Currently it seems appropriate to distinguish between at least three dimensions of liberalism and conservatism: economic, social, and foreign policy or defense (Harrigan 2000).

The majority of people are not "pure" in their ideological beliefs (Harrigan 2000; Hero 1969; Lipset, 1963). Although Campbell et al. (1960) did not find much issue consistency among American voters, Nie et al. (1979: 123) in *The Changing American Voter* suggested greater issue consistency in the American public including the finding that "liberals on traditional issues tend to be more liberal on new issues; conservatives are more conservative on these issues."

The meanings of liberalism and conservatism have certainly changed over time (Harrigan 2000; McKenna and Feingold 2007). Early American liberals like Thomas Jefferson favored less government, while conservatives like Alexander Hamilton preferred government support of economic enterprise. Currently, however, conservatives fear more government leads to interference in people's private lives, too much bureaucracy, regulation of both people and businesses, and high taxes. On the issue of foreign policy, conservatives now tend to support greater military expenditures and favor government involvement to protect people from internal subversion and to fight the war on terrorism. Progressive liberals or New Politics liberals who were critical of the Vietnam war question whether the United States is or should be the leader of the free world and criticize U.S. involvement in Iraq and Afghanistan (McKenna and Feingold 2007: xviii–xxiv).

In terms of labeling oneself as liberal or conservative, few Americans consider themselves radical or extreme liberals or conservatives. A plurality of citizens thinks of themselves as moderate or middle-of-the-road (Dye 2003: 45; Harrigan 2000: 91). In the United States, liberals are more likely to support the Democratic Party, whereas conservatives support the Republican Party. The exit poll data shown in Table 7.3 illustrate how strongly one's ideology influences one's vote. At least 80 percent of liberals supported Democratic candidates in 2000, 2004, 2006, and 2008, whereas 78 to 84 percent of the conservatives supported Republicans. Moderates were much more equally divided but supported Democrats in 2006 and Obama in 2008.

Party Identification

Party identification, closely related to liberalism–conservatism, is another key political attitude that predicts voting preferences. Interpreting party identification is very complex and begins with the question: "Are party identifications relatively fixed features on the political landscape?" (Johnson 2006: 329). Early U.S. studies answered yes; party identification is stable over time: "Identification is characterized as a simple loyalty, learned early and largely unimpaired by subsequent learning" (330). Only extraordinary events would bring about change (Campbell et al. 1960: 151). An alternative approach though is that party identification is "a readily updated sum of preferences" (Johnson 2006: 329), or drawing on Fiorina, "a 'running tally' of retrospective evaluations based on reactions to current political happenings" (Niemi and Weisberg 2001: 322).

Recent studies suggest that partisanship is more changeable than originally believed and party preference is affected by political as well as social variables (Johnson 2006; Niemi and Weisberg 2001). It is not clear just how dramatic events must be to bring about change and whether the change is transitory or has lasting effect. Niemi and Weisberg (2001: 334) conclude that "the question becomes whether the amount of change that occurs is better characterized as large enough to be meaningful or small enough to be ignored under normal circumstances, and this is where analysts differ in their interpretations." Another key question yet to be resolved is: "What does 'Independent' really mean?"

According to Johnson (2006: 347–348), U.S. studies indicate there is strong support for partisanship influencing opinions and values, evaluations of candidates, and their positions on issues and on the vote itself, but the evidence is much murkier cross-nationally. While the precise interpretation of party identification varies, the CNN exit poll data shown in Table 7.3 strongly shows that partisanship influences voting with 86 to 93 percent of those loyal to a party voting for its candidates. Independents were nearly equally divided between parties in 2000 and 2004 but more favorable to the Democrats in the 2006 off-year election and the 2008 election.

U.S. PRESIDENTIAL ELECTIONS

The United States has an election system based on plurality of votes to win the presidency or a seat in the House of Representatives or Senate. Every four years, voters cast their ballots for the presidential candidate, but that does not end the presidential process because the United States uses an Electoral College system. Each state has as many electors as it has members of Congress, and the presidential nominee who wins the plurality of votes in the state, in most cases, garners all the electoral votes from that state. Perhaps somewhat surprisingly, there have been eighteen presidential elections in which the winner did *not* receive a majority of the popular vote. Table 7.4 provides Electoral College vote and popular vote results during the last half

Table 7.4 Popular Votes and Electoral College Votes in Presidential Elections 1960–2008			
	Popular Vote	**Percentage of Popular Votes**	**Electoral College Vote**
1960			
Kennedy (D)	34,226,731	49.7	303
Nixon (R)	34,108,157	49.5	219
Other (D)	503,331	0.8	15
1964			
Johnson (D)	43,129,566	61.1	486
Goldwater (R)	27,178,188	38.5	52
Other	336,838	0.45	
1968			
Nixon (R)	31,785,480	43.4	301
Humphrey (D)	31,275,166	42.7	191
Wallace (Ind)	9,906,473	13.5	46
Other	244,756	0.4	
1972			
Nixon (R)	47,169,911	60.7	520
McGovern (D)	29,170,383	37.5	17
Other	1,378,260	1.8	1
1976			
Carter (D)	40,830,763	50.1	297
Ford (R)	39,147,793	48.0	240
McCarthy (Ind)	756,691	0.9	
Other	820,642	1.1	1
1980			
Reagan (R)	43,904,153	50.7	489
Carter (D)	35,483,883	41.0	49
Anderson (Ind)	5,720,060	6.6	49
Other	1,405,717	1.7	

Table 7.4 Popular Votes and Electoral College Votes in Presidential Elections 1960–2008 (*Continued*)

	Popular Vote	Percentage of Popular Votes	Electoral College Vote
1984			
Reagan (R)	54,455,075	58.8	525
Mondale (D)	37,577,185	40.6	13
Other	620,582	0.6	
1988			
G. H. W. Bush (R)	48,886,077	53.4	426
Dukakis (D)	41,809,074	45.6	111
Other	899,638	1.0	1
1992			
Clinton (D)	44,909,326	43.0	370
G. H. W. Bush (R)	39,103,882	37.4	168
Perot (Ind)	19,741,657	18.9	
Other	670,149	0.7	
1996			
Clinton (D)	47,402,357	49.2	379
Dole (R)	39,198,755	40.7	159
Perot (Reform)	8,085,402	8.4	
Nader (Green)	684,902	0.7	
Other	905,807	0.9	
2000			
G. W. Bush (R)	50,455,156	47.9	271
Gore (D)	50,992,335	48.4	266
Nader (Green)	449,077	2.7	
Buchanan (Reform)	617,321	0.4	
Other	537,179	0.6	
2004			
G. W. Bush (R)	62,040,610	50.7	286
Kerry (D)	59,028,439	48.3	251
Other	1,224,499	1.0	1
2008			
Barack Obama (D)	69,499,303	52.8	365
John McCain (R)	59,950,037	45.6	173
Ralph Nader	739,057	0.6	
Bob Barr	523,720	0.4	
Other	746,688	0.6	

Sources: Congressional Quarterly, *Presidential Elections, 1789–2000*, and Dave Leip's Atlas of U.S. Presidential Elections, 2004 and 2008 Results, http://www.uselectionatlas.org

century. As shown, Kennedy, Nixon, Clinton (twice), and G. W. Bush did not receive 50 percent of the vote. G. W. Bush did not win a plurality of the votes, but he did receive a majority of the Electoral College votes. In the 1800s, three other presidential candidates (J. Q. Adams, Hayes, and Harrison) did not receive a plurality of votes but became president. Over time there has been considerable conflict about the Electoral College system. Textbox 7.2 presents a discussion of the positive and the negative aspects of the Electoral College.

Edsall and Edsall (1995) studied the impact of race and taxes on American politics from 1968 to the early 1990s. They argue that during this period the Republican Party won five of the six elections and that the traditional New Deal cleavages that benefited Democrats were disappearing. From the 1930s to the 1960s Democrats benefited from the votes of two major swing groups: (1) the white, Euro-Americans, frequently Catholic in the north; and (2) the lower-income southern whites and white working and lower middle classes. The rights revolutions, which have advocated for various rights for minorities, women, immigrants, gays and lesbians, welfare recipients, and the criminally accused, have been resented by many in these two groups. School busing and affirmative action led to a great deal of ideological debate and resentment about the role of government and its remedies for segregation and discrimination. Many whites feel threatened by the perceived advances of minorities and the increases in taxes to support welfare recipients who they believe are not worthy of support because they are unwilling to work, engage in welfare fraud, and so on. The Republican Party has attracted these voters, and these gains have helped them win five presidential elections (see Table 7.4). In 1992, however, Clinton broke this cycle when he defeated George H. W. Bush and was reelected in 1996. We note that unlike traditional Democrats, Clinton ran on a more centrist platform that included support for welfare reform and the use of the death penalty.

TEXTBOX 7.2

Should We Abolish the Electoral College?

The 2000 election brought home to many Americans that they do not directly elect the president of the United States, and on a few occasions Electoral College vote and popular vote are not the same. Some argue that the Electoral College has provided more benefits than disadvantages while others argue that it is an anachronistic institution. Hardaway, a professor of law, counted 704 efforts to change or eliminate the Electoral College (Lyman 2006).

Pro

The Electoral College should be abolished because it can alter the outcome of an election. In the wake of the 2000 election, a New York law professor suggested the time was appropriate for change: "We now have the best chance ever to junk [this] anachronistic and dangerous eighteenth-century system. The public should demand that Congress begin a process of constitutional amendment that would eliminate that system, root and branch, and substitute for it the direct election of the president and vice presidency by a plurality of the national popular vote" (Lazare 2003: 100).

The Electoral College violates the principle of democracy that values political equality. The votes of some citizens are favored over others depending on in what state one resides. Candidates often focus on a select list of key battleground states, ignoring many voters. Edwards (2007: 41) argues that the mechanisms allocating electoral votes among the states, the differences in turnout by state, and the role of the size of the House of Representatives result in an inherently unjust procedure. (Remember that the number of electoral votes per state is based on the number of representatives in the House plus the two senators. Every state, small or large, begins with two votes based on its senators, resulting in malapportionment.)

Direct election of the president will encourage candidates to campaign throughout the nation and may increase turnout as well. One vote will be as valuable as the other regardless of location. Such a change will require a constitutional amendment that should allow for a plurality of voters to determine the winner. It would no longer be possible for someone to win with fewer popular votes than another candidate. Finally, abolishing the Electoral College eliminates the possibility that electors would not support the candidate who has won their state.

Con

The Electoral College has benefited the U.S. political system more than it has harmed it. For example, it has helped preserve a two-party system rather than encourage minor parties and minority candidacies that would fragment U.S. society. The current arrangement prevents runoff elections among the two top candidates and channels political struggles into state-by-state contests for the most votes. Runoff elections could result in low voter turnout that may not be representative of the people's will (McKenna and Feingold 2007).

The Bush and Gore 2000 election would have resulted in much greater confusion if there had not been an Electoral College. Requests from both sides for recounts, challenges in every state, and hundreds of lawsuits would have plagued the court system (Edwards 2007; Posner 2004). According to Gregg (2007: 45), "Abolishing the Electoral College would dismantle the firewalls protecting all of us from a quadrennial national nightmare that would turn over our elections to lawyers and judges."

The Electoral College system has stood the test of time and evolved as American politics have developed. It has always given our nation a president. It has ensured that the interests of rural America have been represented as well as those of larger urban areas (Gregg 2007) and has given power to small states as well as large ones. Finally, the system also protects against voter fraud and maintains the principle of federalism.

Elections during the Twenty-First Century

2000 PRESIDENTIAL ELECTION   Elizabeth Dole's bid for the Republican presidential nomination in 1999 "was the longest and most serious bid by a woman for a major party's presidential nomination in the previous two decades" (Heldman, Carroll, and Olson 2005: 315). Heldman et al. examined the print media coverage of her bid for the nomination by comparing her coverage with that of five males including G. W. Bush. Dole was the number two candidate in the public opinion polls initially, but did not receive the amount of media attention consistent for someone with that much support in the polls. Heldman et al. suggested that gender biases existed, including the press paying greater attention to her personality traits and appearance. She ended her candidacy seven months after she entered the race and before the primaries started.

In 2000 G. W. Bush was elected president and won back the White House for the Republicans in one of the most controversial elections in American history. Much of the

Democratic National Convention delegates unveil a banner on 26 July, 2004, at the Fleet Center in Boston, Massachusetts. The banner recalled the mired 2000 election that made the hanging chad a popular term.

Credit: ROBYN BECK/AFP/Getty Images

controversy focused on the state of Florida, where Bush's brother was governor, and especially on Palm Beach County. Some voters there, confused by the maligned "butterfly ballot," ended up voting for Buchanan when they meant to vote for Gore. Adams and Fastnow (2002: 191) point out: "It was clear that if only a small fraction of Gore supporters in Palm Beach County—roughly one quarter of 1 percent of his voters in the county—mistakenly cast their vote, the confusion from the Palm Beach County ballot would have cost Gore the presidency." The closeness of the Florida election[6] prompted a mandatory recount, and concerns over paper ballots with "hanging chads" also raised questions about voters' intentions.

Florida law allowed the Gore/Democratic side to seek a recount in four key counties. This prompted a hard-fought, partisan, legal battle that started in the Florida Supreme Court, moved on to the U.S. Supreme Court, was remanded to the Florida Supreme Court, and was ultimately decided in the U.S. Supreme Court, which on December 12, 2000, reversed the Florida Supreme Court, stating that though some voters were being denied equal protection, there was not sufficient time to correct the problem (Brigman 2002). Whether the U.S. Supreme Court was correct or not, its decision was final and Gore conceded the election.

The U.S. Commission on Civil Rights (2001) investigated the 2000 Florida general election finding that, although blacks comprised about 11 percent of the voters, they cast about 54 percent of the ballots that were rejected. Poorer counties, especially those with significant numbers of people of color, were more likely to use voting systems with higher spoilage rates. In addition, the system of purging voters from the rolls seemed to proceed from "the premise of guilty until proven innocent." The Florida state election apparatus, despite having early signs of a large influx of new voters, did not respond with an appropriate array of measures to avoid the chaos that occurred, which resulted in widespread problems on Election Day: the inability to reach central offices (commonly due to busy signals) and to certify voters, long lines, unprepared and untrained workers, and accessibility problems.

If disenfranchised felons in Florida had been permitted to vote in the 2000 election, Al Gore would likely have won the Electoral College vote and the presidency. It is estimated that there were about 827,000 disenfranchised felons in that state alone, and if one assumes about 27 percent of the felons would have turned out, Gore would have carried the state by more than eighty thousand votes (Manza and Uggen 2006: 192). The Florida electoral reform law adopted after the 2000 election still did not address the issue of felon purges, language assistance, and removing barriers for persons with disabilities who came to the polls.

While much of the focus of the 2000 election was on Florida, the national voting results with the blue and red state projections were also quite interesting. The Democrats won much of the Northeast, with New York having thirty-three Electoral College votes and Pennsylvania twenty-three; a large part of the northern Midwest (Illinois, Michigan, Wisconsin, Minnesota, and Iowa); and the West, where California had the largest number of Electoral College votes (fifty-four). The Republicans were victorious in the West (except for the coastal states), the South (with Bush's home state of Texas having thirty-two Electoral College votes), and both the East Coast and the interior. As Table 7.4 shows, Bush received less of the popular vote (47.9 percent—500,000 fewer votes than Gore) but garnered 241 (50.4 percent) of the Electoral College votes.

2004 PRESIDENT ELECTION   In the 2004 election, the results were not nearly as controversial, although there were some concerns expressed about polling procedures, particularly in Ohio. G. W. Bush captured the majority of the popular vote (50.73 percent) and 286 of the Electoral College votes. Following the September 11, 2001 attacks on New York City and Washington DC, Bush began a "war on terror" involving a U.S.-led invasion of Iraq that toppled Saddam Hussein's reign and military campaigns against the Taliban in Afghanistan. National security issues thus played a key role in citizens' voting in 2004.

Campbell (2004) identified three key fundamentals that help explain election outcomes, and applied them to the 2004 election. First, public opinion about the candidates at the outset of the campaign tilted toward Bush. Second, early objective indicators of the economy indicated a benefit for Bush, but the economy actually worked somewhat to Kerry's advantage. Third, Bush was advantaged because he was the incumbent. Generally, voters thought Kerry was too liberal more than that they believed Bush was too conservative. According to the exit polls, the ratio was 1.6 conservatives for every liberal, which suggested that ideological labels were important.

On the other hand, Weiner and Pomper (2006) suggest that the "war on terror" benefited Bush slightly, but his conduct of the Iraq war and his economic record seemed to hurt him. Party identification was the most significant factor even though Democrats slightly outnumbered Republicans. Bush received 93 percent of all Republican votes while Kerry won 89 percent of all Democratic votes. In addition, Republicans appear to have turned out in greater numbers. Turnout increased nationally, including among the young who supported Kerry 55 to 45 percent, but Christian evangelicals increased their pro-Republican votes with 77 percent favoring Bush. Bush was also regarded as a stronger leader, less likely to change his mind, and more moral than Kerry. Weiner and Pomper conclude that party identification is a key variable, but unlike what Campbell et al. (1960) suggested in *The American Voter,* partisanship is deeply rooted in long-term policy issues and much less on loyalties and attachments to parents and various social groups.

2006 MIDTERM ELECTION   In 2006 the Republican support declined with Republicans losing six governorships and six seats in the Senate. The 2006 exit poll data shown in Table 7.3 illustrate the importance of ideology and party identification in shaping voting. The Democrats convincingly gained control of the House of Representatives and barely had a majority in the Senate but still found it difficult to bring about change on the issue of the war in Iraq and Afghanistan. The Democrats selected Representative Nancy Pelosi as the first woman to serve as Speaker of the House.

2008 PRESIDENTIAL ELECTION   The 2008 election will certainly not be remembered for its closeness but will be remembered as the first one in which a black man (technically the son of a black man from Kenya and a white woman from Kansas) was elected president of the United States. Barack Obama, only forty-seven years old, ascended rapidly in politics in spite of his lack of experience and what many cited as his lack of substance about the issues in many of his campaign speeches. Obama, president of the *Harvard Law Review*, had spent eight years in the Illinois State Senate and only four years as a U.S. Senator.

In the announcement of his candidacy for the Democratic nomination for president in February 2007, Obama portrayed himself as a candidate for change as he criticized the government in Washington DC for its cynicism, petty corruption, and "smallness of politics" that divided the country. "The time for that politics is over," he stated, "It is through. It's time to turn the page" ("The Presidency of Barack Obama" 2009: 5). It is this framing of bringing "change" to the political process that would facilitate his campaign in the primaries and then in his contest with Republican nominee John McCain. The Obama campaign was also able to effectively utilize the Internet to his competitive advantage including raising funds and texting his supporters about who would be his vice presidential choice.

Many candidates initially ran for the Democratic nomination, but the three who did well in the first contest, the Iowa caucus in January 2008, became the leading candidates. In that caucus Obama received the most support followed by John Edwards and then Hillary Clinton. In other words, the frontrunners were a black man, a white man, and a white woman. Eventually Edwards and other candidates dropped out narrowing the competition to Obama and Clinton. Clinton was able to remain competitive until the last primary elections in June 2008.

As Clinton's campaign was struggling, more and more charges of "sexist news coverage" surfaced (Seelye and Bosman 2008). Seelye and Bosman point out that not many in the media perceived any need to change their reporting although Katie Couric, the first woman solo anchor of an evening news broadcast, posted a video on the CBS Web site and stated, "Like her or not, one of the great lessons of that campaign is the continued—and accepted—role of sexism in American life, particularly in the media" (2). Much of the media defended themselves by arguing that their coverage was fair. For example, Phil Griffin, senior vice president of NBC news and the executive in charge of MSNBC, acknowledged that a few mistakes had occurred, but they had been corrected so that overall the coverage was fair. He believed the Clinton campaign was especially trying to attract support from women and possibly used the idea of unfair coverage to secure their support (2).

A look at the Pew Research Center's Project for Excellence in Journalism[7] sheds some light on the coverage of the candidates in the primaries and the election although it doesn't necessarily help determine if sexism per se existed. Early in the campaign in 2007, before any caucuses or primaries, the Pew Project for Excellence in Journalism and the Joan Shorenstein Center on the Press, Politics and Public Policy (Pew Project for Excellence in Journalism 2007) reported that Barack Obama was getting the most positive and the fewest negative stories among the four candidates. The percentage of all stories favorable to Obama was 46.7 percent compared to 26.9 percent for

Clinton, 27.8 percent for Giuliani, and only 12.4 percent for McCain. Some articles were neutral, but 15.8 percent of the Obama articles were negative compared to more than one-third for Clinton and Giuliani and nearly half for McCain. Democrats received more positive coverage than Republican candidates.

Table 7.5 includes information about media exposure from January 6, 2008, through June 15, 2008 (Pew Project for Excellence in Journalism 2008a). As Table 7.5 shows, Obama received more media exposure in fifteen of the twenty-three time periods identified. McCain generally

Table 7.5   Media Exposure of Obama, Clinton, and McCain Over Time from January 6 to June 15, 2008

	Percentage of Candidate Exposure in Main Stories about the 2008 Campaign		
	Barack Obama	**Hillary Clinton**	**John McCain**
Jan. 6–11	31.9	37.0	23.7
Jan. 14–20	27.8	29.0	23.5
Jan. 21–27	41.3	40.3	16.9
Jan. 28–Feb. 3	34.0	32.0	37.4
Feb. 4–10	40.2	41.1	42.3
Feb. 11–17	55.5	56.9	34.3
Feb. 18–24	56.8	49.9	38.4
Feb. 25–Mar. 2	69.0	58.2	28.5
Mar. 3–9	57.6	59.9	25.6
Mar. 9–16	67.1	50.8	15.3
Mar. 17–23	71.6	30.3	16.8
Mar. 24–30	53.5	63.3	23.6
Mar. 31–Apr. 6	55.7	55.4	30.0
Apr. 7–13	46.2	55.8	34.7
Apr. 14–20	75.6	59.1	24.1
Apr. 21–27	70.1	63.9	17.1
Apr. 28–May 4	69.4	40.7	14.2
May 5–11	66.9	70.0	11.7
May 12–18	67.5	53.1	27.3
May 19–25	62.4	42.9	41.0
May 26–June 1	65.9	45.2	36.1
June 2–8	77.5	59.6	21.0
June 9–15	77.2	10.4	54.9

Source: Pew Project for Excellence in Journalism (2008a), see http://www.journalism.org/node/11540. Concerning methodology used, see Pew Project for Excellence in Journalism (n.d.) on http://www.journalism.org/about_news_index/methodology.

Credit: The Pew Research Center's Project for Excellence in Journalism, "Media Exposure over Time" based on the report "PEJ Campaign Coverage Index: June 9–15, 2008. Obama Makes More News Than McCain, But It's Not All Good," http://www.journalism.org/node/11537.

received less coverage than either Obama or Clinton. These results do not, however, give us any indication of the extensiveness of the coverage or whether the coverage was positive or negative.

In early January 2008, when Obama won the Democratic Iowa Caucus, the press seemed to immediately start to count Clinton out. Jurkowitz (2008a) reported that so widespread was the belief Obama would couple his Iowa win with a win in New Hampshire that two respected newspapers were running headlines all but predicting a second Obama victory. However, contrary to expectations, Clinton won and the media searched for explanations. One of the explanations was "that Clinton humanized herself during the Portsmouth, New Hampshire event where she became emotional and teary-eyed while discussing her campaign" (2).

Bystrom (2008) examined a major newspaper in Iowa, the *Des Moines Register,* and another in New Hampshire, the *Concord Monitor,* regarding their coverage of the Iowa caucus and the New Hampshire primary. Both newspapers endorsed Clinton but said positive things about Obama. Clinton received a little less coverage than did Obama in the *Des Moines Register* but considerably more in the *Concord Monitor.* More of Clinton's coverage was negative compared to that of Obama and Edwards. More than 60 percent of articles about both of the men were positive while only 33 percent of Clinton's were. Also Clinton was less likely to receive issue-oriented coverage. Bystrom points out that when women have less issue coverage, they are more likely to be seen as less qualified. Stories about Clinton were more likely to be stories about her personality traits, political scandals, character and ethics, family, and previous record and experiences. Bystrom (26) argues that both "Clinton's more negative, often sexist, and less issue-focused coverage" and "Obama's overwhelmingly positive coverage" were factors in Obama's victory in the Democratic presidential nomination process. This finding is consistent with previous literature that found that in the 1980s and 1990s female political candidates were covered less equitably than male candidates, including the way Elizabeth Dole, Republican nominee for president in 1999, was treated (Bystrom 2008; Heldman et al. 2005; Kahn 1996).

Dimitrova and Geske (2009) used content analysis of the *New York Times* and *USA Today* to examine how Clinton was portrayed by news media at the time of the New Hampshire primary. The articles covered the week before and the week after "Clinton's tears" in New Hampshire. Articles were coded to determine if they used a family frame, a masculinity frame, or a beauty frame. The masculinity frame was used most frequently; it included portraying Clinton as tough, powerful, independent, uncompromising, or authoritative. Family and beauty framings were rarely used. Being "teary-eyed" does not fit the masculinity framework, but the way it was framed by the media helped reinforce the frame as typically masculine as media suggested that Clinton would continue to fight and be aggressive (Dimitrova and Geske 2009). This may be a somewhat different image of Clinton than in her 2000 senatorial campaign when her media coverage included frequent comments on personal appearance and her marital relationship with former President Bill Clinton (Bystrom et al. 2004). Interestingly enough, Obama's coverage tended to focus more on traditionally feminine traits such as honesty, warmth, and sincerity with neither toughness nor aggressiveness being associated with Obama. Although framing women in masculine terms may help them compete with their male opponents, such framing could have negative consequences if voters perceive women as too aggressive (Dimitrova and Geske 2009).

The idea of Clinton's toughness was also supported by Rem Rieder, editor of *American Journalism Review,* who stated, "She had a long track record in public life as a serious person and a tough politician, and she was covered that way" (Seelye and Bosman 2008). In addition, in March 2008, Jurkowitz (2008b) pointed out how the media, including pundit David Gergen, was questioning Obama's toughness, maintaining, "He's got to be a lot tougher and more aggressive" (1). On the other hand, Clinton was noted for "aggressively attacking Obama" (1–2), and a *New York Times* story characterized her as in "happy-warrior mode" (3). Obama faced other problems, including needing to distance himself from Reverend Jeremiah Wright and Obama's own statement in which he labeled some white working-class voters as "bitter" ("The Presidency of Barack Obama" 2009: 6). Ultimately though by June 3, 2008, it was clear that Obama had sufficient numbers of delegates to win the Democratic nomination for the presidency.

Shortly thereafter Clinton ended her campaign in which she had received about 18 million votes. However, many of her supporters, especially females, were unhappy with Obama and more than one-third of them believed Clinton's gender had harmed her candidacy (Pew Research Center for the People & the Press 2008a). By June 2008, as the primaries were ending, public opinion also seemed to believe there was media bias. The Pew Research Center for the People & the Press (2008b) reported that many more people believed that the press had favored Obama (37 percent) than Clinton (8 percent). Another 40 percent indicated that the reporting was not biased. In a breakdown by party affiliation, 45 percent of Republicans, 40 percent of Independents, and 35 percent of Democrats perceived bias for Obama.

Once it was clear that Obama and McCain were the candidates of their parties, attention turned to who their choices for vice president would be. Obama chose Senator Joseph R. Biden (D-Del.), who seemed to be a relatively safe choice with decades of experience, especially in foreign affairs. McCain countered by selecting Sarah Palin, the Republican governor of Alaska. She received strong support from conservative Republicans but had only a few years of experience. She first attracted a great deal of media attention and interest, but also made mistakes during some political interviews ("The Presidency of Barack Obama" 2009).

From September 8 to October 16, the media stories seemed to be more positive toward Obama and very negative about McCain. Based on an analysis of 857 stories from forty-eight news outlets, 36 percent of the Obama stories were positive, 35 percent neutral or mixed, and 29 percent negative. For McCain almost six out of ten stories were negative and only 14 percent were positive (Pew Project for Excellence in Journalism 2008b). Since the economy was most people's number one concern, McCain made what some regard as a major mistake when he claimed, "The fundamentals of our economy are strong" ("The Presidency of Barack Obama" 2009: 8). A positive for McCain certainly was his political experience, but the fact that he was seventy-two years old likely did not benefit him. McCain struggled financially to mount a national advertising campaign while Obama's campaign raised $750 million, hundreds of millions greater than McCain and more than John Kerry and G. W. Bush combined raised in 2004 ("The Presidency of Barack Obama" 2009).

Figure 7.2 provides a sample ballot in the 2008 election while Table 7.4 shows that Obama won quite strongly with almost 53 percent of the vote compared to McCain's 46 percent. He clearly won the Electoral College vote as well. Table 7.1 indicates that although the total population of voting age in the 2008 election was higher than ever before, the percentages of those actually voting and registered were a little lower than in the 2004 election. According to Table 7.2 and the CNN exit polls, Obama had strong support from those making $50,000 or less and those who were members of unions. His strengths were from the groups with the least and the most education, and females were more likely than males to support Obama. Protestants, especially white Protestant born agains and evangelicals, were the religious groups least likely to support Obama. Those who attended church frequently were also less likely to vote for Obama. Although Democratic candidates had previously received very strong support from African Americans, Obama, not surprisingly, received an even higher percentage (95 percent). Obama did very well among other minorities as well, with 67 percent of the Latino/a vote and 62 percent of the Asian vote. Although Obama received only 43 percent of the white vote in the exit polls, he did slightly better than Kerry who received only 41 percent and Gore with 42 percent of the white vote.

FIGURE 7.2   Official Absentee Ballot for Story County, Iowa, in the 2008 Election

This official ballot for the state of Iowa shows seven candidates other than Obama and McCain running for president. In the United States the two-party system, however, makes it very difficult for candidates other than the Democratic and Republican ones to win. See Table 7.4 for the final results of the presidential election.

Although not shown in Table 7.3, the CNN exit poll also asked if the race of the candidate was a factor in the election, but only 19 percent said it was a factor at all. In addition only 2 percent indicated it was the most important factor. Interestingly among those 2 percent, 58 percent voted for Obama ("CNN Election Center 2008 President Exit Polls" 2008). A similar question was asked concerning whether age was a factor, and only 2 percent identified it as most important and another 13 percent as important. Among those people, 77 percent supported Obama. About two-thirds of young people (ages eighteen to twenty-four and also twenty-five to twenty-nine) supported Obama, and McCain received a majority of votes only from those sixty-five and older. About half of those surveyed believed McCain would continue G. W. Bush's policies. Being associated with an unpopular incumbent president certainly did not benefit McCain ("CNN Election Center 2008 President Exit Polls" 2008).

It is apparent from the CNN exit poll results about political attitudes in Table 7.3 that Obama strongly captured the vote of those who believed health care and Iraq were the most important issues. He also received 53 percent of the vote from those who identified the economy as a most important concern. Among those who believed terrorism was the most important concern, McCain did extremely well. In addition to picking up strong majorities of support from liberals and Democrats, Obama did well among moderates and Independents.

In summarizing the results of the election, Nagourney (2008: 1) argued the following:

> The election of Mr. Obama amounted to a national catharsis—a repudiation of a historically unpopular Republican president and his economic and foreign policies, and an embrace of Mr. Obama's call for a change in the direction and the tone of the country. But it was just as much a strikingly symbolic moment in the evolution of the nation's fraught racial history, a breakthrough that would have seemed unthinkable just two years ago.

Two major questions involving this election are what role race played in the election and what are the implications of having a black president. Clearly these are difficult questions that we cannot answer definitively, but we can shed some light on them. Bobo and Dawson (2009: 4) recognize that Obama's election as the first black president is "as much an achievement defined by race as it is an achievement that signals a potential for the transcendence of race." The authors point out that national surveys have documented an increase in the willingness of whites to vote for a black candidate if nominated by their party.

Bobo and Dawson (2009: 5) identified four ways the Obama campaign "had to navigate a quite treacherous field of racial division." First, they argued that Obama had to deal with the negative stereotypes of blacks in spite of the fact that those images are now expressed with greater subtlety than previously. Second, new types of racism have emerged, including "shared collective racial resentments" (7) such as the sentiment that "blacks have no compelling grounds to make special claims or demands on society" (7). According to this view advocated by many whites, blacks should not need special entitlements such as affirmative action to succeed. Third, the collective racial resentment toward those perceived as receiving special advantages has political relevance. Bobo and Dawson found that "as collective racial resentments increase, so do the chances of identifying as a Republican and of voting for the Republican presidential candidates, particularly among white Americans" (8). Fourth, Obama adopted a strategy that tried to move beyond both white resentment and black anger to focus on overarching common problems facing the United States.

The 2008 CNN exit polls ("CNN Election Center 2008 President Exit Polls" 2008) asked respondents what would happen to race relations in the next few years. Fourteen percent indicated they thought race relations would get much better, 33 percent, get somewhat better; 34 percent, stay the same; 10 percent, get somewhat worse; and 5 percent, get much worse. Examining data from a June–July 2008 Gallup/*USA Today* survey, Hunt and Wilson (2009) reported that African Americans especially perceived that an Obama victory would have symbolic significance rather than lead to substantial racial progress. Hispanics were the most likely to believe that an Obama victory would result in concrete societal changes benefiting blacks' careers and opportunities in politics. Supporting the idea of the symbolic importance of the victory, William Julius Wilson in an interview with Henry Louis Gates (2009: 21) pointed out, "Blacks feel more proud of themselves, and this may help to undermine the defeatist feeling, especially among young kids who see this powerful symbol of Black progress."

Bobo and Dawson (2009: 12) do not rule out some kind of transformation in race relations ultimately, but they maintain that "the notion that Obama has fundamentally transcended race and opened the post-racial epoch in the American experience is easy to dismiss." They caution that winning the election does not necessarily lead to the kinds of changes Obama advocates. Wilson supports their argument that the United States is not a postracial society; rather race remains a very important factor due to the "lingering racism in American society . . . [and] a disproportionate number of Black people concentrated at the very bottom of the economic ladder" (Gates 2009: 20).

Winant (2009: 49) too recognizes that Obama needs to continue to deal with the "realities of structural racism in the United States and the problem of exercising executive power in an endemically racial state." He characterizes Obama as a " 'practical idealist,' a true pragmatist" (49).

Barack Obama, left, joined by his wife Michelle, takes the oath of office from Chief Justice John Roberts to become the forty-fourth president of the United States at the U.S. Capitol in Washington DC on January 20, 2009.

Credit: Jae C. Hong/AP Wide World Photos

In looking toward what an Obama administration could do, Winant (63) posed the following two alternatives:

> The new president was elected on the premise of *change,* a sanitized term for democ-ratization and egalitarianism. He takes office poised between two possibilities: first, the prospect of radical reform, greater popular participation and deeper democracy, progressive redistribution of resources and greater social justice; and second, the real threat that popular aspirations both in the United States and abroad will be crushed by "normal politics," by business as usual.

Depending on what Winant means by "normal politics," a third alternative might be possible with the Obama administration bringing about moderate reform rather than more radical reform. His administration is dealing with the economy, health care, social security reform, infrastructure concerns, immigration, possible terrorist threats, and the wars in Iraq and Afghanistan, to name many of the most pressing problems facing the nation.

An October–November 2009 Pew poll showed that 95 percent of blacks viewed Obama favorably but only 56 percent of whites did, a decline of 20 percent from just before the inau-guration. Also the percentage of blacks and whites who believed Obama's election would lead to improved race relations declined dramatically (Kelly 2010). Then in a January 2010 special election, Massachusetts voters elected Republican Scott Brown to fill the Senate seat of the late Edward M. Kennedy. Independent voters appeared especially important in Brown's victory that seemed a repudiation of Obama and Democratic Congressional leaders and their handling of issues such as health care and unemployment (Nagourney 2010). At the end of December 2009 the unemployment rate remained at 10 percent (Irwin 2010).

Obama's approval rating was below 50 percent for much of 2010. Obama acknowledged that he and his advisers had underestimated the effects of the recession when they formulated the stimulus package. However, many economists believe that the stimulus bill coupled with bank bailouts and aggressive actions by the Federal Reserve were significant in preventing full-scale depression ("Barack Obama" 2010). In addition to the $787 billion stimulus bill, the health care bill based in March 2010 and the financial regulatory reform measure passed in July 2010 tend to be viewed as victories for Obama. Obama signed the bill to repeal the military's "don't ask, don't tell" policy on gays in the armed forces. Also Obama received the Nobel Peace Prize in 2009 and appointed two female judges, Sonia Sotomayor and Elena Kagan, to the U.S. Supreme Court through 2010 ("Barack Obama" 2010). On the other hand, in spite of the economic stimulus, the unemployment rate remained near 10 percent in 2010. Also, the record-breaking oil leak of British Petroleum in the Gulf of Mexico did not help the economy or Obama's popularity. Some of his promised actions either were slow to develop or have not occurred in 2010 including immigration reform and a system to limit carbon emissions.

In response to economic issues, especially the stimulus bill, the Tea Party Movement emerged as a very diffuse, conservative, grassroots political movement that could be character-ized as either antigovernment or pro-limited government. It has no charter or governing council and tends to be critical of both the Republican and the Democratic establishment (Scherer 2010; "Tea Party Movement" 2010). Scherer (2010: 28) describes the movement as engaging in a "backlash against elites." During the 2010 primaries, the Tea Party Movement put forth a num-ber of candidates for positions in the House of Representatives and Senate. Among the Tea Party Movement's successes were winning seven Republican primaries for the U.S. Senate. At times Tea Party candidates were victorious over candidates handpicked by Republican leaders in

Washington DC. Midterm primary elections in general tend to have low turnout that could advantage a small but impassioned movement putting forth its candidates. The Tea Party Movement seemed to channel an important part of mainstream frustration (Scherer 2010). Sarah Palin, former governor of Alaska and vice presidential candidate on the Republican ticket in 2008, campaigned for many Tea Party candidates and seemed to energize the movement ("Tea Party Movement" 2010).

2010 MIDTERM ELECTION   As with the primaries, midterm or nonpresidential elections have smaller turnout of voters than presidential ones, and the 2010 election was no exception. Also often the party that controls Congress and the presidency loses seats in off-year elections. The Republican Party gained majority control of the House of Representatives and increased its presence in the Senate. Based on results through November 5, 2010, Republicans gained at least sixty more seats in the House and six more seats in the Senate. Since 1912 when the number of Representatives in the House was set at 435, only Presidents FDR in 1938, Warren G. Harding in 1922, and possibly Woodrow Wilson in 1914 experienced greater off-year losses for their parties ("Biggest Midterm Losses" 2010: 9A). In more recent times one could compare the Obama Democratic loss of seats to the Reagan and Clinton ones. For example, in 1994 the Democrats lost fifty-four seats in the House and eight Senate seats (Von Drehle 2010). Both Clinton and Reagan easily won second terms in spite of these losses.

One can stress the "historic nature of what the GOP accomplished in this election" (Balz 2010) or one can view it as "simply a return to the [center-right] norm" reversing the Democratic wave of 2006–2008 (Krauthammer 2010). Republican leadership viewed the election results as a clear repudiation of Obama's economic policies and health care legislation. Obama, on the other hand, attributed the results to voters' perceptions that the economic recovery was too slow or that government was too intrusive in people's lives (Balz 2010; "Obama More Open to Tax Cuts, Refuses to Budge on Health Law" 2010).

In some ways the findings from the CNN national exit poll of more than seventeen thousand voters in November 2010 are similar to the exit polls in 2008, but in other ways they are quite different. Racial minorities, Latinos/as, women, and younger people still continued to favor Democrats while whites, men, and older people supported Republicans ("CNN Politics Election Center House Exit Polls" 2010). However, African Americans and youth were much less likely to vote in 2010 so that whites increased their percentage of voters from 74 percent in 2008 to 78 percent in 2010. A majority of women no longer supported Democratic candidates (Balz 2010). Protestants, especially white Protestants and white evangelicals, continued to favor the Republican Party.

There was a dramatic swing in the vote of Independents who supported Republicans by a margin of 18 percent in 2010 while they had favored Democrats by 8 percent in 2008. Independents may have voted Republican but they were not supportive of either party when asked in exit polls how they viewed the two parties. More specifically 58 percent of Independents indicated they viewed Democrats unfavorably and 57 percent viewed Republicans unfavorably (Balz 2010). Regarding ideology, only 20 percent of those polled considered themselves liberal and 90 percent of these liberals supported the Democratic candidate. On the other hand, 41 percent considered themselves conservative and 84 percent of them supported Republican candidates ("CNN Politics Election Center House Exit Polls" 2010). Voters have thus turned toward the conservative side compared to 2008.

Although divisions between Democrats and Republicans are significant, the splits between traditional Republicans and Tea Party candidates may also not be easily resolved. The Senate election in Alaska illustrates this division. In the primary, Tea Party candidate Joe Miller defeated

Lisa Murkowski, the Republican Senator. Murkowski then decided to run a write-in campaign and appears to have won although the vote count has been challenged. Victorious Senate candidates supported by the Tea Party Movement included Rand Paul (Kentucky,) Ron Johnson (Wisconsin), Marco Rubio (Florida), and Mike Lee (Utah). ABC News published a list of U.S. House candidates supported by the Tea Party. According to that list, forty-six of those candidates won seats in the House, eighty-four did not, and seven contests had not yet been decided (Srikrishnan et al. 2010). Four in ten voters in the 2010 midterm elections indicated support for the movement in exit polls ("Tea Party Movement" 2010). Defeats for the Tea Party Movement in Senate races in Nevada and Delaware especially led some politicians and media members to suggest that more traditional Republican candidates could have been victorious in those states ("Tea Party Movement" 2010).

At this point it is too early to determine the impact of this election on politics. Some believe that the Republicans controlling the House and Democrats controlling the Senate provide important checks and balances and this encourages the Republicans and Democrats to work together to formulate policy, but others fear gridlock with little, if anything, being accomplished. Whether Democrats and Republicans will work together and how Tea Party members of Congress will work with other Republicans are two of the major issues likely to be discussed at least until the 2012 election.

CONCLUSION

The pluralist theoretical framework emphasizes the value of voting and elections, while the elite and class or Marxist perspectives question their significance. Much of the work cited in this chapter supports a pluralist viewpoint assuming the importance of democratic elections. The rational voter image emphasizes the significance of issues in voting while postmodernism holds that class influences are declining and politics are increasingly chaotic. Studies of turnout have considered individual, structural, socioeconomic, and political cultural factors. Structural variables related to the electoral system including proportional representation, number of parties, and compulsory voting have had significant influence on turnout cross-nationally. Felon disenfranchisement has uniquely affected turnout in the United States, a country with historically low turnout. Whether the United States will develop a significant trend toward increasing turnout remains to be seen.

One major school of thought stresses sociological influences on voting preferences. Various social cleavages are examined by focusing on group influences based on social class, gender, race, religion, and sexual orientation. Social classes exhibit behavioral similarities and class awareness as they share similar occupations, incomes, and lifestyles. Within the racial, religious, and lesbian, gay, bisexual, transgender (LGBT) groupings, members potentially share a sense of peoplehood and historical identification that can affect their voting. Those who favor a postmaterial or postmodern approach believe that the relevance of religious and class cleavages is declining, but others challenge this, suggesting realignments rather than dealignments. In the United States, more professionals have become Democrats, while skilled workers' political preferences are volatile. Racial cleavage remains strong as do divisions based on sexual orientation. Generally speaking, minorities tend to support liberal or leftist parties.

According to the second approach, issues and political attitudes shape voting. Issues vary by context and national history but can be divided into economic, social, and foreign policy concerns. In the United States currently, economic problems, including jobs, social inequalities, health care, moral values, terrorism, and the wars in Iraq and Afghanistan are key issues. Liberal or conservative ideology and party identification are very strong measures of political attitudes predicting voting behavior.

Although much is known about how people vote, less is known about why some turn out and vote a certain way and others do not. If political parties and candidates present clear issue differences, voters are much more likely to be issue oriented. Most of the comparative analyses of voting have been done in advanced industrial societies, but even predicting voting patterns across these societies has not yielded consistent results and trends. Political sociologists need to extend their attention to a greater variety of countries and also engage in comprehensive in-depth studies of selected nations to understand the dynamic process of voting.

Endnotes

1. We draw heavily on Alford and Friedland's book *Powers of Theory* for our discussion of the pluralist, elite/managerial, and class frameworks.

2. For a list of felony disenfranchisement rules for various states, see http://www.sentencingproject.org/pubs_05.cfm, and click on "Felony Disenfranchisement in the United States."

3. The term *Hispanic* is used interchangeably with Latino (male) and Latina (female) here.

4. The scale was 1 = liberal to 3 = conservative.

5. In addition to Chinese, Japanese, and Korean Americans, the term *East Asian Americans* includes Filipino, Asian Indian, Vietnamese, Cambodian, Laotian, and Hmong Americans.

6. For a symposium on election 2000, see Dobratz, Buzzell, and Waldner (2002: 173–260). The Brigman (2002) article contains a "Chronology of Major Legal Developments in the 2000 Presidential Election in Florida."

7. For a detailed discussion of the methodology used, see Pew Project for Excellence in Journalism (n.d.)

References

Adams, Greg D. and Chris Fastnow. 2002. "A Note on the Voting Irregularities in Palm Beach County." Pp. 189–199 in *Sociological Views on Political Participation in the 21st Century*, volume 10, *Research in Political Sociology*, edited by Betty A. Dobratz, Timothy Buzzell, and Lisa K. Waldner. Amsterdam: Elsevier (JAI).

Alford, Robert R. and Roger Friedland. 1985. *Powers of Theory: Capitalism, the State, and Democracy*. Cambridge, NY: Cambridge University Press.

Baker, Peter and Carl Hulse. 2010. "Deep Rifts Divide Obama and Republicans." *New York Times* November 3. Retrieved November 4, 2010 from www.nytimes.com/2010/11/04/us/politics/04elect.html?ref=elections.

Balz, Dan. 2010. "Tuesday's Results Are Open to (careful) Interpretation." *Washington Post* November 4. Retrieved November 5, 2010 from http://www.washingtonpost.com/wp-dyn/content/article/2010/11/03/AR2010110305921.html?wpisrc=nl_cuzhead.

"Barack Obama." 2010. *New York Times Topics*. Updated October 6. Retrieved October 23, 2010 from http://topics.nytimes.com/top/reference/timestopics/people/o/barack_obama/index.html.

Best, Shaun. 2002. *Introduction to Politics and Society*. London: Sage Publications.

"Biggest Midterm Losses." 2010. *Des Moines Register* November 4: 9A.

Blais, Andre. 2006. "What Affects Voter Turnout?" *Annual Review of Political Science* 9: 111–125.

Bobo, Lawrence D. and Michael C. Dawson. 2009. "A Change Has Come: Race, Politics, and the Path to the Obama Presidency."*Du Bois Review* 6(1): 1–14.

Brigman, William E. 2002. "The Chad Legal Wars: The Role of the Courts in the 2000 Presidential Election." Pp. 223–260 in *Sociological Views on Political Participation in the 21st Century*, volume 10, *Research in Political Sociology*, edited by Betty A. Dobratz, Timothy Buzzell, and Lisa K. Waldner. Amsterdam: Elsevier (JAI).

Brooks, Clem and Jeff Manza. 1997. "Social Cleavages and Political Alignments: U.S. Presidential Elections, 1960 to 1992." *American Sociological Review* 62: 937–946.

Brooks, Clem, Jeff Manza, and Catherine Bolzendahl. 2003. "Voting Behavior and Political Sociology: Theories, Debates, and Future Directions." Pp. 137–173 in *Political Sociology for the 21st Century*, volume 12, *Research in Political Sociology*, edited by Betty A. Dobratz, Lisa K. Waldner, and Timothy Buzzell. Amsterdam: Elsevier (JAI).

Brooks, Clem, Paul Nieuwbeerta, and Jeff Manza. 2006. "Cleavage-Based Voting Behavior in Cross-National Perspective: Evidence from Six Postwar Democracies." *Social Science Research* 35: 88–128.

Budge, Ian and Dennis Farlie. 1983. *Explaining and Predicting Elections: Issue Effects and Party Strategies in Twenty-Three Democracies.* London: George Allen & Unwin.

Burrell, Barbara. 2004. *Women and Political Participation.* Santa Barbara, CA: ABC-CLIO.

Bystrom, Dianne. 2008. "Gender and U.S. Presidential Politics: Early Newspaper Coverage of Hillary Clinton's Bid for the White House." Paper for American Political Science Association, August 28–31. Boston, MA.

Bystrom, Dianne, Mary Christine Banwart, Lynda Lee Kaid, and Terry A. Robertson. 2004. *Gender and Candidate Communication.* New York: Routledge.

Campbell, Angus, Philip E. Converse, Warren E. Miller, and Donald Stokes. 1960. *The American Voter.* New York: John Wiley & Sons, Inc.

Campbell, James E. 2004. "The Presidential Election of 2004: The Fundamentals and the Campaign." *The Forum* Vol. 2, Iss. 4, Article 1. Available at http://www.bepress.com/forum.

Chavez, Maria L. 2004. "Overview." Pp. 1–56 in *Latino Americans and Political Participation*, edited by S. A. Navarro and Armando Xavier Mejia. Santa Barbara, CA: ABC-CLIO.

Chi, Tsung. 2005. *East Asian Americans and Political Participation.* Santa Barbara, CA: ABC-CLIO.

Clark, Terry Nichols. 2001. "What Have We Learned in a Decade on Class and Party Politics?" Pp. 9–38 in *The Breakdown of Class Politics*, edited by Terry Nichols Clark and Seymour Martin Lipset. Washington, DC: Woodrow Wilson Center Press.

Clark, Terry Nichols and Seymour Martin Lipset (editors). 2001. *The Breakdown of Class Politics.* Washington, DC: Woodrow Wilson Center Press.

Clegg, Roger. n.d. "Felon Disenfranchisement Is Constitutional, and Justified." Retrieved September 8, 2006 from www.constitutioncenter.org/education/ForEducators/Viewpoints/FelonDisenfranchisement IsConstitutional,AndJustified.shtml.

"CNN Election Center 2008 President Exit Polls." 2008. Retrieved September 15, 2009 from http://www.cnn.com/ELECTION/2008/results/polls/#val=USP00p1 (through p. 6).

"CNN Politics Election Center House Exit Polls." 2010. Retrieved November 5, 2010 from http://www.cnn.com/ELECTION/2010/results/polls/#USH00p1 (through p. 8).

Congressional Quarterly. 2002. *Presidential Elections, 1789–2000.* Washington, DC: CQ Press.

Dalton, Russell J. and Martin P. Wattenberg. 1993. "The Not So Simple Act of Voting." Pp. 193–218 in *Political Science: The State of the Discipline II*, edited by Ada W. Finifter. Washington, DC: American Political Science Assoc.

Dimitrova, Daniela V. and Elizabeth Geske. 2009. "To Cry or Not to Cry: Media Framing of Hillary Clinton in the Wake of the New Hampshire Primary." Paper presented in May to the International Communication Association (ICA), Chicago.

Dobratz, Betty A., Timothy Buzzell, and Lisa K. Waldner (editors). 2002. *Sociological Views on Political Participation in the 21st Century,* volume 10, *Research in Political Sociology.* Amsterdam: Elsevier Science (JAI).

Domhoff, G. William. 2006. *Who Rules America?* 5th Edition. Boston: McGraw-Hill.

Downs, Anthony. 1957. *An Economic Theory of Democracy.* New York: Harper.

Dye, Thomas R. 2003. *Politics in America.* 5th Edition. Upper Saddle River, NJ: Prentice Hall.

Edsall, Thomas B. and Mary D. Edsall. 1995. "Chain Reaction." Pp. 403–420 in *American Society and Politics*, edited by Theda Skocpol and John L. Campbell. New York: McGraw-Hill.

Edwards III, George C. 2007. "Yes, Why the Electoral College Is Bad for America?" Pp. 40–44 in *Taking Sides: Clashing Views on Political Issues.* 15th Edition, edited by George McKenna and Stanley Feingold. Guilford, CT: McGraw-Hill Companies.

Evans, Geoffrey. 1999a. "Class Voting: From Premature Obituary to Reasoned Appraisal." Pp. 1–20 in *The End of Class Politics? Class Voting in Comparative Context*, edited by G. Evans. Oxford, UK: Oxford University Press.

———. 1999b. "Class and Vote: Disrupting the Orthodoxy." Pp. 323–334 in *The End of Class Politics? Class Voting in Comparative Context*, edited by G. Evans. Oxford, UK: Oxford University Press.

Farrell, David M. 2001. *Electoral Systems: A Comparative Introduction.* New York: Palgrave.

Garcia, John A. and Gabriel Sanchez. 2004. "Electoral Politics." Pp. 121–172 in *Latino Americans and Political Participation*, edited by S. A. Navarro and Armando Xavier Mejia. Santa Barbara, CA: ABC-CLIO.

Gates, Jr., Henry Louis. 2009. "A Conversation with William Julius Wilson on the Election of Barack Obama." *Du Bois Review* 6(1): 15–23.

Gregg, Gary L. 2007. "No, the Electoral College Is Good for America." Pp. 45–48 in *Taking Sides: Clashing Views on Political Issues*, 15th Edition, edited by George McKenna and Stanley Feingold. Guilford, CT: McGraw-Hill Companies.

Hamilton, Richard F. 1972. *Class and Politics in the United States.* New York: John Wiley & Sons, Inc.

Harrigan, John J. 2000. *Empty Dreams, Empty Pockets: Class and Bias in American Politics.* New York: Longman.

Heldman, Caroline, Susan J. Carroll, and Stephanie Olson. 2005. "'She Brought Only a Skirt': Print Media Coverage of Elizabeth Dole's Bid for the Republican Presidential Nomination." *Political Communication* 22: 315–335.

Hernandez, Raymond. 2007. "Hispanic Voters Gain New Clout with Democrats." *New York Times* June 10. Retrieved October 12, 2009 from http://www.nytimes.com/2007/06/10/us/politics/10hispanics.html.

Hero, Jr., Alfred O. 1969. "Liberalism–Conservatism Revisited: Foreign vs. Domestic Federal Policies, 1937–1967." *Public Opinion Quarterly* 33: 399–408.

Hout, Michael, Jeff Manza, and Clem Brooks. 1999. "Classes, Unions, and the Realignment of U.S. Presidential Voting, 1952–1992." Pp. 83–96 in *The End of Politics?* edited by Geoffrey Evans. Oxford, UK: Oxford University Press.

Hull, Elizabeth A. 2006. *The Disenfranchisement of Ex-Felons.* Philadelphia: Temple University Press.

Hunt, Matthew O. and David C. Wilson. 2009. "Race/ Ethnicity, Perceived Discrimination, and Beliefs about the Meaning of an Obama Presidency." *DuBois Review* 6 (1): 173–191.

Inglehart, Ronald. 1997. *Modernization and Postmodernization.* Princeton, NJ: Princeton University Press.

Inglehart, Ronald and Pippa Norris. 2000. "The Developmental Theory of Gender Gap: Women's and Men's Voting Behavior in Global Perspective." *International Political Science Review* 21: 441–463.

Irwin, Neil. 2010. "Economy Loses 85K Jobs in Dec., Unemployment Rate Stays Pat at 10 Percent." *Washington Post* January 8. Retrieved January 8, 2010 from www.washingtonpost.com/wp-dyn/content/article/2010/01/08/AR2010010800453_pf.html.

Jackman, Robert W. 1987. "Political Institutions and Voter Turnout in the Industrial Democracies." *American Political Science Review* 81: 405–424.

Johnson, Richard. 2006. "Party Identification: Unmoved Mover or Sum of Preferences?" *Annual Review of Political Science* 9: 329–351.

Jurkowitz, Mark. 2008a. "New Hampshire Teaches National News Media a Lesson." Pew Project for Excellence in Journalism, January 9. Retrieved October 1, 2009 from http://www.journalism.org/print/9267.

_____. 2008b. "Media Admire Clinton's Resilience, Question Obama's Toughness." Pew Project for Excellence in Journalism. Retrieved September 30, 2009 from http://www.journalism.org/sites/journalism.org/files/3-11report.pdf.

Kahn, Kim Fridkin. 1996. *The Political Consequences of Being a Woman.* New York: Columbia University Press.

Kaufmann, Karen and John B. Petrocik. 1999. "The Changing Politics of American Men: Understanding the Sources of the Gender Gap." *American Journal of Political Science* 43: 864–887.

Kelley, Jr., Stanley and Thad W. Mirer. 1974. "The Simple Act of Voting." *American Political Science Review* 68: 572–591.

Kelly, Erin. 2010. "Time Tempers Optimism on Race." *Des Moines Register* January 18: 1A, 16A.

Key, Jr., V. O. 1966. *The Responsible Electorate.* Cambridge, MA: Harvard University Press.

Knoke, David. 1974. "A Causal Synthesis of Sociological and Psychological Models of American Voting Behavior." *Social Forces* 53: 92–101.

Kostadinova, Tatiana. 2003. "Voter Turnout Dynamics in Post-Communist Europe." *European Journal of Political Research* 42: 741–759.

Krauthammer, Charles. 2010. "A Return to the Norm." *Washington Post* November 5. Retrieved November 5, 2010 from http://www.washingtonpost.com/wp-dyn/content/article/2010/11/04/AR2010110406581_pf.html.

Lazare, Daniel. 2003. "Yes. The Velvet Coup." Pp. 100–106 in *Taking Sides: Clashing Views on Controversial Political Issues.* 13th Edition, edited by George McKenna and Stanley Feingold. Guilford, CT: McGraw-Hill/Dushkin.

Lazarsfeld, Paul F., Bernard Berelson, and Hazel Gaudet. 1968. *The People's Choice.* 3rd Edition. New York: Columbia University Press.

Lewis-Beck, Michael S. and Charles Tien. 2002. "Presidential Election Forecasting: The Bush–Gore Draw." Pp. 173–187 in *Sociological Views on Political Participation in the 21st Century,* volume 10, *Research in Political Sociology,* edited by Betty A. Dobratz, Timothy Buzzell, and Lisa K. Waldner. Amsterdam: Elsevier (JAI).

Lipset, Seymour M. 1959. "Democracy and Working-Class Authoritarianism." *American Sociological Review* 24 (August): 482–501.

_____. 1963. *Political Man.* Garden City: Doubleday and Company.

Lyman, Rick. 2006. "Innovator Devises Way around Electoral Colleges." *New York Times* September 22. Retrieved October 12, 2009 from http://www.nytimes.com/2006/09/22/us/politics/22electoral.html.

Manza, Jeff and Clem Brooks. 1998. "The Gender Gap in U.S. Presidential Elections: When? Why? Implications?" *American Journal of Sociology* 103: 1235–1266.

Manza, Jeff, Clem Brooks, and Michael Sauder. 2005. "Money, Participation and Electoral Politics." Pp. 201–226 in *The Handbook of Political Sociology,* edited by Thomas Janoski, Robert Alford, Alexander Hicks, and Mildred A. Schwartz. Cambridge: Cambridge University Press.

Manza, Jeff and Christopher Uggen. 2006. *Locked Out: Felon Disenfranchisement and American Democracy.* Oxford, UK: Oxford University Press.

Marger, Martin. 2008. *Social Inequality.* 4th Edition. New York: McGraw-Hill.

McKenna, George and Stanley Feingold (editors). 2007. *Taking Sides: Clashing Views on Political Issues.* 15th Edition. Guilford, CT: McGraw-Hill Companies.

Medoff, Rafael. 2002. *Jewish Americans and Political Participation.* Santa Barbara, CA: ABC-CLIO.

Milbrath, Lester and M. L. Goel. 1977. *Political Participation.* Chicago: Rand McNally College Publishing Co.

Miller, Warren E. and J. Merrill Shanks. 1996. *The New American Voter.* Cambridge, MA: Harvard University Press.

Morgenstern, Scott and Javier Vazquez-D'Elia. 2007. "Electoral Laws, Parties, and Party Systems in Latin America." *Annual Review of Political Science* 10: 143–168.

Müller, Walter. 1999. "Class Cleavages in Party Preferences in Germany—Old and New." Pp. 137–180 in *The End of Politics?* edited by Geoffrey Evans. Oxford, UK: Oxford University Press.

Nagourney, Adam. 2008. "Obama Elected President as Racial Barrier Falls." *New York Times* November 4. Retrieved September 26, 2009 from http://www.nytimes.com/2008/11/05/us/politics/05elect.html.

_____. 2010. "A Year Later, Voters Send a Different Message." *New York Times* January 20. Retrieved January 24, 2010 from www.nytimes.com/2010/01/20/us/politics/20assess.html?th=&emc=th&pagewanted=print.

Neuman, William Lawrence. 2005. *Power, State, and Society: An Introduction to Political Sociology.* New York: McGraw-Hill.

Nie, Norman H., Sidney Verba, and John R. Petrocik. 1979. *The Changing American Voter.* Cambridge, MA: Harvard University Press.

Niemi, Richard G. and Herbert F. Weisberg (editors). 1976. *Controversies in American Voting.* San Francisco: W. H. Freeman and Company.

_____ (editors). 2001. *Controversies in Voting Behavior.* 4th Edition. Washington, DC: CQ Press, a Division of Congressional Quarterly Inc.

Nieuwbeerta, Paul and Nan Dirk DeGraaf. 1999. "Traditional Class Voting in Twenty Postwar Societies." Pp. 23–56 in *The End of Politics?* edited by Geoffrey Evans. Oxford, UK: Oxford University Press.

"Obama More Open to Tax Cuts, Refuses to Budge on Health Law." 2010. *Des Moines Register* November 4: p. 9A.

Orey, Byron D'Andra and Reginald Vance. 2003. "Participation in Electoral Politics." Pp. 183–240 in *African Americans and Political Participation,* edited by Minion Morrison. Santa Barbara, CA: ABC-CLIO, Inc.

Orum, Anthony. 1983. *Introduction to Political Sociology: The Social Anatomy of the Body Politic.* Englewood Cliffs, NJ: Prentice-Hall.

Pew Project for Excellence in Journalism. n.d. "Methodology." Retrieved October 1, 2009 from http://www.journalism.org/about_news_index/methodology.

_____. 2007. "The Invisible Primary—Invisible No Longer: A First Look at Coverage of the 2008 Presidential Campaign." October 27. Retrieved October 1, 2009 from http://www.journalism.org/node/8187.

_____. 2008a. "Media Exposure over Time." Table retrieved September 30, 2009 from www.journalism.org/node/11540.

_____. 2008b. "Winning the Media Campaign: How the Press Reported the 2008 General Election." October 22. Retrieved September 27, 2009 from http://www.journalism.org/node/13307.

Pew Research Center for the People & the Press. 2008a. "McCain's Negatives Mostly Political, Obama's More Personal: Overview." May 29. Retrieved October 1, 2009 from http://people-press.org/report/425/mccain-obama-negatives.

_____. 2008b. "Many Say Coverage Is Biased in Favor of Obama." June 5. Retrieved October 1, 2009 from http://pewresearch.org/pubs/862/campaign-news-interest.

Piven, Frances Fox and Richard A. Cloward. 2000. *Why Americans Still Don't Vote and Why Politicians Want It That Way.* Boston: Beacon Press.

Posner, Richard A. 2004. "No. Electoral College Reform." Pp. 107–112 in *Taking Sides: Clashing Views on Controversial Political Issues,* edited by George McKenna and Stanley Feingold. Guilford, CT: McGraw-Hill/Dushkin.

"The Presidency of Barack Obama." 2009. *New York Times Topics.* Updated September 10. Retrieved September 26, 2009 from http://topics.nytimes.com/top/reference/timestopics/people/o/barack_obama/index.html

Ringdal, Kristen and Kjell Hines. 1999. "Changes in Class Voting in Norway, 1957–1989." Pp. 181–202 in *The End of Politics?* edited by Geoffrey Evans. Oxford, UK: Oxford University Press.

Rock the Vote. 2006. "Young Voter Turnout Surges in 2006." Released November 8. Retrieved June 10, 2007 from www.rockthevote.com/pdf/RTV-2006-release.pdf

Scheingold, Carl A. 1973. "Social Networks and Voting: The Resurrection of a Research Agenda." *American Sociological Review* 38: 712–720.

Scherer, Michael. 2010. "It's Tea Time." *Time* September 27, 176 (#13): 26–30.

Schulman, Mark A. and Gerald N. Pomper. 1975. "Variability in Electoral Behavior: Longitudinal Perspectives of Causal Modeling." *American Journal of Political Science* 19: 1–18.

Seelye, Katharine and Julie Bosman. 2008. "Media Charged with Sexism in Clinton Coverage." *New York Times* June 13. Retrieved September 29, 2009 from http://www.nytimes.com/2008/06/13/us/politics/13women.html.

Sulzberger, A. G. 2010. "Ouster of Iowa Judges Sends Signal to Bench." *New York Times* November 3. Retrieved November 4, 2010 from http://www.nytimes.com/2010/11/04/us/politics/04judges.html?ref=elections.

Srikrishnan, Maya, Jared Pliner, Jennifer Schlesinger, Joshua Goldstein, and Huma Khan. 2010. "ABC News: Which Tea Party Candidates Won?" ABC News, November 3. Retrieved November 5, 2010 from http://abcnews.go.com/CleanPrint/cleanprintproxy.aspx?1289015540250.

"Tea Party Movement." 2010. *New York Times Topics.* Updated November 5. Retrieved November 5, 2010 from http://topics.nytimes.com/top/reference/timestopics/subjects/t/tea_party_movement/index.html.

Theodorson, George A. and Achilles G. Theodorson. 1969. *A Modern Dictionary of Sociology.* New York: Crowell.

Therborn, Goran. 1978. *What Does the Ruling Class Do When It Rules?* London: New Left Books.

Uggen, Christopher, Jeff Manza, and Melissa Thompson. 2006. "Citizenship, Democracy, and the Civic Reintegration of Criminal Offenders." *Annals of the American Academy of Political and Social Science* 605: 281–310.

U.S. Census Bureau. 2005. "Table A-1. Reported Voting and Registration by Race, Hispanic Origin, Sex and Age Groups: November 1964 to 2004." Retrieved May 25, 2007 from www.census.gov/population/socdemo/voting/tabA-1.xls.

———— (Holder, Kelly). 2006. "Voting & Registration in the Election of November 2004." P20–556, *Current Population Reports*, March.

U.S. Commission on Civil Rights. 2001. "Rights Commission's Report on Florida Election." *Washington Post* June 5. Retrieved June 10, 2007 from http://www.washingtonpost.com/wp-srv/onpolitics/transcripts/ccrdraft 060401.htm.

Utter, Glen and James L. True. 2004. *Conservative Christians and Political Participation.* Santa Barbara, CA: ABC-CLIO, Inc.

Von Drehle, David. 2010. "The Party Crashers. How a New Breed of Republican Candidates Tapped into Voter Rage and Upset the Establishment." *Time* November 8, 176 (19): 38–46.

Weakliem, David L. 2001. "Social Class and Voting: The Case against Decline." Pp. 197–223 in *The Breakdown of Class Politics*, edited by Terry Nichols Clark and Seymour Martin Lipset. Washington, DC: Woodrow Wilson Center Press.

Weakliem, David L. and Anthony F. Heath. 1999. "The Secret Life of Class Voting." Pp. 97–136 in *The End of Politics?* edited by Geoffrey Evans. Oxford, UK: Oxford University Press.

Weiner, Marc D. and Gerald M. Pomper. 2006. "The 2.4% Solution: What Makes a Mandate?" *The Forum* Vol. 4, Iss. 2, Article 4. Available at http://www.bepress.com/forum.

Winant, Howard. 2009. "Just Do It: Notes on Politics and Race at the Dawn of the Obama Presidency." *DuBois Review* 6 (1): 49–70.

Wood, Erika and Neema Trivedi. 2007. "The Modern-Day Poll Tax: How Economic Sanctions Block Access to the Polls." *Clearinghouse Review: Journal of Poverty Law and Policy* 41 (1,2): 30–46.

Social Movements

BRANDON HOFSTEDT[1] AND THE AUTHORS

During the March on Washington for Jobs and Freedom on August 28, 1963, Dr. Martin Luther King, Jr. (1963) declared from the steps of the Lincoln Memorial, "I have a dream that my four little children will one day live in a nation where they will not be judged by the color of their skin but by the content of their character." In 1969, Students for a Democratic Society, a student activist movement in the United States, protested the Vietnam War by staging a demonstration in New York's Central Park, and some of its members chanted, "Burn cards, not people," and "Hell, no we won't go" as they threw their draft cards into a bonfire. In 1988, more than a thousand protestors from ACT-UP (AIDS Coalition to Unleash Power) and other groups and individuals sympathetic to lesbian, gay, bisexual, and transgender (LGBT) issues stormed the Maryland offices of the Food and Drug Administration (FDA), leading to a one-day shutdown. On January 9, 1993, in Pulaski, Tennessee, the birthplace of the Ku Klux Klan, white separatists paraded and chanted, "What do we want? White Power! When do we want it? Now!" What do these events have in common? They are all part of social movement activity that is designed to bring about change in the United States.

Why study social movements? Depending on your interests, there are a variety of answers. According to Goodwin and Jasper (2003: 4–5), studying social movements

- helps one understand why people protest and what they want to accomplish;
- helps one to learn more about politics, including existing public policies;
- sheds light on major sources of change and conflict in society;
- aids one in finding out more about human action or social theory about human behavior and beliefs;
- provides information about technical changes and their advantages and disadvantages;

269

- promotes changes in values and fosters new visions of society;
- helps one recognize that certain movements may want to restrict social change because they believe it would disrupt society or be harmful to certain members of society;
- aids in understanding the moral basis of society or the "moral sensibilities" that guide our actions.

Perhaps you have participated in a social movement and you have your own beliefs about those who also participated and about the success of the movement.

In this chapter, we argue that social movements are a key part of the study of politics and of the relationship between society and politics even though some have maintained that movements are part of irrational, nonpolitical behavior. In their book on political participation, Milbrath and Goel (1977) followed the traditional political science usage of categories at that time and placed social movements under the label *unconventional political behavior*. Conventional activities were regarded as normal or legitimate. Today most political sociologists' views of social movement participants have changed, as political sociologists emphasize the rational elements of social movements.

One of the numerous definitions of social movements is that they are "organized efforts to promote or resist change in society that rely, at least in part, on noninstitutionalized forms of political action" (Marx and McAdam 1994: 73). A significant focus of movements tends to be institutionalized political activities, including lobbying, writing letters to politicians, supporting political party candidates, and so on, as well as noninstitutionalized activities, such as protests, street demonstrations, marches, and so on. Diani (2000) criticizes certain characteristics used to define social movements, including noninstitutionalized behavior and the distinction between public protest and conventional political participation. His synthetic definition of a social movement is "a network of informal interactions between a plurality of individuals, groups and/or organizations, engaged in a political or cultural conflict, on the basis of a shared collective identity" (165).

Reverend Martin Luther King, Jr. waves from the Lincoln Memorial to participants of the Civil Rights Movement's March on Washington. He delivered his famous "I Have a Dream" speech on August 28, 1963, from this spot.

Credit: © Hulton-Deutsch Collection/CORBIS

della Porta and Diani (2006: 20) suggest that the social process of movements is marked by three key mechanisms:

- Involvement in conflictual relations with clearly identified opponents,
- Linkages through dense informal networks, and
- Shared collective identity.

Meyer and Kretschmer (2007: 540–541) have identified several key characteristics about social movements:

- Although movements make demands for change in public policy, they also make claims that affect the culture and values of society.
- Social movements provide outlets for expressing constructed social and political identities.
- Discussing specific starting and ending points of a movement is difficult. Many are deeply rooted in society, leaving significant legacies.
- Generally, committed individuals and established organizations make up a social movement. Different people and groups in a movement share certain goals but may differ on various issues. Thus factions can develop within the movement.
- Social movements develop their own cultures but are not completely separated from mainstream politics and culture. Therefore there is a reciprocal relationship between movements and the larger society, with each contributing support and ideas to the other.

A social movement is comprised of social movement organizations (SMOs). An SMO is an ambiguous concept; however, it can be defined as "a complex, or formal, organization that identifies its goals with the preferences of a social movement or a countermovement and attempts to implement those goals" (McCarthy and Zald 1997: 153). For example, the Civil Rights Movement has been composed of many organizations, including the Southern Christian Leadership Conference (SCLC), the National Association for the Advancement of Colored People (NAACP), the Congress of Racial Equality (CORE), and the Student Nonviolent Coordinating Committee (SNCC). SMOs are very difficult to label or define, in part because of their variety and the type of characteristics of these organizations and how formal or informal the SMOs are, that is, whether they focus more on mobilizing people and public support (time) or on more tangible resources (e.g., money) and whether they are hierarchical (centralized with power at the top) or horizontal (with democratic input). SMOs may also be concerned mainly with challenging the political powerholders or they may focus on the needs of their constituencies (those whose interests they promote). For example, rape crisis centers and shelters for abused women emerged from the women's movement (della Porta and Diani 2006: 140–144).

In this chapter, we discuss social movements; however, at times our discussion applies to other forms of contentious politics as well. We first examine the theoretical frameworks, look at old and new social movements and other approaches to the study of social movements, including a possible synthesis, consider the life cycle of social movements, note transnational movements, and conclude arguing that social movements are an important part of political sociology.

THEORETICAL FRAMEWORKS

Theories related to social movements do not typically use the formal labels of pluralist, elite, and class frameworks; however, there are definite associations between social movement frameworks and political sociology frameworks we have already discussed in our earlier chapters. We discuss McAdam (1982) especially because he has drawn important connections between political sociology's views of power and selected social movement frameworks.

Pluralism and the Classical Collective Behavior Model of Social Movements

Pluralists may find it difficult to explain why people engage in social movements when they could instead join a group that is participating in "rational, self-interested political action" (McAdam 1982: 6) in a relatively open democratic political system. Pluralists tend to value moderate democratic participation, and generally speaking, noninstitutionalized tactics such as demonstrations and violent activities are viewed as a deviant form of political behavior in healthy democracies. Those who have grievances may indicate problems of political representation or blockages to individual opportunity. Too much political participation in movements may signal a breakdown in consensual political culture. At times, though, social movements may use more institutionalized means, such as working with interest groups to encourage parties to adjust to the demands of previously unrepresented groups or to foster the creation of new political parties (Alford and Friedland 1985: 9, 25, 83). Pluralists believe that the challenging groups who use institutionally provided means (e.g., elections, lobbying) rather than "the tactics of the streets" are likely to be successful (Gamson 1975: 12). Pluralists tend to use the classic *collective behavior model*, which focuses on stress, strain, and breakdown as factors encouraging social movement participation. We discuss this in detail in the section on the life cycle of movements.

Elite Theory and Resource Mobilization

While the pluralist model relies on social–psychological approaches to movements, the elite framework provides a political and organizational focus. The capacity of elites to rule may be threatened by social movements that could fragment the state. Noninstitutionalized social movements could suggest "an ill-constructed state structure or strategic failures of control by state elites" (Alford and Friedland 1985: 25).

Because the masses lack power, resources, and political influence, their movements are at a great disadvantage when they try to change the political system. Therefore the masses need resources from key elites for their movement's success, including money, publicity and space, people resources such as leadership and access to networks, and societal resources such as legitimacy and name recognition (Jenkins and Form 2005). This framework clearly considers movements as political phenomena and focuses on the contributions of external groups to the movement. *Resource mobilization* defines social movements as conscious actors making rational decisions (della Porta and Diani 2006: 15). If selected elites support a movement, it is likely that such a movement does not greatly challenge the political system (McAdam 1982).

McCarthy and Zald (1997: 151–152) identify several characteristics of the resource mobilization approach, including: (1) aggregation of resources (e.g., money and labor) for collective pursuits in dealing with conflict; (2) at least minimal organization to ensure resource aggregation by SMOs; (3) recognition of the importance of individual and organizational involvement outside the SMOs; and (4) an emphasis on costs and benefits for explaining individual and organizational involvement in social movement activities.

Class Framework or the Political Process Model

Buechler (2002: 12) and others suggest that the *political process model* may be a branch of resource mobilization, but McAdam (1982) argues that it is distinct from resource mobilization and that the political process model fits very well with the class or Marxist framework, and we agree with him. In modern industrial societies, economic problems within the capitalist system encouraged the growth and development of working-class struggle. Although working-class political participation in the early 1900s may have occurred more in the workplace (e.g., strikes, destruction of machines), it has shifted more to the state and its representative bodies (e.g., Congress, Parliament) for debates on employment, welfare, and the fair distribution of resources (Alford and Friedland 1985: 346).

Both resource mobilization and political process models have wealth and power concentrated in the hands of a few organizations and individuals; however, the political process model is more likely to disagree with the idea of elite inevitability. Insurgent groups are able to mobilize, form social movements, and have success. If indigenous organizations contribute significant resources, they are more likely to challenge the system by demanding reform. The political process model especially stresses the importance of political opportunities for a successful movement.

McAdam's (1982: 40) political process model identifies three factors that are needed to generate social insurgency: (1) the degree of *organizational readiness* within the aggrieved population, (2) the *structure of political opportunities* that exist in the more general sociopolitical environment, and (3) the collective evaluation of the chances for successful insurgency or insurgent consciousness. *Cognitive liberation* occurs when people "collectively define their situations as unjust and subject to change through group action" (McAdam 1982: 51). As shown in Figure 8.1, indigenous organizational strength, expanding political opportunities, and shared cognitions join to facilitate movement emergence, which we will discuss in greater detail later in the chapter. Like resource mobilization, the political process model sees SMOs as acting rationally; thus, both models have similarities with the rational choice model that we will examine next.

Rational Choice

Olson's (1965) *The Logic of Collective Action* recognized the difficulties in getting people involved in group action and the need for selective incentives that would reward those who participated in movements more than those that did not. Olson's model, though, is based on the belief that individuals have quite narrow self-interests (often economic). Now there is greater awareness of the importance of social rewards like meeting like-minded people, gaining new friendships, and the moral satisfaction of fighting for a just cause (della Porta and Diani 2006: 100–103; Goodwin and Jasper 2003: 6–7, 91). In spite of this, a free-rider problem exists because people who don't participate in

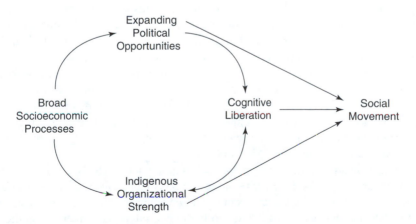

FIGURE 8.1 A Political Process Model of Movement Emergence

Source: McAdam, 1982: 51

Credit: *Political Process and the Development of Black Insurgency, 1930–1970* by McAdam. The University of Chicago Press © 1982 by The University of Chicago.

a social movement can also enjoy the benefits of a movement's accomplishments (e.g., gaining the right to vote, increased civil liberties, or cleaner air) without the risk of participating.

Citizen groups find it difficult to mobilize and engage in collective action due to a number of factors, including, according to Dowding (2001: 38), "the relative costs of taking part in collective action, the size and interactiveness of the group, the number of non-rival demands, whether the affected interests involve potential losses or potential gains, . . . the quality of personnel in a group." Dowding (38) also argues that in a capitalist system "capitalists are systematically lucky because the welfare of everyone is dependent upon the state of the economy and capitalism is the motor of the economy." In general the rational choice model thus examines both the incentives and benefits and the costs of movement involvement.

Postmodern

Although industrial society marked a rather clear distinction between public and private spheres, the end of the twentieth century and the start of the twenty-first century may well mark a blurring of the boundaries between these two spheres as suggested in the postmodern and postindustrial discourse (della Porta and Diani 2006: 49). The growing differentiation in lifestyle also makes social identities even more problematic. Youth movements and LGBT movements may illustrate the possibility for oppositional countercultures to develop.

In the global age of information technology, the state declines in significance and people search for a kind of community in their work, religion, or social movements, but rarely do they completely commit themselves to any one of these (Karp, Yoels, and Vann 2004). Postmodern politics moves from party politics to single-issue and local movements, which results in a "social and political system in which everything is open to negotiation and everything is subject to change" (Best 2002: 65). We will now discuss *old social movements (OSMs)* and *new social movements (NSMs)* and suggest in very broad strokes how OSMs are more likely in modern societies and NSMs are more likely in postmodern nations.

OLD AND NEW SOCIAL MOVEMENTS

Beginning around the 1960s in Europe and the United States, a distinction was drawn between OSMs and NSMs. Some scholars believe that there was a decline in social movements that was based on economic or class interests and an increase in movements related to identity issues, quality of life, or democratic procedures. The new movements tend to occur in postindustrial rather than industrial societies (Best 2002; Goodwin and Jasper 2003). Whereas resource mobilization and the political process frameworks have concentrated on the organizations of social movements and the political opportunities available from the state, theorists concentrating on NSMs often downplay movements that engage in politics at the state level and focus on movements that involve cultural conflicts in society (Nash 2000: 127). Table 8.1 provides a comparison between the characteristics of OSMs and NSMs.

Although there are several different ways of thinking about NSMs, Buechler (1995, 2002) argues that there are two major different versions of NSM theory. One is the neo-Marxist political view that suggests very strong connections between the advanced stage of capitalism and the development of NSMs. This perspective is macro in orientation, remains focused on the state, and recognizes the complexities of the class structure in advanced capitalism. NSMs are often supported by the new middle classes, especially white-collar public-sector employees (Best 2002: 147) who are not tied to the corporate profit motive and are not employed in the corporate world (Pichardo 1997: 416–417). Working-class movements can also be effective, though. Power is

Table 8.1	Characteristics of Old and New Social Movements	
	Social Movements	
Characteristics	**Old Social Movements**	**New Social Movements**
Politics	More class-based	More non-class-based, highly fragmented, cultural
Time Period	Industrial, modern	Postindustrial, postmodern
Sphere of Influence	Political	Cultural
Issues	Wages, job security, benefits, control at work	Peace, environment, human rights, identity
Role of the State	Major target of movement activity	State is one of the possible targets of activity
Action Orientation	High, mainly directed at influencing state policy	More diverse action not directed at the state alone, symbolic action in civil society
Identity	More public, ownership of property, means of production	Personal, who one is, ethnic, racial, gender, sexual orientation
Supporters	Working class	New middle classes, students, unemployed
Ideology	Based on class relation to ownership of means of production	Socially constructed nature of grievances
Organization	Centralized, bureaucratic	Informal networks

Sources: Best 2002; Buechler 1995, 2002; Johnston et al. 1994.

viewed as systemic and centralized under advanced capitalism (Buechler 1995: 457). Buechler's (1995, 2002) second version of NSM theory is post-Marxist, cultural, and focuses on everyday life and civil society rather than the state. In this approach, power and resistance are decentralized and diffuse. Nonclass identity concerns, such as gay rights or gender equality, define those who belong to NSMs. In addition, this theory identifies "the central societal totality as an information society whose administrative codes conceal forms of domination" (Buechler 2002: 16).

Hamel and Maheu (2001: 261) examined movements about collective identity that they consider are *beyond* NSMs as these movements involve resistance to new forms of domination and are more globally oriented. According to Hamel and Maheu "social movements continually challenge the institutions of late modernity that they are also helping to define" (261). Labor movements typify the older social movements, whereas NSMs often focus on direct democracy and are more diverse and heterogeneous. The more current forms of collective action tend to be more fragmented, complex, and diverse than NSMs. Fragmentation involves a process of dissolution that can involve the "break-up of overarching identities and institutions," as can be seen in the collapse of the Soviet Empire, the growth of regionalist and separatist movements, and the development of various different identities and subcultures (Schwarzmantel 2001: 386–387). The World March of Women in the Year 2000, which advocated the improvement of living conditions for women, is an example of such a movement. In addition to signing support cards, there were world rallies or demonstrations that may have ultimately contributed to the development of a cosmopolitan citizenship (Hamel and Maheu 2001: 266). We now turn to a more detailed description of an environmental example of an NSM.

Smart Growth Movements as New Social Movements

Smart growth is a community-oriented planning philosophy. It encompasses a number of general principles, including comprehensive city planning, protection of natural environment, and promotion of social equity. In recent years, smart growth principles have been adopted by community SMOs interested in fighting against urban sprawl, stopping environmental degradation, and improving quality of life. These smart growth SMOs become the spearhead organization of a broader smart growth social movement. Typically, smart growth movements emerge in response to contentious land-use issues such as "big box" retail developments (e.g., Wal-Mart) or large suburban housing developments. Smart growth movements target the interests of local real estate developers by pressuring local elected officials to halt poor development initiatives and to implement a comprehensive land-use plan that adheres to smart growth principles.

According to smart growth advocates, the issue over land-use decisions is sparked by new commercial or residential development. For them, the central concern regarding new development relates to potential changes in overall quality of life. Quality of life can include many things, but for smart growth supporters it usually refers to investing in existing infrastructure, preserving existing businesses, protecting the natural environment, reducing future tax burdens, reducing traffic congestion, creating walkable communities, encouraging mixed-use development, and incorporating the character of the community into new development. For example, one issue that may be seen as problematic is the proposed location of a new development, perhaps located on the outskirts of town, in a flood plain, on existing farmland, or in a wildlife refuge. Smart growth proponents may argue that a given development is a threat to the environment because it eats up valuable farmland or destroys the natural environment. If the development is not within city limits or not close to other types of developments, smart growth supporters may suggest that it may lead to relying more on automobiles, which will also threaten the environment. Supporters may also suggest that a badly planned community will result in major issues with traffic congestion, hurting the environment as well as the character of the community.

In addition, smart growth movements are concerned with land-use designations that are not seen as being in the best interest of the entire community. Movement participants may argue that a parcel of land is best suited for planned industrial rather than commercial or residential uses. The basic assumption is industrial development brings high-paying, quality jobs, as opposed to the low-paying service jobs associated with commercial developments. Another concern of smart growth proponents is commercial developments, such as "big box" retailers, that are a threat to existing businesses—especially small, independent businesses—in the community. A sprawling development may also raise concerns over increased tax burden, including costs related to new infrastructure, the continued maintenance of the infrastructure, building new schools, and expanding fire and police protection. Finally, smart growth advocates may question how local city officials make their decisions—in the interests of a few (such as developers and large land owners) as opposed to the overall interests of the community.

Smart growth movements are often met with stiff opposition from community leaders and groups that can be referred to as pro-growth supporters. Pro-growth supporters may also develop into a coalition of individuals and groups called a pro-growth countermovement. Table 8.2 compares the smart and pro-growth movements.

Criticisms of New Social Movements

Several scholars maintain that, especially in the United States, "new movements" are really not that new because movements such as the temperance movement, women's movement, and religious

Table 8.2	Characteristics of Pro-Growth and Smart Growth Movements	
	Pro-Growth Collective Action Frames	**Smart Growth Collective Action Frames**
Economy	Free market Individual choice	Regulate market
Planning and Development	Minimal/no planning Market-driven solutions	Comprehensive planning Community-driven solutions
Built Environment	Build new	Reinvest in old
Sprawling Development	New tax revenue	New costs
Community Decision Making	Individualism Exclusion	Collectivism Inclusion
Environment	Environment to be developed Immediate return	Environment to be protected Long-term effects
Jobs	New jobs	Quality jobs
Group	Represent majority	Represent majority
Opposition	Vocal minority	Elite interest

movements all existed in the nineteenth century (Buechler 1995; Calhoun 2000; Goodwin and Jasper 2003). For example, Diani (2000: 163), argues that social movements have a difference in emphasis rather than incompatible ideas. Calhoun (2000: 150) also argues that the increase in NSMs does not mean the end to movements that emphasize political and economic issues. Thus, the newness of these movements may be overstated.

Although there is considerable questioning among sociologists about the distinctiveness of NSMs and the relevance of the label, Buechler (1995: 459–460) contends that something relatively new could happen in collective mobilization, and that could well focus on the issue of identity that may be related to the blurring of the distinction between public and private. Pichardo (1997: 425) agrees with this and points out that the contributions of the NSM framework are in the areas of identity, culture, and the civic sphere, which have previously been neglected in the study of social movements.

OTHER APPROACHES TO MOVEMENTS

One of the many other ways to look at the development of theories about social movements is to classify theories as structuralist, rationalist, or culturalist (McAdam 1999; Walder 2006). The first way examines the social organization of society by focusing on the existing patterned social relationships. Structuralists explain the political choice of movement participation by looking at what is happening in society, the activist's social position, and membership or social ties to formal organizations that could influence them to participate. For example, people are more likely to protest when societal ties weaken and they feel less attached to institutions and mainstream organizations or when educational or career opportunities are blocked (Flam 2005: 31). Both the resource mobilization and political process approaches tend to fit the structuralist approach. As previously noted, a rationalist examines the movement's strategies and the benefits or costs that will be incurred by participation. Resource mobilization and political process also have rationalist components. A culturalist stresses how the activists' perceptions about participating fit with their beliefs and values (Walder 2006). In this classification approach, collective identity and framing are key concepts. The study of emotions also directs our attention toward the micro level, that is looking especially at individuals. We consider collective identity first, then framing, and finally emotions, noting though that all three in reality are complexly tied to one another.

Collective Identity

Polletta and Jasper (2001) claim that sociologists turn to collective identity to fill gaps in the dominant political process and resource mobilization frameworks. The structuralist explanations of political process and resource mobilization focus on *how* rather than *why* and depend on rational explanations of individual action. However, reasons to participate in movements related to one's identity seem to be a significant alternative to participating in a movement due to material incentives. In addition, examining identity issues helps explain how interests in a movement actually emerge. Studying collective identity also allows one to better understand the cultural impact of social movements.

McAdam (1994) also recognizes that resource mobilization and the political process model did not give enough attention to the cultural or ideational dimension of social action, although he does include the importance of cognitive liberation in his discussion of black insurgency. "Mediating between opportunity and action are people and the subjective meanings they attach to their situations" (McAdam 1988: 132). Taylor and Whittier (1995: 353) maintain that collective identity is an important concept for all social movements. It is generally assumed that people seek collective identity due to "an intrinsic need for an integrated and continuous social self" (Johnston, Larana, and Gusfield 1997: 279).

Taylor and Whittier (1995) point out that resource mobilization and political process theories focus more on the macro level, which results in downplaying the importance of group grievances. They argue that more attention needs to be paid to how networks transform their members into political actors. *Collective identity* is viewed as the shared definition of a group that is based on members' common interests, solidarity, and experiences. Three key concepts that help us better understand collective identity are boundaries, consciousness, and negotiation.

Boundaries refer to the physical, psychological, and social structures that lay the foundation for differences between the dominant group and the challenging group. Lesbian feminists, for example, adopted two types of boundary strategies. First, the creation of separate distinct institutions such as rape crisis centers and feminist bookstores, and second, the formation of a distinct women's culture that included values such as egalitarianism, collectivism, and cooperation. *Consciousness* involves an ongoing process by which members come to realize the significance of their common interests, experiences, and membership in the collectivity in opposition to the dominant system. For some lesbians, developing group consciousness may result in establishing a lesbian identity that makes political alliances with gay men unlikely. *Negotiation* refers to the ways by which social movement activists try to change symbolic meanings and negative definitions into more positive evaluations. They resist the negative evaluations that devalue them and argue for fair treatment. Boundaries, consciousness, and negotiations all interact to illustrate how lesbian feminist communities develop a collective identity that facilitates women engaging in various actions challenging the dominant political and social system. Taylor and Whittier argue that their model of collective identity can apply to a wide variety of social movements, both old and new.

Jenkins and Gottlieb (2007: 2) argue that identity conflict can be both positive and negative. On the one hand, working toward a broader definition of citizenship and fighting for minority rights and democratic reforms can lead to a more just and equitable society. On the other hand, identity conflicts could destroy social trust and a sense of security while promoting ethnic hatred. Movement organizations are involved in identity work to generate feelings of solidarity and loyalty. Activists try to recruit additional supporters by framing or packaging identities that distinguish "us" from "them" (Polletta and Jasper 2001). We now turn to the framing aspect of the culturalist perspective that involves highlighting the positive aspects of a movement.

Framing

The concept of *frame* is taken from Goffman, who refers to "schemata of interpretation" that enable people "to locate, perceive, identify, and label" things that occur (taken from Snow et al. 1986: 464). Snow and Benford (1992: 137) define a frame as "an interpretive schemata that simplifies and condenses the 'world out there' by selectively punctuating and encoding objects, situations, events, experiences and sequences of actions within one's present or past environments." Social movements "frame, or assign meaning to and interpret, relevant events and conditions" (Snow and Benford 1988: 198). Leaders of social movements try to get people to believe their version of the world. "Because social reality is complex enough to allow for completely different interpretations of what is happening, one situation can produce a variety of definitions, sponsored by competing actors" (Klandermans 1991: 9). Both della Porta (1992) and Snow et al. (1986) emphasize how people's perceptions are shaped by the frames they use to understand events. For della Porta (1992), the events themselves are not objective but can be misinterpreted or fabricated, and there are multiple realities.

Snow et al. (1986) identify four types of frame alignment processes: frame amplification, frame extension, frame transformation, and frame bridging. *Frame amplification* refers to focusing, clarifying, or invigorating an interpretive frame. Common values amplified are justice, democracy, liberty, and equality. Beliefs can also be amplified, for example, the stereotyped images about antagonists or the seriousness of a problem or issue. *Frame extension* occurs when the boundaries of the primary framework of the movement are extended to include interests or points of view that are incidental to the primary objectives but of considerable importance to potential supporters of the movement. *Frame transformation* exists when the programs, causes, and values of the movement are not in line with conventional society, and the movement tries to gather support by professing new values and redefining activities and events so that they are now "seen by the participants to be something quite else" (474). *Frame bridging* involves linking two or more ideologically congruent but structurally unconnected frames regarding a particular issue or concern.

Hunt, Benford, and Snow (1993: 11) point out that framing concepts are used to illustrate how "ideology or belief systems are interactional accomplishments that emerge from framing processes." Ideology is continually being constructed, interpreted, and reinterpreted. Zald (1996) notes that movement groups become involved in framing contests in which they try to persuade possible recruits, authorities, and bystanders of the correctness of their cause. They may create master frames that dominate over other movement-specific action frames so that "their punctuations, attributions, [and] articulations may color and constrain those of any number of movement organizations" (Snow and Benford 1992: 138). Gamson and Meyer (1996: 283), however, point out that

> the degree to which there are unified and consensual frames within a movement is variable and it is comparatively rare that we can speak sensibly of *the* movement framing. It is more useful to think of framing as an internal process of contention within social movements with different actors taking different positions.

Benford (1993) analyzed frame disputes within the nuclear disarmament movement by focusing on diagnostic, prognostic, and frame resonance disputes. Diagnostic framing revolves around the question of what is reality and considers the identification of a problem, whom to blame, or what are the causal forces. Prognostic framing, on the other hand, considers how to change the reality, with emphasis on solutions. Frame resonance involves the extent to which frames will strike a responsive chord or seem credible and thus encourage people to get involved in the movement. Benford found that almost all frame disputes in the nuclear disarmament movement were between different movement factions (moderate, liberal, and radical) rather than within one faction, with the greatest number of frame disputes between moderates and radicals. Textbox 8.1 identifies the frames used by and about white separatist groups.

As the framing perspective developed, Benford (1997) offered his own "friendly" critique of the framework. First, he was concerned about the lack of systematic empirical studies because of

---

TEXTBOX 8.1

The Framing of the White Separatist Movement

The white separatist movement has been known by several labels, including *white supremacist, white power, neo-Nazi, white nationalist*, and *racialist*. Drawing on their interviews with white separatists, Dobratz and Shanks-Meile (2006) found that movement members themselves do not agree on the appropriate labels. Of 139 people interviewed, only six did not use any of the following: *white separatist, racialist*, or *white power*. Sixty-three used all three terms. Another forty used both *white separatist* and *racialist*. (*Racialist* is typically interpreted as love of one's race.) Some resent the label *white supremacist,* such as Ingrid who referred to it as "a term the enemy has coined to smear a legitimate movement that is nationalist rather than 'supremacist.'" Others consider themselves supremacists because they believe that the white race is supreme mentally, physically, and even biblically (especially if supporters embrace the religious belief of Christian identity). Generally movement supporters favor a diagnostic frame that sees minorities as a threat to the white race, pointing out that whites will soon become a minority in the United States. Their prognostic frame calls for the creation of a white separatist state or homeland possibly in the Northwest that would allow whites to live in harmony without minorities polluting their race through intermarriage.

Those who oppose the movement most frequently frame it as a white supremacist one, noting how its members negatively label blacks as niggers, Jews as kikes, and the government as ZOG (Zionist Occupied Government). The organizations in the movement are framed as hate groups and the Ku Klux Klan burns crosses rather than lights them. In order to achieve frame resonance, white separatists try to transform the stigmas of racist and white supremacist to discussions of love, pride, and preservation of the white race and heritage. Berbrier (1998) suggests that white separatists have developed a master frame he calls "Kultural Pluralism" that portrays white racial activism and racism as everyday routine behavior engaged in by normal people who are proud of their race and cultural heritage. Dobratz and Shanks-Meile (2006) argue that the movement itself is too divided to have a well-defined master frame. Dobratz and Shanks-Meile support the appropriateness of Gamson and Meyer's (1996: 283) point that consensual or master frames may not exist, and the master frame is infrequent in that there is only one movement framing. One might think that the white separatist movement fits the description of a new social movement that is searching for identity, and in several ways it does, but this movement really started in late 1865, less than a year after the Civil War ended when the Ku Klux Klan was founded in Pulaski, Tennessee. Thus, like the women's movement, it has a long history and illustrates that identity movements have existed for a long time in the United States.

White separatists engage in a variety of social movement activities. In January 2007, members of the National Socialist Movement protested by burning books and articles they considered anti-white publications.

Credit: Photo by Lisa K. Waldner

the underdevelopment of frame analytic methods. Put another way, how does one operationalize frames? Second, he noted that the empirical studies had been more descriptive than analytical, with numerous frames identified rather than a few generic frames that could be applied across movements. Emphasis has been placed on frames as static objects rather than as dynamic processes being constructed, negotiated, contested, reconstructed, and transformed. The framing of elites in movements has been overemphasized to the detriment of examining rank-and-file movement members, potential members, bystanders, and others. Another problem is the tendency to reify frames, by which Benford (1997: 418) means "the process of talking about socially constructed ideas as though they are real, as though they exist independent of the collective interpretations and constructions of the actors involved." This results in some authors writing as though social movements frame issues when in reality only particular activists or other participants do. In addition, sometimes the role of human agency, as well as the role of emotions, is neglected. At other times the tendency has been to reduce interaction and collective action to individual-level explanations. Finally, there has also been the inclination to oversimplify or treat movements as monolithic rather than as interactive processes that are negotiated in movement participants' everyday involvements.

We now turn to one of Benford's specific criticisms and focus on the role of emotions in social movements. Polletta and Jasper (2001: 299) have observed that there is still a lot to learn about collective identities and "we know little about the emotions that accompany and shape collective identity."

Emotions

Supporters of the resource mobilization approach reacted against the social–psychological collective behavior approach that devalued movement participants as being involved in irrational behavior. Therefore, these supporters emphasized the continuities between institutional politics and social movements, but they "ignored emotions and implicitly accepted the assumptions of rational choice theory, embracing the false dichotomy of emotions and rationality" (Aminzade and McAdam 2001: 21). Further, Aminzade and McAdam (23) argue that in the United States and Europe, the dominant culture has seen emotions as not only irrational but also as illegitimate in political decision making. However, as they and Oliver, Cadena-Roa, and Strawn (2003) point out, rationality versus emotion is a false dichotomy. People, including movement activists, can be both rational and emotional in their decision making. As Jasper (1998: 407) notes, "General affects and specific emotions are a part of all social life as surely as cognitive meanings and moral values are. What is more, they are relatively predictable, not accidental eruptions of the irrational." Aminzade and McAdam (2001: 18) also "see episodes of contention typically involving both heightened emotions and an increase in rational, instrumental action."

Goodwin and Jasper (2003: 7) acknowledge that, although a number of complex emotions are associated with social life in general, they are especially clear in social movements where organizers may try to arouse anger and compassion possibly by playing on fears and anxieties. Other important emotions include excitement, hope for the future, and dedication to the cause.

> Emotions do not merely accompany our deepest desires and satisfactions, they constitute them, permeating our ideas, identities, and interests. . . . Recently, sociologists have rediscovered emotions, although they have yet to integrate them into much empirical research outside of social psychology. (Jasper 2003: 154)

Emotions can be divided into primarily affective and primarily reactive ends of a continuum, with others in between. Hatred and love as well as trust and hostility are primarily affective emotions relevant to protest, whereas anger and grief are primarily reactive. Emotions that are in between include compassion, enthusiasm, resentment, and resignation (Jasper 2003).

Goodwin, Jasper, and Polletta (2001: 11–12) have identified four different possible explanations of emotions. The first is biological, which focuses on the degree to which emotions are innate or instinctive. The second explanation is psychological and examines the "personality structure," including whether one has a positive or negative feeling about a politician. The third is more social–structural but also interactionist. For example, relationships involving power differences, especially in one-on-one engagements, may influence attempts to recruit another person to join a movement. The fourth approach maintains that emotions are culturally or socially constructed. Our culture influences what are considered socially appropriate means to express our emotions. Emotions relevant to social movements frequently tend to be more constructed than others. Fear of someone lunging at you from the dark requires much less cognitive construction than fear of the policies of the World Trade Organization or the joy and hope from participating in a social movement that can possibly result in a better society (12–13).

Emotions can be important building blocks for other social movement concepts. For example, opportunities, identities, networks, and frames are linked closely to emotions. Injustice frames draw upon feelings of indignation and outrage (Goodwin et al. 2001: 14). As Gamson (1992: 32) points out, "Injustice focuses on the righteous anger that puts fire in the belly and iron in the soul." The participants' emotions influence the course of development of a social movement while the movement's development and its victories and failures influence the participants' emotions. In addition, characteristics of the state (e.g., how open or closed it is to protest) and the behavior or actions of the government or political elite (repressive or tolerant) influence the prevailing emotions of a movement (Flam 2005: 32). It is also important to realize the significance of the emotional reactions of the public to the mobilization attempts of the movement and whether a movement's (re)framing of the issues has been effective (Flam with King 2005).

The study of emotions needs to be integrated into the field of political sociology, including that of social movements and contentious politics because "an analysis that ignores the emotional dimensions of attachments and commitments is incapable of explaining activists' determination in the face of high risk and their willingness to endure suffering and self-sacrifice" (Aminzade and McAdam 2001: 21).

TOWARD A SYNTHESIS OF STRUCTURALIST, RATIONALIST, AND CULTURALIST FRAMEWORKS

Although generally taking a structuralist approach in his landmark book, *Political Process and the Development of Black Insurgency 1930–1970*, McAdam (1999) critiques the structuralist, rationalist, and culturalist interpretations of social movements in the second edition of his book. Even though structuralists have emphasized the role of formal and informal organizations, including people's network ties in recruiting people to social movements, they have not generated a social–psychological explanation for why people join movements. The role of individual decision-making is undermined; the individual is acted upon rather than showing human agency.

McAdam generally recognizes the importance of incorporating a culturalist viewpoint, but culturalists need to reflect more on the "process by which existing collective identities get redefined so as to serve as the motivational basis for emergent action" (1999: xxxiv). In addition, culturalists need to ground their framework in a theory of human action and motivation. Rationalists, on the other hand, fail to explain the origins of their individual interests or preferences for social movement activity because they tend to assume relatively fixed and well-defined interests of people, thus making it difficult to understand why someone would join an NSM.

In his effort to combine concepts and ideas from the structuralist, culturalist, and rationalist perspectives and to extend our knowledge of contentious politics, McAdam identifies three key concepts: expanding political opportunities and threats, mobilizing structures, and framing or using other interpretive processes to develop a synthetic explanation of social movements. As political opportunities and threats increase or decline, the power relations are subject to change. Informal and formal collective vehicles such as churches, civil rights organizations, and neighborhood block parties may encourage people to organize, pursue their concerns, and look for solutions. The shared meanings developed through framing and other interpretive processes help link the political opportunities and structures to actual social movement participation. Participants need to share their grievances often about some perceived social injustice and believe that they can improve their situations and/or their cause in general. As McAdam (1999: xi) points out, "It is not the structural changes that set people in motion, but rather the shared understandings and conceptions of 'we-ness' they develop to make sense of the trends."

In his model, which attempts to combine or synthesize elements from the three frameworks, McAdam recognizes the importance of both institutionalized political groups and the previously unorganized new actors that can be mobilized to participate in politics. In uncertain political times, established political leaders, such as elites, political party leaders, and government officials, may be divided over political goals and policies that result in elite contention. This contention opens up political opportunities for SMOs to develop and form new courses of political action called popular contention. In this model, institutionalized and noninstitutionalized politics join together to form possibilities for social change. In addition, both the state or other elite actors and the challenging group(s) go through similar stages of interpretive processes, attribution of threat or opportunity, appropriation of existing organizational or collective identity, innovative collective action, and development of shared perception of environmental uncertainty that can result in the emergence of contentious politics (McAdam 1999: xv–xxx). (More discussion of movement emergence follows in the next section.)

Numerous other attempts to integrate key social movement concepts from different frameworks have been proposed, including some qualitative and quantitative analytical approaches (see Jenkins and Form 2005: 241–242 for more details). Oliver et al. (2003: 225–226) also discuss the need for integrating structural and constructionist or culturalist theories associated with social psychology and cultural sociology. They point out that movements formulate rational and strategic actions *and* also use cultural memories, values, and moral principles to define and redefine situations. Broad macrostructural processes such as economic crises, population pressures, and shifting political alignments clearly shape contentious politics, but the starting points of contention are rooted in the collective interpretations and behavior of individuals responding to such environmental structural changes (McAdam 2001: 223–224). Much more work remains to be done in synthesizing the various theoretical perspectives to give us a more complete understanding of social movements. To advance our knowledge of what happens as social movements develop, we now turn to a more specific discussion about the emergence, mobilization, and decline of social movements.

THE LIFE CYCLE OF SOCIAL MOVEMENTS

Social movement theorists commonly address a number of questions regarding the life cycle of social movements. What factors facilitate the emergence of a social movement? Of these potential factors, which help or hinder the social movement after it has emerged? What factors influence whether a movement is successful? What happens after a social movement has either succeeded or failed? The answer to each of these questions can be quite complex. As a result, a common starting point is to assume that social movements do not truly have a beginning and an end.

In the real world, it seems social movements start and stop all the time. For example, many identify the start of the modern Civil Rights Movement in the United States as 1955 when the Montgomery Improvement Association, led by Dr. King, began the Montgomery Bus Boycotts. However, this assumption disregards decades of work done by civil rights activists who fought for African American civil and human rights. Similarly, some would argue that the Civil Rights Movement ended in the late 1960s or the early 1970s. In particular, some target the assassination of Dr. King on April 4, 1968, as the end, if not the beginning of the end of the Civil Rights Movement. Again, this assumption fails to recognize the important social movement activity that occurred after Dr. King's death and continues to this day. Regardless of what one identifies as the beginning or the end of the Civil Rights Movement, the peak of social movement activity in the Civil Rights Movement began in the early 1950s (e.g., *Brown v. Board of Education,* the killing of Emmett Till, and the Montgomery Bus Boycott) and continued through the end of the 1960s (e.g., Freedom Summer, the Civil Rights Act of 1964, the Voting Rights Act of 1965).

We will assume the following: social movements go through a complex lifecycle; they seem to have a start and an end, although the start is not a definitive one and the end may have many lingering remnants that morph into another cause; what appears to be the start and the end instead marks the peak(s) of social movement activity; and the emergence, mobilization, and decline of social movements involve many different factors. For our purposes, we will discuss these components as the life cycle of social movements.

Social Movement Emergence and Mobilization

The traditional view of social movement emergence deals with three main areas of research: social breakdown, political opportunity structures (POSs), and existing conditions of social organization. Breakdown, opportunity, and social organization relate to the external factors that help give rise to social movement activity. These same factors help or hinder the mobilization of social movements once they do emerge. Once an aggrieved population has emerged, there are other important factors that influence the mobilization of potential adherents. In particular, mobilization strength is strongly affected by the interpretive or framing processes that work as a mechanism of "micromobilization" to attract like-minded individuals and to convert those who may have differing opinions.

STRAIN, CONFLICT, AND BREAKDOWN   Social movement theorists argue that social movements emerge as a response to strain or breakdown in social order (Kornhauser 1959; Smelser 1962). Social breakdown has been discussed in many different ways, including social conflict, structural strain, and social disorganization. Social breakdown comes out of a Durkheimian tradition and has structural functionalist roots, which suggests that under normal conditions of social organization a sufficiently large number of individuals will have their needs, wants, and concerns met by the social structure. If the social structure becomes strained or begins to break down, a progressively larger number of individuals start to feel marginalized. In other words, because the social system is not working for a large group of people anymore, social breakdown, whether real or perceived, leads to feelings of relative deprivation. This, in turn, helps fuel the emergence of collective social action.

Research has found that disruptions in social organization are a factor in the emergence of social movements. In his study of a prison riot in New Mexico in 1980, Useem (1985) used in-depth interviews with prison guards and inmates to reconstruct the social organization of the prison. The data depict how changes in the structure of the prison over the prior decade helped foster the riot. Useem writes: "During the 1970s, the State Penitentiary changed from a relatively benign and well-run institution, to one that was harsh, abusive, painfully boring, and without the 'regulatory mechanisms' that had been in place in the early 1970s" (685). The study points to the importance of explaining social movement emergence in relation to the disruption of social routines and expectations.

Social movement research has also explored the role of conflict and competition in gaining control and power. NSM theorists, such as Alain Touraine and Manuel Castells, have contributed extensively to this discussion. Social movement emergence and mobilization are seen as resulting from rising conflict and competition. For example, Castells (1983) argues that social movements emerge as a result of the imposition of a hegemonic order that conflicts with urban social realities and identities. Castells (1977) gives specific attention to what he calls *urban social movements* and *urban ideology. Urban ideology* is a system of interlocking values and ideas that empower some groups while subordinating others. When the subordinated group identifies this urban ideology, similar to Marx's false consciousness, collective action is highly unlikely. It is not until the hegemonic order conflicts with an urban social reality that movements emerge (Castells 1983).

In an in-depth examination of the rise and fall of the Mission Coalition Organization (MCO) in San Francisco (1967–1973), Castells (1983) argues that the emergence of the MCO resulted from urban renewal efforts prior to 1967. Most important was the role played by the San Francisco Redevelopment Agency (SFRA), a development organization that proposed redevelopment initiatives that coincided with urban renewal efforts related to two primary Bay Area Rapid Transit (BART) stations in the heart of the Mission neighborhood. The rise of the MCO was due largely to the negative views that Mission residents held of previous SFRA-lead redevelopment decisions. Many residents felt that SFRA redeveloped areas largely to benefit private business elites, not to benefit local residents. There were also major concerns over SFRA's previous redevelopment initiative, which resulted in the displacement of many Mission residents.

The new redevelopment initiative was viewed as posing the same threat of urban displacement and gentrification. The proposal of two new transit-oriented redevelopment projects in combination with SFRA's history of displacement in the neighborhood helped fuel the rise of the MCO (Castells 1983).

Similar to Castells, Touraine (1981, 1985) suggests that social movements emerge as a result of the dominant social organization. Touraine assumes that new forms of social organization, referred to as the *postindustrial society*, have given rise to new forms of social movements. These social movements are new because the nature of their conflict, their desired outcomes, and even their makeup are unique from any other movement of the past. They are defined less by attributes held by a group but more by resistance to dominant forms of power (Touraine 1981). Touraine argues the cause of conflict is for control of historicity or "the capacity to produce an historical experience through cultural patterns" (1985: 778). Self-production of society, or societal actors acting against other actors within the social order to control historicity, creates order (Touraine 1977, 1981). Thus Touraine (1985) identifies the conflict over controlling and defining historical experiences as the central conflict of the NSM. The need or want to gain the capacity to control historicity is recognized only when the system of domination that separates those who have the capacity to control historicity from those who do not is uncovered (Touraine 1981). The problem, however, is that domination is masked by the new order of postindustrial societies. By controlling information and knowledge, individuals who are in power are able to subordinate individuals who falsely identify with the new social order (Touraine 1981). Once this system of domination is uncovered, the likelihood of the emergence of collective mobilization increases significantly.

POLITICAL OPPORTUNITY STRUCTURES   Breakdown, strain, and conflict are far from the sole determinants of social movement emergence and the subsequent strength of collective mobilization. Over the last thirty years, social movement research has pointed to the importance of avenues for social movement activity embedded in social structure. These avenues are referred to as *political opportunity structures* (POSs). Eisinger (1973: 25) defines political opportunity as "the degree to which groups are likely to be able to gain access to power to manipulate the political system." In a study examining riot behavior in forty-three American cities, Eisinger found that protest activity was positively related to POSs found within these different cities.

An excellent application of the concept of political opportunity by Jenkins and Perrow (1977) compared two farm workers organizations, the National Farm Labor Union (NFLU) and the United Farm Workers (UFW), between 1946 and 1972. The organizations experienced drastically different levels of success. On the one hand, the NFLU encountered a political environment where it received little financial and political support from key allies, such as organized labor, and also confronted a deeply partisan opposition that was not at all friendly to the organization's concerns and where elected officials strongly supported agribusiness over labor concerns. The UFW, on the other hand, amassed political and financial capital from a very sympathetic political environment and experienced much more open and neutral public authorities. Governmental elites were deeply divided over the concerns and well-being of farm workers. Organized labor was much stronger and openly spoke out against agribusiness public policy. The central argument of Jenkins and Perrow supports resource mobilization theory because it points to the importance of political environmental factors, which can help or hinder social movement mobilization efforts over the internal makeup of the SMO.

As we previously discussed, in his seminal work *Political Process and the Development of Black Insurgency, 1930–1970*, McAdam (1982) put forth a critical advancement in social movement theory that attempts to bring together discussion of structural strain, breakdown, and grievance theories with resource mobilization theory and POSs referred to as the *political process model*. The political process model sees the emergence and mobilization of social movements as a result of expanding and contracting political opportunities that are dependent upon broad-scale structural changes, cleavages of elite power, existent social organization, and cognitive liberation of aggrieved populations. The emergence and mobilization of social movements are largely dependent on a combination of external factors and internal movement characteristics. Political opportunities, in conjunction with existent indigenous organization and subjective "transformation of consciousness" (51), lead to movement emergence. Once a sufficiently organized population has realized a shared grievance and identified and acted upon a political opportunity, the possibility for continued movement development or potential movement decline are impacted by a fourth factor, "shifting control responses of other groups to the movement" (59). Whereas recognized threat and seized opportunity impact the ability for a movement to emerge, the combination of the state's capacity for repression, elite allies, and strength of other competing groups explains whether a movement will succeed or fail. McAdam's original model has undergone a number of changes over the last twenty-five years, and each of the model's main components has received a great deal of attention as well.

First, the relative openness and closure of institutionalized politics can vary regionally and nationally, as can the capacity and propensity for repression by the state. In a comparison of antinuclear movements in four democracies, Kitschelt (1986) found that both strategies and outcomes of social movements are determined largely by the domestic POS. In other words, it is not solely the type of strategy (e.g., disruptive protest tactics) that shapes outcomes; it is also the established and institutionalized political structure that is either more open and responsive (e.g., United States and Sweden) or closed and unresponsive (e.g., France and West Germany). In addition, it is the weak (e.g., United States and West Germany) or strong (e.g., France and Sweden) state capacity to repress political demands that shapes strategies and impacts potential movement outcomes. There is also evidence that strategies, tactics, and social movement outcomes appear to vary across transnational, regional, national, state, and local political settings.

Also, expanding and closing opportunities are highly related to the relative stability or instability of elite alignments. Jenkins, Jacobs, and Agnone (2003) found that from 1948 to 1997 governmental divisions in the United States affected expanding opportunities for civil rights protest. The frequency of civil rights protest was more prominent when northern Democrats increased in strength and Republican presidential incumbents experienced difficult Cold War pressures. A compromise was essentially forced, which resulted in more opportunities for civil rights protesters to successfully attain movement goals. The presence or absence of elite allies is closely related to divisions in elite arrangements (Amenta and Zylan 1991; Jenkins et al. 2003; Meyer and Minkoff 2004).

Despite claims that social movement emergence is related to objective POSs, some researchers have been able to show social movement mobilization in the absence of any POS. Kurzman (1996) argues that the perception of POSs is just as important as actual structural opportunities. In a study of the 1979 Iranian revolution, Kurzman found that in the absence of objective structural opportunities, insurgents were still able to mobilize against an Iranian state. In essence, the Iranian insurgents perceived that POSs existed, which led to the creation of political opportunities and the eventual overthrow of the Iranian monarchy. Roscigno and Danaher (2001) examined the role of radio stations in the mobilization of textile workers in the South from 1929 to 1934. In an area of the country where organized labor was nearly nonexistent and local elites had strong influence on the content of local newspapers and could easily bypass new organized labor laws, a large number of textile workers still mobilized against their employers through organized walkouts and strikes. The authors found that proximity to radio stations was significantly correlated with worker mobilization.

In a final example, Einwohner (2003) found very similar results in a study of Jewish resistance in the Warsaw ghetto during World War II, where structural opportunities were nonexistent. However, Einwohner also found that the perception of lack of opportunity was also strongly present, and suggested that the emergence of Jewish resistance was facilitated by the view that resistance was equivalent to honor.[2] Taken together, one can deduce that in order for a social movement to emerge, there must be the perception of threat and opportunity as well as existing mobilizing structures and objective structural opportunities (Goldstone and Tilly 2001).

EXISTENT SOCIAL ORGANIZATION: MOBILIZING STRUCTURES AND NETWORKS   The level and strength of prior organization with a given population is equally as important to social movement emergence and mobilization as POS. An aggrieved population must have a sufficient level of existent social organization to mobilize successfully. Without prior social organization in place, a group of individuals is highly unlikely to mobilize. Social movement scholars have addressed the importance of social organization by looking at a number of areas, including established and sympathetic organizations and high levels of social capital or networks of formal and informal associations.

Broadly speaking, social movement theorists have discussed prior levels of social organizations as mobilizing structures. Mobilizing structures are "those collective vehicles, informal as well as formal, through which people mobilize and engage in collective action" (McAdam, McCarthy, and Zald 1996: 3). Mobilizing structures, like indigenous organizations from McAdam's (1982) original model, refer to available resources, networks of communication, and existent indigenous organizations that allow for and guide social movement activity. Once the movement has emerged and groups have organized, SMOs become the main "collective vehicles" for organizing potential adherents, guiding movement tactics, and attaining movement goals. In short, efforts by SMOs "influence the overall pace and outcome of the struggle" (McAdam et al. 1996: 13). For example, the leaders of the Congress of Racial Equality (CORE) staged fund-raising activities after the Montgomery Bus Boycott that allowed them to increase their staff and expand their work in the South (McAdam 1982: 148). As part of a social movement's chances for success, both the tactics employed by SMOs and the goals of SMOs are paramount. Groups that use disruptive tactics and have a single and nondisplacing goal have more favorable outcomes than groups that focus on multiple goals and call for displacing or removing antagonists from power (Gamson 1990: 41–46).

Although mobilizing structures play an important role in social movement mobilization, the capacity to mobilize cannot be realized without the establishment of formal and informal social networks. Networks influence the flow of financial (money) and human capital (leadership and membership base). Social networks also impact the avenues of communication, which in turn influence such things as the ability to quickly mobilize movement participants across a broad area. An early study of the role of communication networks by Petras and Zeitlin (1967) found that mobilization and participation in and around rural mining towns in Chile increased as individuals moved closer to mining towns. The opposite was true for those who were farther away from the mining towns. In an examination of the role of internal social organization to the sit-in movements of the 1960s, Aldon Morris (1981) found that both black southern churches and colleges provided resources and communication networks that were crucially important to the emergence and mobilization of the sit-ins. In particular, the majority of leadership was drawn from black churches and colleges in the South.

Existing social organization not only affects the ability of a social movement to tap into important leadership networks and to quickly disseminate information to a broad coalition of individuals but also plays a central role in the recruitment of rank-and-file social movement participants. Social movements have been found to recruit an overwhelming majority of followers from preexisting, informal friendship and family networks and from individuals' links with other groups in which they had previously participated (Snow, Zurcher, and Ekland-Olson 1980). The recruitment of individuals who have prior attachment to sympathetic or like-minded organizations (Gould 1991) is of crucial importance. In addition to affording opportunities for recruitment of members and using communication as a means to quick mobilization, social networks also create salient collective identities and socialize social movement participants (Passy 2001).

COLLECTIVE ACTION FRAMES The framing perspective argues that mobilization of potential social movement supporters is related to whether frames created by SMOs connect on a social–psychological level with potential adherents.[3] In other words, do the collective action frames resonate with social movement participants? In order for frames to resonate, they must be seen as credible and salient (Benford and Snow 2000). The focus is on how "a critical mass of persons collectively define the situation as ripe and persuade others on an ongoing basis that their version of reality rings true" (Benford 1993: 199).

Snow and Benford (1988) make clear distinctions among a number of framing processes. As noted previously diagnostic framing is the process of meaning construction that identifies and defines a given problem while prognostic framing occurs after a problem has been identified and offers a solution to the problem (Snow and Benford 1988). Also important though is *motivational framing,* the process of frame construction that links the problem and resolution to actualized collective action, or the frames that get individuals to act for a cause (Snow and Benford 1988). Whether a frame resonates with potential adherents and motivates them into action is dependent on the credibility and salience of that frame. Frames are credible when they are seen as consistent, articulated by a reliable source, and empirically verifiable (Benford and Snow 2000). Consistency between frames and SMO claims and frames and SMO actions is associated with higher frame resonance (Zuo and Benford 1995). Frames resonate with more intensity when the articulator, such as an expert, elected official, or the media, is seen as legitimate. There must also be a "fit between the framings and events in the world" (Benford and Snow 2000: 620). In addition, frame salience includes three aspects: centrality, experiential commensurability, and narrative fidelity (Benford and Snow 2000). *Centrality* refers to how important and relevant a frame is to a given population and suggests that the more central a frame to a given community the greater likelihood of mobilizing potential adherents. *Experiential commensurability,* or how applicable a frame is to the daily life of potential adherents, suggests "the more experientially commensurate the framings, the greater the salience, and the greater the probability of mobilization" (Benford and Snow 2000: 621). *Narrative fidelity* suggests newly created frames that align with the "cultural narrations" of a target population and therefore carry cultural significance, are more salient, and increase mobilization. Taken together, one can make the argument that mobilization of potential adherents is largely dependent on the identification of a legitimate problem, the suggestion of a realistic solution, and the evidence of opportunity for change.

Social Movement Outcomes, Influence, and Decline

Outcomes are difficult to identify because they can vary greatly, "extending from state-level policy decisions to expansion of a movement's social capital to changes in participants' biographies" (Cress and Snow 2000: 1064). One of the primary areas of study for social movement outcomes is goals. Goals are the intended target or direct outcome of an SMO. You may recall that resource mobilization theory suggests that an SMO's ability to effectively attain its goals is directly related to resources available (McCarthy and Zald 1977). Essentially, SMOs that utilize available resources will achieve positive social movement outcomes. Successful goal attainment, therefore, does not rest on the aggrieved populations as much as on the resources available to that population (Jenkins and Perrow 1977).

Generally speaking, social movement researchers have addressed outcomes as a much more complex issue than simply as goal attainment. In a study of fifteen homeless SMOs in eight U.S. cities, Cress and Snow (2000) tracked SMO-related outcomes and found that the presence of diagnostic and prognostic frames are a vibrant indicator of movement outcomes that identify the presence of one or both in five out of the six pathways to successful outcomes. Cress and Snow (1996, 2000) also suggest that an important addition to collective action frames on successful outcomes is the role of a viable SMO, or the combination of organizational survival, frequency of meetings, and campaigns. In another study of social movement outcomes, Halebsky (2006) found successful outcomes to be positively associated with evidence of widespread opposition, broadly framed threats to the community, positive coverage of the SMO by the media, lack of countermovement forces, and missteps by the movement antagonist.

We will discuss a number of important factors that influence the success or failure of a social movement. These factors play a crucial role in effecting the longevity of a social movement, the rise and sustained peak of action, the decline or eventual demise of a social movement, and so on. We will discuss these factors such as the makeup of internal SMO characteristics, the employment of strategies and tactics, and the makeup of the social and political context.

SOCIAL MOVEMENT ORGANIZATION CHARACTERISTICS AND RESOURCES   Resource mobilization theory surfaced in an attempt to remove a problematic feature of strain theories: deciphering whether grievances caused by strain were in fact objective reality or perceived threats. Stripping away much of this ambiguity, resource mobilization theory suggests that an SMO's ability to mobilize and influence measurable outcomes is connected to and shaped by the resources available to the SMO. In other words, effective SMOs can attain goals through attracting and maintaining adequate resources such as time, money, and movement adherents (McCarthy and Zald 1973, 1977; Oberschall 1973; Tilly 1978). McCarthy (1987) found that two diametrically opposed social movements, pro-life and pro-choice, both relied heavily on valuable resources to launch successful mobilization efforts. However, the resources they tapped into were very different. Pro-choice organizations relied heavily on financial capital collected by a vast number of supporters, whereas pro-life organizations received little financial contributions but had a broad and strongly committed volunteer base.

STRATEGIES AND TACTICS   McAdam (1983) suggests that with the introduction of new tactics comes a heightened level of mobilization followed by increases in movement success. Gamson (1990) also found that disruptive tactics, such as violence, are positively associated with successful movement outcomes. For example, the role of women's groups between 1890 and 1920 in transforming the educational lobbying system was due in large part to the use of innovative tactics. Because women were barred from voting, these women's rights groups were forced to identify different means of creating a new system that replaced "voting as the central act" with "the rise of a political regime in which groups claiming to represent categories of persons presented specific demands to legislatures, using the leverage of public opinion, lobbyists, and expertise rather than sheer numbers of votes" (Clemens 1993: 791). More recent discussions on the role of tactics on movement outcomes have added the dimension of resourcefulness.

Discussed as strategic capacity, strategies increase chances of successful outcomes with access to more resources, originality, and timeliness (Ganz 2000).

Even the most contrasting of social movements (e.g., the white separatist movement versus the Civil Rights Movement) use and share a common repertoire of tactics. The common use and copying of one another, in a sense, help social movements live on. The Civil Rights Movement was particularly innovative when it came to tactics and strategies, such as sit-ins and freedom rides, that were used by aggrieved populations. This tactical innovation (McAdam 1983) in part helped with the ultimate success of this movement. The innovative use of resources made the Civil Rights Movement so influential on other social movements throughout the latter half of the twentieth and the beginning of the twenty-first century. Similar to the preexistence of social organization, we assume that social movements, even after they appear to have disappeared, still have the potential to have some level of influence.

SOCIAL AND POLITICAL CONTEXT   We will focus on the importance of the social and political context and how this impacts social movement outcomes. For example, Amenta, Carruthers, and Zylan (1992), in a study of movement outcomes and the role of political context, found that in sympathetic political environments, or environments with both existing civic organizations that hold political capital and with elites whose interests align with movement concerns, successful SMO outcomes are more likely to occur. However, when these elements are absent, either the SMO does not succeed or more disruptive tactics are necessary to mediate successful outcomes. Furthermore, political context is related to structural changes that encourage protest, influence a favorable political environment, and offer elite support (Meyer and Minkoff 2004). Finally, long-term social movement outcomes (e.g., number of black voters registered, votes cast for black candidates in statewide elections, the number of black candidates running for office in the late 1960s and early 1970s, and the number of black elected officials) is reactive to episodes of local repression and is highly correlated with strength of local infrastructure (Andrews 1997).

Social movement research has also explored the role of countermovements in relation to mobilization and social movement outcomes (Meyer and Staggenborg 1996). Countermovements are "networks of individuals and organizations that share many of the same objects of concern as the social movements that they oppose . . . [but] . . . make competing claims on the state of matters of policy and politics and vie for attention from the mass media and broader public" (1632). Countermovements are likely to emerge when (1) the original social movement shows signs of success, (2) elite interests are threatened by the original social movement's successes, and (3) the countermovement has elite support in the political arena (Meyer and Staggenborg 1996). Interaction between movements and countermovements strongly influence and shape the political environment where "the opposing movements create ongoing opportunities and obstacles for one another" (Meyer and Staggenborg 1996: 1643). The relationship between movements and countermovements is characterized by success of one side sparking the other side and so on, effectively prolonging the conflict. However, without successes, neither movements nor countermovements can sustain mobilization and will decline (1647). We will now briefly examine the likelihood of success of violent tactics in social movements.

SUCCESS AND VIOLENT TACTICS   First of all, it is important to recognize that success of movements in general is typically very difficult to define and measure. Some movements are really involved in bringing about social change whereas others may achieve only symbolic victories, such as having a piece of legislation passed that is not enforced (Burstein, Einwohner, and Hollander 1995: 283). Six types of policy responsiveness have been identified, including:

1. government access—whether movement supporters testify in congressional hearings,
2. agenda—whether a bill is considered by the legislature,
3. policy—whether the desired legislation is passed,
4. output—whether the legislation is actually enforced,
5. impact—whether the legislation does what it is intended to do,
6. structural—whether the system is changed so that the movement has more influence (284).

Determining the success of a movement is difficult in part because it assumes that social movements are homogeneous phenomena when in reality there may be disagreements within a movement regarding its goals, and so on. Movement participants as well as observers and scholars studying movements may disagree about the success of an individual movement. With this in mind we will look briefly at the literature on violence in social movements.

Tilly's (1978) resource mobilization approach maintains that movement participants select their methods on the basis of what resources are available at a particular time; collective violence should be viewed as a normal activity in a struggle for power. In his work on group violence, Gurr (1989: 13) pointed out that violence is often an effective tactic in gaining recognition and concessions, particularly if it is the result of a prolonged social movement. Gamson's (1975: 81) analysis of fifty-three challenging groups supports this finding, although Gamson cautions that the relationship between violence and successful outcomes is not simple. Violence needs to be studied as an instrumental activity designed to advance the goals of the movement group. Participants use violence because they believe it will promote their cause. Giugni (1999) points out that other authors using Gamson's data but employing more sophisticated techniques have basically supported Gamson's findings.

Piven and Cloward (1977) studied four lower-class protest movements during the mid-twentieth century and believed that violence or disruptive activity was effective. They argue, "It is not formal organizations but mass defiance that won what was won in the 1930s and 1960s" (xv). They recommend strategies that escalate the momentum and impact of disruptive politics (37). Instead, what tends to happen is that the leaders of the disruptive movement try to create formal organizations and ask for resources from the elites. Elites sometimes offer resources and encourage the movement organizations that have emerged to "air grievances before formal bodies of the state" (xxi). These are symbolic gestures rather than means to provide meaningful change. Insurgents "leave the streets" (xxi) and many of the organizations fade away. Piven and Cloward conclude that "As for the few organizations which survive, it is because they become more useful to those who control the resources on which they depend than to the lower-class groups which the organizations claim to represent. Organizations endure, in short, by abandoning their oppositional politics" (xxi).

Various authors have found that disruptive tactics or the use of force helps a movement accomplish its goals (Guigni 1999: xvii). Still other authors challenge the success of violent tactics, especially in the area of strike activity, where evidence suggests that labor violence and violent strikes may be less successful than peaceful ones (Burstein et al. 1995; Giugni 1999: xvii). Giugni (1999: xviii–xxi) suggests that the success of violence and disruptive tactics likely depends on the circumstances under which they are adopted. As discussed previously, such factors as the availability of political opportunities, the institutional characteristics of the political system (e.g., representative democracy, authoritarian leader), the tendency of rulers to repress protest activity, the ability of the movement to develop innovative and disruptive tactics, and the cultural climate may be key in determining whether violence is acceptable. As noted earlier, movements are often not homogeneous entities and may exhibit little agreement about what goals are most significant and what constitutes success. While movements are rational efforts to bring about change, their actual effects, whether positive or negative, also may not have been what the movement participants wanted (unintended consequences).

Repression: The State's Reaction to Movements

One of the areas that clearly links social movements with the nation-state is repression. (For a detailed discussion of the state, see Chapter 2.) Earl (2006) suggests that until the last decade or so research on repression lagged behind that of many other topics of social movement studies. She argues that what motivates research on repression has been a desire to understand how nonmovement actors influence the form and level of protest. The study of repression has focused on violent coercive state-based acts rather than on the actions of private actors (e.g., a countermovement), or acts that are less violent, such as channeling, "where carrots and sticks are used to encourage or discourage certain types of actions on the part of protesters" (130). Channeling includes things such as cutting off funding to SMOs or making it difficult to obtain a permit to hold a protest. Earl further argues that repression should be more appropriately labeled *protest control.*

Tilly and Tarrow (2007: 214) define repression as "action by authorities that increases the cost—actual or potential—of an actor's claim making." Davenport (2000: 5–7) points out that many people use the term *repression* in various ways, and notes three different types. The first and the most common use fits the *negative sanctions tradition,* which generally refers to nonviolent behavior that involves limiting civil and political rights such as censorship, propaganda campaigns, imposition of martial law, and mass imprisonments. The second tradition involves violations of human rights, including murder, torture, arbitrary imprisonment, and forced disappearance. The third area is state terror, which includes force/violence or the threat of it to obtain compliance because of fear. (See Chapter 9 for a discussion of terrorism.) Political sociologists, including social movement scholars, are becoming more and more interested in the topic of repression, in part because states have been recognized as "the number-one killers of their own citizens, and they also significantly influence the decision of their citizens to engage in contentious behavior against states" (3).

Social movements can be perceived by the state or its authorities as threatening. A variety of conditions determine the perceived level of threat. For example, if the objectives of the movement threaten the actual structure of the state as opposed to the allotment of some resources (more benefits), the more likely the state feels threatened and will use repression. If there are unexpected events, the introduction of new strategies or unexpectedly high levels of involvement among protesters, the greater the perceived threat (Davenport 2000: 3–5).

If the political leaders of a state are able to maintain control of the military and the police, then the government can likely suppress any social movement if it is willing to apply that much force. Put another way, there is generally a major imbalance in power between the state and the movement. Public opinion and possible disagreements among the elite may influence the extent of repression. While repression can certainly weaken protest, it is possible that it may backfire and anger and outrage participants and observers so that the protest is accelerated (Goodwin and Jasper 2003: 268). Studies show that, when facing repression, dissidents have run away, fought harder, or simply done nothing. Dissent increases the likelihood of state coercion (Davenport 2000: vii–viii). As Davenport (2005) points out, mobilization and repression have very broad-ranging implications on citizens' lives.

TEXTBOX 8.2

Why Social Movements Matter

One of the most difficult tasks for social movement theorists is identifying how social movements actually make a difference and how they create social change. In general, there are three areas of agreement about how social movements make a difference. Social movements can influence political, cultural, and social changes. Political changes include gaining (a) acceptance (i.e., recognition by formal political bodies, representation in decision-making processes) and/or (b) new advantages (i.e., ability to set/influence political agenda, influence public policy, or influence long-term systemic change [Gamson 1975, 1990]). Cultural changes include influencing (a) attitudes, opinions, and values of the general public, (b) systems of knowledge or traditions (Earl 2000, 2004), or (c) the emergence of collective identities (Polletta and Jasper 2001). Finally, social changes include influencing (a) an individual social movement participant (i.e., shaping their life path, occupation, political involvement) or the life course patterns of large blocks of people (e.g., influence of the 1960s on the life chances and life goals of the Baby Boomers [Giugni 2004]) and (b) changes in social networks and the flow of social capital (Diani 1997).

To demonstrate how social movements matter, let us examine the case of three localized "smart growth" movements. First, in 2003 in Ames, Iowa, a group of local citizens upset with a proposal for a new mall formed an SMO called the Ames Smart Growth Alliance (ASGA). The group led the charge against the proposed development and promoted planned growth that balanced economic, social, and environmental concerns. In 2005 in Brunswick, New York, after the local newspaper ran an article about a proposal for a new Wal-Mart Superstore and after learning about the proposal of four large residential developments, seventeen people formed Brunswick Smart Growth (BSG). BSG became the lead organization against the various proposals by voicing concern over the adverse effect these developments would have on the "town's rural character." Finally, in 2001 in Centreville, Maryland, a local developer proposed the development of thirty condominiums on land at the headwaters of the Corsica River referred to as the "Wharf" property. Approximately sixty local area residents came together to speak out against the proposal and formed the Citizens for Greater Centreville (CGC).

One thing these three local social movements had in common was that in some way or another they all "mattered." For example, all three social movements experienced some sort of political success. The combination of the three cases suggests that a strong and vibrant social movement organization with a clear identification of the problem and possible solution is important for political success. In addition, the sociopolitical environment must be favorable toward the movement; that is, there must be (1) a period of crisis such as the experience of rapid development or environmental degradation, (2) open POSs such as responsive public officials, favorable state laws, nonpartisan elections, sympathetic elites, and instability in local leadership alignments, and (3) public opinion must be either supportive or at least ambiguous toward the issue. In the case of CGC, the group's message was simply "Don't Develop the Wharf." The group argued to turn the property into a public space for all citizens to use to enjoy the waterfront. CGC was well organized with committed leadership and a clear division of labor and was able to raise a substantial amount of money. In addition, CGC had very favorable POSs. First, Maryland state laws are restrictive of development along the Chesapeake Bay and its tributaries. Second, the town had just recently dealt with rapid residential development that nearly doubled the city population. The influx of people due to this new development strained the city's sewer treatment plant resulting in the dumping of raw sewage into the Corsica River—the discovery of which led to regional and national media attention, criminal investigation, and state and federal sanctions. Finally, CGC had a number of sympathetic individuals on the local town council as well as the town's planning commission. The combination of these social movement controlled and environmental factors afforded CGC and its members the opportunity to influence public policy and sway the city's planning agenda, gain important representation in decision-making bodies, and most importantly, stop the proposed development and force the county to buy the land to develop as a public park.

Second, as noted before, social movements can influence cultural changes. Typically, this refers to changes in attitudes, values, and opinions; the emergence of new collective identities; or changes to tradition or knowledge. Here we will only explore collective identity. Of the three social movements, only BSG displayed a unique and cohesive collective identity. The members of BSG and supporters of the movement had developed a distinct smart growth identity by emphasizing activism and political involvement. This identity was embraced by movement supporters and was demonized by movement antagonists. Cultural outcomes related to collective identity appeared to be the result of lack of POSs, highly organized SMO, and a clear message. From the very beginning, BSG pushed vigorously for major reform and to overhaul the town's comprehensive plan in hope of emphasizing "appropriate" and "affordable" growth options for the town. Movement supporters were met with stiff opposition at nearly every turn. First, none of the town board members were sympathetic toward the goals of the movement; in fact, most were outright hostile. Also, BSG maintained a devoted group of core activists, regular meetings, a clear division of labor, and organized campaign efforts. And, from the outset, BSG was fighting the proposed developments on the grounds that the cumulative effects of the projects threatened the town's "rural character" and the only plausible and equitable solution was to reform the town's comprehensive plan policy. The group's clear goals and committed members helped attract participants, and the adversarial political environment posed many unique and difficult challenges for BSG. The combination of these factors provided a situation where group members found support and pride in their efforts and threat and confrontation within the town political structure culminated in a strong sense of collective identity.

Finally, regarding social changes, ASGA was very successful. Here we will focus solely on changes in social capital, that is, the ability to develop and foster new partnerships based on trust and open communication with local leaders and organizations. In the case of ASGA, the group became an important "go to" organization for questions about growth and development within the local community and was actively sought out by other nonprofit and activist groups for input and guidance on local issues. Equally as important, a number of the movement's leaders were appointed or asked to take up other leadership positions in the local community. ASGA's success can be attributed to a combination of factors including viability of the organization, high levels of sustained participation by movement supporters, and regular coverage by the local media. Like BSG, ASGA was a fairly active organization with a clear division of labor, regular group activity, and a committed core of individuals. The broader movement was also able to quickly and effectively mobilize supporters for protests, letter-writing campaigns, city council meetings, and so on. Last, but not least, ASGA was regularly in the local newspaper—this included scores of letters to the editors, guest editorials, and quotes from and about the organization. This is noteworthy because the concerns of the ASGA and movement leaders were regularly included in the pages of the local newspaper. This coverage by the media helped legitimize the group and its concerns.

GLOBALIZATION AND TRANSNATIONAL MOVEMENTS

We are now becoming more and more aware of the idea of global interdependence and that "social action in a given time and place is increasingly conditioned by social actions in very distant places" (della Porta and Kriesi 1999: 3). Globalization has resulted in cross-national similarities in protest mobilization. There is diffusion, or spreading, of direct interpersonal and interorganizational ties among movements and participants and a diffusion of information about movements from the mass media. For example, the antiapartheid movement outside of South Africa called for a boycott of South African products, and this mobilization influenced the political relationships between South Africa and various Western nations.

Wallerstein (2004: 91) invented the term *antisystemic movements* to bring together the two concepts of social movements and national movements. Both these types of movements have been formed because of the development of the capitalist world system and the evils of capitalism. They resist the existing modern world system and include the possibility of overthrowing the system. Two major antisystemic movements have fundamentally changed politics and society. The first was the world protest of 1848 supported initially by urban workers in France that spread to rebellions in another ten nations (Robbins 2008; Wallerstein 2004). The second major transnational movement was that of 1968 and was characterized in the United States by the student protests over the Vietnam War, university demonstrations including the killing of students at Kent State and Jackson State by the National Guard, and the protests at the Democratic National Convention in Chicago where demonstrators were beaten and arrested by police. Elsewhere uprisings occurred, even in places as diverse as France, Italy, Czechoslovakia, Japan, and Mexico (Robbins 2008).

According to Wallerstein (2004: 87) the attack on the World Trade Center in New York and the Pentagon in Washington DC on September 11, 2001, signaled a turning point in political alignments as well as illustrated by world political chaos. Those on the right supported the American display of military strength and attempted to undo some of the changes in the areas of race and sexuality that were associated with the world movement of 1968. For Wallerstein the system is in crisis with many acts of violence and yet it also functions in its customary pattern. He maintains that across the world people "are more aware, more willing to struggle for their rights, more skeptical about the rhetoric of the powerful" (Wallerstein 2004: 89). The growth of transnational movements has been due, at least in part, to the increase in problems that transcend national borders including large-scale pollution and transnational migration (Rucht 1999).

Police and demonstrators are in a melee near the Conrad Hilton Hotel on Chicago's Michigan Avenue on August 28, 1968, during the Democratic National Convention. Student protests at the Democratic National Convention resulted in the arrests of many demonstrators.

Credit: © Bettmann/CORBIS

Rucht (1999) identifies several key problems that transnational movements may face. In spite of the fact that modern communications technology makes it easier for movement participants to contact each other and share knowledge, it may be increasingly difficult to achieve coordination and agreement of these groups and "if too many concerns and actors compete with each other the audience becomes highly selective, or even bored" (217). As these organizations become more institutionalized and professionalized, they may become more bureaucratized and more interested in maintaining the organization rather than making major transnational changes. In other contexts, the movement organizations may overestimate how successful they can be and ultimately disappoint themselves and their sympathizers. There is a clear need for more research to determine the impact of various transnational movements on the world.

CONCLUSION: SOCIAL MOVEMENTS AS PART OF POLITICAL SOCIOLOGY

McAdam (2001) believes that the way sociologists study politics has reinforced the distinction between contentious politics (e.g., social movements, revolutions, and peasant rebellions) and the more routine forms of institutionalized politics (e.g., voting, party politics, lobbying) in part because most scholars concentrate their work on only one of these two areas. He finds this both "unfortunate and analytically untenable" (230) because it downplays the links between the two:

> For it tends to obscure the dynamic and reciprocal relationships that almost always characterizes the link between routine political processes and episodes of contention. The point is, the latter always occur in an institutionalized political context and typically are set in motion by more routine, political processes. In turn, these episodes have the potential to reshape the formal systems of politics in which they are embedded. (230)

In reality, social movement scholars have concentrated on studying insurgents, and mainstream political sociologists have concentrated on the state. We agree with McAdam that political sociologists need to explore the relationships between the two topics in order to integrate social movements with studies of the state.

In their article, "Challengers and States: Toward a Political Sociology of Social Movements," Amenta et al. (2002: 47) also find the disconnect between the mainstream political sociologists studying the state, voting, and so on, and the typical social movement theorist who "rarely relies on political sociological insights into states." Put another way, much of the social movements' literature focuses on political opportunity rather than considering the state. Drawing on McAdam, Amenta et al. consider various dimensions of political opportunity that influence movements such as how open or closed the institutionalized political system is, the stability of elite alignments, the presence of elite allies, and the state's capacity and propensity for repression. For example, states that are not democratic, have divisions among elites, and experience a decline in their repressive capacity could well encourage revolutionary movements.

While states and the political opportunities associated with states influence social movements, social movements also influence states. The challenging movement may gain increased influence over the political process, such as winning the right to vote for minorities, women, or the disenfranchised poor. The challenger can obtain numerous benefits that could range "from greater respect through official governmental representations to having the group represented by the challenger recognized in state policies" (Amenta et al. 2002: 74). Labor struggled for the rights to form unions and bargain collectively. At another level, activists pushed the U.S. Census

Bureau to allow for more than one category on racial-background questions. In general Amenta et al. argue that researchers in this area need to focus more on movements as challengers trying to gain collective goods through states.

Oliver et al. (2003: 213–214) point out that since the 1960s, protest can be seen as an important addition to democratic politics and an important influence in the transition from authoritarian to democratic nation-states. The study of social movements has significant ties to political sociology as well as cultural sociology, social psychology, and organizational sociology. Those who study social movements view it as "politics by other means" and recognize that noninstitutional and institutional politics are intertwined and interdependent.

In Chapter 1 we drew on Coser's definition of political sociology as centered around the two key concepts of power and conflict. We also discussed how the state is the legitimate source of power and how at times it is willing to use coercion with or without force to control protest. It was also suggested that political sociologists should examine the role of rule breakers more thoroughly. These emphases on coercion, dominance, protest, conflict, and rule-breaking help link social movements and more broadly contentious politics to the state and thus to political sociology. In addition, if as Weber (1946: 78) argues, politics "means striving to share power or striving to influence the distribution of power, either among states or among groups within a state" then social movements and their organizations clearly should be an integral part of what political sociologists study.

As Jenkins and Form (2005: 322) suggest "bringing social movements into the core of political sociology promotes a better understanding of the processes that generate change." We argue that the subarea of social movements is a key component of political sociology itself, just like elections, political culture, political socialization, and so on. Politics involves the study of power, and social movements attempt to gain power and to influence the state, sometimes using protest and violence as mechanisms of influence just as voters go to the polling places and deposit ballots in ballot boxes.

Endnotes

1. Brandon Hofstedt is Assistant Professor of Sustainable Community Development at Northland College.
2. Note this is what we refer to as *collective action frames,* specifically *motivational frames.*
3. See earlier description for a more thorough discussion of collective action frames.

References

Alford, Robert R. and Roger Friedland. 1985. *Powers of Theory: Capitalism, the State, and Democracy.* Cambridge, NY: Cambridge University Press.

Amenta, Edwin and Yvonne Zylan. 1991. "It Happened Here: Political Opportunity, the New Institutionalism, and the Townsend Movement." *American Sociological Review* 56: 250–265.

Amenta, Edwin, Bruce G. Carruthers, and Yvonne Zylan. 1992. "A Hero for the Aged? The Townsend Movements, the Political Mediation Model, and U.S. Old-Age Policy, 1934–1950." *American Journal of Sociology* 98(2): 308–339.

Amenta, Edwin, Neal Caren, Tina Fetner, and Michael P. Young. 2002. "Challengers and States: Toward a Political Sociology of Social Movements." Pp. 47–84 in *Sociological Views on Political Participation in the 21st Century,* volume 10, *Research in Political Sociology,* edited by Betty A. Dobratz, Timothy Buzzell, and Lisa K. Waldner. Amsterdam: Elsevier (JAI).

Aminzade, Ron and Doug McAdam. 2001. "Emotions and Contentious Politics." Pp. 14–50 in *Silence and Voice in the Study of Contentious Politics,* edited by R. Aminzade, J. Goldstone, D. McAdam, E. Perry,

W. Sewell, Jr., S. Tarrow, and C. Tilly. Cambridge: Cambridge University Press.

Andrews, Kenneth T. 1997. "The Impacts of Social Movements on the Political Process: The Civil Rights Movement and Black Electoral Politics in Mississippi." *American Sociological Review* 62: 800–819.

Benford, Robert D. 1993. "Frame Disputes within the Nuclear Disarmament Movement." *Social Forces* 71: 677–701.

_____. 1997. "An Insider's Critique of the Social Movement Framing Perspective." *Sociological Inquiry* 67: 409–430.

Benford, Robert D. and David A. Snow. 2000. "Framing Processes and Social Movements: An Overview and Assessment." *Annual Review of* Sociology 26: 611–639.

Berbrier, Mitch. 1998. "'Half the Battle': Cultural Resonance, Framing Processes, and Ethnic Affectations in Contemporary White Separatist Rhetoric." *Social Problems* 45: 431–450.

Best, Shaun. 2002. *Introduction to Politics and Society*. London: Sage Publications.

Buechler, Steven M. 1995. "New Social Movement Theories." *Sociological Quarterly* 36: 441–464.

_____. 2002. "Toward a Structural Approach to Social Movements." Pp. 1–45 in *Sociological Views on Political Participation in the 21st Century*, volume 10, *Research in Political Sociology*, edited by Betty A. Dobratz, Timothy Buzzell, and Lisa K. Waldner. Amsterdam: Elsevier (JAI).

Burstein, Paul, Rachel L. Einwohner, and Jocelyn A. Hollander. 1995. "The Success of Political Movements." Pp. 275–295 in *The Politics of Social Protest*, edited by J. Craig Jenkins and Bert Klandermans. Minneapolis: University of Minnesota Press.

Calhoun, Craig. 2000. "'New Social Movements' of the Early Nineteenth Century." Pp. 129–154 in *Readings in Contemporary Political Sociology*, edited by Kate Nash. Malden, MA: Blackwell.

Castells, Manual. 1977. *The Urban Question*. London: Edward V. Arnold.

_____. 1983. *The City and the Grassroots*. Berkeley: University of California Press.

Clemens, Elisabeth. 1993. "Organizational Repertoires and Institutional Change: Women's Groups and the Transformation of U.S. Politics, 1890–1920." *American Journal of Sociology* 98(4): 755–798.

Cress, Daniel M. and David A. Snow. 1996. "Mobilization at the Margins: Resources, Benefactors, and the Viability of Homeless Social Movement Organizations." *American Sociological Review* 61: 1089–1109.

_____. 2000. "The Outcomes of Homeless Mobilization: The Influence of Organization, Disruption, Political Mediation, and Framing." *American Journal of Sociology* 105(4): 1063–1104.

Davenport, Christian. 2000. "Introduction." Pp. 1–24 in *Paths to State Repression*, edited by Christian Davenport. Oxford, UK: Rowman and Littlefield.

_____. 2005. "Introduction: Repression and Mobilization: Insights from Political Science and Sociology." Pp. vii–xii in *Repression and Mobilization*, edited by C. Davenport, H. Johnston, and C. Mueller. Minneapolis: University of Minnesota Press.

della Porta, Donatella (editor). 1992. *Social Movements and Violence*. CT: JAI Press.

della Porta, Donatella and Mario Diani. 2006. *Social Movements*. 2nd Edition. Malden, MA: Blackwell.

della Porta, Donatella and Hanspeter Kriesi. 1999. "Social Movements in a Globalizing World: An Introduction." Pp. 3–22 in *Social Movements in a Globalizing World*, edited by Donatella della Porta, H. Kriesi, and D. Rucht. New York: St. Martin's Press.

Diani, Mario. 1997. "Social Movements and Social Capital: A Network Perspective on Movement Outcomes." *Mobilization* 2(2): 129–147.

_____. 2000. "The Concept of Social Movement." Pp. 155–176 in *Readings in Contemporary Political Sociology*, edited by Kate Nash. Malden, MA: Blackwell.

Dobratz, Betty A. and Stephanie Shanks-Meile. 2006. "The Strategy of White Separatism." *Journal of Political and Military Sociology* 34: 49–79.

Dowding, Keith. 2001. "Rational Choice Approaches to Analyzing Power." Pp. 29–39 in *The Blackwell Companion to Political Sociology*, edited by Kate Nash and Alan Scott. Malden, MA: Blackwell.

Earl, Jennifer. 2000. "Methods, Movements, and Outcomes: Methodological Difficulties in the Study of Extra-Movement Outcomes." Pp. 3–25 in *Research in Social Movements, Conflicts, and Change*, volume 22, edited by Patrick Coy. Stamford, CT: JAI Press Inc.

_____. 2004. "The Cultural Consequences of Social Movements." Pp. 508–530 in *The Blackwell Companion to Social Movements*, edited by David A. Snow, Sarah A. Soule, and Hanspeter Kriesi. Malden, MA: Blackwell Publishing.

_____. 2006. "Introduction: Repression and the Social Control of Protest." *Mobilization* 11: 129–143.

Einwohner, Rachel. 2003. "Opportunity, Honor, and Action in the Warsaw Ghetto Uprising of 1943." *American Journal of Sociology* 109(3): 650–675.

Eisinger, Peter K. 1973. "The Conditions of Protest Behavior in American Cities." *American Political Science Review* 67: 11–28.

Flam, Helena. 2005. "Emotions' Map: A Research Agenda." Pp. 19–40 in *Emotions and Social Movements*, edited by Helena Flam and Debra King. London: Routledge.

Flam, Helena with Debra King. 2005. "Introduction." Pp. 1–18 in *Emotions and Social Movements*, edited by Helena Flam and Debra King. London: Routledge.

Gamson, William A. 1975. *The Strategy of Social Protest*. 1st Edition. Homewood, IL: Dorsey Press.

_____. 1990. *The Strategy of Social Protest*. 2nd Edition. Belmont, CA: Wadsworth.

_____. 1992. *Talking Politics*. Cambridge: Cambridge University Press.

Gamson, William A. and David S. Meyer. 1996. "Framing Political Opportunity." Pp. 275–290 in *Comparative Perspectives on Social Movements: Political Opportunities, Mobilizing Structures and Cultural Framings*, edited by Doug McAdam, John D. McCarthy, and Mayer Zald. Cambridge: Cambridge University Press.

Ganz, Marshall. 2000. "Resources and Resourcefulness: Strategic Capacity in the Unionization of California Agriculture, 1959–1966." *American Journal of Sociology* 105(4): 1003–1062.

Giugni, Marco. 1999. "Introduction: How Social Movements Matter." Pp. xiii–xxxiii in *How Social Movements Matter*, edited by Marco Giugni, Doug McAdam, and Charles Tilly. Minneapolis: University of Minnesota Press.

_____. 2004. "Personal and Biographical Consequences." Pp. 489–507 in *The Blackwell Companion to Social Movements*, edited by David A. Snow, Sarah A. Soule, and Hanspeter Kriesi. Malden, MA: Blackwell Publishing.

Goldstone, Jack A. and Charles Tilly. 2001. "Threat (and Opportunity): Popular Action and State Response in the Dynamics of Contentious Action." Pp. 179–194 in *Silence and Voice in the Study of Contentious Politics*, edited by Ronald R. Aminzade et al. Cambridge: Cambridge University Press.

Goodwin, Jeff and James M. Jasper. 2003. *The Social Movement Reader: Cases and Concepts*. Malden, MA: Blackwell.

Goodwin, Jeff, James M. Jasper, and Francesca Polletta. 2001. "Why Emotions Matter." Pp. 1–24 in *Passionate Politics: Emotions and Social Movements*, edited by Jeff Goodwin, James Jasper, and Francesca Polletta. Chicago: University of Chicago Press.

Gould, Roger V. 1991. "Multiple Networks and Mobilization in the Paris Commune, 1871." *American Sociological Review* 56: 716–729.

Gurr, Ted Robert. 1989. "The History of Protest, Rebellion, and Reform in America." Pp. 11–22 in *Violence in America: Protest, Rebellion, Reform*, volume 2, edited by Ted Robert Gurr. Newbury Park, CA: Sage.

Halebsky, Stephen. 2006. "Explaining the Outcomes of Antisuperstore Movements: A Comparative Analysis of Six Communities." *Mobilization: An International Journal* 11: 443–460.

Hamel, Pierre and Louis Maheu. 2001. "Beyond New Social Movements." Pp. 261–270 in *The Blackwell Companion to Political Sociology*, edited by Kate Nash and Alan Scott. Malden, MA: Blackwell.

Hunt, Scott A., Robert Benford, and David Snow. 1993. "Identity Fields: Framing Processes and the Social Construction of Movement Identities." Paper presented at Midwest Sociological Society, Chicago. (Published 1994 Pp. 185–208 in *New Social Movements: From Ideology to Identity*, edited by Enrique Larana, Hank Johnston, and Joseph R. Gusfield. Philadelphia: Temple.)

Jasper, James M. 1998. "The Emotions of Protest: Affective and Reactive Emotions in and around Social Movements." *Sociological Forum* 13: 397–424.

_____. 2003. "The Emotions of Protest." Pp. 153–162 in *The Social Movements Reader*, edited by Jeff Goodwin and James M. Jasper. Malden, MA: Blackwell.

Jenkins, J. Craig and William Form. 2005. "Social Movements and Social change." Pp. 331–349 in *The Handbook of Political Sociology*, edited by Thomas Janoski, Robert Alford, Alexander Hicks, and Mildred A. Schwartz. Cambridge: Cambridge University Press.

Jenkins, J. Craig and Esther E. Gottlieb. 2007. "Identity Conflicts and Their Regulation." Pp. 1–21 in *Identity Conflicts: Can Violence be Regulated?*, edited by J. Craig Jenkins and Esther Gottlieb. New Brunswick, NJ: Transaction Publishers.

Jenkins, J. Craig, David Jacobs, and Jon Agnone. 2003. "Political Opportunities and African-American Protests, 1948–1997." *American Journal of Sociology* 109: 277–303.

Jenkins, J. Craig and Charles Perrow. 1977. "Insurgency of the Powerless: Farm Worker Movements (1946–1972)." *American Sociological Review* 42: 249–268.

Johnston, Hank, Enrique Larana, and Joseph R. Gusfield. 1994. "Identities, Grievances, and New Social Movements." Pp. 3–35 in *New Social Movements: From Ideology to Identity*, edited by Enrique Larana, Hank Johnston, and Joseph R. Gusfield. Philadelphia: Temple.

_____. 1997. "Identities, Grievances, and New Social Movements." Pp. 274–295 in *Social Movements: Perspectives and Issues*, edited by Steven M. Buechler and F. Kurt Cylke, Jr. Mountain View, CA: Mayfield.

Karp, David, William C. Yoels, and Barbara Vann. 2004. *Sociology in Everyday Life*. Long Grove, IL: Waveland Press.

King, Martin Luther, Jr. 1963. Excerpt from Martin Luther King's "I Have a Dream Speech." http://infoplease.com/ipa/A0874987.html.

Kitschelt, Herbert P. 1986. "Political Opportunity Structures and Political Protest: Anti-Nuclear

Movements in Four Democracies." *British Journal of Political Science* 16(1): 57–85.

Klandermans, Bert. 1991. "The Peace Movement and Social Movement Theory." Pp. 1–39 in *International Social Movement Research*, volume 3. Greenwich, CT: JAI.

Kornhauser, William. 1959. *The Politics of Mass Society.* Glencoe, IL: Free Press.

Kurzman, Charles. 1996. "Structural Opportunity and Perceived Opportunity in Social-Movement Theory: The Iranian Revolution of 1979." *American Sociological Review* 61: 153–170.

Marx, Gary T. and Douglas McAdam. 1994. *Collective Behavior and Social Movements: Process and Structure.* Englewood Cliffs, NJ: Prentice Hall.

McAdam, Doug. 1982. *Political Process and the Development of Black Insurgency 1930–1970.* 1st Edition. Chicago: University of Chicago.

——. 1983. "Tactical Innovation and the Pace of Insurgency." *American Sociological Review* 48: 735–754.

——. 1988. "Micromobilization Contexts and Recruitment to Activism." Pp. 125–154 in *International Social Movement Research*, volume 1, edited by B. Klandermans, H. Kriesi, and S. Tarrow. Greenwich, CT: JAI.

——. 1994. "Culture and Social Movements." Pp. 36–57 in *New Social Movements*, edited by Enrique Larana, Hank Johnston, and Joseph R. Gusfield. Philadelphia: Temple.

——. 1999. *Political Process and the Development of Black Insurgency 1930–1970.* 2nd Edition. Chicago: University of Chicago.

——. 2001. "Harmonizing the Voices: Thematic Continuity across the Chapters." Pp. 222–240 in *Silence and Voice in the Study of Contentious Politics*, edited by R. Aminzade, J. Goldstone, D. McAdam, E. Perry, W. Sewell, Jr., S. Tarrow, and C. Tilly. Cambridge: Cambridge University Press.

McAdam, Doug, John D. McCarthy, and Mayer N. Zald. 1996. *Comparative Perspectives on Social Movements.* New York: Cambridge University Press.

McCarthy, John D. 1987. "Pro-Life and Pro-Choice Mobilization: Infrastructure Deficits and New Technologies." Pp. 49–66 in *Social Movements in an Organizational Society*, edited by Mayer N. Zald and John D. McCarthy. New Brunswick, NJ: Transaction.

McCarthy, John D. and Mayer N. Zald. 1973. *The Trend of Social Movements in America: Professionalization and Resource Mobilization.* Morristown, NJ: General Learning Press.

——. 1977. "Resource Mobilization and Social Movements: A Partial Theory." *American Journal of Sociology* 82(6): 1212–1241.

——. 1997. "Resource Mobilization and Social Movements." Pp. 149–172 in *Social Movements: Perspectives and Issues*, edited by Steven M. Buechler and F. Kurt Cylke, Jr. Mountain View, CA: Mayfield.

Meyer, David S. and Kelsy Kretschmer. 2007. "Social Movements." Pp. 540–548 in *21st Century Sociology: A Reference Handbook*, edited by Clifton Bryant and Dennis L. Peck. Thousand Oaks: Sage.

Meyer, David S. and Debra C. Minkoff. 2004. "Conceptualizing Political Opportunity." *Social Forces* 82: 1457–1492.

Meyer, David S. and Suzanne Staggenborg. 1996. "Movements, Countermovements, and the Structure of Political Opportunity." *American Journal of Sociology* 101: 1628–1660.

Milbrath, Lester and M. L. Goel. 1977. *Political Participation.* Chicago: Rand McNally.

Morris, Aldon D. 1981. "Black Southern Student Sit-in Movement: An Analysis of Internal Organization." *American Sociological Review* 46: 744–767.

Nash, Kate (editor). 2000. *Readings in Contemporary Political Sociology.* Oxford: Blackwell.

Oberschall, Anthony. 1973. *Social Conflict and Social Movements.* Englewood Cliffs, NJ: Prentice-Hall.

Oliver, Pamela E., Jorge Cadena-Roa, and Kelley D. Strawn. 2003. "Emerging Trends in the Study of Protest and Social Movements." Pp. 213–244 in *Political Sociology for the 21st Century*, volume 12, *Research in Political Sociology*, edited by Betty A. Dobratz, Lisa K. Waldner, and Timothy Buzzell. Amsterdam: Elsevier (JAI).

Olson, Mancur, Jr. 1965. *The Logic of Collective Action.* Cambridge, MA: Harvard University Press.

Passy, Florence. 2001. "Socialization, Connection, and the Structure/Agency Gap." *Mobilization* 6: 173–192.

Petras, James and Maurice Zeitlin. 1967. "Miners and Agrarian Radicalism." *American Sociological Review* 32: 578–586.

Pichardo, Nelson. 1997. "New Social Movements: A Critical Review." *Annual Review of Sociology* 23: 411–430.

Piven, Frances Fox and Richard A. Cloward. 1977. *Poor People's Movements.* New York: Vintage Books.

Polletta, Francesca and James M. Jasper. 2001. "Collective Identity and Social Movements." *Annual Review of Sociology* 27: 283–305.

Robbins, Richard H. 2008. *Global Problems and the Culture of Capitalism.* Boston: Pearson.

Roscigno, V. J. and W. F. Danaher. 2001. "Media and Mobilization: The Case of Radio and Southern Textile Worker Insurgency, 1929 to 1934." *American Sociological Review* 66(1): 21–48.

Rucht, Dieter. 1999. "The Transnationalization of Social Movements." Pp. 206–222 in *Social Movements in a Globalizing World*, edited by Donatella della Porta, H. Kriesi, and D. Rucht. New York: St. Martin's Press.

Schwarzmantel, John. 2001. "Nationalism and Fragmentation Since 1989." Pp. 386–395 in *The Blackwell Companion to Political Sociology*, edited by Kate Nash and Alan Scott. Malden, MA: Blackwell.

Smelser, Neil J. 1962. *Theory of Collective Behavior.* New York: Free Press.

Snow, David A. and Robert D. Benford. 1988. "Ideology, Frame Resonance, and Participant Mobilization." *International Social Movement Research* 1: 197–217.

_____. 1992. "Master Frames and Cycles of Protest." Pp. 133–155 in *Frontiers in Social Movement Theory*, edited by Aldon D. Morris and Carol McClurg Mueller. New Haven, CT: Yale University Press.

Snow, David A., E. Burke Rochford, Jr., Steven K. Worden, and Robert D. Benford. 1986. "Frame Alignment Processes, Micromobilization, and Movement Participation." *American Sociological Review* 51: 464–481.

Snow, David A., Louis A. Zurcher, Jr., and Sheldon Ekland-Olson. 1980. "Social Networks and Social Movements: A Microstructural Approach to Differential Recruitment." *American Sociological Review* 45: 787–801.

Taylor, Verta and Nancy E. Whittier. 1995. "Collective Identity in Social Movement Communities." Pp. 344–357 in *American Society and Politics*, edited by Theda Skocpol and J. L. Campbell. New York: McGraw-Hill.

Tilly, Charles. 1978. *From Mobilization to Revolution.* Reading, MA: Addison-Wesley.

Tilly, Charles and Sidney Tarrow. 2007. *Contentious Politics.* Boulder, CO: Paradigm Publishers.

Touraine, Alain. 1977. *The Self-Production of Society.* Chicago: University of Chicago Press.

_____. 1981. *The Voice and the Eye: An Analysis of Social Movements.* Cambridge: Cambridge University Press.

_____. 1985. "An Introduction to the Study of Social Movements." *Social Research* 52(4): 749–787.

Useem, Bert. 1985. "Disorganization and the New Mexico Prison Riot of 1980." *American Sociological Review* 50: 667–688.

Walder, Andrew. 2006. "Ambiguity and Choice in Political Movements." *American Journal of Sociology* 112: 710–750.

Wallerstein, Immanuel. 2004. *World-Systems Analysis.* Durham, NC: Duke University Press.

Weber, Max. 1946. "Politics as a Vocation." Pp. 77–81 in *From Max Weber*, edited by H. H. Gerth and C. Wright Mills. New York: Oxford.

Zald, Mayer N. 1996. "Culture, Ideology, and Strategic Framing." Pp. 261–274 in *Comparative Perspectives on Social Movements*, edited by Doug McAdam, John D. McCarthy, and Mayer N. Zald. Cambridge: Cambridge University Press.

Zuo, Jiping and Robert D. Benford. 1995. "Mobilization Processes and the 1989 Chinese Democracy Movement." *The Sociological Quarterly* 36(1): 131–156.

Violence and Terrorism

The study of political violence falls within the sphere of political sociology yet the study of war (Turner 2007), terrorism, and other political violence "remains compartmentalized and incomplete" (Hooks and Rice 2005: 567), despite ongoing global bloodshed. In the case of war, scholars argue that this blind spot results from classical social thought obscuring war (Hooks and McLauchlan 1992b) and a failure to integrate war into social science theory (Hooks and McLauchlan 1992a) rather than a failure of researchers to investigate. In the case of terrorism and other violence, the failure results from focusing on the domestic rather than the international arena in which nation-states operate (Hooks and Rice 2005). Exclusively focusing on "the state" as the unit of analysis potentially inhibits sociologists from contributing to the discussion and possible resolution of some of the most important issues of the twentieth and twenty-first centuries including human rights abuses, genocide, and military atrocities (Hooks and Rice 2005) as well as the role of warfare in bringing about globalization (Black 1998). Notable exceptions to this domestic bias are globalization scholars and World Systems (WS) theorists.

Scott (2004) disagrees somewhat with Hooks and McLauchlan (1992b), and calls the sociological neglect of war paradoxical given the degree of war making over the twentieth century and the importance of war in early sociological thought, including Marx's ideas regarding the importance of war for accumulating capital and Weber's definition of state that emphasizes a monopoly over the use of violence. Contemporary sociologists have not contributed to these discussions at the same level as political scientists and international relations specialists (Senechal de la Roche 2004; Tiryakian 2005), yet an essential requisite for the continuing relevance of political sociology is coming to terms with the importance of war making and militarism (Hooks and Rice 2005). In this chapter we provide an overview of some of the most important insights offered by political sociologists and other social scientists on political violence including genocide, war, terrorism, and promising future empirical and theoretical trends.

POLITICAL USES OF HATE

Hatred of other groups serves a myriad of political purposes, including consolidating power, claims-making, deflecting blame, and justifying a leader's self-interest (Levin and Rabrenovic 2004). Power is consolidated when leaders eliminate political rivals from either their inner circle or a challenger group. Sometimes nationalistic groups use cultural ideas of superiority to rally members of an ethnic group behind them to claim territories (e.g., Hitler's 1938 annexation of the Sudetenland). Finger-pointing by leaders to deflect attention away from the causes of economic or political turmoil is also a common political strategy as illustrated by Hitler's successful scapegoating of Jews. Finally, some leaders use hate to appear more politically relevant. The treatment of minority groups varies and can include repression, oppression, or genocide.

GENOCIDE

Over 1 million Armenians, 6 million Jews, 1 million Tutsis and moderate Hutus, 10,000 ethnic Albanians, almost 2 million Cambodians, and millions and millions under Stalin were just *some of the victims* of genocide from the twentieth century (Jones 2006). We begin the twenty-first century with the ongoing violence in the Darfur region of Sudan that has claimed the lives of hundreds of thousands and has displaced many more (Genocide Intervention Network 2007). Genocide is a form of political violence directed by the state against its own citizens and is a type of state terrorism as it "must be conducted with the approval of, if not direct intervention by, the state apparatus" (Horowitz 2002: 14). State terrorism is a broader topic and will be discussed in subsequent sections of this chapter.

Defining Genocide

The United Nations (UN) defines genocide as "acts committed with the intent to destroy, in whole or part, a national, ethnical, racial, or religious group" and includes murder, causing serious bodily

Skulls from a mass grave of Khmer Rouge victims in a glass memorial tower at Cheoung EK ("Killing Fields") outside Phnom Penh, Cambodia.

Credit: Photo by Alyssa Levy

or mental harm, deliberately inflicting conditions that bring about physical destruction, imposing birth prevention measures, and forcefully transferring children from one group to another (Jones 2006: 12–13). Some sociologists believe the definition of group should be expanded to include social class (Horowitz 2002). In terms of outcomes, the UN definition is less restrictive as it is not necessary to kill every member of a targeted group or to kill anyone at all (Jones 2006). Imposing birth control measures and sexual violence to discourage reproduction accentuates the vulnerability of women in these types of conflicts (Turner 2007).

An alternative definition is "a form of one-sided mass killing in which a state or other authority intends to destroy a group" (Chalk and Jonassohn 1990: 23). This definition differs in two fundamental ways. First, it leaves open the possibility of a myriad of identities that could be targeted by those practicing genocide. Second, it excludes the suppression or elimination of culture that is reflected in practices such as birth prevention measures and the transfer of children from their parents. The former argue that another term, such as "ethnocide," could be substituted for the suppression of language, religion, or culture and a definition that enhances conceptual clarity is needed for research and theory development. On the other hand, it can be argued that the impact of genocide is much greater than the loss of life. In "I am Not a Witness," Native American poet Deborah Miranda (1999: 73) discusses the eradication of her ancestors from Southern California. Lines such as "I found photographs of bedrock slabs pocked by hundreds of acorn grinding holes, but the holes are empty, the stone pestles that would curve to my grip lie dead behind museum glass" and "Some of our bones rest in 4000 graves out back behind the mission" reveal both the cultural and human loss caused by genocide.

Ethnic cleansing is a related term that has been used to describe events in Darfur, Bosnia-Herzegovina, and Kosovo (Jones 2006). Ethnic cleansing is a strategy that includes killing males of fighting age, expelling women, children, and older men into a neighboring territory, and instilling hate and fear to ensure that the area remains free of members from the targeted group. Ethnic cleansing is but one of many genocidal strategies demonstrated throughout human history.

There are political ramifications from labeling killing as genocide. In 2007 the Turkish government recalled its ambassador from Washington to protest a nonbinding resolution passed by the U.S. House of Representatives' Foreign Relations panel that declared the killing of Armenians by Ottoman Turks (1915–1917) as genocide. Passing the resolution was risky given the "war on terror" with 70 percent of air cargo destined for Iraq including fuel, water, and other supplies going through Turkey ("Turkey's Ambassador in U.S. Ordered Home" 2007).

Conditions for Genocide

In the film, *Hotel Rwanda,* Hutu extremist groups refer to the Tutsis as cockroaches. Leaders may dehumanize a group to deflect blame for societal problems. Dehumanization is part of an organized campaign that paints the targeted group as subhuman or evil. Dehumanization is less necessary when targets are not members of perpetrator society as outsiders are often viewed as inferior. Even if political leaders are successful in demonizing a group, implementing mass killings also involves both coercion and centralized control (Chalk and Jonassohn 1990).

Sociological Causes of Genocide

Modernity, ethnic conflict, the aftereffects of colonialism, and the disruption of economic and political systems that previously unified a society, albeit superficially, are potential causes of genocide. Although genocide researchers do not equally embrace all of these ideas, they provide a starting point for investigating the societal context of genocide. What is problematic is applying these ideas to a variety of social and historical contexts.

MODERNITY Zygmunt Bauman (2000) contends that four features of modernity: nationalism, scientific racism, technology, and bureaucratic rationalization are requisites of genocide. Nationalism is "an ideological movement for attaining and maintaining the autonomy, unity, and identity of a nation" (Smith 1991: 74). Nationalism can be expressed in activities as diverse as genocide in Kosovo or "silence of an American audience" when the *Star Spangled Banner* is played (Schnee 2001: 1). As noted in Chapter 2, nationalism is not inherently negative and can be a means of combating globalization (Jones 2006; Schnee 2001) by providing societies with a sense of national identity and unifying symbols. However, when national ideology is based on perceptions of group superiority, it can result in genocide and other forms of state violence.

Scientific racism is the overlay of an empirical cloak to justify old prejudices and antagonism. The "other" is seen as a virus or pathology that must be quarantined from the superior group and then removed like a diseased body organ. Scientific racism differs from "old racism" in that the justification for prejudice and discrimination is based on the so-called scientific evidence such as that used by the early twentieth-century eugenics movement. *Deadly Medicine,* published by the Holocaust Memorial Museum, is a history of the use of medicine, genetics, anthropology, and other social science disciplines to justify anti-Semitism and genocide. The use of scientific racism is alive and well with white supremacy groups using Herrnstein and Murray's book *The Bell Curve* and other scholarship to justify discrimination. Along with justification, technology and bureaucracy are also required to transform the state into an efficient killer. Bauman's (2000) analysis of the Holocaust contends that modern technology, including efficient transportation and execution equipment, was a product of industrialization and increasing bureaucracy.

A key characteristic of bureaucracy is both specialization and fragmentation of tasks. This affords those doing the killing a degree of psychological distance. "One did not commit murder per se. Rather, one operated a railroad switch, or dropped a few cyanide pellets into a shaft" (Jones 2006: 290). Jones notes two criticisms of Bauman's modernity theory: (1) there is no real substantive distinction between modern genocide that occurred during the Holocaust and premodern forms such as Genghis Khan's invading Mongrel forces and (2) the Rwanda genocide. In Rwanda, Hutus managed to kill over 1 million people in twelve weeks using guns and machetes without the benefit of a centralized bureaucracy to organize the killings or modern technology. Unlike organized bureaucratic killings, these were not impersonal, as murders were public and face to face (Jones 2006). Jones' criticism is this: If Bauman's point is that it is much easier to kill in a bureaucracy where individuals can perceive themselves as a mere "cog in the machine" and ultimately not responsible, how then could the Hutus kill much more quickly and intimately than the Nazis? Scott (2004) contends that social instability combined with weak state power results in ethnic wars that lead to genocide. In the case of the Holocaust, killing was orchestrated and controlled by the state. In the case of Rwanda, one did not need to wait for the bureaucratic memo. It was more of a free-for-all where any Hutu could grab a machete and kill using ethnic divisions as justification, and the state was powerless to intervene.

ETHNIC CONFLICT Nationalism is often related to ethnic conflict. James McKay (1982) describes a mobilization perspective that views ethnic conflict as arising from a deliberate effort to mobilize individuals around ethnic markers such as customs, language, common history, origins, and other shared symbols. Individuals in all societies practice what is called "ethnic work" (Henslin 2002), which can be as innocuous as German-Americans celebrating Oktoberfest or Mexican-Americans participating in Cinco de Mayo celebrations. When ethnic symbols are mobilized for political or economic advantage, this can lead to ethnic nationalism that, in its extreme form, can result in genocide. Ethnic nationalism is not always negative

---

TEXTBOX 9.1

Get Involved

The Genocide Intervention Network (http://www.genocideintervention.net) was started by a group of students at Swarthmore College in 2004 in response to the genocide occurring in the Darfur region. Presently this is an international network that engages in a variety of political activities including fund-raising for African peacekeepers in the region and pressuring organizations to divest any funds invested in Sudan. High school and college students may start chapters of the student arm of this group called Stand (http://www.standnow.org). There are over eight hundred campus chapters. Check if your school has a chapter or consider creating one.

Amnesty International (http://www.amnestyusa.org) has a broader focus on human rights abuse that includes advocacy against genocide and state terrorism as well as the use of the death penalty and the rights of sexual minorities (lesbians, gays, bisexuals, and transgendered) who are routinely killed in some countries.

(Kourvetaris 1997) as movements for autonomy and civil rights can be a positive force when led by those advocating for peace. A strong and autonomous state can reduce ethnic nationalism but states that are not neutral can worsen the situation by enacting policies that lead to more tension and violence (Haque 2003).

COLONIALISM   Imperial colonialism is where a core or developed state exploits a more peripheral region through extracting raw materials and/or cheap labor or subordinates an indigenous population and separates them from a ruling power for an extended period of time. Imperialistic rule involves political, economic, and cultural control. Though all types of colonialism have been linked to genocide and other types of repression, internal colonialism is considered to have the strongest tie (Jones 2006). Non-Arab Muslims in Darfur, the Chinese in Tibet, and Russians in Chechnya are considered either current or potential examples of genocide caused by imperial colonialism (Jones 2006).

WAR MAKING

Some see no distinction between war, genocide, and terrorism because all of these involve violence and are motivated by political goals. Henderson (2004) argues that it is too simplistic to state that the only difference between war and terrorism is that war claims more lives and is fought by governments. Rather, the distinction is whether the killing of civilians is a goal or an outcome. Although, civilians die as a result of war, armies generally abide by the principle of avoiding civilian targets. Terrorists see the killing of civilians as a necessary goal and this is even more the case with "new terrorism" in the age of globalization (Martin 2007).

Theoretical Views on War Making

In Chapter 2, Tilly's (1990) argument about the relationship between war making and state making was introduced. Briefly, Tilly contends that the rise of nation-states took place within two settings, "capital intensive" and "coercive intensive," that are defined in part, by the resources available for war making and the difficulty extracting those resources from local capitalists. Others have also theorized on the emergence of European states and the role of the military, including Rasler and Thompson (1989) and Porter (1994). Even though there are important differences between these three works (Kestnbaum 1995; Kestnbaum and Skocpol 1993), all

U.S. Marine Brandon Haugrud in Fallujah, Iraq (2006)

Credit: Photo courtesy of Brandon Haugrud (Lisa Waldner's son)

share a view that war making influenced the emergence and organization of the nation-state, and they use the European experience to illustrate these linkages.

Hooks and McLauchlan (1992a) offer an institutionalist view of U.S. war making (1939–1989) that emphasizes the role of both bureaucracy and technology. Two ideas are fundamental, including: (1) the military is composed of a number of bureaucracies situated within the larger state and (2) technology shapes war making. Three periods in U.S. war making (1939–1989) are identified including: (1) mass industrial warfare, (2) strategic nuclear bombing, and (3) strategic nuclear missiles. Although the type of technology defines the three phases, the key is not technology but political battles over selection that illuminates social influences on war making. Shifts between weapons or warfare modes are not determined by what is technologically possible but by political processes determining what is available for development and deployment. Each branch of the military competes with one another and with civilian agencies for resources. This competition is contextualized by both the international and the domestic political climate (Hooks and McLauchlan 1992b). Civilian agencies shape the military and vice versa. Consider the power of the military. It is not simply a matter of the state extracting resources at the behest of the military. The state, through the Pentagon, "has wielded sufficient infrastructural power to dominate scientific research and technological development and has actively intervened in the production process" (762). Civilian agencies also impact the military. For example, the geographic distribution of military bases after World War II was influenced by congressional clout (Hooks 1994). In 1992, Hooks and McLauchlan predicted that there would be difficulty in maintaining U.S. military superiority due to record trade deficits and a declining U.S. share of the world's gross domestic product. As a result, the U.S. military can no longer count on the ability to extract resources from the world's dominant economy that will rely increasingly on imported goods. This warning seems even more appropriate given recent economic problems exacerbated by globalization. What else does the future hold?

Future of War Making

Wars between nation-states and civil wars are on the decline, but nonstate actors are becoming increasingly important. International relations specialists Englehart and Kurzman (2006) offer the following reasons for a decline in intrastate and interstate war making: increased world trade; the spread of democracy; more international bodies that mediate disputes; international norms that discourage war; and a single hegemonic state military power—the United States. They also note that there are four reasons why the decline of war may fuel nonstate political violence including terrorism: downsizing of armies, liquidation of weapons, decline in foreign aid, and vulnerable security.

The downsizing of organized state armies means that there are multitudes of unemployed individuals who have the skill set and willingness to commit violence for pay. A decline in war also results in excess weapons that are at risk for being sold to terrorists. A reduction in foreign aid has weakened some governments, increasing vulnerability to challenges by local warlords. The Afghan government does not have much control over things beyond Kabul, and Yemen is a haven for terrorist groups (e.g., Al Qaeda) precisely because the government lacks strong internal control. Even for stronger states, military downsizing in the new era of "world peace" has the unintended effect of increasing vulnerability to outside challengers.

The future of war is potentially more widespread global conflict where nation-states are replaced by larger entities that engage in conflict over both territory and scarce resources (Huntington 1996). Edward Tiryakian argues that there is currently a third type of global conflict characterized by nations giving "partial support to one major combatant, the U.S., which made a de facto declaration of war" against terrorism "in the 2002 [G.W. Bush] presidential State of the Union speech" (2005: 23). Terrorists have an ideology, networks of supporters in a variety of countries, and the nation-state itself may sponsor these networks or possess weapons of mass destruction.

New Wars

Bryan Turner (2007) contends that "new war" is a recent conceptual innovation in military sociology to capture how warfare has changed, including the treatment of civilians. "Old wars" involve military conflict between armies trained and supplied by nation-states. Attacking a civilian population interfered with the primary objective of directly engaging the opposing army. International law governing the treatment and protection of civilians was compatible with old war military objectives. With new war, violence of all types toward civilians, including sexual violence, becomes a "functional activity" compatible with war making because the end goal is the destruction of civil society. While the rape of civilians was not uncommon during old wars (Brownmiller 1975), Turner argues that it was unplanned.

In new war, causalities shift from military personnel to civilians, and sexual violence, especially raping and killing women, occurs because it both prevents reproduction of the targeted population and sends civilian males of the same population a profound political message—that they are unable to protect women. Children are an additional vulnerable population, treated like "cheap and biddable combat troops" (Turner 2007: 6 of 15). Another consequence of new warfare is the decreasing efficacy of military techniques and institutions of nation-states. Turner argues that "tanks are relatively useless against suicide bombers mingling in urban crowds on urban subways" (6 of 15) and that this new style will replace the old because nuclear wars between nation-states cannot be pursued without the risk of annihilating both parties. The targeting of civilian populations and the use of tactics like suicide bombing suggest that terrorism is a staple of new wars. New wars are also conceptualized as ethnic conflict with ethnic cleansing and genocide as strategies for gaining control of the state. These wars are believed to be a direct result of globalization's weakening of the nation-state (Kaldor 1999, cited in Scott 2004), which is discussed more fully in Chapter 10.

TERRORISM

In Chapter 8 we considered that social movements initiate terrorism. This can be conceptualized as part of a continuum of nonconventional political protest (della Porta 2004). Terrorism is a strategic fundamental to war making and state making (Lauderdale and Oliverio 2005); yet, everyday discourse on terrorism differentiates between rational and patriotic actors engaged in war and evil, irrational terrorists. This view also impacts scholarship with "terrorism studies," conceptualizing this phenomenon as pathological compared to more institutionalized means of political protest (della Porta 2004). This distinction is false as states are not typically created in peaceful ways and even democracies cannot claim the moral high road on the use of terrorism. Because terrorism has replaced communism as "public enemy number one," some of the issues we raise may be troubling. Sociology though is a discipline that asks "impertinent questions" (Nielsen 1990) by critically challenging "taken-for-granted" views. We hope to raise questions that encourage further exploration as you come to your own conclusions about terrorism.

Until the September 11, 2001 attacks, U.S. sociologists had little interest in terrorism (Senechal de la Roche 2004; Turk 2004), and sociological research in this area was waning (Oliverio and Lauderdale 2005). Reasons for sociology's relative silence include difficulties in data collection and a bias toward studying social movements and protest organizations (Bergesen and Lizardo 2004). Post-9/11 interest has increased among sociologists specializing in social movements (Senechal de la Roche 2004) but not significantly among general political sociologists. We expect this to change with the call for research issued by sociologists

---

TEXTBOX 9.2

Was the Boston Tea Party (BTP) an Act of Revolution or Terrorism?

The East India Company (EIC) was authorized by the British Parliament (Tea Act of 1773) to export 1.5 million pounds of tea to sell in the American colonies. The EIC was facing financial ruin due to mismanagement, and this act of Parliament exempted it from paying duties and tariffs and allowed its tea to be sold directly to American merchants at a cheaper price. This undercut tea smuggling from Holland that had almost completely taken over the American market. In fact, John Hancock, a signer of the Declaration of Independence, smuggled Dutch tea (Brinkley 2010). It was assumed that Americans would buy the cheaper tea, the EIC would be saved from bankruptcy, and the authority of Parliament to impose a tax would be upheld. Besides creating an unfair advantage (EIC lobbyists had much influence in the British Parliament), it also gave the EIC a monopoly over tea distribution. The potential for other monopolies as well as renewed resentment of past policies of taxing colonists without representation united the conservative mercantile class and the more radical patriots. Past taxation imposed included: the Sugar Act of 1764 (taxes on sugar, coffee, and wine), the Stamp Act of 1765 (all printed matter including playing cards), and the Townshend Act of 1767 (glass, paper, paints, and tea). The Stamp Act was passed to pay for protecting the colonists from the Native Americans. Although the Stamp Act and others were repealed, the tax on tea was upheld as a symbol of Parliamentary authority. One of the groups protesting the Stamp Act was the Sons of Liberty led by Samuel Adams. This group was an underground organization that had previously used physical violence and intimidation against British stamp agents and prevented American merchants from ordering British goods. Three ships loaded with EIC tea landed in Boston but were prevented from unloading their cargo. If the tea was not unloaded in twenty days, it could be seized and used to pay custom taxes. On December 16, 1773, the Sons of Liberty, who did not want to drink tea that had been taxed, disguised themselves as Mohawk Indians and boarded each of the tea ships. Armed with axes, 342 crates of tea were opened and then dumped into the sea over a three-hour period. When they were finished, they swept the decks and made each ship's first mate attest that only the tea was damaged. The British responded by closing Boston Harbor, sending more soldiers (four regiments), and replacing the colonial governor, thus ending colonial self-government (Intolerable Acts of 1774).

Revolution

The BTP was one of the events that sparked the American Revolution and is revered worldwide as an important example of principled resistance. Because the colonists were trying to secure basic human rights—indeed their inalienable rights—their actions are an example of a justified revolt against an oppressive government (Jaggar 2005). Furthermore, no one was physically harmed due to the actions of the BTP participants. Revolution can be distinguished from terrorism because it has a broader base of support and there is some ability to create a new government to replace the one that was overthrown (Henderson 2004). There was a broad base of support among the colonists to resist what was perceived to be unfair treatment, and the founding fathers were able to constitute a democratic republic to replace British rule. Henderson further argues that prior acts of terrorism may create the conditions for revolution, and revolution may be accompanied by terrorist acts. Even if the BTP is an example of terrorism, terrorist actions that are part of a revolution are different from terrorist actions that perpetrate violence for the sake of creating fear regardless of the political goals of those involved. The actions of the BTP participants were not to incite fear in innocent civilians, but voice concerns that an oppressive government had previously refused to hear.

Terrorism

Historically, violence has been defined as justified as a response to oppressive and corrupt governments (Oberschall 2004), and the BTP certainly is an example of colonists resisting repression. Bergesen's (2007) definition of terrorism seems to fit the BTP. There were perpetrators (the Sons of Liberty) and victims as the tea thrown overboard belonged to the EIC. The financial backers of the EIC also suffered a loss. One might also argue that the ship crews were also victimized in that they were held captive with threat of physical harm if they interfered with the destruction of the tea. The target, however, was not the crew or the EIC but the British government because the participants were trying to influence a taxation policy that they perceived as unfair. Butko's (2006) definition also seems to have been met as this violence was politically motivated and innocent civilians (ship crew) were threatened with violence. Furthermore, the colonists knew that their actions were illegal because they disguised themselves as Mohawk Indians to prevent being identified and tried for treason. Regardless of representation, it seems unfair to expect the British government to foot the entire bill for providing military protection to the colonists. The Sons of Liberty was simply a terrorist organization using illegal physical violence and intimidation for political and economic gain. Consider that John Hancock gained economically because the cheaper and legal EIC tea was no longer a threat to the market share captured by the illegally smuggled Dutch tea.

Which View Is Correct? You decide, but consider the possibility that both terrorism and revolution are not mutually exclusive. In other words, actions can be both. A sociological view enables us to strip away hegemonic views that connote the American Revolution with good and terrorism with evil.

Sources: http://www.bostonteapartyship.com/history.asp, http://www.theamericanrevolution.org/hevents.asp, http://www.pbs.org/ktca/liberty/chronicle_boston1774.html, http://www.boston-tea-party.org/darthmouth.html, and http://www.americanrevwar.homestead.com/files/TEAPARTY.HTM

(e.g., Hooks and Rice 2005) and the increased attention by several sociology journals. While sociological research and theories are not well suited for explaining one-time events such as the 9/11 attacks, they can and should be used for examining general patterns (Neuman 2007). Although it is easy to fault American sociologists for failing to take notice, Figure 9.1 illustrates that the number of deaths in North America from domestic terrorism was relatively low pre-9/11 compared to the Middle East.

Political scientists Walter Enders and Todd Sandler (2006: 10) describe a sociological approach to terrorism as studying the "norms and social structure within terrorist organizations." We find this description of sociology's contribution to the study of terrorism much too limiting. There are many additional sociological questions that researchers have posed, including but not limited to: how does society define terrorism, what is labeled as terrorism, what factors increase its likelihood, how do individuals become terrorists, what role do the media play in promoting or discouraging terrorism, and how can terrorism be prevented (Turk 2004).

Defining Terrorism

There are more than one hundred definitions of terrorism and few concepts are considered as ideological (della Porta 2004) or contentious in this post-9/11 environment (Butko 2006; Kinloch 2005).

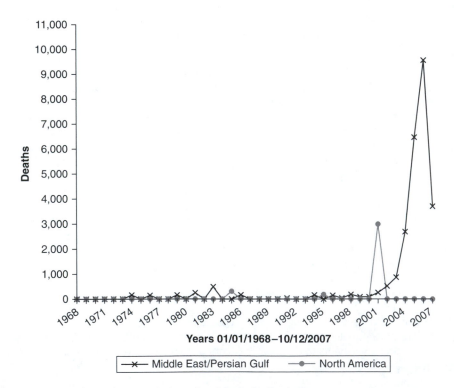

FIGURE 9.1 Comparison of Domestic Terrorism Deaths by Region

Source: This graph was created using the Terrorism Knowledge Base (TKB) at http://www.tkb.org. Data from January 1968 to September 2007. Formerly operated by the Memorial Institute for the Prevention of Terrorism where you can find other terrorism-related information at http://www.mipt.org.

Problems with contemporary definitions include a lack of international consensus, historical changes in usage, and inconsistent use by both media and government[1] (Miller and File 2001). The original use was popularized during the French Jacobin government's "Reign of Terror" when thousands of citizens were guillotined to deter critics. As one philosopher writes, "it is worth remembering that the original case was one of politically motivated violence carried out by a government against its own citizens" (Jaggar 2005: 202). In contrast, the U.S. Department of State, Office of the Coordinator for Counterterrorism defines terrorism as "premeditated, politically motivated violence perpetrated against noncombatant targets by subnational groups or clandestine agents, usually intended to influence an audience" (2006). Whereas some believe that academic researchers and government officials have come close to a definitional consensus (Bergesen and Han 2005), we believe that there are some important distinctions between official and social scientific definitions.

Although Bergesen and Han (2005) acknowledge the importance of state terrorism, the U.S. Department of State omits violence committed by a government against its own citizens such as the 2007 crackdown ordered by the ruling military junta of Myanmar (Burma) against antigovernment protesters, killing 138 persons and detaining over 6,000 including Buddhist monks (Casey 2007). In contrast, researchers are interested in both state and substate actors, and current sociological definitions of terrorism tend to include both (e.g., Tilly 2004).

Substate terrorism includes individuals such as Timothy McVeigh and Terry Nichols who are responsible for the bombing of the Alfred P. Murrah Federal Building in Oklahoma City, Oklahoma, on April 19, 1995, and networks such as Al Qaeda. Regardless of whether the focus is on state or substate actors, there are three common elements for a social scientific definition including the actual or threatened use of violence, political aims of those committing violence, and the threat of or actual harm to innocent civilians (Butko 2006). Threats tend to be overlooked by official definitions but are important because of the potential to influence audience behavior through fear (Gibbs 1989). Think of all the inconveniences associated with air travel and the billions of dollars spent annually on security[2] because of the continued *threat* of terrorism. While many of the current air travel restrictions are a reaction to 9/11 and related events, we continue to modify our behavior on the premise that terrorists will strike again.

Terrorism undermines two pillars of democracy: personal security and tolerance (Matthew and Shambaugh 2005). Perceptions of security are lowered by both threats and actual incidents. We have advocated for a social scientific definition that is broader than those used by some government agencies. Yet, conceptual clarity necessitates that researchers distinguish terrorism from other acts of violence such as homicide or suicide.

Political aim separates terrorism from general physical violence. The motives of the 9/11 hijackers cannot be known with absolute certainty—was it political or merely revenge for some perceived transgression? (Senechal de la Roche 2004). However, researchers as well as government officials infer motive when they classify incidents as terrorism. della Porta reminds us that terrorists' political goals are varied and include "gaining consent, rather than merely terrorizing" (2004: 2 of 8).

Albert Bergesen agrees that terrorism has a political motivation but argues that the distinguishing feature lies with the difference between target and victim because "the victim is merely the means to affect the target. . . . In all other forms of violence, the victim is the target" (2007: 112). For example, the victims of the 9/11 terrorist attacks were innocent people who were killed or maimed, but the target was the U.S. government and public opinion regarding its Middle East policy. In other types of violence, the victim and the target are the same.

Victims are connected to targets because victims are citizens of a specific country or are affiliated with a business or other target. This connection is a means of influencing the behavior of both victims and targets to instill fear (Beck 2007). The political sphere is about gaining and using power to force others, including nation-states, to do one's bidding. Targets, then, are a means to obtain some political goal, and terrorism is an attempt to exercise power. Another aspect of power is who decides what constitutes terrorism?

Labeling Terrorism

Researchers use specialized knowledge and criteria when classifying and organizing data, however, labeling something a *terrorist attack* has political ramifications. One of the most important sociological insights in the study of terrorism is the realization that this label is socially constructed (Turk 2004), but this goes beyond the cliché "one man's terrorist is another man's freedom fighter." Labeling someone a *terrorist* rather than a *liberator* and the inability of the labeled party to renegotiate an alternative meaning signifies the ability of the labeler to stigmatize the actions of others (Gibbs 1989). For example, Bangladesh labeled government critics as *media terrorists* or *intellectual terrorists,* signifying the willingness of some states to use fighting terrorism as a justification for eliminating political criticism and opposition (Khondker 2008). Bangladesh is not alone. Governments often describe terrorism in terms of "cowardly, criminal acts of desperate, extremist minorities bent on revenge against powerful national elites" (Kinloch 2005: 136) and communicate these labels to the global community through official lists. Groups and individuals on these lists may face financial and legal obstacles. The U.S. State Department has three designations including Terrorist Exclusion List (TEL), Foreign Terrorist Organization (FTO), and Other Terrorist Organization (OTO)[3] (Terrorism Knowledge Base 2007). An explicit intent of designating a group as an FTO is to "stigmatize[s] and isolate[s] designated terrorist organizations internationally" (U.S. Department of State, Office of Counterterrorism 2005).

Sometimes labeled groups use the media to attack the terrorist label. The Revolutionary Armed Forces of Colombia (FARC) demanded that the European Union (EU) remove FARC from its list. The EU joined the United States in designating FARC as a terrorist organization in 2002. Raul Reyes,[4] a FARC commander, argued in a letter "We are a political military organization that has taken up arms against state violence to seek deep social transformations" ("FARC Writes: Stop Calling Us Terrorists" 2007). The point is that similar acts of political resistance are defined differently and may be celebrated or condemned and that groups seeking redress against alleged state terrorism are at a disadvantage in the labeling process.

Refugees lacking the protection of national citizenship may be the most disadvantaged group of all, therefore any actions toward self-determination are outside the law; this results in the transformation from refugee to "terrorist" (Ukai 2005). Furthermore, other institutions may act to reify the government label. For example, the American media typically does not label official military attacks as terrorist even when civilians are victimized, although attacks by nonstate guerilla forces, even when the targets are military, are termed *terrorist* (e.g., the Israeli–Palestinian conflict) (Jaggar 2005). Similarly, the definition of terrorism used by the U.S. Department of Defense includes attacks against American military targets (Enders and Sandler 2006). Because the state or government has a monopoly on legitimate power, we ask the question posed by other sociologists: "under what conditions will the state define acts of deviance as acts of terrorism?" (Oliverio and Lauderdale 2005: 166).

Oliverio and Lauderdale note that labeling is the result of a hegemonic process or a society's dominating view that is beyond question or reproach. It is a taken-for-granted view of the world that most accept rather than critically question. The American hegemonic view is that Western civilization is superior to all others and that those who attack it are evil, irrational, and fanatical. Furthermore, the mental image most Americans tend to associate with terrorism is not one of a government victimizing its own citizens but individuals committing violence against the state. Not surprisingly, this view parallels all of the different definitions used by U.S. government agencies. We are not suggesting that terroristic violence is justifiable or excusable, however understanding it necessitates looking beyond hegemonic views.

The significance of hegemony comes from the work of Antonio Gramsci (1971), who argues that the ruling elite may use coercion but is also able to use consensual means because the ruling elite uses its position to define concepts such as equality, justice, and terrorism. This occurs because those who rule "have a monopoly over moral and intellectual discourse, and this—backed by coercive might—allows them to create, construct or label 'others' within the global system as the enemy or the 'terrorists' " (Butko 2006: 149).

The international relations literature uses a non-Gramscian notion of hegemony that is also useful for understanding labeling. In this context, *hegemony* refers to a dominant nation-state (Evans 2008). The United States is a hegemonic state, meaning that it has the power to internationalize and enforce terrorist classifications (Butko 2006), and this is a source of frustration for those who are wary of the influence of Western civilization and specifically, the United States (Abi-Hashem 2003). An example is the UN Counter Terrorism Statement and Action Plan. Nowhere in this document is reference made to terrorism committed by the state against its own citizens. In fact, citizens committing terrorism against their government, regardless of the reason, may find themselves at a disadvantage in the asylum-seeking process. UN member states agree "to take appropriate measures, before granting asylum, for the purpose of ensuring that the asylum seeker has not engaged in terrorist activities and, after granting asylum, for the purpose of ensuring that the refugee status is not used in a manner contrary to the provisions set out in paragraph 1 of this section" (United Nations 2006). Even hegemonic states enact terrorism policies that do not seem to fit with their respective national interest. Although it makes sense for the United States to restrict individuals such as those who bombed the *USS Cole* at a Yemen navel port in 2000, this policy also restricts those who fought against their own governments as a U.S. ally.

Hegemonic discourse may also foster prejudice and discrimination as *Middle Eastern* is becoming synonymous with terrorist (Oliverio and Lauderdale 2005). This, of course, has implications for how we view and treat persons who appear Middle Eastern regardless of the likelihood that these individuals will engage in terrorist activities and reminds us of the point made earlier, that responses to terrorism may erode democracy (Matthew and Shambaugh 2005) because when states balance the need for security against civil liberties, it is always those in the minority who have the most to lose (Zedner 2005). Consider that those who are not Muslim and have no Muslim connections have no risk of being arrested and detained as an enemy combatant in a military jail (Dworkin 2003).

While the labeling perspective challenges us to consider the power of the labeler and the consequences of being labeled, Albert Bergesen (2007) asserts that terrorism is not only a label but also a specific type of violence that can and should be distinguished from other forms of violence, including that arising from the practice of "contentious politics" (Tilly and Tarrow 2006). Although hegemonic discourse may favor emphasizing substate over state actors, researchers need conceptual clarity (Gibbs 1989) to develop explanatory models of both state and substate terrorism.

Types of Terrorism

Currently, there are three main categories of terrorism, including state or regime, state sponsored, and substate. Furthermore, we often divide terrorism into domestic and international, with domestic meaning that all the parties involved are from the same country in which the terrorist incident took place. In contrast, international or transnational terrorism occurs when an incident involves victims, perpetrators, citizens, or governments of two or more nations (Enders and Sandler 2006).

TEXTBOX 9.3

The Repercussions of Being Labeled a Terrorist

Xo Chia Vue is a former CIA recruit who fought against the Laos government during the Vietnam War with other Hmong tribe members (a hill tribe of northern Laos) recruited by the CIA beginning in 1961 to stop the spread of communism. For fourteen years he fought against the Laotian government on behalf of the United States including assisting in the rescue of two American pilots and the evacuation of the remains of third pilot of a plane that crashed into a mountain in 1971. Because Xo Chia Vue is classified as a terrorist for activities committed against the Laotian government, he is barred from entering the United States. His two granddaughters are also ineligible because they provided "material support" by cooking for him while he evaded Laotian authorities in the jungle. Vue's only hope for entry is a legislative change or a waiver. As of 2006, only three waivers have been granted and are available only to those who provided material support and not to terrorists themselves (Husarska 2006). While Vue's granddaughters are eligible for waivers, he is not. Should Vue and others like him be granted a waiver?

Pro

While Vue is certainly a terrorist, he was an agent of American-sponsored terror. The United States should support individuals who risked their lives on behalf of U.S. policies. Furthermore, the United States should reject rigid policies that disallow the investigation of the context in which terrorist activities took place. Should the United States have barred the French resistance fighters who fought against the Nazi Vichy regime? Barring evidence that would make him ineligible under other criteria, he should be admitted. This law also fosters gender discrimination by failing to recognize that women from other societies may not have the ability to refuse to provide the kinds of services that are defined as "material support." Vue's granddaughters should also be welcomed.

Con

Allowing any terrorist to enter the United States (regardless of the targeted regime) undermines credibility with the larger global community. Isolating and stigmatizing terrorists and terrorist groups is one of the tools of the "war on terror" and the United States needs the cooperation of other nations to achieve the objective of a safer nation and world. Otherwise, other nations will give safe haven to criminals who threaten U.S. security. Although Vue's past service is appreciated and valued, a policy barring any terrorist from entering member countries strengthens global cooperation and must not be undermined by the circumstances of any one man. Nor can the United States provide entry to every individual who assists the U.S. government. Reviewing every case would only result in the substitution of the subjective "one man's terrorist is another man's freedom fighter" for an objective standard.

What Do You Think?   What other arguments could be made for either the pro or con positions? Which view is correct? More examples of barred individuals can be found at http://www.worldaffairsjournal.org/2008%20-%20Summer/full-Husarska.html.

Update: In October 2007, The U.S. Departments of State and Homeland Security announced that certain Hmong groups that provided material support to terrorist organizations prior to December 31, 2004, are exempt from laws that bar them from entry into the United States or becoming legal, permanent residents ("Some Hmong to Get Waiver on 'Terrorist' Designation" 2007). This waiver does not apply to those labeled as *terrorists* (U.S. Department of State, Office of the Spokesman 2007). For more information on policy regarding immigration and terrorism, see Garcia and Wasem (2007).

STATE OR REGIME TERRORISM   The state has a monopoly on the legitimate use of power and sometimes uses this against its own citizens to further political goals. Josef Stalin, Adolph Hitler, Pol Pot, and more recently, Saddam Hussein, as heads of authoritarian or totalitarian regimes, have used violence both at home and abroad to further political goals. There is some disagreement whether violent actions perpetrated by a state against its own citizens should be called terrorism (Enders and Sandler 2006), with scholars from the "rejectionist school" declining to apply the label precisely because the state has a monopoly on authority (Sandhu 2001). Sandhu argues that perpetuating the myth that all political terrorism is committed by substate actors conceals atrocities committed by the state including ruling by fear through kidnapping, assassination, torture, genocide, and forced imprisonment without trial.

Generally, domestic variables associated with the use of state terror include state strength, level of political self-mobilization, social organization density in civil society, economic structure, and political culture or structure. Generally, weak states are more likely to resort to terrorizing their own citizens (Schmid and Jongman 1988), because strong governments have legitimacy and opt instead for less extreme repression such as internment camps during times of civil unrest (Cohen and Corrado 2005). When stronger governments use terrorism, victims tend to be unpopular or distrusted segments of society (Duvall and Stohl 1988).

Using the historical cases of Chile, El Salvador, and Brazil, Petras (1987) asserts that both higher levels of social movement activity in nondemocratic societies and density of individuals in interconnecting political activity networks are associated with an increase in state repression. When wealth is sufficiently unequal, the state may resort to torture to quell those who demand change, which threatens the economic and political status quo (Cohen and Corrado 2005). In contrast, liberal democracies with welfare programs and other mechanisms for transferring wealth are able to mitigate poverty and other conditions that lead to political unrest among citizens, which reduces the need for repressive tactics. Authoritarian regimes often employ institutionalized torture systems with trained torturers, written rules and policies, and a physical infrastructure—in short, a torture bureaucracy.

Liberal democracies not only have less need to use torture but also may pressure other states to stop using it as a social control mechanism. Globalization enhances the reach of liberal democracies and is hypothesized to decrease the usefulness of state torture because of the "needs and requirements of an interdependent global economy" (Cohen and Corrado 2005: 105) with both agrarian- and industrial-based economies susceptible to international pressure. Potential loss of foreign markets, access to debt relief, and the need for economic growth all discourage torture. Liberal democracies may block access to their markets and influence global organizations (e.g., International Monetary Fund and World Bank) to block credit or debt relief to offending nations.

Besides government, the media also play an influential role by utilizing an extensive global network to publicize atrocities so that nations and organizations in a position to pressure an offending regime can do so. New technological developments allow individuals and groups to directly appeal for help when global media are blocked, as was seen during the anti-Iranian government protests in 2009 when most news initially were available only through Twitter and Facebook ("Crackdown in Iran" 2009). The ability to pressure repressive governments depends on the degree of economic dependency, which is lessened with the availability of alternative markets. For example, Cuba was able to mitigate some of the impact of the U.S. embargo because it had the Soviet Union as a trading partner. The fall of the Soviet Union has limited alternative markets that human rights violators can turn to when pressured by liberal democracies.

Economic relationships alone cannot predict whether a liberal democracy will pressure a repressive regime (Cohen and Corrado 2005). Other important variables include extreme religious fundamentalism and specific crisis events. For example, Russia's use of torture against Checheyan rebels was ignored by the United States and its allies because they feared the spread of Muslim fundamentalism and potential political instability in a region where multinational corporations had large investments in energy infrastructure (Cohen and Corrado 2005). Sometimes the United States not only ignores repressive regimes but actively supports them.

James Petras argues that the United States was a driving force behind authoritarian regimes in the 1970s and 1980s that resulted in the "growth and proliferation of state terror networks" (1987: 315) that were supported by both Republican and Democratic administrations. He contends that there is a bilateral relationship between the center and client state. The client state receives training, financing, and other support to create and maintain a torture infrastructure. The center state receives support for economic and political policies that benefit the elite of both center and client state. Though there is no doubt that the United States has supported authoritarian regimes for a variety of reasons (Carr 2006; Gareau 2004; Huggins 1987; Lauderdale and Oliverio 2005; Robinson 2004), Petras' analysis may not be currently relevant in a post-Soviet era with the economic transformation of China and increasing global interdependency.

While Petras argued that support of a global terror network coincides with a "decline in economic levers in imperial foreign policy" (1987: 317), Cohen and Corrado (2005) counter that economic policy is a powerful tool to coerce repressive state regimes to end the use of torture. Robinson (2004) contends that U.S. interests explain why there has been a shift from past support of authoritarian governments to democratic ones although he argues full democracy is not being supported but rather, polyarchy.

If global dependency decreases the likelihood that a regime will resort to torture, the reverse must also be true with isolated regimes more likely to use it (Duvall and Stohl 1988). Because of the disinterest of the international community, torture is also more likely to occur in "less strategically or economically useful" areas (Cohen and Corrado 2005: 126) with recent examples including Cambodia under Pol Pot, and Darfur. Because more lives have been lost to regime terror than terrorism committed by substate nationals (Henderson 2004), it is imperative that more attention be paid to this topic. While there is no consensus on whether regime terror constitutes terrorism, what is less contentious is the acknowledgment that some nations support terrorist groups.

STATE-SUPPORTED TERRORISM   Nations sometimes aid terrorist groups to further their political goals (Sandhu 2001). The downing of Pan Am Flight 103 over Lockerbie, Scotland, on December 21, 1988, killed 270 persons including everyone on board. Libya was accused of aiding the individuals responsible for this attack and eventually agreed to turn two Libyan intelligence agents over for trial and to pay financial reparations to victims' families. As of this writing, nations labeled by the U.S. State Department as engaging in state-sponsored terror include Cuba, Iran, Sudan, and Syria (U.S. Department of State, Office of the Coordinator for Counterterrorism 2010). North Korea was delisted in 2008 after it granted greater access for nuclear site inspections (Richter 2008). Libya was removed in 2006 for cooperating in the "global war on terror" including the ending of its weapons program (U.S. Department of State, Bureau of Consular Affairs 2007). While still on the list, Sudan is described as continuing "to take significant steps to cooperate in the War on Terror" and Venezuela, though not considered a "state sponsor," is "certified by the [U.S.] Secretary of State as 'not fully cooperating' with U.S. counterterrorism efforts" (U.S. Department of State, Office of the Coordinator for Counterterrorism 2007). Affected nations face restrictions on arms sales, U.S. exports, economic assistance, loss of diplomatic immunity, and other miscellaneous financial restrictions.

Some have argued that the United States is also a sponsor of terror for historically supporting groups that have undermined democratically elected governments in South and Central

America (Lewellen 1990; Montiel and Anuar 2002; Petras 1987) as well as communist ones. Quoting the philosopher Derrida, "the reason of the strongest is always the best", Ukai argues that "when one looks closely at what it means to be called a rogue state [a government that supports terrorism], it is not very difficult to see that those who coined the term and impose it on others are rogue states themselves" (2005: 247). This is obviously a controversial statement that challenges hegemonic beliefs that researchers may have and need to set aside to study terrorism.

SUBSTATE TERRORISM   Individuals and organizations that commit violence against the state to challenge state power are engaged in counterhegemonic political violence (Butko 2006). Currently, radical Islamic fundamentalists are challenging Western hegemony. Yet, to focus only on Muslims is misleading because historically they are only one of many groups that have perpetrated violence against Western democracies and their allies. Between 1968 and 1990, terrorists tended to be either leftists adhering to communist ideology (e.g., Red Army Faction—Germany, Shining Path—Peru, Weathermen—the United States) or ethno-nationalists (e.g., Irish Republican Army—Northern Ireland, Palestine Liberation Organization—West Bank/Gaza). More recently there has been a shift from secular to religious, fundamentalist groups (Enders and Sandler 2006; Martin 2007; Schmid and Jongman 1988; Terrorism Knowledge Base 2007), although out of all groups tracked since the 1960s, the majority are communist or socialist (see Figure 9.2). Homegrown terrorism or citizens attacking their own governments such as Timothy McVeigh or the 1960s Weathermen are often overlooked in contemporary terrorism discussions. Other shifts or changes since the 1990s include the use of loose networks instead of a classic hierarchical organizational structure, decreased specificity in the demands made by terrorist groups, more global dispersion of targets, increased difficulty in identifying motive as fewer groups claim

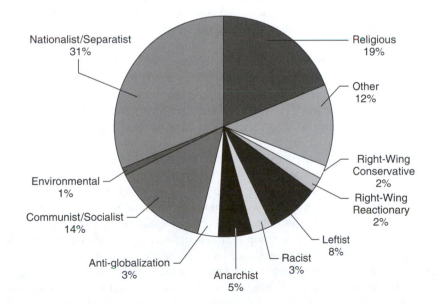

FIGURE 9.2 Terrorist Groups by Type

Source: This graph was created using the Terrorism Knowledge Base (TKB) at http://www.tkb.org. Data from January 1968 to September 2007. Formerly operated by the Memorial Institute for the Prevention of Terrorism where you can find other terrorism-related information at http://www.mipt.org.

responsibility, and violence that is less discriminating in terms of victims (Bergesen and Han 2005). Some argue that terrorism in the age of globalization or "new terrorism" differs from older forms because it is characterized by asymmetrical warfare, the use of high-yield weapons, and religious motivation (Martin 2007). We will discuss some of these trends in the following sections.

The classic organization of a substate terrorist group is a pyramid structure with the apex occupied by a few top leaders who plan overall strategy and policy. The next level is the *active cadre* or a larger group of individuals who perform attacks. There may be several smaller groups within this level that specialize in certain operations such as bomb making, intelligence gathering, and surveillance. The next larger level is made up of *active supporters* who provide intelligence, safe houses, communication, and other support activities. Active members divide themselves into cells to preserve secrecy. A cell has only a few members whose activities and identities are known only to identical cell members. The cell leader may communicate with only one other cell. On the bottom are *passive supporters* who may provide money and voice support for terrorist goals (Frasier, as cited in Henderson 2004). In reality, most groups have fewer than fifty members, and these individuals may shift between different levels. Furthermore, most terrorist groups have little public support, although there may be sympathy with group ideology. While the cell structure maintains secrecy and helps protect the identities and plans of other cells, it makes communication and coordination with other cells difficult (Henderson 2004).

More modern terrorist groups consist of a small number of individuals who commit actions in the name of the group[5] and communicate using Web sites maintained by unaffiliated but sympathetic supporters. One example is Earth Liberation Front (ELF), an alleged international ecoterrorism group, which advocates for animal rights and targets both the timber industry and urban sprawl with the recent destruction of luxury apartments and condominiums in New York City. Groups such as ELF hardly exist or function as an organization, with no central structure or membership and decision making concentrated at the local cell level (Henderson 2004; Terrorism Knowledge Base 2007). More militant white separatist groups in the United States have advocated the use of leaderless resistance, which is a modified version of the communist cell structure (Dobratz and Shanks-Meile 1997). The leaderless strategy not only makes intelligence gathering more difficult but also may shield a national office from both the legal and financial consequences of actions attributed to renegade cells.

Charles Tilly (2004) notes that it is important to distinguish between different types of terrorist actors and by doing so realize the broad spectrum of entities, ideologies, and circumstances involved with terrorism. Tilly's (2004, 2005) self-described crude typology is divided among two dimensions: degree of specialization (i.e., specialists, nonspecialists) and location of attacks (i.e., home territory, outside home territory). Specialists are members of military forces that may be part of a government, nongovernment, or antigovernment forces.

Conspirators are specialists who operate by striking targets away from the home base. Intelligence or military agents such as those in Libya who masterminded the Lockerbie bombing would fit here although this constitutes a small number of actual incidents. Like conspirators, *zealots* also operate away from the home base but are not specialists or part of an organized military force such as the 9/11 hijackers. This group inflicts a significant amount of terrorism that occurs away from a group's home base and can include exiles who return to their homeland to attack their enemies. For example, some young Somali males raised in the United States are returning to Somali to train with Al-Shabaab, a terrorist group with ties to Al Qaeda, and have subsequently died in Somali committing suicide bombing attacks (Walsh and Meryhew 2009). *Autonomists* include political groups that launch attacks on targets within their own territories without becoming specialists in coercion. Because specialists are members of an organized military force, nonspecialist autonomists commit substate terrorism. *Militias* include specialist groups that are involved in incidents inside their own territory. Specialists who are part of a government force commit state terrorism, whereas organized antigovernmental forces engage in substate terrorism. *Ordinary Militants* engage in other types of protests but from time to time engage in terrorist attacks either at home or abroad. In the case of the disappearing Somali youth, counterterrorism experts fear these individuals may not stay in Somalia but return to their adopted homeland and commit terrorism (Walsh and Meryhew 2009). Tilly's typology suggests that individuals can shift between these five types through changing social relations between activists as well as between activists and their targets.

An example of a terrorist group operating in the United States is the antiabortion group, Army of God, whose most infamous member, Eric Robert Rudolph, was charged with the 1996 Centennial Olympic Park bombing in Atlanta, the 1997 bombings at a gay nightclub and an abortion clinic in the Atlanta area, and the 1998 bombing of a clinic in Birmingham, Alabama (Terrorism Knowledge Base 2007). Using Tilly's typology, classifying Rudolph as an autonomist or an ordinary militant would depend on whether he had also engaged in other forms of nonterrorist antiabortion protest, such as picketing. Recognizing that terrorism is one of many political and apolitical options that rational actors may *simultaneously* employ (Tilly 2004, 2005) reinforces the uselessness of conceptualizing terrorists as "crazy, irrational fanatics." While this latter hegemonic attribution reinforces how different we are from "them," it does nothing to enhance the understanding of terrorism or the development of counterterrorism policies and tactics.

Despite a renewed focus on terrorism by politicians, law enforcement, and academics, a 2007 Gallup poll suggests that only 5 percent of the public believes it is the most pressing problem facing the United States; the economy and the Iraq war rank higher (Gallup Poll News Service 2007) (see Figures 9.3 and 9.4). This makes some sense because most terrorism does not take place in our backyard but overseas in the Middle East. Yet, understanding how terrorists

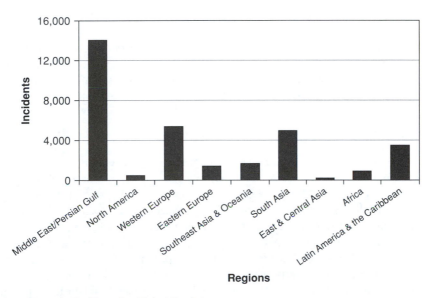

FIGURE 9.3 Terrorist Incidents by Global Region

Source: Graph created using the Terrorism Knowledge Base (TKB) at http://www.tkb.org. Data from January 1968 to September 2007. Formerly operated by the Memorial Institute for the Prevention of Terrorism where you can find other terrorism-related information at http://www.mipt.org.

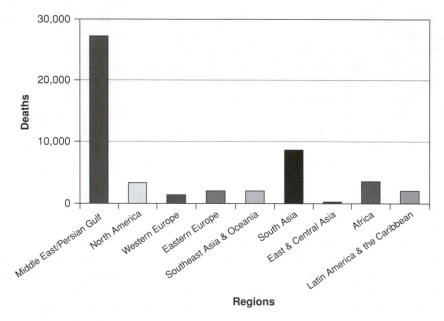

FIGURE 9.4   Deaths by Region Including Both Domestic and International Terrorism

Source: Graph created using the Terrorism Knowledge Base (TKB) at http://www.tkb.org. Data from January 1968 to September 2007. Formerly operated by the Memorial Institute for the Prevention of Terrorism where you can find other terrorism-related information at http://www.mipt.org.

operate and their motivations as well as structural conditions that create and foster terrorism is the only way to reduce the carnage.

Sociological theories provide a framework for moving beyond a pathological perspective and toward answers backed by empirical data. A sociologist asks "what social, economic, and political conditions create terrorism?" Although the "sociology of terrorism" might be in its infancy (Bergesen and Lizardo 2004), current theories are being applied in new and innovative ways.

TERRORISM AND SOCIOLOGICAL THEORIES

There is some disagreement about whether a general theory of terrorism is desirable and/or achievable. Some contend that terrorism should be separated from other forms of political violence (Bergesen and Han 2005; Black 2004; Bergesen and Lizardo 2004; Senechal de la Roche 2004). Given broad definitions of terrorism (Senechal de la Roche 2004) and important distinctions between substate, state, and state-sponsored terror, it seems unlikely that a single theory could explain all types. Even developing a single theory of substate terrorism seems problematic as "a remarkable array of actors sometimes adopt terror as a strategy, and therefore no coherent set of cause and effect propositions can explain terrorism as a whole" (Tilly 2004: 11).

Others argue against a distinct theory of terrorism because current theories of political confrontation should be applicable to all types of political action because "terrorism is only one of several modes of confrontation ranging from peaceful and conventional political actions to extremes of group violence" (Oberschall 2004: 26). Furthermore, those adopting terror often alternate with other political strategies and even inaction as only a small number of terrorists choose terror alone (Tilly 2004, 2005). If developing a single theory of terrorism is difficult, why assume that other theories that lump terrorism with other forms of non institutionalized or unconventional political behavior will be successful? Tilly (2005) explains that terrorism is a strategy that includes interacting political actors. To understand why terrorism is selected over other choices, we must analyze it as a type of political process. This debate is likely to continue but in the interim, several current theories are being applied, including Collective Action Theory, Political Economy, WS, a Framing perspective, and Categorical Terrorism.

Collective Action Theory

According to Oberschall (2004), four dimensions must be met for collective action to take place: discontent, ideology, ability to organize, and political opportunity. First, there must be prevalent dissatisfaction that cannot be alleviated through conventional political means as elites are either unwilling or unable to provide relief. Second, the aggrieved must collectively define that their complaints are legitimate. Third, individuals must have the capability to recruit, raise funds, provide leaders, communicate, and make decisions. Both social movement and terrorist groups are often built out of preexisting networks. For example, Islamic terrorists use the network of religious schools and mosques as well as family groups for recruiting (Oberschall 2004; Smelser 2007) just as Red Brigade (an Italian Marxist–Leninist group) members knew each other from the university where they participated in leftist politics or factories where they worked (Carr 2006).

Liberal democracies report higher levels of terrorism[6] (Enders and Sandler 2006) because political opportunities are greater with civil liberties make organizing easier by protecting free speech, the dissemination of information, and the right of association. Finally, political opportunities are expanded when there is strong public support for terrorist activities, political allies that are sympathetic to the cause, a supportive international climate, and outside state support or sponsorship of terrorism (Oberschall 2004).

Political Economy

This perspective is a more interdisciplinary approach and is useful for answering questions such as why liberal democracies are more prone to terrorism, what is the net impact of media coverage or do the benefits of coverage justify the risks, and what is the trade-off the public will accept between declining civil liberties and increased protection. Sometimes called rational choice, this approach argues that terrorists engage in terrorism because it is a cost-effective means for a weaker party to challenge a stronger opponent. The public tolerates both the economic and noneconomic costs of airline security because we perceive that the benefits outweigh the cost.

Due to the 9/11 attacks, the public is much more accepting of the key provisions of the USA PATRIOT (Uniting and Strengthening America by Providing Appropriate Tools Required to Intercept and Obstruct Terrorism) Act, including increased electronic surveillance, expanded wiretapping, reduced immigration rights, and the suspension of habeas corpus or demonstrating just cause for imprisonment or detention (Enders and Sandler 2006). Although the U.S. Supreme Court rejected the right of the G. W. Bush administration to suspend habeas corpus for Guantánamo Bay detainees (*Boumediene v. Bush*), the court was closely divided in a 5–4 decision with those in the minority believing that the court overreached in matters best left to the president and the military. Associate Justice Scalia warned, "The nation will live to regret what the court has done today" as it "will almost certainly cause more Americans to be killed" (Savage 2008). The British too seem more accepting of privacy intrusion with the introduction of "bobby-cams" strapped to the helmets of police officers on top of the already existing video surveillance network using 4 million closed-circuit cameras with the typical resident being videotaped as much as three hundred times daily (Satter 2007). In the case of wiretapping without warrants, there is little evidence of effectiveness (Lichtblau and Risen 2009), raising the issue of just how long the U.S. public will continue to tolerate the intrusion.

A political economy approach assumes that all actors are rational because decisions are based on a cost-benefit analysis. Governments must weigh the costs of conceding to demands (encouraging attacks from counter groups) against the cost of future attacks. If the cost of a future attack exceeds the cost of conceding, a government may give in to demands. Suicide bombings have become more commonplace[7] because these kill more victims than other methods and raise the anxiety level of targets. Suicide bombings occur in liberal democracies because elected officials perceive pressure to protect lives although making concessions encourages future attacks (Enders and Sandler 2006). Not everyone agrees with a rational choice interpretation. Recent work using the context of the Palestinian–Israeli conflict contends that suicide bombings are not cost-effective given the degree of repression that results after each attack, but that new attacks are instigated due to a "cultural logic of retaliation," which perpetuates the cycle of violence (Brym and Araj 2006). In other words, the continued use of suicide bombing is motivated by the need to exact revenge from the Israeli government.

World Systems Perspective

Some argue that international terrorism is best studied from a WS perspective (Bergesen 1990). *WS analysis* refers to a set of related theories from a variety of contributors (Hall 2002). By comparing the current wave of terrorism with the political unrest of the mid-1800s, Bergesen and Lizardo (2004) suggest a common set of international conditions conducive to international terrorism including hegemonic decline, globalization, empire or colonial competition, and autocratic semiperipheral zones.

Hegemonic decline is the rise and fall of dominant states. History reveals a pattern of rising and falling empires with no region permanently dominant. Hegemonic decline is inevitable "as the world-economy moves to a new center based on more advanced production techniques" (Bergesen and Lizardo 2004: 47). Political entities that cannot adapt to changing global economic conditions will be replaced by political structures that can. These transitions from one hegemonic center to another are not peaceful as there is no process for transferring advantage. A new power center emerges with the destruction of the former hegemonic state.

If the WS perspective is correct, the ability of the United States to maintain its hegemonic position will depend on maintaining its production advantage. Whether it can continue to do so is unclear with some arguing that the United States is in a state of decline that began with the Vietnam conflict (Hall 2002; Wallerstein 2003) and coincides with the current economic downturn (Bergesen and Lizardo 2004; Wallerstein 2003). What does all of this have to do with terrorism? Bergesen and Lizardo (2004) suggest a number of possibilities, including signaling a power struggle, the differentiation of war and terrorism, the role of semiperipheral zones, and trigger events.

Hegemonic decline results in global instability. Outbreaks of international terrorism may be analogous to a "canary in the mineshaft" that signals the onset of state-to-state power struggles between a declining hegemonic power and other entities vying for control (Bergesen and Lizardo 2004). For example, there was a period of international terrorism (1880s–1914) that preceded World Wars I and II (1914–1945).

The semiperiphery exists between powerful core nations and the economically undeveloped periphery. The periphery supplies both cheap labor and raw materials to core economies. This exploitation enables those residing in the core (e.g., the United States, Japan, the United Kingdom) to have a standard of living that is subsidized off the backs of those living and working in the periphery (e.g., Bangladesh, Vietnam). Although jobs are provided, workers are paid poorly with little job security or access to benefits such as health care. Deskilling or breaking down complex tasks that previously were performed by skilled workers into less complicated tasks that can be performed by unskilled laborers results in no transfer of technology to the periphery. This and the lack of capital (land, buildings, equipment, etc.) render it impossible for a periphery nation to set up competing industries. The semiperiphery (e.g., Indonesia, Taiwan, and the Middle East) is not as developed as the core but more so than the periphery. This middle group has many functions including deflecting anger away from the core, as the existence of a semiperiphery suggests that development and a higher standard of living is possible over time.

Bergesen and Lizardo argue that international terrorism erupts in the semiperiphery including Arab-Islamic states. Explanations for this trend include a weakening of the hegemonic state that allows those living in the semiperiphery to resist dictatorial rulers, a decline in support from core states to dependent states in the semiperiphery, and backlash against the hegemonic state. An alternative role of the semiperiphery is to provide a trigger event for a power struggle between competing core states. An example of such a trigger may have been the assassination of the Austrian Archduke and heir to the throne, Franz Ferdinand, by Gavrilo Princip, a Bosnian Serb student and member of Young Bosnia, a group that advocated for independence from Austria–Hungary, which lead to the outbreak of World War I. Weaknesses of this approach include a lack of historical evidence for the existence of terrorism during the Spain hegemonic era preceding the Thirty Years' War (1618–1648), a failure to identify a specific link between hegemonic decline and the onset of terrorism, and exactly why terrorism originates in the semiperiphery rather than the periphery (Bergesen and Lizardo 2004).

Framing

As previously discussed, the framing perspective was developed by social movement theorists to recognize that individuals actively produce and maintain meaning (Snow et al. 1986) as opposed to merely transmitting movement ideology. Diagnostic framing articulates what is wrong with society, government, or some other aspect of social life, and attributes responsibility (Snow and Byrd 2007). Diagnostic frames are not fixed or static but change over time. In applying diagnostic framing to Islamic terrorist groups, Snow and Byrd suggest that there is some evidence for a shift from blaming Westernization and the United States to a more inwardly based frame that focuses on oppression and inequality against Muslims within their own countries.

Once groups articulate diagnostic frames (i.e., what's wrong and who's to blame?), prognostic frames offer solutions to grievances. Frame alignment occurs when organizers and potential members share a common definition of both "what is wrong" and "what needs to be done" (Snow et al. 1986). Yet in Snow and Byrd's examination of both the Iranian revolution and the recent Sunni–Shi'a conflict in Iraq, they note that solutions do not flow neatly from diagnoses and are often contested.

Although groups may be successful in aligning diagnostic and prognostic frames, this does not automatically translate into individuals who will readily act on behalf of the movement. As Snow and Byrd argue, the problem of motivational framing is moving constituents "from the balconies to the barricades" (2007: 128). Motivational frames must encourage people to take action despite incurring risks in light of the possibility of receiving the same benefits by doing nothing (i.e., free-rider effect). In their review of writings on Islamic terrorist movements, Snow and Byrd note that clerical leaders frame action as a religious and moral duty but this is not always sufficient. In the case of Palestinian suicide bombers, the appeal of special rewards, both spiritual and worldly, is especially motivating.

The use of framing as an analytic tool promises a more nuanced and complicated view of social movements because the three core framing tasks can vary both within and among movements. For example, when comparing two movements, a diagnostic frame may not be as important as a prognostic frame and even within a movement, the importance of different types of frames may shift over time as a reaction to the task at hand or the type of social control or support encountered (Snow and Byrd 2007). Diagnostic framing may not be as important when members are recruited from preexisting networks as organizers can assume more shared values and beliefs and thus devote more energy to prognostic and motivational frames (Jasper and Poulsen 1995). There may also be differences between frames, in the level of both development and coherence. While diagnostic and prognostic frames might be well developed and cohesive, mobilization frames may not be. Finally, frames may vary in relevance as perceived by their intended audience. Because of these potential differences, Snow and Byrd note that it is possible to find differences in both the "spread and mobilization efficacy of a number of movements within the same category" (2007: 130) including Islamic terrorist groups such as Al Qaeda or Hezbollah.

Categorical Terrorism

Jeff Goodwin's (2006) theory of categorical terrorism proposes to explain violence or threats of violence against noncombatants or civilians. Goodwin argues that terrorists do not attack civilians indiscriminately. Because terrorists are interested in gaining the support of some segments of the population, terrorists direct violence toward "complicitous civilians" (2006: 2037) or persons who benefit from the actions of the state, support the state, and/or are perceived as having an influence on state policy. According to Goodwin, the goal of categorical terrorism is to influence complicitous civilians to stop supporting the state or to demand changes favored by the terrorists such as a policy change. Goodwin identifies three factors that he believes influence the decision to use categorical terrorism.

Most importantly, categorical terrorism is used when combatants perceive that there are complicitous civilians or those who "benefit from, support, demand or tolerate *extensive and indiscriminate state violence or state terrorism* [emphasis Goodwin's] against the revolutionaries and their presumed constituents" (2006: 2039). A second factor is having a large and unprotected group of complicitous civilians. When the target group is smaller or well protected because of wealth or social status, violence is less likely. A third factor is the lack of political alliances between revolutionaries and their supporters and the complicitious civilians. When ties or alliances do exist between supporters of categorical terrorists and civilian targets, violence is discouraged because targeting complicitious civilians would jeopardize a potential political ally. Goodwin acknowledges that his ideas need more rigorous empirical testing; yet, he provides an interesting framework for connecting terrorist decision making with structural factors. All of the theories reviewed suggest various causes of terrorism. The next section reviews some of the more popular ideas discussed by social scientists.

CAUSES OF TERRORISM

Sociological theories generate questions that can be tested by empirical data. Gathering such data can be difficult as terrorist events are performed by a small number of individuals operating in relative secrecy and not directly accessible to sociologists (Bergesen and Lizardo 2004; Smelser 2007). Identifying terrorist events to study is difficult because this depends on identifying the motive (Beck 2007; Tilly 2004) in an era when increasingly groups do not make public claims of responsibility (Schmid and Jongman 1988) and violence may be due to vengeance or retribution (Senechal de la Roche 2004: 2). Social scientists as well as government officials are forced to use more indirect methods such as the posting of Web site videos and background information on group ideologies. All of these sources are helpful but this information is limited and sometimes even misleading. In this next section we review recent empirical findings. Because the literature focuses on substate actors, we do as well but acknowledge the seriousness of state and state-sponsored terror.

della Porta (2004) argues that understanding terrorism involves dynamics that operate at three levels, including micro, meso, and macro. Microdynamics is a more social psychological approach that focuses on the characteristics of individuals involved in terrorist organizations. The mesodynamic level is concerned with group characteristics, whereas the macrodynamic level is more focused on societal or institutional conditions that foster political violence. A sociological approach to terrorism tends to favor the macrodynamic level with calls for examining the political, social, and economic context in which it takes place (Oliverio and Lauderdale 2005); yet, all three approaches provide valuable information.

Microdynamic and Social Psychological Variables

A microdynamic or psychological approach focuses on individual personality characteristics including low self-esteem, lack of personal trust, self-destruction, narcissism, or emotional disturbance (Kinloch 2005). Unfortunately, there is little consensus on what psychological traits define terrorists, with most experts agreeing that terrorists are essentially normal (de Zulueta 2006). Irving Horowitz's (1973) study of the biographical details of terrorists in the 1970s suggest that most are male, young, middle class, economically marginalized, self-destructive, willing to self-sacrifice, and lack a well-defined ideological persuasion. Whether this applies to today's more religiously motivated terrorists is unknown.

della Porta argues that focusing on militant characteristics fails to address the question, "how can isolated and marginalized individuals translate strains into collective action?" (2004: 3 of 8). It is not that psychological or more microdynamic approaches are unhelpful, as this approach aids in understanding why members stay (della Porta 2004). For example, there is some evidence that individuals recruited into Al Qaeda are encouraged to cut off ties with friends and family who do not share their extreme fundamentalist views (de Zulueta 2006). Because of extreme isolation, terrorist groups became the only reference for members (della Porta 2004). Contemporary research emphasizes collectively held beliefs, perceptions of the group, and the risks and benefits of staying or leaving. Fully understanding these issues necessitates a shift from the individual to the group.

Mesodynamic

This type of explanation is interested in group characteristics such as shared ideologies and how groups are able to attract and keep resources, including money, members, and leaders. An additional area of inquiry is how groups adapt their ideology, strategies, and structures to the external environment. della Porta (2004) argues that isolation, a feature of clandestine groups, limits the ability to adapt.

Individuals who are more socially isolated and believe it is easier to stay with a terrorist group than to leave are more likely to do so. Perceptions shared among group members include believing that society is unjust, can be changed, should be changed, and it is one's duty to do so (Moghaddam 2003). Other views collectively held by terrorists include believing that the world can be divided into good and evil, that the ends of terrorism justify the means, that terror is necessary, and that engaging in terrorism is a form of self-improvement (Moghaddam 2003). Using framing terminology, individuals share diagnostic and prognostic frames.

SOCIALIZATION OF TERRORISTS   The vast majority of persons who suffer from poverty and oppression do not become terrorists although they may be passive supporters according to Frasier (Henderson 2004). What experiences increase the likelihood of an individual becoming a terrorist and how do groups socialize members? Terrorists are not born but are a product of the social and cultural environment in which they are enmeshed. Groups such as families and other socialization agents may socialize members to be more susceptible to framing by terrorist groups. Staub (2003) argues that terrorists are more likely to have childhoods characterized by extreme pain, suffering, and harsh treatment with few opportunities for warmth and affection from caring adults who modeled other ways of working for change. Socialization is a lifelong process that influences our daily interactions. Smelser's (2007) review of the literature suggests that networks are important, with people being influenced by friends, family, in-laws, and other associates.

COLLECTIVE IDENTITY   Others have argued that the need for a functioning collective identity can explain a proclivity for terrorism (Taylor and Louis 2003). *Collective* identity is defined as "a description of the group to which individuals belong against which they can articulate their unique attributes" (172). Sociologists refer to reference groups as the collective against which we evaluate ourselves. Taylor and Lewis argue that individuals can have a variety of collective identities because we belong to a variety of different groups, including ones defined by ethnicity, gender, work, and leisure, but the cultural group, which may or may not include religion, has special relevance. This cultural collective identity specifies both what is valued in society and the acceptable means for obtaining achievement and recognition. The significance of collective identity is that one cannot have a personal identity without the collective to serve as a backdrop. Furthermore, a functioning collective identity exists only when there is a means to achieve valued goals.

Although Osama bin Laden comes from a privileged family in Saudi Arabia and is highly educated, because he had no opportunity to achieve his ambitions, he constructed a new collective identity based on blaming the West and specifically the United States for the economic deprivation that exists in the Arab world (Taylor and Lewis 2003). Some of the 9/11 hijackers as well as the Russian revolutionaries known as People's Will (responsible for the assassination of Tsar Alexander II in 1881) were highly educated and came from the middle or upper social classes (Carr 2006) although this does vary within the group, with followers having less education and status compared to leaders (Smith 2002). Social alienation may also be relevant to understanding motivation (Smelser 2007). The London bombers also were not poor but their social alienation may have been an outcome of having no sense of belonging (Turner 2007).

Though much more empirical evidence needs to be gathered to document whether collective identity issues and/or social alienation are relevant explanatory variables, the importance placed on the interaction between individuals and structural forces within their environment such as the disconnect between cultural goals and opportunity structures to achieve those goals is interesting. Merton's (1968) strain theory of deviance may be one lens through which we can view terrorism and the connection between individual actions and structural forces.

STRAIN THEORY   Briefly, Robert Merton argues that deviance, or the violation of cultural norms, occurs because of a break between cultural goals such as achievement and culturally accepted means to achieve those goals, such as education or employment. This disconnect is called strain, and results in four types of deviance including the ritualist, rebel, retreatist, and innovator (Merton 1968). Of these, the innovator and the rebel are especially relevant to terrorism.

Innovative deviance occurs when individuals accept cultural goals but reject the means to achieve those goals. A classic example is a drug dealer who accepts goals such as accumulating wealth but rejects the accepted means of achieving this goal through education or hard work. A terrorist may accept cultural goals of achievement but may use terrorism as a means of success. In his examination of forty neo-Nazi terrorists, criminologist Mark Hamm (2004) argues that celebrity is the goal for many.

In contrast, the rebel rejects both societal goals and means and tries to actively replace both. Theodore Kaczynski, the Unabomber, sent mail bombs to airlines and universities for over eighteen years before being detected. In his manifesto published in 1995 by the *New York Times* and *Washington Post*,[8] he argued that the bombs were necessary to call attention to the evils of modern technology. He rejected cultural goals and the means to achieve them by resigning from the University of California, Berkeley, faculty and subsisting in a remote Montana shack by occasionally doing odd jobs. He actively tried to replace societal goals and means by sending mail bombs (Oleson 2005).

Employment is another traditional means of achieving success that is blocked for some individuals. Neil Smelser's (2007) review of motivational factors notes that terrorists are often unemployed and reside in countries not of their origin. Opportunity structures may be more difficult to traverse for individuals who are trying to adapt to different cultures and turning to terrorism may be one outcome of failing to assimilate. Whether Merton's theory can be applied cross-culturally to Islamic militants or other terrorist groups remains to be seen, but is an interesting line of inquiry that has been applied to the Italian terrorist group, Brigate Rosse (Ruggiero 2005). With strain theory, Merton attempts to connect individuals to larger societal forces, including culture. Structural factors operate outside the control of both groups and individuals and constitute what della Porta (2004) refers to as a macrodynamic level of analysis.

Macrodynamic or Structural

This level seeks to discover how social, economic, and political forces create and sustain violence. This is not to say that the social structure of a society is *solely* responsible for creating terrorists. We agree with Hallett (2003: 65) that "one cannot say that the terrorists' social milieu 'creates' him. To do so is to deny the terrorist his individuality, his moral agency." Disagreeing with Hallett, Black asserts that "every form of violence has its own structure" whether it is dueling, lynching, feuding, or terrorism, and that "structures kill and maim, not individuals or collectivities" (2004: 15). Regardless of which perspective is correct, we must acknowledge that some social contexts are more conducive to terrorism than others and that there are outside social forces that influence and contribute to individual behavior. Although recognizing the importance of phenomena operating on all three levels, della Porta (2004: 7 of 8) argues that political violence occurs when institutions are unable to direct conflict into a "peaceful decision-making process" and that interactions between social movements and the state are important for understanding the emergence of terrorist organizations.

Structural conditions that breed terrorism include a lack of political power, severe economic stress, rapid social change, perceived threats to national interests, and political conflict (Taylor and Louis 2003). A political climate supportive of the goals of the terrorist group is also associated with activity. For example, Beck (2007) found that ecoterrorism in the United States tends to occur in areas that primarily vote Democrat and have a "youth bulge" defined as 20 percent or more of the population between the ages of fifteen and twenty-four. Islamic societies with a youth bulge are experiencing an upswing in terrorism (Hallett 2003).

Marsella (2003) argues that terrorism will continue unless the root structural causes, including global poverty, racism, oppression, and political instability are addressed. Similarly, Smelser argues that dispossession is a key predisposition for terrorism and is defined as "perceptions on the part of the group that it is systematically excluded, discriminated against, or disadvantaged with respect to some meaningful aspect of social, economic, and political life to which it feels entitled" (2007: 16). Globalization may feed perceptions of exclusion and deprivation because through instant communication and increased tourism it has become increasingly possible to compare one's life to those living in more developed countries and to also attribute blame to those perceived as "fattening at the expense of the plundered majority of earth inhabitants" (Galkin 2006: 79).

Only a small minority of the world's population lives in relative comfort. Wealthy nations, including the United States, are perceived to be the source of global poverty because consumption of cheap goods and services is based on the exploitation of others, which fuels anger and resentment. Globalization has created more economic inequality that lead working-class Arabs to embrace militant Islam (Martin 2007; Toth 2003). Furthermore, globalization is not only an economic phenomenon but also a social one, through the exporting of cultural values and beliefs. There is a positive association between violent actions directed at the United States and global economic interaction through foreign direct investment and the expansion of world culture through international nongovernmental organizations (INGOs) affiliated with the UN (Lizardo 2006). INGOs enhance lives by pressuring governments to abide by International Human Rights treaties, but as noted by Wiest (2006), this expansion of world culture has empowered both human rights activists and those who use violence against the state.

GLOBALIZATION   Globalization has contributed to the spread of Western values such as individualism, materialism, and liberalism that challenge Islamic fundamental views that stress collectivism and authoritarianism. Increasingly, globalization has come to mean Westernization and Americanization (Martin 2007; White 2003). Westernization is perceived as threatening traditional hierarchies, including family and religious structures, which leads to rising levels of violence. Some of the most popular expressions of the argument predicting violence motivated by religion in response to Westernization are Samuel Huntington's *Clash of Civilizations* thesis (1993, 1996) and Benjamin Barber's *Jihad vs. McWorld* (2001). Although Huntington's arguments have been severely criticized, others argue that this does not mean that the problems outlined by Huntington are unfounded (Galkin 2006; Martin 2007; Turner 2007). In *Jihad vs. McWorld,* Barber agrees that resentment of Westernization breeds the development of religious fundamentalist opposition but unlike Huntington, he comes to the conclusion that McWorld will "win" because in the end, Jihad must use the same strategies.

It is not simply a matter of clashing values but the perception that Western values are penetrating the entire globe through mass media and commercial exports such as Hollywood films and music. Every society values the very things that make it unique including values, beliefs, and customs. Although terrorism is an extreme response to cultural identity threats, consider how perceived threats to American culture evoke passionate debate over issues like bilingualism and workplace accommodations and proposals such as the one to build a fence across the U.S.–Mexico border. Though none of these responses are as extreme as terrorism, surely we can identify with the feelings of those who wish to protect their way of life while still condemning terrorist actions.

America, Love It or Leave It

Credit: Photo by Karl Wagenfuehr and used under licensing agreement with http://creativecommons. org/licenses/by-sa/2.0/.

Some may argue that avoiding Westernization is as simple as forgoing Hollywood films and other cultural products. However, as a structural force, the effects of globalization are beyond the making of individual choices; refusing to see a film does not immunize someone from Westernization, because globalization forces an interdependency through a variety of systems, including transportation, telecommunications, and transnational capital flow through organizations dominated by the West (e.g., World Bank) (Marsella 2003). Not all researchers agree that a Western homogenization of culture is an outcome of globalization (Robertson 1992).

While globalization is considered a grievance that is a root cause of terrorism, the changes in international terrorism are also a reflection of globalization. For example, terrorist networks working across national boundaries resemble global business networks. Terrorists operate with no regard for national boundaries, and demands and pronouncements made by terrorist groups decreasingly reflect a specific national interest (Bergesen and Han 2005). Just as globalization has made it easier for people and goods to flow across borders, it has also simplified transportation for terrorists who freely mingle with tourists (Galkin 2006). Martin (2007) argues that access to the media via the Internet and more integrated economies defines "new terrorism." This differs from older forms through the use of asymmetrical methods, including the use of high-yield weapons and religious motivation for violence.

Asymmetrical methods have transformed terrorism from the use of "armed propaganda" (Martin 2007: 7 of 15) into a mode of warfare that enables terrorists to confront a much larger and seemingly more powerful enemy using creative tactics (e.g., using an airliner as an armed missile in the 9/11 attacks). Launching a cyber attack that can disrupt communications and financial transactions is a new threat enabled by globalization. While terrorists have always had access to bombs and guns, the weapons of today (e.g., AK-47 rifles and plastic explosives) are much more destructive than their predecessors (Martin 2007). The potential to acquire weapons of mass destruction (e.g., radiological, chemical, biological, and nuclear) also dramatically increases the killing potential. Martin argues that although terrorists in the past killed civilians, they tended to constrain themselves to symbolic targets. With new terrorism, the entire population is viewed as a legitimate target. Those religiously motivated may be less disturbed by the targeting of civilians, believing that these actions will please God no matter how violent and destructive.

POLITICAL OPPRESSION   Political oppression is also considered an important structural factor but its relationship with terrorism is not clear-cut. Oppression of a subnational group by powerful central governments (e.g., China, Chechnya, perceived treatment of the Palestinians by the Israelis) results in some groups using terrorism as a means for calling attention to their oppression as well as exacting revenge. Many Arabs and Muslims believe that the West is biased against them and the perceived disproportionate support given to Israel is considered proof (Galkin 2006; Marsella 2003).

CIVIL LIBERTIES   Although oppression might be a grievance that might motivate terror, the existence of civil liberties in a target area is a structural condition that increases the likelihood of an attack. Democracies are prone to terrorist attacks precisely because the freedoms inherent within them protect terrorist groups. For example, Palestinian suicide bombers perceive political oppression as a result of their experiences living in the West Bank and Gaza Strip but carry out their attacks within Israel, a democratic society, by targeting Israelis who are going to work, waiting for the bus, or shopping (Enders and Sandler 2006).

SECURITY   Nations such as Iraq and Afghanistan are unstable and lack the ability to provide basic services including security. Terrorism is seen by some as a response to the ongoing instability. Citizens may tolerate and assist armed terrorist groups operating in their area because some security is better than none at all.

Many of the structural factors mentioned in this section including political instability, globalization, and clash of cultural values are linked to Westernization. Grievances are often motivators for terrorism but are not sufficient causes for violence (Black 2004; Schmid and Jongman 1988) because other response options exist, including protest and inaction (Tilly 2004). Black (2004: 16) describes terrorism as "self-help, the handling of a grievance with aggression." What then explains whether individuals with grievances caused by structural factors will engage in this sort of self-help?

GEOMETRY   According to Black, a grievance must be accompanied by "the right geometry—a particular location and direction in social space" (2004: 18). Relying on the work of Senechal de la Roche, Black argues that terrorism is more likely when social distances are great (e.g., indigenous persons resisting colonial rulers) and less likely when not. For example, terrorism is less likely when grievances are individual rather than collective and when conflict originates between adversaries that share social space, such as members of a community or a shared ethnicity. Subnational terroristic conflict is also less likely to be initiated by social superiors against those with less or equal social power. Terrorism is more likely when a collective has a shared grievance against an entity with more social power and this collective is socially distant due to differing ethnicities or societal membership.

Social geometry must also be accompanied by physical opportunities that Black argues were not common until the twentieth century. Noting that terrorists often try other political strategies first, Goodwin (2006, 2007) contends that the turn to "categorical terrorism" is more likely when potential victims are perceived as complicit in the oppression of the aggrieved group and unlikely to convert.

Black's analysis may explain why WS theorists have failed to find evidence of terrorism during the Spain hegemonic era preceding the Thirty Years' War as this predates the technological advances that have allowed civilians of differing social positions to come into frequent physical contact.

"Terrorism arises only when a grievance has a social geometry distant enough and a physical geometry close enough for mass violence against civilians" (Black 2004: 21). Recall that another weakness of WS is the failure to explain why terrorism develops in the semiperiphery as opposed to the periphery.

Although the periphery and the semiperiphery share both greater social distance and grievances against the core, the semiperiphery might provide more opportunities for physical contact with potential targets. Theoretical models that incorporate both a WS perspective and a social geometric view of collective violence could become a powerful tools for explaining the structural causes of international terrorism.

RESPONDING TO TERRORISM

Terrorism is difficult to combat for a variety of reasons. As William Crotty argues, "authoritarian governments . . . are likely to persevere; repression will continue; poverty, ignorance, fear of modernity, and religious zealotry will not disappear; and military action over any prolonged period of time is costly, debilitating to the nation relying on it, and potentially destructive to the democratic values it has been enlisted to serve" (2005: 523). While military action and counter intelligence or security seems to be the primary U.S. method for combating terrorism, other options exist, including diplomacy, economic sanctions, humanitarian aid (Crotty 2005), and other methods of peacemaking and peacebuilding (Wagner 2006). Ultimately, terrorism cannot be eliminated without removing social and political motivators (Galkin 2006).

Using the context of Muslim attacks against the West, removing social and political motivators would require that grievances be addressed, including global poverty and political oppression. For some, this is considered the only real hope of ending violence (de Zulueta 2006). Any action requires the long-term financial commitment of several nations and with the exception of military action is unlikely to show any short-term improvement. While military action has immediate short-term effects, its use as a primary means of combating terrorism is unlikely to have sustainable positive effects and may in fact be counterproductive by fueling more terrorism (Butko 2006). We address several potential state responses to terrorism including increasing security and repression, eliminating political opportunities, alleviating structural causes, and peacebuilding.

Security and Response

Henderson (2004) distinguishes between two types of substate terrorism; *systematic* that is based on global disparities such as poverty and other economic, political, and cultural issues, and *idiosyncratic* or groups that have absolute views on a specific issue such as abortion or animal rights. The response to terrorism depends on which type is involved because strategies that will work with one type will not necessarily work with another. For example, antiabortion terrorist groups will stop their violence only if laws are changed, rendering abortion illegal. Barring that, the only appropriate response seems to be intelligence gathering and the hardening of targets or rendering them less susceptible to attack. Preventing and responding to terrorist attacks is a complicated process with a bureaucratic structure that poses many organizational and technological challenges. For example, in the United States, technology is often antiquated and the federal bureaucracy is complex, with agencies such as the Federal Bureau of Investigation (FBI) and Central Intelligence Agency (CIA) resistant to sharing turf.

The merging of security functions into the Department of Homeland Security (DHS) was intended to improve disaster responsiveness. But even within DHS there are a myriad of agencies, including Federal Emergency Management Agency (FEMA), Immigration and Customs Enforcement (ICE), Transportation Security Administration (TSA), Customs and Border Protection, the Coast Guard, and the Secret Service. These agencies have different organizational cultures that can be hard to mesh, and congressional oversight often pulls agencies in different directions with a potential for mission creep or straying from intended mandates (Kettl 2004). While Kettl contends that it makes sense to subsume FEMA into DHS because the needs and priorities of first responders are similar for both terrorism and natural disasters, this analysis predates FEMA's flawed response to Hurricane Katrina. Security and repression are less controversial strategies when applied to idiosyncratic groups. Our subsequent discussion will consider possible responses to terrorism committed by nonidiosyncratic groups.

Repression

The repression paradigm is a typical government response to terrorism (Martin 2006). Some have termed current U.S. policies as an example of a *garrison state* with treatment of immigrant detainees by the ICE and the FBI as an example of state-initiated violence (Franz 2005). While everyone is aware of the atrocities committed by the U.S. military at Abu Ghraib prison in Iraq, examples of abuse of Arab and Muslim immigrant detainees in the United States documented by the Department of Justice include beating, withholding of halal (Islamic dietary laws) food, and denial of access to family members and legal assistance (Franz 2005). The treatment of immigrant detainees, the indefinite confinement of enemy combatants at the U.S. Naval base in Guantánamo Bay, Cuba (prior to the U.S. Supreme Court decision), alleged torture of detainees, and the expanded surveillance powers of the USA PATRIOT Act can be considered outcomes of what Giorgio Agamben (2005) calls the "state of exception."

Historically, states of exception occur when regimes are faced with extraordinary crises such as the 9/11 terrorist attacks. These extraordinary events provide the justification needed for extreme measures such as the curtailing of civil liberties. The USA PATRIOT Act (Wong 2006) as well as the British equivalent (Zedner 2005) was adopted with little challenge. While the public initially supported the increased surveillance and other curtailments of civil rights after 9/11, poll data suggest that this support has declined (Best, Krueger, and Ladewig 2006; Matthew and Shambaugh 2005).

The danger of a state of exception is its potential to turn democracies into authoritarian regimes. Consider some of the more controversial aspects of the USA PATRIOT Act, including "sneak and peek" warrants (authorities may search the premises without an owner present and delay notification), roving wiretaps (allows wiretapping without the prior establishment of cause), and the ability to easily obtain medical, employment, and educational records as well as DNA samples (Wong 2006). Robert Weiss contends that U.S. society has the ingredients for "conservative totalitarianism" (2006: 135) given the history of state-sanctioned torture combined with other violent proclivities. This is one potential outcome of the state of exception.

Agamben believes that the state of exception is becoming the basis for modern state power in the West. The extraordinary measures that are used to respond to crises, such as the suspension of habeas corpus, become the rule rather than anomalies. The implication for democracies is that legal protections previously guaranteed to all are at the whim of law enforcement and other judicial processes—no longer a guarantee. In a state of exception, a citizen is at risk of becoming a *homo sacer,* or someone stripped of all legal and civil protections (Agamben 1998). Creators of the Index of Democracy argue that security- and terrorism-related concerns along with a decline in political participation and weakness in government functioning are having a "corrosive effect on some long-established democracies" (Economist Intelligence Unit 2008: 1).

As noted by Lauderdale and Oliverio (2005), Dwight D. Eisenhower, former U.S. President and Army General, warned of state ability to inappropriately use power to bring about change by evading government checks and balances. What Eisenhower termed the *Military–Industrial Complex* is alive and well with secret CIA prisons and the use of private security contractors for jobs including interrogation. Military personnel prosecuted for Abu Ghraib contend that CIA interrogators, army military intelligence, and private contractors encouraged them to soften up prisoners (Meixler 2004). Additionally, private security firms operating in Iraq have been immune from criminal prosecution. An incident where thirteen Iraqi civilians were allegedly killed in 2007 by Blackwater USA employees prompted U.S. Secretary of State Condolezza Rice to order security cameras installed in all vehicles and to have U.S. State Department diplomatic security guards ride with Blackwater conveys (Lee 2007). Blackwater USA (now XeServices LLC) is only one of many nonstate private security companies under scrutiny, including two investigated for Abu Ghraib abuses (Lauderdale and Oliverio 2005). When nonstate actors commit abuses against civilians that are financed by the state, it constitutes state-sponsored terror.

Not everyone agrees that a state of exception exists, because although liberal democracies initially respond to terrorism by giving security precedence over the importance of human rights and civil liberties, these practices are moderated over time with the pendulum forced toward the center (Matthew and Shambaugh 2005). Whether this describes what will ultimately happen to policies involving the "war on terror" is uncertain, but many have a vested interest in maintaining the status quo of citizen fear and repression justified by the promise of increased security.

Sociologists ask, "Who benefits from fear?" and besides the terrorists, there is the state and business. It is easier for the state to be unfettered from legal obligations such as warrants and speedy trials. Security companies benefit from fear of terrorism just as alarm companies benefit from the public's fear of crime (Zedner 2005). An example is the aftermath of the anthrax scare in 2001 that raised new fears about bioterrorism.

According to the authors of *Marching Plague: Germ Warfare and Global Public Heath,* the public should fear the institutions (e.g., military, government, business) benefiting from the weaponization of germs more than they should fear the specter of bioterrorism itself. They contend using germs is not an effective military strategy due to the inability to control weather conditions and the limited efficacy of germs in a single indoor space. They argue that terrorists have "more profoundly symbolic and terrible ways to kill" that are readily available (Critical Art Ensemble 2006: 32).

Alleviating Structural Causes

Galtung and Fischer (2002) call for dialogue and global education as the first step toward addressing structural causes that breed grievances and ultimately terrorism. A political and economic development approach suggests that in the long run, substate terrorism will only subside by reducing the gap between developed nations and developing ones, or the haves and the have-nots. Henderson (2004) refers to global disparities as the *engine that drives terrorism* and predicts that dislocation due to global warming and population and immigration pressures are future engines to consider. Marsella (2003) argues that rogue nations foster terrorism both within and beyond national borders and encourage diplomacy and economic development as a means of diffusing precursor economic and political conditions.

It is impossible to stall or reverse globalization and Westernization. But actions could mitigate some of the grievances associated with it. For example, educating Westerners on the numerous contributions made by Arabs and Muslims to world culture and celebrating those contributions may reverse perceptions of ethnocentrism and reduce resentment toward the West. Perhaps more importantly, curbing the inequality in developing countries that comes with globalization may also eliminate grievances.

Eliminating Political Opportunities

If Oberschall (2004) is correct, eliminating political opportunities should curtail terrorism. In the case of international or transnational terrorism, he argues that policy initiatives such as pressuring governments not to provide a safe haven for insurgents as well as reducing the flow of resources from citizens of other countries to terrorist groups (e.g., much of the cash raised by the Irish Republican Army was from U.S. citizens) should go a long way in curbing violence. Oberschall acknowledges that states agreeing to enact policies aimed at reducing political opportunities may insist that target states also engage to bring about a more peaceful political solution and that this response is the first best choice for eliminating violence.

Peacebuilding

Terrorism based on ideology, or what Henderson (2004) terms *old terrorism*, can be addressed by supporting the peace process as established in Northern Ireland, Sri Lanka, and Spain. Oberschall (2004) suggests that while no terrorist group has been successful in the overthrow of a government, they have ceased their activities when they have attained their goals, including on some occasions, power-sharing agreements with governments. Governments that attempt to negotiate with terrorists have a more successful outcome when they do not insist on cease-fires and other absolutes to terrorist activities. Like Tilly (2004), Oberschall recognizes that terrorist groups often have a variety of individuals who may practice both terrorism and conventional politics. To insist on a complete moratorium puts the most violent faction of an insurgency in charge. Thus, peacekeeping is unlikely to bring about a long-term solution to the problem (Wagner 2006).

Peacemaking involves dealing with basic needs such as providing security and economic resources to an aggrieved group as well as negotiating solutions to previous injustice. Current peacemaking efforts tend to deal with narrowly defined issues such as the control of a specific piece of land or who can send representatives to a governing body. Long-term peacemaking solutions need to deal with the basis of the conflict (Wagner 2006) such as the loss of land experienced by the Palestinians, treatment of the Palestinians by the Israeli government (e.g., razing the homes of family members of suspected terrorists), and the right of Israel to exist as a Jewish state. Like peacekeeping, Wagner argues that peacemaking will not result in an end to terrorism because peacemaking proposals do not build in a mechanism for withstanding future conflicts.

Peacebuilding involves alleviating the causes of grievances as well as developing *realistic empathy* between antagonists. Wagner explains this does not mean one has to agree or sympathize with the other party but to understand their perspective. True understanding comes from trying "to walk in another person's shoes" or what sociologists call role-taking (Mead 1934). In applying realistic empathy to the Palestinian–Israeli conflict, Wagner suggests that Palestinians might then be able to understand Israel's real need for security precautions and that Israelis might begin to see why Palestinians are angry over the loss of their homeland and their current need for autonomy and self-determination. Terrorism is less likely when aggrieved parties come to view the target group as potential allies. Goodwin (2007) notes that the African National Congress (ANC) did not resort to terrorism in their antiapartheid struggle in South Africa because they came to see whites as potential allies despite the fact that these same whites were benefiting from the apartheid system.

THE FUTURE OF TERRORISM

The demonization of terrorism results in this label being used for every evil act of violence in society and when a term is overused, the "sin of the ism" will disappear (Ukai 2005: 249). While terrorism may cease to be useful as a social science concept, the behaviors themselves are still a concern. What do social scientists predict for the future of terrorism? As expected, there is no single view, with both pessimists and optimists making predictions.

Optimistic View

Black (2004) argues that increasing technology, including transportation and electronic communication, has made physical geometry less relevant and social geometry even more so. Terrorism increased because of opportunities for those with great social distance to have closer physical contact. Eventually, technology will reduce terrorism because of the potential to decrease social distance due to greater global intimacy. Black's argument is based on the premise that terrorism occurs because of differences in cultural values and having greater contact over time will dissipate these differences. In the case of American targets, political scientist John Mearsheimer (2008) disagrees by arguing that terrorists do not hate Americans because of who they are but terrorists do hate American policies. Citing the *Wall Street Journal,* Noam Chomsky (2003) argues that a survey of post-9/11 attitudes of nonterrorist Muslims with money (e.g., bankers, professionals) found that there was much support for U.S. policies in the wake of 9/11 as well as admiration for American freedoms, but there was also deep resentment of U.S. support for repressive and corrupt regimes. Black's prediction is unlikely if terrorism is due to anger over U.S. foreign policy.

Pessimistic View

Terrorism works best when it inhibits the target's behavior, enhances the standing of perpetrators with allies, and influences third parties to cooperate with terrorist organizations (Tilly 2004). Terrorism will continue because there will always be weaker parties with grievances trying to level the playing field and the inability of multiple governments to effectively coordinate their antiterrorist policies (Enders and Sandler 2006). If we concede that a world without terrorism or the threat of terrorism is highly unlikely, what can we expect to happen in the next few decades? Some predictions have been made, including:

1. Domestic terrorism will continue to overshadow transnational terrorism
2. Terrorists will continue to change tactics, venues, and targets as a means of adapting to counterterrorism
3. Attacks waged by religious groups will continue to be more deadly per incident.
4. Terrorists will continue to use the Internet as a means of coordination and communication.
5. Economic targets will continue to be vulnerable. (Enders and Sandler 2006: 256–257)

FUTURE DIRECTIONS

Research

Albert Bergesen and Yi Han (2005) urge sociologists to consider two issues as they conceptualize and implement future research. First, use a comparative approach that captures which international conditions are associated with terrorism and the cycles or waves of terrorism that occur. They note that the current cycle is similar to that of 1878–1914, which they describe as a leftist, anarchist-inspired wave preceding World War I.

Second, transnational terrorism needs a more nuanced conceptualization that accounts for different degrees of internationalism. For example, they note that the 9/11 attacks involved perpetrators from abroad attacking a foreign target on its own turf, which is a much more aggressive attack than perpetrators attacking targets on the home turf of the perpetrators or going abroad to attack foreign interests that are located in neither the home turf of the perpetrators nor targets. This conceptualization does away with the domestic and international split. Domestic terrorism is simply the least international of the four types (see Figure 9.5). This is important because Bergesen and Han (2005) believe that domestic terrorism should not be construed as a special

Victim		
Perpetrator	*Home*	*Away*
Home	Assassination of Egyptian President Sadet (1981)	Bombing of U.S. Marine Barracks in Beirut (1985)
Away	World Trade Center/Pentagon Attacks (2001)	U.S. Embassies Bombed in Nairobi and Dar es Salaam (1998)

FIGURE 9.5   Location of Perpetrator and Victim in Terrorist Incidents

Source: Based on Bergesen and Han (2005)

category of political violence although they do acknowledge that goals, recruitment tactics, and other issues might significantly differ between the four types. They suggest that researchers should ask three types of questions that are posed at different levels of analysis.

The first level inquires about organizations, ideologies, demands made, and types of violence used, such as are recruitment tactics different for different types of "international" terrorism? The second level uses the wave cycles (1870s–1914 and 1968–present) as the unit of inquiry, with researchers examining wave development and indicators of a life cycle. Finally, the third level should explore whether waves of terrorism are historically unique or whether cycles are similar.

CONCLUSION

Drawing on Max Weber's "Science as a Vocation" and "The Meaning of 'Ethical Neutrality' in Sociology and Economics," political scientist Jeffrey Isaac argues that social scientists have an obligation to provide analysis of significant events, including war. However, in times of war and civil unrest, the freedoms scholars depend upon, such as the ability to "inquire, communicate, and publicize" (2004: 476), are jeopardized. In Agamben's words, this is another outcome of state of exception democracies and it is up to scholars to "mobilize their theories to explain how and why those conflicts are unfolding" even if doing so discloses facts that are "inconvenient" to government "its critics, the media, terrorist organizations, rogue states, and clerical ideologues alike" (479). Disclosing "inconvenient facts" is the heart of sociology and essential for a critical analysis needed to challenge hegemonic notions (Lauderdale and Oliverio 2005) that are based on ideology and prejudice rather than scientific truth. Isaac contends that scholars have been impacted in numerous ways, including limitations on the free movement of scholars and students, surveillance that undermines the privacy of library and Internet users, and the emergence of campus "watchdog" groups such as "Middle East Watch."

Another concern is the misuse of scientific data and theories to justify the dehumanization and mistreatment of others, including alleged terrorists. As German scientist Benno Müller-Hill writes, "science is about knowledge and truth. So, we must ask ourselves, how could German scientists support anti-Semitism and the racial measures of the Nazis?" (2004: 485). In *Deadly Medicine,* Müller-Hill provides a detailed account of how some non-Jewish academics benefited from the anti-Semitism of the National Socialists even if they did not agree with it (and of course others did). Ethical scientists never let ideology or personal self-interest cloud their use of data or justify violence against others rooted in perceptions of superiority–inferiority.

Human history is replete with examples of violence perpetrated by nation-states against civilians, including their own citizens. While we live at a time when conventional war making is at an all-time low, violence does continue in less conventional but equally brutal forms, including genocide and terrorism. While most acts of terrorism occur overseas, domestic prevention measures are a continuing concern as the very protections afforded to citizens of a liberal democracy can also be used by terrorists to hide their activities. The continuing need for intelligence gathering and other security measures needs to be balanced against protecting civil liberties lest we come to live in a society that no longer resembles the democratic principles upon which it was founded. We predict that terrorism, war, and genocide will remain a significant topic of discussion in years to come and that political sociologists will increase their contributions to the understanding of this complex phenomenon.

Endnotes

1. The U.S. State Department (CIA uses the same definition) has a different definition than the Department of Defense. The DHS defines terrorism as any activity that (1) involves an act that (a) is dangerous to human life or potentially destructive of critical infrastructure or key resources; and (b) is a violation of the criminal laws of the United States or of any State or other subdivision of the United States; and (2) appears to be intended (a) to intimidate or coerce a civilian population; (b) to influence the policy of a government by intimidation or coercion; or (c) to affect the conduct of a government by mass destruction, assassination, or kidnapping (http://www.dhs.gov/xprepresp/committees/editorial_0566.shtm). The FBI defines it as "the unlawful use of force or violence against persons or property to intimidate or coerce a government, the civilian population, or any segment thereof, in furtherance of political or social objectives" (http://www.fbi.gov).

2. The U.S. Air Transport Association estimates that compliance with post 9/11 security measures costs U.S. airlines $4.5 billion annually ("Relief Effort" 2007).

3. A potential immigrant belonging to a group on the TEL would be excluded from immigrating to the United States. It is illegal to knowingly provide material support or resources to any group labeled an FTO.

Alien members of such groups are excluded from the United States, and banks and other financial institution that become aware that they are holding funds of an FTO must maintain possession and report assets to the U.S. Treasury (http://www.state.gov/p/nea/rls/rm/2007/91522.htm).

4. Raul Reyes was killed by Columbian security forces on March 1, 2008 ("Columbian Forces Kill FARC Leader" 2008).

5. Because it is becoming less common for terrorist groups to take responsibility (Schmid and Jongman 1988), this has implications for counterterrorism actions but also for researchers developing theories and explanations of terrorism.

6. Authoritarian governments are less likely to report terrorist activities (Enders and Sandler 2006).

7. There has been an increase in the number of women who take part in suicide bombings although women have been active in terrorist movements including the ones at the turn of the twentieth century.

8. Publishing the Unabomber's manifesto was a controversial decision, as government officials were reluctant to give him a forum for his views. In hindsight it appears this was the right thing to do as Kaczynski's brother noted the similarities between the manifesto and his brother's letters and turned him in to the FBI.

References

Abi-Hashem, Naji. 2003. "Peace and War in the Middle East: A Psychopolitical and Sociocultural Perspective." Pp. 69–89 in *Understanding Terrorism*, edited by F. M. Moghaddam and A. J. Marsella. Washington, DC: American Psychological Association.

Agamben, Giorgio. 1998. *Homo Sacer: Sovereign Power and Bare Life*. Translated by Daniel Heller-Roazen. Stanford, CA: Stanford University Press.

_____. 2005. *State of Exception*. Translated by Kevin Attell. Chicago: Chicago University Press.

Barber, Benjamin. 2001. *Jihad vs. McWorld*. New York: Random House.

Bauman, Zygmunt. 2000. *Modernity and the Holocaust*. Ithaca, NY: Cornell University Press.

Beck, Colin J. 2007. "On the Radical Cusp: Ecoterrorism in the United States, 1998–2005." *Mobilization* 12: 161–176.

Bergesen, Albert J. 1990. "Turning World-System Theory on its Head." *Theory, Culture, and Society* 7: 67–81.
_____. 2007. "Three-Step Model of Terrorist Violence." *Mobilization* 12: 111–118.

Bergesen, Albert J. and Yi Han. 2005. "New Directions for Terrorism Research." *International Journal of Comparative Sociology* 46: 133–151.

Bergesen, Albert J. and Omar Lizardo. 2004. "International Terrorism and the World-System." *Sociological Theory* 22: 38–52.

Best, Samuel J., Brian S. Krueger, and Jeffrey Ladewig. 2006. "The Polls—Trends: Privacy in the Information Age." *Public Opinion Quarterly* 70: 375–401.

Black, Donald. 2004. "The Geometry of Terrorism." *Sociological Theory* 22: 14–25.

Black, J. 1998. *War and the World: Military Power and the Fate of Continents 1450–2000.* New Haven, CT: Yale University Press.

Brinkley, Douglas. 2010. "The Spark of Rebellion." *American Heritage* 59: 32–34.

Brownmiller, Susan. 1975. *Against Our Will.* New York: Simon and Schuster.

Brym, Robert J. and Bader Araj. 2006. "Suicide Bombing as Strategy and Interaction: The Case of the Second Intifada." *Social Forces* 84: 1969–1986.

Butko, Thomas. 2006 "Terrorism Redefined." *Peace Review* 18: 145–151.

Carr, Matthew. 2006. *The Infernal Machine: A History of Terrorism.* New York: The New Press.

Casey, Michael. 2007. "Groups Struggle to Tally Myanmar's Dead." *Associated Press*, October 1.

Chalk, Frank and Kurt Jonassohn. 1990. *The History and Sociology of Genocide.* New Haven, CT: Yale University Press.

Chomsky, Noam. 2003. *Hegemony or Survival: America's Quest for Global Dominance.* New York: Henry Holt.

Cohen, Irwin M. and Raymond R. Corrado. 2005. "State Terrorism in the Contemporary World." *International Journal of Comparative Sociology* 46: 103–131.

"Columbian Forces Kill FARC Leader." 2008. *News Services*, March 2.

"Crackdown in Iran." 2009. News Services, June 21.

Critical Art Ensemble. 2006. *Marching Plague: Germ Warfare and Global Public Health.* Brooklyn, NY: Autonomedia.

Crotty, William. 2005. "International Terrorism: Causes and Consequences for a Democratic Society." Pp. 523–531 in *Democratic Development and Political Terrorism*, edited by W. Crotty. Boston: Northeastern University Press.

della Porta, Donatella. 2004. "Terror against the State." In *The Blackwell Companion to Political Sociology,* edited by K. Nash and A. Scott. Blackwell Publishing. Blackwell Reference Online. Retrieved August 18, 2009 from http://www.blackwellreference.com/subscriber/tocnode?id=g781405122658_chunk_g978140512265821.

Dobratz, Betty A. and Stephanie L. Shanks-Meile. 1997. *White Power, White Pride: The White Separatist Movement in the United States.* New York: Twayne.

Duvall, Raymond D. and Michael Stohl. 1988. "Governance by Terror." Pp. 231–269 in *The Politics of Terrorism.* 3rd Edition, edited by M. Stohl. New York: Marcel Dekker.

Dworkin, R. 2003. "Terror and the Attack on Civil Liberties." *New York Review of Books:* 50.

Economist Intelligence Unit. 2008. "The Economist Intelligence Unit's Index of Democracy 2008." *Economist.* Retrieved July 22, 2009 from http://graphics.eiu.com/PDF/Democracy%20Index%202008.pdf.

Enders, Walter and Todd Sandler. 2006. *The Political Economy of Terrorism.* Cambridge, NY: Cambridge University Press.

Englehart, Neil and Charles Kurzman. 2006. "Welcome to World Peace." *Social Forces* 84: 1957–1967.

Evans, Peter. 2008. "Is an Alternative Globalization Possible?" *Politics & Society* 36: 271–305.

"FARC Writes: Stop Calling Us Terrorists." 2007. *Star Tribune* September 7: A10.

Franz, Barbara. 2005. "Letter from America: Still Land of the Free." *Borderlands* 4(1).

Gallup Poll News Service. 2007. Most Important Problem, September 24. Retrieved September 25, 2007 from http://www.galluppoll.com/content/?ci=1675&pg=1.

Galkin, Alexandr. 2006. "Globalization and the Political Upheavals of the 21st Century." *Social Sciences* 37: 67–82.

Galtung, Johan and Dietrich Fischer. 2002. "Preventing Terrorism." *Social Alternatives* 21: 67–68.

Garcia, Michael John and Ruth Ellen Wasem. 2007. "Immigration: Terrorist Grounds for Exclusion and Removal of Aliens." *CRS Report for Congress.* Congressional Research Service. Retrieved October 26, 2010 from http://fpc.state.gov/documents/organization/96472.pdf.

Gareau, Frederick. 2004. *State Terrorism and the United States: From Counterinsurgency to the War on Terrorism.* London: Clarity Press.

Genocide Intervention Network. 2007. "Darfur." Retrieved October 10, 2007 from http://www.genocideintervention.net/educate/darfur.

Gibbs, Jack P. 1989. "Conceptualization of Terrorism." *American Sociological Review* 54: 329–340.

Goodwin, Jeff. 2006. "A Theory of Categorical Terrorism." *Social Forces* 84: 2027–2046.

_____. 2007. "'The Struggle Made Me a Nonracialist': Why There Was so Little Terrorism in the Antiapartheid Struggle." *Mobilization* 12: 193–203.

Gramsci, Antonio. 1971. *Selections from the Prison Notebooks.* Edited by Q. Hoare and G. N. Smith. New York: International Publishers.

Hall, Thomas D. 2002. "World Systems Analysis and Globalization Directions for the Twenty First Century." Pp. 81–121 in *Theoretical Directions in Political Sociology for the 21st Century*, volume 11, *Research in Political Sociology*, edited by B. A. Dobratz, T. Buzzell, and L. K. Waldner. Oxford: Elsevier (JAI).

Hallett, Brian. 2003. "Dishonest Crimes, Dishonest Language: An Argument about Terrorism." Pp. 49–68 in *Understanding Terrorism*, edited by F. M. Moghaddam and A. J. Marsella. Washington, DC: American Psychological Association.

Hamm, Mark S. 2004. "Apocalyptic Violence: The Seduction of Terrorist Subcultures." *Theoretical Criminology* 8: 323–339.

Haque, M. S. 2003. "The Role of the State in Managing Ethnic Tensions in Malaysia." *American Behavioral Scientist* 47: 240–266.

Henderson, Harry. 2004. *Global Terrorism*. New York: Facts on File.

Henslin, James. 2002. *Essentials of Sociology*. 4th Edition. Boston: Allyn & Bacon.

Hooks, Gregory. 1994. "Regional Processes in the Hegemonic Nations: Political, Economic, and Military Influeunces on the Use of Geographic Space." *American Sociological Review* 59: 766–772.

Hooks, Gregory and Gregory McLauchlan. 1992a. "Reevaluating Theories of U.S. War Making: Technology and Bureacracy in Three Eras of Strategic Planning, 1939–1989." *Social Science Quarterly* 73: 437–456.

———. 1992b. "The Institutional Foundations of Warmaking: Three Eras of U.S. Warmaking, 1939–1989." *Theory and Society* 21: 757–788.

Hooks, Gregory and James Rice. 2005. "War, Militarism, and States: The Insights and Blind Spots of Political Sociology." Pp. 566–584 in *The Handbook of Political Sociology*, edited by T. Janoski, R. Alford, A. Hicks, and M. A. Schwartz. Cambridge: Cambridge University Press.

Horowitz, Irving L. 1973. "Political Terrorism and State Power." *Journal of Political and Military Sociology* 1: 147–157.

———. 2002. *Taking Lives: Genocide and State Power*. 5th Edition. New Brunswick, NJ: Transaction Publishers.

Huggins, Martha K. 1987 "U.S.-Supported State Terror: A History of Police Training in Latin America." *Crime and Social Justice* 27–28: 149–171.

Huntington, Samuel P. 1993. "The Clash of Civilizations." *Foreign Affairs* 72(3): 22, 48.

———. 1996. *The Clash of Civilizations and the Remaking of World Order*. New York: Touchstone, Simon and Schuster.

Husarska, Anna. 2006. "A Bum Deal for the Hmong." *Star Tribune* December 20: A23.

Isaac, Jeffrey C. 2004. "Social Science and Liberal Values in a Time of War." *Perspectives on Politics* 2: 475–483.

Jaggar, Alison M. 2005. "What Is Terrorism, Why Is It Wrong, and Could It Ever Be Morally Permissible?" *Journal of Social Philosophy* 36: 202–217.

Jasper, James M. and Jane D. Poulsen. 1995. "Recruiting Strangers and Friends: Moral Shocks and Social Networks in Animal Rights and Anti-Nuclear Protests." *Social Problems* 41: 493–512.

Jones, Adam. 2006. *Genocide: A Comprehensive Introduction*. London: Routledge.

Kestnbaum, Meyer. 1995. "Review of *War and the Rise of the State: The Military Foundations of Modern Politics* by Bruce D. Porter." *Contemporary Sociology* 24: 360–361.

Kestnbaum, Meyer and Theda Skocpol. 1993. "Review: War and the Development of Modern National States." *Sociological Forum* 8: 661–674.

Kettl, Donald. F. 2004. *Homeland Security and American Politics*. Washington, DC: Congressional Quarterly Press.

Khondker, Habibul H. 2008. "Globalization and State Autonomy in Singapore." *Asian Journal of Social Science* 36: 35–56.

Kinloch, Graham C. 2005. "Towards a Sociology of Terrorism: Concepts, Theories, and Case Studies." *International Journal of Contemporary Sociology* 42: 155–166.

Kourvetaris, George A. 1997. *Political Sociology: Structure and Processes*. Boston: Allyn & Bacon.

Lauderdale, Pat and Annmarie Oliverio. 2005. "Introduction: Critical Perspectives on Terrorism." *International Journal of Comparative Sociology* 46: 3–10.

Lee, Matthew. 2007. "Rice Issues New Rules for Blackwater." *Associated Press*, October 6.

Levin, Jack and Gordana Rabrenovic. 2004. *Why We Hate*. Amherst, NY: Prometheus Books.

Lewellen, Ted C. 1990. "State Terror and the Disruption of Internal Adaptations by CIA Covert Actions." *Scandinavian Journal of Development Alternatives* 9: 47–65.

Lichtblau, Eric and James Risen. 2009. "U.S. Wiretapping of Limited Value, Officials Report." *New York Times* July 11. Retrieved July 13, 2009 from http://www.nytimes.com/2009/07/11/us/11nsa.html.

Lizardo, Omar. 2006. "The Effect of Economic and Cultural Globalization on Anti-U.S. Transnational Terrorism 1971–2000." *Journal of World Systems Research* 7: 144–186.

Martin, Brian. 2006. "Instead of Repression." *Social Alternatives* 25: 62–66.

Martin, Gus. 2007. "Globalization and International Terrorism." In *The Blackwell Companion to Globalization*, edited by G. Ritzer. Blackwell Publishing. Blackwell Reference Online. Retrieved March 27, 2009 from http://www.blackwellreference

.com/subscriber/tocnode?id=g9781405132749_chunk_g97814513274937.

Marsella, Anthony J. 2003. "Reflections on International Terrorism: Issues, Concepts, and Directions." Pp. 11–48 in *Understanding Terrorism*, edited by F. M. Moghaddam and A. J. Marsella. Washington, DC: American Psychological Association.

Matthew, Richard and George Shambaugh. 2005. "The Pendulum Effect: Explaining Shifts in the Democratic Response to Terrorism." *Analysis of Social Issues and Public Policy* 5: 223–233.

McKay, James. 1982. "An Exploratory Synthesis of Primordial and Mobilization Approaches of Ethnic Phenomena." *Ethnic and Racial Studies* 5: 395–420.

Mead, George Herbert. 1934. *Mind, Self, and Society*. Chicago: Chicago University Press.

Mearsheimer, John. 2008. "Why the Bush Administration's Attempt at Empire Died So Quickly in Iraq." Presented at *American Empire and the Exportation of Democracy*, Midwest Faculty Seminar, University of Chicago, October 30–November 1.

Meixler, Louis. 2004. "U.S. Prison Commander Says No to Plan to Close Abu Ghraib, Interrogations Will Continue." *Associated Press*, May 8.

Merton, Robert K. 1968. *Social Theory and Social Structure*. 2nd Edition. New York: Free Press.

Miller, M. and J. File. 2001. *Terrorism Factbook*. Peoria, IL: Bollix Press.

Miranda, Deborah. 1999. "I am Not a Witness." In *Indian Cartography*. Greenfield Center, NY: Greenfield Review Press.

Moghaddam, Fathali M. 2003. "Cultural Preconditions for Potential Terrorist Groups: Terrorism and Societal Change." Pp. 103–117 in *Understanding Terrorism*, edited by F. M. Moghaddam and A. J. Marsella. Washington, DC: American Psychological Association.

Montiel, C. J. and M. K. Anuar. 2002. "Other Terrorisms, Psychology, and Media." *Journal of Peace Psychology* 8: 201–206.

Müller-Hill, Benno. 2004. "Reflections of a German Scientist." Pp. 485–499 in *Deadly Medicine*. Washington, DC: United States Holocaust Museum.

Neuman, W. Lawrence. 2007. *Basics of Social Research*. 2nd Edition. Boston: Pearson.

Nielsen, Joyce M. 1990. *Sex and Gender in Society: Perspectives on Stratification*. 2nd Edition. Prospect Heights, IL: Waveland Press.

Oberschall, Anthony. 2004. "Explaining Terrorism: The Contribution of Collective Action Theory." *Sociological Theory* 22: 26–37.

Oleson, J. C. 2005. "Evil the Natural Way: The Chimerical Utopias of Henry David Thoreau and Theodore John Kaczynski." *Contemporary Justice Review* 8: 211–228.

Oliverio, Annmarie and Pat Lauderdale. 2005. "Terrorism as Deviance or Social Control: Suggestions for Future Research." *International Journal of Comparative Sociology* 46: 153–169.

Petras, James. 1987. "The Anatomy of State Terror: Chile, El Salvador, and Brazil." *Science and Society* 51: 314–338.

Porter, Bruce D. 1994. *War and the Rise of the State: The Military Foundations of Modern Politics*. New York: Free Press.

Rasler, Karen and William R. Thompson. 1989. *War and State Making: The Shaping of Global Powers*. Boston: Unwin Hyman.

"Relief Effort." 2007. *Airline Business* May 21. Retrieved September 28, 2007 from http://www.flightglobal.com/articles/2007/05/21/214120/airports-special-relief-effort.html

Richter, Paul. 2008. "N. Korea Is Off Terrorism List, but Questions Linger." *Los Angeles Times* October 12.

Robertson, Roland. 1992. *Globalization: Social Theory and Global Culture*. Thousand Oaks, CA: Sage Publications.

Robinson, William. 2004. "What to Expect from US 'Democracy Promotion' in Iraq." *New Political Science* 26: 441–447.

Ruggiero, Vincenzo. 2005. "Brigate Rosse: Political Violence, Criminology and Social Movement Theory." *Crime, Law and Social Change* 43: 289–307.

Sandhu, Amandup. 2001. "Algerian Conflict: An Exercise in State Terrorism." *Journal for the Study of Peace and Conflict* 1–15.

Satter, Raphael G. 2007. "Bobby-cam Takes British Surveillance to a New Level." *Associated Press*, July 14: A3.

Savage, David G. 2008. "In Historic Ruling, Gitmo Detainees Win Day in Court." *Star Tribune* June 13: A1, A3.

Schmid, Alex P. and Albert J. Jongman. 1988. *Political Terrorism*. Amsterdam: North-Holland Publishing Company.

Schnee, Walter. 2001. "Nationalism: A Review of the Literature." *Journal of Political and Military Sociology* 29: 1–18.

Scott, Alan. 2004. "The Political Sociology of War." In *The Blackwell Companion to Political Sociology*, edited by K. Nash and A. Scott. Blackwell Publishing. Blackwell Reference Online. Retrieved August 18, 2009 from http://www.blackwellreference.com/subscriber/tocnode?id=g9781405122658_chunk_gs978140512265819.

Senechal de la Roche, Roberta. 2004. "Toward a Scientific Theory of Terrorism." *Sociological Theory* 22: 1–4.

Smelser, Neil. 2007. *The Faces of Terrorism: Social and Psychological Dimensions*. Princeton, NJ: Princeton University Press.

Smith, Anthony D. 1991. *National Identity*. London: Penguin.

Smith, M. B. 2002. "The Metaphor (and fact) of War." *Peace and Conflict: Journal of Peace Psychology* 8: 249–258.

Snow, David A. and Scott C. Byrd. 2007. "Ideology, Framing Process and Islamic Terrorist Movements." *Mobilization* 12: 119–136.

Snow, David A., R. Burke Rochford, Jr., Steven K. Worden, and Robert D. Benford. 1986. "Frame Alignment Processes, Micro-mobilization, and Movement Participation." *American Sociological Review* 51: 464–481.

"Some Hmong to Get Waiver on 'Terrorist' Designation." 2007. *Associated Press*, October 27.

Staub, Ervin. 2003. "Understanding and Responding to Group Violence: Genocide, Mass Killings, and Terrorism." Pp. 151–168 in *Understanding Terrorism*, edited by F. M. Moghaddam and A. J. Marsella. Washington, DC: American Psychological Association.

Taylor, Donald M. and Winnifred Louis. 2003. "Terrorism and the Quest for Identity." Pp. 169–186 in *Understanding Terrorism*, edited by F. M. Moghaddam and A. J. Marsella. Washington, DC: American Psychological Association.

Terrorism Knowledge Base. 2007. The Memorial Institute for the Prevention of Terrorism. http://www.tkb.org.

Tilly, Charles. 1990. *Coercion, Capital, and European States, AD 990–1990*. Oxford and Cambridge, MA: Basil Blackwell.

_____. 2004. "Terror, Terrorism, Terrorists." *Sociological Theory* 22: 5–13.

_____. 2005. "Terror as a Strategy and Relational Process." *International Journal of Comparative Sociology* 46: 11–32.

Tilly, Charles and Sidney Tarrow. 2006. *Contentious Politics*. Herndon, VA: Paradigm Publishers.

Tiryakian, Edward A. 2005. "From the Welfare State to the Warfare State." *Contexts* 4: 23–24.

Toth, James. 2003. "Islamism in Southern Egypt: A Case Study of a Radical Religious Movement." *International Journal of Middle East Studies* 35: 547–572.

Turk, Austin T. 2004. "Sociology of Terrorism." *Annual Review of Sociology* 30: 271–286.

"Turkey's Ambassador in U.S. Ordered Home." 2007. *Star Tribune* October 12: A3.

Turner, Bryan S. 2007. "The Futures of Globalization." In *The Blackwell Companion to Globalization*, edited by G. Ritzer. Blackwell Publishing. Blackwell Reference Online. Retrieved March 27, 2009 from http://www.blackwellreference.com/subscriber/tocnode?id=g9781405132749_chunk_g978140513274939.

Ukai, Satoshi. 2005. "The Road to Hell Is Paved with Good Intensions: For a Critique of Terrorism to Come." Translated by Thomas LaMarre. *Positions* 13: 235–252.

U.S. Department of State, Bureau of Consular Affairs. 2007. "Consular Information Sheet." Retrieved August 8, 2007 from http://travel.state.gov/travel/cis_pa_tw/cis/cis_951.html.

U.S. Department of State, Office of Counterterrorism. 2005. "Fact Sheet: Foreign Terrorist Organizations: FTOs." Retrieved September 12, 2007 from http://www.state.gov/s/ct/rls/fs/37191.htm.

U.S. Department of State, Office of the Coordinator for Counterterrorism. 2006. "Country Reports on Terrorism." April 28. Retrieved September 1, 2007 from http://www.state.gov/s/ct/rls/crt/2005/64337.htm.

_____. 2007. "Country Reports on Terrorism." April 30. Retrieved September 1, 2007 from http://www.state.gov/s/ct/rls/crt/2006/82736.htm.

_____. 2010. "State Sponsors of Terror." Retrieved October 26, 2010 from http://www.state.gov/s/ct/c14151.htm.

U.S. Department of State, Office of the Spokesman. 2007. "Secretaries of State and Homeland Security Exercise Discretionary Authority Relating to Material Support to Benefit Certain Montagnards from Vietnam." Retrieved October 28, 2007 from http://www.state.gov/r/pa/prs/ps/2007/oct/93814.htm.

United Nations. 2006. "UN Plan to Counter Terrorism." Retrieved September 18, 2007 from http://www.un.org/terrorism/strategy-counter-terrorism.html#resolution.

Wagner, Richard V. 2006. "Terrorism: A Peace Psychological Analysis." *Journal of Social Issues* 62: 155–171.

Wallerstein, Immanuel. 2003. *The Decline of American Power*. New York: The New Press.

Walsh, James and Richard Meryhew. 2009. "Jihad Draws Young Men across Globe Back to Somalia." *Star Tribune* December 2. Retrieved October 25, 2010 from http://www.startribune.com/templates/fdcp?1288042820151.

Weiss, Robert P. 2006. "The American Culture of Torture: A Review Essay." *Social Justice* 33: 132–137.

Wiest, Dawn. 2006. "A Story of Two Transnationalisms: Global Salafi Jihad and Transnational Human Rights Mobilization in the Middle East and North Africa." *Mobilization* 12: 137–160.

White, John Kenneth. 2003. "Terrorism and the Remaking to American Politics." Pp. 37–63 in *The Politics of Terror: The U.S. Response to 9/11*, edited by W. Crotty. Boston: Northeastern University Press.

Wong, Kam C. 2006. "The Making of the USA PATRIOT ACT II: Public Sentiments, Legislative Climate, Political Gamesmanship, Media Patriotism." *International Journal of the Sociology of Law* 34: 105–140.

Zedner, Lucia. 2005. "Securing Liberty in the Face of Terror: Reflections from Criminal Justice." *Journal of Law and Society* 32: 507–533.

de Zulueta, Felicity. 2006. "Terror Breeds Terrorists." *Medicine, Conflict, and Survival* 22: 13–25.

CHAPTER
10

Globalization

Both the shift from an agrarian economy to an industrialized one characterized by mechanized production and efficiency and the pull of the city have transformed our institutions, including the polity. Globalization is to the twenty-first century what urbanization and industrialization were to the nineteenth and twentieth centuries. Like urbanization and industrialization, globalization also creates and necessitates more interconnectedness and interdependence between geographic areas and artificially created political units. Geographic disparity, where some locations are more influential than others, is one of the political outcomes of globalization (Martin 2007; Robinson 2007). This transformation has not gone unnoticed by sociologists, with a significant increase in research and writing on globalization issues (Hall 2002; Robertson and White 2007). Regardless of whether globalization will continue to dominate the sociological agenda, sociologists are credited with being the first to notice this phenomenon and its effects (Guillén 2001; Robertson and White 2007).

By challenging sociologists to question whether society is the largest unit of analysis (Robertson and White 2007; Robinson 1998, 2001), globalization calls into question the "core organizing principles of modern social science—namely, the state, society, political community and the economy" (McGrew 2007: 2 of 23). Like political scientists, political sociologists are especially interested in the question of state sovereignty or the impact of globalization on the power of the state. Indeed, Weber's notion of state characterized by a monopoly on the use of legitimate power *linked to a specific territory* (Heydebrand 1994) may become obsolete, and indeed some are calling for a rejection of the Weberian conception of state (e.g., Robinson 2001).

Both in Chapters 2 and 9, we raised the issue of the state as the preferred unit of analysis or methodological focus. Globalization raises this issue as well (Nash and Scott 2001; Ohmae 1990; Robinson 2001; Sklair 1999), yet the idea that globalization is transformative is not universally accepted (McGrew 2007) as there are globalization skeptics.

Most scholars are not skeptics and view globalization and its many processes as "the defining issue of our time" but what *globalization* means (Hall 2002; Held and McGrew 2002; Robertson and White 2007; McMichael 2005: 587; Robinson 2007; Sklair 1999; Staples 2008) or how it will affect the state is not clear. In this chapter, we consider the following questions: What is globalization? How do sociological theories explain it? What are the implications for the nation-state? What is the relationship between globalization and exporting democracy? How do anti-globalization movements aid our understanding of globalization? What does the future hold? Because globalization is currently considered one of the most contested and debated topics in sociology and indeed the social sciences (Guillén 2001; Kellner 2002; McGrew 2007; Robinson 2001, 2007), there are different answers to these questions.

WHAT IS GLOBALIZATION?

Smith argues that *globalization* is "one of those faddish neologisms that is frequently invoked but rarely defined" (2007: 1). The lack of conceptual clarity is also due to contradictory usage (Robertson 1992), the failure to distinguish globalization from related terms (e.g., Kearney 1995; Sklair 1999), and a split between those who emphasize the economic dimension of globalization and those who define it more broadly (Robertson and White 2007). The economic dimension is important to political sociologists because of the potential impact on the state. The social or cultural dimensions are also important but ironically have not received as much attention from sociologists (Robertson and White 2007).

Defining Globalization

There are several sociological definitions of globalization but many emphasize that globalization (1) is a combination of several processes (Ritzer 2008; Robertson and White 2007); (2) involves different societal facets or dimensions (e.g., cultural, social, economic, political, and demographic [Manning 1999; Robertson and White 2007; Robinson 2007; Turner 2007]); (3) transcends political nation-state boundaries with cross-border exchanges involving people, goods, money, and culture (Guillén 2001; Held, McGrew, Goldblatt, and Perraton 1999; Robinson 2007; Staples 2008); (4) results in an increasing level and depth of interconnectedness (Robertson and White 2007; Turner 2007); (5) is a decoupling between space and time (Giddens 1990) or alternatively the compression of both time and space (Arrighi 1999; Harvey 1989; Robertson 1992; Smith 2007); and (6) results in an increasing consciousness of the world as a single space (Robertson 1992; Robertson and White 2007; Turner 2007).

In *Global Families*, Karraker defines globalization as "involve[ing] the motion and absorption of goods and capital, politics and power, information and technologies worldwide. But globalization also involves the transmission of pollution, crime, and other social problems across and beyond national, regional, and special borders" (2008: 13). This definition underscores the proverbial double-edged sword of globalization. Though the so-called positive impacts of globalization such as new technologies, easier travel and communication, and more widespread access to goods have the potential to make the world relatively smaller and to improve the standard of living in every corner of the globe, they also create undesirable problems and thus create a double-edged sword. Capitalists also are not immune from experiencing both the promise and the curse of globalization. "With the click of a mouse, capital can be moved to low-wage and low cost parts of the world. But the very arrangements that make exit easier also create new and more fragile interdependencies. Outsourcing is also two-sided. One one hand, it loosens the dependence of employers on domestic workers. On the other hand, it binds employers to many other workers in far-flung and extended chains of production . . ." that "depend on complex systems of electronic communication and transportation that are themselves acutely vulnerable to disruption" (Piven 2008: 7).

Critique of the Term

The multifaceted nature of globalization and the many different ways the term is used create confusion and ambiguity (Nassar 2005). For example, an environmental activist might criticize economic or corporate globalization but advocate environmental globalization or worldwide standards for air and water purity. The fact that one can be for some aspects of globalization while against others is summed up by political scientist Charles Lipson (2008), who remarked, "people that hate globalization talk on their Nokia while driving a Volvo." Indeed, *globalization* has become a "negative buzzword, something to employ as a source of blame for each and every 'problem' on the planet—indeed, in the cosmos" (Robertson and White 2007: 9 of 11).

That many different phenomena are being cast under the globalization umbrella has not gone unnoticed or unchallenged (Giulianotti and Robertson 2007). Scott and Marshall explain:

> It is undoubtedly true that, on a planet in which the same fashion accessories . . . are manufactured and sold across every continent, one can send and receive electronic mail from the middle of a forest in Brazil, eat McDonald's hamburgers in Moscow as well as in Manchester, and pay for all of this using a MasterCard linked to a bank account in Madras, then the world does indeed appear to be increasingly "globalized." However, the excessive use of this term as a sociological buzzword had largely emptied it of analytical and explanatory value. (2005: 250)

For sociological research on globalization to have value, globalization needs to be "defined as something tangible and concretely measured and . . . clearly differentiated from other precise phenomena—e.g., neoliberalism" (Brady, Beckfield, and Zhao 2007: 317). Breaking down globalization into its various conceptual dimensions is one way to enhance the understanding of a complex phenomenon. Nassar (2005) identifies interdependence, liberalization, universalization, Westernization, and capitalism as components of globalization.

Components of Globalization

INTERDEPENDENCE   *Interdependence* simply means we live in an interconnected world where we need each other to survive. Interdependence is not a new phenomenon. In *The Division of Labor in Society*, Emile Durkheim argued that the shift from mechanical to organic solidarity as a basis of social order was due to a division of labor that led to interdependence, exchange of services, and reciprocity of obligations (Durkheim 1964[1893]). The difference in this "age of globalization" is the shift from being dependent on others who live in our community to those from afar. For example, Americans wear clothes sewn in Chinese and Mexican factories (to name a few), eat food grown in locations hundreds or even thousands of miles away, and interact with telephone customer service representatives in India. Indeed, this textbook was copyedited by a team in India that communicated with your authors over e-mail.

Everyone is more vulnerable when depending on others, and interdependence due to globalization is more fragile and easily disrupted (Piven 2008). With interdependence comes interconnectedness, which can result in problems that were once localized or isolated spreading to other areas. Interdependence also has a cultural component as the ability to communicate and interact depends upon having a common language. Nassar (2005) argues that English, French, Spanish, Chinese, and Arabic are global languages and may be evidence of an emerging global culture (Waters 1995). Because the United States is considered a singular world power, some argue that

English is becoming the *lingua franca* of the world (Alasuutari 2004). However, many scholars disagree and conclude that there is not one global language or emerging global culture (Guillén 2001).

LIBERALIZATION   Liberalization or neoliberalism is not globalization, but the ideological justification of economic globalization or the free movement of capital and goods without governmental inference in the forms of tariffs, price controls, taxes, and the like (Chomsky 2003; Robertson and White 2007). This has political implications because economic globalization is often seen as an "irreversible, law-like global process" to which there is no alternative but to enact neoliberal policies (Alasuutari 2000: 262). Globalization commentators refer to this belief as "there is no alternative" or TINA (e.g., Evans 2008).

Neoliberalism is usually associated with political conservatives (Wallerstein 1998), and those who advocate it often call themselves neoconservatives (Klein 2007). It is a libertarian ideology more influential in the fields of economics and political science that became prominent in the 1980s and promotes the rights of individuals against the coercive state (Scott and Marshall 2005). The state is viewed as the enemy of the free market because in addition to interference, it often competes by providing services (e.g., postal delivery, education, Social Security) considered best left to the private sector. The drive to privatize services such as Social Security would result in minimizing or even eliminating the welfare state.

On the international side, neoliberalization is associated with the spread of capitalism and free market ideologies. Some perceive International Financial Institutions (IFIs) such as the International Monetary Fund (IMF), the World Bank, and the World Trade Organization (WTO) as promoting American neoliberalism at the expense of less-developed economies through the endorsement of the "Washington Consensus" (WC). The WC is a list[1] of economic policies, including the abolishment of barriers to foreign investment and privatization of state services, free trade, and reductions in "unnecessary" government spending, in other words, a neoliberalist agenda for economic reform.

The IMF, World Bank, and GATT (General Agreement on Tariffs and Trade, the forerunner of the WTO) were created in the aftermath of World War II, in 1944, at the UN Monetary and Financial Conference in Bretton Woods, New Hampshire. The IMF and World Bank are sometimes called Bretton Woods institutions. U.S. President Franklin D. Roosevelt and U.K. Prime Minister Winston Churchill believed that the economic shocks of the 1930s contributed to World War II. As a result, forty-three charter member nations contributed to create the World Bank[2] and the IMF[3] (Robbins 2008). Both institutions are headquartered in Washington, DC, and coordinate with each other.

The WTO[4] officially came into being in 1995 but grew out of the 1986–1994 Uruguay rounds of GATT negotiations. The WTO has 153 member nations and is a forum for settling trade disputes, including intellectual property rights. The WTO views its role as a means of liberalizing trade between nations as well as providing a forum for negotiation and mediation. Member countries are contractually obligated to follow WTO agreements or the ground rules for international commerce.

How power is allocated in some of these organizations is often criticized by development experts and other critics (e.g., see The Bretton Woods Project at http://www.brettonwoodsproject. org/item.shtml?x=320869) as developed countries with stronger economies have more power. According to the World Bank, the five largest shareholders (France, Germany, Japan, the United Kingdom, and the United States) each appoint an executive director, whereas the other 179 member countries are represented by 19 executive directors. The IMF allocates a quota based on the relative size of each member's economy. The quota determines several other factors, including the country's financial obligation to the IMF, voting power, and ability to obtain financing from the IMF. Although the quota system has been reformed to give more voice to developing countries, developed countries such as the United States, Japan, France, and the United Kingdom still have more influence. Figure 10.1, produced by the IMF, portrays pre- and postreform influence.

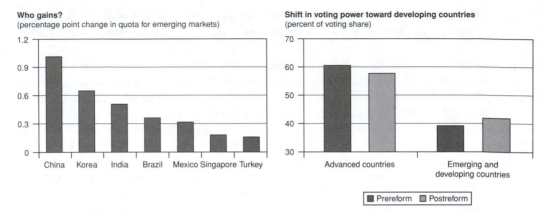

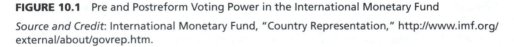

FIGURE 10.1 Pre and Postreform Voting Power in the International Monetary Fund

Source and Credit: International Monetary Fund, "Country Representation," http://www.imf.org/external/about/govrep.htm.

In contrast, the WTO does not have an executive board or an organization head, and decision making is by consensus. The creation and evolution of organizations that need not answer to a specific nation-state and that, at minimum, create more economic and financial interconnectedness and interdependency provide some evidence of globalization.

Naomi Klein's *The Shock Doctrine: The Rise of Disaster Capitalism* is a scathing critique of American neoliberalism. Klein argues that capitalists, and some corporations, profit when disasters strike, from the privatization of the New Orleans public school system in the aftermath of Hurricane Katrina[5] to the Iraqi invasion.[6] Others, such as Nobel Prize–winning economist Milton Friedman, see neoliberal economic policies as a positive development. To the extent that neoliberal policies are blamed for inequality in developing countries, globalization may be a grievance used by some to justify terrorism.

UNIVERSALIZATION Nassar (2005) terms *universalization* as the potential weakening of state sovereignty with corporations and nongovernmental organizations (NGOs) challenging the state. However, this terminology contradicts the fact that corporations depend on states to enforce treaties and trade agreements (Nassar 2005) and also need a strong state for capital accumulation and to both repress and appease dangerous classes (Wallerstein 2003). We will examine these arguments more closely when we discuss the political implications of globalization.

WESTERNIZATION Globalization is accused of homogenizing culture with Hollywood films, television shows, and Western music distributed worldwide. This is related to Waters' (1995) notion of an emerging global culture albeit a Westernized one. Although scholars do not believe a global culture is emerging, many non-Westerners resent Westernization and this is cited as a grievance justifying terrorism. The diffusion of culture is not a new or unique phenomenon. Culture changes over time and is influenced by ideas and practices developed by others. The Greeks first developed democracy, and the English language contains many words with foreign origins. Samuel Huntington's *Clash of Civilizations* (1993, 1996) thesis and Benjamin Barber's *Jihad vs. McWorld* (2001) are perhaps the most well-known treatises predicting conflict between the Western and Muslim worlds due to Westernization enabled by globalization. The main difference between these two perspectives is that whereas Barber argues the divide is between consumer capitalism (McWorld) and retribalization linked with religious fundamentalism (Jihad), Huntington sees conflict between civilizations or Western versus Islamic (Alasuutari 2000).

While Arabs and Muslims are usually the first groups Americans associate with the resentment of Westernization, the French have long resented the British and American influence on their culture, including English words creeping into the French language, such as *le t-shirt*. These words are called *franglais* (a combination of français or French and anglais or English). The Toubon Laws or Loi Toubon (1994)—named after the Minister of Culture, Jacques Toubon—mandates government communication in French and bans the use of foreign words in business and advertising without a French translation.

Despite The French Academy or L'Académie Française's efforts to create French expressions for English words including *software* (*logiciel*) and *e-mail* (*courriel*), French manufacturers often borrow English phrases, contributing to the proliferation of franglais. Business, including the automotive, engineering, energy, telecommunications, and information technology industries, has promoted the use of franglais. While no one will be arrested for saying *anti-lock braking system* instead of *anti-blocage de sécurité* or *car showroom* instead of *salle d'exposition*, businesses that do not provide French translations of English text pay fines ("Franglais Resurgent" 2008). Music is also restricted, with a law (1996) mandating that "at least 40 percent of all songs played on the country's 1,300 FM stations be French songs" (Murphy 1997).

Cultural diffusion is not one-way or unilateral; ethnic restaurants are an example of other cultures impacting American culture. What is considered profoundly different though is the more pronounced degree of penetration with satellite television and cable networks such as CNN infiltrating all parts of the world and the perceived accompanying ethnocentrism with American ways being promoted as more modern or progressive. Galkin (2006) argues that Westernization has a corrosive impact on religious, cultural, and linguistic traditions and, specifically, that Islamic countries have been some of the prime victims of globalization. A competing view contends that instead of global influences overpowering the local or more traditional, the global and local combine creating something new or "glocal" (Robertson 1992).

CAPITALISM Some see globalization as simply a way to expand the reach of capitalism by exploiting less wealthy countries by building sweatshop factories where workers are paid only pennies a day or extracting cheap raw materials at the expense of the environment. In the United States, many see globalization as migration that brings illegal immigrants and the outsourcing of well-paying jobs to companies in developing nations, which benefits company stockholders at the expense of American workers. Globalization also allows developed countries to flood external markets with cheap imports such as food, forcing indigenous farmers out of business and increasing inequality.

One of the engines of global capitalism is the transnational corporation (TNC), also known as the MNC or multinational corporation. TNCs are involved in cross-border exchanges and their global reach has dramatically increased (Sklair 1999). TNCs are powerful, with some corporations having assets and resources that rival those of many smaller nation-states (Sklair 1999). Finally, the CEOs or top-level managers of TNCs make decisions that affect the lives of citizens but they are not accountable to those whose lives are impacted by these decisions (Staples 2008). For example, drug affordability is a huge problem in developing countries trying to deal with infections such as HIV (see Textbox 10.1). Drug companies have been resistant to lowering the cost of drugs, citing the need to recoup research and development costs. Capitalism is an important component of several theories of globalization, including World Systems Theory, Global Capitalism, and postmodernism.

> ## TEXTBOX 10.1
>
> ### Transnational Corporations and Fighting HIV
>
> According to the World Health Organization (WHO), it is estimated that over 25 million people have died of AIDS since 1981 and that there are currently 33 million living with the disease, of which 2 million are children. In Africa alone, there are 11.6 million AIDS orphans (UNAIDS 2008 Report of the Global AIDS Epidemic 2008). The sheer numbers prove this is a pressing global problem. One suggested way to fight AIDS is to sell affordable HIV drugs through either licensing the manufacture of cheaper generic drugs or negotiating with drug companies for cheaper pricing. This has lead to many disputes in the past, including:
>
> - GlaxoSmithKline and the Russian government over the price of Combivir (Wang 2009).
> - Roche and the Korean government over the price of Fuzeon (Tong-hyang 2009).
> - South Africa and the U.S. government over a plan to allow South African companies to manufacture drugs patented by U.S. pharmaceutical companies (BBC News 1999).
> - Glaxo and the Indian drug company Cipla over a plan to manufacture a generic version of HIV infection-fighting drugs (Kamath 2000).
>
> Nations that are members of the WTO risk violating the TRIPS agreement (Trade-Related Aspects of Intellectual Property Rights) if they do not honor drug company patents. According to the WTO, TRIPS patent protection for twenty years is necessary to reward drug companies that invest in research and development. The WTO claims there are some public health safeguards built into TRIPS, including compulsory licensing where a country authorizes the manufacture of a patented invention without the owner's permission (with compensation) and parallel imports (product produced by a patent owner is imported from another country where the price is lower). Critics argue that persons living in impoverished countries still do not have the resources to pay and that much of the cost of drugs is attributable to the monopoly of pharmaceutical giants (Evans 2008). Currently, differential pricing is touted as a method of providing access for the needy while still protecting intellectual property rights. Under differential pricing, companies charge different prices in different markets (WTO News 2001), so richer Americans would pay more for a drug than someone in Zimbabwe. Despite the public health provisions in TRIPS, former U.S. President Clinton has argued that "American companies have been too harsh" in lobbying the U.S. government to restrict the manufacture of generics ("Clinton Announces New Programs to Train 150,000 Indian Doctors" 2005). The Indian government has also succumbed to pressure by passing a new patent law that prevents Indian generic-drug companies from manufacturing recently patented medications to be in compliance with TRIPS. The notion that companies need to be compensated for expensive research and development is somewhat disputed by the practice of patenting herbal remedies with no compensation to indigenous persons (Hawthorne 2004).
>
> ### Impertinent Questions
>
> 1. Globalization as a project legitimizes neoliberal policies (McMichael 2005) such as TRIPS. Does the framing of this issue as a property right deliberately obscure the plight of millions of people in poor countries?
> 2. It is estimated that in 1998 the U.S. pharmaceutical industry lost $500 million because of insufficient patent protection (Håkansta 1998). Are the financial losses of TNCs a legitimate reason to limit generic manufacture and licensing?
> 3. Ideological dominance is one way that TNCs exercise power (Evans 2000). If policymakers side with TNCs, is this an example of Gramscian hegemony? If so, what ideology legitimizes this?
>
> *Sources*: UNAIDS 2008 Report of the Global AIDS Epidemic. http://www.avert.org/worldstats.htm.
> BBC News: September 18, 1999. World: Africa AIDS Drug Trade Dispute Ends. http://news.bbc.co.uk/2/hi/africa/450942.stm.
> World Trade Organization: WTO News. http://www.wto.org/english/news.

THEORETICAL PERSPECTIVES ON GLOBALIZATION

It is difficult to divide globalization scholars into mutually exclusive theoretical camps. Hardt and Negri are considered postmodern, yet Robinson (2007) classifies these scholars under the heading "global capitalism." Manuel Castell's network theory is considered separately but his work also has a postmodern feel with an emphasis on how information technology will transform production and consumption. A postmodern classification also fits those emphasizing the compression of space and time (e.g., Giddens 1990; Harvey 1990). Therefore, do not consider this discussion definitive. Rather, understand that some theorists fit multiple categories and that any classification oversimplifies a very complicated body of scholarship.

World Systems Theory (WST)

World Systems Theory is a predecessor of more recent theories of globalization (Robinson 2007). The first volume of *The Modern World System* (Wallerstein 1974) is a "milestone" by recognizing that nation-states are components of a larger system (Kearney 1995). Although Wallerstein does not approve of the concept of globalization (Robinson 2007; Wallerstein 2000), WST is a "cohesive theory of globalization organized around a 500 year time scale corresponding to the rise of a capitalist world-economy in Europe and its spread around the world" (Robinson 2007: 5 of 16). The use of *world* should not be confused with that of *global* as the world system of the sixteenth century did not encompass the entire globe. The "world system" truly became global only in the late twentieth century (Hall 2002). Yet, this process began centuries ago (Wallerstein 2003) and is transitioning the world system to a postmodern era (McMichael 2005).

Two periods are crucial to understanding globalization. The first is 1945 to the present, which represents one Kondratieff cycle or K wave of the world economy. A K wave is an approximately fifty-year cycle in prices with both an A (economic expansion) and a B (economic downturn) phase. The A phase went from 1945 through 1967/1973. The current B phase began at the end of the A phase and will continue for several more years. When writing about the Asian financial crisis of the late 1990s Wallerstein argued:

> The financial collapse of the southeast Asian states and the four dragons [Hong Kong, Singapore, South Korea, and Taiwan] was followed by the disastrous interference of the IMF, which exacerbated both the economic and political consequences of the crisis. . . . The world holds its breath, waiting for it to hit the United States. When this occurs we shall then enter into the last subphase of this Kondratieff B-phase. (2003: 57)

Are the subprime lending housing crisis, the onset of the credit crunch in 2008, and the financial bailout of Wall Street all indicators of the last stage of the current B phase? If so, will there be another phase of economic expansion? Of this latter question, Wallerstein says *yes* but argues that the systemic crisis of capitalism will interfere.

The period 1450 to the present represents the entire life cycle of the world economy and specifically the capitalist world system. This life cycle can be divided into three phases: the genesis, normal development, and "terminal crisis" (Wallerstein 2003: 46), which may last over fifty years and end about 2050 (Robinson 2007; Wallerstein 2000). For Wallerstein, the world system is transitioning into something else that will result in a struggle between two camps. The first will want to retain the advantages of the status quo. The second will want a more democratic and egalitarian system. This transition will be characterized by more chaotic economic swings and violence as state structures continue to experience declines in legitimacy. While this sounds like a bleak forecast, Wallerstein insists that because the outcome is "intrinsically uncertain," it is "open to human intervention and creativity" (2003: 68).

What role will the United States play in this transition? Hegemonic cycles are related to but different from K waves. Non-Gramscian hegemony[7] occurs when a state dominates another without overt coercion but through its sheer economic and political power. Once power peaks, hegemony is lost or diminished, resulting in intense inter-state rivalry and competition. Hegemons come to power through a global war (global as in world system). Currently, the United States is in a state of hegemonic decline, which corresponded with the beginning of the B-phase of the K cycle. Another nation or political entity will topple the United States and become the new hegemonic power. While a "milestone," WST is criticized as a theory of globalization for not being a theory of social change that focuses on the late twentieth and early twenty-first centuries and not having a concept of global in the WST literature (Robinson 2007).

Theories of Global Capitalism (GC)

Global Capitalism theorists share with WST an emphasis on historical analysis of large-scale macroprocesses and are critical of capitalism. Robinson (2007) argues that GC differs from WST in three fundamental ways. First, GC theorists argue that globalization is a new stage in the evolution of capitalism. Second, GC theorists perceive a new global system of production and finance fundamentally different from earlier forms of capitalism. Finally, GC theorists argue that globalization cannot be understood with a framework that emphasizes the nation-state or an inter-state system. Rather, national states (as opposed to nation-states) are linked into a transnational state (TNS) network with a transnational global capitalist class. This group consists of executives of transnational corporations (TNC), global bureaucrats (e.g., IMF and World Bank heads), politicians, and other business elites (Sklair 2000).

TNCs have advantages in global trade with the ability to provide both material rewards and sanctions and have ideological dominance. For example, defenders of the interests of the transnational class use terms such as *free trade, intellectual property rights,* and *competitiveness* in ways that frame TNCs as working for the common good rather than for stockholders. Furthermore, those opposing TNCs are labeled as not understanding the rules of the game or pursuing their own interests at the expense of others (Evans 2000).

Robinson's (2007) GC theory emphasizes the transnational state apparatus or network of both supranational political and economic institutions (e.g., Trilateral Commission, WTO) and national state apparatuses "that have been penetrated and transformed by transnational forces" (6 of 16). As part of a transnational state apparatus, a national state will serve global rather than national interests. A transnational class exists that forms divisions both across and within borders. Additionally, Robinson argues that transnational production transforms national economies linked through trade and finance to global circuits of production and capital accumulation. Evidence that GC researchers use to support the existence of a transnational class includes increases in foreign direct investment (FDI), the number of TNCs, mergers and acquisitions across national borders, the existence of global financial systems, and the number of interlocking of positions within the global corporate structure (Robinson and Harris 2000). Like postmodernists, GC scholars agree that technology is impacting production, creating new patterns of capital accumulation (Robinson 1998).

Postmodern Views on Globalization

The postmodern view predicts dramatic consequences for all social institutions, including the state. Postmodernists believe that capitalism is being defined by post-Fordism (Kellner 2002) or the ways in which work has been reorganized to adapt to the technological and market environment of the late twentieth and twenty-first centuries (Scott and Marshall 2005). Post-Fordism is associated with the decline of state regulation and the rise of global markets and corporations and is characterized by different patterns of consumption and production (Milani 2000). Corporations operating in a postmodern world must be flexible by adapting to a constantly changing market. Flexibility includes an increase in using temporary, part-time, and home-based workers. Also, workers producing a single product need not be located at the same place or even at a traditional factory production site. Because of information technology (IT), "postmodernity has no need for physical movement. These changes have a significant effect upon the nature of economic, cultural, and political life. The world is being reconstituted into a single social space and life has become delocalized" (Best 2002: 204). The use of IT dramatically increases "the flow, rapidity, intensity, and volume of communications" and greatly expands the number of international arenas in which we participate (Karp, Yoels, and Vann 2004: 376). IT has compressed both time and space (Giddens 1990; Harvey 1990), shaping local events by phenomena occurring hundreds or even thousands of miles away. This delocalization is one of the hallmarks of globalization.

Sassen (1991) contends that globalization is enabling a new spatial order based on networks of global cities (e.g., New York, Tokyo, London) that provide specialized services for moving capital in a global economy. These "producer services" might be financial, such as banking or other corporate services such as insurance, real estate, design, and accounting. In a modern economy, global cities have been transformed from their role as producers (manufacturing, Fordist production) to producer service centers (post-Fordist) while production may take place in a developing or third world economy where pay is minimal and benefits nonexistent.

In *Empire* and *Multitude*, Hardt and Negri (2000, 2004) contend that the global capitalism of today is distinctly different from previous eras of imperialism and capitalist expansion. The nation-state is withering away and is transitioning into Empire. This entity is decentralized and accepts no boundaries of any kind, including geographic, political, cultural, and economic. Unlike other theories of globalization that view a transnational capitalist class as a key agent of globalization, Hardt and Negri identify no such agent but conceive Empire as a power structure that is not centered anywhere yet is everywhere as it faces resistance from networked citizens or the multitude (Robinson 2007). *Empire* is criticized for being ahistorical, lacking convincing empirical data (Arrighi 2003; Tilly 2003), and failing to distinguish politics and the state from the economy (Steinmetz 2002). Yet these writers have been very influential, impacting scholars in various disciplines, including sociology.

Network Society

Castells (1996, 1997, 1998) uses "network society" to conceptualize a global economy and culture grounded in communications and IT. Briefly, he argues that technological innovations, including the computer, have allowed for changes in communications and information processing, resulting in a new "technological paradigm" (Castells 2000). Capitalism used this technology to create a new system of "information capitalism" or the new economy (Robinson 2007). Castells (2000) characterized the new economy as informational, global, and networked using information technologies that are fundamentally different from previous technological innovations (e.g., printing press and the assembly line).

Although Castells' network theory shares with WST, GC, and postmodern approaches an analysis of capitalism (Robinson 2007), it proposes that technological change and not capitalism drives globalization. For example, the internationalization of the economy could never have occurred had it not been for advances in telecommunications and IT. IT has made the flexible production of a post-Fordist world possible; information itself is a commodity. Production has also changed by shifting from centralized large corporations to decentralized networks that comprise organizational units of different sizes. Similar to postmodernism, a network society approach also emphasizes flexible production and the power of technology to communicate and transport people, goods, and information over large distances in shorter periods of time.

In contrast to Network Society Theory and other accounts that stress the importance of technological innovation for globalization, GC theorists, such as Robinson, argue that this is a mistake. Rather, "technological change is the *effect* [emphasis Robinson's] of social forces in struggle" (2001: 169) to get around barriers hampering the further development of capitalism created by nation-states. A network society perspective also contends that technological innovations have political implications for the regulatory and welfare functions of the state. We will discuss these insights in a subsequent section.

Cultural Theories of Globalization

There is no such thing as "Globalization Theory" (McGrew 2007), yet there are theories of global culture (Robinson 2007) that seek to explain cultural aspects of globalization. These theories can be distinguished from WST because of the emphasis on culture rather than economics and, unlike WST, global culture approaches do not view cultural globalization as an outcome of economic globalization (Waters 1995). Robertson (1992), one of the main proponents of cultural theories of globalization, argues that economic globalization has received most of the attention and that other important social and cultural dimensions, especially religion, have been ignored. Some of the long-term cultural developments that Robertson deems important include the rise in world religions, the globalization of sport, the spread of human rights, the unification of global time, and the spread of the Gregorian calendar (Turner 2007). There are different kinds of cultural theories, which are divided into subcategories, including homogeneity, heterogeneity, and hybridization (Robinson 2007).

As a phenomenon, globalization consists of two separate and indeed contradictory processes: homogeneity and differentiation (Kellner 2002; Scott and Marshall 2005) or heterogeneity. Global capitalism promotes both homogeneity and heterogeneity (Robertson 1992). While homogeneity emphasizes global sameness, heterogeneity emphasizes difference. Non-Westerners often feel threatened by the potential homogenization of culture brought about through Westernization. Even hybridization or the fusion of two different cultural practices may be seen as threatening and contributing to the loss of cultural distinctiveness.

Proponents of homogenization agree that convergence is taking place or that the world is becoming more uniform or similar. For example, Ritzer coined the term *McDonaldization* to refer to "the process by which the principles of the fast-food industry are coming to dominate more and more sectors of the American society as well as the rest of the world" (2008: 1). Homogenization researchers also look for evidence of an emerging global culture (Waters 1995 as cited in Scott and Marshall 2005). In contrast, heterogeneity highlights cultural clash (e.g., Huntington and Barber) and resistance to globalization. Finally, hybridization emphasizes the continual evolution of culture and the melding of different cultural forms (Appadurai 1996). For example, how democracy is practiced is influenced by other factors, including culture.

Robertson (1992, 1994) has contributed to the heterogeneity–homogeneity discussion through his concept of "glocalization": an interaction between the local and the global to produce highly localized responses to global phenomena. He defines *glocalization* as "'real world' endeavors to recontextualize global phenomena or macroscopic processes with respect to local cultures"

(1992: 173–147), in other words, how human beings reconstitute and redefine a global phenomenon and give it a local flavor. "Glocalization registers the societal *co-presence* (emphasis Giulianotti and Robertson 2007: 168) of sameness and difference, and the intensified interpenetration of the local and the global, the universal and the particular, and homogeneity and heterogeneity."

Although glocalization emphasizes heterogeneity over homogenization, Ritzer explains that it is not an issue of the local dominating the global or vice versa but rather "the global and the local interpenetrate, producing unique outcomes in each location" (Ritzer 2008: 166). Using the conceptual lens of glocalization, the penetration of local culture through Hollywood movies and CNN is less of a concern as it is only one input that combined with local influences creates a unique point of view (Ritzer 2008). Ritzer argues that glocalization minimizes or dismisses fear about homogenization or the loss of cultural distinctiveness and proposes "grobalization," a combination of globalization and growth.

Ritzer also argues that glocalization ignores the ambitions of nations and other organizations to dominate other parts of the world to increase power, influence, and profits (Ritzer 2007; 2008). Grobalization is driven by three subprocesses, including Americanization, capitalism, and McDonaldization. In contrast to glocalization, grobalization is a deterministic force, where the global overpowers and dominates the local and limits the ability of individuals to act and react. Unlike glocalization, where news outlets such as CNN are combined with local influences to create a unique point of view, grobalization views CNN and its Arab counterpart, Al-Jazeera, as "grobal media powers" (2008: 168) that "define and control what people think in a given locale" (2008: 167). Ritzer's concept of grobalization is a counterbalance to glocalization or an overly optimistic view of globalization. Central to Ritzer's ideas is McDonaldization, which is not globalization in itself but is one of the "major motor forces of globalization" (2008: 166) and has four elements: efficiency, calculability, predictability, and control.

McDonaldization Thesis

ELEMENTS OF MCDONALDIZATION   Efficiency occurs because the production process is deskilled or broken down into smaller steps that all workers follow. A McDonald's hamburger is not made by one person but by several, each going through the steps of one part of the process, from toasting the bun, grilling the meat, dressing the burger, and selling to a customer. Calculability is concerned with the quantitative aspects of the production process or how quickly and cheaply products are made and delivered. Quality becomes defined by quantity: How many burgers were sold, and how many seconds does it take to place and receive an order in a drive-thru?

Ritzer argues that calculability has also affected politics. As a result of calculability, poll ratings have become more important. Political speeches and the news stories about politics have become shorter as well. As a result, speechwriters create "sound bites" that are more likely to be shown on television or reported by the media.

Predictability refers to the notion that a product will taste the same no matter where it is made, as the same production steps are followed. Do Democrats or Republicans really offer different outcomes, or is there predictability no matter who is in charge? Finally, Ritzer argues that managers, through a limited menu and strictly defined jobs, control both workers and customers. Are voters' choices constrained by a two-party system that offers little choice? An elite theoretical view of voting argues that voting does not offer the masses a real choice but manipulates citizens into believing that they actually have a voice (Alford and Friedland 1985). Ritzer uses McDonald's as a metaphor for the increasing importance of the four elements at the expense of other criteria (e.g., quality, equity). Table 10.1 summarizes the similarities and differences between the major theoretical perspectives and view of globalization.

Table 10.1	Theories of Globalization
Theory	**Main Ideas**
World Systems Theory	Is globalization occurring? Yes. Is it novel? No. What is the main focus? Economic and political systems. What causes it? Capitalism.
Global Capitalism	Is globalization occurring? Yes. Is it novel? Yes. What is the main focus? Economy. What causes it? Capitalism, formation of transnational capitalist class. Technological innovation is needed to get around barriers imposed by the nation-state to continued capitalistic development.
Postmodern	Is globalization occurring? Yes. Is it novel? Yes. What is the main focus? The role of technology in meeting the demands of a more flexible market. What causes globalization? Capitalism with post-Fordist production and consumption patterns.
Network Society	Is globalization occurring? Yes. Is it novel? Yes. What is the main focus? The role of information technology. What causes it? Technological innovation. Information is also a commodity that can be bought and sold.
Cultural Theories of Globalization	Is globalization occurring? Yes. Is it novel? Yes. What is the main focus? Cultural changes that are not an outcome of economic changes. What causes it? Global capitalism promotes both homogeneity and heterogeneity.

GLOBALIZATION DEBATES

Clearly, world systems, postmodern, and cultural globalization theories emphasize different aspects of globalization and therefore provide different answers to the many different questions asked by globalization researchers. In the next section, we review some of the main points of contention and debate, including (1) is globalization occurring? (2) what is the evidence? and (3) what is the impact? These questions have been extensively debated in the social science literature (Guillén 2001; Robinson 2007), and there is no shortage of opinions depending on what aspect of globalization is considered and the theoretical perspective of the researcher.

Is Globalization Occurring?

Not everyone agrees that globalization is occurring and those who do often disagree on its significance. There are three globalization camps: skeptics, hyperglobalists, and transformationists.

SKEPTICS   Hirst and Thompson (1996) are considered one of the best documented (Guillén 2001) cases for what Karraker (2008) and others (Başkan 2006) call the skeptic (e.g., Boyer and Drache 1996; Hirst and Thompson, 1992, 1996) and Guillén (2001) the "feeble view" of globalization. Briefly, skeptics argue that the importance of globalization has been overexaggerated and that globalization is neither unprecedented nor novel but a new phase of Western imperialism (Başkan 2006). Because both trade and foreign investment are concentrated in the markets of Western Europe, North America, and Japan, the economy is becoming more international, but not yet truly global.

Skeptics argue that local governments still control their own economies and that domestic investment is greater than foreign investment and that most TNCs still locate their assets, owners, and top-level management in their home countries (Guillén 2001). Sklair (1999) disagrees, arguing that TNCs may have "home" nations but they are developing global strategies and there is no evidence that TNCs are loyal to their home nations. Skeptics also believe that the cultural homogenization caused by globalization is a myth and that we have instead a clash of civilizations (Başkan 2006). However, skeptics tend to pay more attention to economic rather than political or cultural issues (Başkan 2006). In contrast to skeptics, both hyperglobalists and transformationists agree that globalization is occurring.

HYPERGLOBALISTS   Hyperglobalists (e.g., Hardt and Negri 2000; Ohmae 1995) believe that other aspects of social life are affected by the increasingly global nature of capital and marketplaces. Finance and the production and distribution of goods and services are more transnational and are less encumbered by borders. Hybridization results when global forces interact with national institutions such as the economy and the state. The result will be a more denationalized and a more single world society with transnational networks of production, trade, and finance replacing national economies (Başkan 2006). Like skeptics, hyperglobalists also emphasize economic rather than political or cultural globalization (Başkan 2006).

TRANSFORMATIONALISTS   Transformationists (e.g., Giddens 2000; Ritzer 2007, 2008) agree that globalization is occurring and argue that the world is becoming more interconnected across not only economic and political systems but also cultural and other social systems. Transformationalists view global society as "more uncertain, risky, and stratified" (Karraker 2008: 14), with some individuals and societies benefiting more than others from open markets and cross-border flows. Transformationalists disagree with hyperglobalists on the question of a more unified world society. Rather than unity, there will be strife and conflict as some will benefit from globalization at the expense of others (Başkan 2006; Karraker 2008). Skeptics, hyperglobalists, and transformationalists disagree not only on whether globalization is occurring but also on the meaning of some of the structural transformations taking place. Table 10.2 summarizes the similarities and differences between the three globalization camps.

What Is the Evidence for Globalization?

Some of the globalization indicators cited by Waters (1995) include (1) the recognition of the world as a single place or shared consciousness (Robertson and White 2007); (2) the proliferation of global organizations (e.g., WTO, UN, IMF, Catholic Church) and events (e.g., Olympics, IKA Culinary Olympics, World Games); (3) global patterns of consumption or the worldwide importing and exporting of goods and services; (4) the spread of world tourism; (5) cooperation among many nations to provide solutions to world problems (e.g., global warming, pollution, AIDS, crime, and human trafficking); and (6) the emergence of a global, cultural system.

Table 10.2	Three Globalization Camps
Globalization View	**Main Ideas**
Skeptic	Is globalization occurring? No.
	Is it important? No.
	Is it novel? No. What is called "globalization" is just a new phase of Western imperialism.
	Is the nation-state important? Yes, as it still controls economic activities occurring within its sphere.
	Is the state impacted? No.
	Is homogenization occurring? No, but there is cultural clash.
	What is the main focus? Economic impacts.
Hyperglobalist	Is globalization occurring? Yes.
	Is it important? Yes.
	Is it novel? Yes, historically unprecedented.
	Is the state important? No, world is transforming into a denationalized space.
	Is the state impacted? Yes, the state cannot control economic activity within its sphere.
	Is homogenization occurring? Yes.
	What is the main focus? Economic impacts.
Transformationalist	Is globalization occurring? Yes.
	Is it important? Yes.
	Is it novel? Yes, historically unprecedented.
	Is the state important? Yes.
	Is the state impacted? Yes, being transformed but not the end of sovereignty.
	Is homogenization occurring? No, world is not becoming more unified but more stratified and dangerous.
	What is the main focus? Economic and political impacts.

ECONOMIC GLOBALIZATION Economic globalization has increased especially among affluent or wealthy democracies (Brady et al. 2007). Economic indicators cited by Guillén (2001) include foreign investment as a percentage of the world Gross Domestic Product (GDP), or the total value of all goods and services produced in a given year, and trade including exports plus imports of goods and services as a percentage of GDP. Between 1980 and 1998, FDI was 2.5 percent greater. Trade did not grow as fast as foreign investment, but it increased from 40 percent of GDP (1980) to 42.3 percent (2008), which is somewhat down from a high of 45.2 percent in 2000. Huber and Stephens (2005) also note an increase in trade flows for most countries.

FINANCIAL GLOBALIZATION Financial globalization is examined using indicators such as currency exchange turnover and both cross-border bank credit and assets as a percentage of the world GDP. Guillén (2001) claims that this dimension of globalization has grown the fastest and some use these indicators as proof that the sovereignty of the state has been diminished although others believe this claim has been overstated (Brady et al. 2007).

SOCIAL AND POLITICAL GLOBALIZATION   Indicators of cross-border social exchange include tourism and international telephone calls (Guillén 2001). Data from the World Tourism Organization suggest that international tourist arrivals as a percentage of the world population increased from 6.2 percent in 1980 to 13.8 percent in 2008, with more growth projected in 2010 after a decrease in 2009 due to struggling economies (UNWTO World Tourism Barometer 2010). In 2008, international calling was estimated to have grown to 384 billion minutes ("International Phone Calls Up 12% in 2008" 2009). Of course, the Internet is another medium for communication and information exchange. The number of Internet hosts also increased from 213 sites in 1980 to over 681 million in 2009 (Internet Systems Consortium 2009). The percentage of the world population using the Internet increased from 0.3 percent in 1995 to 28.7 percent in 2010; the highest degree of penetration is in North America and the lowest is in Africa (Internet World Stats 2010). According to the Union of International Associations, the number of international organizations also increased from approximately fourteen thousand in 1980 to over fifty-seven thousand by 2004 (*Yearbook of International Organizations* 2004/2005) and is considered an additional indicator of globalization (Guillén 2001).The very existence of the modern rationalized nation-state, which has been adopted by most nations, is also an example of globalization and a key feature of world society (Essary 2007; Waters 1995). An example of where globalization is not having an impact is in the number of nation-states. According to the UN, in 1980 there were 154 UN member countries, which increased to 192 in 2006 and has remained so as of 2010 (http://www.un.org). A World Bank study identifies 209 states and territories (Kaufmann, Kraay, and Masstruzzi 2007). Guillén (2001) argues that increases in the number of nation-states are due to the importance of nationalism.

While the increase in the number of nation-states is viewed as evidence against globalization, there has been a substantial increase in the growth and influence of IFIs, including the IMF, World Bank, and other international organizations such as the European Union (EU) and the WTO (Huber and Stephens 2005). Huber and Stephens note that the creation of the EU is historically without precedent and has shifted many areas of decision making away from the nation-state. This raises an important point; it is not only the number of organizations but also the expanding role of supranational organizations including IFIs. See Table 10.3 for a summary of globalization indicators.

IMPACT OF GLOBALIZATION ON THE NATION-STATE

Perhaps the outcome most debated by political sociologists is the impact of globalization on the nation-state. with a variety of opinions on whether the state will continue to exist, its importance, strength, and capacity. We review some general observations made by a variety of globalization scholars and then examine these questions in the context of the withering state debate, weak–strong state thesis, and competing globalizations views or the skeptic, hyperglobalist, and transformationalist. Finally we review how different theoretical perspectives view the state.

Rotberg (2003) contends that states are important—not despite of but because globalization is increasing state capacity and capability. Yet, in calling universalism a component of globalization, Nassar (2005) assumes that a weakened state is an outcome of globalization. Indeed, much of the globalization literature suggests that the state is losing its power to TNCs and NGOs (Alasuutari 2000) although some contend that this argument is ideological and made by those who would like to see a weaker state (e.g., neoliberals) and are making a TINA type of argument (Khondker 2008). Other sociologists are concerned about globalization's impact on the state and express concern especially in areas such as trade, security, arms control (Paquin 2002; Pakulski 2001), and immigration (Janoski and Wang 2004). In a more nuanced argument, some contend that the state is adapting to changing conditions (Ó Riain 2000) or that the state is being redefined but has not lost its significance (Sassen 1996).

Table 10.3	Globalization Indicators					
Indicators	**1980**	**1985**	**1990**	**1995**	**2000**	**2009**
Nation-States with UN Membership (number)	154	159	159	185	189	192
Internet Hosts (number)	213[a]	1,961	313,000	4,852,000	29,670,000	681,064,561
Internet Users as a Percentage of the Population	NA	NA	NA	0.3	5.9	28.7
International Organizations (number)	14273	25124	26656	41722	50373[b]	57964[d]
International Tourist Arrivals (% world population)	6.2	6.7	8.6	9.9	11.2	13.8[e]
Exports + Imports of Goods and Services (% world GDP)	40	38.8	38.9	42.9	45.2[c]	42.3[f]
International Calls (minutes per million $ world GDP)	NA	1354	1600	2174	2345	2934[g]

Sources: Table modified from Guillén (2001) with other figures provided by the United Nations: http://www.un.org/en/members/growth.shtml; Internet Systems Consortium Internet Hosts Domain Survey: https://www.isc.org/solutions/survey/history; Internet World Statistics: http://www.internetworld.stats.com/stats.htm; U.S. Census Bureau, International Database: http://www.census.gov/ipc/www/idb/worldpop.php; Union of International Associations: http://www.uia.org/statistics/organizations/ttb199.php; World Tourism Organization: http://www.unwto.org/index.php, http://www.unto.org/facts.eng.pdf/historical/ITA_1950_2005.pdf; International Telecommunication Union: http://www.itu.int/ITU-D/ict/statistics/at_glance/KeyTelecom99.html; *UN Statistical Yearbook.*
[a]1981.
[b]1999/2000 *Yearbook of International Organizations.*
[c]1998. Data 1980–2000 is from Guillén (2001).
[d]2004. Data from the *Yearbook of International Organization.*
[e]2008.
[f]2004.
[g]2006. Data for 1985–1995 from Guillén (2001), who notes that his data excluded international calls from cellular phones. It is not clear whether data from the International Telecommunications Union excluded cellular phones.

Withering State Debate

Waters (1995) describes two camps in the "withering state debate": realists and modernists. Realists reject a declining state argument and argue that the state is still the primary institution for organizing politics (e.g., McGrew 1992). In contrast, for modernists such as Held (1991) and Ohmae (1995), the decline of the state is already occurring, with a shift toward a type of world governance or in the case of Hardt and Negri (2000), Empire. A new position is also emerging: those who believe that the nation-state is still important but it is being redefined (Ó Riain 2000; Sassen 1996) and even transformed. Robinson (1998, 2001) posits that the nation-state is transforming into the national state, which is part of a transnational state apparatus (TNS) but this is different from a global state or Empire. Cultural theories of globalization also view the state as changing but do not theorize a national state or TNS network. As an example of a modernist position, we review Held's argument as summarized by Waters (1995).

First, Held contends the nation-state is in decline and will be replaced by some sort of world government because globalization makes it more difficult for governments to control both the flow of trade and ideas. As a counter argument, we note some governments have effectively restricted the flow of ideas by blocking politically sensitive Internet sites[8] (e.g., Iran,

China). Second, Held argues that state power is also diminished by transnational corporations (TNCs). Third, areas that have formally been considered under the domain of states (e.g., defense, communications, and economic management) must be coordinated between governments. Fourth, states have surrendered their sovereignty rights for membership in larger political units (e.g., EU, IMF, WTO, NATO, UN, OPEC). Fifth, a system of global governance is emerging that will further reduce state power. Finally, the previous conditions provide the prerequisites for the emergence of a supranational state that will possess coercive power. While points 5 and 6 are somewhat tentative, there is some evidence that nation-states have surrendered some sovereignty rights to become members of larger political units. Waters (1995) discusses some of the historical events that have resulted in this loss.

Waters notes that the treaty of Westphalia[9] established three principles, one of which is *rex est imperator in regno suo,* or that the state is not subject to external authority. The Nuremberg tribunal, which punished German leaders for atrocities committed during World War II, was a breach of Westphalia and allowed the Allied nations to legitimize the defeat of the axis powers and to punish their leaders. Westphalia was circumvented by appealing to human rights, which has continued to be a method for states to intervene as the 1948 UN Human Rights Declaration justifies intervention when human rights are at stake.

Similar to human rights, environmental concerns have also impacted state sovereignty as we have redefined parts of the planet as "global commons" outside the control of any one nation-state, including outer space, Antarctica, the high seas, the airwaves, and the atmosphere. In the case of both human rights and environmental concerns, a global normative culture promoted by grassroots organizations, social movements, and international NGOs (Delanty and Rumford 2007) pressures states to comply.

Strong State–Weak State Thesis

The strong state–weak state thesis also raises the question of relevance. Evans (1997) acknowledges that globalization can undermine the state because the neoliberal ideology associated with globalization is against a strong state, yet he believes that the "eclipse of the state" is not likely because the higher rates of cross-border exchanges associated with globalization depend upon having a strong state. Furthermore, he argues that having a strong state may give the same a competitive advantage in the global market (65). Although Evans appears to be taking the realist side of this debate, most scholars are not pure realists or modernists but take a more nuanced position. For example, while still positing a strong state argument, Evans also believes that TNCs have a dominating influence in the international arena.

Ó Riain (2000) disagrees with the notion that with globalization comes a weaker state as "globalization does not consist of an inevitable march to a neoliberal order but is a political contested process in which different state-market models of interaction come into conflict locally, nationally, and transnationally" (188) and that states must balance these activities against the interests of their citizens. States play a crucial role in three ways, by (1) enabling the construction of markets by guaranteeing the rules of commerce, (2) creating new markets, and (3) shaping market strategies (Ó Riain 2000). Weiss (2000) agrees, arguing that globalization and state power are not linked, so globalization advances only with the loss of state power. Alasuutari (2000) argues that the state is still very powerful for identity construction as the nation-state is for most of us our most important cultural system.

Different theoretical camps provide different answers on whether the state is weakened by globalization. We begin our analysis by comparing the skeptic, hyperglobalist, and transformationalist views and then compare and contrast different theoretical perspectives, including

World Systems, Global Capitalists, postmodernism, Network Society, and Cultural Globalization theoretical perspectives.

Competing Globalization Camps

The skeptic, hyperglobalist, and transformationalist camps also take a stance on the question of diminishing state power. Başkan (2006) describes skeptics as denying that the state is being undermined due to the increasing internationalization of the economy. In direct opposition, hyperglobalists such as Ohmae (1995) believe the state is in decline because it no longer is able to control economic activities. Başkan describes hyperglobalists as pointing to the increasing influence of IFIs and global elite that are not controlled by any single nation-state as evidence of the decline in state power. Contrary to the hyperglobalists, Brady et al. (2007) note that many studies have concluded that international financial managers are not effectively monitoring or responding to states engaged in fiscally questionable policies (Mosley 2003) and that the influence of these managers is overstated (Wilensky 2002). Transformationalists (e.g., Giddens 1998) take a position somewhere in the middle. They agree with skeptics that the state power is not being diminished but argue that state power is being transformed precisely because of the rise in the number of IFIs and other international governance institutions. The state is still important precisely because there is currently no other alternative to the nation-state (Smith 1995).

Theoretical Views on State Power

WORLD SYSTEMS THEORY   World Systems Theory contends that capitalists need strong states to succeed, but states are increasingly suffering from the loss of legitimacy (Wallerstein 2003). States are necessary for companies to acquire capital and appease and repress the "dangerous classes" by providing legitimizing ideology that encourages the have-nots to wait and be patient. Wallerstein (1999) asks: What is the point of accumulating capital if you cannot hold on to it? Capitalists need the state, yet opposition to the state has been growing worldwide. Wallerstein believes the masses are questioning the ability of states to maintain order and transform society. Wallerstein (2003) describes a vicious cycle where individuals confront fears about their own security by taking back this function (e.g., private citizens patrolling the border and "detaining" illegals) from the state. This in turn breeds more chaos, fueling fears as states become increasingly unable to handle the situation, inciting more people to "disinvest" from the state. States losing legitimacy also lose power to execute functions for sustaining capitalism (e.g., controlling the dangerous classes). Because there are more players due to globalization, no group has the power to make decisions alone. Using the analogy of a car, Wallerstein writes:

> A wise chauffeur might drive quite slowly under these difficult conditions. But there is no wise chauffeur . . . and the very fact that these decisions are being made by a large number of actors, operating separately and in each his or her own immediate interests virtually ensures that the car will not slow down . . . Consequently, what we may expect is recklessness. As the world-economy enters a new period of expansion, it will thereby exacerbate the very conditions that have led it into a terminal crisis. At the same time, we may expect the degree of collective and individual security to decrease, perhaps vertiginously, as state structures lose more and more legitimacy. And this will no doubt increase the amount of violence in the world-system. This will be frightening to most people; as well it should be. (2003: 67)

In summary, WST views the state as an important political institution that serves many functions necessary for capitalism but the state is losing power in light of a legitimacy crisis in face of ever chaotic economic swings as capitalism continues to run its course. Because the nation-state is still considered primary and not transforming into another entity, WST views states from the more realistic point of the withering state debate continuum.

GLOBAL CAPITALIST THEORISTS   William Robinson (2001) rejects the strong-state and competing weak-state theses, arguing that globalization scholars need to move beyond this dualism by developing the concept of a transnational state or TNS. Globalization is a new stage in the development of world capitalism, but it does not mean the rejection of the state. The state is neither primary nor obsolete but is being transformed and absorbed by the larger structure of the TNS.

Briefly, Robinson argues that the state and the nation-state do not necessarily share the same boundaries, and the fusion of the two concepts has negatively impacted the ability of scholars to detect the "increasing separation of state practices from those of the nation-state" (2001: 157). He argues (as we have in Chapter 2), that *nation* and *state* are analytically distinct concepts. He contends that the social science literature shares a nation-state centrism that mistakenly assumes that phenomena associated with the TNS are an international expression of the nation-state system (1998, 2001). A global capitalist (GC) perspective recognizes that no regions of the world are outside the sphere of global capital and rejects a Weberian view of the state in favor of understanding the state both as a set of class power relations and as a political institution. According to Robinson, Weber's mistake was focusing only on the state as a political institution.

Because of the globalization of capital, the state is being transformed into the TNS. First, class relations are becoming globalized, with capitalists from different countries comprising a transnational capitalist class that differs from a national capitalist class by being involved in global (as opposed to local or national) production and managing global circuits of capital accumulation. This class also has a global identity rather than a link to a specific territory. The role of the TNS is to maintain and perpetuate the hegemony of this transnational capitalist class. The TNS is a network of national states that have been integrated, as well as the rise of supranational economic and political institutions.

National states have been reorganized by the rise of the transnational class. Both processes are necessary for the TNS: (1) the transformation of nation-states into national states and (2) the rise of supranational institutions. Globalization then, does not involve the diminishing or withering away of national states but does involve a transformation as the national state is a component of a larger TNS. These national states are "neoliberal states" that provide services essential for global capitalism, including (1) adopting fiscal and monetary policies enabling macroeconomic stability; (2) providing infrastructure needed for global commerce, including transportation, education, and communication; and (3) providing security through both direct force and ideological persuasion.

Like Marxist-based theories of class, GC recognizes a contradiction within the national state as it becomes difficult to maintain social cohesion at the same time national economies are becoming more integrated. This failure results in the loss of legitimacy. Marxist views of the state theorize the capacity for states to respond to these crises without constraints imposed by the capitalist class. Robinson also poses similar questions regarding the TNS: (1) "Is it possible for TNS cadre to acquire enough autonomy from transnational capitalists to act independent of their short-term interests?" and (2) "Can the TNS develop a long-term project of global capitalist development beyond these interests?" (2001: 190).

In summary, GC views the state as an important and a powerful political institution that is being transformed into a national state integrated into a TNS. Like WST, the role of the TNS is to perpetuate capitalism despite the challenge of potentially diminishing state legitimacy. Unlike

WST, GC views the state as transforming rather than unchanging and theorizes the role of the TNS as perpetuating the dominance of a TNC. In terms of the withering state debate, GC fits closer to the realist position although it does theorize a transformation from the traditional nation-state into a network of national states or TNS.

POSTMODERN VIEWS   Postmodern theorists are modernists contending that the postmodern condition of the state is the end of sovereignty as the nation-state no longer controls what is going on within its borders (Best 2002; Harvey 1989). "The state is shrinking as its modern role in providing external defense, internal surveillance, and citizenship rights are undermined" (Best 2002: 375). Arms control and nuclear proliferation treaties, the decline in the military elite, the spread of individualistic and libertarian philosophies, and membership in organizations such as NATO all have undermined the defensive function of the state (Best 2002; Pakulski 2001) as well as other state capacities.

International agreements and membership in international organizations diminish state capacity to respond to economic crises such as unemployment (Pakulski 2001). Even if states maintain the ability to act unilaterally, global problems such as AIDS, pollution, illegal drugs, and human trafficking are beyond the control of an individual state. The ability of INGOs and supranational organizations to pressure other states into following international norms (e.g., human rights) also is a threat to state sovereignty.

In combination with global norms, the worldwide reach of the mass media also decreases the capacity of the state to use violence against its own citizens to maintain order. To do so anyway is politically risky (Best 2002). For example, consider the 2009 protests in Iran after the reelection of President Mahmoud Ahmadinejad and the resulting clash between civilians and the police. The killing of a young nonprotesting Iranian woman resulted in an international public outcry after a video of her killing was released on the Internet[10] (Fathi 2009).

For Hardt and Negri, perhaps the two most popular postmodernists, the nation-state is not only in a state of decline but is being replaced by "a national form of sovereignty, a global empire" (2004: 3). This global empire is conceptualized as a pyramid composed of several tiers. At the apex of control is the only remaining superpower, the United States. At a subordinate level within this first tier are the other nations that comprise the G8.[11] These principals, along with the United States, control IFIs. The second tier includes TNCs and other less powerful nation-states that are subordinate to the interests of TNCs. Finally, the last tier, which is the broadest and represents people, is made up of religious and media organizations, NGOs, and other entities comprising global civil society. Hardt and Negri note that individuals themselves or collectively, the multitude, cannot advocate for themselves but must seek representation through other mechanisms, such as membership in organizations. In this respect, multitude is analogous to a pluralist view that posits that citizens exercise power through organization membership. Although the United States may enjoy a privileged position within Empire, this is not a return to old-style European imperialism. "Imperialism is over. No nation will be world leader in the way modern European nations were" (2000: xiv).

In summary, unlike WST and GC, a postmodern perspective views the nation-state as becoming irrelevant. Other organizations and entities are replacing the nation-state and creating a structure of global governance. This is different from Robinson's GC perspective of the TNS, where nation-states transform into national states as a building block of the TNS. Like GC, supranational political and economic organizations are also important.

NETWORK SOCIETY   Network Society Theory directly addresses the issue of state capacity. The capability to gather and process information with the help of technology has expanded the regulatory capacity of the state. However, this same technology has made the flow of information bidirectional, enabling civil society to keep the state's regulatory activities in check without damaging state effectiveness to work on behalf of public interest. Because of this ability of civil society, perceptions of state bureaucratic detachment and authoritarianism act to delegitimize its power. This in turn brings about pressure for institutional reform with the goal of creating a more responsive and flexible government (Castells 1989).

In sum, while the state regulator role has been enhanced, the ability of civil society to keep the state in check has also increased. The same technological advances that have enabled global trade also enable strategies that protest the excesses of globalization. Although not considered a network society theorist, Evans makes this point quite well when he asks, "Why shouldn't the burgeoning growth of communications and movement across national boundaries create new global strategies aimed at well-being and equity at the same time that it stimulates transnational finance and trade?" (Evans 2000: 230). Because Network Society Theory views the state as important and primarily focuses on the impact of information technology on both state capacity and civil society, it falls closer to the realist camp in the withering state debate.

CULTURAL THEORIES OF GLOBALIZATION   Robertson and White (2007) question the framing of the state debate. They contend that the nation-state is an "aspect" of globalization rather than something that globalization a priori diminishes, as we cannot talk about globalization "were it not for the existence of nation-states" (6 of 11) because as the result of globalization the nation-state is the global norm for organizing the exercise of political power. For Robertson and White, the issue is not about the decline of the nation-state but the *changing nature* (emphasis Robertson and White) of the state. As an example of how central the nation-state is, cultural theorists point to the impact of migration on societal debates about the nature of national identity as one cannot have national identity without a nation. Yet, cultural theorists do not believe that the nature of the nation-state is static.

Robertson (1992) views globalization in five stages. Stage 1, the "germinal phase" (1500–1750) is characterized by the expanding influence of the Catholic Church, the spread of the Gregorian calendar, and the beginning of modern geography. In the "incipient stage" or stage 2 (1750–1875) the modern nation-state was established. The "take-off stage" or stage 3 involves conceiving the world in terms of four reference points (nation-state, the individual, an international single-society, and a single humanity). Stage 4 is the "struggle for hegemony phase" including World War II, the cold war, and the emergence of the United Nations. In the "uncertainty phase" or stage 5, international relationships are more complicated, global media are available, and there is recognition that environmental problems are global rather than local. Giulianotti and Robertson (2007) have added a sixth stage, characterized by more pronounced local global penetration; yet it is unclear what the implications may be for the nation-state. Clearly, cultural theory does not fit the modernist view of the demise of the nation-state. Rather, Robertson contends that the state will be transformed but does not go as far as Robinson (1998, 2001) in defining the future of the nation-state. Because the nation-state is still important, we place cultural theorists such as Robertson closer to the realist side of the withering state debate.

In conclusion, there is a great deal of dissent and debate regarding changes to the nation-state. Most theorists do not take a strict realist or modernist stance in the withering state debate but do view the nation-state as transforming or changing. We agree with Delanty and Rumford, who write,

> The notion of the decline of the nation-state . . . should be replaced by the idea of the continued transformation of the nation-state. The idea of a zero-sum situation of

states disappearing in a global world of markets or replaced by global structures of governance, on the one side, or as in the neo-realist scenario the survival of the so-called Westphalian state as a sovereign actor must be rejected. (2007: 3 of 13)

Despite the differences, all the theories reviewed have something interesting to add to our understanding of globalization. Besides the question of the nation-state, other aspects of political globalization include public policy, the welfare state, and nationalism. Table 10.4 summarizes theoretical views regarding the impact of globalization on the state.

Public Policy

The debate on the potential weakening of the state emphasizes the declining ability of states to mitigate the effects of globalization as some argue that economic globalization and the accompanying involvement of nation-states in international agreements diminishes the ability of states to influence economic performance, unemployment, as well as the allocation of rights and privileges (Pakulski 2001). Blackman disagrees by arguing that precisely because of the growth in global trade flow, nation-states are not irrelevant "because there is an imperative to invest heavily in education and training, research and development and infrastructure to position open economies" to capitalize on these global trade flows (2007: 3 of 14).

Blackman contends that the nation-state is still relevant; not only because it needs to enact policies to gain a competitive advantage but also because the globalized economy is the product of an international order based on nation-states. Far from eroding or ending the role of nation-states,

Table 10.4 Differing Theoretical Views of the Impact of Globalization on the State	
Theory	**Views toward the State**
World Systems Theory	Capitalism needs a strong state.
	The state is losing legitimacy.
	The role of the state is to repress and appease the dangerous classes and to legitimize ideology that supports global capitalists.
Global Capitalism	State is transforming into national states that are absorbed into a transnational state apparatus.
	National states are neoliberal states that provide macroeconomic stability, infrastructure enabling global commerce, providing security through coercion and ideological persuasion in support of transnational elite.
Postmodern	The state is irrelevant and in decline.
	The governing structure is becoming global.
Network Society	State is still relevant.
	The state is increasing its regulatory capacity through technology.
	Civil society has an increasing ability to monitor the state, keeping it in check.
Cultural Theories of Globalization	Globalization resulted in the spread of the modern nation-state.
	The nation-state is being transformed.
	Politics is becoming "McDonaldized."

globalization is redefining but not curtailing it. For example, many consider the EU as an example of an outcome of globalization, European integration. Yet, Blackman asserts that the EU is a creation of democratic nation-states and not globalization. While the EU gives member states some latitude in determining policies to mediate some of the negative impact of globalization, choices are more constrained in an interconnected environment. Yet, Blackman argues that some nation-states are increasingly using their policy systems as a means to better situate economies for growth by investing in education, research and development, health, and infrastructure. He argues for conceptualizing the nation-state as a major player that still can significantly impact the lives of its citizens and for rejecting the neoliberal ideology calling for a smaller state that accompanies globalization.

> What governments do makes a difference in the globalized economy. The neoliberal discourse that links globalization and its benefits to small government is just that: a discourse that reflects the power and interests of those for whom small government is advantageous. This is never likely to be true for most people because of the need for smart public policies that have real impact across key sectors . . . [e.g., education] and because democracies are unlikely to tolerate the extent of income inequality that globalization will fuel without intervention. (Blackman 2007: 8 of 14)

Blackman is arguing that states can and *should* buffer their citizens. While Blackman sees the role of the welfare state expanding in times of globalization, others forecast welfare state retrenchment as a globalization outcome. Globalization researchers should continue to examine the impact of globalization on how the state both regulates and administers policy (Brady et al. 2007).

Welfare State

Welfare states view economic globalization and neoliberalism as a threat because of pressure from IFIs to open markets in what has traditionally been defined as public service (e.g., water, sanitation, fire protection) despite lacking evidence that welfare states are bad for economic growth (Blackman 2007). Brady et al. (2007) describe three arguments concerning the impact of globalization on the welfare state: expansion, retrenchment, and curvilinear.

The expansion thesis suggests that the volatility and uncertainty accompanying globalization causes expansion of the welfare state, whereas the retrenchment thesis suggests that governments cut back on benefits as a means of staying globally competitive to attract markets. The retrenchment thesis is connected to hyperglobalization. Proponents of this view argue that the emergence of a single global market and competition has eliminated the latitude previously afforded nation-states. The imposition of neoliberal policies means that governments must reduce intervention such as unemployment benefits because extending benefits raises production costs (Huber and Stephens 2005). The curvilinear thesis argues that globalization initially causes expansion of the welfare state but eventually leads to retrenchment.

What is the empirical evidence? The effect of globalization on the open market is highly disputed. Just because there is a parallel trend toward both globalization and declining state intervention does not mean there is a causal relationship (Huber and Stephens 2005). The consensus emerging among researchers is that globalization has only a small effect on the welfare state and is far less influential that other political forces (Brady et al. 2007). While welfare rollbacks have occurred in some areas, this was due more to adopting neoliberal ideology (Huber and Stephens 2005) rather than globalization per se. Citing Iverson (2001), Brady and colleagues argue that welfare state growth is still likely due to an aging population that pressures politicians to maintain these programs. Similar to Huber and Stephens (2005) Brady and associates argue that "globalizations' effects on the welfare state might be better understood as a socially constructed discursive device that legitimizes calls for efficiency and undermines calls for egalitarianism" (2007: 319). In other words, it is not economic globalization per se that impacts the welfare state but neoliberal policies that are enacted to respond to what is perceived by some as an inevitable and unstoppable process where there is no alternative (TINA) but to contract the welfare state. While economic globalization has received most of the research attention, globalization also impacts culture. In the next section, we examine research on cultural globalization and national identity.

Nationalism

Nationalism is a sense of identity collectively shared by people who define themselves as belonging to or being citizens of a specific state. If globalization results in homogeneity or cultural convergence, we might expect diminishing nationalism. On the other hand, globalization may be perceived as threatening cultural uniqueness, including national identity, motivating a rise in nationalism. What is the relationship between globalization and nationalism?

Başkan (2006) reviews some of the differing positions on the relationship between globalization and nationalism. On one hand, he describes hyperglobalists who view globalization as a threat to national identity because it eliminates borders, leading to a decline in the importance of the nation-state (e.g., Ohmae 1995). Because the nation-state is the basis for nationalism (Başkan 2006), its decline should coincide with decreasing nationalism. A hyperglobalist asks whether nationalism will remain an effective way of mobilizing people in a globalized world.

Başkan also describes an alternative argument, specifically, that nationalism will rise as a form of resistance to any perceived cultural loss or threat. In other words, if homogeneity is a globalization outcome, will this spark a nationalism resurgence to resist homogeneity (Jones 2006; Schnee 2001)? Certainly the sense of nation that persists despite the global flow of capital is some evidence in favor of this view. However, whether resistance to globalization is the motivating cause of persistent nationalism is unclear.

Political psychologist Catarina Kinnvall (2004) makes a transformationalist rather than a skeptic or hyperglobalist argument by declaring that globalization increases uncertainty and insecurity, potentially fueling the growth of local identity. Specifically, globalization encourages the rejection of traditional power structures. Once traditional means are rejected, these need to be replaced to prevent insecurity. The combination of religion and nationalism provides a particularly powerful way of responding to times of rapid change and insecurity. Nationalism, then, is like any other aspect of culture being transformed by globalization and breeding the "new nationalism" (Kaldor 2004) or national identity motivated by uncertainty and insecurity brought on by globalization.

Using the Nationalist Action Party of Turkey (MHP), Başkan (2006) examines the methods used by an ultranationalist political party to include globalization as part of its political discourse as well as how globalization impacted its political success. The MHP drew its supporters from those feeling the most threatened by globalization, including farmers and low-income workers. However, as part of a majority government coalition, MHP supported Turkey's membership in the EU as well as the implementation of economic programs in collaboration with the IMF. As a result, some supporters were alienated and left the party. MHP's political discourse was in line with a skeptic view defining globalization as primarily an economic process that does not undermine the authority of the nation-state. MHP party ideology also promoted a strong Turkish identity and love for the state. Although MHP tried to ally itself with voters who were worried about how the negative impacts of globalization would affect them, it alienated its political base by pursuing policies that enhanced globalization. Its appeal to voters was aimed toward those with a hyper-globalist or a transformationalist view but it pursued the course of a globalization skeptic.

The resurgence of nationalism as an outcome of globalization possibly occurs as a response to the loss of traditional structures. Sometimes those structures are authoritarian, oppressive, and undemocratic. If democracy is viewed as Westernization and an attempt to homogenize culture, nationalism as well as other forms of resistance may rise. Democracy is one aspect of neoliberalization or the ideology justifying some of the WC policies seen by developing nations as benefitting the haves at the expense of the have-nots. Does globalization explain the spread of democracy? Just what type of democracy is being spread? What explains the role of the United States in exporting democracy and is it successful?

DEMOCRACY AND GLOBALIZATION

Francis Fukuyama (1992) famously declared the "end of history" thesis or the idea that liberal democracy is fated to triumph over authoritarian political forms because of the human need for expression or "thymos" that leads to the perfect political state, democracy. According to Fukuyama, now that democracy has become globally accepted, we have reached "the end of history." Others disagree, arguing that the end of the cold war and the fall of former communist regimes has not brought about the end of history, but "political anarchy, tribal warfare, genocide, and ethnic and religious warfare" (Erler and Wood 2009: 122). Despite the criticism, there has been a large increase in the number of democratic states (Blackman 2007), with many scholars discussing "waves of democracy" (Huntington 1991; Markoff 1996) and attributing this political outcome to globalization.

How widespread is democracy? Citing figures from the *Wall Street Journal*, Kathleen Schwartzman (1998) contends that worldwide the number of democracies rose from 25 percent in 1974 to 66 percent by 1996. In 2008, the number of authoritarian regimes was approximately 31 percent, which suggests that 69 percent of nations were democracies of some sort (*Economist* 2008), representing a 3 percent increase from 1996 and more significantly, a 44 percent increase from 1974. Yet, not all democracies are created equal and U.S. involvement in exporting democracy is not without criticism. What is the relationship between globalization and democracy?

The worldwide spread of democracy is a political and cultural outcome of globalization as well as part of the neoliberal project (Hall 2002). Although globalization is a double-edged sword, Kellner (2002) acknowledges the "progressive features" of globalization, including the Internet. Expounding on the possibilities provided by technology, Francis Fox Piven (2008) foresees globalization as expanding both the availability and accessibility of "popular power." Hardt and Negri (2004) have stressed the possibilities of democratic transformative struggle within Empire through "multitude." Although they argue that the current biggest threat to democracy is global war, and that Empire, enabled through globalization, involves "new mechanisms of control and constant conflict," globalization also includes "the creation of new circuits of cooperation and collaboration that stretch across nations and continents and allow an unlimited number of encounters" (xiii). Does globalization enable the spread of democracy, and is it actually spreading?

Is Democracy Spreading?

The percentage of countries categorized as "non-authoritarian" is at an all-time high. In the 1960s and 1970s, many social scientists doubted the resilience of democracies, noting the success of authoritarian regimes in the former Soviet bloc to control opinion and dissent, the preponderance of "presidents for life" in Africa after colonialism, and authoritarian regimes and practices in both Latin America and Asia (Markoff 1996). Beginning in the mid-1970s and continuing into the 1990s was the reversal of this trend, with the fall of communism and the endorsement of democracy in what is called the "third wave" (Huntington 1991; Markoff 1996). It seems an inescapable conclusion that democracy is becoming a global political standard. Yet, we have not come to "the end of history" as there is a wide variation in the quality of political life under the "democracy" umbrella. How do social scientists differentiate between different "democracy" types and what accounts for the third wave?

As we have seen in Chapter 2, there is a wide variation under the democracy umbrella with "low quality" democracies failing to provide basic services (Markhoff 2005) and democracy often co-exists with anti-democratic forces and conflict (Markoff 1996, 2005). To differentiate, between various levels, the *Economist* (Economic Intelligence Unit 2008) uses an "index of democracy" consisting of sixty indicators that fall into five categories, including electoral process, civil liberties, government functioning, political participation, and political culture. From these indicators, index scores ranging from 10 through 0 are calculated with higher scores equated with democracy. Index scores are broken down into ranges to classify nations into four categories: full democracies, flawed democracies, hybrid regimes, and authoritarian regimes.

In 2008, 70 percent of the 167 countries examined were not "authoritarian," but only 18 percent of nations are full democracies (e.g., the United States, Western European countries, and Japan) meaning that only 14.4 percent of the world's population currently experiences democratic rights and protections. About 30 percent of nations are categorized as flawed democracies (e.g., India, South Africa, Israel, and Brazil), and 22 percent are hybrid regimes (e.g., Turkey, Russia, and Pakistan). The final 30 percent of regimes are classified as authoritarian regimes (e.g. Cuba, Kuwait, and China). The authors of the 2008 report contend that although the third wave of democratization was impressive, and that almost half of the world's population lives under democracy "of some sort," the spread of democracy appears "to have come to a halt" (Economic Intelligence Unit 2008). Yet, there seems to have been substantial improvement since 1974. What role has globalization played?

Role of Globalization

Markoff (1996) contends that governing elites pay attention to what is happening to their counterparts in other areas, sometimes resulting in political convergence. Weaker states may attempt to become successful by modeling themselves after stronger ones or strong states may impose their political organization on weaker states. To explain the "third wave," Schwartzman (1998) contends that scholars examining the role of global connections tend to focus on six main categories, including favorable international climate, global industrialization and development, global shocks, a shifting global hegemon, world system cycles, and foreign intervention. The next section is based mostly on Schwartzman's (1998) summary.

FAVORABLE INTERNATIONAL CLIMATE   This is a type of domino argument suggesting that as one nation falls away from an authoritarian system of government others follow suit. Clearly linking this to globalization, Huntington (1991) argues that expansion of global communications and transportation started the domino cascade. Schwartzman criticizes this argument because it fails to answer several questions, including what caused the first domino to fall, and why did this not occur earlier after the Greeks first developed democracy? Further, Schwartzman contends that it does not seriously consider social, economic, and political processes operating at both global and domestic levels. She concludes that the international climate argument does not contribute much to our understanding.

GLOBAL INDUSTRIALIZATION AND DEVELOPMENT   Global industrialization and development promotes democratization through technological innovations in communication and transportation and industrialization, contributing to a growth in both the middle and working classes and global growth undermining nondemocratic states. The role of communication and transportation in spreading democracy is criticized because networks that can spread democratic ideals can also spread fascism. In other words, networks are content neutral. Furthermore, this argument does not explain the initial introduction of democratic ideas. However, the growth in middle and working classes has the advantage of explaining why democracy is the preferred regime as "revolution and democracy offer the best opportunities for workers to satisfy their material needs" (Schwartzman 1998: 167).

GLOBAL SHOCKS   This explanation posits that economic shocks create a legitimacy crisis for nondemocratic regimes because an intolerable gap is created between what a state promises and what it is able to deliver, resulting in a loss of legitimacy and possible overthrow. While democratic states also face a loss of legitimacy during economic crisis, citizens do not overturn the state but vote incumbents out of office. How might the recent 2008–2009 economic crisis impact democracy? Rather than arguing that shocks will put only nondemocratic states at risk with democratic ones experiencing only a change in administration, Kekic (2007) argues that nations with "emerging markets" and "fragile democratic institutions" face a higher risk of slipping back into authoritarianism because free market capitalism and Western ideology may be blamed for the economic crisis.

SHIFTING GLOBAL HEGEMON   World Systems Theory posits that a shift in the global hegemon is one of the factors important for understanding the third wave. Schmartzman notes that Wallerstein (1991) does not agree that the collapse of Eastern Europe is a triumph of Western democracy. Rather, the breakup of the former Soviet bloc is the result of the decline in the hegemonic power of the United States because the old war standoff allowed both the United States and the Soviet Union to maintain dominance over their sphere of influence. German and Japanese economic competition challenged U.S. hegemony. With U.S. decline, the Soviets also lost their hold on the Eastern bloc, resulting in a wave of democratic transitions.

WORLD SYSTEM CYCLES   According to WST, democracy has occurred more in the semi-periphery than the periphery as the former is impacted more severely by the shock waves of the B-phase. Summarizing Wallerstein (1984), the semi-periphery had systems of labor control (e.g., tenancy or sharecropping) that were best maintained under authoritarian regimes. Transitioning to democracy actually works to maintain the power of the capitalist class because it provides a way to peacefully organize a contentious working class. Schwartzman argues that "the B-phase world-system perspective seems to offer the greatest insights in deciphering the deeper significance of the Third Wave of democraticization" (1998: 179).

FOREIGN INTERVENTION   This literature emphasizes the positive role played by the United States in promoting democracy and also examines the historic cases of former British colonies. Schwartzman correctly notes that the United States has a long history of ignoring nondemocratic regimes when there is a strategic interest at stake such as access to resources or geographical positioning. Why then the democratic shift? The short answer is that it must meet the needs of the hegemonic power. Yet, this leaves an important question unanswered: "from where comes this good will?" (Schwartzman 1998: 172). This argument posits that a certain type of democracy provides a less contentious method for dominant nations to control their interests. In the next section, we examine some arguments for why the United States has shifted its foreign policy from supporting nondemocratic regimes to exporting democracy.

Exporting Democracy

Although Westerners view the exporting of democracy positively, others view this as threatening traditional structures resulting in the loss of privilege or security (Kinnvall 2004). Recently, the United States invaded Iraq and is supporting Iranian NGOs in the hope that civil society will rise up against this regime (Esfandiari and Litwak, 2007). The United States has previously tolerated various authoritarian regimes. What explains the shift in its foreign policy, and does globalization play a role?

Robinson (1996) posits that the rise of global capitalism requires new forms of transnational control and that the United States, as a dominant nation in a highly stratified international system, is encouraging the replacement of coercive means with consensual ones. On behalf of an emerging transnational elite, the United States is promoting polyarchy or "a system in which a small group actually rules and mass participation in decision-making is confined to leadership choice in elections carefully managed by competing elites" (623–624).

Robinson criticizes polyarchy for focusing on the process of democracy (e.g., elections) and not the outcome, resulting in a system characterized by inequality. Because the process is "democratic," polyarchy legitimizes inequality much more effectively than authoritarianism. Furthermore, the removal of dictatorships and other forms of authoritarian government "preempts more fundamental change" such as a more fair or equitable distribution of resources (1996: 626). Robinson (1996, 2004) argues that American foreign policy began promoting polyarchy in the 1980s and 1990s to circumvent change that would mitigate inequality. Polyarchy assists elites by securing power over the state apparatus to bring it into the global economy.

What does any of this have to do with globalization? Polyarchy provides the basis for "Gramscian hegemony in a transnational setting" (Robinson 1996: 627), where a dominant class gains the permission of the ruled to be dominated through active adoption of legitimizing ideology (Gramsci 1971). Transnational domination becomes hegemonic when justification ideology is accepted in both core and periphery regions. Globalization has spread transnational hegemony into periphery regions such as former colonies in Africa. Promoting democracy is combined with neoliberalism, enabling the transnational capitalist class to overcome disparate monetary, fiscal, and industrial policies. Polyarchy works better than authoritarianism because it is a more "durable form of social control" (Robinson 1996: 627) that promotes stability. Polyarchy is also better equipped to deal with the social dislocation and political reorganization that accompanies entrance into the global economy and the need to deal with popular demands pressuring elites to reinstate barriers that provided some protection against undesirable economic impacts of globalization. Textbox 10.2 focuses on the issue of democracy promotion in Iraq.

Despite the criticism of U.S. foreign policy, few would argue that citizens are better off under authoritarian regimes. The transition to democracy, even if imperfect, is an improvement over nondemocratic government and so globalization is considered essential for creating democracy as a global norm. Yet, globalization is criticized for perpetuating many global ills including inequality, environmental degradation, and the homogenization of culture. Antiglobalization movements are the main resistance against the perceived negative effects of globalization.

ANTIGLOBALIZATION MOVEMENTS

Globalization may appear to be natural, inevitable, and/or logical but we are cautioned not to think of globalization as either because it is a human phenomenon and thus can be altered (Evans 2005). Those who oppose globalization may be against the ideology, actual globalization, or both (Hall 2002). Antiglobalization or counterhegemonic globalization is the "globally organized project of transformation aimed at replacing the dominant (hegemonic) global regime with

TEXTBOX 10.2

Exporting Democracy to Iraq

According to Index of Democracy ratings, Iraq is not a full or even a flawed democracy but a hybrid regime, with a 2007 index score of 4.0 (10 is fully democratic) and an overall ranking of 116 out of 167 countries (*Economist Intelligence Unit* 2008). *Hybrid regime* is a classification applied to countries with a score ranging from 5.9 to 4.0. Iraq is on the low end of the scale, just above the demarcation for authoritarian or nondemocratic regimes. While democracy is a slow process even in the United States (just ask African-Americans and women), what is the prognosis for Iraq to develop as a democracy? According to Erler and Wood (2009), the prospects for democracy "are dim" because the Iraqi government lacks both the desire and the might necessary to sustain democracy on their own. In their criticism of U.S. foreign policy, Erler and Wood argue that the invasion of Iraq was "always ill-advised," that the goal was "imprudent and reckless," and that the strategy was "poorly conceived and executed" (131). Is there any substance to the accusations? Erler and Wood argue that there is a theological–political problem in Iraq. Specifically, that sectarian–religious division (with secular Kurds, Shia, and Sunni Muslims) is incompatible with constitutional democracy that requires the free exercise of religion. Assuming that major theological differences between the Shia and Sunni Muslims could ever be resolved, there is still the problem of the minority Kurds. Furthermore, the fact that the government of Iraq cannot provide security makes it difficult to engage in the deliberations necessary to create and sustain democracy. Finally, they argue that the proportional representation system that was created has resulted in an unstable coalition government incapable of competently ruling. Robinson (2004) accuses U.S. "democracy promotion" as catering to the interests of the transnational elite and the global capitalist system. Furthermore, he asserts that it is polyarchy that is being promoted and not true democracy. Although Saddam Hussein was a brutal dictator who killed and tortured his own people, taking a critical perspective requires us to ask some impertinent questions.

- Who else (besides potentially Iraqis) benefits from democracy promotion in Iraq?
- Does the United States have the right to interfere in the internal affairs of another country?
- What is being promoted: democracy or polyarchy?
- Can democracy be successfully exported to nations that do not share the Western values (e.g., freedom of religious expression) upon which constitutional democracy has been based?

one that maximizes democratic political control and makes the equitable development of human capabilities and environmental stewardship its priorities" (Evans 2008: 272). In sum, these movements promote access to political power and equitable opportunities for all, responsible land and resource management, and resistance to global domination.

Drawing on Karl Polanyi's ideas of the "double movement," Evans (2008) argues that the status quo is not sustainable because giving priority to self-regulating markets cannot endure over the long run. Perhaps the most well-known antiglobalization demonstration in the United States is the "Battle of Seattle" (November 29, 1999 to December 3, 1999), resulting in the arrest of over 500 demonstrators, 2.5 million dollars in property damage (Special Reports: The WTO Legacy), and the closing off of over twenty-five city blocks to contain the protests. What types of organizations or entities have risen to combat generic globalization?

Evans (2000) discusses three types of counterhegemonic globalization: transnational advocacy networks, transnational consumer/labor networks, and the labor movement. First, he reviews what Keck and Sikkink (1998) have termed "transnational advocacy networks" that tend to focus on issues such as human rights, environmental protection, and women's rights. Groups

November 30, 1999—Seattle, WA—Marchers occupied Pike Street in front of the Paramount Theater keeping the WTO from holding its opening ceremony. The conference start, which was scheduled for 10 am, was postponed until noon, and then cancelled as one of the largest protests in Seattle's history unfolded.

Credit: Newscom

falling into this category have networks of activists that are motivated by ideals and values and gain leverage by the spread of norms. With widespread adoption, these ideas become cultural norms. Ironically, transnational advocacy networks oppose globalization but take advantage of cultural globalization to gain political leverage to bring about a more equitable and sustainable planet (Evans 2005, 2008).

Transnational consumer/labor networks are antiglobalization entities that pursue corporations exploiting third-world workers (e.g., low pay, no benefits, harmful working conditions). They share with advocacy networks the goal of establishing and spreading global norms but target corporations using consumer boycotts (e.g., Nike shoes). Finally, the labor movement is also counterhegemonic as it tries to spread and sustain "core labor standards" including the right to unionize. Citing Keck and Sikkink (1998), Evans (2000) notes that antiglobalization advocacy networks are effective if they can accomplish three tasks, including transmitting information, invoking norms, and shifting political venues.

Transmitting information is "simple but crucial" (Evans 2000: 232) because punishment does not occur unless others have knowledge of a transgression. Invoking norms or standards allows local groups to connect with global allies, creating a sense of unity and power. Finally, the successful use of "venue shifting" allows local groups to draw in global allies who use political leverage to force change. This often involves connecting those who are not always natural allies. Evans explains:

> While organizations like the World Bank and the WTO appear from the outside to be titanically powerful representatives of the "new world order," they are in fact politically vulnerable, not because they are attacked by environmentalists or labor activists, but because these groups can so easily muster "strange bedfellows" as allies from the ranks of conservatives . . . . Distrust of government in any form, combined

with deep-seated xenophobia, turns any institution of global governance into the enemy for so many conservatives, despite the fact that the transnational corporate constituents who finance the campaigns of these conservatives are acutely aware of the need for stable and global governance. (2000: 239)

Global alliances must be constructed in combination with local organizing and in the case of transnational consumer/labor networks; the connection between products and exploitation needs to be made clear by "forcing affluent customers to acknowledge that what are for them marginal gains are bought at the price of real misery" (Evans 2000: 237). Prior to the successful boycott of Nike, consumers were unaware of the impact on workers including low wages and harm from inhaling glue fumes.

This discussion has focused on progressive antiglobalization activity. To assume all antiglobalization activity is progressive would be a mistake, as many movements have their share of "irresponsible nilhists" and that the alternative could be more authoritarian and oppressive (Evans 2005). Yet, these movements challenge the TINA belief and remind us that human intervention is always a possibility. What do sociologists predict for the future? As usual, there is a great deal of contention and debate. Table 10.5 summarizes the types of antiglobalization organizations.

FUTURE OF GLOBALIZATION

Future Trends

PESSIMISTIC VIEW   The state will not disappear but "meaner, more repressive ways of organizing the state's role will be accepted as the only way to avoid the collapse of public institutions" (Evans 1997: 64). Wallerstein (2000) foresees a world system characterized by more chaotic economic swings and more violence as state structures continue to experience declines in legitimacy. Bryan Turner has criticized sociologists for having an overly optimistic view and puts forth one of the bleakest views of the future. His "neo-Malthusian sociology of globalization" (2007: 3 of 15) proposes examining the connections between (1) environmental damage due to waste and resource depletion, (2) radical politics grounded in fundamentalist religion, (3) new wars and youth alienation, (4) rising importance of human rights responses to failed states, and (5) the importance of religious ideas including those that motivate violence. Only a few of his several predictions are reviewed here.

First, Turner argues that global governance needed to regulate local conflicts and regional wars will require systems of domination and regulation that cannot be provided by states.

Table 10.5   Antiglobalization Entities

Type	Goals	Strategy
Transnational Advocacy Networks	Promote human rights, environmental protection, and women's rights	Create and spread global norms
Transnational Consumer/Labor	Establishes global norms	Target corporations through consumer boycotts
Labor Movement	Establishes core labor standards (e.g., outlaw child labor and promote the right to organize)	Network with labor organizations

Source: Evans (2000)

Second, dwindling environmental resources too depleted to support population growth will require the exploitation of outer space as states will struggle to maintain natural resources for their populations. The struggle for scarce resources will lead to war and increase tension between developing and developed countries. The surplus of unemployed and underemployed men will be a major factor in the development of new wars.

Consistent with others (e.g., Martin 2007), Turner predicts religious fundamentalism will continue to grow and replace political ideology as a motivator for violence as radical religion is attractive to the socially alienated, including the legions of unemployed and underemployed men displaced in the world economy. Globalization will render catastrophes more "general, immediate, and profound" because the world is more interconnected but lacks an effective global governance strategy (Turner 2007: 12 of 15) as the UN is weak and unwilling to step in unless backed by the United States but it is unlikely that the latter can continue to act as either "a global policeman, or a global doctor."

In this bleak future it is "the world of Mad Max with roaming armies of displaced men in search of gasoline, armaments, and drugs, where small fortified hamlets of the rich and powerful would seek shelter, and secure religious meaning from their cults and prophets" (Turner 2007: 12–13 of 15). The global neo-Malthusian crisis of spreading infectious diseases, roaming displaced and socially alienated men, drug dependency, environmental degradation, civil disruption, war lords, and the like will drain away both economic resources and democratic civil liberties and it is unlikely that the spread of human rights will stem this tide.

OPTIMISTIC VIEW   While Piven does not view globalization as resulting in the "dawn of global democracy or global socialism" (2008: 12), she argues that globalization can be harnessed for positive reform. In the case of human rights, access to globalized media and communication has allowed some to reframe their relationship with the nation-state by connecting with international allies that pressure repressive nation-states (Kearney 1995). Wallerstein has a gloomy forecast but also argues for the possibility of positive human intervention. Hardt and Negri deplore the transition into Empire but also proclaim the democratic potential residing within the "multitude." Globalization is happening but it is neither positive or negative nor monolithic or inevitable (Guillén 2001). While globalization has undesirable social problems throughout the globe, the same networks can spread global standards for human rights, freedom, and environmentalism.

Future Sociological Research on Globalization

Robertson and White (2007) contend that although sociologists were the first to initiate discussion of globalization, researchers have often ignored the social dimension of globalization. Furthermore, while there has been much theorizing about globalization, there is a paucity of empirical data (Staples 2008), with affluent democracies overrepresented in globalization research (Brady et al. 2007). What does exist is often subjected to misleading statistical analysis and interpretation (Babones 2007). We need more concrete empirical data on globalization, but books stressing "grand theorizing" sell much better than those stressing empirical data on a more narrowly defined geographic region (Alasuutari 2000). If true, this is a rather ironic if not scathing critique of a discipline that prides itself on the objective collection and interpretation of empirical data. Why might collecting data be difficult?

Globalization is a difficult phenomenon to study. Researchers not only struggle with competing definitions (Babones 2007) but the phenomena itself is "fragmented, incomplete, discontinuous . . . and in many ways a contradictory and puzzling process" (Guillén 2001: 238). Even answering one of the most fundamental questions, when did globalization begin, is difficult due to a lack of appropriate data. Babones (2007) argues that the tremendous number of academic books and papers on globalization renders a definition impossible to agree on, and agreement is not even desirable for theory development. Yet, this lack of agreement creates methodological problems because researchers tend to measure globalization in whatever way may best fit the data but not necessarily the way that is in line with the theoretical perspective underlying the research. Babones writes, "one suspects the plurality or even the majority of the hundreds of articles . . . use globalization more as a rhetorical backdrop than as a variable to be operationalized and measured" (2007: 2 of 15). In short, future research needs to follow the rules of sound methodology, including grounding the research in theory and measuring variables in ways that fit theoretical definitions. If correct, much of the research on economic globalization in particular may be problematic, making tentative any conclusions that are drawn.

CONCLUSION

There is a great deal more disagreement than agreement among political sociologists regarding the existence, duration, and impact of globalization. Alasuutari (2000) has criticized sociologists for confusing cause and effect in their examination of globalization. Using the compression of time and space as an example, if this is an effect of globalization, what is the cause? Sociologists are criticized for saying *globalization*! If the compression of time and space is a characteristic of globalization, what causes that? Is it technological innovation, the needs of capitalism, or something else? Readers of this chapter have a variety of answers to choose from depending upon which theoretical perspective seems most convincing.

It may well be a long time before sociologists have a theory of globalization but that is not to say that efforts to understand globalization have been fruitless. We have reviewed many interesting theoretical ideas and sociological questions that will continue to stimulate research for decades to come. To quote Guillén (2001), globalization is not "civilizing, destructive, or feeble" but is a real phenomenon that is transforming every social institution, including the nation-state in ways that have both positive and negative consequences for all. Whether the nation-state is transforming into a national state as part of a TNS or a type of global governance system such as Empire, or something else, is unknown. Regardless, political sociologists will be there to observe, explain, and critique the transformation.

Endnotes

1. The Washington Consensus is a ten-point list: (1) impose fiscal discipline, (2) reform taxation, (3) liberalize interest rates, (4) raise spending on health and education, (5) secure property rights, (6) privatize state-run industries, (7) deregulate markets, (8) adopt a competitive exchange rate, (9) remove barriers to trade, (10) remove barriers to direct foreign investment (from John Williamson's 1989 formulation as cited by Ferguson 2008).

2. The World Bank has 184 member countries and consists of both the International Bank for Reconstruction and Development (IBRD) and the International Development Association (IDA). According to its Web site (http://www.worldbank.org), "the IBRD focuses on middle income and creditworthy poor countries, while IDA focuses on the poorest countries in the world. Together we provide low-interest loans, interest-free credits and grants to developing countries for a wide array of purposes that include investments in education, health, public administration, infrastructure, financial and private sector development, agriculture, and environmental and natural resource management."

3. The International Monetary Fund (IMF) has 185 member countries. According to its official Web site (http://www.imf.org) the IMF works "to foster global monetary cooperation, secure financial stability, facilitate international trade, promote high employment and sustainable economic growth, and reduce poverty around the world."

4. The WTO (http://www.wto.org) has 153 members and views its role as a means of liberalizing trade between nations as well as providing a forum for negotiation and mediation. Critics of the WTO

accuse the organization of emphasizing property rights rather than issues related to workers. Evans (2000) observes that labor ought to be considered a trade-related issue because the lack of "core labor standards" can lead to unfair advantage by nations allowing child labor and preventing workers from organizing for better wages. The WTO defends itself against these accusations by arguing that "the WTO has never ruled on child labour because the issue has never come up for a ruling. Countries' efforts to deal with child labour problems have never been challenged in the WTO" (http://www.wto.org/english/thewto_e/minist_e/min99_e/english/misinf_e/03lab_e.htm).

5. Prior to Hurricane Katrina, 123 public schools were run by the school board. Post Katrina has only four public schools with thirty-one charter schools run by private organizations. Forty-seven hundred members of the New Orleans teachers union were fired, with only a few rehired by the charter schools at reduced salaries (Klein 2007).

6. Halliburton, the company run by former Vice President Dick Cheney (1995–2000), is involved in providing logistical support, which includes building and running military bases, to the U.S. military. Blackwater (now Xe Services) is a private security firm accused of killing Iraqi civilians. Companies such as Health Net and IAP Worldwide Services benefited from the then U.S. Secretary of Defense Donald Rumsfeld's expansion of the privatization of services. IAP received the contract to take over many services at the Walter Reed military hospital. Klein (2007) claims at the start of the 2003 U.S. invasion of Iraq there was one contractor for every ten U.S. soldiers. By 2007 this ratio became 1 contractor for every 1.4 U.S. soldiers.

7. *Non-Gramscian hegemony* refers to domination of one nation by another. Characterizing the United States as a global hegemon is an example of this. In contrast, *Gramscian hegemony* refers to the relationship between two classes where one class or group within that class exercises control by gaining the consent of the dominated group. In other words, the dominated agree that they should be dominated. Adopting the ruling class ideology legitimizes domination (Robinson 1996).

8. Green Dam-Youth Escort software is an Internet filtering software developed by the Chinese to be installed on all new computers sold in China. The Chinese government describes it as a method to protect youth by blocking "unhealthy" Internet content. The software would automatically download updated lists of banned content. Critics have argued that it also blocks users from content critical of the Chinese government. The Chinese government has delayed enforcement (Wines 2009). China has previously been criticized for blocking access to politically sensitive information during the 2008 Olympic Games ("IOC Agrees to Internet Blocking at the Games" 2008). Iran also uses software to block politically or religiously offensive Web sites and blogs and threatened to shut down the Internet for legislative elections in 2008 to "ensure that the government had unimpeded Internet service for the elections, even though the governments' Internet lines had been upgraded" ("Iranian Users Face Blockage During Coming Election" 2008).

9. The treaty of Westphalia, also known as the "Peace of Westphalia" signed in 1648, ended the Thirty Years, War in Europe. It established the right of nation-state sovereignty, or the principle that nation-states have the right of political self-determination and should be free from interference in internal affairs from other nation-states.

10. Neda Agha-Soltan, an Iranian bystander, was killed in June 2009 during an antigovernment protest. She was not an active protestor but had decided to watch the demonstrations with her singing instructor. They were trying to get home after being caught up in a clash in central Tehran. She was shot in the heart and died after saying "It burned me." Her killing was captured by video and posted on the Internet (Fathi 2009).

11. The G8 is an international forum represented by the governments of Canada, France, Germany, United Kingdom, Italy, Japan, Russia, and the United States.

References

Alasuutari, Pertti. 2000. "Globalization and the Nation-State: An Appraisal of the Discussion." *Acta Sociologica* 43: 259–269.

———. 2004. "The Principles of Pax Americana." *Cultural Studies* 4: 246–249.

Alford, Robert and Roger Friedland. 1985. *Powers of Theory*. Cambridge: Cambridge University Press.

Appadurai, A. 1996. *Modernity at Large: Cultural Dimensions of Globalization*. Minneapolis: University of Minnesota Press.

Arrighi, G. 1999. "Globalization, State Sovereignty, and the Endless Accumulation of Capital." Pp. 53–73 in *States and Sovereignty in the Global Economy*, edited by D. Smith, D. Solinger, and S. Topik. London, UK: Routledge.

———. 2003. "Lineages of Empire." Pp. 29–42 in *Debating Empire*, edited by G. Balakrishnan. New York: Verso.

Babones, Salvatore. 2007. "Studying Globalization: Methodological Issues." In *The Blackwell Companion* to *Globalization*, edited by G. Ritzer. Blackwell Publishing. Blackwell Reference Online. Retrieved March 27, 2009 from http://www.blackwellreference. com/subsriber/tocnode?id=g781405132749_chunk_g 97814051327499.

Barber, Benjamin. 2001. *Jihad vs. McWorld*. New York: Random House.

Başkan, Filiz. 2006. "Globalization and Nationalism: The Nationalist Action Party of Turkey." *Nationalism and Ethnic Politics* 12: 83–105.

BBC News. 1999. "World: Africa Aids Drug Trade Dispute Ends." September 18. Retrieved July 27, 2009 from http://news.bbc.co.uk/2/hi/africa/450942.stm.

Best, Shaun. 2002. *Introduction to Politics and Society*. Thousand Oaks, CA: Sage.

Blackman, Tim. 2007. "Globalization and Public Policy." In *The Blackwell Companion to Globalization*, edited by G. Ritzer. Blackwell Publishing. Blackwell Reference Online. Retrieved June 23, 2009 from http://www.blackwellreference.com/subscriber/ uid=54/tocnode?id=g9781405132749.

Boyer, R. and D. Drache (Editors). 1996. *States against Markets: The Limits of Globalization*. London: Routledge.

Brady, David, Jason Beckfield, and Wei Zhao. 2007. "The Consequences of Economic Globalization for Affluent Democracies." *Annual Review of Sociology* 33: 313–334.

Castells, Manuel. 1989. "The Informational Mode of Developing and the Restructuring of Capitalism." Pp. 260–284 in *The Castells Reader on Cities and Social Theory*, edited by Ida Susser. Oxford: Blackwell.

_____. 1996. *The Rise of the Network Society*. Oxford: Blackwell.

_____. 1997. *The Power of Identity*. Oxford: Blackwell.

_____. 1998. *End of Millennium*. Oxford: Blackwell.

_____. 2000. "Materials for an Exploratory Theory of the Network Society." *British Journal of Sociology* 51: 5–24.

Chomsky, Noam. 2003. *Hegemony or Survival*. New York: Owl Books.

"Clinton Announces New Programs to Train 150,000 Indian Doctors; India's HIV Statistics Disputed." 2005. *The Body Pro* May 27. Retrieved July 27, 2009 from http://www.thebodypro.com/content/ art8478 .html00?ts=pf.

Delanty, Gerard and Chris Rumford. 2007. "Political Globalization." In *The Blackwell Companion to Globalization*, edited by G. Ritzer. Blackwell Reference Online. Retrieved March 27, 2009 from http://www.blackwellreference.com/subscriber/tocno de?id=g9781405132749_chunk_g78140513274924.

Durkheim, Emile. 1964 [1893]. *The Division of Labor in Society*. Translated by George Simpson. New York: Free Press.

Economic Intelligence Unit. 2008. "The Intelligence Unit's Index of Democracy 2008." *The Economist*.

Retrieved July 22, 2009 from http://graphics.eiu. com/PDF/Democracy%20Index%202008.pdf.

Erler, Edward J. and Gary Wood. 2009. "Is Democracy Exportable? The Case of the United States in Iraq." Pp. 121–131 in *Global Politics in the Dawn of the 21st Century*, edited by A. Kalaitzdis. Athens: ATINER.

Esfandiari, Haleh and Robert S. Litwak. 2007. "When Promoting Democracy is Counterproductive." *The Chronicle of Higher Education* (October 19): B7–B9.

Essary, Elizabeth H. 2007. "Speaking of Globalization: Frame Analysis and World Society." *International Journal of Comparative Sociology* 48: 509–526.

Evans, Peter. 1997. "The Eclipse of the State? Reflections on Stateness in an Era of Globalization." *World Politics* 50: 62–87.

_____. 2000. "Fighting Marginalization with Transnational Networks: Counter Hegemonic Globalization." *Contemporary Sociology* 29: 230–241.

_____. 2005. "Counterhegemonic Globalization: Transnational Social Movements in the Contemporary Global Political Economy Integration." Pp. 607–629 in *The Handbook of Political Sociology*, edited by T. Janoski, R. Alford, A. Hicks, and M. A. Schwartz. Cambridge: Cambridge University Press.

_____. 2008. "Is an Alternative Globalization Possible?" *Politics & Society* 36: 271–305.

Fathi, Nazila. 2009. "In a Death Seen Around the World, a Symbol of Iranian Protests." *New York Times* June 23. Retrieved July 15, 2009 from http://www. nytimes.com/2009/06/23/world/middleeast/23neda .html.

Ferguson, Niall. 2008. *The Ascent of Money*. New York: Penguin Press.

"Franglais Resurgent." 2008. *The Economist* September 11. Retrieved January 15, 2009 from http://www. economist.com/world/europe/displaystory.cfm?story_ id=12208926.

Fukuyama, Frances. 1992. *The End of History and the Last Man*. New York: Oxford.

Galkin, Alexandr. 2006. "Globalization and the Political Upheavals of the 21st Century." *Social Sciences* 37: 67–82.

Giddens, Anthony. 1990. *The Consequences of Modernity*. Stanford, CA: Stanford University Press.

_____. 1998. *The Third Way: The Renewal of Social Democracy*. Cambridge: Polity Press.

_____. 2000. *Runaway World: How Globalization Is Reshaping Our Lives*. New York: Routledge.

Giulianotti, Richard and Roland Robertson. 2007. "Recovering the Social: Globalization, Football, and Transnationalism." *Global Networks* 7: 144–186.

Gramsci, Antonio. 1971. *Selections from the Prison Notebooks*, edited by Q. Hoare and G. N. Smith. New York: International Publishers.

Guillén, Mauro F. 2001. "Is Globalization Civilizing, Destructive, or Feeble? A Critique of Five Key

Debates in the Social Science Literature." *Annual Review of Sociology* 27: 235–260.

Håkansta, Carin. 1998. "The Battle on Patents and AIDS Treatment." *Biotechnology and Development Monitor* 34: 16–19.

Hall, Thomas D. 2002. "World-Systems Analysis and Globalization: Directions for the Twenty First Century." Pp. 81–122 in *Theoretical Directions in Political Sociology for the 21st Century*, volume 11, *Research in Political Sociology*, edited by B. A. Dobratz, T. Buzzell, and L. K. Waldner. Amsterdam: Elsevier/JAI.

Hardt, Michael and Antonio Negri. 2000. *Empire*. Cambridge: Harvard University Press.

_____. 2004. *Multitude: War and Democracy in the Age of Empire*. New York: Penguin Books.

Harvey, David. 1989. *The Condition of Post-modernity: An Enquiry into the Origins of Cultural Change*. New York: Blackwell.

_____. 1990. *The Condition of Post-Modernity*. London: Blackwell.

Hawthorne, Suzanne. 2004. "Wild Politics: Beyond Globalization." *Women's Studies International Forum* 27: 243–259.

Held, David. 1991. "Democracy and the Global System." Pp. 197–235 in *Political Theory Today*, edited by D. Held. Cambridge: Polity.

Held, David and Anthony McGrew. 2002. *Globalization and Antiglobalization*. Cambridge: Polity.

Held, David, Anthony McGrew, D. Goldblatt, and J. Perraton. 1999. *Global Transformations*. Stanford University Press: Stanford, CA.

Heydenbrand, Wolf (editor). 1994. *Max Weber: Sociological Writings*. The German Library, volume 60. New York: Continuum.

Hirst, P. and G. Thompson. 1992. "The Problem of Globalization: International Economic Relations, National Economic Management, and the Formation of Trading Blocks." *Economy and Society* 21: 357–396.

_____. 1996. *Globalization in Question*. London: Polity.

Huber, Evelyne and John D. Stephens. 2005. "State Economic and Social Policy in Global Capitalism." Pp. 607–629 in *The Handbook of Political Sociology*, edited by T. Janoski, R. Alford, A. Hicks, and M. A. Schwartz. Cambridge: Cambridge University Press.

Huntington, Samuel P. 1991. *The Third Wave: Democratization in the Late Twentieth Century*. Norman: University of Oklahoma Press.

_____. 1993. "The Clash of Civilizations." *Foreign Affairs* 72: 22, 48.

_____. 1996. *The Clash of Civilizations and the Remaking of World Order*. New York: Touchtone, Simon and Schuster.

"International Phone Calls up 12% in 2008." 2009. March 21. Retrieved July 3, 2009 from http://www.itfacts. biz/international-phone-calls-up-12-in-2008/12924.

Internet Systems Consortium. 2009. "Internet Host Count History." Retrieved November 5, 2010 from http://www.isc.org/solutions/survey/history.

Internet World Stats. Usage and Population Statistics. 2010. Retrieved November 5, 2010 from http://internet worldstats.com/stats.htm.

"IOC Agrees to Internet Blocking at the Games." 2008. *New York Times* July 30. Retrieved July 15, 2009 from http://www.nytimes.com/2008/07/30/business/worldbusiness/30iht-olymedia.4.14895767.html?scp=1&sq=IOC%20agrees%20to%20%20internet%20blocking&st=cse.

"Iranian Users Face Blockage during Coming Election." 2008. *New York Times* March 3. Retrieved July 15, 2009 from http://www.nytimes.com/2008/03/03/world/africa/03iht-tehran.4.10662595.html?scp=1&sq=iranian%20users%20face%20blockage&st=cse.

Iverson, T. 2001. "The Dynamics of Welfare State Expansion: Trade Openness, De-industrialization, and Partisan Politics." Pp. 45–79 in *The New Politics of the Welfare State*, edited by P. Pierson. New York: Oxford University Press.

Janoski, Thomas and Fengjuan Wang. 2004. "The Politics of Immigration and National Integration." Pp. 607–629 in *The Handbook of Political Sociology*, edited by T. Janoski, R. Alford, A. Hicks, and M. A. Schwartz. Cambridge: Cambridge University Press.

Jones, Adam. 2006. *Genocide: A Comprehensive Introduction*. London: Routledge.

Kaldor, Mary. 2004. "Nationalism and Globalisation". *Nations and Nationalism* 10: 161–177.

Kamath, Gauri. 2000. "Cipla Stops Exports to Ghana over Glaxo Allegations." *Economic Times*. Retrieved July 29, 2009 from http://www.cptech.org/ip/health/c/india/economictimes11032000.html.

Karp, David A., William C. Yoels, and Barbara H. Vann. 2004. *Sociology in Everyday Life*. 3rd Edition. Long Grove, IL: Waveland Press.

Karraker, Meg Wilkes. 2008. *Global Families*. Boston, MA: Pearson.

Kaufmann, Danile, Aart Kraay, and Masimo Masstruzzi. 2007. *Governance Matters IV*. Washington, DC: The World Bank.

Kearney, M. 1995. "The Local and the Global: The Anthropology of Globalization and Transnationalism." *Annual Review of Anthropology* 24: 547–565.

Keck, Margaret and Kathryn Sikkink. 1998. *Activists beyond Borders: Advocacy Networks in International Politics*. Ithaca, NY: Cornell University Press.

Kekic, Laza. 2007. "The Economist Intelligence Unit's Index of Democracy." *Economist*. Retrieved, January 2, 2008 from http://www.economist.com/media/pdf/DEMOCRACY_INDEX_2007_v3.pdf.

Kellner, Douglas. 2002. "Theorizing Globalization." *Sociological Theory* 20: 285–305.

Khondker, Habibul Haque. 2008. "Globalization and State Autonomy in Singapore." *Asian Journal of Social Science* 36: 35–56.

Kinnvall, Catarina. 2004. "Globalization and Religious Nationalism: Self, Identity, and the Search for Ontological Security." *Political Psychology* 25: 741–767.

Klein, Naomi. 2007. *The Shock Doctrine: The Rise of Disaster Capitalism.* New York: Picador.

Lipson, Charles. 2008. "America as Anti-Empire." Presented at the "American Empire and Exportation of Democracy." *Midwest Faculty Seminar,* University of Chicago, October 30 to November 1.

Manning, S. (editor). 1999. Introduction [To special issue on globalization]. *Journal of World Systems Research* 5: 137–141.

Markoff, John. 1996. *Waves of Democracy.* Thousand Oaks, CA: Pine Forge Press.

_____. 2005. "Transitions to Democracy." Pp. 384–403 in *The Handbook of Political Sociology*, edited by T. Janoski, R. Alford, A. Hicks, and M. A. Schwartz. Cambridge: Cambridge University Press.

Martin, Gus. 2007. "Globalization and International Terrorism." In *The Blackwell Companion to Globalization*, edited by G. Ritzer. Blackwell Publishing. Blackwell Reference Online. Retrieved March 27, 2009 from http://www.blackwellreference .com/subscriber/tocnode?id=g9781405132749_chunk_ g97840513274937.

McGrew, Anthony. 1992. "Conceptualizing Global Politics." Pp. 1–29 in *Global Politics*, edited by A. McGew and P. Lewis. Cambridge: Polity.

_____. 2007. "Globalization in Hard Times: Contention in the Academy and Beyond." In *The Blackwell Companion to Globalization*, edited by G. Ritzer. Blackwell Publishing, 2007. Blackwell Reference Online. Retrieved January 16, 2009 from http:// blackwellreference.com/subscriber/tocnode?id=g9 781405132749_chunk_g97814051327493.

McMicheal, Phillip. 2005. "Globalization." Pp. 587–606 in *The Handbook of Political Sociology*, edited by T. Janoski, R. Alford, A. Hicks, and M. A. Schwartz. Cambridge: Cambridge University Press.

Milani, Brian. 2000. *Designing the Green Economy: The Postindustrial Alternative to Corporate Globalization.* Lanham, MD: Rowman and Littlefield.

Mosley, L. 2003. *Global Capital and National Governments.* Cambridge: Cambridge University Press.

Murphy, Cullen. 1997. "The Spirit of Cotonou." *The Atlantic Monthly.* January. Retrieved January 14, 2009 from http://www.theatlantic.com/issues/ 97jan/french/french.htm.

Nash, Kate and Alan Scott. 2001. "Introduction." Pp. 1–6 in *The Blackwell Companion to Political Sociology*, edited by K. Nash and A. Scott. Malden, MA: Blackwell Publishers.

Nassar, Jamal R. 2005. *Globalization & Terrorism.* Lanham, MA: Rowman and Littlefield Publishing.

Ó Riain, Seán. 2000. "States and Markets in an Era of Globalization." *Annual Review of Sociology* 26: 187–214.

Ohmae, Kenichi. 1990. *The Borderless World.* New York: Harper Business.

_____. 1995. *The End of Nation-State. The Rise of Regional Economies.* London: HarperCollins.

Pakulski, Jan. 2001. "Postmodernization, Fragmentation, Globalization." Pp. 375–385 in *The Blackwell Companion to Political Sociology*, edited by K. Nash and A. Scott. Malden, MA: Blackwell Publishers.

Paquin, Stéphane. 2002. "Globalization, European Integration and the Rise of Neo-Nationalism in Scotland." *Nationalism and Ethnic Politics* 8: 55–80.

Piven, Frances Fox. 2008. "Presidential Address: Can Power from below Change the World?" *American Sociological Review* 73: 1–14.

Ritzer, George. 2007. *The Globalization of Nothing 2.* Thousand Oaks, CA: Pine Forge Press.

_____. 2008. *The McDonaldization of Society.* 5th Edition. Thousand Oaks, CA: Pine Forge Press.

Robbins, Richard H. 2008. *Global Problems and the Culture of Capitalism.* 4th Edition. Boston, MA: Pearson.

Robertson, Roland. 1992. *Globalization: Social Theory and Global Culture.* Thousand Oaks, CA: Sage Publications.

_____. 1994. "Globalisation or Glocalisation?" *Journal of International Communication* 1: 33–52.

Robertson, Roland and Kathleen E. White. 2007. "What Is Globalization?" In *The Blackwell Companion to Globalization*, edited by G. Ritzer. Blackwell Publishing, Blackwell Reference Online. Retrieved June 23, 2009 from http://www.blackwellreference .com/subscriber/tocnode?id=g9781405132749_chun k_g9784051327494.

Robinson, William I. 1996. "Globalization, the World-System, and 'Democracy Promotion' in U.S. Foreign Policy." *Theory and Society* 25: 615–665.

_____. 1998. "Beyond Nation-State Paradigms: Globalization, Sociology, and the Challenge of Transnational Studies." *Sociological Forum* 13: 561–594.

_____. 2001. "Social Theory and Globalization: The Rise of a Transnational State". *Theory and Society* 30: 157–200.

_____ 2004. "What to Expect from US 'Democracy Promotion' in Iraq." *New Political Science* 26: 441–447.

_____. 2007. "Theories of Globalization." In *The Blackwell Companion to Globalization*, edited by G. Ritzer. Blackwell Publishing. Blackwell Reference Online. Retrieved January 16, 2009 from http://www. blackwellreference.com/subscriber/tocnode?id=g978 1405132749_chunk_g97814051327498.

Robinson, William I and Jerry Harris. 2000. "Towards a Global Ruling Class? Globalization and the Transnational Capitalist Class." *Science and Society* 64: 11–54.

Rotberg, Robert I. (editor.) 2003. *State Failure and State Weakness in a Time of Terror.* Washington: Brookings Institution Press.

Sassen, Saskia. 1991. *The Global City.* Princeton, NJ: Princeton University Press.

_____. 1996. *Losing Control? Sovereignty in an Age of Globalization.* New York: Columbia University Press.

Schnee, Walter. 2001. "Nationalism: A Review of the Literature." *Journal of Political and Military Sociology* 29: 1–18.

Schwartzman, Kathleen C. 1998. "Globalization and Democracy." *Annual Review of Sociology* 24: 159–181.

Scott, John and Gordan Marshall. 2005. *Oxford Dictionary of Sociology.* 3rd Edition. Oxford: Oxford University Press.

Sklair, Leslie. 1999. "Competing Conceptions of Globalization." *Journal of World Systems Research* 5: 144–163.

_____. 2000. *Globalization: Capitalism and Its Alternatives.* New York: Oxford University Press.

Smith, Anthony D. 1995. *Nations and Nationalism in a Global Era.* Cambridge: Polity Press.

Smith, David A. 2007. "Politics and Globalization: An Introduction." Pp. 1–23 in *Politics and Globalization*, volume 15, *Research in Political Sociology*, edited by H. Prechel. Elesevier/JAI: Amsterdam.

"Special Reports: The WTO Legacy." *Seattlepi.com.* Retrieved July 14, 2009 from http://www.seattlepi.com/wto.

Staples, Clifford L. 2008. "Cross-Border Acquisitions and Board Globalization in the World's largest TNCs, 1995–2005." *Sociological Quarterly* 49: 31–52.

Steinmetz, George. 2002. "*Empire* by Michael Hardt and Antonio Negri." *American Journal of Sociology* 108: 207–210.

Tilly, Charles. 2003. "A Nebulous Empire." Pp. 26–28 in *Debating Empire*, edited by G. Balakrishnan. New York: Verso.

Tong-hyang, Kim. 2009. "Patients Given No Say in AIDS Drug Dispute." *The Korea Times.* Retrieved July 27, 2009 from http://www.koreatimes.co.kr/www/news/biz/2009/06/127_47153.html.

Turner, Bryan S. 2007. "The Futures of Globalization" in *The Blackwell Companion to Globalization*, edited by G. Ritzer. Blackwell Publishing. Blackwell Reference Online. Retrieved March 27, 2009 from http://www.blackwellreference.com/subscriber/tocnode?id=g9781405132749_chunk_g978140513274939.

UNAIDS. 2008. "Report of the Global AIDS Epidemic". Retrivied July 27, 2009. http://www.avert.org/worldstats.htm.

UNTWO World Tourism Barometer. 2010. "Interim Update." Retrieved November 5, 2010 from http://unwto.org.

Wallerstein, Immanuel. 1974. *The Modern World System.* New York: Academic.

_____. 1984. *The Politics of the World Economy: The States, the Movements, and the Civilizations.* Cambridge: Cambridge University Press.

_____. 1991. *Geopolitics and Geoculture: Essays on the Changing World-System.* Cambridge: Cambridge University Press.

_____. 1998. *Utopistics.* New York: The New Press.

_____. 1999. "States? Sovereignty? The Dilemma of Capitalists in an Age of Transition." Pp. 20–34 in *States and Sovereignty in the Global Economy*, edited by D. Smith, D. J. Sollinger, and S. C. Topik. London and New York: Routledge.

_____. 2000. "Globalization or the Age of Transition?" *International Sociology* 15, 249–265.

_____. 2003. *The Decline of American Power.* New York: The New Press.

Wang, Shirley S. 2009. "Glaxo Says No to Russia on Cutting Price of HIV Drug." *The Wall Street Journal* June 12. Retrieved July 29, 2009, from http://blogs.wsj.com/health/2009/06/12/glaxo-says-no-to-russia-on-cutting-price-of-hivdrug.

Waters, Malcolm. 1995. *Globalization.* New York: Routledge.

Weiss, Linda. 2000. "Globalization and State Power." *Development and Society* 29: 1–15.

Wilensky, H. L. 2002. *Rich Democracies.* Berkeley: University of California Press.

Wines, Michael. 2009. "After Outcry, China Delays Requirements for Web-Filtering Software." *New York Times* July 1. Retrieved July 15, 2009 from http://www.nytimes.com/2009/07/01/technology/01china.html?sq=internet.

WTO News. 2001 Press Releases. "Experts: Affordable Medicines for Poor Countries Are Feasible." April 11. Retrieved July 27, 2009 from http://www.wto.org/english/news_e/pres01_e/pr220_e.htm.

Yearbook of International Organizations. 2004/2005. Union of International Associations (http://www.uia.org).

CREDITS

Photo Credits

Text Credits

INDEX